CW01237872

contents

Foreword	SP.3
The Author	SP.4
Introduction	SP.5
Colour Plates	
Emotionally	SP.13
E-bay and Collecting	SP.17
The New Top 100	SP.21
Where Are They Now?	SP.121-122
Special Edition Index	SP.123-125
The Clubs	13
Frank Wilson No.1	15
So What's The Story?	16
Dateline	17
No. 2 to No. 100	18-116
No. 101 to No. 200	117-166
No. 201 to No. 300	167-216
No. 301 to No. 400	217-266
No. 401 to No. 500	267-316
Bubbling Under	317
Essential CD Purchases	324
Colour Plates	325-334
Charts By Year	335
Other Top Tens	369
Index	421

Pictured: Jackie Day, *a legendary artiste whose recordings have been packing allnighter dancefloors since the 60's - tracks like her Modern records classic 'Before It's Too Late' and her Phelectron outing 'Naughty Boy' remain very popular today. Picture courtesy: Ian Clark.*

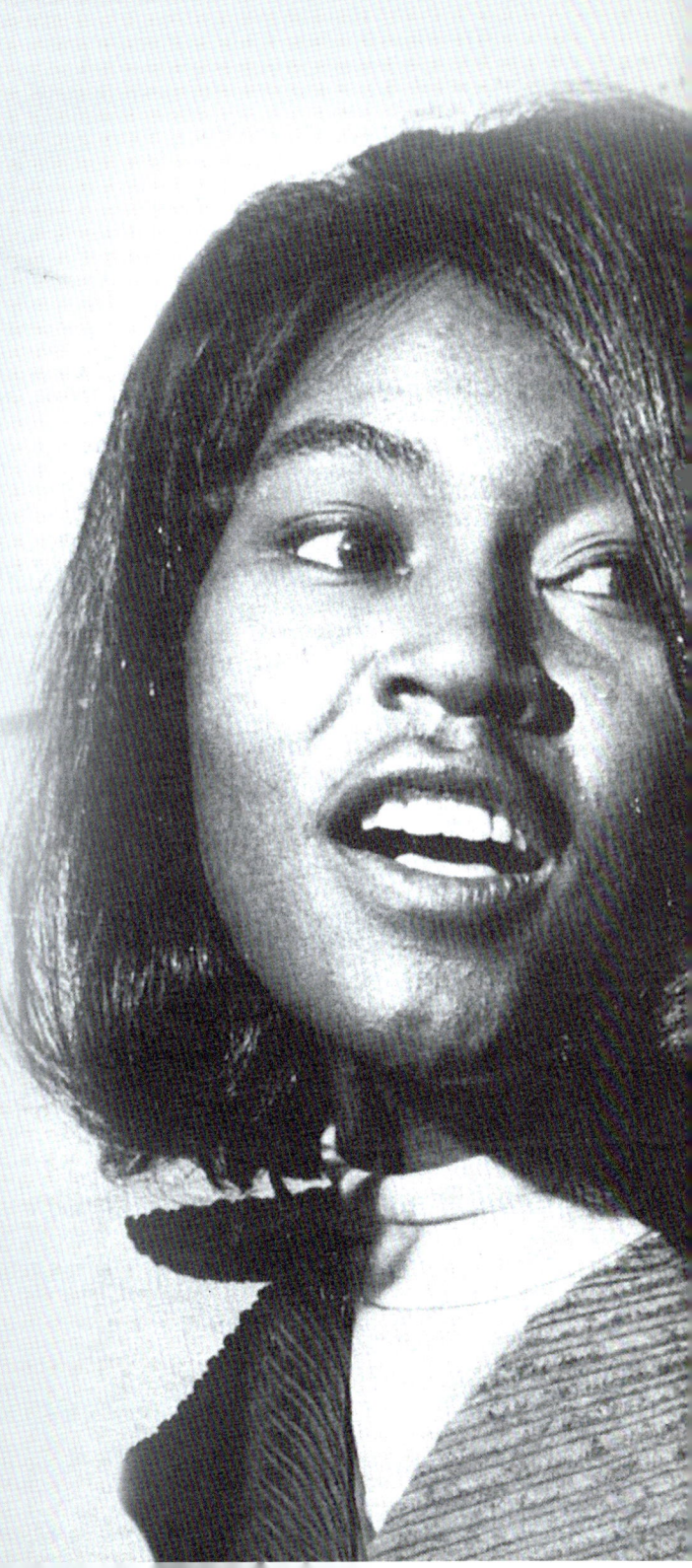

The Northern Soul Top 500 Special Edition

The Northern Soul Top 500 Special Edition

production credits
Written and edited by Kev Roberts.

Additional material and editing by Dave Carne.
Photograph and illustration captions by Kev Roberts and Dave Carne.
Book and cover design by Dave Carne at CWP, 015396 23619.
Printed and bound in Great Britain by: Hi-Tec Print.

Published by: The KRL Group,
PO Box 909, Worksop, Nottinghamshire S80 3YZ, UK.
www.goldsoul.co.uk

UK distribution by Gardner's Books, Eastbourne, Sussex
and Worldwide by Ibex Distribution +44 (0)1782 281777

Sources of additional information:

The In-Crowd (Bee-Cool), Billboard Book of Top 40 Hits (Billboard), Behind The Hits (Bob Shannon), Joel Whitburn, Soul Music (Hugh Gregory), Sound Of The City (Charlie Gillett), Soul Harmony Singles (Beckman, Hunt and Kline), Joel Whitburn's American Top 40, John Manship's Rare Record Price Guide, Rock and Roll Thru' 1969.

Photographs and illustrations courtesy of:

Kev Roberts, Tim Brown, Martin Koppel, Raymond 'Ginger' Taylor, Pete Whitney and Dave Carne, Blues and Soul, Mark Crooks, The LA Black Music History, Derek Allen, Rob Smith, Richard Searling, Ian Levine, Ian Clark and Martin Alsop.

Record labels courtesy of Tim Brown and many other collectors across the UK.

First published in the UK in © 2003 Kev Roberts, all rights reserved.

A CIP catalogue record for this book is available from the British Library.

ISBN 0-9539291-1-6

Also still available: The Northern Soul Top 500 (ISBN 0-9539291-0-8)

No part of this publication may be reproduced, stored in a retrieval system or transmitted in any form or by any means, electrical, mechanical, photographically, digitally or otherwise without the express prior permission of the copyright proprietor thereof.

The Northern Soul Top 500 Special Edition

foreword

I had been producing records independently for around 18 months in the early early 60's when I came to work for Motown. During that time I had written and produced a song for Ike and Tina Turner with another recording quickly following for their backing group the Ikettes. Things were starting to roll, especially following a song I had written for Stevie Wonder entitled 'Castles In The Sand'.

At that time Brenda Holloway, a new young beautiful and talented songstress with Motown was having an incredible impact on my desire to become a popular songwriter and producer. I thought that the only thing that stood in my way was sufficient opportunity to realise my dream.

Shortly after I secured a position as a producer with Motown, Berry Gordy Jnr. invited me to move to Hitsville, USA in Detroit from my base of operations in Los Angeles and I jumped at the opportunity! Within weeks I was there in the studio, producing a song on 'Smokey' Robinson! After Smokey's' record came out I started to work with Marvin Gaye, The Four Tops, Diana Ross, The Supremes, The Marvellettes, The Originals, Kiki Dee, Jimmy Ruffin and Eddie Kendricks.

Now besides being one of America's top five producers I also ranked number one in Britain - thanks! At this point my work as both a songwriter and producer with these great artists had already sold over 35 million records worldwide! Later, lost in all of my success with Motown was a song that Berry had originally intended to release on me as an artist, it was entitled 'Do I Love You (Indeed I Do)'. Prior to producing all these other artists I had been doing a bit of songwriting around the Los Angeles area and often became the vocal vehicle for my own material.

Now standing backstage at the Fox Theatre in Detroit, Michigan one night in 1966 a decision was made that changed my life in more ways that I could have imagined. It was decided between myself and Berry that, rather than becoming a recording star myself, I would instead concentrate on being a writer and producer for Motown stable of awesome talents.

Berry then ordered that all of the masters with my voice on be destroyed and overdubbed another artist (Chris Clark sic.) on my backing track!

Somehow, and I don't know how, a copy surfaced in England and was played in the clubs... The rest is, one might say, history!

It seems to me that England is made up of people who are by nature explorers, discoverers and pioneers. I should therefore have not been surprised to find that 'Do I Love You' has been caught up in the phenomenon called 'Northern Soul' which has been secretly bubbling under in the North of England for quite sometime but is now seeping slowly into the rest of the world.

How did I become such an integral part of such an occurance? It has to be supernatural, it has to be God because I knew nothing of it until just a few years ago!

A producer/promoter from London called me up enquiring whether I had any idea where he might get his hands on an original recording of 'Do I Love You' - of course I didn't! I had NO idea an original still existed! Though today I consider it to be one of my life's great achievements!

Since this discovery, I have done countless interviews for the print and electronic medias with regard to this unique musical uprising known as 'Northern Soul' and my own part in it. What have I learned about it personally? Northern Soul is a love affair, some callously suggest that it is just American music that never made it. But if you are in love with it you know that it is music that has found a true home in the hearts of those who have found it to be for them a 'treasure'.

I'm honoured to be included in this book and happy that Kev has asked me to write this foreword to his work which chronicles the experiences, history and most importantly harmonies of this grand odyssey known affectionately in England as Northern Soul.

Frank E. Wilson

Writer and Artist behind 'Do I Love You (Indeed I Do)'

The Northern Soul Top 500 Special Edition

the author

Kev Roberts started collecting records in 1968. Becoming a disc jockey in 1973, he was one of the originals at Wigan's legendary Casino where he DJed weekly for several years before embarking on a successful music and radio career - ultimately spending 2 years living and working in New York at the end of the 70's.

His launch into the music business realised many production credits including Mai - Tai, the late, great Edwin Starr, Bizzare Inc, Altern 8, Linda Lewis plus hits as diverse as Mistura and Andy Stewart. He is the Managing Director of the KRL Group, a music and media company based in the North Midlands. Over the airwaves, he has worked for many independent local radio stations including a long stint at Magic 828 in Leeds and has long been the voice of many radio programmes during weekends - a classic Northern tune is never far away from the decks of his national shows for radio stations like Solar on Sky Digital and Saga, (one of today's big 'regionals' in the Midlands). Kev was a key partner in the development of Soul music on CD, compiling over 100 titles for Goldmine/Soul Supply, Sony, BMG, Connoisseur Collection amongst others.

Kev is also a very active promoter of Northern Soul events in the UK and abroad and is partner in the Togetherness organisation with fellow ex-Casino DJ Richard Searling. Togetherness is behind the UK's biggest and most successful Northern Soul promotions the King's Hall Allnighter in Stoke is by far the biggest in the UK. Meanwhile its annual Fleetwood Weekender attracts over 2,000 Northern Soul fanatics from around the globe for 3 days and nights of dancing heaven.

Currently, Kev holds several directorships and media interests, and through his consultancy business has created new radio brands and many compilation albums. Married to Sam, with two children, he cites Soul, travel, radio, Italian food and Sheffield Wednesday as his personal vices!

2003 saw Kev celebrate 30 years of DJing, and with the increasing popularity of of Northern Soul and his unerring enthusiasm no doubt we'll see him celebrate 60 years in the business in the future!

Kev would like to thank the following family, friends and contacts that have contributed their thoughts to this book on what is still, the greatest underground music cult the world has ever seen...

Samantha Hallam-Roberts, Richard Searling, Martin Alsop (for his great shots), Ian Levine, Bill Snow, Alison Holden, Tony Delahunty, Rob Smith, Derek Allen, Anthony Beeby, Paul Robey, Carl Kingston, Gavin Stearn, Simon White, Chris King, Martin Koppel and Tim Brown. Plus all those who contributed images of their fantastic rare 45s.

This book is dedicated to Kev's many inspirational past masters...

In the United Kingdom from the 60's: DJ's Paul Harrison, Laurie and Tony Prince and in the 70's DJ's Ian Levine, Tony Jebb, Alan Day and Sgt., Army Bill Kemp. And Stateside, from the 70's: DJ's Hy Lit, Jerry Blavat and Don Steele and from the 80's DJ's John Hook, Dick Heatherton (Joey's brother) and Jeff Thomas

The Northern Soul Top 500 Special Edition

'The Crowd Is In Tonight - Lined At The Door'...

The return of the monster event has been a feature of the Northern Soul scene post-millennium. Here around 1750 Soul fans pack into Manchester's Ritz to watch Freddie Gorman of The Originals perform 'Take Me Back' during Richard Searling's 50th birthday celebration.

The Northern Soul Top 500 Special Edition

introduction

Northern Soul is more than merely a musical form, it is a feeling, a spirit that mixes a working class youth culture with a irresistable desire to discover as much about Soulful dance music as possible.

The 'Northern Soul' name is defined by the popularity of certain Soul records amongst the youth of the North of England, not the fashion driven South, and not the USA. The movement developed the late 60's at clubs like Manchester's Twisted Wheel and the Mojo in Sheffield and was subsequently named as definate genre in 1970. Interest level gathered momentum as other legendary clubs like the Torch and the Mecca opened their doors - the sound becoming more defined and focussed as DJ's and collectors discovered powerhouse obscurities on magical labels like Ric-Tic, Thelma, Cameo-Parkway and Mirwood.

Throughout its 70's boom period, all nighters were commonplace across the UK as youngsters flocked to this very special scene. Many venues of the time have their place in the role of honour but the undoubted focal point for the new mass following was Wigan's Casino from 1973 until its final closure in 1981.

Following the Casino's sad closure, the 80's saw the Northern scene in a period of uncertainty, musical change and development at venues like Leicester, Stafford, Hinckley, Morecambe and London's 100 Club. Despite being on a small scale, the scene flourished, developing a new momentum that started to draw back the faithful from years past.

The Scene Hots Up

By 1990 things were really hotting up, revival was imminent and the golden era ready for a renaissance. Younger promoters were now more experienced and the old guard were returning, events were better-promoted, sound systems upgraded and better venues were now being booked. Finally popularity really took off with the advent of many well-compiled CD's from the likes of Goldmine/Soul Supply. Initially purchased for 'old-time's sake' by now long-married couples, they proved an irresistible reminder of a wonderful youth - and with babysitting no-longer a problem it was time to dig out the dancing shoes again.

Post millennium the scene has attained monster proportions. There are many major local Soul nights to satisfy the large numbers returning, though this HAS meant that fewer now travel long distances - resulting in the development of many very regional sounds.

As ever in a scene of such intense passion, tension is still high with 'hardcore' collectors and event organisers never really seeing eye to eye over the popularity-versus-quality/soulfulness debate. Raised voices continue to coerce innocent bystanders into 'taking a stand' - often perhaps losing sight of the fact that care deeply though we do, it should be FUN too.

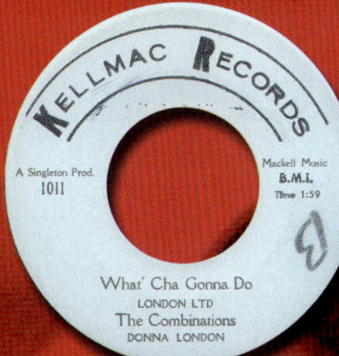

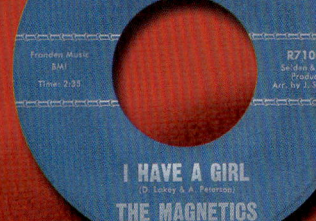

Wonderful rarities!... Classic floorpackers that everyone's after in the New Millennium!

Right: The Originals. Their triumphal appearance at Richard Searling's 50th Birthday Allnighter has been key in the re-evaluation of their output, prompting many album tracks from the 60's and 70's to now be fully appreciated by collectors and dancers alike.

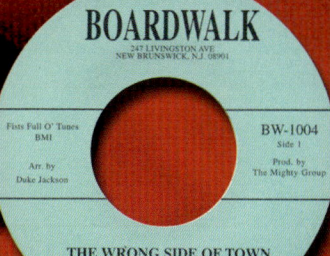

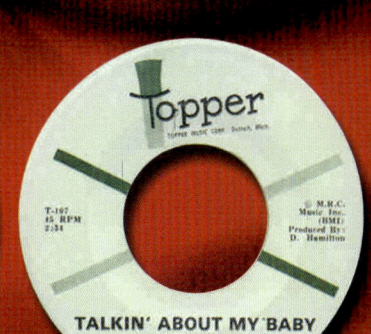

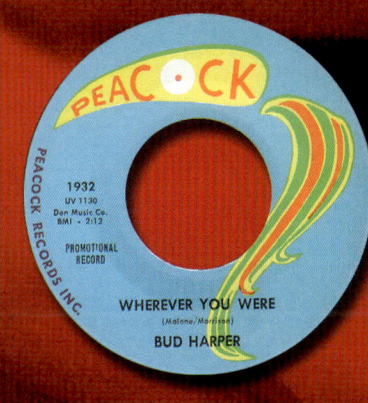

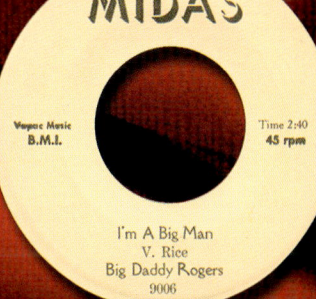

Wonderful rarities!... Classic floorpackers that everyone's after in the New Millennium!

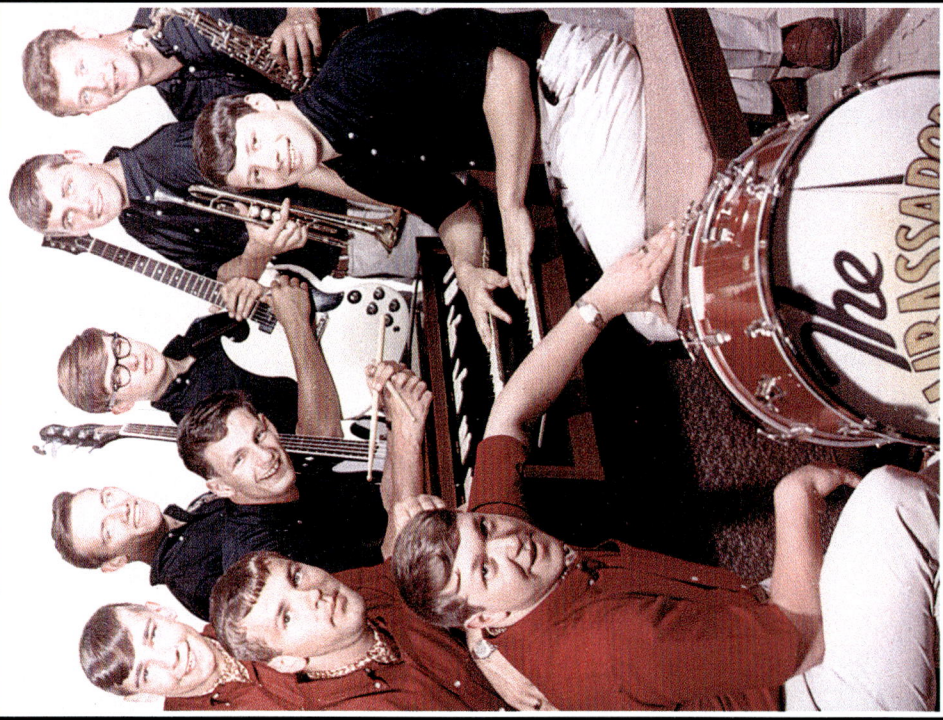

Patti and the Emblems, top. The Ambassadors, bottom, the group behind 'Too Much Of A Good Thing' on Pee Vee.

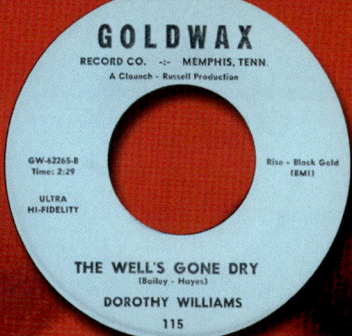

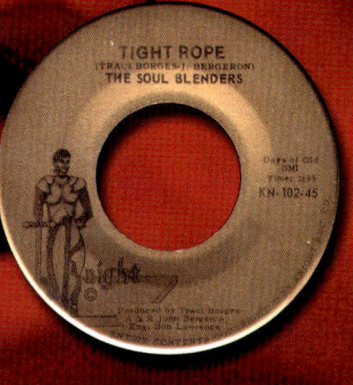

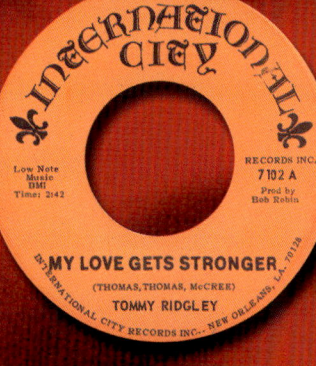

Wonderful rarities!... Classic floorpackers that everyone's after in the New Millennium!

Gladys Knight: More than any other artist, working solo or with the Pips, Gladys Knight has seen a massive rise in popularity at allnighters with FOUR tracks featured in the New Millennium Top 100.

Of particular note have been Ms. Knight's superb unissued cuts for Motown which have surfaced in recent years.

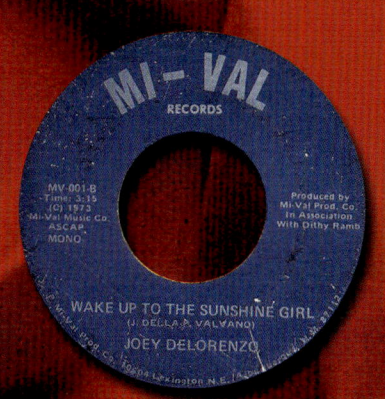

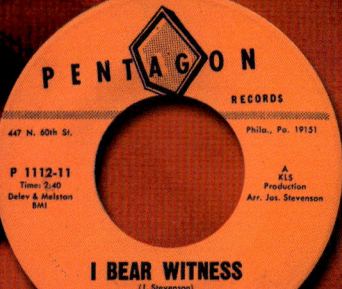

Wonderful rarities!... Classic floorpackers that everyone's after in the New Millennium!

Sandi Sheldon: Long-time mystery artiste, Sandi was finally tracked down by DJ legend Ian Levine after many years of searching.

A series of incredible live appearances followed, along with confirmation that the lady was in fact, as long suspected, a vocalist on The Vonettes' allnighter classic 'Touch My Heart'.

What was even more surprising was that the lady had in fact recorded quite a catalogue both as a backing singer for close friend Van McCoy and under various names as a solo artist - best known of which is Tuff act Kendra Spotswood (actually her real name).

Opposite: Learning to 'Do The Duck' at Fleetwood Weekender with the assistance of Sandi Sheldon and Willie Hutch.

Inset, opposite: Getting older - but the feet still work!... After all 'Dancing is a part of life'.

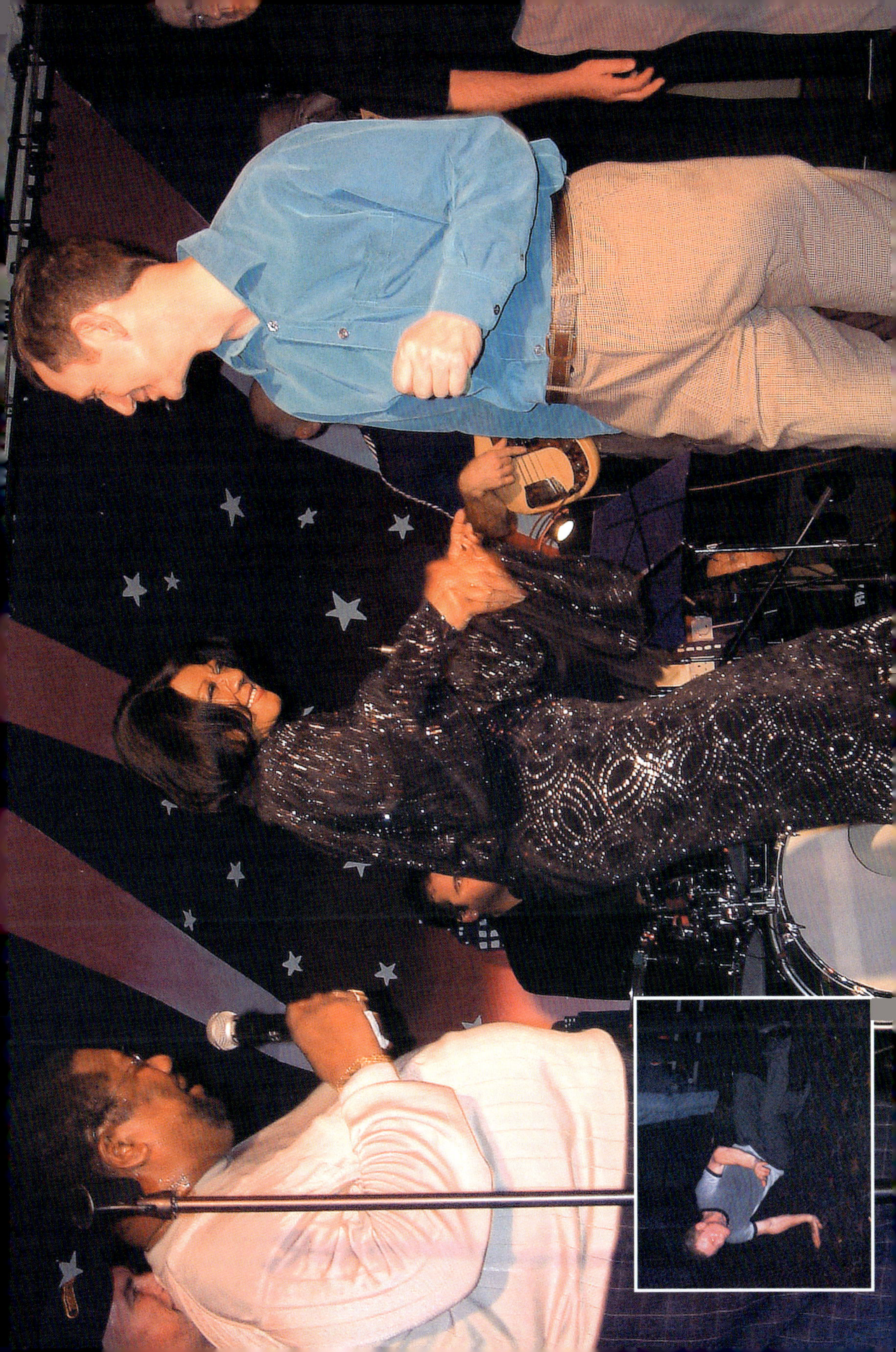

Collector's items don't get much better than this - the British collector's Holy Grail.

SKO-FIELD
SK-23-2-A
SOUL SOUND
THE JOKERS
RENESS RECORDS
RRC-10919
THINK IT OVER BABY
GROOVETTES
ULTRA-CITY
70-317B
SMALLEST MAN ALIVE
THE BLACK EYED PEAS
VULCAN
V 100
I'M GONNA WALK
MICKEY LANAY
OKeh
45 RPM
4-7319
LET MY HEART AND SOUL BE FREE
TAN GEERS
GEMINI
RECORDS
UNDER THE STREET LAMP
THE EXITS
1004
SOUL
NIGHT
DISCOTECA
Star Club
KISS F.M.
THURSDAY 3rd SEPTEMBER
TONIGHT
SUBOPTIK CREW
LIVE DISCO MUSIC
WEST END

'Prince' Philip Mitchell during a draining performance at Fleetwood.

Despite rocketing prices, vinyl collecting is still very brisk at allnighters.

Packin' them in at Manchester's Ritz Allnighter - post millennium the 'faithful' have returned in droves.

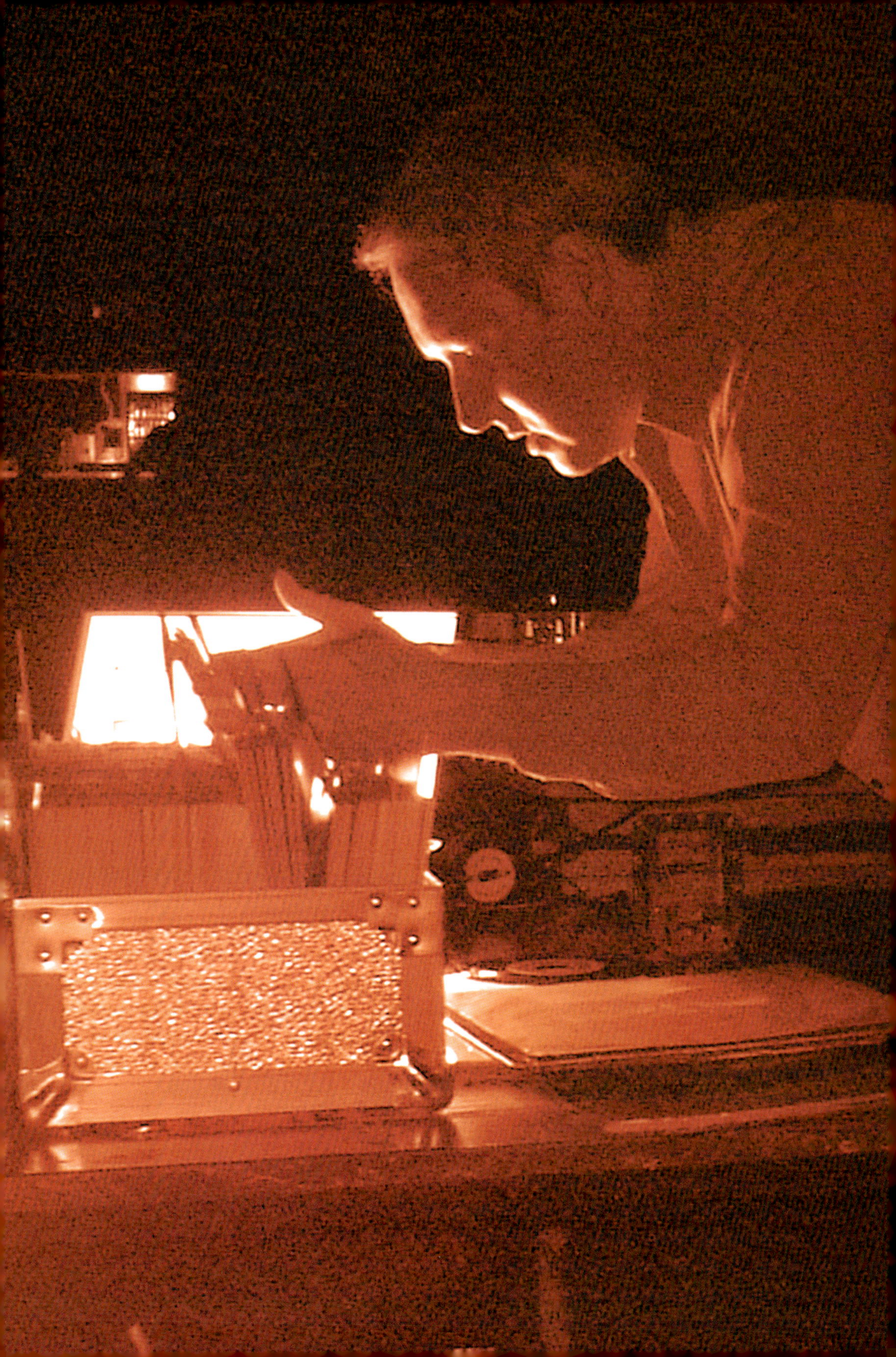

A Healthy Scene

It must be said that the scene is still in fine fettle although the tribal warfare breaking out on the internet looks like prime material for a Hollywood melodrama! To quote a close American friend of mine after I described the exact makeup of the scene *'my god, it's a movie of the week!'*

Joking apart though, tensions DO run pretty high over the most minor and unsubstantiated detail. Today instead of collecting being an enjoyable hobby, many find they have to run the gauntlet of shadowy, venomous individuals who hide in dark corners spouting off stupid second rate obscenities toward each other!

The Importance Of Promoters

It must not be forgotten that it is the hard working entrepreneurs take the financial risks to put the venues on that keep the pot boiling. Yet they are so often frowned upon by the 'that's not right' brigade - most of whom never actually put their money where their mouth is.

Northern Soul is a most interesting and desirable creature, and while purists and self-appointed authorities chase an unattainable holy grail, it is the general punter that is now deciding what, and who, is doing it right.

To quote one, sadly now dead, Northern Soul fan talking at the time
about the rumpous that surrounded the now legendary Stafford allnighter...

"Everyone argues over
Northern Soul
because they care SO MUCH about it - the day they don't argue about the scene is the day to start worrying - coz that's the day people don't care about it - and... when they don't care the scene will die"

For better or worse, the reality is that the VAST MAJORITY of top notch Northern Soul WAS discovered 25 to 30 years ago. And, though great previously undiscovered sounds DO still occasionally turn up, today's scene is split into the following categories:

10% Unknown discoveries ....Usually from acetate or studio tapes, many from the Motown vaults.

10% R'n'B ....Often verging on Black Rock'n'Roll - much of which doesn't sound anything like the R'n'B from the days of the early Twisted Wheel and would NEVER have been played in the 'golden era'.

30% 70's and Modern ....After the heated controversy of past years Modern is at long last gaining widespread acceptance.

10% 60's re-discoveries ......Minor spins of years gone by (good and bad) that simply didn't make it in the day.

40% 'Classic' oldies ....At the end of the day a great sound is simply a great sound - even if it is well known 40%.

The Internet

Today the internet plays a major role in the scene - offering chat rooms and rare soul links to satisfy every pallet. The grass roots soul fan now has a voice and a forum to be heard... and about a time too! The only real down side of chat rooms is that many tend to be treated as second class Soul fans by an elitist few.

Still, we are talking the most important underground scene of all time and with so many wanting an 'in', it's hardly surprising the movement is shrouded in suspicion and rumour.

Today the source of all those great sounds, the good old USA is at last fully aware of the UK Northern Soul scene. America has its own Soul scene with fans, collectors and dealers perfectly placed to search their homeland for the good stuff.

Britain remains as committed as ever to collecting rare Soul vinyl with E-Bay and UK dealers reporting brisk business... Indeed during a trip to Florida recently, I ran into an old contact of mine who revealed that a British collector, who was actually on his honeymoon, arrived at the dealers house with newlywed and suitcases in tow! The groom, with priorities well fixed in his mind, promptly went through a couple of thousand Soul 45's before finally acknowledging his new wife! All those records - you could say he reached pre-nuptual orgasm!

And the end of the day the Northern Soul scene knows no bounds, it keeps growing and growing. The unerring passion, intensity and all round craziness that made it unique is alive and kicking and today continues to bewilder outsiders as much as it did 30 years ago.

The New Sounds

The task of compiling my initial published material was relatively easy. As a young DJ in 1973, I debuted on the scene with 500 golden nuggets that quite literally fell into my lap.

Back in those days, most spinners had the same 100 'hot' plays interspersed with another hundred 'fringe' floorshakers. Musically the style was fairly crude to say the least, typically Motown-esque, loud, VERY fast and with a straight 4/4 beat.

I found writing up the first 500 over the scene's first 30-year history a joyous experience as I was reminded of just how incredibly good many of the sounds that today are largely forgotten were - especially at the time. Narrowing down the batch was hard though - there just have been SO MANY great dancers over the years quite frankly it was nearly a 'Top 1,000'!

Why then attempt to follow up the all-time greats with new (in my view sometimes substandard) tracks? In answer, look no further than our first 50... The Northern Soul scene has changed DRAMATICALLY during the last 5 years, the main reasons being a huge injection of new and returning blood, as a result nearly every town 'North of Watford' has a 'Soul' night of some description.

Today the finer, classier sides tend to be from unreleased acetates, studio tapes or previously unissued CD cuts... RARE Soul today is insanely rare! Where in the past there might have been only 50 or a 100 copies of a big sound - now the top spins are in the hands of less than a dozen Brits (many of whom don't DJ).

Local 'Do's'

Quite different from the big national events like Togetherness' Stoke allnighter, the local gatherings have seized the opportunity to make their mark with their own spins, hence many of the fabulous 50 the result of popularity at a 200 to 300 people get together in towns like Bury, Kettering, and Cannock... The movement has certainly hit the suburbs! Promoters have abandoned the young, hip, overcrowded city centres in favour of a more relaxed, friendly scene in the small town.

Major events have benefitted from these well run Soul nights however and have spread far and wide from their traditional North West home with the huge weekend events in Fleetwood pulling well over 2,000 - a definite throwback to the 70's! Most today's Northern enthusiast tend to stay local, travelling only occasonally to a 'big' event - quite the opposite of 30 years ago when Crewe, Wigan and Nottingham would be frequented in the same weekend!

Sure, a healthy 200+ are still wearing out serious shoe leather EVERY week round the country, but the majority have singled out their favourite venue and support it alone for the most part.

Comparing the past with today's scene is tricky though, the venues of the 70's were generally below average in décor and sophistication. Today, the overall presentation is paramount when choosing your Soul event. Thousands have enjoyed the new found professionalism behind gigs like the Kings Hall, Stoke supplying major security and up £20k in sound systems. And for the first time the toilets are half way decent! Backing group to the top acts, Snake Davies and the Suspicions have revitalised the live music scene too... Remember all those glorious acts in the 70's that fell down due to the 'rock' band that backed them?

The General Public's Fascination With The Scene

If you are toying with making a night of it, you will find most promoters have truly got their act together. The UK's general public as a whole seem fascinated with Northern Soul at the moment with the result that there is in fact more TV and radio coverage today than ever before. I must say that the current variety in music is absolutely great with the all-time greats fused with many Modern classics interspersed with more specialised genres such as 'crossover' and 'R'n'B'.

Today good times are top of the agenda for the masses - but always check out the musical profile of a venue before travelling, there are one or two renegades out there who avoid the all-time winners in favour of a more obscure play lists. At the end of the day it has to be said that the promoter has every right to champion more esoteric musical themes, however the ordinary punter can be disappointed if he or she is after a good old dance to 'Night Owl', 'Heartaches Away My Boy' or 'Do I Love You'.

The return of so many has also meant that many collections have been reactivated. As a result vinyl prices have sky rocketed, with £200/300 quite normal for reasonably easy to find turntable hits.

The scene toady is still based around DJ's, although a very popular jock in the North West may be practically unheard of to the Cambridge or Morden (Surrey) lot!

We have moved on dramatically in recent years, at the end of the day that is why I have written another chapter charting our remarkable scene. The Northern Soul Top 500 - Special Edition charts the popularity post-2000. I hope you find your particular favourites listed in all their glory. ENJOY!

Kev Roberts

October 2003

Kev Roberts, just 16 years old on his first night as a DJ at the legendary 'Heart Of Soul'... Wigan Casino. 2003 saw Kev celebrate his 30th anniversary as a Northern Soul DJ.

emotionally...

Wherever you travel to each weekend, 'politics' is almost bound to rear its head. The basis for the scene's term refers primarilly to two areas - firstly, hypocritical jealousy over success and secondly, heartfelt disagreement over musical tastes - usually in conflict with the greater whole.

In many there seems to be an ingrained jealousy toward the Soul fan-turned-entrepreneur, who for the most part have fallen into moneymaking schemes through market forces - ie they've simply done the job of promoting properly. 'Politics' go back to the scene's roots in the early 70's when the majority of Soul music events WERE promoted sold by local businessmen with little real interest in the music. As a result controversy in the press and at grass roots level raged between venues in competition with each other.

During the early 80's the first signs of friction came by the way of DJ Chris King, who cleverly packaged the legendary Ric-Tic Revue for a live appearance in Hinckley, Leicestershire. King promoted a truly memorable evening and followed through with several well put together all nighters. It did not stop a serious wave of sniping however, with CK being singled out as a 'money maker'.

According to the minority hardcore making money is wrong, even though financial stability is essential to continue events when the going gets tough. A decade or so before there was no problem when businessmen Chris Burton, Tony Petherbridge (RIP) successfully promoted all nighters with the full support of hardliners.

Many a DJ or well known face on the scene has received hideous, unfair criticism over the years. Record dealers are essential to supply the scene with new discoveries, all-time greats, hot in-demanders. But if one particular dealer is 'raking it in big time' the comments in certain dark corners can be pretty distasteful.

A recent debacle in the capital witnessed such distasteful behaviour from a bunch of childish and spiteful individuals that almost it pushed me into giving up promoting altogether to concentrate on broadcasting... However several top pro's talked me out of it in the end.

Conflicting, but genuinely held musical opinions are indeed healthy however, but 'market forces' are oblivious to a small minority who simply cannot accept one of their own making money out of their beloved scene. If a promotion is done right surely there is nothing wrong with the people behind it making money at it. According to detractors promoting a soul night is fairly easy right?...

You are a local soul fan and spot a gap in the market. The hall costs £75, equipment £100, no security! DJ's £50, £20 flyers, £50 ad in the Togetherness magazine. Total outlay: £295.

Hey! 180 have turned up at £3 each. Total income: £540 - success!

The Northern Soul Top 500 Special Edition

Profit? You do the math. The new promoter is congratulated - it's beers all round. But woe betide if he quits his £20k p.a. plus company car job to 'work the scene' full time. Northern Soul is not alone in this attitude, it is seems to be a British thing that rears its head rather too frequently.

The fact of the matter is that Northern Soul event organisers promote venues because first and foremost they LOVE the scene and its music. They do it from the heart and if they make £50 or £1,000 at the end of the night, so what? You don't see detractors patting a promoter on the back when he's making a loss and doing it anyway - but they seem to line up to snipe if he turns a good profit.

Regionally, the scene has changed dramatically. Areas considered dormant 30 years ago have emerged as formidable players, whilst other traditional hotbeds have faltered in recent times.

To illustrate, I have listed below five 'stonking' venues pre-millennium which have now quietened, closed or seen continuing success - compared with five current packers of today.

Pre-millennium	Post-millennium
1. Lowton	1. Junction 11, West Midlands
2. Albrighton	2. Ritz, Desborough
3. Brighouse	3. Annesley, Nottingham
4. Normanton	4. Ponds Forge, Sheffield
5. Winsford	5. Longfield Suite, Prestwich

The North West is still very much the strong hold with major events such as the King Georges Hall, Blackburn and the Longfield Suite, Manchester with large feeders like Bury Town Hall.

Again musically, the great North West is the most progressive, while the Midlands has a 50/50 split of Oldies and R'n'B with Modern.

Right: *Despite the influx of Modern Soul, R'n'B and previously unissued cuts, today's scene is very much dominated by the all-time classic oldies like Rose Batiste's (right) 'Hit And Run' c/w 'I Miss My Baby' for Revilot.*

Pictured left: *The consumate professional... Detroit legend JJ Barnes gives his all at Togetherness' Fleetwood Northern Soul Weekender, Autumn 2002. Recent years have seen a number of unissued floor packing gems surface from the great man.*

Confused? Don't be, this 'One-derful', 'Mar-v-lus' scene of our's has evolved into a desirable well-attended music genre that knows no bounds. In the general public's eyes a new image of super-coolness has developed, making Northern Soul a desirable association for forward thinking brand managers and record companies - just think about those KFC commercials!

The tricky part is attempting to second-guess the future. If anyone had told me the likes of Driza Bone's 'Pressure' could be deemed a 'classic' on the maple wood sprung dancefloors, I would have certainly called them crazy as recently as 5 years ago!

Today with the great mass of events the really popular turntable hits are the ones that are accessible to the Soul Night jocks. Unless you are a serious collector first and a DJ second any singles over £500 are now fairly redundant for DJs, except at the big one-offs like Fleetwood, Cleethorpes, and Stoke. Due to the geographical nature and age of the mass Northern culture, local gigs generate their own hits. Unlike the past when many travelled simply to hear a single track, today big all-nighter popularity or ind3eed rarity is not necessary for a sound to smash.

In a nutshell, today's scene encompasses a varied range of sounds that aren't always popular (or even played at all) everywhere. The 90's influx of CD's has made certain tracks very popular indeed, with some mega-spins that were little heard because of extreme rarity getting widespread exposure at even the smallest local events.

My prediction is that Northern and Modern are so close today in servicing the dancefloor that many new releases will soon become instant classics. Yes, the days of 'Sliced Tomatoes' and 'Pretty Little Girl Next Door' could find themselves totally out of focus real soon.

The energy level of our beloved scene never ceases to amaze me, and while the zimmer frame remains a little way off, the monthly blowout is still the favourite for most Northern fans!

Collecting, dancing, socialising or just a plain good time - whatever you're looking for from the scene, it is still as fulfilling and beautiful as ever. 35 years on Britain has made Soul a worldwide musical force to be reckoned with, of that we can be very proud indeed... Keep on keeping on!

The KFC effect: *The latest piece of vinyl to show a massive rise in popularity as a result of a dusting from the Colonel's special cripsy southern coating has been 'Sock It To 'Em J.B.'. Played since the days of the Twisted Wheel it was released in the UK on Red Atlantic as a direct result of demand from the Soul scene of the late 60s.*

e-bay and soul collecting

Collecting Northern Soul has never been a more serious passtime. In 2003 45's casually change hands for 3 and 4 figures daily as collectors compete for the few copies available of increasingly scarce tracks. Unfortunately the escalating prices have however forced many into surrender and the 5" silver disc has for many replaced the delicious vinyl they once owned.

It's not simply wealthy British collectors in the running though, worldwide interest in Northern Soul has inevitably sent prices absolutely spiralling out of control. Specifically on-line market place, E-Bay has developed a dedicated Northern Soul collector following, allowing interest worldwide to flourish as it puts far flung collectors in touch with particulalry hard to find releases.

During 2002, Don Gardner's immortal 'Cheatin' Kind' hit the magic 10 grand while Narbay's great 'Believe It Or Not' scored £112 - NOT on the original La Beat release but on a UK Grapevine reissue! (Which I'm sure MANY readers of this book own themselves).

With the incredible rate at which prices can jump price guides have today become fairly worthless. Sure, a copy of a regular 45 with no serious demand that's priced at £50, generally stays that figure for a while . But should it pick up extensive club plays the guide price becomes obsolete as it races in demand - Big Daddy Roger's Midas release 'I'm A Big Man' being is perfect example, once £15 it was recently listed for £350. And it's not just 60's - Ace Spectrum's minor hit from '75 should technically be worth around £20 - max, but it regularly commands £75 but peaked at £150 when it was most popular.

These prices however reflect demand and collectors voice their choice daily. The buzz around certain sounds created by internet chat groups encourage other collectors into chasing particular items. But it has to be said that the regular punter may never hear that track out at a venue, and since the dancer votes with their feet, if it ain't got a good beat it may fall flat on the floor.

DJ's are caught up in a difficult situation. While wishing to 'move forward' - many current 60's discoveries cannot match up to the first great wave of the 70's - hence the switch to newer styles such as R'n'B and Modern sounds.

Edwin Starr RIP: *Charles Hatcher aka. Edwin Starr sadly passed away in 2003. A true friend to the Northern Soul scene since the 60's and the man who recorded more Northern classics than any other, he was the legendary artiste behind the greatest live performances at Wigan Casino, The Torch and the Twisted Wheel.*

The Northern Soul Top 500 Special Edition

Prices go up, up, up...

To highlight the hard financial facts of collecting post millennium, let's take a look at 10 individual 45's and the growth in collectability over the last 25 years... And bear in mind that, with the discovery of additional copies, many of these have become LESS rare than in the 70's.

		1977	2003
1.	Lillie Bryant **'Meet Me Halfway'** Tay-Ster	£60	£1,200
2.	Bobby Kline **'Say Something Nice To Me'** MB	£40	£500
3.	Mel Britt **'She'll Come Running Back'** FIP	£40	£800
4.	Seven Souls **'I Still Love You'** Okeh	£30	£400
5.	The Ringleaders **'Baby What Has Happened To Our Love'** M-Pac	£10	£300
6.	Rubin **'You've Been Away'** Kapp Demo	£40	£250
7.	Don Gardner **'Cheatin' Kind'** Sedgrick	£150	£10,000
8.	Sandi Sheldon **'You're Gonna Make Me Love You'** Okeh	£50	£500
9.	The Magnetics **'Lady In Green'** Bonnie	£200	£2,000
10.	Jimmy 'Bo' Horn **'I Can't Speak'** Dade	£5	£800

The Dealers

Retailing highly collectable 45's has changed dramatically in recent times. Top dealers no longer need to travel to gigs to sell their esoteric gems - and many big spending collectors no longer go to events at all... Today three clicks and an obscurity is sold on the internet - generally for 50% above the going rate. The professional dealer becomes richer overnight - wheeling and dealing in the comfort of his own home or office and realising a much higher value for his wares.

Cheatin' Kind... 2002 saw this stunning, but elusive piece of vinyl top £10,000!

FINALLY for the new or uninitiated collector here's a few dealer sales prompters that I see all the time on their prime turkey cuts!... Watch dem pennies on these darlings - unfortunately 'Should Go Massive' on a sleeve almost always refers to the seller's bank balance!

1. **'BIG FOR SOUL SAM'** *(actually Sam's probably never actually heard it, variations on this theme include 'BIG FOR RICHARD SEARLING', 'BIG FOR TERRY DAVIES' etc., etc.)*

2. **'GOING MASSIVE'** *(not popular at the moment - and VERY MUCH I doubt it ever will be)*

3. **'LEVINE BIGGIE'** *(yeah back in '74! A SPECIAL WARNING - beware this could be the infamous one-time Mecca spin 'Maisie Douts')*

4. **'ON MANSHIP'S LIST FOR £XX -ONLY 50 FROM ME'** *(John's probably never actually heard it)*

5. **'BUY NOW BEFORE THE PRICE DOUBLES'** *(quick! I have 300 in stock)*

6. **'ONLY 2 KNOWN IN THE COUNTRY'** *(sorry typing error - that should have read 'COUNTY')*

7. **'STORMING WIGAN TYPE DANCER'** *(reminiscent of GARY LEWIS AND THE PLAYBOYS - only a bit MORE poppy)*

8. **'PLAYED EXTENSIVELY ON THE KEV ROBERTS' SHOW'** *(particularly close to my own heart this one - however I'm still waiting for someone to send me the audio as I'VE probably never heard it)*

1973-2003... Thirty years after the opening of Wigan's legendary Casino allnighter and its legacy is VERY MUCH alive and kicking - and now not simply around the UK - but around the globe! Picture courtesy: Mark Freeman.

The Northern Soul Top 500 Special Edition

The Northern Soul Top 500 Special Edition

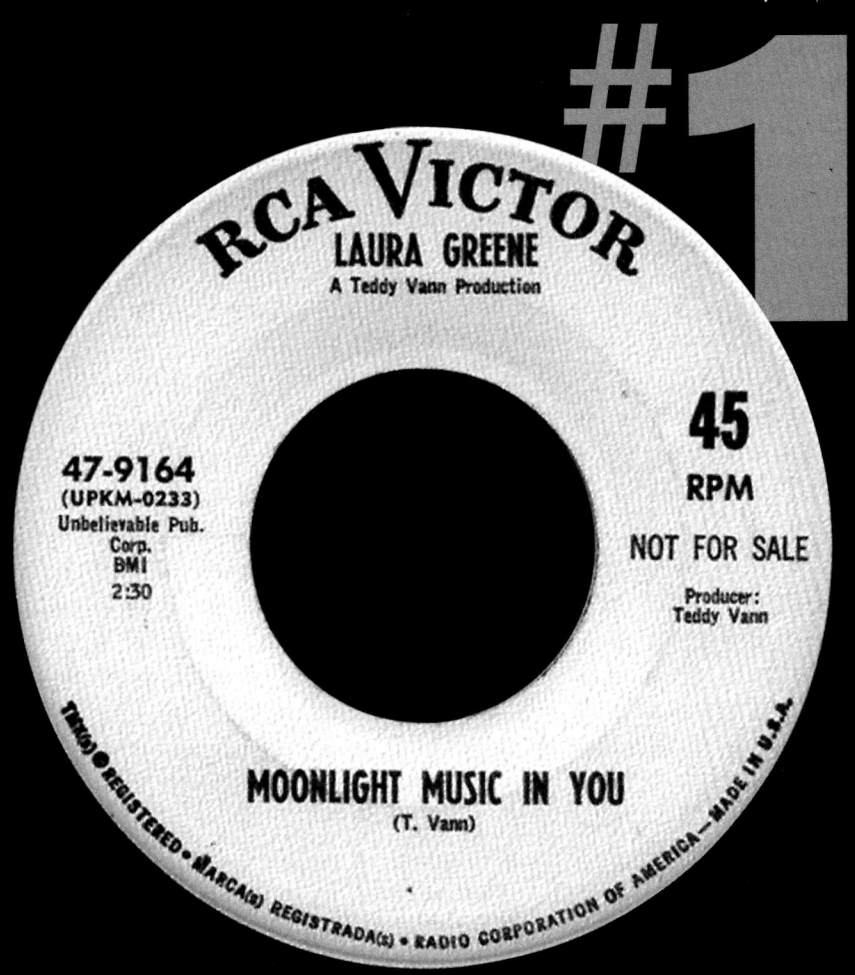

#1

Artist: Laura Greene
Title: Moonlight, Music In You
Label: RCA Victor
Value: £100

'oh, by the way, did your bring your guitar?... take a bow colonel sanders!'

Few Northern Soul 45s can have seen such a meteoric resurrection in their fortunes as this Wigan classic from the RCA Victor stables of the mid-60s.

Needless to say Laura's new found popularity has (along with several other classic spins, including our all-time Number 1 'Do I Love You') been the result of relentless TV exposure through Kentucky Fried Chicken's 'Soul Food' advertising campaign.

Most collectors will of course have noticed that this well known tune by Teddy 'Colored Man' Vann was cut and pasted into the backing of several other classics. The best known being the instrumental 'After The Session' and Frankie and the Classicals' great 'What Shall I Do' (some copies of which also include a spoken intro). 'Moonlight Music In You' was itself also recorded by Anita Humes' group, The Essex, on Bang records.

A long-standing £10-£20 sound that has been reissued several times, today pure demand has pushed this relatively common piece of vinyl up and over the ton!

The Northern Soul Top 500 Special Edition

#2

Artist: **Ace Spectrum**
Title: **Don't Send Nobody Else**
Label: **Atlantic**
Value: **£75**

'the pinnacle of the new breed of turntable hits'

Purchased as a new release in 1975, the 'never hard to find' outing from a vastly underrated outfit was first widely exposed Northern wise by Bolton DJ Bob Hinsley. A well respected spinner, Hinsley understood the need to play accessible singles. Everyone loved it, hence the scramble for available copies. The result meant just about every jock had one to play, which always results in mass appeal. The scene is possibly the only one whereby prices are determined by dance floor popularity. And in isolated cases this 45 has reached in excess of £150!

What's in the groove, well, a delightful lilting piano led intro over a soft disco beat with vocals that range somewhere between Timothy Wilson and Eddie Kendricks. Several versions exist including Millie Jackson and The Dynamic Superiors. But this is it, the absolute dog's b*******. The track symbolises the popularity of Northern in 2003. There are even a few intro bars for anthemic clapping which adds to the atmosphere of the 1975 Atlantic minor hit. Irresistible for all ages, it's the inevitable way forward to cover newcomers and seasoned veterans.

The group led by Rudy Gay made their debut on Atlantic in 1974, taking a full 29 years to achieve world wide recognition.

The Northern Soul Top 500 Special Edition

#3

Artist: **Driza Bone**
Title: **Pressure**
Label: **4th and Broadway**
Value: **£10**

'the 90's are coming'

When compiling the first top 500 pre-millennium, the thought of a 90's single even making the chart would have been unthinkable.

The British outfit recorded their masterpiece in 1992 with the sole aim of charting pop wise. The recording fell perfectly into the lap of the buoyant Modern scene, which in turn was lent to the Northern fraternity.

The sheer availability made it so popular it has crossed over to the over 30's revival nights. And sits comfortably in between a Motown and Philly tune.

The lead even toured recently as 'Driza' and wowed a few gigs, the act even have the distinction of scoring a second entry in the 500, confirming the fact that Northern has moved forward to very new territory indeed.

The Northern Soul Top 500 Special Edition

#4

Artist: **Bettye Swann**
Title: **Kiss My Love Goodbye**
Label: **Atlantic**
Value: **£100**

'a stunning piece of philly soul'

'Make Me Yours' will forever be at the forefront of personal choice among long term collectors. And with the scene changing course dramatically in the last five years Swann's 70's masterpiece confirmed a new vibe within the Northern hierarchy.

Producers Phil Hurtt and the late Tommy Bell were straight out of studio one at Sigma Sound possibly working with the likes of the Spinners before working on the B list, which included Bettye Swann.

The song itself is infectious, with Ms. Swann wailing out the title aided competently by the usual strong backup.

It did not take long for DJ's to hear of the discs emerging popularity, which in turn prompted a scramble for copies at around £10, a throw.

Absolutely monstrous, with a freshness that should carry it through the next decade at least.

The Northern Soul Top 500 Special Edition

#5

Artist: **Gladys Knight**
Title: **If You Ever Get Your Hands On Love**
Label: **Motown**
Value: **£20**

'a mesmerising motowner from the vaults'

For over 50 years the Georgia peach of Motown has stunned the world with her vocal prowess. The vaults of Hitsville have generated another masterpiece by way of this 1966 five star thrill seeker.

During the 65-67 periods and pre 'grapevine', Knight must have recorded reels upon reels of tracks with the record company 'losing'sight, once her first biggie (the original of Marvin's epic) hit pay dirt.

Gladys tears out of the stalls at such a pace she might pass out.

This is old school, with a supreme vocalist rasping through the beat of its time with real vigour.

An absolute dance floor monster that no serious dancer should be without.

The Northern Soul Top 500 Special Edition

#6

Artist: **Clarence Carter**
Title: **Messin' With My Mind**
Label: **Ichiban**
Value: **£35**

'grits 'n' chitlins head north'

Wonderfully handled by the former 'Mr. Candi Staton' as he surprises the UK with a mid to up tempo take on Otis Clay's Echo recording, also cut by Barbara Carr, that's even available on 12". A definite sign of the times - Carter doesn't even break sweat over a bubbling backbeat that's laced with synth chords and stabs.

What's ironic, is that the UK release promoted in the 80's to the dance market found favour in Northern circles - ever the genre for picking up chart failures.

Coming full circle, the groove is irresistible, drawing from CC's southern roots with a neat hook that dancers can pick up on fairly easily.

Clarence 'Looking For Fox' Carter is of course legendary in Southern soul circles, somehow I feel he would be disinterested in his North of England popularity. A real piece of longevity.

The Northern Soul Top 500 Special Edition

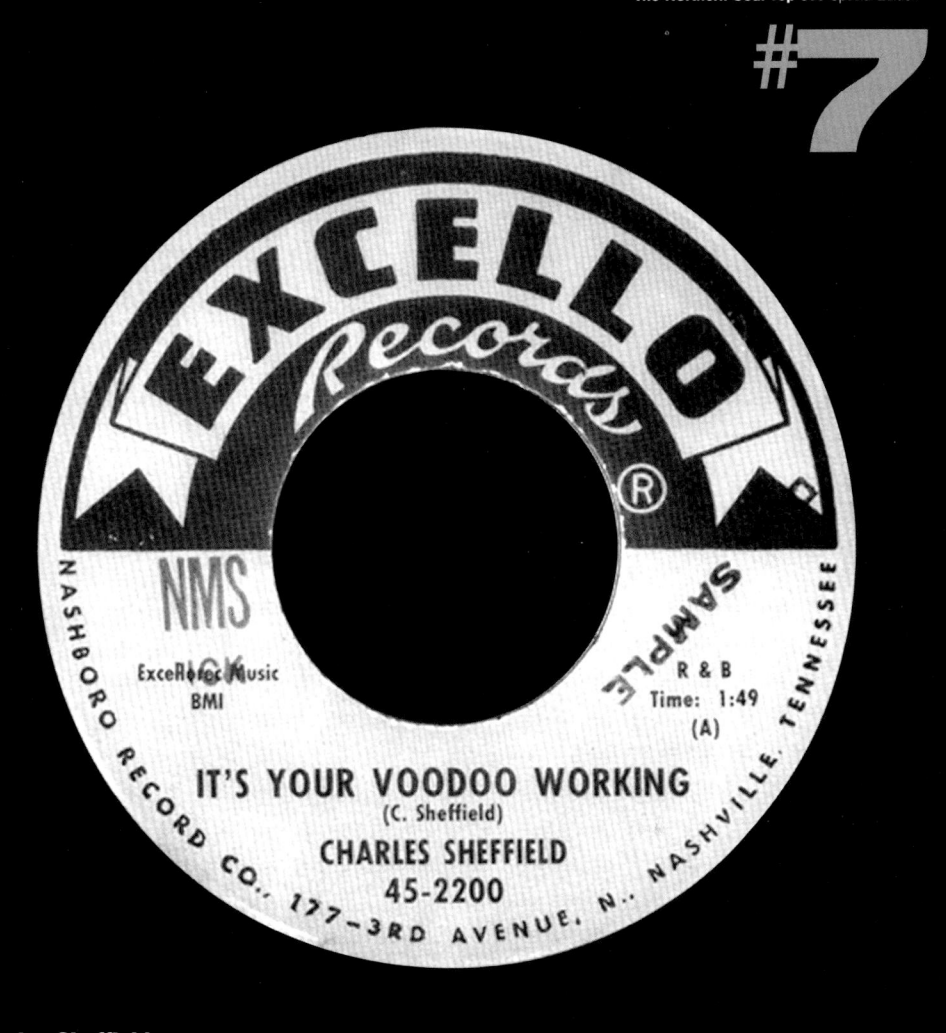

#7

Artist: **Charles Sheffield**
Title: **It's Your Voodoo Working**
Label: **Excello**
Value: **£400**

'rhythm and blues epic'

Most R'n'B titles that infiltrate the scene don't work. Charles Sheffield's 1961 Excello workout is an exception.

Coming off like Benny Spellman's - 'Fortune Teller', the percussion/piano led intro has just enough time for dancers to leap on the maple wood before CS gruffs his way in to your shoe leather.

DJ/Collector Carl Willingham spotted the potential long ago and exposed the very short anthem to the North. A standard on the Rock 'n' Roll scene three decades ago, the former £10 item has soared in value due to the scene's popularity and a helping hand from Carl.

The Northern Soul Top 500 Special Edition

#8

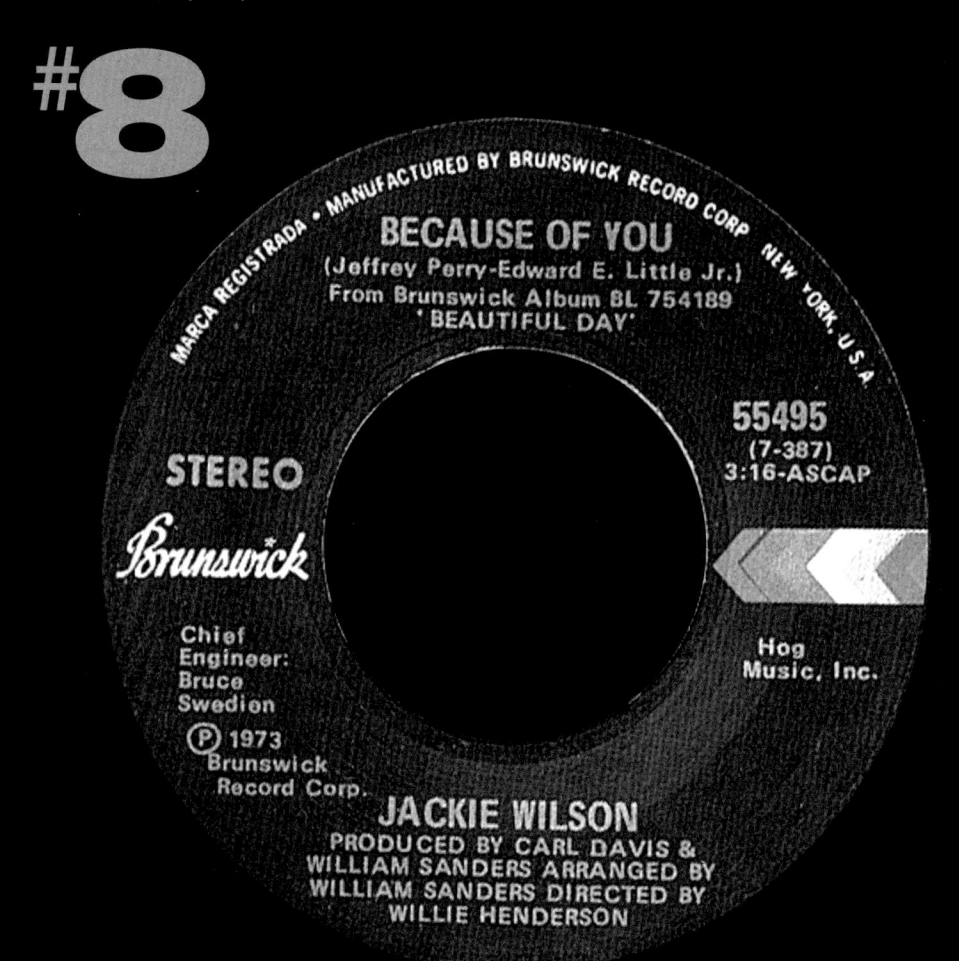

Artist: **Jackie Wilson**
Title: **Because Of You**
Label: **Brunswick**
Value: **£30**

'superiority at the most senior level'

Inevitably the master would return with his 70's catalogue ripe for the pickin'.

You could select a wealth of up-tempo tracks from the great man, but the scene adopted 'Because of You'. And what a superb groove it is with the usual full orchestra intro setting the scene for Jackie to take charge and deliver another performance that beggars belief.

He truly was the soul daddy and could sing anything... Hell, I am writing this on Christmas Day 2002 while listening to his seasonal epic from 1963.

My initial tome featured many of Wilson's 60's floorshakers, had he lived, the scene would have no doubt benefited almost annually from new recordings...

Can you imagine JW still around, recording today and living in the UK?

The Northern Soul Top 500 Special Edition

#9

Artist: **The Brothers**
Title: **Are You Ready For This**
Label: **RCA**
Value: **£20**

'studio 54 comes to blackburn'

A revived 45 from the heart of the North West with DJ's such as Ginger Taylor and Terry Davies probably re-spinning the 1977 groove as a throwaway filler.

The disc 'that nobody wants' has soared to popularity making a mockery of so called 'biggies', many of which are merely weak, badly produced, but super-rare 60's cuts or nondescript rhythm and blues.

The Warren Schatz production melts the hearts of today's dancer to perfection. Agreed, you almost expect to see Travolta laying down the talc, but the groove is unstoppable regardless of any negativity from hardliners.

Spin-offs include Revelation's vocal version. If like me you dance on one leg, take a load off and feast your eyes as the floor jams up worse than the drive from Manchester to Birmingham!

The Northern Soul Top 500 Special Edition

#10

Artist: The Phonetics
Title: Just A Boy's Dream
Label: Trudel
Value: £1,200

'doo wop meets motown in a joyous romp'

Straight out of the marines were two hopeful performers Willie Hutch and Lamont McLemore who eventually went on to follow very different paths.

The group, lost on a much bigger stage of gooey girl trio's and male quartets cut a low-key release out of Los Angeles. The scene itself has been aware of the monster for nigh on 15 years - yet it required serious effort from one or two DJ's to really make it happen.

This heavily doo-wop influenced male harmony led chugger features Willie M. Hutchinson on lead - showing off his incredible range even then. McLemore later joined Fifth Dimension after a brief spell on Bronco with The Versatiles (who were basically the same group).

The part I like about Northern Soul is when a track that missed out first time around is finally aired with conviction, displacing the many third division new 'discoveries' that are heading into Nowhere's-Ville.

The Northern Soul Top 500 Special Edition

#11

Artist: Jimmy Ruffin
Title: He Who Picks A Rose
Label: Motown
Value: £20

'a rivetting slab of unreleased detroit'

DJ Chris King was given the go ahead to listen to unreleased source masters and compile two CD's for Polygram's (now Universal) budget label Debutante.

A cache of superb finds was discovered with Ruffin's alternate vocal to The Temptations' 'I Gotta Find A Way'. Quite why JR's magnificent performance remained in the can is a great mystery... Did they really have SO MUCH great stuff locked away?...

The answer is YES, as the visit to California by CK proved. Despite British popularity and his brother's success, Ruffin was always a 2nd division player at Hitsville, which is shameful considering he recorded one of the biggest selling singles ever in 'What Becomes Of The Broken Hearted'.

Chart position number 11 not only goes to JR but also to CK for unearthing a wealth of unreleased masters that most of us had no idea existed!

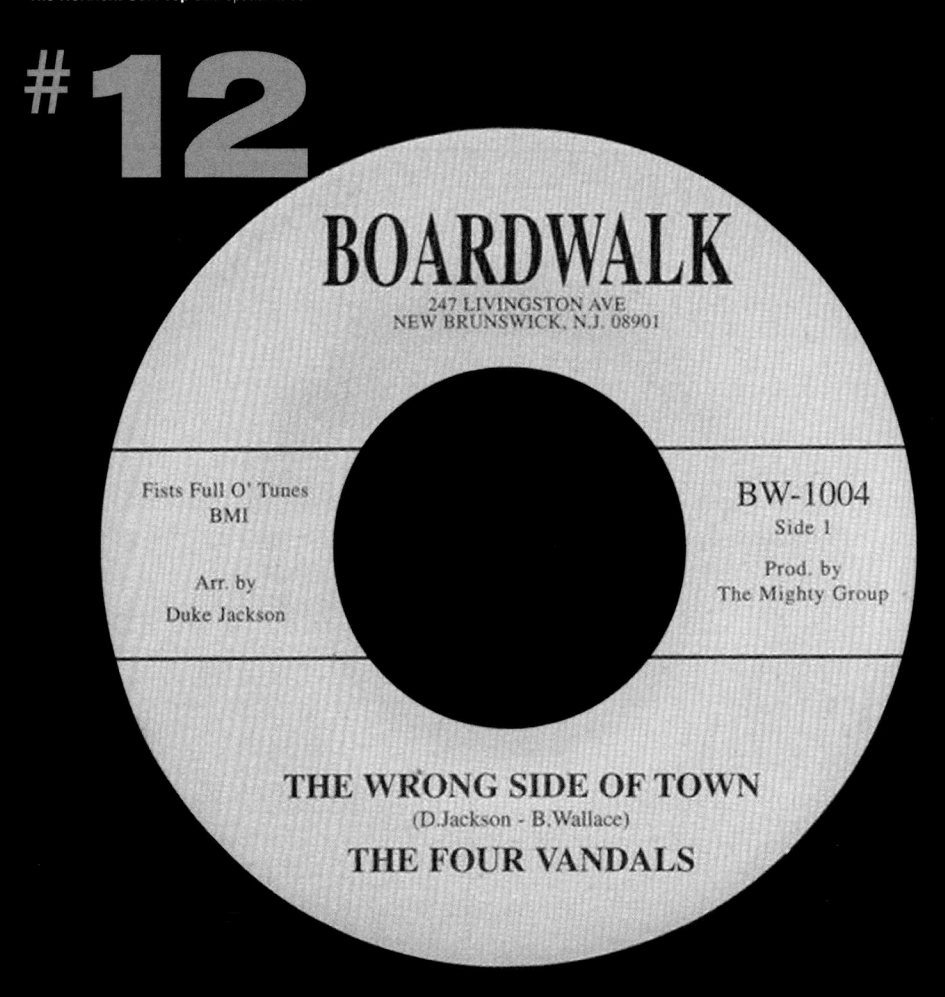

#12

BOARDWALK
247 LIVINGSTON AVE
NEW BRUNSWICK, N.J. 08901

Fists Full O' Tunes
BMI

Arr. by
Duke Jackson

BW-1004
Side 1

Prod. by
The Mighty Group

THE WRONG SIDE OF TOWN
(D.Jackson - B.Wallace)
THE FOUR VANDALS

Artist: **The Four Vandals**
Title: **The Wrong Side Of Town**
Label: **Boardwalk**
Value: **£100**

'the mystery movie of the week'

If the scene is to be conned (Footsee) then it has to be done well. After all eagle eyed collectors are too long in the tooth to be sold a dummy. Sometimes however, while waiting for the jury's verdict, the dancefloor will make up its own mind regardless of dealer/collector approval.

OK, here's the deal. DJ Ian Levine claims to have found the single in the early 70's. A couple of dealers 'found' the single within a few months of each other.

The claim being that they were recorded and pressed by Levine and then planted carefully in the hands of US dealers and the saga roles on!

The tale is destined for Hollywood at this stage. But as Paramount or Fox pictures would surely be as confused as the rest of us. However nothing can detract from the fabulous 'Wall of Sound'-meets-Jimmy James-meets-George Smith's 'I've Had It' tune, coupled with the rippling 'I'm on the wrong side of town' chorus.

Whatever it is (and it AIN'T from New Brunswick!) it rocks - that's for sure! ...If authentic as IL suggests, then it's a full on tip-top discovery ...If a tailor made, it's damn good, and you're staring at one of the best scams since Ocean's 11!

The Northern Soul Top 500 Special Edition

#13

Artist: **Joanie Sommers**
Title: **Don't Pity Me**
Label: **Warner Brothers**
Value: **£200**

'the old pop style is still with us'

Northern Soul would never be the same without a Lynn Randell or Lainie Hill to sing a long to. 60's hit maker Sommers was staring at anonymity unless her Warner Bros. deal finally kick started.

Her 'Johnny Get Angry' had propelled her to Lesley Gore type status. Sadly this 45 bombed, leaving the UK to activate this sugar coated cookie to melt in the mouths of most females.

Love 'em or hate 'em there will always be a poppy Holly St. James type sound kicking around the boundaries of the scene. It's a confusing problem for international collectors - the way old Blighty categorises such twee popsters' output as 'soul' classics!

The Northern Soul Top 500 Special Edition

#14

Artist: Joe Tex
Title: I Wanna Be Free
Label: Dial
Value: £60

'joe hits early with this spin'

Texan Joseph 'Joe Tex' Arrington, who sadly passed away in 1982, has long been associated with Northern Soul.

His perennial 'Show Me' was played as a brand new release at the Twisted Wheel and remained popular through the days of the Torch despite becoming a major hit on for Atlantic in the UK. His other Dial cuts also started to see plays at the Torch, particularly 'You Better Believe It', Joe has also entered the original Top 500 with yet another Dial release, 'Under Your Powerful Love' - though his biggest pop hit came with 'Don't Want To Bump No More With No Big Fat Woman' - a comedy cut predictably popular with fans of chart music, it hit a couple of times in the UK.

Current biggy 'I Wanna Be Free' is actually a much earlier release than the well known and largely overplayed classics, but today's taste for R'n'B has seen this relatively common release rocket in value.

The Northern Soul Top 500 Special Edition

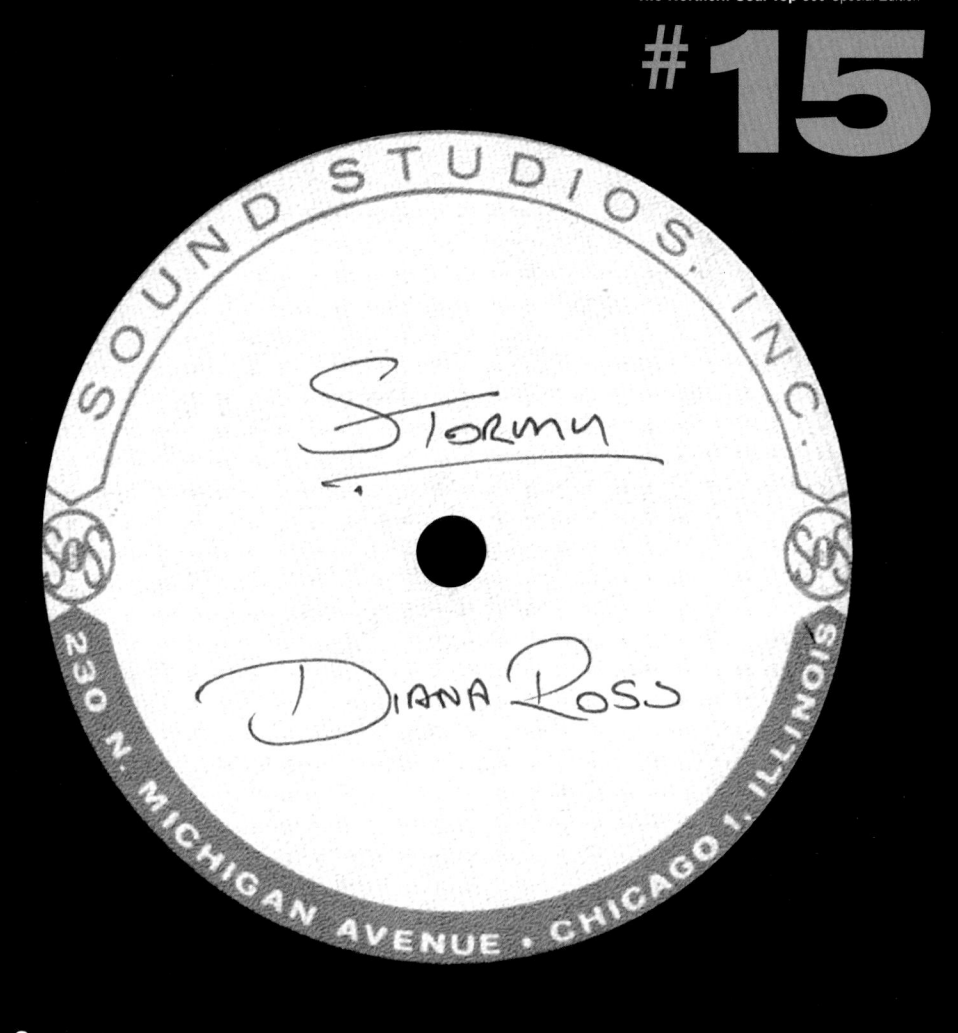

#15

Artist: **The Supremes**
Title: **Stormy**
Label: **Motown**
Value: **£10**

'the soul version of the classics IV'

Originally on a promo cd, the pop standard from Jacksonville's Classics IV was obviously chosen at the start of the session in 1968. During the final rundown, the A & R team felt there was more than enough material for a new Supremes material hence the exclusion of number 15 .

Unusually for the scene, the track is almost 'west coast'in design. Very tuneful and extremely groovy, Ross works it as know more than a demo. But the fascination with unreleased Motown means that almost anything with a backbeat is considered playable.

Showing the new diversity of the scene, Stormy transformed from a cd only track to a limited 45 in the UK around five years ago.

The Northern Soul Top 500 Special Edition

#16

- Artist: **Barbara Lynn**
- Title: **Movin' On A Groove**
- Label: **Jet Stream**
- Value: **£100**

'the left handed guitar swapped for horns'

Ms. Ozen's association with the North dates back to the late 60's with her Tribe output being of particular interest. Her signing to Atlantic rippled the dance floors with 'Take Your Love And Run' and 'You're Losing Me'.

During the 90's a track recorded for Huey P. Meaux's Jet Stream reactivation a decade before, re-affirmed Lynn's popularity with DJ's.

During her visit to the Togetherness Soul Weekender, Barbara performed her latest Northern winner to a 1,500 audience, who in turn warmed to the newest anthem, catapulting it to massive popularity.

Neat horns and backing vocals steer Barb into a comfortable performance. Not her best work, but certainly the most refreshing.

The Northern Soul Top 500 Special Edition

#17

Artist: **Gladys Knight and the Pips**
Title: **No One Can Love You More**
Label: **Tamla Motown**
Value: **£40**

'gladys kicks ass once again'

The unreleased Motown material is legendary. Imagine then, the surprise at this previously US unreleased cut found on the flip of the 'Take Me In Your Arms And Love Me'.

The softly spoken intro explodes into a fully charged super turbo-dance groove.

The modern effect switching out of Detroit to LA just about allows both pre and over 35's to gig together on this one.

Gladys cruises the track with consummate ease and tells the tale sweetly with occasional yelling and hollering. One wonders if Millie Jackson might have seized the opportunity to record the Pam Sawyer almost tune. Anyway, Jobete and company confined it to the tape store until the magic men from the North took charge and spun it vigorously for the past decade.

The Northern Soul Top 500 Special Edition

#18

Artist: **The Montclairs**
Title: **Hey You, Don't Fight It**
Label: **Arch**
Value: **£700**

'the irrepressible phil perry'

The Arch label symbolises the famous landmark of St. Louis. When discovered by Ian Levine as far back as 1973, almost 1,000 copies were there for the taking in a small record store in the city.

Known as a 'last hour' shuffler at the famous Blackpool Mecca venue, the disc was hidden for a two decades before collectors brought it, once again, to the forefront of the scene. Would I have played it back in the day? You betcha!... But due to a lack of availability I had to settle for sloppy seconds.

In terms of the soul and dance content it is superb. A light intro develops into a wailing Perry led romp with the harmonies zipping in and out of the track followed by the hook 'hey you'. The value has sky rocketed. The single itself owes a lot to DJ Pete Haigh who kept the momentum going simply by forever talking about it. Thanks Pete!

The Northern Soul Top 500 Special Edition

#19

YES I'M IN LOVE
(Harrison, Holman, Kinnebrew)

Promotion Copy
Not For Sale

E 601
Bridgeport
Music, Inc.
(BMI)
Time: 2:45
(E 2562)

UNIQUE BLEND
A Holman & Associates Production
For Eastbound Records, Inc.
℗ 1972 EASTBOUND
RECORDS, INC.
DISTRIBUTED BY JANUS RECORDS N.Y., N.Y.

EASTBOUND RECORDS

Artist: **Unique Blend**
Title: **Yes I'm In Love**
Label: **Eastbound**
Value: **£300**

'doo wop is back, 70's style'

A typical discovery by the Blackpool shuffle crew in the mid 70's, which hung around the collector's scene for nigh-on two decades before the crossover development focused its attention on the 1973 Detroit outing.

With tempos changing dramatically, DJ's flipped back to known titles that lacked exposure first time around. UB's love anthem fitted the bill perfectly with the piano and horns collectively arranged to perfection.

The classy mover settles perfectly for old timers and newcomers alike to do the business without much need for the customary talc.

A second release on Eastbound failed miserably too.

The Northern Soul Top 500 Special Edition

#20

Record label shown:
GEMINI STAR RECORDS
David Gay — BMI
8939-BW
30,008
Time: 2:38
I DON'T KNOW ABOUT YOU
(David Henry)
THE CONSTELLATIONS
Arranged by Richard Tee
Produced by Pat Jaques
DISTRIBUTED BY AMY RECORDS, N.Y.C.

Artist: **The Constellations**
Title: **I Don't Know About You**
Label: **Gemini Star**
Value: **£350**

'burying the motown sound with a new flavour'

In similar vein to Unique Blend, the New York outfit score with a 1968 harmoniser that shoots directly towards soul group buyers of the era. Unfortunately the sound was confined to a select group of collectors on both sides of the pond.

A 1973 discovery, the single hung around in the cheap boxes alongside their other popular cut 'I Didn't Know How To' at many a gig before re-inventing itself in the last decade.

Fused somewhere in-between Northern and the crossover scene, the 45 has the classy edge of an Intrigues, Steelers, and other like-minded groups of their generation. Lead by Keith Rose, the group also recorded for Violet, Smash and Dionne Warwick's Sonday label.

The Northern Soul Top 500 Special Edition

#21

Artist: **The Trends**
Title: **Thanks For A Little Lovin'**
Label: **ABC**
Value: **£200**

'a major reactivation'

Chicago has always played a massive part in securing major label releases for up and coming talent. ABC's head of Artist and Repertoire urban wise was Johnny Pate. He handled everything from the Impressions to non-hits like Earl Jackson.

The Trends were one of the super finds, and Pate took no time in cutting several sides with them. Led by Eddie Dunn, the group had nine singles altogether, making them long-standing veterans of the industry without having a hit.

The popularity has endured an almost self-build: when as far back as the mid 70's it received a lukewarm attention. Sensibly, the top spinners have championed the cause well, and we get off our butts on a weekly basis to the strains of 'Thanks for a little lovin' baby'

The Northern Soul Top 500 Special Edition

#22

Artist: **Martha Reeves**
Title: **No One There**
Label: **Tamla Motown**
Value: **£30**

'martha delivers another classic'

Motown is in fifth gear and cruisin" 'with new discoveries, reactivations and unreleased tape finds. The fascination has now spread to the 70's and in particular the UK only releases which appear to be harder to find than if released in the US.

For a time, 'Love Guess Who' a missed 45 from 1970 was the focal point of Martha's latest Northern hit. But, more recently this sublime emotional mid tempo effort has captured the hearts and minds of the Tobi, Jimmy and Dean brigade.

At the time of writing, Reeves' catalogue is under construction. The word from Martha herself is, many unreleased songs will accompany the all time greats.

As part of the movie 'Standing In The Shadows Of Motown' she proves a wonderful ambassador for the label. Messrs. Gordy and Ross, are you paying attention?

The Northern Soul Top 500 Special Edition

#23

Artist: **Chairmen Of The Board**
Title: **Bless Your Heart**
Label: **Surfside**
Value: **£15**

'the general rocks the world - one more time'

In February of '02, General Johnson guested on my weekly radio programme. The usual evergreens from his vast repertoire were immediately under discussion. The parting shot was GJ promoting his latest offering stateside 'Timeless'. A copy was promptly mailed from Atlanta and it sat desk bound for 10 days before I previewed it during a short journey to Nottingham.

By the time track 5 kicked in, I was in a state of delirious enthusiasm as my 30 years in the industry told me 'this is the new A/C mother of all mothers'.

The scene at this time had nothing new in the pot, so a very welcome side indeed was promo'd on a vinyl 45 for the UK market. Instinctively I became head cook and bottle washer by way of playing it on the air, servicing it to fellow club DJ's, doing the mail out and securing a UK release on Expansion!

The General is not only a friend but also one of the all time greats who burns 'em every week at the endless gigs he performs in the US. What total refreshment this really is.

The Northern Soul Top 500 Special Edition

#24

Artist: **Barbara McNair**
Title: **Baby A Go-Go**
Label: **Motown**
Value: **£20**

'motown's vegas showgirl in fine fettle'

From the initial haul of unreleased cuts discovered in the mid-90, McNair's output revealed some real stomping dancers as opposed to the schmaltz that BG cornered her into a full-on big beat with Jamerson and crew walking through the production with consummate ease.

With the Funk Brothers on hand it's hardly surprising that any of the label's investments had, at one time a 'super groove' session.

A new tape find recently has unearthed yet another version - with different lyrics, but this jerky romper has certainly been a star mover during the last 5 years.

Check out the Hullabaloo DVD currently in circulation. A gorgeous Barb vocalises the epic 'You're Gonna Love My Baby'.

The Northern Soul Top 500 Special Edition

#25

Artist: **Bobby Womack**
Title: **Home Is Where The Heart Is**
Label: **Columbia**
Value: **£20**

'the king of soul... any soul'

The legend is never far away from any chart and the last decade proved fruitful for Womack's 70's catalogue. I distinctly remember the work of art as a new visitor to the famous Highland Room in the mid 70's.

Now it's the turn of the revived Northern scene to wax lyrical on another master class in vocal superiority. A rock guitar led intro stuns a first time listener into confusion before BW mini raps over strings. A walloping back beat with anthemic chorus and the guvnor' reaffirming even then that the King of Soul is back!

The sheer availability of copies have meant maximum turntable exposure, especially at the country's many soul nights.

SP. 45

#26

The Northern Soul Top 500 Special Edition

Artist: Ketty Lester
Title: Some Thing's Are Better Left Unsaid
Label: RCA Victor
Value: £50

'boy meets girl meets northern'

'Love Letters' hitmaker was bound to have some form of emotional beat ballad tucked away in her 'nipper' catalogue alongside. This early 90's find received both UK and US releases. Stylistically the track is all too familiar, rubbing shoulders with McNair, Hill, Legend etc. It is a good song though, with Lester combining easy-listening pop with a slight tinge of soul.

Ketty struggled to make it after the big hit, however she did record a couple of in-demanders, most notably Wheel sound 'West Coast' on Capitol and 'Show Me' on Pete.

Never a favourite of the author - but one that the girls sing a long to while their male counterparts strut and wriggle on the welcoming Maplewood.

The Northern Soul Top 500 Special Edition

#27

HARTH1

harthon

Promotional Copy - Not for Resale

Side A

Copyright in this sound recording is owned by Weldon Arthur McDougall III/ Universal Love

World Of Happiness

A previously unreleased Harthon recording licensed to Goldmine/Soul Supply Limited
Recorded at Virtue Sound, Philadelphia, PA, U.S.A.
© 1966

GOLDMINE SOUL SUPPLY

Artist: **Ann Robinson**
Title: **World Of Happiness**
Label: **Harthon**
Value: **£30**

'thumping unreleased philly soul'

When well-known collectors Rob Thomas and Andy Rix discovered a Virtue acetate of this remarkable side, the scene was set for the best find of the decade!

Fortunately Goldmine, the UK CD reissue specialists, had a license deal with Harthon boss Weldon McDougall allowing the UK label to press 200 demo 45's to help in the promotion of the gem. A true anthem was born which today still figures in most DJ playlists.

In typical Philly-meets-Detroit style, Robinson wails up a storm. Originally the acetate was credited to 'Cindy Scott' a fellow PA recording artist, the correct labelling finally being applied after several years' extensive research.

Copies are drying up fast, so get one double quick!

The Northern Soul Top 500 Special Edition

#28

TAMLA MOTOWN PRESENT THE ISLEY BROTHERS
STEREO — MFP 50014
℗ 1972 — SMFP 50014 A 33⅓

1. BORN TO LOVE YOU (Hunter—Stevenson)
2. SAD SOUVENIRS (Stevenson)
3. MY LOVE IS YOUR LOVE (FOREVER) (Wonder—Hunter)
4. GREETINGS (Cecchino—Costenzo)
5. NEVERMORE (Stevenson)
6. AIN'T THAT REAL SATISFACTION (Stevenson)

Jobete Carlin Music Ltd., NCB

Artist: **The Isley Brothers**
Title: **My Love Is Your Love (Forever)**
Label: **Motown**
Value: **£10**

'yet another classic performance from ronnie'

Originally on a budget UK only LP from the 70s, more recently the track surfaced on the bizarrely titled 'Greatest Hits' CD!

Most aspiring jocks had the customary slate cut before the 'limited 45' drenched parts of the North.

In simple terms it's fantastic. And one wonders how the group could have so little success at Hitsville - stateside, the group from Ohio only had real chart success much later on their own T-Neck label.

A beautiful song handled delicately by Ronnie Isley that glides dancers around the maplewood with a sort of classy overtone.

Can we please have a box set on the group- Universal... Anyone???

The Northern Soul Top 500 Special Edition

#29

Artist: **Gladys Knight**
Title: **Pieces Of A Broken Heart**
Label: **Motown**
Value: **£30**

'it's motown time again'

Without wishing to turn the book into the Motown show, I did indicate in Volume 1 that many unreleased Hitsville masters were slowly surfacing and here's another testament of fact.

Recorded in 1965 during the 'Just Walk In My Shoes' period, Gladys tears up the script on this one and simply 'goes for it'. The resulting performance is awesome to say the least. Discovered by 'ace tape ferret' Chris King who should be crowned for his tenacity and passion in bringing such magnificent material to the UK. More recently there have also been a couple of versions by Brenda Holloway doing the rounds.

A word of praise to the Pips who conjure up a few precious moments in the art of background vocal styling

The Northern Soul Top 500 Special Edition

#30

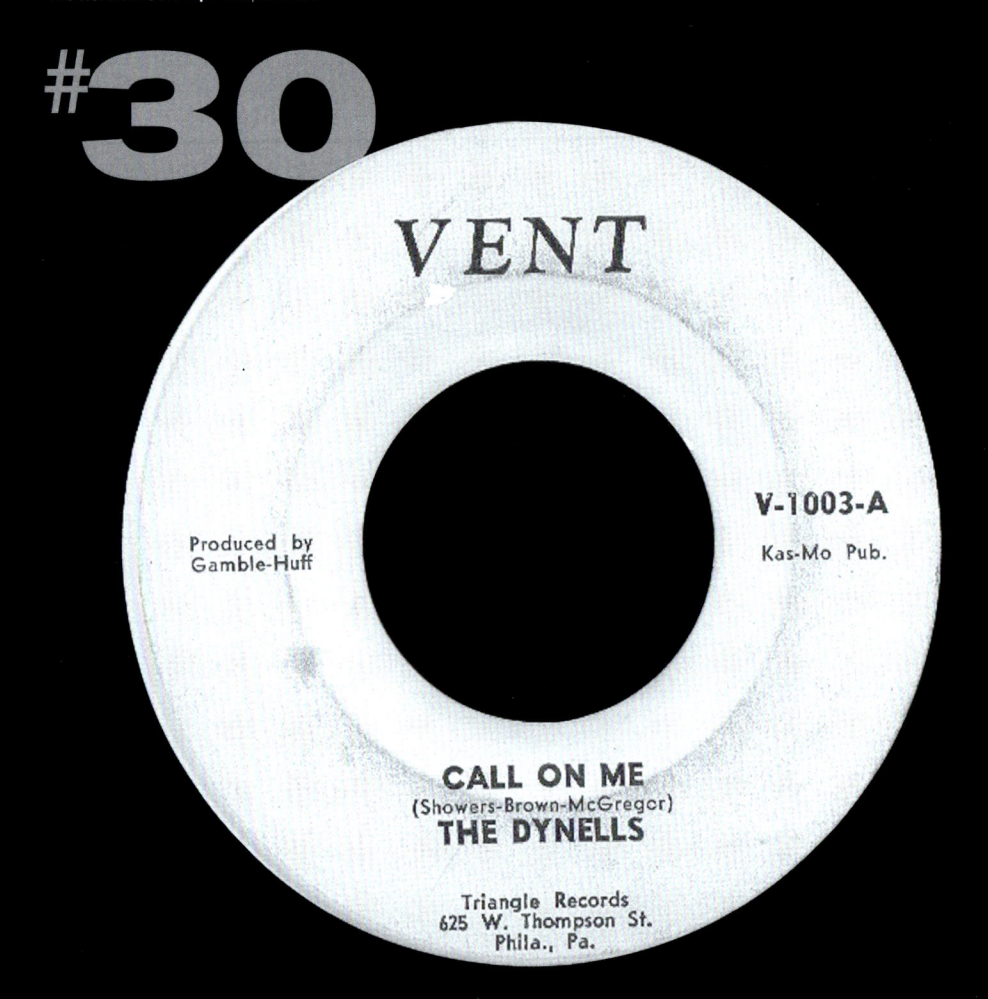

VENT

Produced by Gamble-Huff

V-1003-A
Kas-Mo Pub.

CALL ON ME
(Showers-Brown-McGregor)
THE DYNELLS

Triangle Records
625 W. Thompson St.
Phila., Pa.

Artist: **The Dynells**
Title: **Call On Me**
Label: **Vent/Atco**
Value: **£200**

'northern fused with crossover = dance floor hit'

The all-original £3 single back in the 70's finally got the breaks and sits comfortably among the new hierarchy of collectables.

Known in the trade as a 'grower', it took 25 years for the Philadelphia outfit to achieve some recognition. Originally on the local Vent label (check out the Ethics sides on the same label) the master was picked up by Atlantic for release on their Atco label.

Recorded in 1968, it's a typical group thing with the hook being sung at the end of each line. So by the time the fade out is upon us, you can't help humming the line 'Call On Me'. Simple eh!

The Northern Soul Top 500 Special Edition

#31

Artist: Brothers Guiding Light
Title: Getting Together
Label: Mercury
Value: £75

'sublime 70's mover'

A minor disco hit in the early 70's for Philly based BGT. Many copies were to be found on the East Coast. But as always, they're long gone, being snapped up by eager collectors from the UK and dance music completists worldwide.

The groove is typically Sigma, with clever vocal arrangement in a throwback to the doo-wop styling of earlier times.

Producer Bud Ross sent me the alternate take (featured on Goldmine's Northern Soul Of Philadelphia Volume 3), which sounds great too.

Group wise they need no introduction to hardened collectors, as they passed off as The Dreamlovers too, recording for Columbia, Cameo, Warner Bros and Mercury.

The Northern Soul Top 500 Special Edition

#32

Artist: **The Detroit Spinners**
Title: **I Just Want To Fall In Love**
Label: **Atlantic**
Value: **£30**

'a top tune from the 80's!'

DJ's such as Terry Jones had long championed the side on the Modern scene, however the bigger picture emerged by way of its Northern counterpart and much larger audience potential.

A Michael Zager production instantly conjures up visions of handclapping, chanting disco. Nothing could be further from the truth as the group flex vocal tissue all over a solid bass tingling East Coast sounding piece of art. The hook is solid, and it's easy to see why it was overlooked first time out. John Edwards confirming his status as a major league front man. Rap, D Train, Kashif etc were shaping up to take R'n'B to a new level, leaving the old timers just off base in slightly dated mode.

Still, better late than never!

The Northern Soul Top 500 Special Edition

#33

Artist: **Patrice Holloway**
Title: **Stolen Hours**
Label: **Capitol**
Value: **£75**

'a rich vein of form for ms. holloway'

The comments from many West Coast contacts are that Patrice should have rocketed to stardom in a key position at Motown. Certainly the CV looks impressive with fine sides for Capitol before teaming up with Charlie's Angel Cheryl Ladd for the TV group Josie and the Pussycats, as well as fronting the Belles for Mirwood.

Her backing and guide vocal studio work is second to none with producers such as Frank Wilson utilising her services at almost every opportunity.

Her sister Brenda scored at Motown while Pat languished in the reserves working on Wilson's West Coast projects like 'Lonely Boy' (backing sister Brenda), 'Keep On Rolling' and 'Touch Of Venus'.

'Stolen Hours' has surpassed the earlier discoveries such as 'Love And Desire' and 'Ecstasy', creating a real buzz for the lady's output. We know Brenda, but where's Patrice? Come on girlfriend-get in touch!

The Northern Soul Top 500 Special Edition

#34

Artist: Venecia Wilson
Title: This Time, I'll Be Lovin' You
Label: Top Top
Value: £100

'a better disguise than lon chaney'

Ian Levine roared back onto the scene amidst fury from the hardliners. Not only did he revamp many forgotten or never played first timer's, he put noses out of joint big style by first championing the equally infectious Four Vandals 'discovery' and then a '1966' obscurity by Venecia Wilson.

...Well FIRSTLY, no one had ever seen the 45 until 3 years ago. AND the label discography shows no trace either.

From a fan's point of view, the track is a delightful vocal version of a pop track on Jamie titled 'Hey Girl'. The melody is a take on Pet Clark's 'Downtown' with a sort of West Coast 60's rhythm track. Vocally, Wilson shrills through OK.

As for finding it in a used 45 store in Chicago? Stick to the CD methinks!

Shrouded in mystery - YES. Top Dancer - YES

The Northern Soul Top 500 Special Edition

#35

Artist: **Jackie Day**
Title: **Naughty Boy**
Label: **Phelectron**
Value: **£1,500**

'a rip snorting stomper'

Jackie guested on my show in 2002 and revealed the label financiers back in 1965. Why, it was none other than Johnny Cochran the famous defence lawyer behind the OJ Simpson case.

Day went on to record epic sides for Modern and Paula most of which received extensive turntable action in the early 70's.

The single must have been her debut and amazingly was our last discovery in the lady's repertoire. This must be one of the finest dancers from the West Coast with the piano led intro working off the bass drum prior to a blaze of horns and Ms.Day's echo chamber vocal. The song is fairly routine but oooo that groove. You need two cans of talc for this baby!

The Northern Soul Top 500 Special Edition

#36

Artist: **Bud Harper**
Title: **Wherever You Were**
Label: **Peacock**
Value: **£150**

'nitty gritty city soul'

Harper stood out as a magnificent vocalist 'Mr.Soul' and 'Let Me Love You'.

The revived Stafford sound 'Wherever You Were' is in keeping with today's 'R'n'B vibe'. A strong emphasis on verse and chorus, Bud checks in and out of the typical southern style rhythm of the time with a sort of Johnny Ace-meets-James Carr-meets-Joe Tex.

A superlative 45 now getting the widespread recognition it deserves.

Recorded in Houston in 1965, this release pre-dates his Twisted Wheel classic 'Mr.Soul'.

The Northern Soul Top 500 Special Edition

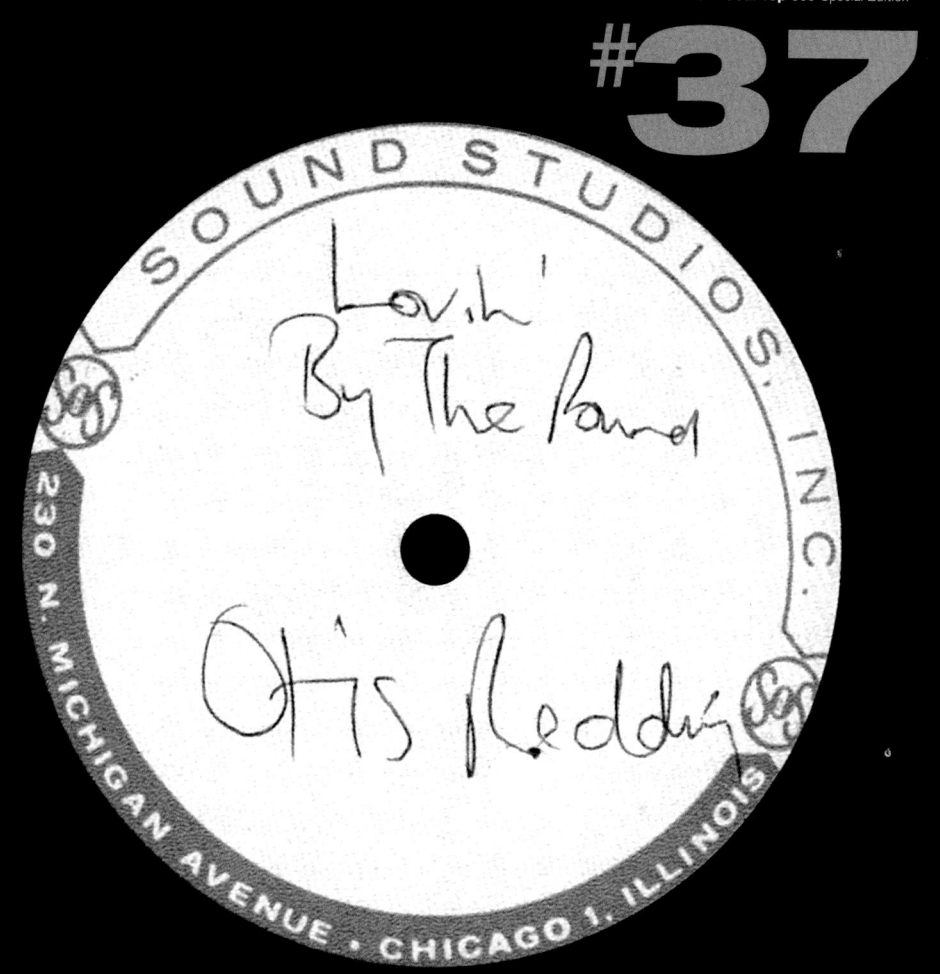

#37

Artist: **Otis Redding**
Title: **Lovin' By The Pound**
Label: **Volt CD**
Value: **£12**

'a killer from the great man'

Lost somewhere in the tape vault, this 1966 recording surfaced a few years ago on Kent's 'Do The Crossover Baby' Stax compilation - along with similar cut William Bell's 'Bark At The Moon' - prompting various DJ's to grab a slate and start working it.

You can pretty much imagine how strong it is with Otis roaring his head off on this powerhouse dancer with the usual trademarks from the Memphis Horns.

Ace records did a superb job in collating the unreleased tapes in Berkley, California shortly after Fantasy acquired the Stax deal... Just to hear Otis on a cut like this must be worth the plane fare alone!

SP. 57

The Northern Soul Top 500 Special Edition

#38

"FROM THE VAULTS" VARIOUS ARTISTS

NR 4014T1 SIDE TWO — NR 4014T1B

1. WHAT MORE COULD A BOY ASK FOR - THE SPINNERS (J. Bristol - H. Fuqua) 2:40
2. IT'S FANTASTIC - SMOKEY ROBINSON & THE MIRACLES (William Robinson - R. Rogers - W. Moore - D. Whited) 2:32
3. DROP IN THE BUCKET - MARY WELLS (William Robinson) 2:20
4. THE LONELY HEART AND LONELY EYES OF LONELY ME - GLADYS KNIGHT & THE PIPS (I. J. Hunter) 2:55
5. UNDECIDED LOVER - MARTHA REEVES & THE VANDELLAS (N. Whitfield) 2:11

℗ © 1979 Motown Record Corporation / Trademark Motown Record Corporation

Natural Sounds For Natural People — NATURAL RESOURCES

Artist: **The Detroit Spinners**
Title: **What More Can A Boy Ask For**
Label: **Motown LP**
Value: **£15**

'everything a northern fan could hope for'

If on a 45 promo and one copy known, you would be staring at 5 grand's worth of single. Quite simply, this has to be the most immaculate unreleased Motown track of the 60's.

Bobby Smith is on lead and oozes class has the group take charge of a 'this old heart of mine' meets 'i'll always love you'.

Although very available on CD and LP, who knows the heights the track would have achieved on a 45.

Remember, these were Motown's rejects, so god help the likes of The Antellects or The Dynells. Absolutely stunning!

The Northern Soul Top 500 Special Edition

#39

Artist: **Angie Stone**
Title: **I Wish I Didn't Miss You Anymore**
Label: **Arista**
Value: **£5**

'the track that changed the scene'

The Northern scene has long played new releases. Why, back in the day it was customary to play the latest Johnny Johnson or Jimmy James single.

The difference here is that Stone's take on the O'Jays' 'Back Stabbers' is aimed directly at the mainstream 'R'n'B' audience.

Pleasing though it is to hear it, I personally can't see where it fits in the 35 years of scene's history. Still, if choices must be made, I will take it any day over 3rd rate pop rarities such as Larry Trider or some of the non-descript 50's singles currently being portrayed as Northern.

Stone has since hit big time with her album and while she's hardly interested in this particular chart placing, her cool Philly vibed epic may have changed the views of hardened collectors who have difficulty coming to terms with the phrase 'by request'.

SP. 59

The Northern Soul Top 500 Special Edition

#40

Artist: **Bobby Day**
Title: **Pretty Little Girl Next Door**
Label: **RCA Victor**
Value: **£150**

'the real roots of soul coming to the fore'

Recorded around 1962, the 'Rockin' Robin' man voices a teen song with Chuck Jackson type vigour. The idea was good, but never it was destined never to win the hearts of fans of Paul Anka or Tommy Sands.

The soul content is magnificent, the beat okay and all round production is classy.

My personal feeling is that here is a sound that's 'past its sell by date'.

Championed heavily by top collector Tim Brown, the single has hero worship attached to it in many parts of the North West. However, currently plays ARE in decline and one wonders if such a rarity would have charted so high if discovered during the golden era.

The Northern Soul Top 500 Special Edition

#41

Artist: **The Tangeers**
Title: **Let Your Heart And Soul Be Free**
Label: **Okeh**
Value: **£400**

'a flip side waiting to happen'

30 years ago, 'What's The Use Of Me Trying' was a non-starter in my DJ box, very much one of the weaker Okeh singles. However market forces have changed the value considerably over the years. But, it is the wisdom of the record collector who flipped it and played the less well known side at the smaller venues that has brought it to the ultimate attention of much larger audiences.

Sources report only two singles from the group. The first being a cover of a Bacharach and David song 'This Empty Place' for Scepter and this juicy double sider for Okeh.

Now one of the rarest and in demand 45's from the legendary label, a UK limited 45 was issued by Sony as a promotional disc for their 'Best Of Soul Time' double CD, which yours truly happily compiled for them.

#42

The Northern Soul Top 500 Special Edition

Artist: Patrinell Staten
Title: A Little Love Affair
Label: Sepia
Value: £3,000

'gospel hooked crossover'

A collector's dream find as the extremely rare disc from Seattle surfaced around 5 years ago. Certainly not the most instant of dancers, the gospel roots and shuffly beat from around 1969, is a refreshing thirst quencher in the dry oasis of real Northern discoveries.

Amazingly Patrinell has been tracked down and interviewed - know doubt she was very surprised at the singles popularity - not least the price tag!

If discovered in the 70's it would have commanded no more than £50. But such is the love affair for super rare 60's discoveries that the choir member from the state of Washington enters the great hall of fame for magnificent soul failures.

The Northern Soul Top 500 Special Edition

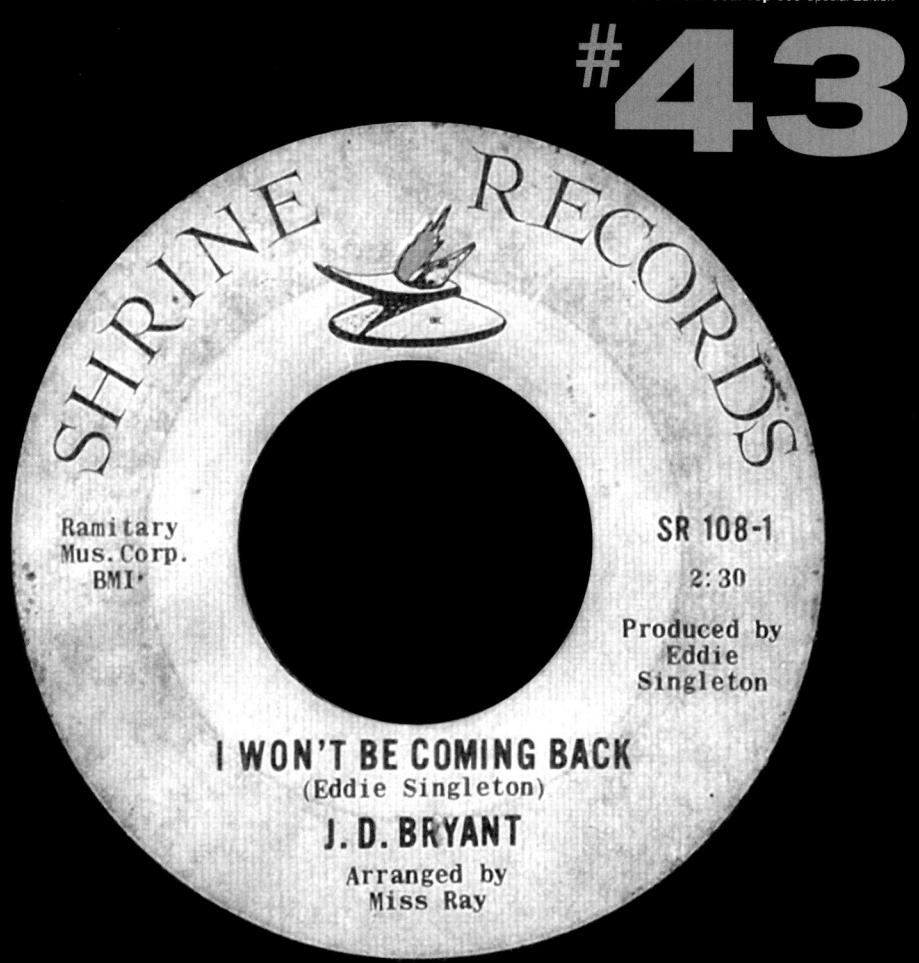

#43

Artist: JD Bryant
Title: I Won't Be Coming Back
Label: Shrine
Value: £5,000

'a super find by the author'

Back in 1982 I had returned from a 12 month stint in the US to discover to my horror that the beloved 'on the four's' stompers were a little out of style.

At the time, shortly after Wigan's final demise, the Northern scene was hanging on by a thread. Demand for the old favourites was at a standstill... Still not to worry, I had amassed more than 12,000 45's to add to my collection.

Boo-boo number one came as I allowed 'friends' Jim Wensiora and Mark 'Butch' Dobson to come over once in a while and buy or trade assorted unknowns. JW, being well aware of the new demand for big beat ballads, eyeballed Bryant's DC masterpiece and promptly paid me a smacking £125... Poor old KR, figuring it was rare - but not that wonderful, did the deal.

I originally found it in New York in 1981, and paid the princely sum of 50 cents! Amazingly I also found other killer Shrine rarities Eddie Daye, Ray Pollard and Shirley Edwards in the same load!

The Northern Soul Top 500 Special Edition

#44

Artist: **Gene Chandler**
Title: **Let Me Make Love To You**
Label: **20th Century**
Value: **£10**

'the commonest can be the best'

Chandler made a controversial appearance at the Fleetwood Weekender in 2001. His stage presence is still as good as ever but forgot most of the lyrics to one or two of his 60's Northern classics (admittedly he never performed them otherwise).

Thank heavens then for this easy to find mid-pacer from 1980. We knew it years ago, but didn't need to activate the side as we had bigger fish to fry. Still, better late than never as Gene troops on with a fabulous piece of Chicago soul that gets both scenes married off to the sunset.

Smooth as silk, as competent as you like and easy to find. That probably explains the popularity.

The Northern Soul Top 500 Special Edition

#45

Record label shown:
wand
254 W. 54 ST., NEW YORK, N.Y.
WND 1196
(61153)
Big Buck's Inc.
Our Children's (BMI)
Time: 2:14
Audio Engineer: Michael Wright
** STOP SIGN **
(M. Wynn - B. O'Connell - J. Sechleer)
MEL WYNN & THE RHYTHM ACES
Producer: Julian Gill & Bob Di Lorenzo for Hy Mizrahi Prod. Recorded At Scepter Studios, N.Y.C.

Artist: **Mel Wynn and the Rhythm Aces**
Title: **Wand**
Label: **Stop Sign**
Value: **£10**

'it's a mecca rap'

Long-time Wand also ran 'Stop Sign' has been kicking around in collectors' cheapy sales boxes forever. Never a front runner on the scene 'Stop Sign' clearly attempts to hook into New York's late 60's electric hip soul sound coming from labels like Fatback and the likes of Flame 'n' King.

In 2003 the few on the scene who would even remember this minor Mecca spin would never have expected it to return to popularity... And how were they to know that some 18 year old UK rap artist would not only heavily sample the original track but would cover it AND have a major hit with it?

How did Abs come across 'Stop Sign'? Your guess really is as good as mine.

The Northern Soul Top 500 Special Edition

#46

Artist: Etta James
Title: Seven Day Fool
Label: Argo
Value: £60

'an old-time sound deservedly receiving accolades'

Peaches rides in with a cut from her 'Second Time Around' LP which saw release in 1962. Perhaps surprisingly co-written by Berry Gordy, this basic R'n'B track, recorded for the Chess brother's Argo imprint, has caught on big style.

Born Jamsetta Hawkins in Los Angeles and world famous for her shock of peroxide hair and songs like 'Security', 'Tell Mama' and current biggie 'Mellow Fellow'.

If you are having difficulty accepting new trends within the scene, take a listen to this, ostensibly a newie it was certainly known way back in the 60s ...wild baby!

The Northern Soul Top 500 Special Edition

#47

Boss-Nova
Anthor Music
B.M.I.

Time 2:30
45 r.p.m
5001-B

My Baby's Been Cheating
(I Know)
Corthen-Neal-Coldert
A. C. Reed & His Band

produced by Colbert Productions, Chicago

Artist: **AC Reed & His Band**
Title: **My Baby Been Cheatin' I Know**
Label: **Cool**
Value: **£150**

'exceptional blues orientated stomper'

This one's 'straight outta the box' as the industry would say. A kick-ass stomper that typifies the best of Northern Soul.

Popular at Stafford and the 100 Club of the 80s, AC Reed wouldn't have been out of place at the Wheel or Torch, and while the grit out ways the smooth, Reed's delivery and enthusiasm delivers a full-on green light around the dancefloor entrance.

Recording for Nike records with a popular urban classic 'Boogaloo Tramp' Reed fell from grace in his native Chicago soon after.

The Northern Soul Top 500 Special Edition

#48

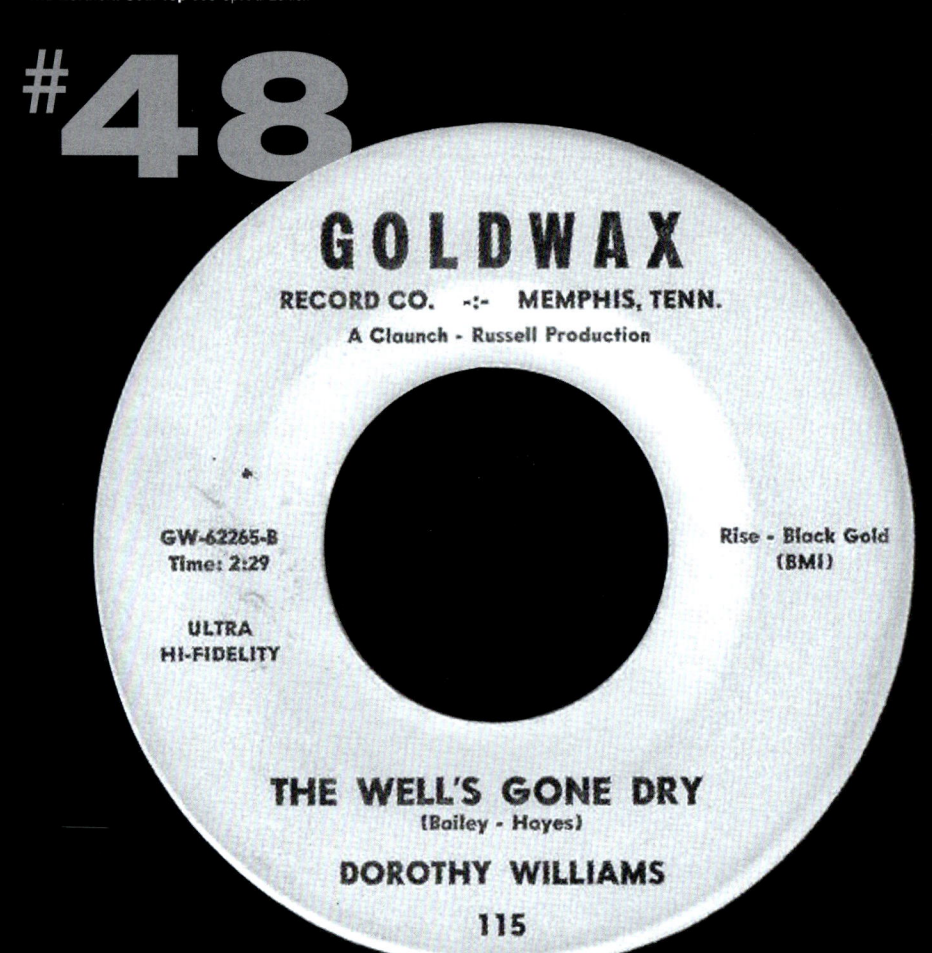

Artist: Dorothy Williams
Title: The Well's Gone Dry
Label: Goldwax/Band Box
Value: £200/£250

'rolling rhytmn and soul'

Despite being best known worldwide as the seminal Deep Soul label, Quinton Claunch's legendary Memphis based Goldwax imprint has spawned innumerable Northern legends from Quinton's protegé James Carr, the Ovations and Gospel legend OV Wright as well a more recently discovered unissued monster Spencer Wiggins' 'Let's Talk It Over' (original Top 500 #264).

Goldwax is best known on our scene for hard edged R'n'B Club classics like 'That's What I Want To Know' (original Top 500 #267), and though in a similar vein 'The Well's Gone Dry' is rather more of a roller than the rest making it a great dancer.

A well known item amongst R'n'B collectors for some years now, this blue label release is yet another once cheap track that has seen its dancefloor popularity drive the price skyward.

The Northern Soul Top 500 Special Edition

#49

Artist: Bobby Reed
Title: The Time Is Right For Love
Label: Bell
Value: £700

'a double sided spectacular'

Reed first surfaced in the mid 60's on Eddie Singleton's legendary Shrine label. The unreleased material is of particular interest with 'You Are' a neat local release from 1967 that got a national release on Brunswick a close second.

With a career almost over as early as 1967 Reed kept a door knockin' finally securing a one off deal in 1972 with Bell.

The resulting session spawned two classics. The 'Time Is Right' backed with 'If I Don't Love You'. With the emerging Modern scene stealing a march, its elder brother has adopted the side into the Northern family.

This one no longer needs a chewy rusk, more a juicy steak. A different, but brilliant rarity.

The Northern Soul Top 500 Special Edition

#50

Artist: Sidney Joe Qualls
Title: I Don't Do This
Label: 20th Century LP
Value: £40

'the chicago soulster hits the mark'

Originally on LP before a limited UK release from Expansion finally made it available to a much wider audience. As with many of the Top 500, this Chicago recording first found a home on the Modern soul dancefloors.

A track of long standing popularity, eventually the groove has found favour on Northern dancefloors and achieving legendary status ever since. The 7" re-issue certainly helped this Joe Tex-ish bounder, as horns and bass line bubble along in the backing. Qualls is responsible for several other goodies too, most notably for Dakar.

The sound seems to be here to stay, and while the likes of April Stevens are confined to the local gig, this has serious longevity.

The Northern Soul Top 500 Special Edition

#51

- Artist: **Sam Moore**
- Title: **Plenty Good Lovin'**
- Label: **Expansion**
- Value: **£6**

'wow, a stunning unreleased tape'

One half of the famed battlers 'Sam and Dave', Mr Moore hoped to revitalise his career with a stunning album recorded in 1970... At the time though it never saw the light of day.

Finally getting an outing in 2002 the album contained 'Plenty Good Lovin'' which is quite simply a classic! A conga led intro sets the stage before the backing vocals weave in and out, leading into a wonderful mid to up tempo soul sensation.

Perfect for radio, clubs and bar mitzvahs. Moore proves what 'carrying a song' is all about. He squeals in all the right places as the song works up to a crescendo finish.

The good folks at Expansion stayed ahead of the game by releasing a vinyl 7", which has further added to the popularity.

The Northern Soul Top 500 Special Edition

#52

Artist: **The Jokers**
Title: **Soul Sound**
Label: **Sko-field**
Value: **£600**

'stomping - but a 'soul sound'?...'

A fairly typical 'where the hell did this one come from' side, that often surprises the fringe Northern soul fan. First breaking big a few years ago, this sound remain very popular indeed the North West courtesy of DJ's Ginger Taylor and Terry Davies.

My own personal view is one of sheer anguish! The recording is shallow and uneventful and I have to say one of the worst singles known to man!

...But apart from that, it's bloody well HUGE!

The Northern Soul Top 500 Special Edition

#53

MIDAS

Vapac Music
B.M.I.

Time 2:40
45 rpm

I'm A Big Man
V. Rice
Big Daddy Rogers
9006

Artist: **Big Daddy Rogers**
Title: **I'm A Big Man**
Label: **Midas**
Value: **£150**

'just what did the daddy mean by "drop a couple of planks on you"?'

First played on the Mod scene of the mid 80s, this powerhouse R'n'B outing laced with wailing horns and suitably salacious lyrics is a cracker.

Championed by Mark 'Big Daddy' Bicknell following a triumphal first play at Hinckley around 1990, its popularity and price tag has grown inexorably.

This is a brilliant peace of Windy City Rhythm 'n' Soul from the same stable as the Inspirations' 'Your Wish Is My Command'.

Once a £15 sound - if ever there was case for buying Northern Soul as an investment then this is it!

#54

Artist: **Channel 3**
Title: **The Sweetest Thing**
Label: **Dakar**
Value: **£150**

'a perfect investment'

We bought it as a new release and no doubt re-sold the group gem several years later, citing that Northern was in decline... Dumb move brother, it's rarer than we thought and perfect for today's split scene.

Channel 3 consisted of former members of local groups such like The Ideals and the Notations, and was led by Jerome Johnson.

Male harmony leads the song down a fresh Windy City road, never once stopping at the 7-11 for a pit stop. A mega spin constantly in focus, the one time low-ball investment has matured handsomely and is helping many owner cash in a very valuable piece of stock.

The Northern Soul Top 500 Special Edition

#55

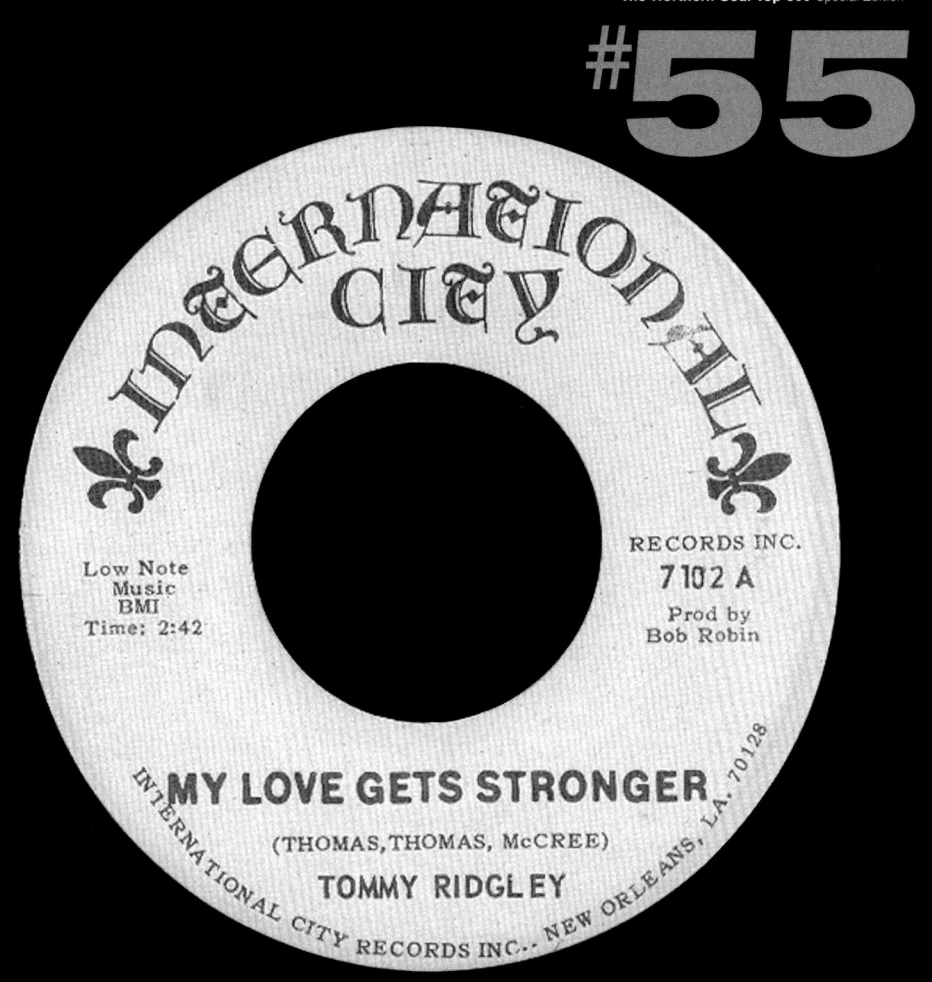

Artist: **Tommy Ridgely**
Title: **My Love Is Getting Stronger**
Label: **International City**
Value: **£750**

'long time grower hits its peak'

New Orleans has played a major role in Northern. Mostly, the grooves have a gritty edge as opposed to a smoother sound of say Detroit or Los Angeles.

Ridgley's low key outing was spun by a variety of first wavers in the 70's. It really failed on the big stage. But as the 22 carat stuff dried up, it re-appeared as a solid bona fide rare 'un. Girls and more girls weave in the chorus with Tommy boy delivering tuneful, memorable verses too.

His career never took off and tried everything in his early years recording for local labels Ric and River City.

One can imagine him as the local bar singer in the French Quarter, with record execs signing him every 2 or 3 years. Judging by his delayed output of releases, which certainly would answer a few anorak type questions.

#56

The Northern Soul Top 500 Special Edition

Artist: **Bill Harris**
Title: **Am I Cold, Am I Hot**
Label: **RCA**
Value: **£150**

'van mc coy reigns supreme'

A pleasurable experience anytime listening to a VM disco track with soulful roots. Without wishing to show my age, I remember the track being played on WWRL the big AM Urban station in New York as a new release.

'Am I Cold' boasts long-standing popularity on the scene and Harris also scored with 'Uptown Saturday Night' for Warner Bros. But this sublime tale of 'never knowing where a guy stands' is executed perfectly by a very under estimated singer. Van's trademarks are all in place, and one wonders if Faith, Hope and Charity or even the Stylistics have cut a version.

Played during the famous last hour at Blackpool Mecca in the mid 70's, the 45 got revived a decade or so ago, and has moved along nicely ever since.

The Northern Soul Top 500 Special Edition

#57

Artist: **The Four Tracks**
Title: **Like My Love For You**
Label: **Mandingo**
Value: **£700**

'moving up to the heavyweight division'

DJ's and collectors fall in love when confronted by an obscurity such as this.

The song is good, vocal remarkably sounding like a youthful Carl Carlton, with a back beat that 'gets the night going'. First spun in the early 70s by Les Cokell to total disinterest and hideously under valued in the early 80's, I had the misfortune to let go of 'known investment'.

Thankfully it gets better with every play. And one that gets regular workout in most major Northern cities. The flip side is the oddly titled 'Voo Doo Man'

The Northern Soul Top 500 Special Edition

#58

THINK IT OVER BABY
(Billy Jackson)
GROOVETTES
and THE BOB REED ORQUESTRA
Prod. by B. Reed & U. Dozier

Artist: **The Groovettes**
Title: **Think It Over Baby**
Label: **Reness**
Value: **£1500**

'a serious rarity from la'

Finally getting the recognition it deserves...

This Los Angeles pounder from 1966 sees another hopeful girl group aided by the great Bob Reed's significant orchestral arrangement.

'Think It Over Baby' first came to the attention of serious collectors and soul fans in the early 80's. However whilst it became a popular spin in the south, due to the masses vacating the movement during that decade and its incredible rarity, the track failed to achieve the status.

Reed himself has been contacted directly by several 'dealers' during the last 10 years enquiring about this cut... I wonder why!

The Northern Soul Top 500 Special Edition

#59

Artist: **Jimmy Bo Horne**
Title: **I Can't Speak**
Label: **Dade**
Value: **£800**

'spanking great crossover'

Henry Stone's Dade label functioned locally in the Miami area for many years. The early days produced acts like Nat Kendricks and the Swans who found fame on the scene with 'I Can't See Him Again' notoriously mis-spelt as the Twans.

Horne and Stone stayed together successfully throughout the 70's. But the real collectable is the 1968 recording on the famous label named after Florida's Dade county.

Smooth as you like, the accepted tempo entices the shufflers to hip jiggle while poring scorn on beer towels ad backdrops. So... when will we hear S&M disco classic 'Spank' being spun?

SP. 79

The Northern Soul Top 500 Special Edition

#60

expansion

Side B
LP EXP 4

SOUL CHASERS
VARIOUS ARTISTS
1. VALERIE CARTER - TRYING TO GET TO YOU (4.08)
(E. Record) Produced by James Newton Howard
Publisher: Rondor Music (London) Ltd. ℗ 1978 Sony Music Entertainment Inc. Licensed courtesy of Sony Music
2. GLORIA SCOTT - (A CASE OF) TOO MUCH LOVE MAKIN' (3.51)
(Tom Brock) Produced by Barry White
Publisher: January Music Corp./Sa-Vette Music (BMI)
℗ 1974 Casablanca Records Inc. Licensed courtesy of Polygram Special Products
3. COLLINS AND COLLINS - TOP OF THE STAIRS (4.38)
(Nickolas Ashford/Valerie simpson) Produced by John Davis
for Palm Music/Monster Productions Inc.
Publisher: Island Music Ltd.
℗ 1980 A&M Records Inc. Licensed courtesy of A&M Records Ltd.
4. HIGH FASHION - I WANT TO BE YOUR EVERYTHING (3.35)
(Kashif/G. Ballard) Produced by Jaques Fred Petrus/Mauro Malawski
Publisher: MCA Music Ltd.
℗ 1982 Capitol Records Inc.
Licensed courtesy of EMI Records UK
33 rpm

Artist: **Gloria Scott**
Title: **A Case Of Too Much Of Lovemaking**
Label: **Casablanca**
Value: **£100**

'great songs are still in style'

Scott was signed to the late Neil Bogart's Casablanca imprint. A few minor plays on 'What Am I Gonna Do' was about it.

But tucked neatly away on her album, is a tremendous song that scores instantly. A long orchestral intro quivers, before Scott sweetly purrs over the big LA production. Undoubtedly Lisa Stansfield's cover version, a massive hit, has been key in ressurecting the popularity of this widely CD reissued track.

Released as a seven inch in Australia, the song has become so popular of late that cover versions are springing up faster than kangaroos at Wigan pier.

The Northern Soul Top 500 Special Edition

#61

Artist: **Paul Thompson**
Title: **Special Kind Of Woman**
Label: **Stax**
Value: **£1000**

'the rarest stax release?'

Long known and popular with collectors and 'connoisseurs', Paul Thompson's 1970 release epitomises the term 'Cross Over'.

Discovered by DJ Richard Searling, 'Special Kind Of Woman' is arguably the rarest Stax release - certainly the most sought after, today its massive popularity has driven the cost of an always pricey record right through the roof... On paper around a £1000 - you still have to FIND a copy for sale!

A typically Muscle Shoals lazy beat and comfortable style DID hold this back from full dancefloor popularity in the past, but changing tastes post millennium definitely approve of the track today.

By the way has anyone else noticed the startling similarity between Paul Thompson's and Eddie Holland's voice?

#62

The Northern Soul Top 500 Special Edition

Artist: **The Magnetics**
Title: **I Have A Girl**
Label: **Ra-Sel**
Value: **£2,000**

'an outstanding philly walloper'

Detroit influenced many Philadelphia soul sides. Harthon and Arctic are just two labels that locked in their production teams to the conveyer belt of success. Others simply had a stab themselves and invariably failed.

The Magnetics (no relation to the Detroit or Chicago groups of the same name) found themselves studio bound in 1965. Virtue cut many aspiring singers. And the group and label must have 'champed at the bit'after the final mix down.

Well-produced, sterling vocals, harmonies chanting 'yeah yeah' throughout.

Wow, this is fantastic.

The Northern Soul Top 500 Special Edition

#63

Artist: **The Springers**
Title: **Nothing's Too Good For My Baby**
Label: **Wale**
Value: **£3,000**

'top class sixties soul, that's hard to beat'

Following on from the Magnetics, you can almost play these back to back. That is, if you have five grand!

Thadeus Wales was a local Philly entrepreneur looking for the 'American dream'. The group doubled as The Ethics ('Look At Me Now') on the Vent label but this is by far their rare masterpiece.

Harmony led, the front man peeps out from the shadows briefly to inject additional life into a regular up-tempo beat. And while the song falls way short commercially, the whole experience is tailor made for us.

You can imagine Wales moving house and dumping 487 of the 45s in the dumpster. Then being asked 'what was in those boxes', only to holler across the street, 'oh I made a record once'. A reply was heard, 'did it ever sell'? 'yeah in another life', Thadeus replied!

A regular play for 20 years now, the single has deservedly charted - at last.

The Northern Soul Top 500 Special Edition

#64

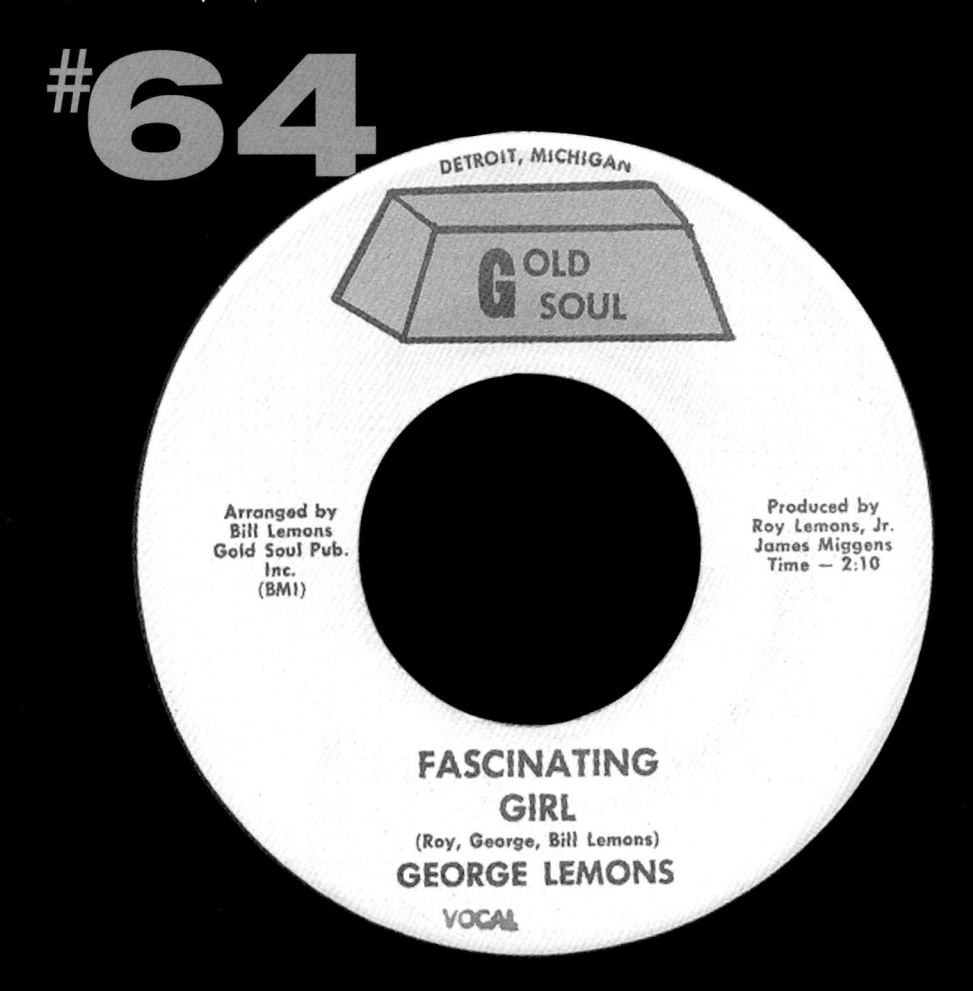

Artist: George Lemons
Title: Fascinating Girl
Label: Gold Soul
Value: £1,000

'this michigan mover delights'

A single I had as early as 1978, complete with business card inserted into the sleeve! Yeah, of course I called up only to receive the usual 'the number you are dialling has been connected'. Drat and triple drat!

Lemons a local Detroit singer, tried his hand at being an entrepreneur. Generally peaking in the mid 80's, the obscurity has being holding its own ever since.

Sadly the disc sank quickly, leaving us unsatisfied. George had entered the Northern soul arena like a pimp with the best hooker on the block. We pull out our 200 dollars only to see the babe withdrawn 'from sale'.

A stonking good effort from the man.

The Northern Soul Top 500 Special Edition

#65

Hillary-Marsupial (BMI) (45-LBJ-610)
PROMOTIONAL COPY

783
Time 2:00
Arr. by Jack Eskew
NOT FOR SALE

GONE WITH THE WIND IS MY LOVE
(L. Barreto)
RITA & THE TIARAS
Prod. by Louis Barreto & Rod Baumgardner

Artist: **Rita and the Tiaras**
Title: **Gone With Wind Is My Love**
Label: **Dore**
Value: **£400**

'massively revived and just as good as ever'

Huge for a couple of years at the end of the 70's, this LA produced Dore release is a Motownesque ditty effectively overslept for the next 20 years.

Finally awakening as an 'underplayed oldie' the single took on a new meaning to jocks and collectors. The dust was wiped away from this rare platter and the vibey intro got the auditoriums rocking once again. A haunting melody sets the scene for a song that Martha Reeves might have recorded and never released.

A slower version by Betty Willis exists too, proving someone had faith in the song at least. As for the UK, we prefer the whole package that is seriously old school.

The Northern Soul Top 500 Special Edition

#66

LEAVE ME ALONE
(Weiss, Edwards Jnr, Maurer)

SUE 790
SR 790-01
TM Music
BMI
3:30
A "JUGGY"
PRODUCTION
FOR PROMOTIONAL
USE ONLY

BABY WASHINGTON

MFG. BY SUE RECORDS, INC., N.Y.

Artist: **Baby Washington**
Title: **Leave Me Alone**
Label: **Sue**
Value: **£75**

'justine hits yet again'

Justine 'Baby' Washington (who also uses the stage name Jeanette) was born in Bamberg, South Carolina around 1940. She soon moved to New York, and started her recording career whilst still at High School in 1956.

Baby Washington has been responsible for many great R'n'B sides for ABC, J&S and of course Sue - as well as recording classics like 'That's How Heartaches Are Made' and the original version of 'I Can't Wait Until I See My Baby's Face'.

'Leave Me Alone' has reached an amazing level of popularity, given that for many a collector it is not only a second rate R'n'B spin but is also a second rate Baby Washington cut too.

The Northern Soul Top 500 Special Edition

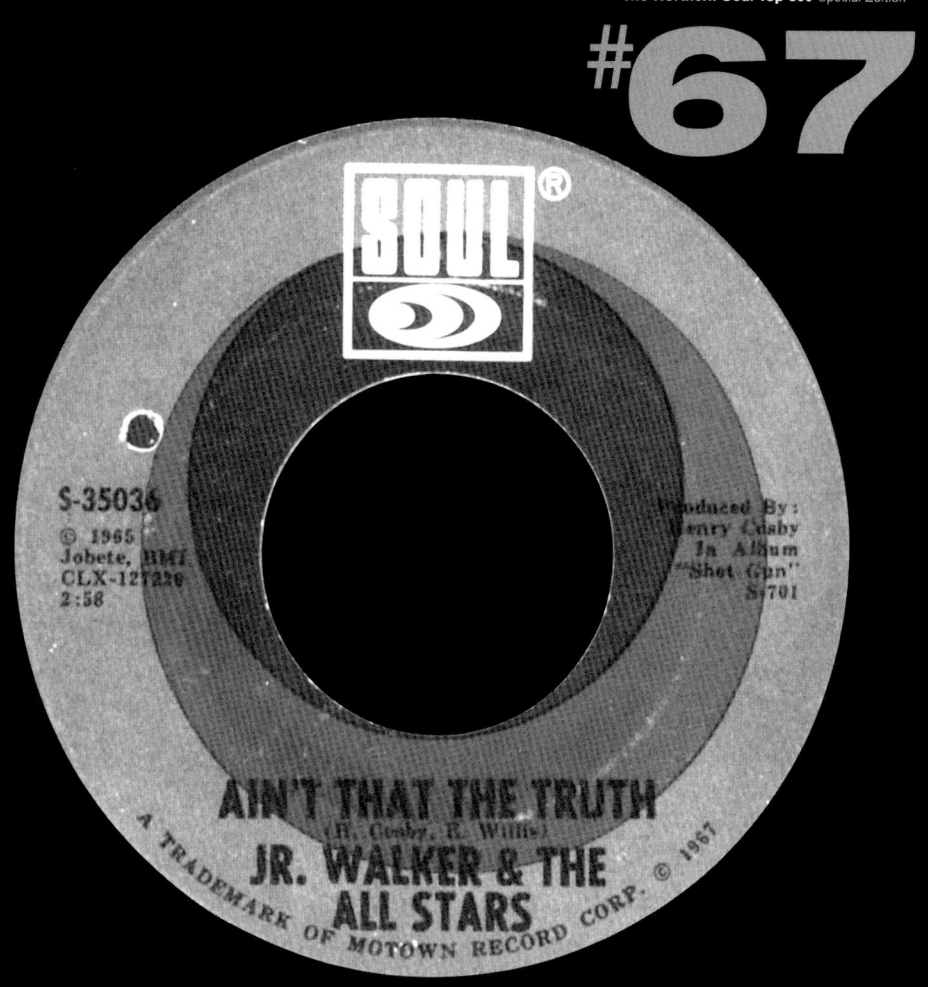

#67

Artist: **Junior Walker an the All Stars**
Title: **Ain't That The Truth**
Label: **Soul**
Value: **£25**

'rockin' sax classic'

Culled from his vast catalogue, Autry De Walt from Battle Creek, Michigan accepts centre stage for one of the groups more raucous efforts.

Staying just behind Edwin Starr and Major Lance in the all time 'UK's best live performances', Walker blows his horn right at us with the chanting 'truth'adding more grits to the otherwise hearty breakfast.

For years it remained the proverbial £5 sound languishing on the B side of 'Shoot Your Shot' before the North West continued his 'Tune Up' revival with this solid non-hit from Motown.

The Northern Soul Top 500 Special Edition

#68

Artist: **Elbie Parker**
Title: **Please Keep Away From Me**
Label: **Veep**
Value: **£300**

'that elbie's been big darn sarf for years mate'

A true icon of the scene, Parker's effort for UA subsidiary Veep has been a standout for nigh on two decades. Not too many singles from this period give us the hook first line: this does, and helps establish a cruising course for the next 2 minutes.

Championed by DJ's such as Mark Bicknell this is a cut of long standing popularity in the South.

The record is a juicy slab of 1966 soul with the unknown Parker getting a one shot deal at making something happen... Well it failed, except for pockets of allnight dancing offering a warm bed for the night.

The Northern Soul Top 500 Special Edition

#69

Artist: **The Volumes**
Title: **Ain't Gonna Give You Up**
Label: **Karen**
Value: **£300**

'ollie mc laughlin can rest easy'

One of the last releases from McLaughlin's classic Karen imprint, Detroit's the Volumes connect with a mid pace chugger from 1970. The group had been the pride of Detroit's unsung heroes during the 60's, with outings on Chex, Jubilee, Astra, Twirl, Inferno, American Arts and Impact. The group remained the same throughout, with Ed Union on lead.

Sometimes eroniously claimed to also be the Detroit Magnetics, rumours persistently swing to the direction of Motown as to a 'session or two', we have no confirmed recordings though at this time.

As dance styles change, top-notch tackle such as this gets a welcoming from all serious purveyors of quality soul. The Volumes were absolutely ACE!

The Northern Soul Top 500 Special Edition

#70

Artist: **Nino Tempo & 5th Avenue Sax**
Title: **Sister James**
Label: **A&M**
Value: **£40**

'april stevens' brother finally hits the northern soul scene'

The scene continues its foray into 'lost hits' - the North West has been the prime mover in popularising this minor hit from 1974.

Nino was born Antonio Lo Tempio in Niagra Falls, New York and achieved considerable success stateside both as a session Saxman for Phil Spector and with sister April 'Wanting You' Stevens, however his solo success didn't come to the 70's, 'Sister James' being a very popular sound in US nightclubs and discos of the time.

At long last DJs are looking to better the quality and more accessible tracks (often on major labels) rather than the frequently sub-standard, yet ultra-rare 1960s cuts that change hands for thousands.

The Northern Soul Top 500 Special Edition

#71

Milestone
MILESTONE RECORDS INC., NEW YORK 10036

PROMOTION COPY
Time—1:55
Amestoy (BMI)
produced by
ALBERT MARX
Productions

7-107-B
(M-45-014)
vocal, with orchestra conducted by PHIL MOORE III

TELL ME, BABY
(Brooks)
KARMELLO BROOKS

Artist: **Karmello Brooks**
Title: **Tell Me Baby**
Label: **Milestone**
Value: **£600**

'northern meets a jazz tingler'

California based Brooks finds the unlikely home of Northern Soul for the incredibly poor selling 'Tell Me Baby'. Released on Jazz label Milestone and obviously better placed on an album, the cut surfaced by the alternative London market that tends to pour scorn on the 'great' oldies.

But with material like this does make a refreshing change. The scarce single, championed by Carl Fortnum, is classy but difficult to dance to, however maybe the tide has turned to welcome the unusual to the scene.

The Northern Soul Top 500 Special Edition

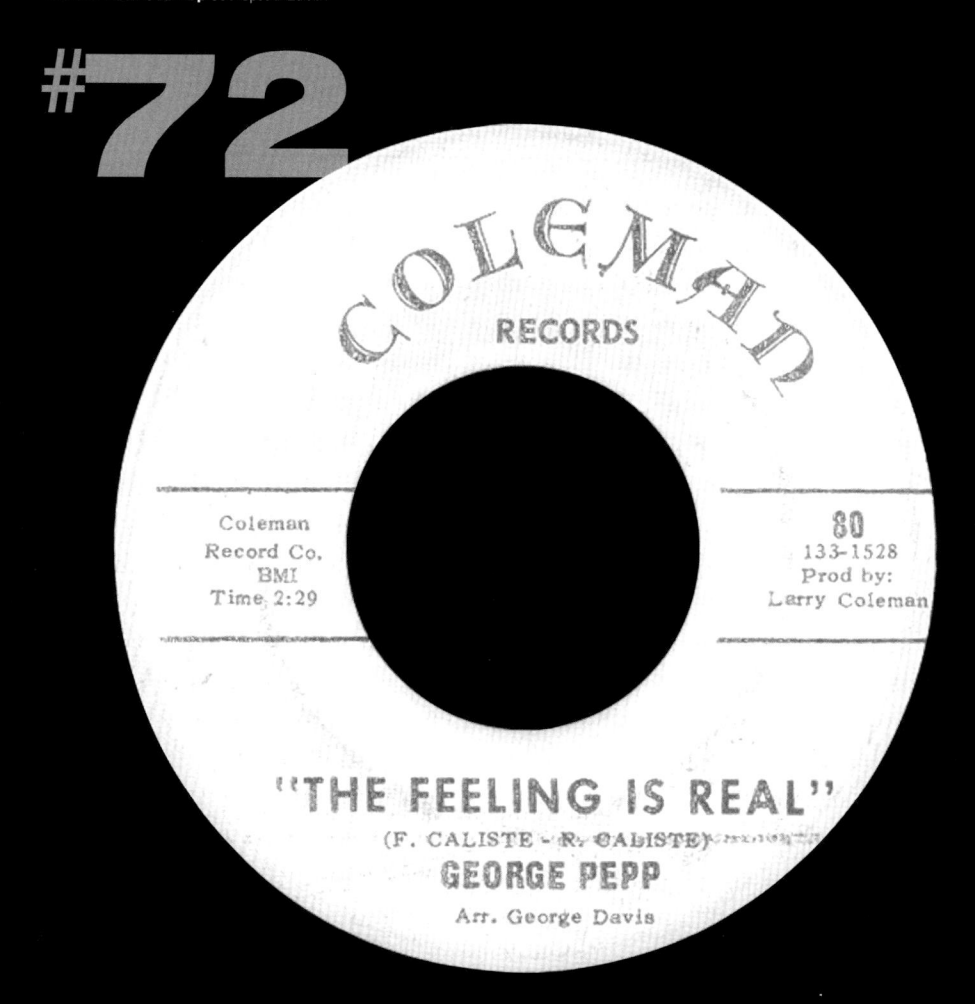

#72

Artist: **George Pepp**
Title: **This Feeling Is Real**
Label: **Coleman**
Value: **£1,500**

'vinyl junkie heaven'

Another ridiculously obscure waxing from New Orleans that captures the very essence of top drawer beat ballads.

Due to the lack of availability of the 45, 'The Feeling Is Real' has taken some time to seep through to mass popularity.

However today no self respecting DJ can enter a top class arena without a Kurt Harris, Roy Hamilton, Lou Johnson and George Pepp somewhere in 'the box'.

The Northern Soul Top 500 Special Edition

#73

Artist: **Walter and the Admerations**
Title: **Man-O-Man (What Have I Done)**
Label: **La-Cindy**
Value: **£1,000**

'a storming old-time northern stomper'

This is a s storming cut that's the B-side of big Wigan Casino spin 'Life Of Tears'. 'Man Oh Man (What Have I Done)' is a cracking old-school Northern track that was strangely neglected in the past... However today this monster spin packs the floor whenever it is played.

Walter and the Admerations are a rather mysterious bunch - with nothing concrete known about the group - the record was released on La-Cindy, the same label that brought us Ernest Mosely's 'Stubborn Heart' (owned by Windy City man Eddie LaShea), though there is of course no guarantee of this and rumours abound that they in fact became Uni label soldier boys 'The Green Berets'.

The Northern Soul Top 500 Special Edition

#74

Artist: **Patti Austin**
Title: **(I've Given) All My Love**
Label: **Coral**
Value: **£200**

'finally reaching dizzy heights'

Overshadowed by 'Take Away The Pain Stain' during Volume 1's countdown, Austin (16 at the time!) marvels with another superb 1966 production from Decca staff member Dick Jacobs.

The workout is slick, as you would expect from a major label with Patti's youthfulness roaring through to the finish line.

You can dance or simply hold a drink in one hand and finger snap with the other. Always superb, the 70's spun many sounds by Ms. Austin but missed out on this classy gem, simply by being in the right place and wrong time.

Goddaughter of Quincy Jones, she started it all off at the age of 4 at the Apollo Theatre, New York.

The Northern Soul Top 500 Special Edition

#75

Artist: Moses Smith
Title: Try My Love
Label: Jamie
Value: £25

'a legendary act resurfaces'

We often wonder what happened to acts that made that one monumental Northern side and then disappeared. Well here's one that got stuck on the tape spool and no one ever bothered to promo it!

If discovered 30 years ago, Smith's former monster may have not reached the heights it has. The problem is the recording. It's almost too good. The stereo effect on the CD nullifies the track's true potential. Recorded in 1967 as part of his deal with Gilda Woods' Dionn label. Jamie records sadly mishandled the promotion of the song, by handing it to collectors instead of DJ's.

The potential was there from the get-go but CD's don't cut it like vinyl, so we are left with a fantastic track in the 'almost'category. Still, top drawer tackle.

SP. 95

The Northern Soul Top 500 Special Edition

#76

Artist: **Soul Bros Inc**
Title: **Pyramid**
Label: **Golden Eye**
Value: **£200**

'the all-original obscurity'

A variety of groups masqueraded as the Soul Bros. Inc. Combos recording for Salem, CUR, SBI and Emblem are just some with the world's most un-original name.

This group are from California, and obviously put their life savings in, as one side's a vocal and the oddly named 'Capricorn XL2' instrumental occupies the flip.

Discovered in the 80's and working its way up the pay scale nicely, the weird 45 has peaked with an enjoyable top 100 placing.

The Northern Soul Top 500 Special Edition

#77

- Artist: **Danny White**
- Title: **Keep My Woman Home**
- Label: **Atlas**
- Value: **£30**

'the old school returns'

One of the very finest Soul/R'n'B workouts from the very early days of the scene. The late Roger Eagle and London counterpart Guy Stevens were key players in launching this magnificent side from 1965.

Released here on Sue (courtesy of label manager Stevens), the single long remained of fringe interest to 'Northern' collectors, until that is, the new wave of collectors sought to 'bring it home'.

Charting in the US, the 'Cracked Up Over You' man paints a work of art with the biggest hog's hairbrush he could find. If you are starting out on the scene or revisiting, check this stormer out at your earliest opportunity!

The NORTHERN SOUL TOP 500 Special Edition

#78

Artist: **Dottie and Millie**
Title: **Talkin' About My Baby**
Label: **Topper**
Value: **£300**

'another dave hamilton special'

A recently spun ditty from Dave Hamilton's 60's Topper label that was unplayed cheapy for years.

Pure sugary Detroit! A personal dislike - it quite simply pales when compared to legendary stablemates Tobi Lark (Legend) and Little Ann - but the disc is definitely on the up, as the insatiable chorus ripples through around two and a half minutes of a major back beat and legendary producer Dave Hamilton's carefully crafted horn arrangements.

A little on the twee side for me, this single is white hot today.

The Northern Soul Top 500 Special Edition

#79

Artist: **Barbara Lynn**
Title: **Trying To Love Two**
Label: **Ichiban**
Value: **£40**

'even a cover is good value from the lady'

When William Bell recorded the original version, it felt so good one could never imagine a cover, except for maybe a cover by Faith No More or other Rock gods.

Imagine our delight upon hearing the song again, this time a decade or so later than Atlanta's favourite soulster. Barb wastes no time in working the irresistible hook - 'trying to love two, sure ain't easy to do'. The song could have been recorded in any decade and is 'ready made' for urban living.

The left handed guitar works a treat as anyone who has seen her perform it can testify. Destined for classic status, what it lacks in romper value of 'movin on a groove' makes up the shortfall with a breezy, emotional soul trip Texan style.

The Northern Soul Top 500 Special Edition

#80

NU-TONE RECORDS

Mecosta Music
BMI - 2:30

1211
Produced by
Duane Johnson

YOU CAN'T GO
(L. Duggan)
LONNIE LESTER
210

Artist: **Lonnie Lester**
Title: **You' Can't Go**
Label: **Nu-Tone**
Value: **£80**

'cookin the grits
to perfection'

Chicago is the base for a neat blues and soul workout from two single man Lester. He worked with Chuck Danzy on a fairly common 45 before going solo on this impressive number 80.

From the opening line of 'wait a minute baby' you know the guy means business. And totally in keeping with the dance floor, the performance reigns supreme, challenging the 2nd division players such as Bobby McClure, Rodger Collins etc to the play offs.

What surprises us, is the total lack of support from the record company, as one would expect this to have gained a lot of airplay in the mid-60's. Still it's the US loss and this cut which has been around since the 70s, seeing its first real popularity at Stafford, is our gain.

The Northern Soul Top 500 Special Edition

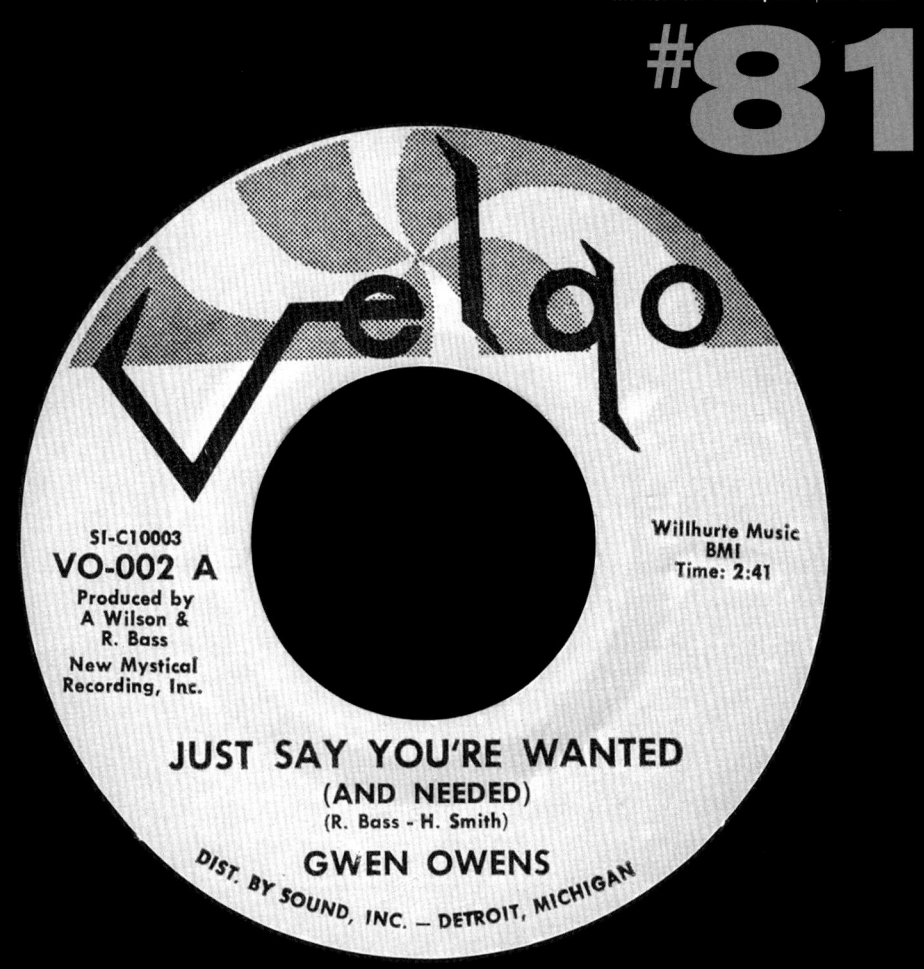

#81

Artist: **Gwen Owens**
Title: **Just Say You're Wanted And Needed**
Label: **Velgo**
Value: **£800**

'amazingly missed in volume 1'

With so many to compile in my first effort, it comes as no surprise that certain evergreens were overlooked initially and have rallied themselves and ready to stamp their delayed authority.

A corking Detroit dancer from 1966 released on Larry Lick's Velgo imprint.

Owens was 15 at the time and recorded one other single on the same label. She finally resurfaced in 1974 after moving to LA, with another 'dance hit' by way of 'You Better Watch Out'.

Many of the initial pressings are faulty with a serious skip towards the fade out. That probably explains the withdrawal and extreme rarity - to top that off there is a white DJ copy in circulation. Don't even ask the price!

Gwen was in the UK recently, and coupled with our entry to Volume 2, 2003 looks brighter for Ms. Owens.

The Northern Soul Top 500 Special Edition

#82

Artist: **The Originals**
Title: **Don't Stop Now**
Label: **Motown LP**
Value: **£20**

'finally acknowledged as a true classic'

When DJ Richard Searling did the unbelievable and brought his favourite act to the UK to celebrate his 50th birthday, the scene refreshed itself with a deeper look at this incredible group's output.

Led by Freddie Gorman they released their first single 'Good Night Irene' in 1966. Most group members, which included Ty Hunter at various times, had either been solo or worked in other bands. The final success of this revived 'Portrait' album track from Marvin's favourite group is very much down to the band's UK champion Richard S.

The group is also distinguished in having performed on Frank Wilson's last Motown production project - the multi-million selling 'Down To Love Town' - an all-time disco classic.

Soft and gentle intro with an almost fairy tale type theme, the track kicks in with those enormous harmonies. The hook is great and with Crathman 'CP' Spencer's controlled lead, the all round production is exquisite.

This should have been a 45 for the 'Soupy Sales'!

The Northern Soul Top 500 Special Edition

#83

Artist: **The Futures**
Title: **Party Time Man**
Label: **Philadelphia International**
Value: **£100**

'rising from the ashes of the misplaced 70's'

OK so you bought it as a new release... The problem though, was that you flogged it for a couple of quid coz nobody daring to play it, until now.

The track is immaculate and full of Sigma Sound's tricks of the trade. Frank Washington leads the group into a Trammps type performance with vocals flying all over the final mix down.

Released in 1978, it just wasn't quite disco enough and pre-jazz funk. And with Northern on its way out, the little devil to go.

Still, the long lost stray as been found, fed and watered, and booming out of a set of Peavey speakers at a gig near you!

The Northern Soul Top 500 Special Edition

#84

Achievement RECORDS

SIDE 1
Stereo
45 RPM

ART 10011

TALK OF THE GRAPEVINE
(I. Levine, J.J. Barnes, S. Wagner)
JJ BARNES
© Kastlekat Music/Warner Chappell/Jayfunk Music ASCAP
Produced and Arranged by Ian Levine and Clive Scott
for Tropicana Holdings (Bahamas) Ltd © 1989
Licensed from Tropicana Holdings (Bahamas) Ltd
Distributed by Goldmine/Soul Supply Ltd

Artist: **JJ Barnes**
Title: **Talk Of The Grapevine**
Label: **Achievement**
Value: **£5**

'the very regional of regional'

Recorded in the 80's and then re-mixed just pre-millennium using a Johnny Wyatt take off, this 45 from Ian Levine is certainly tailor made for dancers.

No its not worth very much, but this is strictly for dancers only.

JJ is accomplished in his delivery and there's more than enough enthusiasm from singer and producer to generate a feel good session.

Super big in the East Midlands and spitefully overlooked by parts of the North West due to the disrespect of the producer himself. A travesty of justice!

The Northern Soul Top 500 Special Edition

#85

COLUMBIA
® "Columbia," Marcas Reg.

STEREO   45 RPM

GLADYS KNIGHT & the Pips

BABY, BABY DON'T WASTE YOUR TIME

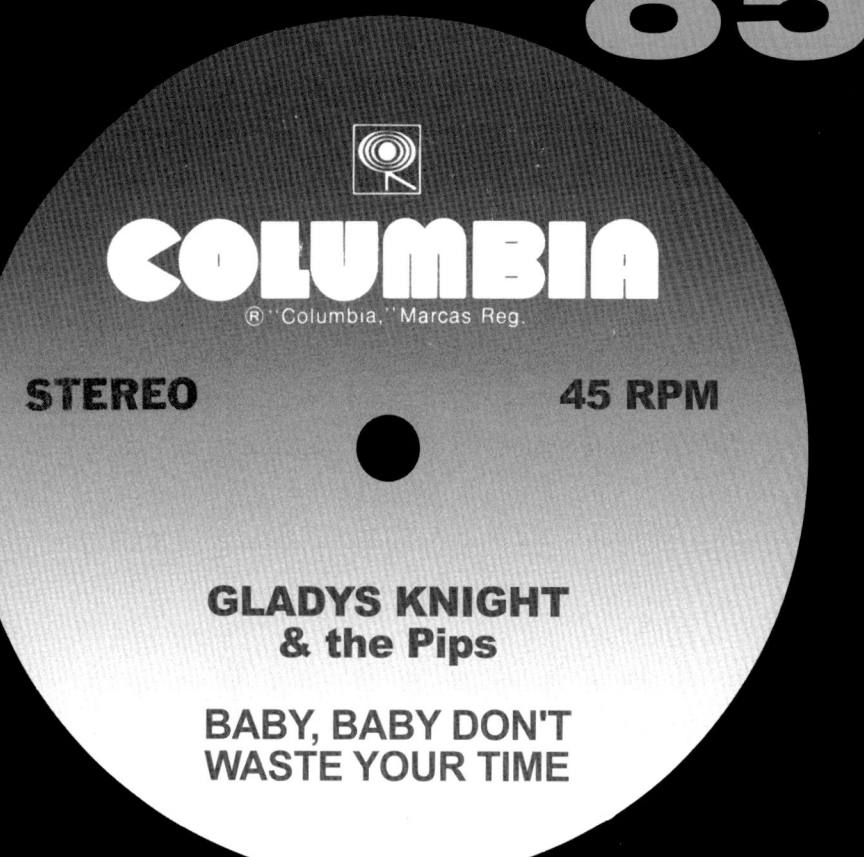

Artist: **Gladys Knight and the Pips**
Title: **Baby, Baby Don't Waste Your Time**
Label: **Columbia LP**
Value: **£20**

'the lady strikes again'

One could be forgiven for thinking that Ms. Knight has somehow hijacked the book for her own end. The reality is she simply has so many cracking dancers in her Motown and Columbia repertoire.

A plodding dance groove from 1980 sees Gladys effortlessly gliding over an adult contemporary LP cut that would have been a single for anyone else.

She is the absolute business, so good in fact she could rock my Baby Pug to sleep!

Extensively featured around the late 90's, the track fuses the Northern and Modern rooms together. If only she would now make an appearance up North!

The Northern Soul Top 500 Special Edition

#86

Artist: **Frank Popp**
Title: **Breakaway**
Label: **Unreleased CD**
Value: **N/A**

'here's a great one I made earlier'

NOT to be confused with either Linda Lloyd, Toni Basil or the Valentines, this 2003 - yes 03 as yet unreleased CD track from Warner Music, Germany has become my biggest play of the moment.

Apparently the vocalist is from Manchester, while Frank Popp is a DJ. Taking the old Soul Communicators track on Fee Bee 'Those Lonely Nights', Popp created a new Northern sound instantly... And yes it IS that good!

Record companies would be licking their chicken flavour lips if only they had their act together!

The Northern Soul Top 500 Special Edition

#87

Artist: **Delegates of Soul**
Title: **I'll Come Running Back**
Label: **Up Look**
Value: **£300**

'a killer investment if made in the 70's'

Superb group harmony from Philadelphia as a former 2nd division collector's item (unless you can find a copy that's NOT water damaged!) finally hits gold.

Not quite Northern enough in the day, but rich in crossover, this Stafford spin is soaring in popularity today and deservedly so.

Collectors will of course recognise the rarity of the label pictured - The Delegates' Up Look release is one of those tracks where, like the Debonaire's 'Lovin' You Takes All Of My Time', practically every copy has a mysteriously after damaged label... Dealers take note - for goodness sake improve the waterproofing in your warehouses!?!!!

The Northern Soul Top 500 Special Edition

#88

Artist: **Joseph Moore**
Title: **I Still Can't Get You**
Label: **Mar-V-Lus**
Value: **£1,000**

'hard hitting late arrival'

If discovered in the golden era there are no doubt collectors would have clamered for a copy. Now we are into a 3rd generation of vinyl freakdom, obscurities such as this Chicago label anthem sit perfectly with little or no competition.

Moore struggled to make any impact, as the label was flying by '66. Consider Johnny Sayles, The Du-ettes, Alvin Cash and you can see the picture - Moore simply got left behind, but how thankful we are that dear old blighty persisted with the exposure of the labels most in demand 45.

The Northern Soul Top 500 Special Edition

#89

Artist: **The Mayfield Singers**
Title: **Don't Start None**
Label: **Mayfield Unreleased**
Value: **£20 recent press**

'one of the best of the best'

A tape find by former Westside records employee Tony Rounce. Who let one or two copies be made, when in reality, 20 or so should have been serviced to the crowd pullers?

An absolutely mind boggling dancer from 1965, with the instrumental already known to many. But this Chicago offering tells it like it is - dance floor wise.

Racing vocals across a 100mph beat. Hey, what more could you ask for?

The Northern Soul Top 500 Special Edition

#90

ETHON RECORDS

Morgie Music (BMI)
(M-E-3034)

101
Time 2:27
Engr.: G. Fernandes

IT WAS TRUE
(McElroy - Bennett)
BIG DON'S REBELLION
Produced by Murray Cohen

Artist: **Big Don's Rebellion**
Title: **It Was True**
Label: **Ethon**
Value: **£1,500**

'becoming so damn popular at the moment'

Big Don's rebellion could well be white, the lead vocalist however is very much a Little Anthony soundalike.

The 45 long knocked around the corridors of the famous Top Dog Allnighter at Stafford for as little as £30... What a fabulous investment!

The weird thing is, dancers are not so ecstatic about this Spectorish group sound, it is collectordom that has more than picked up the slack on this cut.

A neat production from 1966 and currently burning hot at £300 plus.

The Northern Soul Top 500 Special Edition

#91

HOT - LINE

Beauchamp Pub
BMI - 3.37
Arr.: W. Quezergue

907
176-1769

WHO CAN I RUN TO
(R. Washington)
GERRI HALL

Artist: **Gerri Hall**
Title: **Who Can I Run Too**
Label: **Hot-Line**
Value: **£800**

'the last thing you'd expect from the label that spawned donna king!'

A New Orleans bounder for this local gal that delivers a driving performance, that sadly fails in the star quality department.

The tune's a real romper that has the hallmarks of Allen Toussaint or a wannabe soundalike.

The Hot-Line label also boasted early recordings for Al Green, notably 'Get Yourself Together' and 'Don't Leave Me', and of course the evergreen ender 'Take Me Home' by Donna King.

As session singer at Imperial records in the 50s, Hall worked with the likes of Huey 'Piano' Smith before recording for International City and Atco. There are two takes of 'Who Can I Run Too' using the same catalogue number.

The Northern Soul Top 500 Special Edition

#92

Artist: **Cody Black**
Title: **I'm Slowly Molding**
Label: **King**
Value: **£2000**

'seems to have been around forever'

Discovered 3 decades ago and popularised by Pat Brady at Bradford in the 80s - backed up by extensive plays by Roger Banks, Detroit icon Cody scores with yet another sleeper from the famous King imprint.

Brilliant under rated vocals with fierce D-Town back beat sends dancers hopping with delight as Black continues his quest for Northern supremacy with this and killers on Gig and other equally as attractive collectables.

The Northern Soul Top 500 Special Edition

#93

Artist: Dee Dee Sharp
Title: Comin' Home Baby
Label: Cameo
Value: £100

'wickedly in demand by 60's aficionados'

Numerous chancers around the early 60's covered the Mel Torme Mod classic. Sharp's version on the face of it, should be no more than another version, however the groove clicks instantly with dancers and whips 'em up to a frenzy.

It's always difficult to constitute what makes a great Northern side post millennium, this works the 60's beat and soul scene a treat. And, if discovered 2 or 3 years before, Philadelphia's Mrs Gamble would be a top 10 certainty.

The Northern Soul Top 500 Special Edition

#94

Artist: **Jim Gilstrap**
Title: **Run, Run, Run**
Label: **Bell**
Value: **£500**

'reaching out for greatness'

'Discovered' by Ian Levine - although I distinctly remember having the single in the mid-70's and it saw plays in the 80s.

It is difficult to gauge how popular 'Run, Run, Run' really is as hardly any DJ has a copy (Ian's is often claimed to be the only one). Dubs and CDR's are widely in circulation so others can air the 1972 release. Rarity aside the real winning formula is the catchy beat and hook.

Yes, he is indeed the 'Swing Your Daddy' hit maker from 1975, with this his debut 45 for Bell. Impossible to get, unless more copies circulate, the spins will be less frequent ending its current gravy train popularity.

The Northern Soul Top 500 Special Edition

#95

Artist: Keni Lewis
Title: Not The Marrying Kind
Label: Unreleased
Value: N/A

'incomplete, raw and exciting'

Washington DC's favourite songwriter has a demo unearthed by collectors Rob Thomas and Andy Rix. Boy, if this were only complete we would be staring at one of the all time greats.

The fairly worn acetate turned up by Shrine expert Andy Rix has turned into numerous poor quality dubs... But the sheer magnitude of the track has left many of us 'having to play it' - no matter what!

Musically it's straight out of '66, with a typical East Coast production that would have turned into a superb single if pressed on Shrine or similar DC outlets. This could be one we might never see even on compact disc.

The Northern Soul Top 500 Special Edition

#96

Artist: **September Jones**
Title: **I'm Coming Home**
Label: **Kapp**
Value: **£400**

'reeks of 60's quality'

Tip top Detroit effort from 1967. And a single that is every self respecting jocks box. Totally overlooked in the 70's, it first came to prominence a decade ago, gathering pace as a fairly scarce collector's item, DJ action followed inevitably and subsequent CD compilations have aired the side to a much wider audience.

Can't afford a 7" copy? Try Billy Sha Rae's cheapy 'Do It' - sounds identical - if anything better!

The Northern Soul Top 500 Special Edition

#97

Artist: **Driza Bone**
Title: **Real Love**
Label: **4th and Broadway**
Value: **£10**

'a second chart placing'

Well it had to happen. The follow up to 'Pressure' in terms of turntable play, sees another irresistible groove in both Northern and Modern rooms.

Easy to find - it hit the charts a few years ago as many will remember, simple to dance to, wonderful vocals and production. But does it have a place on our beloved scene?... of course it does.

SP. 117

The Northern Soul Top 500 Special Edition

#98

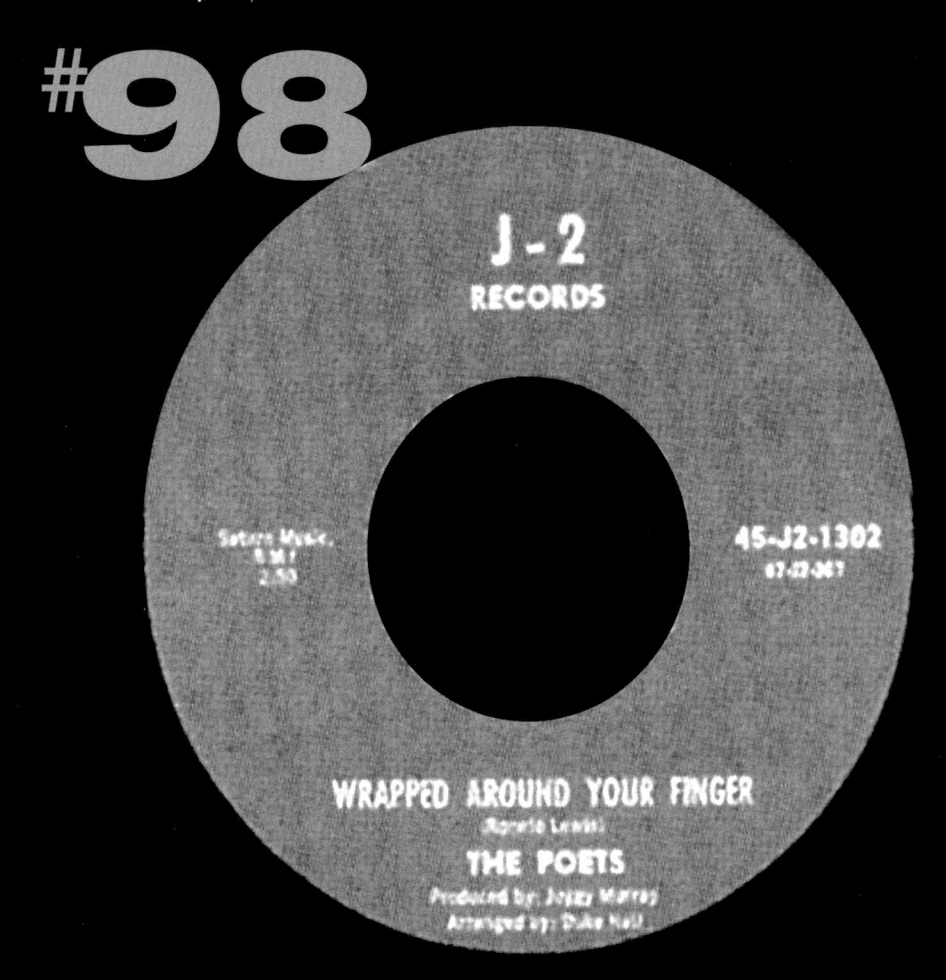

(record label image: J-2 RECORDS — "WRAPPED AROUND YOUR FINGER" (Ronnie Lewis) / THE POETS / Produced by: Juggy Murray / Arranged by: Duke Hall / 45-J2-1302)

Artist: **The Poets**
Title: **Wrapped Around Your Finger**
Label: **J-2**
Value: **£2500**

'a rivetting piece of collectordom'

Formed in 1964, lead singer Ronnie Lewis debuted the group, also featuring Donald McPherson, Luther Simmons Jnr and Tony Silvester on vinyl in November 1965 with this their rarest and perhaps best single recorded for Juggy Murray's Sue subsidiary J-2.

The group moved onto another Sue owned label, Symbol, to achieve Northern immortality with 'So Young' and the Twisted Wheel classic 'She Blew A Good Thing', which of course charted big style in Volume 1. Later the combo moved to Red Bird.

Massively in demand with collectors, the side has reached iconic status with both vinyl junkies and maplewood bouncers.

As a postscript the legendary Cuba Gooding joined the Poets in 1971 and the group's name was changed to ...The Main Ingredient.

The Northern Soul Top 500 Special Edition

#99

Artist: **The Moments**
Title: **You Said**
Label: **Deep**
Value: **£1,000**

'there's more 'moments' groups than you can shake a stick at!'

A candidate for most used name for a soul group has to be that of the Moments. Used by at least seven different outfits before the seventies All Platinum group laid the definitive claim. Virtually all of these groups were male but here on 'You Said' we have a female combo.

Issued on Bill Linton's Deep label out of New York, 'You Said' was released twice with different flipsides – the second of these is much rarer with another winner 'Hey Boy' touted as the A-side instead of 'You Said'.

Recent years have seen massive popularity for this disc with the lengthy note held by the lead singer towards the fade becoming a certain trademark effect.

The Northern Soul Top 500 Special Edition

#100

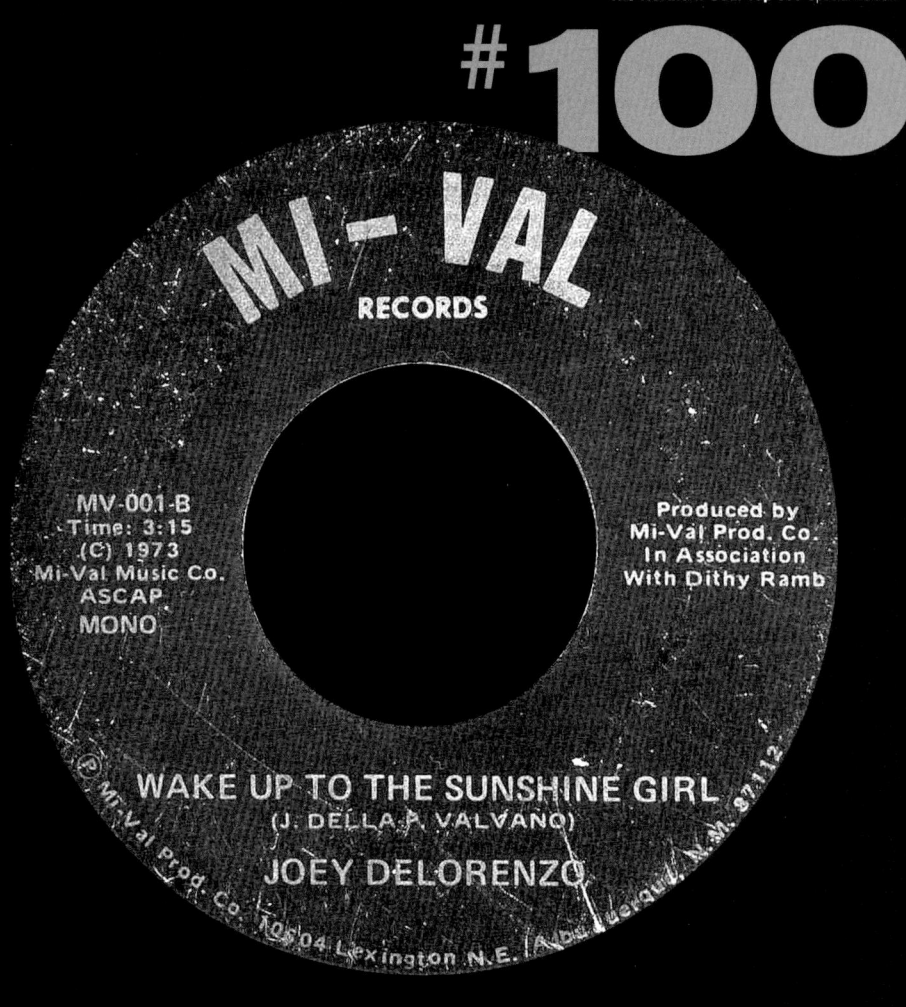

- Artist: **Joey De Lorenzo**
- Title: **Wake Up To The Sunshine Girl**
- Label: **Mi-Val**
- Value: **£1000**

'even the great mike valvano had a rough day!'

Out of 1973, this incredibly rare release is a pure pop belter from New Mexico of all places. Just one of four examples, the copy above belongs to UK collector Pete French.

The late, great Micky Valvano of Mike and the Modifiers and Maltese records fame is behind this blue eyed production.

Today this questionable cut is hugely popular in most Northern arenas, but for the purist the track is about as a poppy as it gets... But at the end of the day we are not discussing string arrangements here, purely how popular it really is.

The Northern Soul Top 500 Special Edition

where are they **now**?

For many years some of the Northern Soul scene's most legendary acts languished in total obscurity, often utterly unaware of the notoriety in the UK. Latterly the efforts of promoters and radio DJ's in tracking down these great artists has paid dividends as more and more are finally tracked down and given the appreciation they have long deserved. Here are a few stars that have surfaced in recent years...

Ruby Andrews

The early days of Ruby Stackhouse were at the independent label, Kellmac out of Chicago. Following her debut with the rare 'Wishing' in 1965, she sang all the backgrounds on fellow signings The COD's and The Combinations.

Background singing on The COD's US hit 'Michael' was a thrill she explained, but when she was told of how incredibly rare the song 'She's Fire' was, she nearly fell through the floor! Detroit producer George McGregor (the man behind 'Hit and Run' etc) took her to ABC, where a cache of gems were recorded. Supremely popular post-millennium are the songs 'I Got A Bone To Pick With You' and 'Merry Go Round'.

Based in Chicago today, Ruby still performs most of her Zodiac recordings. That particular phase of her career is most requested in her homeland. With all these positives apart, the UK has certainly made 'Just Lovin' You' the daddy of 'em all.

The Magnificent Men

In the States very few white acts have enjoyed the popularity with black audiences achieved by the Magnificent Men in the 60's. Whilst their records sold only moderately well in the US, their stardom came late at night on the stages of top black American theatres as word of their dynamic stage act spread, their appeal made them a favourite on the college campuses.

The 'Mag Men' led by the great voice of David Bupp, didn't evolve in the traditional urban surrounding, but from the smaller cities of York and Harrisburg Pennsylvania, and the surrounding towns.

The band's roots in early R'n'B group stylings (which were never recorded to the collector's misfortune) were transformed largely by the Windy-City soul influences more than Philadelphia or New York styles, into the unique style you hear on the band's popular Capitol Northern Soul cuts including the great 'Keeps On Rollin'', an Excellent version of 'Just Walk In My Shoes', 'All You Loving's Gone To My Head' (which was also released on UK Capitol Discotheque '66) and the powerhouse 'I Got News'.

An interesting footnote is that 'Soul Step' a very rare and once VERY popular instrumental released on Treasure in 1964 by 'The Dog's' was in fact by The Magnificent Men - in their earlier form, The Del-Chords!

Left: The Magnificent Men - perhaps the greatest 'Blue-Eyed' Soul group. Led by David Bupp (front) they recorded some top quality tunes for Capitol, including the massively popular album cut 'Keeps On Rollin'.

Judy Street

Judy Street began her singing career at the tender age of 16 working with a 5 piece show group, "Society", travelling widely from Bermuda to Hawaii.

The legendary 'White Pop' Northern Soul classic 'What' was her first venture into recording and was produced by the great HB Barnum. It was recorded in 1969 in Los Angeles and was the 'B' side to 'You Turn Me On' on Strider records.

At only 19 years of age, this recording session was awe-inspiring to her. Not only was there a great rhythm section of musicians, but also an 8 piece string section and a 4 piece brass section.

Also included in that day was a very well known back-ground singing group known as the Blossoms. They were 3 black girls who didn't need parts written out for them, HB just told them what he needed and they layed it down! When it came time to lay down the lead vocals, everything went quite smooth except for HB Barnum reminding Judy that the word was sung 'BAY-BA' not as she was pronouncing it, 'BABEE'.

Settling in California, Judy had her own groups from duos, trios, and quartets. As well working as the lead singer in these groups, she was also the drummer.

In 1991, she and her family moved to the home of country music, Nashville, Tennessee. Tom Stewart is a song writer and singer/guitar player. Her two sons, ages 14 and 11, play piano, saxophone, trumpet, and flute.

In 1996, she sang lead on a song called 'There Is A God' on an album made by the Christ Church Choir. That album was called 'All Praise', though of course for this cut her name is Judy Stewart.

Pictured: Judy Street, though the epitome of 'a White Pop' Northern Soul sounds, her 1969 classic 'What' continues to be much loved. It will of course certainly not be forgotten as it received the 'Tainted Love' treatment by hit-making Northern Soul fans Soft Cell.

Jimmy Conwell

A much loved new visitor to the UK, this multi-talented songwriter and performer's resumé extends very close to the beginning of R'n'B. Jimmy first started working in the late 50's developing one of his great talents, the knack for writing beautiful ballads and hook lines that are out of this world.

During the 60s Mr. Conwell joined a group called The Exits, co-writing the chart busting songs 'Under The Street Lamp' and 'Another Sun Down In Watts' (both of which have become very popular in recent years). He went on to tour with some of his neighbourhood pals... The O'Jays, who were under the same management company as The Exits. As a result of an introduction by friend Len Jewel he next released with Randall Wood's Mirwood label, 'Cigarette Ashes' and, and as we in the UK later learned, as Richard Temple with 'That Beatin' Rhythm', both releases were actually originally destined for Teri-De records.

Jimmy next signed to 20th Century and worked with such great musical icons as Len Jewel, Barry White, Bloodstone, The Stylistics and many more. Moving to the present through all the trials and tribulations that many artists went through in that era, Jimmy proved an absolute storming performer when he finally appeared at Fleetwood Northern Soul Weekender alongside bemused legend Gene 'Duke Of Earl' Chandler.

special edition index

4th & Broadway Records	SP 23
20th Century Records	SP 64, 70, 122
100 Club	SP 8, 67

A

A Case Of Too Much Of Lovemaking	SP 80
A Little Love Affair	SP 62
A&M Records	SP 90
ABC Records	SP 41, 86, 121
Abs	SP 65
Ace Records	SP 57
Ace Spectrum	SP 17, 22
Ace, Johnny	SP 56
Achievement Records	SP 104
After The Session	SP 21
Ain't Gonna Give You Up	SP 89
Ain't That The Truth	SP 87
All Platinum Records	SP 119
All You Loving's Gone To My Head	SP 121
Allen, Derek	SP 5
Alsop, Martin	SP 5
Altern 8	SP 5
Am I Cold, Am I Hot	SP 76
American Arts Records	SP 89
Andrews, Ruby	SP 121
Anka, Paul	SP 60
Ann, Little	SP 98
Another Sun Down In Watts	SP 122
Antellects, The	SP 58
Anthony, Little	SP 110
Arch Records	SP 38
Arctic Records	SP 82
Argo Records	SP 66
Arista Records	SP 59
Arrington, Joseph 'Joe Tex'	SP 34
Astra Records	SP 89
Atco Records	SP 50
Atlantic Records	SP 22, 24, 36, 50, 52
Atlas records	SP 97
Austin, Patti	SP 94
Australia	SP 80

B

BMG Records	SP 5
Baby A Go-Go	SP 44
Baby What Has Happened To Our Love	SP 18
Baby, Baby Don't Waste Your Time	SP 105
Bacharach and David	SP 61
Back Stabbers	SP 59
Band Box Records	SP 68
Bang Records	SP 21
Banks, Roger	SP 112
Bark At The Moon	SP 57
Barnes, JJ	SP 14, 104
Barnum, HB	SP 121
Basil, Toni	SP 106

Batiste, Rose	SP 15
Because Of You	SP 28
Before It's Too Late	SP 1
Believe It Or Not	SP 17
Bell Records	SP 69, 114
Bell, Tommy	SP 24
Bell, William	SP 57, 99
Belles, The	SP 53
Best Of Soul Time	SP 61
Bicknell, Mark 'Big Daddy'	SP 73, 88
Big Don's Rebellion	SP 110
Bizzare Inc	SP 5
Black, Cody	SP 112
Blackpool Mecca	SP 38, 39, 76
Bless Your Heart	SP 43
Bloodstone	SP 121
Blossoms, The	SP 121
Boardwalk Records	SP 32
Bogart, Neil	SP 80
Boogaloo Tramp	SP 67
Borther, The	SP 29
Brady, Pat	SP 112
Breakaway	SP 106
Britt, Mel	SP 18
Bronco Records	SP 30
Brooks, Karmello	SP 91
Brothers Guiding Light	SP 51
Brown, Tim	SP 60
Brunswick Records	SP 28, 69
Bryant, JD	SP 63
Bryant, Lillie	SP 18
Bupp, David	SP 121
Burton, Chris	SP 13
'Butch', Mark Dobson	SP 63

C

CODs, The	SP 121
CUR Records	SP 96
Call On Me	SP 50
Cameo-Parkway/Cameo	SP 8, 51, 113
Capitol Records	SP 46, 53, 121
Capricorn XL2	SP 96
Carlton, 'Little' Carl	SP 77
Carr, Barbara	SP 26
Carr, James	SP 56, 68
Carter, Clarence	SP 26
Casablanca Records	SP 80
Casino, Wigan	SP 5, 8, 11, 12, 17, 19, 21, 63, 93
Castles In The Sand	SP 3
Chairmen Of The Board	SP 43
Chandler, Gene	SP 64, 122
Channel 3	SP 74
Cheatin' Kind	SP 17, 18
Chex Records	SP 89
Cigarette Ashes	SP 122
Clark, Chris	SP 4
Classics IV	SP 35

Claunch, Quinton	SP 68
Clay, Otis	SP 26
Cleethorpes Weekender	SP 16
Cochran, Johnny	SP 55
Cokell, Les	SP 77
Coleman Records	SP 92
Collins, Rodger	SP 100
Colored Man	SP 21
Columbia Records	SP 45, 51, 105
Combinations, The	SP 121
Comin' Home Baby	SP 113
Connoisseur Collection	SP 5
Constellations, The	SP 40
Conwell, Jimmy	SP 122
Cool Records	SP 67
Coral Records	SP 94
Cracked Up Over You	SP 97

D

D Train	SP 52
Dade Records	SP 18, 79
Dakar Records	SP 70, 74
Danzy, Chuck	SP 100
Davies, Terry	SP 29, 72
Davis and the Supsicions, Snake	SP 12
Day, Bobby	SP 60
Day, Jackie	SP 1, 55
Daye, Eddie	SP 63
De Lorenzo, Joey	SP 120
De Walt, Autry (Junior Walker)	SP 87
Debonaire's, The	SP 107
Debutante Records	SP 31
Deep Records	SP 119
Del-Chords, The	SP 121
Delegates of Soul	SP 107
Detroit Spinners, The	SP 52, 58
Dial Records	SP 34
Dionn Records	SP 95
Discotheque '66 (Capitol Records UK)	SP 121
Do I Love You (Indeed I Do)	SP 4, 12, 21
Do It	SP 116
Do The Crossover Baby	SP 57
Dogs, The	SP 121
Don't Send Nobody Else	SP 22
Don't Leave Me	SP 111
Don't Pity Me	SP 33
Don't Start None	SP 109
Don't Stop Now	SP 102
Dore Records	SP 85
Dottie and Millie	SP 98
Down To Love Town	SP 102
Dreamlovers, The	SP 51
Driza Bone	SP 16, 23, 117
Du-ettes, The	SP 108
Dunn, Eddie	SP 41
Dynamic Superiors, The	SP 22
Dynells, The	SP 50, 58

SP. 123

The Northern Soul Top 500 Special Edition

E

E-Bay	SP 10, 17
Eagle, Roger	SP 97
Eastbound Records	SP 39
Echo Records	SP 26
Ecstasy	SP 53
Edwards, John	SP 52
Edwards, Shirley	SP 63
Emblem Records	SP 96
Essex, Anita Humes and the	SP 21
Ethics, The	SP 50, 83
Ethon Records	SP 110
Excello Records	SP 27
Exits, The	SP 122
Expansion Records	SP 43, 70

F

FIP Records	SP 18
Faith, Hope and Charity	SP 76
Fantasy Records	SP 57
Fascinating Girl	SP 84
Fatback Records	SP 65
Fee Bee Records	SP 106
Fifth Dimension, The	SP 30
Flame 'n' King and the Bold Ones	SP 65
Fleetwood Weekender	SP 5, 12, 16, 64, 122
Fortnum, Carl	SP 91
Fortune Teller	SP 27
Four Tops, The	SP 4
Four Tracks, The	SP 77
Four Vandals, The	SP 32
Fox Theatre, The	SP 4
Frankie and the Classicals	SP 21
Funk Brothers, The	SP 44
Futures, The	SP 103

G

Gardner, Don	SP 17, 18
Garvin and the Mighty Cravers, Rex	SP 16
Gay, Rudy	SP 22
Gaye, Marvin	SP 3, 102
Gemini Star	SP40
Get Yourself Together	SP 111
Getting Together	SP 51
Gilstrap, Jim	SP 114
Gold Soul Records	SP 84
Golden Eye Records	SP 96
Goldmine/Soul Supply	SP 5, 8, 47, 51
Goldwax Records	SP 66
Gone With Wind Is My Love	SP 85
Gooding, Cuba	SP 118
Goodnight Irene	SP 102
Gordy, Berry	SP 3, 4, 42, 66
Gorman, Freddie	SP 6, 102
Grapevine Records	SP 17
Green Berets, The	SP 93
Green, Al	SP 111
Groovettes, The	SP 78

H

Haigh, Pete	SP 38
Hall, Gerri	SP 111
Hamilton, Dave	SP 98
Hamilton, Roy	SP 92
Harper, Bud	SP 56
Harris, Bill	SP 76
Harris, Kurt	SP 92
Harthon Records	SP 47, 82
Hatcher, Charles (Edwin Starr)	SP 17
Hawkins, Jamsetta (Etta James)	SP 66
He Who Picks A Rose	SP 31
Heartaches Away My Boy	SP 12
Hey Boy	SP 119
Hey Girl	SP 53
Hey You, Don't Fight It	SP 38
Highland Room (Blacpool Mecca)	SP 45
Hill, Lainie	SP 33, 46
Hinkley Allnighter	SP 8, 13, 73
Hinsley, Bob	SP 22
Hit And Run	SP 15, 121
Hitsville	SP 3, 25, 31, 48, 49
Holland, Eddie	SP 81
Holloway, Brenda	SP 48, 53
Holloway, Patrice	SP 53
Home Is Where The Heart Is	SP 45
Horn, Jimmie 'Bo'	SP 18, 79
Hot-Line Records	SP 111
Humes, Anita	SP 21
Hunter, Ty	SP 102
Hunter, Ty	SP 102
Hurtt, Phil	SP 24
Hutch, Willie	SP 30

I

I Can't Speak	SP 18
I Can't See Him Again	SP 79
I Can't Wait Until I See My Baby's Face	SP 86
I Don't Do This	SP 70
I Don't Know About You	SP 40
I Got A Bone To Pick With You	SP 121
I Got News	SP 121
I Gotta Find A Way	SP31
I Have A Girl	SP 82
I Just Want To Fall In Love	SP 52
I Miss My Baby	SP 15
I Still Can't Get You	SP 108
I Still Love You	SP 18
I Wanna Be Free	SP 34
I Wish I Didn't Miss You Anymore	SP 59
I Won't Be Coming Back	SP 63
Ichiban Records	SP 26, 99
If I Don't Love You	SP 69
If You Ever Get Your Hands On Love	SP 25
Ike and Tina Turner	SP 3
Ikettes, The	SP 3
Impact Records	SP 89
Impressions, The	SP 41
Inferno Records	SP 89
Inspirations, The	SP 73

International City Records	SP 75
Internet	SP 10
Intrigues, The	SP 40
Isley Brothers, The	SP 48
Isley, Ronnie	SP 48
It Was True	SP110
It's Your Voodoo Working	SP 27
I'll Come Running Back	SP 107
I'm A Big Man	SP 17, 73
I'm Coming Home	SP 116
I'm Slowly Molding	SP 112
I've Had It	SP 32
(I've Given) All My Love	SP 94

J

J&S Records	SP 86
J-2 Records	SP 118
Jackson, Chuck	SP 60
Jackson, Earl	SP 41
Jackson, Millie	SP 22, 37
Jacobs, Dick	SP 94
Jamerson, James	SP 44
James, Etta	SP 66
James, Holly St.	SP 33
James, Jimmy	SP 32, 59
Jamie Records	SP 54, 95
Jet Stream	SP 36
Jewel, Len	SP 122
Jobete Publishing	SP 37
Johnson, General	SP 43
Johnson, Jerome	SP 74
Johnson, Johnny	SP 59
Johnson, Lou	SP 92
Jokers, The	SP 72
Jones, Quincy	SP 94
Jones, September	SP 116
Jones, Terry	SP 52
Josie and the Pussycats	SP 53
Jubilee Records	SP 89
Just A Boy's Dream	SP 30
Just Lovin' You	SP 121
Just Say You're Wanted and Needed	SP 107
Just Walk In My Shoes	SP 49, 121

K

KFC (Kentucky Fried Chicken)	SP 14, 21
Kapp Records	SP 18, 116
Karen Records	SP 89
Keep My Woman Home	SP 97
Keep On Rolling	SP 53
Keeps On Rollin'	SP 121
Kellmac Records	SP 121
Kendricks, Eddie	SP 3
Kendricks, Nat	SP 79
Kent Records	SP 57
King Records	SP 112
King, Chris	SP 13, 31, 49, 93
King, Donna	SP 111
Kiss My Love Goodbye	SP 24
Kline, Bobby	SP 18
Knight (and the Pips), Gladys	SP 21, 37, 49, 105

SP. 124

L

La Beat Records	SP 17
La-Cindy	SP 93
LaShea, Eddie	SP 93
Lady In Green	SP 18
Lance, Major	SP 87
Lark/Legend, Tobi	SP 98
Leave Me Alone	SP 86
Lemons, George	SP 84
Lester, Ketty	SP 46
Lester, Lonnie	SP 100
Let Me Love You	SP 56
Let Me Make Love To You	SP 64
Let Your Heart And Soul Be Free	SP 61
Let's Talk It Over	SP 68
Levine, Ian	SP 32, 38, 54, 104, 114
Lewis, Keni	SP 115
Lewis, Linda	SP 5
Lewis, Ronnie	SP 118
Lick, Larry	SP 101
Life Of Tears	SP 93
Like My Love For You	SP 77
Linton, Bill	SP 119
Lonely Boy	SP 53
Look At Me Now	SP83
Looking For Fox	SP 26
Love And Desire	SP 53
Love Guess Who	SP 42
Love Letters	SP 46
Lovin' By The Pound	SP 57
Lovin' You Takes All Of My Time	SP 107
Lynn, Barbara	SP 36, 99

M

M-Pac Records	SP 18
MB Records	SP 18
Magnetics, The	SP 18, 82, 83
Magnificent Men, The	SP 121
Main Ingredient, The	SP 118
Make Me Yours	SP 24
Maltese Records	SP 120
Man-O-Man (What Have I Done)	SP 93
Mandingo	SP 77
Mar-V-Lus Records	SP 16, 108
Mayfield Singers, The	SP 109
McClure, Bobby	SP 100
McDougall III, Weldon	SP 47
McGregor, George	SP 121
McLaughlin, Ollie	SP 89
McLemore, Lamont	SP 30
McNair, Barbara	SP 44, 46
McPherson, Donald	SP 118
Meaux, Huey P	SP 36
Meet Me Halfway	SP 18
Mellow Fellow	SP 66
Memphis Horns	SP 57
Mercury Records	SP 51
Merry Go Round	SP 121
Messin' With My Mind	SP 26
Michael	SP 121
Midas Records	SP 17, 73
Mike and the Modifiers	SP 120
Milestone	SP 91
Mirwood Records	SP 8, 53, 122
Modern Records	SP 1, 55
Mojo Club, The	SP 8
Moments, The	SP 119
Montclairs, The	SP 38
Moonlight, Music In You	SP 21
Moore, Joseph	SP 108
Moore, Sam	SP 71
Motown Records	SP 3, 10, 23, 25, 31, 35, 37, 42, 44, 48, 49, 53, 58, 87, 89, 102, 106
Movin' On A Groove	SP 36
Mr.Soul	SP 56
Murray, Juggy	SP 118
Muscle Shoals	SP 81
My Love Is Getting Stronger	SP 75
My Love Is Your Love (Forever)	SP 48

N

Narbay	SP 17
Naughty Boy	SP 1, 55
Night Owl	SP 12
No One Can Love You More	SP 37
No One There	SP 42
Not The Marrying Kind	SP 115
Notations, The	SP 74
Nothing's Too Good For My Baby	SP 83
Nu-Tone Records	SP 101

O

Okeh Records	SP 18, 61
One-derful Records	SP 16
Originals, The	SP 6, 102
Ovations, The	SP 68
Owens, Gwen	SP 101
Ozen, Barbara (Barbara Lynn)	SP 36
O'Jays, The	SP 59, 122

P

Parker, Elbie	SP 88
Party Time Man	SP 103
Pate, Johnny	SP 41
Peacock Records	SP 56
Pepp, George	SP 92
Perry, Phil	SP 38
Pete Records	SP 46
Petherbridge, Tony	SP 13
Phelectron Records	SP 1, 55
Philadelphia International	SP 103
Phonetics, The	SP 30
Pieces Of A Broken Heart	SP 49
Plenty Good Lovin'	SP 71
Poets, The	SP 118
Pollard, Ray	SP 63
Polygram Records	SP 31
Popp, Frank	SP 106
Portrait Of The Originals	SP 102
Pressure	SP 16, 23, 117
Pretty Little Girl Next Door	SP 16, 60
Pyramid	SP 96

Q

Qualls, Sidney Joe	SP 70

R

RCA Victor Records	SP 46, 60, 76, 21
Ra-Sel Records	SP 82
Rae, Billy Sha	SP 116
Randell, Lynn	SP 33
Real Love	SP 117
Red Bird	SP 118
Redding, Otis	SP 57
Reed & His Band, AC	SP 67
Reed, Bob	SP 78
Reed, Bobby	SP 69
Reeves and the Vandellas, Martha	SP 42, 85
Reness Records	SP 78
Revilot Records	SP 15
Ric Records	SP 75
Ric-Tic	SP 8
Ric-Tic Revue	SP 13
Ridgely, Tommy	SP 75
Ringleaders, The	SP 18
Rita and the Tiaras	SP 85
River City Records	SP 75
Rix, Andy	SP 47, 115
Robinson, Ann	SP 47
Robinson, William 'Smokey'	SP 3
Rockin' Robin	SP 60
Rogers, Big Daddy	SP 73, 17
Rose, Keith	SP 40
Ross, Bud	SP 51
Ross, Diana	SP 35, 42, 3
Rounce, Tony	SP 109
Rubin	SP 18
Ruffin, Jimmy	SP 3, 31
Run, Run, Run	SP 114

S

SBI Records	SP 96
Salem Records	SP 96
Sam and Dave	SP 71
Sands, Tommy	SP 60
Sawyer, Pam	SP 37
Say Something Nice To Me	SP 18
Sayles, Johnny	SP 108
Scepter Records	SP 61
Schatz, Warren	SP 29
Scott, Cindy	SP 47
Scott, Gloria	SP 80
Searling, Richard	SP 5, 6, 81, 102
Second Time Around	SP 66
Security	SP 66
Sedgrick Records	SP 18
Sepia Records	SP 62
Seven Day Fool	SP 66
Seven Souls, The	SP 18
Sharp, Dee Dee	SP 113
She Blew A Good Thing	SP 118
She'll Come Running Back	SP 18
She's Fire	SP 121
Sheffield, Charles	SP 27

The Northern Soul Top 500 Special Edition

Sheldon, Sandi	SP 18	**T**		**V**	
Shoot Your Shot	SP 87	T-Neck Records	SP 48	Valentines, The	SP 106
Show Me (Joe Tex)	SP 34	Take Away The Pain Stain	SP 94	Valvano, Mike/Micky	SP 120
Show Me (Ketty Lester)	SP 46	Take Me Back	SP 6	Vann, Teddy	SP 21
Shrine Records	SP 63, 115	Take Me In Your Arms And Love Me	SP 37	Veep Records	SP 88
Sigma Sound Studios	SP 24, 51, 103	Take Your Love And Run	SP 36	Velgo Records	SP 101
Simmons Jnr, Luther	SP 118	Talk Of The Grapevine	SP 104	Vent Records	SP 50, 83
Singleton, Eddie	SP 69	Talkin' About My Baby	SP 98	Versatiles, The	SP 30
Sister James	SP 90	Tamla Motown	SP 37, 42	Virtue, Frank	SP 47, 82
Sko-Field	SP 72	Tangeers, The	SP 61	Volt Records	SP 57
Sliced Tomatoes	SP 16	Taylor, Raymond 'Ginger'	SP 29, 72	Volumes, The	SP 89
Smash Records	SP 40	Tell Mama	SP 66	Voo Doo Man	SP 77
Smith, Bobby	SP 58	Tell Me Baby	SP 91		
Smith, George	SP 32	Temple, Richard	SP 122	**W**	
Smith, Huey 'Piano'	SP 111	Tempo, Nino & The 5th Avenue Sax	SP 90	Wake Up To The Sunshine Girl	SP 120
Smith, Moses	SP 95	Temptations, The	SP 31	Wale Records	SP 83
So Young	SP 118	Teri-De Records	SP 122	Wales, Thadeus	SP 83
Sock It To 'Em J.B.	SP 16	Tex, Joe	SP 34, 56, 70	Walker and the Allstars, Junior	SP 87
Some Thing's Are Better Left Unsaid	SP 46	Thanks For A Little Lovin'	SP 41	Walter and the Admerations	SP 93
Sommers, Joanie	SP 33	That Beatin' Rhythm	SP 122	Wand Records	SP 65
Sonday Records	SP 40	That's How Heartaches Are Made	SP 86	Wanting You	SP 90
Sony Records	SP 5, 61	That's What I Want To Know	SP 68	Warner Brothers Records	SP 33, 51, 76, 106
Soul Brothers Inc	SP 96	The Sweetest Thing	SP 74	Warwick, Dionne	SP 40
Soul Communicators, The	SP 106	The Time Is Right For Love	SP 69	Washington, Frank	SP 103
Soul Records	SP 87	The Well's Gone Dry	SP 68	Washington, Justine/Jeanette 'Baby'	SP 86
Soul Sound	SP 72	Thelma Records	SP 9	Wensiora, Jim	SP 63
Soul Step	SP 121	Think It Over Baby	SP 78	What	SP 122
Soupy Sales, The	SP 102	This Empty Place	SP 61	What Am I Gonna Do	SP 80
Spank	SP 79	This Feeling Is Real	SP 92	What Becomes Of The Broken Hearted	SP 31
Special Kind Of Woman	SP 81	This Time, I'll Be Lovin' You	SP 54	What More Can A Boy Ask For	SP 58
Spector, Phil	SP 90	Thomas, Rob	SP 47, 115	What Shall I Do	SP 21
Spellman, Benny	SP 27	Thompson, Paul	SP 81	What's The Use Of Me Trying	SP 61
Spencer, Crathum 'CP'	SP 102	Those Lonely Nights	SP 106	Wherever You Were	SP 56
Springers, The	SP 83	Timeless	SP 43	White, Barry	SP 122
Stackhouse (Andrews), Ruby	SP 121	Top Top Records	SP 54	White, Danny	SP 97
Stafford Allnighter	SP 8, 9, 56, 67, 100, 107, 110	Topper records	SP 98	Who Can I Run Too	SP 111
Standing In The Shadows Of Motown	SP 42	Torch, The	SP 17, 34, 67	Wiggins, Spencer	SP 68
Stansfield, Lisa	SP 80	Torme, Mel	SP 113	Williams, Dorothy	SP 68
Starr, Edwin	SP 5, 87	Touch Of Venus	SP 53	Willis, Betty	SP 85
Starr, Edwin	SP 17	Toussaint, Allen	SP 111	Wilson, Frank	SP 4, 5, 102
Staten, Patrinell	SP 62	Trammps, The	SP 103	Wilson, Jackie	SP 28
Stax Records	SP 57, 81	Treasure Records	SP 121	Wilson, Timothy	SP 22
Steelers, The	SP 40	Trends, The	SP 41	Wilson, Venecia	SP 54
Stevens, April	SP 70, 90	Tribe Records	SP 36	Womack, Bobby	SP 45
Stevens, Guy	SP 97	Trudel records	SP 30	Wonder, Stevie	SP 3
Stolen Hours	SP 53	Try My Love	SP 95	Wood, Randall	SP 122
Stone, Angie	SP 59	Trying To Love Two	SP 99	Woods, Gilda	SP 95
Stone, Henry	SP 79	Tune Up	SP 87	World Of Happiness	SP 47
Stop Sign	SP 65	Twans (Swans), The	SP 79	Wrapped Around Your Finger	SP 118
Stormy	SP 35	Twirl Records	SP 89	Wynn and the Rhythm Aces, Mel	SP 65
Street, Judy	SP 122	Twisted Wheel, The	SP 8, 10, 17, 34, 56, 67, 118		
Strider records	SP 122			**Y**	
Stubborn Heart	SP 93	**U**		Yes I'm In Love	SP 39
Stylistics, The	SP 76, 122	Under The Street Lamp	SP 122	You Better Believe It	SP 34
Sue (UK)	SP 97	Under Your Powerful Love	SP 34	You Better Watch Out	SP 101
Sue Records	SP 86, 118	Uni Records	SP 93	You Can't Go	SP 100
Supremes, (Diana Ross and) The	SP 3, 35	Unique Blend	SP 39, 40	You Said	SP 119
Surfside Records	SP 43	United Artists (UA) Records	SP 88	You Turn Me On	SP 122
Swann, Bettye	SP 24	Universal Records	SP 31, 48	You're Gonna Make Me Love You	SP 18
Swing Your Daddy	SP 114	Up Look Records	SP 107	You've Been Away	SP 18
Sylvester, Tony	SP 118	Uptown Saturday Night	SP 76	Your Wish Is My Command	SP 73
Symbol records	SP 118			You're Gonna Love My Baby	SP 44
				You're Losing Me	SP 36

SP. 126

THE TWISTED WHEEL
MANCHESTER

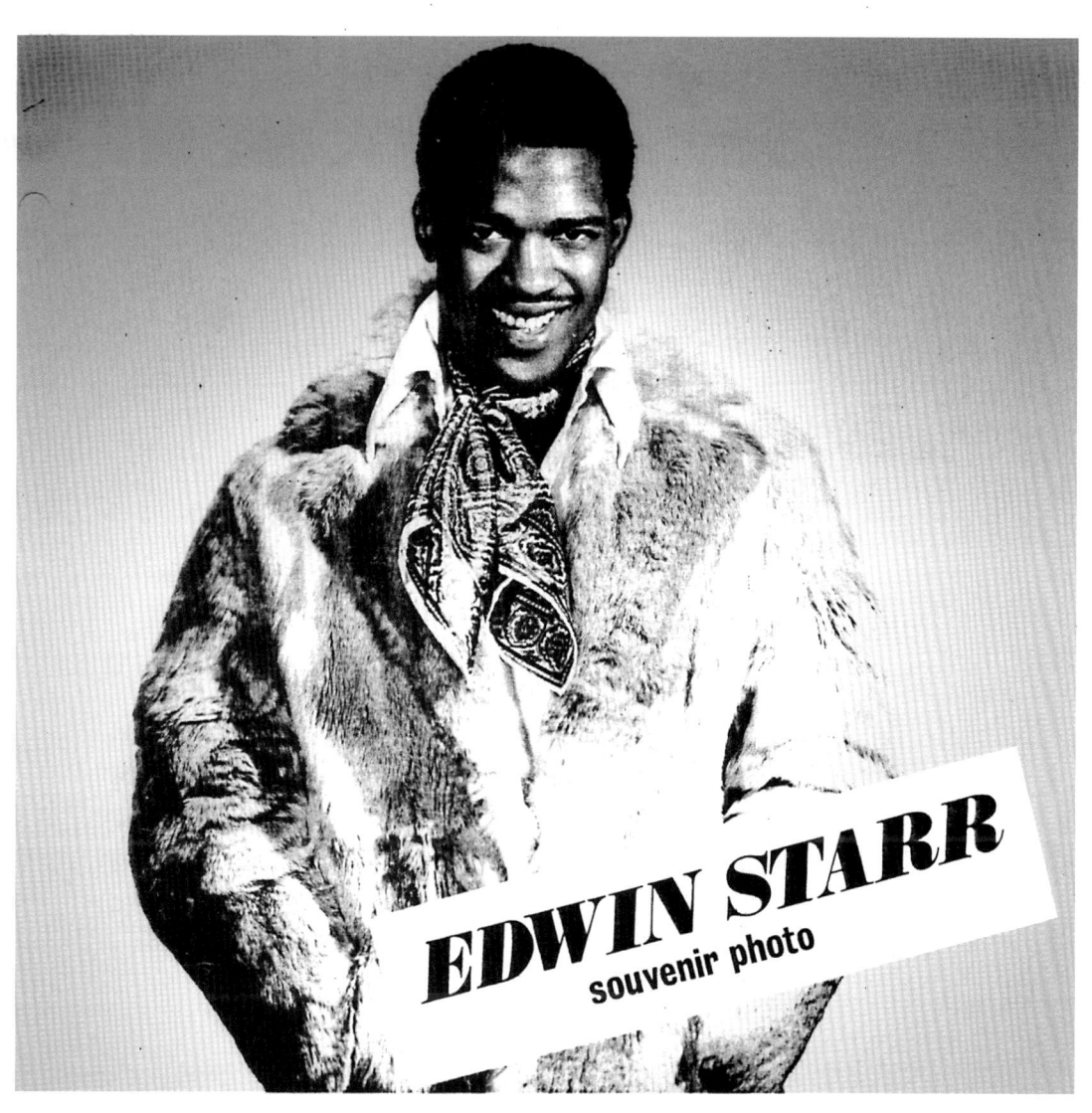

EDWIN STARR
souvenir photo

SATURDAY JAN 30th
SPECIAL SCOOP ATTRACTION
DIRECT FROM AMERICA

"I'M THE ONE WHO LOVES YOU"
(M. Davis)

VOA-4014
(VO-0151)
Groovesville
Music, BMI
Time: 2:38

VOLT

DARRELL BANKS
Produced by: Don Davis
May, 1969

VOLT RECORDS, 926 EAST McLEMORE, MEMPHIS, TENNESSEE 38106

Great unsung hero of Soul music, Darrell Banks whose sadly short career (he was shot dead in highly suspicious circumstances in 1970) produced a number of all-time Northern classics for Revilot, Volt and Atco.

The Northern Soul All Time Top 500

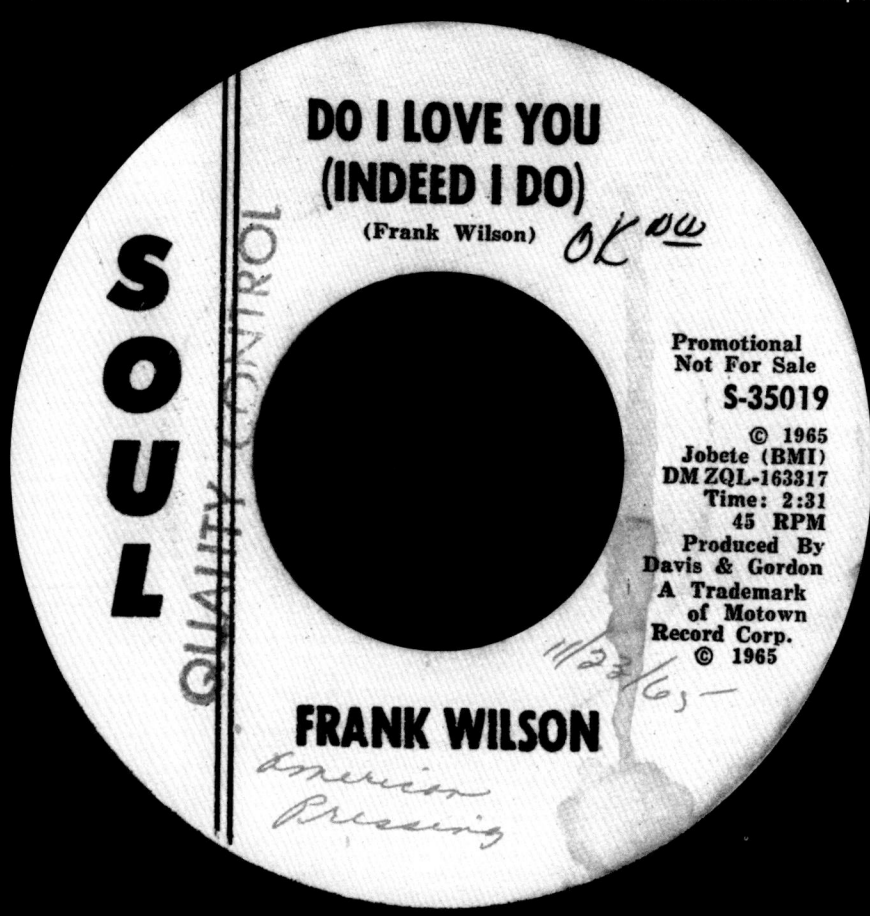

Frank Wilson
Do I Love You (Indeed I Do)

Top 500 Position: **1**
Original Label: **Soul**
Current Value: **£15,000**

'A truly awesome piece of vinyl, and worth every penny of fifteen grand!'

Tim Brown,
Owner of one of the two known copies and MD of Goldmine/Soul Supply Records

The ultimate floorshaker that shook the UK in 1978 and has reached dizzy heights ever since. The most valuable, played and stunning 60's Soul dancer ever made. Recorded in 1965 for Motown's subsidiary SOUL label, the release was shelved as Frank concentrated on his work as a Motown producer.

The flipside 'Sweeter than the day before' was also recorded by Marvin Gaye and Chris Clark, who recorded her own version of 'Do I Love You'.

Frank remained a respected arranger/producer, working with the likes of The Commodores, The Supremes and Brenda Holloway, as well as other great independent label releases, including the Checkerboard Squares and Connie Clark.

There are only two known copies, both are in the UK!

The Northern Soul All Time Top 500

so what's the story?

As one of the former owners of this legendary piece of vinyl I will attempt to shed a little light on the mystery surrounding Frank Wilson's anthem - 'Do I Love You (Indeed I Do)' Soul 35019.

The actual discovery was made by a former researcher Tom Dieperro, a Motown historian who worked for the company in the mid 70's. Low on Tom's list of priorities, the disc and its destiny were about to be turned upside-down when legendary Northern Soul dealer and record producer Simon Soussan finally met up with him. They both shared a love of Detroit and Motown in particular. Dieperro gave a clutch of oddball 45s, including Frank Wilson to Soussan for his collection.

The initial play was enough to send Simon into a frenzy and with his marketing know-how immediately sent acetates to the UK DJs under the guise of Eddie Foster. Understandably it became Northern's biggest ever find and caused much debate as to it's real identity (Simon being notorious for discovering Northern classics and giving them false identities).

The secret was out in 1978 when Soussan offered his collection to Les McCutcheon (an entrepreneur from Weybridge, Surrey who later formed the band Shakatak amongst other chart successes). The fact that it was now owned by a relatively unknown player in Les Mac, and the fact that it's origin was Motown, made collectors give it something of a luke-warm reception.

Whether or not Les got cold feet or simply moved on to pastures new remains unclear but the disc was subsequently sold to Jonathon Woodliffe, a Nottingham DJ who briefly emerged as one of the UKs top collectors.

With a sudden change of heart Jonathon agreed to part company with the record to yours truly, who owned the disc for over 10 years, when my future partner in Goldmine/Soul Supply and reputedly the world's biggest Northern Soul collector offered me the (then) staggering sum of £5,000. At the time I thought that the Northern Scene had bottomed out and I couldn't see prices getting any higher so I agreed to the deal.

Tim Brown has now sold a second copy belonging to Martin Koppel for £15,000, this single voted by collectors and DJ's as the biggest Northern Soul single of all time now belongs to Scots DJ Kenny Burrell.

Ken ya lend us the bus fare te get home?.... Kenny Burrell, right, a popular face and DJ on the scene has recently fulfilled his dream of owning an original copy of 'Do I Love You (Indeed I Do)'... Unfortunately it cost him £15,000 to do it!

Dateline

1977 Tom Dieperro discovers the disc. Simon Soussan acquires the disc from Tom Dieperro in Los Angeles. 1978

1978 Les McCutcheon reputedly paid $500 to Simon for the single. Les loans the single to Russ Winstanley to play. Russ was the key DJ in turning the record into a monster. After a mishap at Wigan Casino the disc accidentally develops an edge warp. Les McCutcheon retrieves the disc from Russ and sells it to Jonathan Woodliffe for a reputed £250.

1979 Jonathan Woodliffe sells the disc to me in an exchange deal valued at £350 for 12", LP's and white demo Funk/Soul releases for his collection.

1989 I sell the disc, warp and all, to Tim Brown for the new world record of £5,000.

1990 The 'only other' copy turns up in Canada with Martin Koppel who acquires an original from former Motown collector Ron Murphy in Detroit. 1996 Tim Brown is offered an earth shattering £15,000 for the ultimate Northern Soul 45.

1999 Scottish DJ and collector Kenny Burrell actually does purchase the only other known copy for the princely sum £15,000 from Martin Koppel through Tim Brown!

Notes

- The single was scheduled for release on the U.S. Motown subsidiary label 'Soul' on November 23rd 1965 (Tim Brown's Birthday!).
- Marvin Gaye had recorded a version of the flip side "Sweeter As The Days Go By". Chris Clark also recorded "Do I Love You".
- The single gained a UK release in 1979.
- A source at Motown/Polygram revealed Wilson's about turn on his vocal debut and quickly convinced Berry Gordy to destroy all existing promo copies.
- Frank Wilson was a reputable writer and producer and has legendary status with Northern Soul collectors for his work with Connie Clark, Mary Love and the Checkerboard Squares amongst others. He is now a church minister in California.

The Northern Soul All Time Top 500

Dobie Gray
Out On The Floor

Top 500 Position: **2**
Original Label: **Charger**
Current Value: **£10**

'My first experience with Northern Soul - this is it!'

Dobie Gray, Artist, USA

Born Leonard Ainsworth, Dobie is a veritable giant amongst Northern fans due to this disc. The groove encapsulates the 60's 'full on' with a stirring LA production and DG's controlled vocal and Spectoresque reverb.

In terms of 'feel good' they do not come much better than this. First released on the US Charger label, the disc was massively imported into the UK during the 70's, finally entering the UK charts in 1975 on Black Magic. Best known for his classic 'The In-Crowd', Dobie went on to record the ultra-rare 'What A Way To Go' for White Whale before topping the charts in the 70's with the country influenced 'Drift Away'.

Yeah, yeah, yeah babe it's out of sight!

The Northern Soul All Time Top 500

Yvonne Baker
You Didn't Say A Word

Top 500 Position: **3**
Original Label: **Parkway**
Current Value: **£200 Demo**
£300 Issue

'This obscure disc I made, still sends a shiver through me even today'

Yvonne Baker, Artist, Philadelphia, USA

The James Bond intro was typical of many 60's 'groovers' of their day. Miss Baker, born Yvonne Mills, was already an experienced hand in the studio, realising a US No. 4 hit in 1962 with 'Let me In', as lead singer of the Sensations. In fact she later teamed up with the group again for a cover of Lorraine Chandler's 'I Can't Change'.

To the North of England this is Yvonne's unsurpassable classic, a moody John Barry type arrangement, precocious Dinah Washington type lead, and a dance beat to die for. When the beloved Casino opened its hallowed doors to this winner it confirmed the new venture's position as No.1. Bizzarely, this original version has never been released on CD or as a vinyl reissue, at least not legally! Apparently, the ownership of the master is as shrouded in mystery as the record itself!

The Northern Soul All Time Top 500

Al Wilson
The Snake

Top 500 Position: **4**
Original Label: **Soul City**
Current Value: **£6 Issue**
£15 Demo

'Fast, funny, and as original as you can get'
Tom Smith, Beatin' Rhythm, Manchester, UK

A kooky 60's song produced by Johnny Rivers and executed to perfection by singer/drummer Al Wilson. The oddity of the disc stems from the pen of Oscar Brown Jnr and together with the basic groove alongside the Jim Webb type orchestration, the song and lyrics sit nicely for dancers and listeners alike.

Wilson hails from Meridian, Mississippi, which could be a contender as a twin town with... WIGAN!

Jimmy Radcliffe
Long After Tonight Is All Over

Top 500 Position: **5**
Original Label: **Musicor**
Current Value: **£20 Issue**
£30 Demo

'The pure emotion of the song is the most precious thing I have ever heard'

Pete Waterman, Record Producer, UK

Jimmy may no longer be with us, but his superlative 1964 recording of Bacharach and David's underrated song means much to all Rare Soul lovers... This is the side that rendered machismo and girl power to mush.

A stylish ballad originally recorded by Jimmy as a demo for its intended artist, Gene Pitney, 'Long After' is similar in style to Chuck Jackson and Roy Hamilton singles of the time.

Imagine the scenario at the all-nighter, you have spent too much money, argued with your best friend, the cloakroom girl AND the 'other half', to top all that the 45 you've bought for £100 is cracked! Jimmy's vocals suddenly appear at ten minutes to eight and Sunday is spent in lustful motion.

The Northern Soul All Time Top 500

James Fountain
Seven Day Lover

Top 500 Position: **6**
Original Label: **Peachtree**
Current Value: **£30**

'A hunk of Northern funk, excuse me while I wriggle on to the dance floor'

Paul Hatton, Soul Fan, Hull, UK

Undoubtedly the 45 that broke the mould in terms of traditional Northern productions. A typical 70's bass drum and melodic piano kick starts a script from James that transforms into a wailing five star piece of Atlanta Soul.

The real credit goes to Ian Levine though, for vigorously challenging the Northern scene to 'look, listen and learn'. Well we did, and became wiser for it.

Label owner, the legendary William Bell, has found himself in the unusual but pleasurable position of releasing a single which bombed in the States but was revered in Europe.

Epitome Of Sound
You Don't Love Me

Top 500 Position: **7**
Original Label: **Sandbag**
Current Value: **£30 Issue**
£100 Demo

'The first of many classic turntable spins from the class of '74'

John Manship, Record Dealer, UK

I suspect a blue eyed Soul effort here, and what a performance. 'You told me that you loved me (told me that you love me) states the lead singer. Nothing too interesting there until you hear the most uplifting performance from Robert Paladino's Epitome of Sound. I can't help thinking the initial release might have caused a stir somewhere on the East Coast of America, largely due to an abundance of copies that were in several record stores in Philadelphia during the 70's.

Backed by the excellent 'Where Were You', in some quarters 'You Don't Love Me' is considered to be the Wigan anthem.

Garnett Mimms
Looking For You

Top 500 Position: **8**
Original Label: **United Artists**
Current Value: **£40 Issue**
£50 Demo

'Hearing it in 1970 and today tells me nothing has changed, it's fantastic!'

Derek Allen, DJ, Leicester, UK

In recent interviews the man from West Virginia is as surprised as any one at his 1966 recording's history. Though originally in R&B group The Gaitors, 'Cry Baby' launched his solo career in '63, but it is 'Looking' that has become the 'anthem'.

Again, totally easy on the ear, the simplistic arrangement confirms, great songs do not need complicating. The 45 has have pounded the speakers at most Northern gigs during the past 30 years, and I for one never tire of it. In keeping with the scene's tradition a disastrous cover version attempt was made in 1979 by the Echoes, co-produced by... Whatsisname!

Frank Beverly and the Butlers
If That's What You Wanted

Top 500 Position: **9**
Original Label: **Sassy/Gamble**
Current Value: **£50 Sassy**
£100 Gamble

'The intro testifies that this really is the business'

Rob Smith,
DJ, Collector, Record Dealer, Nottingham, UK

I remember distinctly the first time I ever heard this at Va-Va's in Bolton, where after a chance meeting with the late Les Cokell, I raced over to the turntables to see a Gamble label spinning at 45 rpm. The following week was spent humming it, and desperately trying to find a copy. Although on Kenny and Leon's outlet, the side's initial release was on Billy Jackson's Sassy label from where most DJ's secured it to play. The truly gifted front man of MAZE, Frank revels in a tip-top production, of which Philadelphia never mind Lancashire should be proud.

Following the initial hi-hats and horn intro, the next 8 bars suggest a heard of elephants are about to run through the auditorium while you're in full flight on the floor.

If you are looking for big time Northern Soul? - THIS IS IT!

The Northern Soul All Time Top 500

Chuck Wood
Seven Days Too Long

Top 500 Position: **10**
Original Label: **Roulette**
Current Value: **£10 Issue**
£15 Demo

'Seven minutes is too long without this one'

Chris Williams, HMV, Stoke-on-Trent, UK

Chuck's finest hour reveals to all that here is a performer who sounds like he's auditioning for Otis Redding. A monster, walloping, racing, looping, bounding, Soul side from '67 (to quote the late James Hamilton) and known to bit part players as the flip to the UK release of 'Footsee', which peaked at No.9 in 1975. You can see the thinking back then, stick a fantastic record with massive credibility on the flip of a in-vogue piece of nonsense!

The record is marvellous and I urge everyone to own it. Chuck may have faded into obscurity but the legacy left by this outing will remind all of us what a totally brilliant track it is. Chuck, welcome to the Top 10!

Billy Butler
The Right Track

Top 500 Position: **11**
Original Label: **Okeh**
Current Value: **£15 Issue**
£25 Demo

'Simply awesome'
Alan Day, DJ, Derby, UK

A super slick, but basic workout from Jerry Butler's brother.

Recorded for the US Okeh label in 1966, this (amazingly) B side was championed by the Soul City record store in London, who subsequently released the single. The hook is in the guitar and piano which bubbles along delightfully for dancers.

The man from Chicago who recorded many fabulous 60's sides finds himself an unlikely hero 3,500 miles away. Collectors trivia-during a reissue by Columbia (Sony) in 1973, they accidentally used the wrong master and pressed the instrumental version!

The Salvadors
Stick By Me Baby

Top 500 Position: **12**
Original Label: **Wise World**
Current Value: **£800**

'A mesmerising performance on such an obscure disc'

Martin Smith, Soul Fan, Herts, UK

The Salvadors, a Chicago group formed in '62 hit us with one of the great intros of all time, with eight bars of a dark, sinister piano, bass and drum melody. The really big venues associated with Northern Soul can rely wholeheartedly on such a side to get the night underway and it is easy to see why.

In rarity terms, the original vinyl 45 is extremely sought after, as very few copies have emerged after the initial finds over 27 years ago.

Played simultaneously at Blackpool Mecca and Wigan Casino.

The Tomangoes
I Really Love You

Top 500 Position: **13**
Original Label: **Washpan**
Current Value: **£500**

'Detroit has produced many things, most notably (in my house)… The Tomangoes'

Steve Crozier, Soul Fan, London, UK

Similar in style to our preceding number, the basis of the scene lives and breathes on such a side as this. The trademarks are all here, a super rare Detroit 45 with a great lead vocal by Geno Washington (the Atac/Do-De-Ri man, NOT the Ram-Jam band singer!), with an almost 'hey this will be popular, someday, somewhere' stamp on the label.

One thing you will discover about Northern Soul is that the roots are based around a production such as this, and while other distractions (ie, quirky pop dancers) diverted us from time-to-time on the dance floor, it is a 45 of this magnitude which gets us focused again on the big picture.

This is Northern Soul of the highest quality - Tomangoes, take a bow!

The Northern Soul All Time Top 500

Tobi Legend
Time Will Pass You By

Top 500 Position: **14**
Original Label: **Amy**
Current Value: **£100 Demo**
£300 Issue

'One of the world's great enders'

Clarence Bennett,
Soul Fan and DJ, Oldham, UK

Recording as Tobi Lark for Dave Hamilton's Topper label, the gal from Detroit realised 20 years post release that Bell records had issued a demo she recorded in 1968.

Under the guise of 'Legend' Tobi's finest hour was captured weekly at the Casino, known as one of the 'three before 8'. 8am being the closure time of the all-nighter.

The song also received long awaited publicity via M People who covered the song several years ago.

All in all the track is one of the true anthems and still carries enough charisma long into the millennium.

Tony Clarke
Landslide

Top 500 Position: **15**
Original Label: **Chess**
Current Value: **£30 Issue**
£150 Demo

'The drum roll instigates the perfect back drop'

Dave Nowell,
Soul Journalist, Blackpool, UK

Once again, if you are someone with a good memory you're likely to challenge the chart position.

All things being equal, it ought to be a Top 10 sound at the very least. Overkill is the key word here, as this explosive dancer from the late TC rocketed it's way into the arena in late '73.

The track hardly got a play in the 80's, but has since reactivated itself to be one of the true giants. If there was any argument as to the voted position, I would almost certainly be on the side of the challenge.

Passing away in 1970, Clarke recorded for Chess, MS, Chicory and Fascination and became an actor, appearing in 'They call me Mr. Tibbs'. 'The Entertainer' on Chess was his only hit.

The Northern Soul All Time Top 500

Larry Williams and Johnny Watson
Too Late

Top 500 Position: **16**
Original Label: **Okeh**
Current Value: **£25 Issue**
£50 Demo

'Amphetamine driven Northern Soul'

Franny Moore, Soul Fan, Leigh, UK

The Northern traditionalists would possibly rate the track as No.1 contender, considering it's dance floor history and, while turntable spins have fallen of late, the nostalgia value in it is unequalled.

Duets are uncommon on the scene, but an exception is made in this case as two seasoned pro's 'tear it up' with a full blown rampant display that Little Richard would be proud of.

Larry sadly committed suicide in 1980, Johnny passed away recently. Williams in particular was a huge influence on the Beatles. What a shame they did not live to see a major Soul night spinning this marvellous gem. From the vaults of Okeh and recorded in 1967, Williams and Watson we salute you.

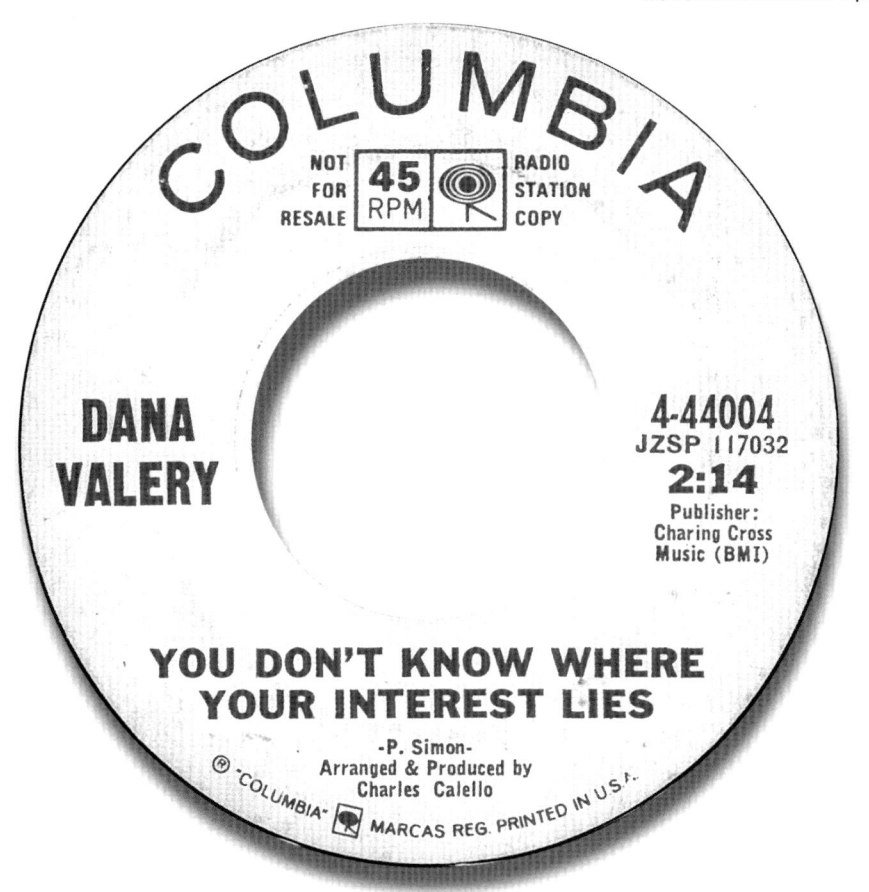

Dana Valery
You Don't Know Where Your Interest Lies

Top 500 Position: **17**
Original Label: **Columbia**
Current Value: **£125 Demo**
£350 Issue

'An adrenaline rush just hits you every time you hear it'

Dave Raistrick,
Record Dealer, Skegness, UK

Many years on, one could question this disc's validity in such an important chart. Dana singing a Simon and Garfunkel song has trademarks of lack of fulfilment Soul-wise, but again the tempo clicked instantly with dancers and it became a truly massive Wigan spin, 25 years on it seems DV has retained a level of credibility.

She later moved to record for Brunswick where 'You Babe' found favour with the UK Soul crowd once more - not bad for a blonde of Italian extraction!

Willie Tee
Walking Up A One Way Street

Top 500 Position: **18**
Original Label: **Nola**
Current Value: **£40**

'Easy does it as Willie tells the tale superbly'

John Abbey, Blues & Soul, UK

Willie Turbiton from New Orleans specialised in recording simplistic lyrics with stunning craft and guile, complimented by that unique Louisiana feel. 'Thank you John', 'Teasin' you' and later 'Please don't go' have their own following, but the winner is 'Walking' which bubbled under the US chart in '66, and remains a classic on both sides of the Atlantic.

The quaintness of tempo lies solely with the artist's vocal control, of which Mr. Tee is a master.

From the Wheel to Keele this masterpiece proudly sits on the top shelf in the Northern Soul Top 500.

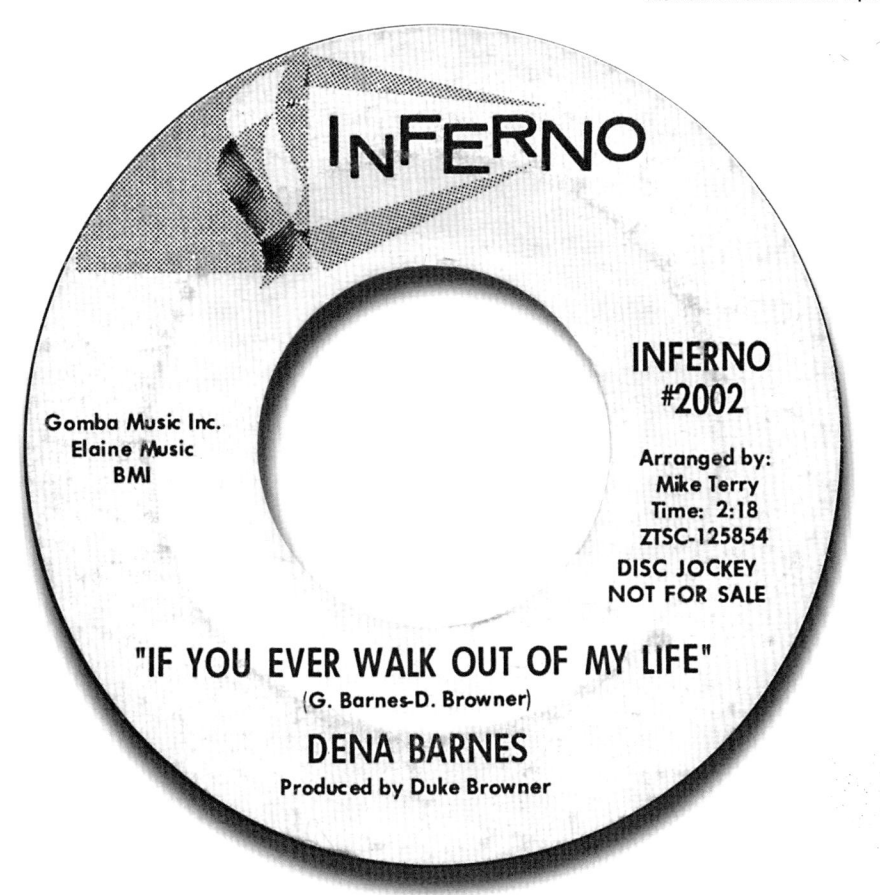

Dena Barnes
If You Ever Walk Out Of My Life

Top 500 Position: **19**
Original Label: **Inferno**
Current Value: **£300 Issue**
£200 Demo

'A timeless piece of sugar coated Soul'

Kev Sowerby, DJ, Penrith, UK

Dena produced just one single for Harry Balk's Inferno label, though there are pressings of 'These Heartaches I Can't Stand', an alternative vocal to Duke Browner's 'Crying Over You' which actually have nothing to do with her!

At a funeral recently of a good friend, the song was broadcast to the congregation which many shed a tear. The moment was poignant, and while the masses grieved, my thoughts also turned to others who had embraced this classic Detroit 45 and made it 'their song'.

Still, it's only a 3 minute piece of black plastic and we should not take it too seriously, but hey, this Northern Soul business is like life and death, except it's far more important than that!

The Northern Soul All Time Top 500

R. Dean Taylor
There's A Ghost In My House

Top 500 Position: **20**
Original Label: **V.I.P.**
Current Value: **£20 Issue**
£30 Demo

'R. Dean's cowboy hat fell off at hearing which of his songs had made the UK charts'

Roger St Pierre,
Journalist, London, UK

Hailing from Toronto, Taylor was the all original session guy for Motown. He occasionally got to write for Mr. Gordy too, as co-author on 'Love Child' for The Supremes and the Canadian also had is own chart success with 'Indiana Wants Me' and 'Gotta See Jane'.

Hang on there RD, 3,000 miles eastbound your throwaway 1965 single for Motown subsidiary VIP is hot in England, in fact it was at No. 3 in the charts (1974)!

The tour, the acclaim, and back to reality. In real terms the 45 is only rarely played at the rarer events, however in the 70's, 'Ghost' pleased many a promoter with the level of spins it demanded.

Archie Bell and the Drells
Here I Go Again

Top 500 Position: **21**
Original Label: **Atlantic**
Current Value: **£6 Issue**
£10 Demo

'The first of many 'handclaps' within the scene... fresh sounding even now'

Carol England,
Soul Fan, Birmingham, UK

Archie Bell from Henderson, Texas was on a roll when a 'out of print' single from 1969 hit the shores of an unsuspecting old blighty. I say on a roll, because he had scored with 3 hits in a row for Atlantic during the late 60's. The 'Tighten Up' man was certainly surprised when 3 years later the single 'Here I go again' was unearthed by DJ's here.

Gamble and Huff had already marked our cards with their new sound, i.e. 'Moody Woman' with Jerry Butler.

In terms of ingredients it has the lot, swirling string intro, fast uptempo beat complimented by the unique vocal that we have come to cherish. Bell of course became a hit maker for the Philly machine, but the US totally missed out on this sensational Soul platter.

Rose Batiste
Hit And Run

Top 500 Position: **22**
Original Label: **Revilot**
Current Value: **£100 Issue**
£150 Demo

'A major felony has been committed... Run onto that dance floor!"

Tot Johnson,
Collector, Stoke-on-Trent, UK

Don Davis formed a label in Detroit called Revilot (the name is Toliver spelt backwards) with a partner Lebaron Taylor (aka Toliver). Together, they released a plethora of gems, aimed at taking on Motown. Unfortunately the gameplan failed but the legacy has been truly embraced by us Brits. 'Hit and Run' is arguably the finest single on the label, certainly the best dancer.

Rose in an interview recently, choked back the tears as she thanked the UK for discovering one of her long lost 45's.

Rose sweetie, thank you for a performance to savour!

The flipside 'I Miss My Baby', vocal to the classic 'Bari Track', is of course superb too!

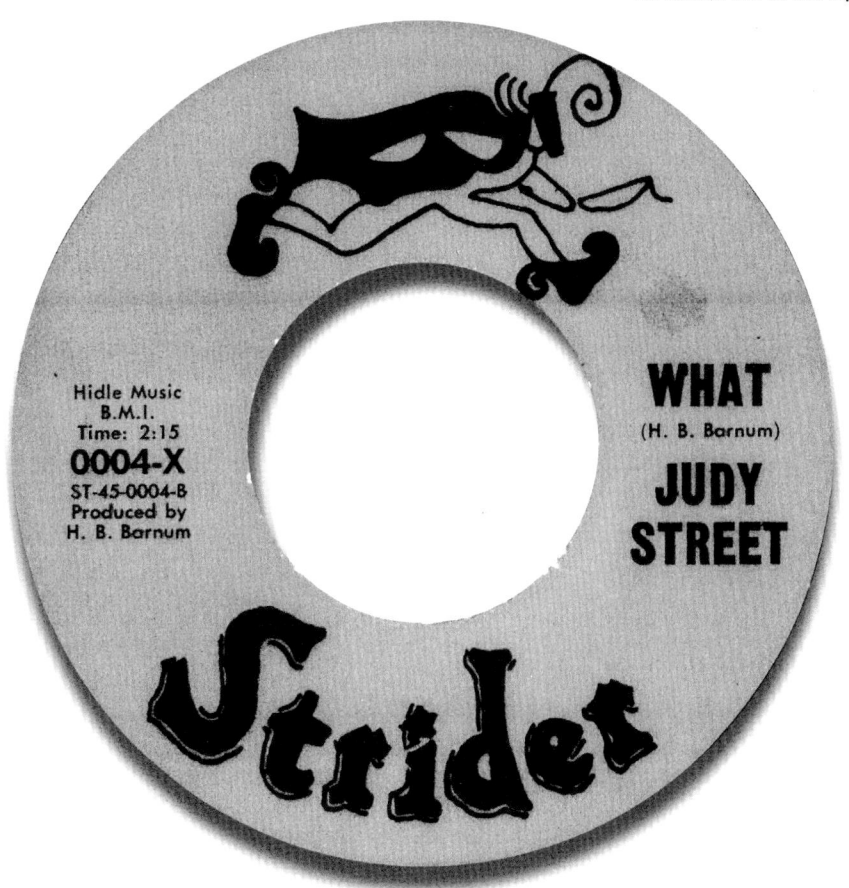

Judy Street
What

Top 500 Position: **23**
Original Label: **Strider**
Current Value: **£100**

'The regionality of sales precluded a chart position'

John Anderson,
owner of Grapevine Records, UK

'What' by Judy Street is an HB Barnum production of late 1966 that almost charted in the UK. The unknown Californian had strong competition from several better known artists who have recorded it over the years (including Britain's Soft Cell, who had chart success with their homage to their own musical roots).

The 'What can I do, what can I say?' chorus is an instant winner and, although considered too poppy by many today, it has undeniably been one of the biggest Northern Soul dance sounds of them all!

Gloria Jones
Tainted Love

Top 500 Position: **24**
Original Label: **Champion**
Current Value: **£15 issue**
£40 Demo

'A great big beautiful romp'
Michelle Vincent, Soul Fan, London, UK

The history of Ms. Jones is well documented, the Soft Cell cover hit even more so. What else can we extract from a US non hit from '65? Well, one key factor to the disc's rating is timing, as initial plays in late '73 mixed perfectly with the 'stomp' sound Wigan was to become famous for.

I would certainly rank it at No.2 behind R. Dean Taylor as the Casino's biggest ever play. In terms of strength, the drum pattern sells it, working dancers to a frenzy, and a mere 2.12 of audio delivers all that's good about the 60's. Gloria recorded for Minit too shortly after her contract with Ed Cobb expired, but those sessions circa 65/66 were the best by a mile, so much so, she enjoys another chart placing later in the book.

Moses Smith
The Girl Across The Street

Top 500 Position: **25**
Original Label: **Dionn**
Current Value: **£100 Demo**
£40 Issue

'The unique vocal sets the song alight'

Rod Hemmings, Soul Fan, Australia

The artist is a mystery, his only other recording being for Cotillion. At least label boss Gilda Woods saw 'hit' written all over it, the problem for label and act though is one of bad timing.

Recorded in '67 in Philadelphia and with the smooth but tense delivery from Smith, I can't help thinking this must have caused a stir somewhere in the Delaware Valley upon release. No, not a fig, many radio contacts have the blank face on this one. So would the real Mr. Smith stand up, we are dying to know who you really are!

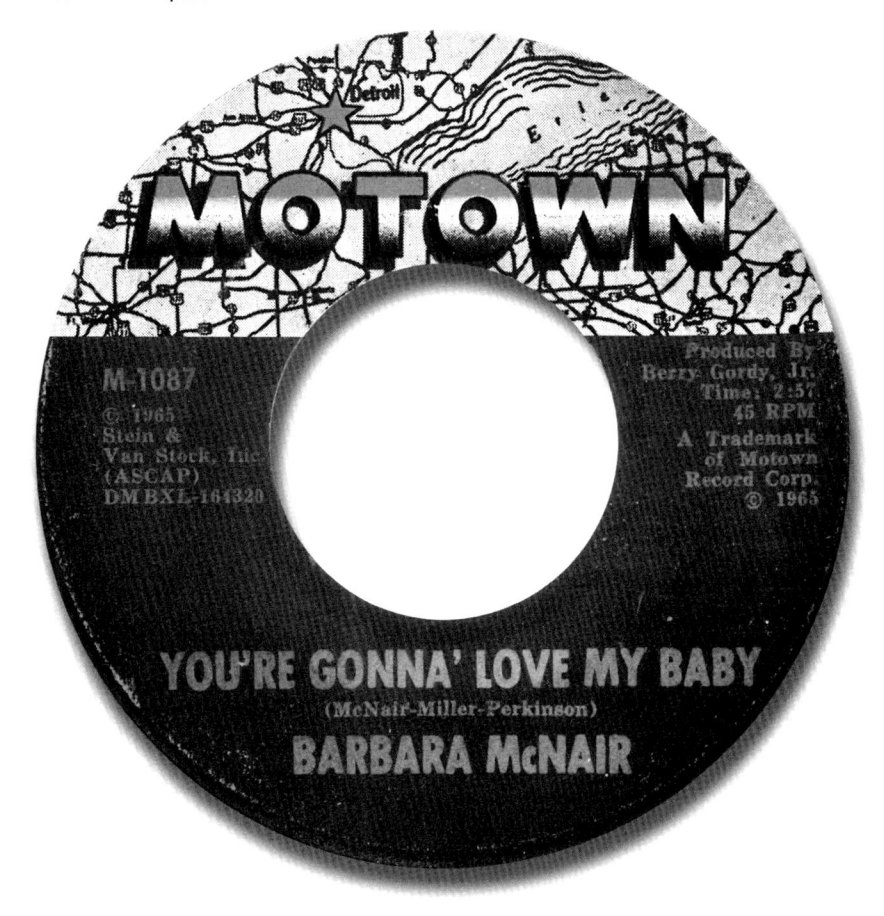

Barbara McNair
You're Gonna Love My Baby

Top 500 Position: **26**
Original Label: **Motown**
Current Value: **£60 Issue**
£100 Demo

'Still sought after by many'

Pete Smith, Record Dealer, Sussex, UK

When a Tobi Legend or Timi Yuro capture the scene's imagination, the songs themselves develop a longevity that many traditional dancers lack. Similarly Barbara was the showgirl at Motown, a sort of Rogers and Hammerstein version of Miss Ross.

With a Berry Gordy production in tow, one should expect a decent chart placing at least. Sadly, it bombed - even worse it's the B side! The UK release fared no better, but the association with Northern finally gave it the acclaim it deserves, albeit North Of Watford.

This wonderful orchestral performance was co-written by Babs herself, who's unreleased 'Baby A Go-Go' is a massive current sound gleaned from a master tape.

Rubin
You've Been Away

Top 500 Position:	**27**
Original Label:	**Kapp**
Current Value:	**£250 Issue**
	£150 Demo

'A delightful over the top performance'

Dale Winton, TV Celebrity

Two stories on this hot blooded piece of ferocity.

Firstly, when aired initially the track became massive and remained so for about a year. Then without notice the 45 was eliminated from most play lists due to the 'reissue' becoming available. Following a 20 year isolation period, apart from collector interest in the super rare 'stock' copy issue on Kapp, the song re-invented itself as the Felix cat food theme.

Obviously, the Northern Soul loving advertising agencies rate it as much as we do! Consequently the popularity now is at an all time high, and deservedly so. Rumours are rife about the identity of the artist, personally I will stick to my own illusion of who he really is.

The Northern Soul All Time Top 500

Mel Britt
She'll Come Running Back

Top 500 Position: **28**
Original Label: **FIP**
Current Value: **£600 Issue**
£800 Demo

'Style and sophistication during a glut of stompers'

Ian Levine,
Filmaker, DJ, Producer, London, UK

Recently discovered living in Grand Rapids, Michigan, Mel has appeared in 'The Northern Soul Story' video.

First discovered by DJ Ian Levine 'the shuffler' as it was known, was an instant hit telling us a great deal about the DJ and Mel's finest hour too!

An extremely sought after disc, even after the influx of around a 100 copies in the seventies. The once common reissues are even scarce today!

Smooth and oh-so classy.

The Checkerboard Squares
Double Cookin'

Top 500 Position: **29**
Original Label: **Villa**
Current Value: **£300**

'The best instrumental ever'

Peter Whitney, Soul Fan, Cumbria, UK

In the early 70's, cover-ups were part and parcel of the scene. One of the first major pseudonyms and in some circles still known as 'Strings-a-go-go', this massive instrumental kicks ass like no other (OK, maybe Mike Post's 'Afternoon Of The Rhino' is a contender) and complete with Frank Wilson style influence, the recording from Los Angeles relates to Detroit perfectly.

Thank heavens the production team relinquished any vocal suggestions! (The Del-Satins' version is a vocal overdub recorded in 1977) leaving us with a legacy of symphonic stomping SOUL.

The Northern Soul All Time Top 500

The Carstairs
It Really Hurts Me Girl

Top 500 Position:	**30**
Original Label:	**Red Coach**
Current Value:	**£25 Issue**
	£75 Demo

'The first time I ever heard a wah-wah in a Northern single'

V. Truman, Soul Fan, Australia

Cleveland Horne and Ray Evans recorded a vintage single for Gene Redd's Red Coach label, it promptly bombed in the US.

A glimmer of hope appeared on the horizon, when in 1974 Ian Levine on vacation in Miami heard the track on a local Soul station. Levine intuitively acquired the single(on a promo at the time) and promptly aired it at his forthcoming gig at the Mecca. Surprisingly the patrons loved it, as the UK was still in the midst of stomp fever and a track of this styling was a considered to subtle and too modern!

Persistent plays by Levine got everybody hooked, including the group themselves who visited the UK recently, and played live at the same venue that first broke it!

Jerry Williams
If You Ask Me

Top 500 Position: **31**
Original Label: **Calla**
Current Value: **£30 Issue**
£40 Demo

'My worst seller to-date in the States!'

Jerry 'Swamp Dogg' Williams,
performer, writer and producer, USA

Legendary writer-producer Swamp Dogg's 'If You Ask Me' coupled with strings and backing vocals drift in and out of Richie Rome's richly textured production.

A UK release in '75 almost realised a hit according to Pye (Disco Demand) label manager Dave McAleer. Fashion was to dominate the labels output, hence the success of Wigan's Chosen Few and The Javells.

In terms of real quality, the single is still being enjoyed by a new army of fans 25 years on.

Lou Johnson
Unsatisfied

Top 500 Position:	**32**
Original Label:	**Big Top**
Current Value:	**£20 Issue**
	£40 Demo

'Yep!... I'm satisfied!'

Derek Howe,
Retailer, Manchester, UK

Lou Johnson was one of Bacharach and David's favourite sons and, although he always remained second in the pecking order to Dionne Warwick. Recording many killer sides for Big Top in the early 60's, this became Lou's 'dance' tune - in the UK at least.

Absolutely perfect for DJ play in as much as use of the thunderous intro to ID the track which whips dancers into a frenzy.

If youth is on your side (lucky you!) you will have missed (for me) the greatest all-nighter ever at The Torch in Tunstall, Stoke-on-Trent, where a playlist would have consisted of maybe 150 winners. Unsatisfied would have been high in the chart even then and, mixed with a cocktail of pharmaceuticals, you most definitely left Hose Street well and truly 'satisfied'

JJ Barnes
Our Love Is In The Pocket

Top 500 Position: **33**
Original Label: **Revilot**
Current Value: **£80 Pink**
£100 Multicoloured

It is hard to find any other record that is as instantaneous as this 1966 outing recorded at the famous United Sound Studios.

Crikey! even Amen Corner recorded it!

The Darrell Banks version is of course brilliant too, but it is JJ on what is for me the most commercial Soul record of the 60's never to be a major hit!

Discovered at Stoke's legendary Golden Torch, DJ Tony Jebb gets most acclaim for plugging this masterpiece to death!

'One of United Sound's premier recorders'

Frank Garcia, Soul Fan, Detroit, USA

Don Thomas
Come On Train

Top 500 Position: **34**
Original Label: **NUVJ**
Current Value: **£15 Issue**
£25 Demo

'A superb 70's sound full of originality'

Bryan Wakelyn,
Collector, Blackpool, UK

Virtually a new release at the time of discovery, but no real problem due to the originality of the waxing. Don Thomas hit the North big in 1975/76, why even UK label DJM picked it up for UK release.

Mixing with the likes of other 70's finds, 'Train' sat rhythmically in sync with other spins, and soon became one of the most requested on the manor. As for Don Thomas, well he slipped back into San Francisco obscurity, probably never knowing the new sexy wriggles his workout had created.

The M.V.P.'S
Turnin' My Heartbeat Up

Top 500 Position: **35**
Original Label: **Buddah**
Current Value: **£100**

'A song's pulse is paramount in a great Northern track, mine races to herculean proportions listening to this!'

Will Harris, BMG/Arista, UK

To any newcomer, the most difficult aspect to understand is the variety of tunes on offer, plus the differential between each track via a dance floor fill.

'Turning My Heartbeat Up' initially appears to have no credence with the scene for the following reasons- 1. It's a rock single from '72. 2. It's a tricky beat and non-traditional.

This is the 'show off' 45, the one where the movers and shakers go for it with energetic twists and turns, leaving onlookers jealous and unfulfilled as claps of appreciation are given to 'dancefloor nomads'. The cultured track deserved more internationally, but again the great Uncle Sam had too many releases of commercial intake to worry about another wannabee searching for stardom.

The Northern Soul All Time Top 500

Sandi Sheldon
You're Gonna Make Me Love You

Top 500 Position:	**36**
Original Label:	**Okeh**
Current Value:	**£200 Issue or Demo**

'A total adrenaline rush'

Adey Pierce,
Record Dealer, Gloucester, UK

To trigger off your real interest in the scene, you need a record that is 'Northern Soul', on this occasion you've found it first hit.

A traditional classic usually needs to engage a 4/4 beat, strong vocal, big city production, all polished off with super gloss. Van McCoy delivers the request with consummate ease, adding to the theory that big time producers make the best records.

The track is quite outstanding and the unknown Ms. Sheldon can quietly be 'well chuffed' at her debut. Van, rest in peace, the legacy you have left us with this soulful adventure leaves a leviathan conquest.

The Vel-vets
I Got To Find Me Somebody

Top 500 Position: **37**
Original Label: **20th Century**
Current Value: **£100**

'The 'woo' in the track is just irresistible'

Steve Jeffries,
Record Dealer, Leicester, UK

Special times at a club centre around invigorating sounds, and this 1967 outing from LA's Vel-Vets captures the very essence of spirit and togetherness.

The track hurtles out of the speakers like Hurricane Andrew and not once does it allow a smidgen of breath.

A trio of gals have simply been given a recording opportunity, and accepted the chance with relish, grasping the mic. and yelling 'n' screaming until producer Jackie Mills is satisfied with the end product. The rest is down to marketing, with which our 'scene' is generally un-interested.

The Northern Soul All Time Top 500

Patti and the Emblems
I'm Gonna Love You A Long, Long Time

Top 500 Position: **38**
Original Label: **Kapp**
Current Value: **£250 Issue**
£75 Demo

'A race against time for dance floor space'

Matt Jahans,
Capitol Soul Club, London, UK

Philly stood tall within the R&B spectrum, churning out countless hits from a variety of production outlets, some however didn't make it but still are quite breathtaking.

The group we focus on here were no strangers to success and one can be forgiven for thinking this is yet another smash for the city of brotherly love. It wasn't and mores the pity as lead singer Patty Russell takes charge of the Leroy Lovett / Frank Bendinelli production and delivers the package beautifully. Many memories are associated with this discovery of the early 70's and it is great to see the more youthful end of the market gagging to hear it at most venues.

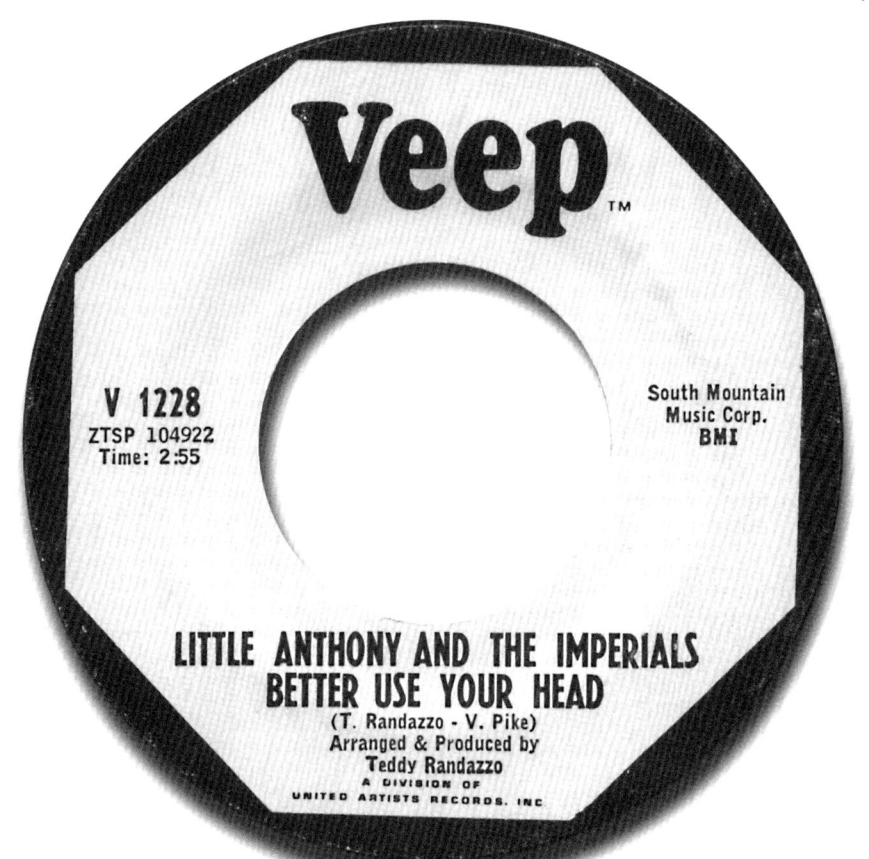

Little Anthony and the Imperials
Better Use Your Head

Top 500 Position: **39**
Original Label: **Veep**
Current Value: **£10**

'A top tune of '75'

Chas Lucas, Soul Fan, Southampton, UK

Consequential to popular belief, a proven winner on the Northern scene often has to realise a kind of distinctiveness. It can be a drum pattern, vibes, or the inevitable hook.

Song 39 is all about vocalising, and who better than Anthony Gourdine, with his unmistakable falsetto lead which scored a series of pop hits as far back as 1958.

Again, we Brits feast on the 'loser', this time the disaster(US wise) is 'Better Use Your Head' a fairly typical Randazzo/Pike production. Soaring to rapturous applause from day one, the soft texture of this Northern classic is summed up astutely by the record buyers, landing the group to a No. 42 position in 1976.

The Northern Soul All Time Top 500

The Casualeers
Dance, Dance, Dance

Top 500 Position: **40**
Original Label: **Roulette**
Current Value: **£20 Demo**
£40 Issue

'Wreaking havoc on the Casino dance floor... Ahhhhhh heaven!'

Chris King, DJ, Nottingham, UK

There was only one venue that could accommodate such a disc and that was the big building in Station Road.

The Casualeers, a New York group, consisted of Arnold Davis, Isiah Love, Jimmy and Ollie Johnson. Production wise it has everything, including the all important 'stomp stomp' feel. Although pop in it's approach (largely due to input of 'Star Wars' themester Meco Monardo) the guys click instantly with the groove and the whole experience is one of joyous fulfilment.

Along with the R. Dean, Javells, and 'Footsee', 'Dance, Dance, Dance' was one of the the biggest songs of '74. The title reveals it's true intention, and we Brits take the challenge gleefully.

Jack Montgomery
Dearly Beloved

Top 500 Position: **41**
Original Label: **Scepter**
Current Value: **£150 Issue**
£100 Demo

'Detroit again, thanks a lot Don Mancha'

Dave Flynn,
DJ and Collector, London, UK

A tale of two sides, firstly the 70's spin being the flip 'Do you believe it'. From the mid-80's our no. 41 came in to play and quite rightly too. Mancha, although a bit part player in Detroit did produce a few excellent sides, but it's the simplistic 'BELOVED' that craves attention. Montgomery is in fact really the writer Marvin Jones, and with other collectables on Barracuda and Revue it is hard to understand why a more successful career was not forthcoming.

An interesting trivia note; Northern Soul fan and friend to the scene Dennis Coffey arranged the orchestration during the session, back in 1966.

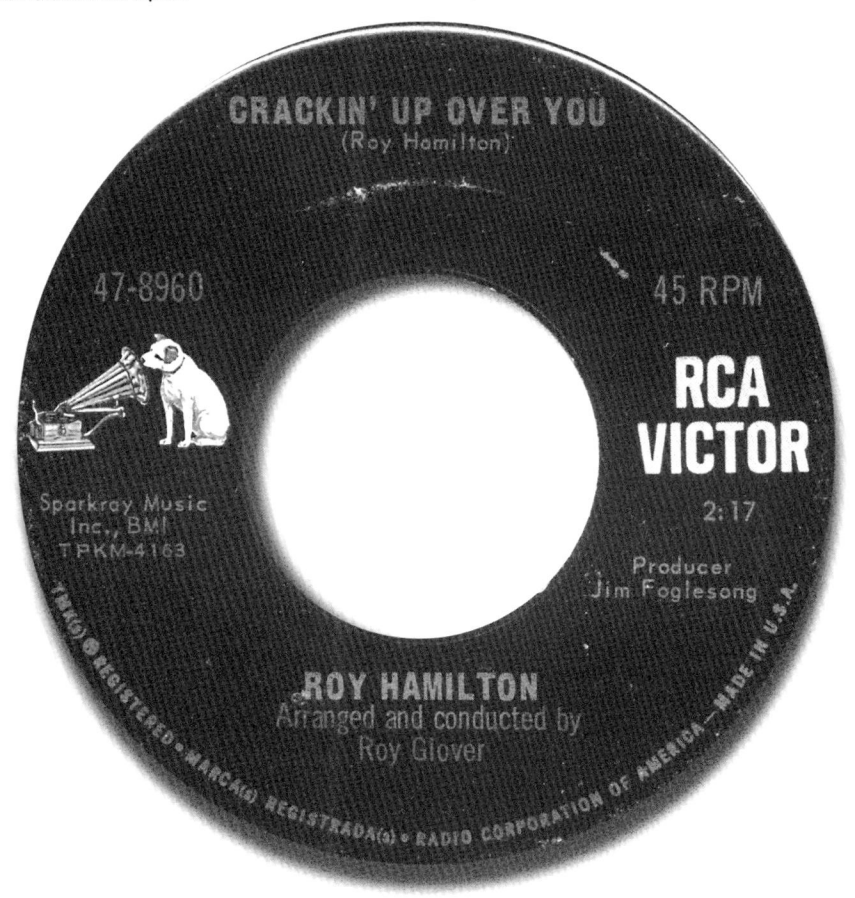

Roy Hamilton
Crackin' Up Over You

Top 500 Position: **42**
Original Label: **RCA Victor**
Current Value: **£60**

'The song gets all over you like a rash, but you don't need any lotion after hearing it'

Eddy Edmundson, Soul Fan, Kendal, UK

Legendary, and requiring little introduction. One of the first major 'niter' sounds, circa 1971.

Total big city anthem from the man responsible for 'Unchained Melody', 'You'll never walk alone' plus a few corkers from the Northern archive.

Roy left us for that great 'gig' in the sky in 1969 and considering he started as a gospel act in 1948 no less. 'Crackin' Up' was one of his final recordings along with 'You Shook Me Up', a enormously popular floorfiller of recent years.

Ironically, a book published in 1999, traced the youth culture surrounding Northern Soul. The title? you guessed it...

Connie Clark
My Sugar Baby

Top 500 Position: **43**
Original Label: **Joker**
Current Value: **£250**

'Frank Wilson on a sojourn from Motown with Chris 'Connie' Clark'

Gary Mellor,
Collector, Swansea, Wales, UK

Written and produced by the legendary Frank Wilson in 1965, 'My Sugar Baby' is not dissimilar to 'Do I Love You' - perhaps unsurprising given Connie's own version under her real name - Chris Clark!

Connie - or rather Chris - remains with Motown to this day in a managerial capacity whilst the Reverand Wilson recorded his own version which sadly languishes in the Motown vaults.

Achieving monster status at the Casino long before anyone made the connection(s) this Joker release is many people's all-time favourite and remains one of the biggest sounds born of a golden era.

The Voices Of East Harlem
Cashing In

Top 500 Position: **44**
Original Label: **Just Sunshine**
Current Value: **£15**

'A generous mix of Gospel and Blackpool'

Bob Hinsley, DJ, Bolton, UK

Wigan Casino had established itself as the new No.1 venue, with Blackpool Mecca pushing it's nose in the air by creating a brand new playlist of current releases mixed with exclusive 60's, in keeping with their one upmanship policy. Silly as it was, the scene became better for it, simply by accepting new but exquisite sides such as this Leroy Hutson/Curtis Mayfield production.

Sounding as fresh as ever, the 1973 release has crossed over to a posse of outlets and, it has the distinction of bridging the North/South divide perfectly. Piano driven, with a Windy City string effect all topped off with customary gospel wails, I'll have this for brunch any day!

Dee Clark
That's My Girl

Top 500 Position: **45**
Original Label: **Constellation**
Current Value: **£30 Issue**
£50 Demo

'A crazy flute driven ditty, that drives 'em wild'

Glenn Bellamy, Dealer, UK

Dee Clark was already established as a hitmaker on both sides of the pond and his 'Hot Potato' side for Constellation, was a 'nearly' song on the UK's dance floors 25 years ago.

The track kicking in at 45, is a strange one to say the least, modelling itself on a former pop hit 'Sugar Shack' by Jimmy Gilmer.

Internationally, the single has acquired cult status on both the Soul and Scooter scenes by receiving more plays than most in the last decade.

Born Delecta Clark in Arkansas, Clark was vastly underrated, and in true nostalgic style, we salute him for giving us a real monster Chicago single. He sadly died in 1990.

The Northern Soul All Time Top 500

Bobby Hutton
Lend A Hand

Top 500 Position: **46**
Original Label: **ABC**
Current Value: **£20**

'Oh so classy'

Carol Smart, Soul Fan, London, UK

To everyone who has heard this Dee Erwin production first played from his album, I can't think of a single contact who does not rate this as one of the great Soul records of all time.

I did not of course use the word Northern, the reason, well I believe it to be the perfect 'Soul' record to dance to, even on the planet Mars!

Hutton, from Chicago, has grown in stature on our scene in recent times due to 'Come See (What's Left Of Me)' recorded for Philips in '69. 'Lend A Hand' though cannot be topped, and probably is the adhesive that held Northern and Modern fans together in more acrimonious times.

Ruby Andrews
Just Loving You

Top 500 Position: **47**
Original Label: **Zodiac**
Current Value: **£80**

'A superb single from a cult artiste'

Roger Williams, Soul Fan, Wirral, UK

Originally recording as Ruby Stackhouse on Kellmac, Andrews' 45 was a heavy hitter in the 80's, spilling nicely into the revival scene of NOW. The track was released on the Zodiac label and bustled around the back of most guys record boxes, until the fateful day, someone plucked up courage to champion the track.

'Just Loving You' caught on instantly, and though we all have experienced Ms. Andrews' various recordings at some time or another, it is the 1969 track recorded in Mississippi that wins the day.

The Vibrations
Cause You're Mine

Top 500 Position: **48**
Original Label: **Okeh**
Current Value: **£40 Issue**
£60 Demo

'A track that could cause serious injury to the dance maniacs...'

Robin McKenzie,
Soul Fan, St Neots, UK

Led by Ricky Owens, who sadly died in 1996, this exceptional Soul group have recorded a couple of classics since their initial hit on Atlantic in 1963.

A strange quirk of fate evolves out of this 'pill poppin' niter anthem. Not wishing to glorify the drugs scene, the flip of the original 45 is called 'I Took An Overdose'. A sombre thought I know but, we have the ultimate dancer here from the real deal-1973.

The track knocks you sidewards by the 4th bar and continues to race against time, leaving you collapsed in a crumpled heap of delight!

Julian Covey
A Little Bit Hurt

Top 500 Position: **49**
Original Label: **UK Island/ US Philips**
Current Value: **£15/£20**

'Dump your holdall next to the Lambretta and Dance, Dance, Dance!'

Rino Sapere, Soul Fan, Italy

Covey, together with his band, The Machine, hails from Sherwood... near Nottingham! A popular R&B band of the mid-sixties they played most of the local clubs and gained a contract with Island.

'A Little Bit Hurt', was also released in the States on Philips and has proved to be a perennially popular tune both on the mainstream Northern scene and the Scooter scene of the seventies, eighties and nineties.

Keyboard driven, the hook and lead vocal combine to deliver an enthralling performance.

The Northern Soul All Time Top 500

Dee Dee Sharp
What Kind Of Lady

Top 500 Position: **50**
Original Label: **Gamble**
Current Value: **£25**

'Gamble and Huff again!...That figures!'

Rob Johnson,
Soul Fan, Dublin, Eire

The production is clinical and arranged by the legendary Bobby Martin and Tommy Bell. All that's required is a vocal of some repute, and who better than the former Mrs. Gamble.

The label owners were just starting to make serious noises in the industry but were still three to four years off the real big time, without any disrespect to their 1968 million seller 'Cowboys to Girls'.

The key motivation here lies with the fresh sounding 'Sigma Studios' input along with a major orchestral backdrop.

The unique piano riff, played by Leon Huff, scurries along to the end, with the vocalist asking 'Tell me, Tell me, Tell me, Tell me!'

Alexander Patten
A Lil' Lovin' Sometimes

Top 500 Position: **51**
Original Label: **Capitol**
Current Value: **£50**

'I wanted this on a British demo so badly

Julian Bentley,
Soul Fan, Manchester, UK

True old school from California produced by James 'Tenafly' McKeachin who has a plethora of great productions to his credit (ie The Furys) and the distinction of being 'Al the DJ' assisting Clint Eastwood in the movie 'Play Misty For Me'

It took a new scene 6,000 miles away in Manchester, UK to discover the track on Capitol (British), which was amazing to say the least as I rate the US copy even harder to find.

In terms of quality, this really is the business, with the usual big city production amidst a tireless vocal from Patten. If you are discovering Northern Soul for the first time, get a load of this!

The Northern Soul All Time Top 500

Chubby Checker
You Just Don't Know
(What You Do To Me)

Top 500 Position: **52**
Original Label: **Parkway**
Current Value: **£350**

'I thought we were supposed to do the twist not the cart wheel'

Dave Clark, Hipshaker, Hampshire, UK

An unlikely source of Northerness from Ernest Evans the twistmaster. Cut in 1965 and, one of his final recordings for Cameo Parkway.

In any event, we are privileged to discover his best work and amazingly the rarest. Coming 'atcha like a whore laced with rocket fuel, the big beat cuts the room up like the finest Harley Street surgeon.

Another 45 where the American issue is exceedingly scarce, suffice to say, the initial find was on the UK Pye distributed Cameo label. One final insult to CC, is that the song is the official 'B' side!

The Northern Soul All Time Top 500

CONSTELLATION
RECORDS, INC.

Disc Jockey
Advance Sample

NOT FOR SALE

C-65-279
VOCAL
A Bill Sheppard
Production

Costoma
Music-BMI
Time: 2:25
Arr. By
Richard Evans

JUST LIKE THE WEATHER
(Richard Parker)
NOLAN CHANCE
C-161

Nolan Chance
Just Like The Weather

Top 500 Position: **53**
Original Label: **Constellation**
Current Value: **£150**

'One of the very first three figure records'
Tony Banks, DJ, Leeds, UK

A massive injection to the scene complete with early tales of the even rarer second issue on Bunky fetching upwards of £200 in 1973!

Vastly underrated Soul act from Chicago works the lyrics a treat, which is just as well as competition in the same market came from Chess by the way of Denise Lasalle's 'A Love Reputation'. Both sides are almost identical, with probably Ms. L gaining most sales locally, as Chance's release is pretty scarce.

Made for the timeless golden era, the relaxed effortless delivery, cleverly builds climatic similies with a love pledge. Born one Charles Davies, he also recorded for Thomas and Scepter.

A vintage production line showing from 'Bunky' Bill Sheppard.

The Northern Soul All Time Top 500

Bobby Paris
Night Owl

Top 500 Position:	**54**
Original Label:	**Cameo**
Current Value:	**£100**

'Wigan's ultimate anthem'

Dave 'Paris' Ibbetson,
Soul Fan, West Yorkshire, UK

Bobby Paris ended up with no less than three huge floor fillers, this being the last of the trio. Originally a B side to 'Tears On My Pillow', the track was released on Cameo in 1966.

The man, it appears, was on a mission from Wigan, with 'Owl' in '66, 'I Walked Away' on Capitol in '67 and 'Per-so-nally' for Tetragrammaton in '68!

A badge was created off the back of the song and no aspiring soulie could be without customary holdall with the 'symbol'

The song is a cover of the Tony Allen hit and Italian-American Paris rasps his way into the Station Road Hall of Fame. Visiting these shores in 1999, he sang his famous three in Blackburn of all places to an amazed but appreciative audience.

Doni Burdick
Bari Track

Top 500 Position: **55**
Original Label: **Sound Impression**
Current Value: **£250**

'Big big Detroit'...

Greg Tormo, Collector, USA

A terrific double sider, but we'll focus on the constantly played one, as the sax lead 'Bari Track' rips into our hearts and minds.

We all knew the vocal version already via Rose Batiste which suffered a lack of turntable play due to it's flipside 'Hit and Run'. Burdick's local tribute is no more than a throw a way jam session, but in Britain it has swarmed consistently over the scene for over 20 years.

It has instant appeal on the floor, and appears to grow in stature year on year, an unusual disc, but white hot!

Dean Courtney
I'll Always Need You

Top 500 Position: **56**
Original Label: **RCA Victor**
Current Value: **£100 Issue**
£50 Demo

'Len Barry's original will always be second best to this incredible cover version'

Chris Toothill, Collector, Manchester, UK

Major labels have the budget to record well, plus manufacture and distribute their products to maximum effect.

Why oh why, did they not do the full monty on this slab of excitement from '67. Nipper looks as bemused on the RCA label as we do about the lack of success of this pure gem.

Rising above the wild and wacky echelons of crude aberrations such as 'My Hearts Symphony' or 'Hawaii 5-0', the side was Wigan all it's own, and while the classy Blackpool Mecca were championing their own cause, here's one that had the 01942 dialling code stamped all over it.

Dean is also a recent visitor to the UK. As per usual, totally gob-smacked at his notoriety 'up North'.

Larry Clinton
She's Wanted

Top 500 Position: **57**
Original Label: **Dynamo**
Current Value: **£1,500 Issue**
£1,000 Demo

'Larry's mesmerising performance is to die for'

John Poole, Collector, Nottingham, UK

From the great Harthon stable in Philadelphia comes one of the last all niter pioneers of the late 70's.

DJ Richard Searling made this song all his own, covering it over to conceal identity.

You can hardly blame a DJ when a track is as good as this, although he didn't have to worry, the record is so scarce that even today there must be less than 20 copies known.

The trademark, well that's simple, a crunching bass driven groove with strong vocals from one-time Lawn recording artist.

Philly cut a lot of stuff like this, but 'She's Wanted' just has that bit extra to satisfy dancers and collectors alike.

Lou Ragland
I Travel Alone

Top 500 Position: **58**
Original Label: **Amy**
Current Value: **£300**

'Part of the new wave of Casino finds that rebuilt the venue's credibility'

Steve Phyllis,
Soul Fan, Nottingham, UK

Slipping neatly into the fold of '74, this super Soul plodder revived the fortunes at the main event, just as the pop influence was starting to infiltrate.

Cleveland based Ragland was no stranger to collectors and for a time his early 70's outing for Warner Bros was gathering pace amongst them. However this remains his ace card which got a release on Bell subsidiary Amy in 1967.

An inventive 45 with Lou and strong backing vox intertwining with each other to hit home a dark and moody song which will always be known as 'Travellin' Man'.

Freddie Chavez
They'll Never Know Why

Top 500 Position: **59**
Original Label: **Look**
Current Value: **£400 Issue**
£200 Demo

'But they'll never know why I love you'... AWESOME!'

Steve Taylor-Collis,
Soul Fan, Jersey, Channel Islands

A Tex-Mex Northern Soul single that is reaping the rewards of almost a play-a gig since '73!

Freddie also doubles as Dave Newman on the same label but it's the 1968 Motownesque kicker that works best for Chavez.

The strength lies in the song, and when even the most energetic are 'out there', they can't help singing along to the effortless solo, similar in range to Bobby Paris.

Tennessee was never a hot bed of uptempo Soul sounds, so it is refreshing to hear one that is original in concept at the very least even though as I said Detroit is in there hovering!

The Seven Souls
I Still Love You

Top 500 Position: **60**
Original Label: **Okeh**
Current Value: **£300 Issue**
£200 Demo

'It took 15 years to break, phew! It was worth the wait'

Roger Stewart,
Record Dealer, London, UK

Massive pop influence as Larry Williams takes charge of the unknown group from LA, who later recorded for Venture and gained a French EP release. The track is a classic... and thanks only to the collectors who continually reminded the scene of it's quality.

I returned from LA in March of '74 clutching Willie Hutch, Obrey Wilson, and a zillion other goodies including this. On the second Saturday of my return I aired it for the first time (unless you know otherwise), it promptly cleared the floor! I could not believe it, and even worse I sold the thing for £3. The notion being at the time that Okeh 45's were not rare.

Oh how gullible we all were, and certainly concerning the longevity of the tracks popularism

Dean Parrish
I'm On My Way

Top 500 Position: **61**
Original Label: **Laurie**
Current Value: **£10 issue**
£30 Demo

'The finest amongst the 'three before eight"

Carl Kingston,
Radio DJ, Leeds, UK

Parrish is apparently living in Sicily and remains unaware of the UK popularity of his sides for Boom and, more importantly of the special place held by 'I'm On My Way' as the last record played at Wigan at 7.57am.

Discovered at Rediffusion in Nottingham in 1971 it became a local cheapie amongst collectors before the Casino's Russ Winstanley made it his own, raising it to the anthem status it has retained ever since.

Together with Brenda Lee Jones' 'You're The Love Of My Life' it also gained a British release on Jonathon King's UK label in the mid 70's.

The Contours
Baby Hit And Run

Top 500 Position:	**62**
Original Label:	**Tamla Motown**
Current Value:	**£20**

'Dennis Edwards is simply magnificent'

Chris Conroy,
Journalist, Preston, UK

Discovered languishing on a budget label LP containing The Contours hits and one other previously unissued cut.

Quite irresistible is this final recording by the group before Edwards joined the Temptations. Many Motown tracks of course should enter our chart, but we'll reserve the right to placement on only the real floorshakers.

Originally recorded in 1966 it was released as a single in the UK in 1974.

The band enjoyed a brief revival via 'Do You Love Me', but the real deal is Dennis Edwards' performance who obviously had the Temps in his sights!

Possibly one of the best Tamla Motown non-hits ever.

Darrell Banks
Open The Door To Your Heart

Top 500 Position: **63**
Original Label: **Revilot**
Current Value: **£10 Issue**
£100 Demo

'The first of the 'legends' in the North of England'

Jan Barker,
Collector, Todmorden, UK

Probably the most respected 45 ever. Discovered shortly after UK release, the sheer quality of the echoes through the corridors of the Northern museum like the golden treasures of Tutankamen.

Born Darrell Eubanks, he died in a shooting incident in 1970 but not without a whole a selection of recordings that are quite frankly - FANTASTIC!

Here's the US hit from 1966, and one often wonders whether the A&R team at Stateside or the preceding promo only London release were just unlucky in not gaining a hit for their respective employers. Back in vogue once again, the track is slightly above a beat ballad, and the whole aura of Darrell's vocal presence is sumptuous.

The Northern Soul All Time Top 500

The Detroit Spinners
I'll Always Love You

Top 500 Position: **64**
Original Label: **Motown**
Current Value: **£8 Issue**
£25 Demo

'It's hard to discount Motown within the scene and this is my personal favourite'

Terry Finn,
Collector, Doncaster, UK

In terms of sheer quality we are staring at a no. 1 single.

Our chart though traces the history of each disc, and though we all love and cherish this 1965 outing from Bobby Smith and the boys, the position allocated is based on the overall success rate on the dance floor.

In the corridors of Hitsville, USA, this is the one that got away, the inch perfect melody being coupled with a killer hook. The 45 has possibly sold more post release than any other non-hit single, and here in Britain we certainly have played our part in it's continuing popularity.

Stunning in the approach, Smith controls the production rather similar to the Isleys - This Old Heart Of Mine, which does not figure in our chart, but symbolises precisely the sound that Northern Soul is based upon.

Earl Jackson
Soul Self Satisfaction

Top 500 Position: **65**
Original Label: **ABC**
Current Value: **£150 Demo**

'My kind of dancefloor satisfaction!'

John Atkinson,
Collector, Burnley

An express train dancer steeped in Torch folklore, Earl Jackson's 1967 demo only release for ABC is nonetheless shrouded in mystery.

Excellent production work by Chicago main man Johnny Pate starts with one of the truly great intros leading you into a stunning vocal performance by this total unknown telling of how he needs some 'Soul Self Satisfaction' because 'since you've been gone I ain't seen nothing but heartache'... supported by heavenly backing vocals and express train instrumentation featuring a bright guitar and powerhouse drums.

Scarce today it is a snip at £150 (even though it's on a major label) for a piece of utterly supreme Northern Soul!

The Northern Soul All Time Top 500

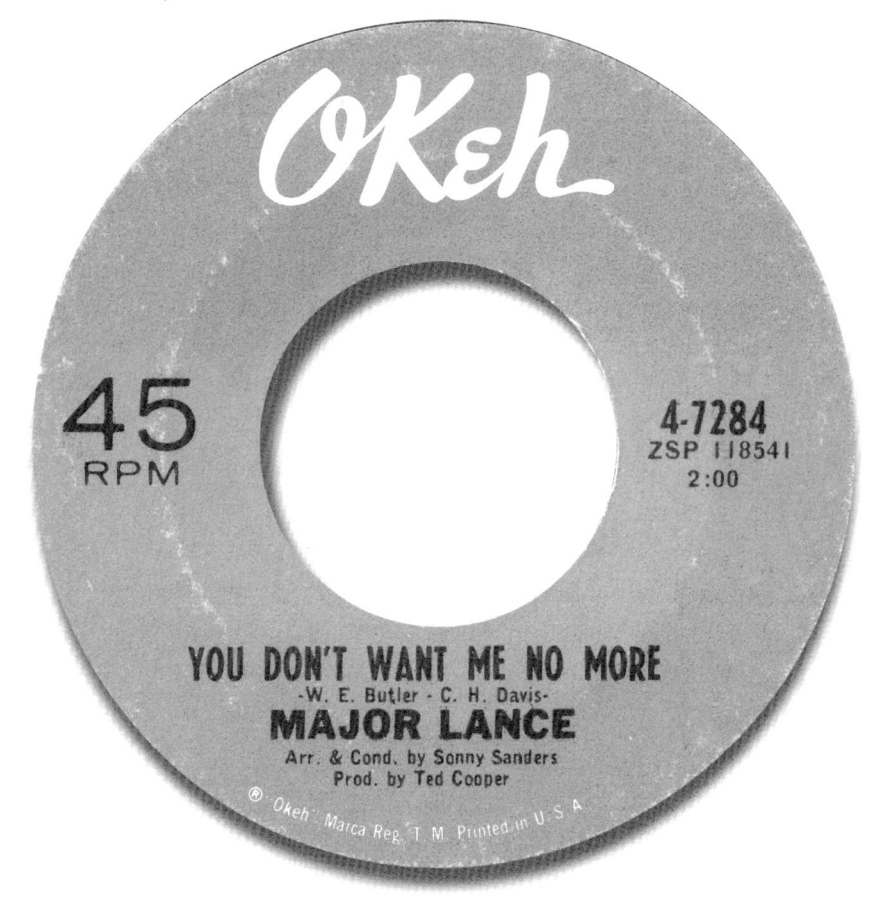

Major Lance
You Don't Want Me No More

Top 500 Position: **66**
Original Label: **Okeh**
Current Value: **£75 Issue**
£100 Demo

'Powerhouse Soul from the Major'
Gary Neale,
Soul Fan, Lancashire, UK

The master of 60's Chicago Soul decided on a real mover with this one. A superlative racer from Okeh that saw Major Lance provide the label with a real 'bomb'. Easy to see the label were clutching at straws with their former 'ace' card, and the main man promptly moved on to Curtom.

The aggressive nature of the production is superb for the UK, and one interesting piece of trivia is the 'B' side 'Wait 'Til I Get You Into My Arms' was recorded by Kenny Carlton on Blue Rock. The Major sadly passed away in 1994.

A Northern treasure that first gained widespread popularity at the Blackpool Mecca.

The Northern Soul All Time Top 500

Bobby Hebb
Love, Love, Love

Top 500 Position: **67**
Original Label: **Philips**
Current Value: **£6 Issue**
£15 Demo

'An exemplary sound'
Paddy Grady,
Merchandiser, Northampton, UK

A Country/Soul singer from Nashville, on whom Philips scored a No.2 in 1966 with 'Sunny'. Jerry Ross was Hebb's producer and well versed in turning black talent into pop stars. Although a 'B' side the flip charted in '66 in the US, while a re-issue of 'Love' scored here in 1972 peaking at No.32.

While Hebb was wrestling with those 'country' roots, Ross supplied him with 'You Want to Change Me' another Northern gem. The real winner though will always be this classic anthem.

Bob Relf
Blowing My Mind To Pieces

Top 500 Position: **68**
Original Label: **Trans-American**
Current Value: **£40**

'Original stuff... and one of the big guns of '73'

Ron Simpson,
Soul Fan, New Zealand

After reigning supreme as the top turntable terror of 1973, the song was re-recorded for the Black Magic label in 1974 and, unknown to them, didn't feature Relf at all, even though he got the vocal credit. All a little confusing, and part and parcel of the scene at that time. Suffice it to say Relf is amused at the cult status of the disc. Many collectors think of him as one half of , this is in fact part fiction - he was the second 'Bob'. He was a key player on the LA music scene, writing many a tune for the Mirwood group of labels, mostly with partner Earl Nelson (aka Jackie Lee), he also recorded as Bobby Angelle on Money, TKO and Imperial records.

His moment of triumph is this epic from 1968 for the independent Trans-American label. The strings make it, and the chorus is about as Northern Soul as you could get.

The Drifters
You Got To Pay Your Dues

Top 500 Position: **69**
Original Label: **Atlantic**
Current Value: **£40 Issue**
£30 Demo

'A rare uplifting Soul groove from, of all people, The Drifters!'

Richard Pack,
Historian, Toronto, Canada

Out of left field comes a contract disputed song from the ever popular Drifters. The word 'THE' was dropped for this 1970 recording, a 'difference of opinion' cited by former lead member-the late Johnny Moore.

The pop influence is there for all to see with Paul Vance and Rupert 'Pina Colada Song' Holmes at the controls.

While the band were in limbo, the UK benefits from a super 'feel good' sound that the label obviously had no intention of promoting. The peak period of it's popularity was the 70's, but it has reared it's head in more recent times. Great to sing-a-long to!

The Invitations
Skiing In The Snow

Top 500 Position: **70**
Original Label: **Dynovoice**
Current Value: **£150**

"The weather's getting cold and snow is piling up on the hill' - a true 60's treasure!'

Jonathon Askew,
Soul Fan, Essex, UK

One had to ponder long and hard about this one. Powered on by Herman Coefield's lead vocal 'Skiing' certainly has a roller coaster feel to it.

Firstly, it was a monster in the early 70's, then a cover by Wigan's Ovation reached No.12 in the UK charts in '75.

That alone should propel either version high into our chart. The group feature again later on with the Wheel classic 'What's Wrong With Me Baby?', but this is the most commercial of their two chart entries.

If you truly dislike the UK pop cover then check out the equally poor US version by the Beach Girls!

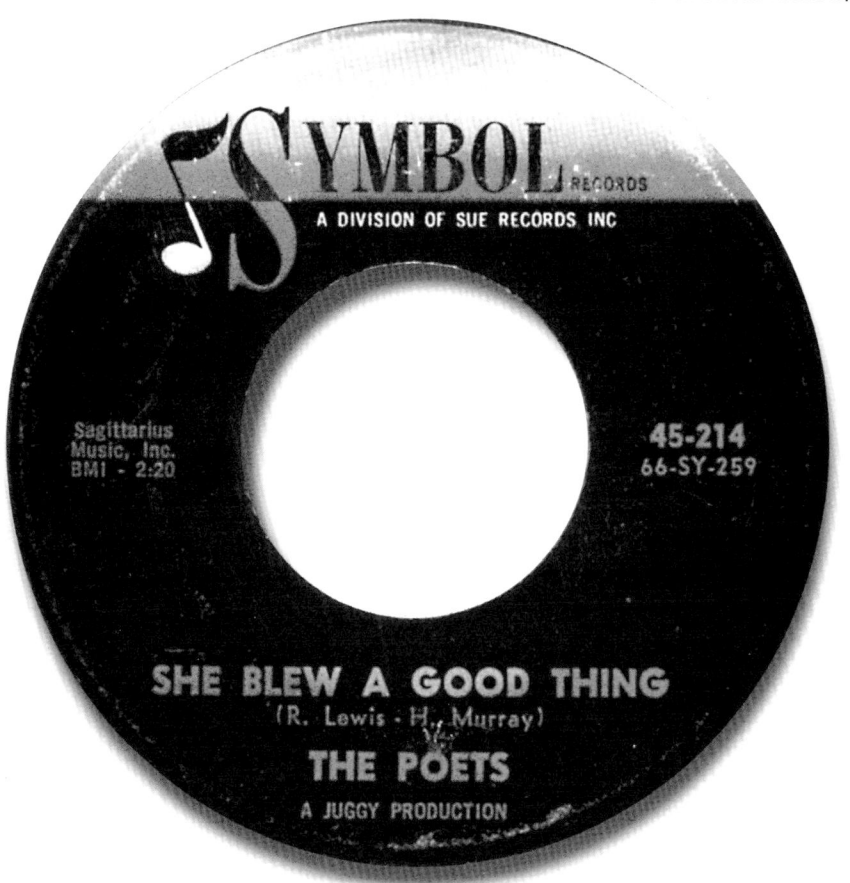

The Poets
She Blew A Good Thing

Top 500 Position: **71**
Original Label: **Symbol**
Current Value: **£10 Issue**
£25 Demo

'A monumental group sound'

Nancy Yahiro,
Collector, Orange County, California, USA

Issued in the UK as the American Poets because of an existing British act signed to Decca. The single, featuring Ronnie Lewis on lead, became a US R&B hit.

The group have had a number of popular Northern sounds and recorded the mega-rare 'Wrapped Around Your Finger' for New York label J-V in 1965.

A totally fantastic single that became massive at the Whitworth Street Wheel in the late 60's, it oozes appeal as the group harmonise perfectly behind Lewis' brilliant lead.

Joy Lovejoy
In Orbit

Top 500 Position: **72**
Original Label: **Chess**
Current Value: **£15**

'One great gallop to find some dancefloor space'

R, Doncaster, UK

Sensational is just one word that springs to mind when hearing this old style 1967 pumper from the little known Joy Lovejoy.

Chess, like Motown, experimented with new upcoming talent periodically, and Lovejoy paraded her wares hopefully, but it wasn't to be. In terms of original Northern Soul roots, this is about as good as it gets with Lovejoy wailing and squealing her way through the extra large Chicago production.

US copies were around in abundance during it's heyday, but try finding it now. Absolutely rivetting and one of my all time personal favourites.

Remember this is the type of track that made us fall in love with Northern Soul.

Lynne Randell
Stranger In My Arms

Top 500 Position: **73**
Original Label: **Epic**
Current Value: **£75 Issue**
£60 Demo

'Wonderful blue eyed Soul effort from the Aussie'

Alan Kline,
New South Wales, Australia

The A side is a cover of a Toys track for Philips, but it's the B side that won the Northern hearts. Co-written by Bob Crewe, a specialist in girl group material, the Spectoresque production proved to be a real winner in the golden era.

Fully atmospheric, Lynne nullifies the old accent, and sounds like she had been part of the Brill Building for years and in fact this single was recorded in New York and NOT Australia as is usually believed.

The single also was released in the UK on CBS, which is incredibly rare.

The Northern Soul All Time Top 500

The Velvet Satins
Nothing Can Compare To You

Top 500 Position: **74**
Original Label: **General American**
Current Value: **£200 Issue**
£100 Demo

'Furious in it's approach, but a totally class act'

Gaynor Coffey,
Soul Fan, Delaware, USA

Can you imagine standing inside a record shop in Jersey City, New Jersey only to be told you have to provide a list before the owner will look for your wants. Imagine a red stock copy of this single sitting on his record player, with the owner saying he liked it! To this day, I still wonder who got THAT record and what on earth was behind the counter!

Let's get back to a total and utterly magnificent rarity from early 1965 and New York's Velvet Satins. A rather moorish slice of slick male vocal, sensational arrangement with piano riffs, old fashioned sax break and just about everything else. I can understand why we all fell for the 45 hook, line and sinker, it's a real shame it came out during the Beatles/Vietnam period, when simple danceable Soul was 'nowhere man'.

Shane Martin
I Need You

Top 500 Position: **75**
Original Label: **Epic**
Current Value: **£50**

'More of that pop-turned-Northern working up a treat'

Belle and Sebastian, Recording Artists, UK

Internationally, confusion often arises with respect to what is a Northern Soul 45.

Imagine say, a collector from Japan trying to understand us Brits, when on one turntable were playing Johnny Sayles or perhaps Maxine Brown. On player No.2 is this little ditty from Martin, written by Jim Webb. It hardly conjures up the ghetto does it!

The scene has many emotional twists and turns and sometimes the whole aura of the groove is the winning factor in the disc's destiny. A smart mover from '68, this is pure dance floor, with 'yer punter dictating to Mr. Rare DJ, that in his or her eyes, this is really where it's at. At least for 2 minutes 5 seconds anyway! 'I Need You' was also released on UK CBS, but is incredibly scarce.

The Tams
Hey Girl Don't Bother Me

Top 500 Position:	**76**
Original Label:	**ABC Paramount**
Current Value:	**£6 Issue**
	£10 Demo

'A No.1 single? Now that's Northern Soul POWER!'

Tania Crossley,
Soul Fan, London, UK

The first No.1 for a single connected to the all nighter scene.

Who could ever forget the legendary group from Georgia led by the Pope brothers forgetting their dance steps on Top Of The Pops in '71! But hardly surprising with the fact that the song was a complete failure in the US on it's inaugural release in '64.

Musically, it is pure 'Sharon and Tracy', but who can argue with a group as legendary as these guys.

Collector wise it's common place, but the roots of its early turntable plays keep it firmly in the minds of even the staunchest of Northern bods!

Lou Pride
I'm Comun' Home In The Morn'un

Top 500 Position: **77**
Original Label: **Suemi**
Current Value: **£1,000**

'Psychedelic Soul - meets Rock - meets Northern'

Mark Sargeant,
Scootering Magazine, Oxford, UK

I feel this particular 45 only received as much play as it did (still does!) because of a similar rhythm to the Case Of Tyme's 'Manifesto'.

A sort of progressive Northern sound, with Pride soulfully riding the groove as if he's Isaac Hayes auditioning for Blood Sweat and Tears.

In and out of fashion for nigh on 20 years, the result being it's new found popularity and current value!

Originally around £20, say hello to £1,000 plus these days, such is the demand.

An out of left fielder, the side has stood the test of time and thoroughly warrants it's chart position.

The Northern Soul All Time Top 500

Paul Anka
I Can't Help Lovin' You

Top 500 Position: **78**
Original Label: **RCA Victor**
Current Value: **£40**

'Paul Anka said the DJ, I remarked 'you're kidding''

Mike Atherton,
Journalist, Sussex, UK

When a seasoned pro like acclaimed pop singer Anka delves into the All Niter arena, one could be forgiven that we have lost the plot completely!

To anyone else who has heard, danced, and owned the masterpiece, you of course know different.

The track is absolutely magnificent, starting with bass n drums followed by melodic vibes and a crunching 1966 dance beat, all topped off with Anka doing it 'his way'!

During the Casino/Mecca race for supremacy, Wigan needed records like this desperately. They were a sort of warning shot to The Highland Room that Station Road meant business, and with 45's like this, it kept the momentum rolling at the newest venue on the manor.

The Four Perfections
I'm Not Strong Enough

Top 500 Position: **79**
Original Label: **Party Time**
Current Value: **£150 Issue**
£200 Demo

'Simply enormous'
Phil Kingswood,
Soul Fan, Mansfield, UK

The single looks and feels Northern, without even playing it! A typical scenario emerges with a wonderfully obscure label from Philadelphia, percussive heavy production and the usual killer hook line that slays you.

One point that many Brits will find interesting is that certain radio DJ's in Philly at the time remember the track well.

Former New Jersey radio DJ Ron Diamond actually played it on his show back in '68!

The City of Brotherly Love had a massive influence on the North of England with both provinces creating their own destiny without the need to follow others.

The Prophets/The Creation
I Got The Fever

Top 500 Position: **80**
Original Label: **Smash/Eric**
Current Value: **£20/£5**

'White psychedelia produces a killer Soul sound'

Rob Matthews,
Soul Fan, Midlands, UK

A long story this, so here is the shortened version. Originally released on Smash in the US, a specialist shop in the UK got Mercury to release it here two years after the initial US release. Apart from a small number of Northern fans who latched on to it in '71, it did in fact peter out fairly quick. Selectadisc, the main importer at the time, were suddenly besieged by collectors wanting to purchase it (Mercury deleting it too soon). The upshot was that they had a contact in the US (Eric records) who obtained the master, and engaged producer Bobby Martin to remix it.

The track was slightly more upbeat and sounded a lot fresher. A UK release on Stateside and subsequent reissues throughout the 70's, have made 'Fever' one of the most spirited and energetic sides ever to hit the North.

The Coasters
Crazy Baby

Top 500 Position: **81**
Original Label: **Atco**
Current Value: **£80**

'The Coasters - dispensing with Rock n Roll for Northern Soul'

Bob Fisher,
Connoisseur Collector, London, UK

Another unlikely rare 45 to infiltrate the scene.

Collector Dave Burton must have been bowled over to discover one of the last recordings for their label Atco.

Cut in '65 with Billy Guy on lead, the song is memorable throughout, as per the hook 'My Heart's Wide Open' (the original cover-up title). Many tracks in the 70's were covered up so as to conceal identity. The thinking behind it was that nobody would be able to find a copy. Such was the intensity of the 'exclusive', the artist was also changed to 'Freddie Jones'.

Back to reality and a truly superb dance anthem as far as the UK is concerned, however it is possibly the group's least successful recording.

The Northern Soul All Time Top 500

Christine Cooper
Heartaches Away My Boy

Top 500 Position: **82**
Original Label: **Parkway**
Current Value: **£150 Issue**
£250 Demo

'That wonderful Parkway label again'
Gary Macklish,
Soul Fan, Leeds, UK

Coming off like a cross between 'Back In My Arms Again' and 'A Lover's Concerto', Christine Cooper was a change of direction for the bubblegum producers 'Super K Productions'.

Years earlier, Cooper had another floor filler by the way of 'S.O.S' also on Parkway, but it's the more Motownesque 'Heartaches' that captures the floor, both were however US sales failures, and her third single for the label promptly flopped stateside too.

Co-written by Richie Cordell of Tommy James fame, the pop influence is there for all to witness, sadly Ms. Cooper fell from grace, the producers though went on to record such inane pop as 'Simon Says' and 'Quick Joey Small' amongst many others!

The Impressions
You've Been Cheatin'

Top 500 Position: **83**
Original Label: **ABC Paramount**
Current Value: **£10 Issue**
£20 Demo

'One of the truly wonderful sounds from the late, great' Curtis Mayfield

Rob Messer,
Record Dealer, Essex, UK

Originally a non hit, gaining late 60's play but dying a death in the 70's, it received a spin or two in the following decade, before returning triumphantly to the past and current years in full working order. Perfect in every way, this is the complete 'dancer' from the 60's with Curtis controlling the whole epic. Mayfield, bless him, was undoubtedly the Steven Spielberg of the Soul business.

The group had a range of members at various times, but included Northern names Jerry Butler, Leroy Hutson and Nate Evans. After his well publicised stage accident of the early 90's Mayfield made a recovery and started recording and performing again, however this genius of melodic Soul with so many hits passed away in 1999.

As for the record itself, well everybody owns a copy don't they?

Harold Melvin and the Blue Notes
Get Out

Top 500 Position: **84**
Original Label: **Landa**
Current Value: **£30 Issue**
£40 Demo

'That 'just hung up the telephone' introduction just kills me!'

Ian Dewhurst,
Simply Vinyl, London, UK

Even without Teddy Pendergrass the group were pretty tasty, relying on more of a collective approach vocally.

The surprise with this dated workout from 1964 is the slow beginning, which just about puts the dancer to sleep except at the last moment the lead leaps out of the trap like the longshot on a hiding to nothing.

The song is produced by 3 Degrees former manager Richard Barrett, and while the group became enormous in the 70's, they can be comforted in the fact that their first serious attempt in the business did nothing but enhance their reputation.

The Dells
Run For Cover

Top 500 Position: **85**
Original Label: **Chess**
Current Value: **£15 Issue**
£25 Demo

'One of our best, but relatively poor sellers'

Chuck Barkesdale,
Dells member, USA

Oh the mighty, mighty Dells! Run For Cover was a poor seller by Dells' standards, selling a paltry 30,000! Played on and off for 30 years or more, it's a mid paced groover which Marvin Junior sails through.

You get the feeling that the lead was begging to do more on the vocal side, being limited as Phil Wright's arrangement created pleasurable but suppressive background vocals.

Either way Junior never fails and we are left with another 24 karat golden nugget from the world's longest surviving vocal group.

The Fascinations
Girls Are Out To Get You

Top 500 Position:	**86**
Original Label:	**Mayfield**
Current Value:	**£15 Issue**
	£25 Demo

'One for the ladies'
Billy Swain, Soul Fan, Nottingham, UK

Originally recording for ABC, the girls signed to Curtis Mayfield's label, released here on Stateside and then Sue, before finally charting at No.32 in 1971 on Mojo.

To Mayfield it was all so simple. Create a melody, write a pop song with a hurricane hook all backed by his ingenious players, and wait for the sales.

Although it did not fair to well stateside, the song is an anthem here, with just about every girl imaginable bopping to the enchanting voices of Bernadine Smith, Shirley Walter, Fern Bledsie and Joann Leavell.

Eddie Foster
I Never Knew

Top 500 Position: **87**
Original Label: **In**
Current Value: **£150**

'One of the great all nighter songs'

Benjamin Rassat, Soul Fan, Lyon, France

On the classier side of dance circa 1974, and one which got the initial play at the Mecca, but found fame at the Casino.

A slick production for this 1967 single from Berkeley, California which became so popular it could have been the first 'musical' tattoo!

A real stunner that you sing a long to, groove to, make love to!

There's little to say except please listen out for it if you like 'em sweet and sassy. Foster incidentally is still knocking around the Bay area and recorded another in demander 'Closer Together', although this one ranks much higher in popularity.

A proven winner, without any real hype.

The Van Dykes
Save My Love For A Rainy Day

Top 500 Position: **88**
Original Label: **Mala**
Current Value: **£100**

'Pure, unadulterated Northern Soul'

Magnus,
Nitty Gritty, Stockholm, Sweden

Texas reigns supreme once again with the much loved Van Dykes who recorded this gem in Dallas, 1966.

Originally a Motown demo and written by Norman Whitfield, you somehow can't help thinking the song was created for Eddie Kendricks and indeed it was recorded by the Temptations and Undisputed Truth. The Van Dykes lead is so reminiscent of Kendricks, I'm quite sure the demo was similar.

In terms of popularity, it qualifies as a real monster in the golden era and, as time has evolved it always commands a full floor whenever it receives an airing.

The Pointer Sisters
Send Him Back

Top 500 Position: **89**
Original Label: **Atlantic**
Current Value: **£60**

'Cleethorpes really made its mark with this one'

Mary Chapman, Promoter, Lincoln, UK

An unlikely spin from Oakland's Pointer Sisters, who recorded this 'hard to find' item in 1972.

Co-written by Richard Caiton, who is no stranger to rare Soul, and produced by Wardell Quezergue in New Orleans.

Preliminaries aside, the new venue of 1975 Winter Gardens, Cleethorpes, broke this full on after being serviced by record dealer John Anderson (Soul Bowl).

A quirky but seriously effective 45, the value and popularity are soaring again. Best get in the queue.

The Northern Soul All Time Top 500

The Yum Yums
Gonna Be A Big Thing

Top 500 Position: **90**
Original Label: **ABC Paramount**
Current Value: **£500**

'A smooth girl group with that little extra'

John Hulme,
Soul Fan, Greater Manchester, UK

Ironically the other version by the Sapphires was the initial playmaker. Largely due to the raucous tempo which suited most back in '74.

As the slowing down process took a toe hold, the Yum Yum's version also discovered around the same time was revisited, and has since become one of the most played 45's of the last 10 years.

A Philadelphia sound, with girl group specialists Ross/Renzetti at the controls, this is a totally superior side that was long overdue a comeback.

Nolan Porter
If I Could Only Be Sure

Top 500 Position: **91**
Original Label: **ABC**
Current Value: **£40**

'The changing face of Rare Soul and much better for it'

Craig Caukhill,
Vital Distribution, London, UK

Here's the scoop, firstly the track is fairly motionless, moody and non-traditional it even gained a UK release well and truly in the middle of the golden era.

Porter had already tasted underground success with another oddity 'Keep On Keeping On' during the Torch era. At the time, I likened it to Norman Greenbaum's 'Spirit In The Sky', with it's weird sound effects. On this selection, he excels his first UK discovery, and I now find myself waiting for a cover version by a major rock act.

This track could form the basis of a massive worldwide hit - attention all major A&R executives!

Hoagy Lands
The Next Line

Top 500 Position: **92**
Original Label: **Laurie**
Current Value: **£20 Issue**
£50 Demo

'A gifted performer'
Jeff Hunter,
Soul Fan, Loughborough, UK

A fantastic record that has remained popular since its first plays in 1971 and perhaps the most sought after of all British collectors' items, worth in excess of £150 on Stateside.

Lands recorded for both MGM and Atlantic before teaming up with New York's Laurie label.

A truly sparkling 7" featuring a fabulous girlie chorus backing up Land's vastly underrated lead. The superb 'Next In Line' was monumentally popular in 71/72 and pure demand from the scene eventually resulted in another UK release.

Lainie Hill
Time Marches On

Top 500 Position: **93**
Original Label: **New Voice**
Current Value: **£300**

'A quaint, subtle song, that you just can't help singing along to'

Laura Jennings,
Soul Fan, Inverness, Scotland

Emotively, the track has it all. A simplistic orchestral arrangement with young female lead capturing the innocent side of the 60's.

An old hand at hitmaking, Bob Crewe saw no reason why this should not attain another chart success for the New Voice label. This one however took a dive - that is until the 1976 when it was discovered by our beloved Northern scene, who embraced it whole-heartedly.

Filed in the DJ box alongside Dena Barnes, Lynne Randell and Nancy Ames, the dancefloor era to which they belong remains a poignant one to many of the scene's female members, who often identify strongly with this type of record.

The Northern Soul All Time Top 500

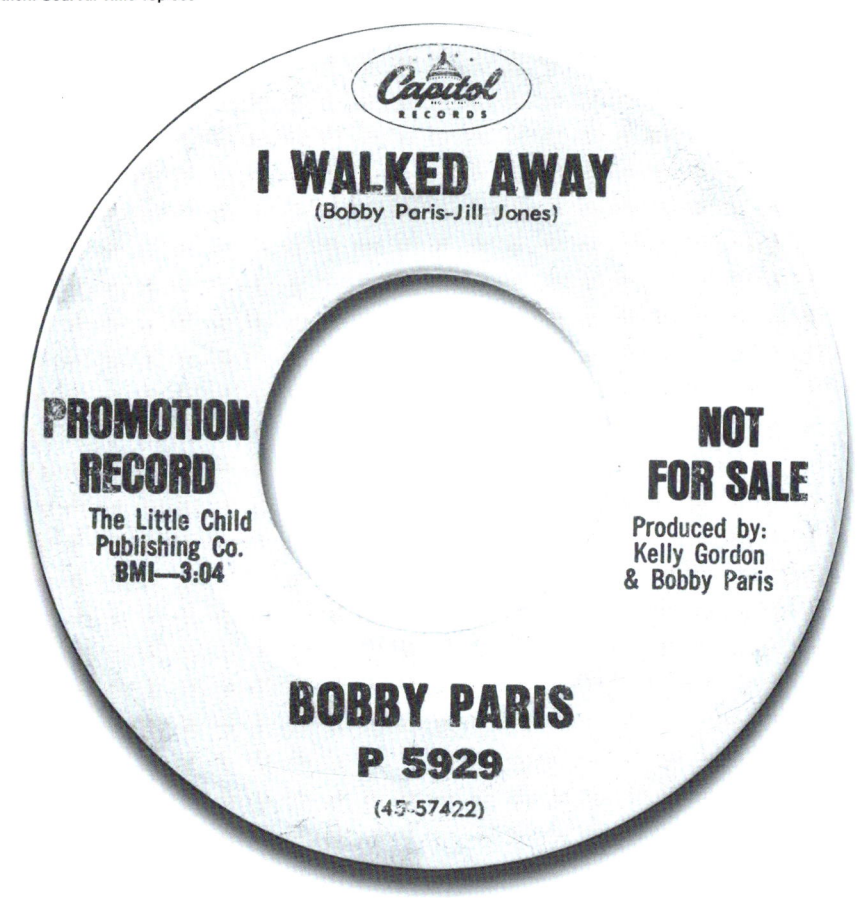

Bobby Paris
I Walked Away

Top 500 Position: **94**
Original Label: **Capitol**
Current Value: **£100 Issue**
£50 Demo

'Bobby Paris is a legend'

Bobby Paris,
recording artist, Los Angeles, USA

The middle part of Paris' trio of Northern classics involves the Capitol label, which was tucked neatly in between his Cameo and Tetragrammaton sides.

While the other two are out and out stompers, 'Walked' reveals itself as an emotive blue eyed rumbler with those ever-so-tearful lyrics.

During the frantic years the disc often got a end of night spin, today it is about as upfront as you can get.

His visit to the UK is well documented, and while we may have questioned his ability as a Soul artist, 'the boy done good' at a recent Soul festival.

Spyder Turner
I Can't Make It Anymore

Top 500 Position:	**95**
Original Label:	**MGM**
Current Value:	**£8 Issue**
	£35 Demo

'In and out of fashion for 30 years, the track thrills to this day'

Richard Moore, Soul Fan, Kent

Dwight D. Turner will be remembered for the amazing rendition of 'Stand by me' in the US, peaking the charts at no. 12 in 1967. As a vocalist from Beckley, West Virginia he had a remarkable range and would probably have been the best warm up man in the business for Otis or Jackie.

His recordings from twelve months earlier at the Terra Shirma studio in Detroit provided us with the masterpiece herein. Played almost constantly since 1970, it reigned supreme at Wigan Casino where DJ Dave Evison reactivated it into a classic revived 45 breaking much of the unwritten 'rarity' rule in the process.

The Northern Soul All Time Top 500

Frankie Valli
You're Ready Now

Top 500 Position: **96**
Original Label: **Smash**
Current Value: **£6 Issue**
£10 Demo

'A monumental pop tune reserved strictly for the scene'

Mick Fitzpatrick,
Soul Fan, County Durham, UK

Arguably the first Northern 45 to chart due to regional demand.

Valli who departed briefly from the Four Seasons, cut two sides for Mercury subsidiary Smash. One upshot being the catchy 'You're Ready Now', which reached No.11 in 1970 in the UK charts. Although recorded in '66, it failed on both sides of the pond, that is until the great North West took it to heart and played it religiously every Saturday.

Valli, born Francis Castellucio, also encountered the scene once again with 'The Night' a veritable Wigan monster in '74/75, which appears later in the chart. In terms of real commercial Northern, this possibly is the forerunner of a generation, and although scorned by purists, if it were not for such sides the scene might never have flourished.

Earl Wright
Thumb A Ride

Top 500 Position: **97**
Original Label: **Capitol**
Current Value: **£25**

'There's a myth among collectors that a vocal exists. Pure fiction, although not a bad idea'

Wayne Smith,
Soul Fan, Greater Manchester, UK

Walking into the Golden Torch in 1972 was a real eye opener. The array of tuneful dancers was unrivalled, and Earl Wright's oddity on Capitol was just another A listed turntable favourite.

The track was a throwaway 'B' side (Wright covering Dylan's 'Rolling Stone' on the 'a' side) and has all the attributes of being a big single for the major. Unfortunately Capitol deemed it an 'easy' single, while North of Watford we took to it like Fred Astaire and Ginger Rogers. This big beat instrumental was produced by Dave Axelrod possibly at their own studios on Vine Street in LA.

The Sapphires
Gotta Have Your Love

Top 500 Position: **98**
Original Label: **ABC Paramount**
Current Value: **£15 Issue**
£25 Demo

'The ultimate one for the girls'

Dave Pointon, Soul Fan, London, UK

The UK HMV label must have been inundated with fantastic Soul cuts such as this, due to their licensing agreement with ABC in the US.

The track flopped but became a minor hit stateside almost surpassing their only hit 'Who Do You Love'.

Carol Jackson had a terrific voice and, complete with George Garner and Joe Livingston on background, they became the darlings of Philadelphia in '64 while returning to glory here in '71. The mid tempo piano lead with Jackson's first line followed by the group yelling 'hold on baby' is pure magic.

With 'Evil One', 'Slow Fizz' etc under their belts, it is difficult to decide on the most prominent side. The judges decision reveals 'Love' to be the most popular, and who's arguing!

Michael and Raymond
Man Without A Woman

Top 500 Position: **99**
Original Label: **RCA Victor**
Current Value: **£300 Issue**
£50 Demo

'An exquisite Detroit monster'

Gary Givens, Soul Fan, Detroit, USA

Pied Piper productions were a key link to RCA's US black music output. Mike Campbell and Raymond Monette are an unusual combination, sounding a lot like another Detroit duo, Bob and Fred.

Dennis Coffey arranged the track which the label released in 1967 only to relegate it to the 'b' side in favour of the old standard 'Walking the Dog'. MWAW is atmospheric to say the least, with an orchestral overture to savour. Not a work of art but close, and pretty darn popular too.

Furthering the Pied Piper connection, Michael and Raymond had a rare single on Giant which, though not as good, is much sought-after by collectors.

The Northern Soul All Time Top 500

Millie Jackson
My Man Is A Sweet Man

Top 500 Position: **100**
Original Label: **Spring**
Current Value: **£6 Issue**
£10 Demo

'Fortunately this is one to dance, not fornicate to!'

Millie Jackson, Artist, USA

A baaaadddd gal from Thompson, Georgia kicks up her heels and goes 'pop' on this minor 1972 hit.

Taken from her first album, it's not hard to understand the appeal of such a track. Gospel delivery over a sort of Philly arrangement complimented with a title hook that is sung more times than almost any song I know (pre-75).

When the calibre of songs such as this are confronting the scene the term 'rare' is relegated to the wastebin, even by the most hardened collectors.

A well seasoned performance by a veritable newcomer (at the time), having previously only released a minor effort for MGM in 1969.

Top 500 Position: **101**
Original Label: **Autumn**
Current Value: **£15 Issue**
£30 Demo

'Humungous Soul'

Chloe Smith,
Soul Fan, Liverpool, UK

Bobby Freeman
I'll Never Fall In Love Again

Written by Sly Stewart, and a side that went even further than the former Northern giant 'C'mon and Swim'.

Absolutely top notch stomping Soul from San Francisco from former lead of the Vocaleers and Romancers.

When in penetrative discussion about the real McCoy this must be almost at the pinnacle. A forceful guitar lead (Larry Graham?) complimented by drums a'plenty and Freeman's wailing climax make a mockery of chart success. Freeman himself realises this as the single is considerably livelier and more upbeat than his original album version. Sly Stone also recorded it, so too did John Lee's Groundhogs.

One of the first big imports after the Wheel's closure in 1970.

Top 500 Position: **102**
Original Label: **Epic**
Current Value: **£50 Issue**
£30 Demo

'One of the sweetest 45's of its generation'

Gail Thompson,
Soul Fan, Stafford, UK

The Poppies
There's A Pain In My Heart

Along with Fern Kinney (Malaco), Rosemary Taylor (ABC) and Patsy McEwan, Dorothy Moore lead this girl group from '66 to minor success with Epic records.

'Pain in my heart' was such an anthem during the 70's largely again to the female crossover appeal.

Dorothy belts out the song with conviction and although producer Billy Sherrill's production is full of Spector'isms, the Jackson, Mississippi born gal reaches beyond the monstrous reverb instigated by Sherrill.

Pop Soul at it's finest!

Top 500 Position: **103**
Original Label: **Island**
Current Value: **£100**

'Jamaican Soul rules'

Lester Sands, Soul Fan, Croydon, UK

Jackie Edwards

I Feel So Bad

One of the original clutch of British-only releases to kick start the scene in the late 60's.

The red and white Island label is synonymous with Ska collectors and Edwards himself was no stranger to the cool Rock Steady scene of that time.

We are focusing though on a song recorded in England with producer Syd Dale in 1966. Basically it's a love song with a beat, but the melody drives it to fulfilment as far as the dance floor goes.

There is a rare duet version too, and I can't help wondering if someone like Brenton Wood was to have recorded it in the US it could have realised more sales for Edwards here.

Top 500 Position: **104**
Original Label: **Ric-Tic/Gordy**
Current Value: **£10 Issue**
£20 Demo

'A fierce instrumental that sounds like Mantovani on acid!'

Gordon Wilton, Soul Fan, Mansfield, UK

The San Remo Golden Strings

Festival Time

Taking the name from the Italian city and titling the song of the annual festival. The end result being Detroit meets Europe and climaxes in rainy Manchester.

The vocal of course is superbly done by Laura Lee, but on this occasion I fancy the instrumental.

With a string arrangement that even Andre Previn would be proud of, the groove is remarkable. I can't help wondering what the angle was. Did Mr. Gordy intend to parade the single as some sort of theme tune at Midem '67?

Either way it's a blockbuster that all and sundry have at one time 'done their back in' to.

Originally on local Detroit label Ric-Tic, Gordy acquired the master from label owner Ed Wingate.

Top 500 Position: **105**
Original Label: **Columbia**
Current Value: **£15 Issue**
£30 Demo

'Discovering a single by the Spellbinders is the highlight for any record collector'

Simon Richards, Soul Fan, Hull, UK

The Spellbinders
Help Me (Get Myself Back Together Again)

Big time production from Van McCoy, song written by Ken Williams and with Columbia records behind it, the scene is set for the group led by Robert Shives.

From the 'git go' the vibes sweetly announce the melody, followed by a massive beat and slick vocal, all topped off with a orchestral crescendo that marries the backing vocals and lead perfectly.

Yep, it's an old timer, but if like me you found yourself recording the ultimate in car tape play, 'Help Me (Get myself back together again) would feature on side 1.

Recorded in 1966, the golden year for 'our' music.

Top 500 Position: **106**
Original Label: **Uptown**
Current Value: **£30 Issue**
£60 Demo

'A rip-roaring corker for this multi-talented lady!'

John Anson,
Soul Fan, Greater Manchester, UK

Gloria Jones
Come Go With Me

The Del-Vikings' Rock'n'Roll classic given a 60's Motown style makeover. Taken from her Uptown album which contains a clutch of Northern anthems 'Come Go With Me' with its massive Lincoln Mayorga and Ed Cobb production is undoubtedly the best floorfiller.

Later her career flourished with the late Marc Bolan and her own creative songwriting and performing talents for the likes of Motown in partnership with Pam Sawyer.

'Come Go With Me' first gained exposure at Hanley's Top Rank allnighter in mid-1973.

Top 500 Position: **107**
Original Label: **Congress /Philtown**
Current Value: **£200 C**
£400 P

'Instant romp-appeal'

Terry Lowe, Soul Fan, Norfolk, UK

The 7th Avenue Aviators/Frankie Karl and the Chevrons

You Should 'O Held On

'Held On' has risen to cult status during the recent years, despite being originally discovered in the 70's, it falls into the category of 'oddities waiting to be re-found', and boy is it sought after!

The way to gauge a 45 in the popularity stakes is when the official value is, say, £150 but you can still easily get 200+.

I remember Barbara McNair's 'You're Gonna...' for Motown some years ago, reaching astronomic proportions for a single that ain't rare. I digress, the 'Aviators' fly up into the top 200 with their one shot wonder.

Frankie Karl, formerly of the Chevrons and the Dreams is the vocal behind both the Kapp release as the 7th Avenue Aviators as well as the Philtown release with the Chevrons.

Top 500 Position: **108**
Original Label: **Musicor**
Current Value: **£150 Issue**
£100 Demo

'Revel in that gospel - and dance sister dance'

Karen Harvey, Soul Fan, Oldham, UK

Marie Knight

That's No Way To Treat A Girl

Gospel singer Knight released a couple of pearlers for Musicor, along with the original version of 'Come Tomorrow' which Manfred Mann scored with and a sublime version of 'Cry Me A River'.

The big city production is pure New York, and Knight attacks the Tony Bruno co-written song full on.

From the first four bars she establishes exactly where the performance is going and spends the balance of the 2.23 yelling and hollering much to the delight of the backing singers who suddenly realise who they are dealing with.

A real butt kicker of anthemic magnitude.

Top 500 Position: **109**
Original Label: **Ric-Tic**
Current Value: **£5 Issue**
£25 Demo

'A dark, enduring Don Davis production classic'

Edwin Starr, Artist, Nottingham, UK

Edwin Starr
Agent Double-O Soul

Charles Hatcher travelled from Cleveland, Ohio to sign a deal with Don Davis's Solid Hitbound productions in 1965.

Before embarking on a breathtaking career(mainly in the UK), he was recording as far back as 1957 with the Futuretones. After a stint with Bill Doggett's combo he secured his first US hit with this super smooth 60's anthem.

It sort of typifies the authenticity of the scene with the bubbling bass line and dramatic intro all pulled together by one of the best live performers ever.

He of course is Edwin Starr, who probably has more influence on the Northern scene, artist wise, than anyone else.

Top 500 Position: **110**
Original Label: **Chess**
Current Value: **£50**

'Ouch! this is really great'

Mitch Reed, Soul Fan, Chicago, USA

The Valentinos
Sweeter Than The Day Before

The intro as so often makes this particular 45.

Co-written by Mary Wells and Cecil Womack, who with his brother Bobby, recorded for Sam Cooke's SAR label before instigating an even more successful career as solo performers.

The track hardly needs an introduction suffice to say, if discovered today it would instantly raise four figures.

Due to the amount of copies floating around in the 70's the turntable play was somewhat muted early on. Two decades on and it's back to the real fighting weight for this Chicago recorded icon of Northern soul.

Interestingly enough the single is possibly bigger now than at its point of discovery.

The Northern Soul All Time Top 500

Top 500 Position: **111**
Original Label: **Tangerine**
Current Value: **£10 Issue**
£25 Demo

'Annie Mae tearing up the dance floor'

Larry Hall, USA

Ike and Tina Turner
Dust My Broom

Anywhere, everywhere this argumentative couple went, the end result was recorded heaven.

Married from 1958-76 (how did it last so long?) the duo recorded for Sue, Tangerine, Pompeii, Loma, A&M, Phil Spector, United Artists, Kent and Modern.

Two outstanding recordings in 1966 bore the brilliant 'Beauty Is Just Skin Deep' and 'Dust My Broom', the latter winning hands down.

Tina, as with all her performances gives an eleven out of ten, and complete with Ray Charles produced thunderous rhythm, the result is an AWESOME update of Elmore James' blues standard!

Top 500 Position: **112**
Original Label: **Ric-Tic**
Current Value: **£10 Issue**
£20 Demo

'Pure genius'

Brain Philips, DJ, Manchester, UK

JJ Barnes
Real Humdinger

This production which developed out of a demo entitled 'Sweet Honey Baby' became one of the first major rarities (at the time) at the Twisted Wheel.

Yet another classic on which Dennis Coffey played bass, he recently commented on how 'up' everyone was on the very first take!

Few would argue that JJ is one of the best loved of Northern Soul heroes with this just one of many many classic sounds from the great man.

Top 500 Position: **113**
Original Label: **RCA Victor**
Current Value: **£100 Issue**
£50 Demo

'Reminds me how my first wife left 'cause I was paying more attention to gear at Wigan than I was to her!'
Big Mick, Soul Writer, Bolton, UK

Beverly Ann
You've Got Your Mind On Other Things

Country singer turned Northern star. I agree it's somewhat bizzare. Songs, for no apparent reason spring out of left field and become 'classics'. Personally, I could never understand why it has remained popular alongside the Joanie Sommers, Holly St. James of this world. I think the emotional side of us takes a bit of a toe hold. The chorus is certainly catchy, the rest belongs where it originated - Nashville.

To top it all, BA scored again on RCA with 'He's Coming Home'.

In a copy of the Togetherness magazine, a photo appeared of Beverly Ann, all kitted out and ready to take on Petula Clark in a 'battle of the sexies'. Well it was in fact Station Road, Wigan where Ms Ann's won her skirmish!

Top 500 Position: **114**
Original Label: **MGM**
Current Value: **£200 Issue**
£100 Demo

'Everything a Northern record should be'
Tony Dent, Soul Fan, Merseyside, UK

The Charades
Key To My Happiness

Discovered around 1973 and surprisingly never reached it's peak until the 90's. There are many reasons for this, the main one being that the first Verve/MGMs turned up on issue (rather than the ones which are principally demos and are harder to find).

Basking in bass, hi-hats, killer vocals and group harmony, this is the business!

Maybe the timing of it was all wrong, it certainly was for the 50's group who planned a comeback but refused to sign for MGM who promptly formed this group - their very own 'Charades' for this '66 release.

If this were your first lesson in Northern Soul, I would insist we start with the letter C for Charades.

Top 500 Position: **115**
Original Label: **Sussex**
Current Value: **£2,000**

'The ultimate rarity that has lived to tell the tale'

Bill Robinson, Soul Fan, Cheshire, UK

Billy Woods
Let Me Make You Happy

A classy outing from former Verve recording artist Billy Woods for Van McCoy productions.

Can a 70's 45 really be worth the amount quoted?

Well, hear it once and you will be hooked regardless of price.

The single has reached a junction of credibility both in price and stature. All that's left to say is, that a dozen copies or so were found in 1974, with a further promo being unearthed in 1981. There are no others known, leaving the label's swan song a delight for anoraks plus the McCoy legacy attaching itself neatly to this wonderful offering.

When a dance beat and lead vocal combine to deliver the line 'wipe those teardrops from your eyes' it's liable to be special, and it is.

Top 500 Position: **116**
Original Label: **Mirwood**
Current Value: **£25 Issue**
£50 Demo

'Travelling to the Catacombs we heard about a great new discovery by Richard Temple'

Les Hare, King Bee Records, Manchester, UK

Richard Temple
That Beatin' Rhythm

Temple is also known as Jimmy Conwell, who was part of the Mirwood/Mira/Keymen set up. Basically the names of Jackie Lee, Bob and Earl etc were a talented bunch of studio guys churning out their own brand of uptempo soul music.

From the piano intro and the spoken words of 'dancin' is a part of life, it's one of the thrills of young America' you know what's coming! The instrumental version 'Cigarette Ashes' had a firm following also, but lyrically it all but sums up Northern soul and the dance floor.

Conwell is still around after being tracked down to appear in the video 'The Northern Soul Story'

Top 500 Position: 117
Original Label: **Perception**
Current Value: **£50 Issue**
£125 Demo

'One of the coolest tracks ever'

Arthur Chisholm, Soul Fan, New York, USA

Otis Smith
Let Her Go

When the Golden Torch in Stoke on Trent closed it's doors in March 1973, it took all of six months for the scene to re-group and witness the opening of one Wigan Casino. During this time a few add-ons to the successful Torch playlist emerged outside of Rubin's 'You've Been Away'. I believe this New York recording from 1970 to be the best discovery during that time. The original label was almost a Jazz outlet and quite why the 60's sounding effort from Smith even got out is a mystery. The fact is, it was released in June 1970 and sold positively zilch!

One even stranger twist is the level of promotion it got. I can reveal whilst being a young record hound in New York in 1975, I just about found copies in every store I visited, leading me to the conclusion that 'somebody, somewhere liked it'.

Top 500 Position: 118
Original Label: **Tie**
Current Value: **£1,000**

'Extremely rare, and oh so good'

Jeff Milton, Soul Fan, Yorkshire, UK

Jon and the Wierdest
Can't Get Over These Memories

On many occasions I have studied the growth of 'really rare' 45's, and concluded that many are undesirable on the dance floor. How refreshing then to see this wonderfully obscure single from Los Angeles.

As for the group name I wonder how many copies are lying in a box of psychedelic collectables?

Front man John is John Hendley who is no stranger to the scene after his mini monster 'My Baby Came From Out Of Nowhere' created a stir.

Emotive and timeless, this four figure treasure which was first spun by Richard Searling as 'Spyder Turner' is pure class.

Top 500 Position: **119**
Original Label: **Hi EP**
Current Value: **£50**

'That driving Hi beat is just Champion!'

Chas Alcock, Soul Fan, Greater Manchester, UK

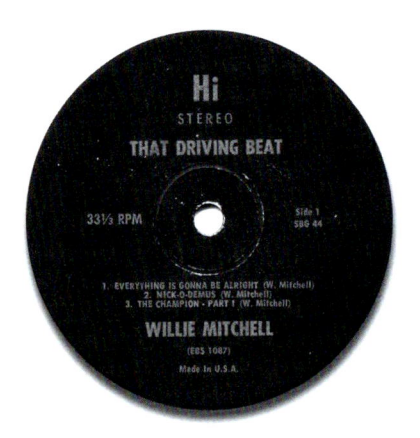

Willie Mitchell

The Champion

Legendary musician/producer Mitchell hardly needs an introduction especially with Al Green in tow during the 70's.

His own brand of instrumental R&B culminated from his big band days in Ashland, Mississippi.

The Champion is taken from the 'Driving Beat' album which is full of essential 60's tracks. The word 'stomper' is synonymous with the scene and, if anyone has heard the term but struggling to fully understand it, simply play this dynamic Memphis boss waxing and you too will be 'stomping'!

DJ John Vincent well and truly 'championed' this epic.

Top 500 Position: **120**
Original Label: **Uptite**
Current Value: **£25 Blue**
£40 Yellow

'A pulsating group sound from the Kyser stable'

Mick Love, Soul Fan, Dublin, Eire

The Superlatives

I Still Love You

In the vein of other stormin' group sounds such as the Tempos, comes a real boss waxing from New Jersey.

Paul Kyser was the local guy who recorded a fair amount of Jersey talent. Along with Robert Banks, Joe Evans, George Blackwell, Kyser was in and out of the studios of Newark and East Orange working with a series of undiscovered groups.

The Superlatives from Newark are not to be confused with the Detroit group of the same name. Lead by Julian Bonaparte with Robby 'Burning Sensation' Lawson on backing vocals. Why is this one-off release on on Uptite so good? Well, the tempo is ferocious, string arrangement tuneful, and as for the lead and background harmony...just awesome. A perfect dancer and quality old school.

Top 500 Position: **121**
Original Label: **20th Century**
Current Value: **£5**

"Reaching For The Best'? What are you taking about?'

Bob Relf, Singer, Los Angeles, USA

The Exciters
Reaching For The Best

How intriguing, the player being played. Key record dealer Simon Soussan invented the fictitious title by artist Bob Relf. Maybe Soussan had it in mind to record, but a creative DJ from Blackpool beat him to it.

Levine, intrigued himself by the title, used the platform to realise his venture into the music industry by utilising the services of the Exciters, who at the time were looking for a record deal.

The upshot of Ian's entrepreneurialism was a fantastic, fresh sounding Northern mover, which to this day remains totally original.

Eventually making the UK charts, the song paved the way for Levine to utilise his knowledge of the scene to great effect in the studio.

Top 500 Position: **122**
Original Label: **UK MGM**
Current Value: **£150**

'We used to hum it at football matches'

John Mahoney,
Soul Fan, Nottingham, UK

Father's Angels
Bok To Bach

Jerry Ross decided to record a church band from Pennsylvania to record a cover of Wilson Pickett's 'Don't Knock It' and release it on his own Heritage label.

Requiring a B side, the band put together a throwaway titled 'Bok To Bach', the result being not a US release, but a UK one, with his licensee MGM.

Four years later the disc was discovered and taken to the Golden Torch, the top allnighter of 1972... every Nighter goer knows the rest.

One final note on the confusion of the influx of 'Heritage label imports' which are common place within the scene. They are in fact reissues, the original 1968 record was only released in Britain.

Top 500 Position: **123**
Original Label: **Musette**
Current Value: **£150**

'Totally storming Northern'

Jackie Lovell, Soul Fan, Preston, UK

Mickie Champion
What Good Am I?

From the outset Mickie Champion is out to kick some ass with a full blooded appeal for her man to stay home.

The futility of the recording session is felt 6,000 miles away as the little label from California had about as much chance for a hit as Sheffield Wednesday have of winning the European Cup!

An absolute Wigan MONSTER, listening in the light of today's all-nighter sounds I am struck by just how much of and R&B sound it is for a period of stomp-driven cuts. Recorded originally with the Nic-Nacs on RPM, Mickie had two and a half minutes to convince us that the record is good, I can reveal it is GREAT!

Top 500 Position: **124**
Original Label: **Hickory**
Current Value: **£10 Issue**
£25 Demo

'I thought it sounded like a Top Ten hit'

Barbara Mills, Artist, Nashville, USA

Barbara Mills
Queen Of Fools

Very strange indeed that a country singer signed to Hickory records, Nashville should find herself in the Northern Hall of Fame.

The track recorded in 1965 actually got a release here, and with a mock Motown beat one obviously imagines a sort of change of direction for the label.

It is authentic and typical of the time of playing (1971/2), plus it has the advantage of a soaring chorus with the background vocalists all chanting 'she's the queen of foooollls', which becomes the 45's focal point.

Although out of step today and somewhat 'cheesy' in comparison to more soulful offerings, that should not detract from the awesome popularity it once had.

Mary Love
You Turned My Bitter Into Sweet

Top 500 Position: **125**
Original Label: **Modern**
Current Value: **£50 Issue**
£80 Demo

'Cute, slick with the most soulful finesse'

Linda Lewis, Artist, London, UK

Mary Love Comer recorded the evergreen in 1965 for Modern in Los Angeles and surprisingly enough it got a UK release courtesy of King.

Published by Jobete and with that in mind we conjure up ideas of that elusive publisher's acetate (Kim Weston, Brenda Holloway?) being used as a door stop at Hitsville in Detroit.

In the UK it was covered twice by Linda Lewis, once on Polydor in 1967 then later on Electricity in 1984.

Perfectly executed by Love who warbles smartly around the Chester Pipkin production, the sugar coated hook is irresistible and works a treat even today, some 32 years since the inaugural play.

The Professionals
That's Why I Love You

Top 500 Position: **126**
Original Label: **Groove City**
Current Value: **£1,000**

'The cream of Detroit rarities'

Tom Hickman, Soul Fan, Grand Rapids, USA

Superb group harmony, an excellent lead and a brilliant song in the Detroit groove... what more could anyone ask for?

This is a sumptuous piece of vinyl that even got a limited gold vinyl release - now there's confidence in a true piece of SOUL perfection! Indeed there were several takes of 'That's Why I Love You'- Goldmine were lucky enough to track them down and compile them all on various CDs... I for one never tire of any of them!

This Groove City release was a brilliant one-shot wonder for the boys, they must have been shattered to see it fail - especially as they clearly felt so confident of well deserved chart success.

Top 500 Position: **127**
Original Label: **Linda**
Current Value: **£150 Issue**
£200 Demo

'Soul Mexican style'

Huggy Boy, KRLA, Los Angeles, USA

The Majestics

I Love Her So Much (It Hurts Me)

A spin off from the Rampart group of labels comes this Doo Wop flavoured effort from East Los Angeles.

The Mexican influence is apparent with soft latino guitar riffs, a neat string arrangement and a raft of 'Tijuana' brass.

Playing in the major league towards the late 70's, the group are one of a series of acts using the same group name.

The song was also released on Warner Bros by David and Reuben.

In terms of danceability, its the trumpets and violins that make it, as the arranger gets 'up and at 'em' and creates a terrific hum along tune right from the off.

Top 500 Position: **128**
Original Label: **Dynamo**
Current Value: **£400 Issue**
£300 Demo

'Real meat and potatoes Detroit Soul'

Martin Koppel, Record Dealer, Canada

Stanley Mitchell

Get It Baby

The most invigorating thing about Richard 'Popcorn' Wylie and Tony Hester is their knack for testing out 'other' versions of newly written material. A classic case being this rampant dancer from Mitchell, who in fact 'raps' his way through (yes it was 1967!) a rippling Detroit groove.

Hester himself cut the demo as 'Down in the Dumps' which also proved itself in the late 70's, after being unearthed on acetate.

Longevity wise we plump for Stanley's raw screecher which is reminiscent of Rex Garvin, Jerry-O etc, and one even Puff Daddy might enjoy!

Top 500 Position: **129**
Original Label: **Amy**
Current Value: **£300 Issue**
£200 Demo

'I used to think he sang 'Too Much Sulphate' but then, of course, that's what I'd had!'

Dave Carne, Soul Fan, Penrith, UK

Morris Chestnut

Too Darn Soulful

Former lead singer of the Bell group, the Attractions and the Soundmasters on Juliet, Morris also recorded with Street Corner Symphony in the 70's.

Sources inform me of a budding TV career, with an appearance in an American hospital drama.

The multi-talented Chestnut really wows us with one of the best nighter sounds EVER. Produced in Los Angeles by Anthony Renfro, this 1967 rarity originally discovered by Ian Levine is today a very sought after piece of vinyl.

Top 500 Position: **130**
Original Label: **Dynamo**
Current Value: **£10 Issue**
£25 Demo

'The Mockingbird duo in fine fettle'

Billy Foster, Soul Fan, Lancashire

Inez and Charlie Foxx

Tightrope

Brother and sister duo from Greensboro', North Carolina who hit paydirt with 'Mockingbird'. The track recorded with Luther Dixon for Dynamo/Musicor is a wonderful piano laden, all horns blazing gutsy workout by Inez.

You can hear the 'performance' as she shrills through the song in a desperate attempt to revive fortunes. The single was released in the UK on Stateside, hence the very early discovery and subsequent all nighter plays.

Every classic Northern in demander needs something to fire off dance floor imagination, and apart from the duo begging to 'walk that tightrope' it's the opening sixteen bars that do it.

The Northern Soul All Time Top 500

Top 500 Position: **131**
Original Label: **Elbejay**
Current Value: **£30**

'Jailer... Bring me Bragg'

Dave Lee, Soul Fan, London, UK

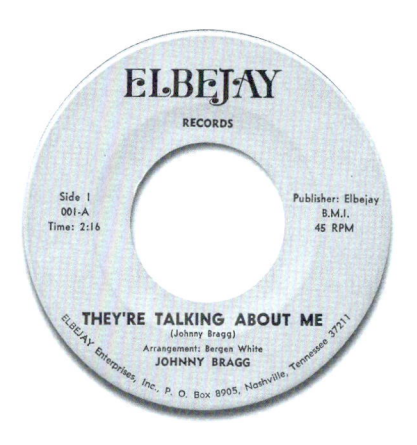

Johnny Bragg

They're Talking About me

Originally a member of the Prisonaires who were famous for recording the original of Johnny Ray's 'Just Walking In The Rain' while serving life sentences.

Bragg apparently recorded this track in Nashville while in the slammer in 1967, modelling it on Jackie Wilson's upbeat style.

Joyously buoyant, the clinky intro sets the scene as to the next 2 minutes. Bragg sings up a storm, and the UK (Especially Wigan Casino where it became an anthem) loves it enough to have demanded his parole, sadly in the US they seem unaware of his real talent.

Top 500 Position: **132**
Original Label: **Calla**
Current Value: **£20 (Short)**
£60 (Long)

'Is it the long or short version?'

Ron Diamond, Los Angeles, USA

Frankie and the Classicals

What Shall I Do?

Almost a national hit when released on Calla in 1967. The origins of the recording derive from Teddy Vann who created a backing track that no less than six other versions(some with different lyrics and song title), with F/C edging the contest.

A former Philadelphia DJ Ron Diamond played it to death upon release and that is where the promotion ended.

The disc received a UK release on Philips which is really scarce, then the subsequent re-issue on Pye's Casino Classics. A rarer long version with spoken intro. exists on another Calla number with a different flip.

Top 500 Position: **133**
Original Label: **Columbia**
Current Value: **£100 Issue**
£150 Demo

'British Gospel?'

Mick Yeats, Soul Fan, Leicester, UK

Solomon King / Levi Jackson

This Beautiful Day

Very strange indeed, as the serious British collectors item attacked under two guises. Firstly as a 'b' side released in 1969. Then as if EMI 'knew something' they re-released it in 1970 under the name of Levi Jackson.

Either way both releases flopped, and during the Torch all nighter heyday it became a part of the furniture. King of course is the hit balladeer on 'She wears my ring', but on this flopped 45 you would think he was auditioning for Stax.

A single that is a credit not only to the scene but to the UK recording industry since Solomon was in fact a Jewish guy from Prestwich, Manchester!

Top 500 Position: **134**
Original Label: **Fusion**
Current Value: **£5**

'In terms of strangeness, this ranks in the Top Ten'

Tilly Rutherford, Soul Fan, London, UK

Mistura, featuring Lloyd Michels

The Flasher

To be associated with a 'great' Northern Soul single is of course satisfying - unless it is a unique single like the Flasher!

Never in my wildest dreams did I envisage this throwaway instrumental being anything more than another 'new release'.

A friend of mine who was mailing 45's to me from the New York disco pool had sent this along with many previous goodies such as Oscar Perry and further oddities like Barnaby Bye. On first hearing I was unimpressed and following a trip to Blackpool Mecca I watched in amazement as DJ Ian Levine aired it for the first time. The rest of course is history as I cut my first record deal in the UK leasing it to Route in 1976, who promoted it well to secure a No.23 hit.

Now that's the strange world of Northern soul!

Top 500 Position: **135**
Original Label: **ABC Paramount**
Current Value: **£100 Issue**
£60 Demo

'A hard-hitting, big label monster'

Pauline Lovell, Soul Fan, West Midlands, UK

The Reflections
Like Adam And Eve

Major label signing the Reflections had hoped to re-capture the form that gave them a US hit in 1964 with 'Just Like Romeo And Juliet'. Timing was all off so it was left to the UK to unearth the non seller and put it to the test.

The upshot was an even bigger 'hit' north of Watford.

Tony Michaels who is no stranger to the scene via his wonderful 'Love The Life I Live' for Golden World sang with conviction but you rarely score twice two years apart with the same theme.

Apart from a further single for ABC the group disbanded, the north of England revelled with 'Adam And Eve' and possibly was the biggest sound of '75.

Top 500 Position: **136**
Original Label: **Revilot**
Current Value: **£15 Issue**
£80 Demo

'Mister Banks singing on a Frank Wilson/Marc Gordon song - it doesn't get better'

Thierry Moulange, Soul Fan, Brussels, Belgium

Darrell Banks
Somebody (Somewhere) Needs You

Co-written by Frank Wilson and Marc Gordon for Motown's publishing arm Jobete.a variety of artists recorded this 1965 classic and its alternate vocals with Banks just edging out the great Ike and Tina Turner version on Loma.

Never a monster on the scene, it sort of just appeared as everyone took it to heart as if 'it had always been around'.

A delectable Don Davis production at his United Sound studio, Banks excels himself over an enduring melody and typical Detroit backing track.

Wilson himself acknowledges the song as 'almost' a hit and with a hook so generous as this, I totally agree.

Along with Spyder Turner's chart entry this remains one of the most affordable and cherished scene 45's... every home should own it!

Top 500 Position: **137**
Original Label: **Music Merchant**
Current Value: **£30**

'Could easily have been the new Supremes single'

Melanie Sawyer, Soul Fan, Detroit, USA

Eloise Laws
Love Factory

With an array of super talented brothers and sisters including Ronnie, Hubert and Debra, Eloise almost had a smash with this in the States. A massive radio hit, but for some reason it failed at the last hurdle.

Conjuring up another vocal find, Holland Dozier Holland released this commercial attempt in 1973, and on the face of it, looks like they should have scored again.

Fair play then to Ian Levine who created 'the hit' albeit super regionally (somewhere north of Wolverhampton) and gave this tremendous Honey Cone style groover a place in our own piece of history making.

Top 500 Position: **138**
Original Label: **ABC**
Current Value: **£10 Issue**
£15 Demo

'An irresistible floor shaker'

John 'Hector' Heathcote,
Soul Fan, Derby, UK

The Shakers
One Wonderful Moment

I often wonder why soft rock writers/producers such as Cashman and Pistilli, would record a mock soul single such as this. Maybe rock stalwarts attempted the soul thing in an attempt to crossover, rather like Sly Stone doing the progressive line. Either way the record is superb, with a stunning intro and on the fours back beat, all topped off with falsetto harmonies and OTT reverb.

The original was lying in wait, searching for a big name to play it, due to a few copies surfacing in the old 'sales and exchange' junk shops of the early 70's.

Old style stomper with mucho dance appeal that ranks alongside the best of 'em for sheer exuberance.

Top 500 Position: **139**
Original Label: **Revilot**
Current Value: **£800**

'A two sider that remains one of the very best from Detroit'

Don Davis, Groovesville, Detroit, USA

Jackie Beavers
I Need My Baby

Manchester proved an unlikely source to hear and learn all about this marvellous discovery. Richard Searling had played it at the Casino, I remember hearing it in Manchester around 1979. Shortly after, the flip side 'A Love That Never Runs Cold' started to get action.

Ten years later hosting a radio programme in the very same city, I'm interviewing Johnny Bristol, who notices I am playing the Beavers disc. The next few minutes are spent listening to JB's account of his friend. Firstly as Johnny and Jacky the pair wrote and sang on the original 'Someday We'll Be Together' (for Harvey Fuqua's Tri-Phi label), which became the departing anthem for Diana Ross and The Supremes. Bristol knew him well and proceeded to reveal all about this character who recorded for Revilot, Sound Stage 7 and Dade amongst others.

Top 500 Position: **140**
Original Label: **Bell**
Current Value: **£1,500**

'A top tune oozing credibility'

Dave Brown,
Philly Archives, Philadelphia, USA

Bernie Williams
Ever Again

The current asking price for the original is quite breathtaking. Before we take a reality check, let's examine the facts...1. The track is excellent. 2. Even though 'Ever Again' is on a major label, it's mega rare.

The situation regarding the discs history is one of turmoil. Firstly Del Val the indie label from Philadelphia produced the track but used Gene Woodbury as the chosen vocalist. The subsequent release flopped. Label owner Joe Stevenson then leased a second version by Bernie Williams, not to be confused with former Blue Notes lead, Bernard Williams well (known for his Harthon recording 'It's Needless To Say') to Bell, that also failed.

UK wise the single has grown and grown reaching a pinnacle rather late in the day.

Top 500 Position: **141**
Original Label: **Cuppy**
Current Value: **£700**

'A superb doo-wop influenced soul shaker'

Ian Thomas, Soul Fan, Swindon, UK

The De-Lites

Lover

Bill Haley decided on a new record label in 1965, naming it Cuppy after his wife.

Resisting the temptation to travel down the rockabilly road, he astutely (or as he thought) followed 'what the kids wanted'. He was half right. The track kicks, great vocals, and lovely hook. Unfortunately the song felt dated even then.

Many years later, cue old Blighty to turntable it to death, and create a showcase for the catchy little number.

Hailing from Chester, PA, the label, band and single disappeared quickly. In terms of collectors, this is a prime contender for the 'most wanted' list.

Top 500 Position: **142**
Original Label: **Warner Brothers**
Current Value: **£75 Issue £100 Demo**

'One of a host of supreme stormers from the girls'

Lawrence Toulan, Soul Fan, Essex, UK

The Apollas

Mr. Creator

Loma and Warner Brothers stalwarts the Apollas, made up of Leola Giles, Ella Jamerson and Dorothy Ramsey recorded many singles and made several US TV appearances. Sadly they didn't quite crack it.

After a wealth of turntable exposure the UK finally succumbed to the charms of 'Mr Creator'. The song which was written by Ashford (Nick not Jack) and Simpson also saw a demo cut by Candy and the Kisses which was scheduled for release on Scepter. With an accomplished production by Dick Glasser this is undoubtedly one of the scene's best girl group sounds.

Top 500 Position: **143**
Original Label: **Audio Arts**
Current Value: **£15 Issue**
£30 Demo

'The strings could have been from a Hitchcock movie'

Graham Coulter,
Soul Fan, Inverness, Scotland

The Incredibles
There Is Nothing Else To Say

A 'bubbling under' hit from 1966 on Madelon Baker's Audio Arts label. The group fronted by Cal Waymon gained a release here on Stateside.

The string ensemble make it and coupled with the 'galloping hoof' effect, Waymon controls the vocal like a seasoned pro.

Unlike the syrupy Wheel sides of the time like 'I'm Gonna Miss You', 'Apple, Peaches Pumpkin Pie' and the like, this was as hotter than fire and became the song you would sing for the rest of the week!

Top 500 Position: **144**
Original Label: **End**
Current Value: **£450**

'A perfect dancefloor anthem'

Richard Searling, DJ, Bolton, UK

Lenny Curtis
Nothing Can Help You Now

Recorded for the New York based End label in 1965, this single has certainly been slow in reaching its full potential having regularly changed hands for £50 for over ten years.

Merely a bit-part player in the Wigan Casino make-up, this track that represents the finale for the legendary Doo-Wop label is now one of the top DJ spins on the scene. Suddenly every collector wants a copy and it is today one of the most sought after 45s in the UK!

Top 500 Position: **145**
Original Label: **Brunswick**
Current Value: **£10 Issue**
£20 Demo

'Regarded as THE version, surpassing Soul Brother No.1'

Bridget Jones, Soul Fan, Newport, Wales, UK

Gene Chandler
There Was A Time

Highly regarded as the definitive version, Gene delivers his own rendition of James Brown's classic, showing the grit and determination side to his game.

Popularised at the Casino via the Mr. M's oldies sessions, the man from Chicago (born Eugene Dixon) has for many a year added the song to his repertoire when touring Europe.

Regarded as a Soul icon, his fan base is high and together with Major Lance and Curtis Mayfield is one of the legendary Windy City soul stars.

Top 500 Position: **146**
Original Label: **Pameline**
Current Value: **£250 green**
£40 orange

'Producer Wylie smiles yet again as another 'B' side is the UK winner!'

Frank Elson, Blues & Soul, 1975

The Detroit Executives
Cool Off

Richard Wylie and Tony Hestor were the eternal optimists, recording at least one other version of each of their creations.

No change here then, as The Ideals (from the same stable) recorded a similar track titled 'mighty lover'.

Cool Off, became one of the first alternate 60's singles to reach a slightly different audience, mainly at Blackpool Mecca, where a more stylish club goer was beginning to emerge. On saying that, the record 'broke out', and to this day is an essential spin for most DJ's.

The Northern Soul All Time Top 500

Top 500 Position: **147**
Original Label: **Stateside**
Current Value: **£5 Issue**
£25 Demo

'Now this is a hit'

Biddu, Songwriter, London, UK

Jimmy James

A Man Like Me

Suddenly from out of nowhere comes a new release (at the time) that revolutionised the scene and put paid to the myth that 'it has to be rare'.

A 45 one could say was 'made for the scene', but it wasn't according to songwriter and producer Biddu.

Apparently he had produced a demo that just felt right, which his client Lenita productions then leased to EMI, promptly releasing the song in November, 1972.

Famous all-night venue the Torch, Tunstall, Stoke-on-Trent latched on to it around 4 weeks prior to release, you can imagine the demand!

According to Jimmy, the song sold in excess of 50,000 copies, but as the sales were all regional (ie THE NORTH) it failed to chart.

Top 500 Position: **148**
Original Label: **Boom**
Current Value: **£30 Issue**
£50 Demo

'Big, gruff Italian New York soul'

Barry Aswith, Soul Fan, Hertfordshire, UK

Dean Parrish

Determination

Parrish remains one of soul's great mysteries. We know so little and have yet to see a photo, but it's still as if we have known him for so long.

Utterly distinctive, the 'northern' hits are legendary with sides for Boom, Musicor and Laurie, eventually ending up on Polydor with a rock band.

Determination is the first of his classics and easily the best dancer. The song is fairly simple with Deano's unmistakable voice rasping through the big NY production.

Released here on Stateside, the man has to be the finest white soul singer of his generation. A duet with Janis Joplin would have changed the course of his career methinks.

Top 500 Position: **149**
Original Label: **Wand**
Current Value: **£40**

'An awesome, ferocious rip-roarer

Carol Poole, Soul Fan, Derby, UK

Al Wilson
Help Me

A crazy, wild dancer from Wilson who fought tooth and nail to get his vocal heard, while DJ's initially plumped for the instrumental.

This is northern soul with a rip roaring intro followed by cooking guitar licks and heavyweight brass riffs.

The Casino rose to the challenge when first exposed, and for a few months this could easily have been the No. 1 single in the country.

Tempos have changed, but 'Help me' is fondly remembered and danced to at many a revival.

Top 500 Position: **150**
Original Label: **Hi**
Current Value: **£8 Issue**
£15 Demo

'A wicked instrumental version of Chuck Berry'

Derek Allen, Soul Fan, Leicester, UK

Bill Black's Combo
Little Queenie

Absolutely massive in the early 70's and one real left field dancer.

The Memphian famous for his work with Elvis, had one of the most formidable bands in the US, and this stone soul workout of Berry's original was worthy of a hit. The plays though came from the north of England and while Black never experienced it's popularity here (passing away in 1965), the track remains one of the really big oldies. As a 'current spin' it was big for quite a while from the late Torch to the early days of Wigan.

Recorded in 1964, the single was released here on London.

Top 500 Position: **151**
Original Label: **Crazy Horse**
Current Value: **£30**

'Obviously in contention for the pop and soul chart'

Rod Law, Soul Fan, Australia

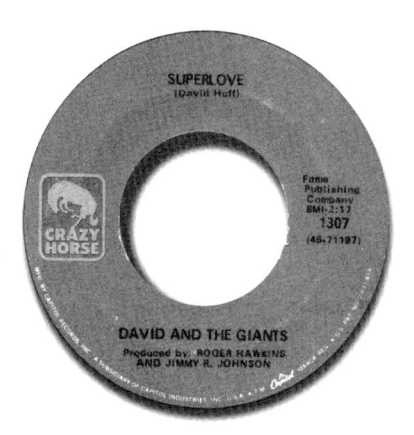

David and the Giants
Superlove

On the crest of a wave in 1974, this pop ditty from David Huff had all the right ingredients from master chef Rick Hall at Muscle Shoals, Alabama using his Soul roots to break into the Top 40. Ironically, three years later Hall did score with the Osmonds' 'One Bad Apple', a similar effort to Superlove.

While Huff, fluffed his chance, those cover-merchants Wigan's Ovation worked their 'magic' over a cute song with masses of dance floor appeal.

The group meanwhile had 'Ten Miles High', another scene fave, unfortunately petering out some 12 months later.

Top 500 Position: **152**
Original Label: **Decca**
Current Value: **£200 Issue**
£100 Demo

'Carribean Soul?'

Keith Walsham, Soul Fan, Merseyside, UK

Johnny Caswell
You Don't Love Me Anymore

Caswell had earlier been discovered by former Danny and the Junior - Johnny Madara. A source recently informed me that Madara is in fact Caswell, who in turn was trying to capitalise on Madara's other new hitmaker Len Barry. They sound remarkably similar. Anyway, the track written by Leon Huff was released by Decca in 1966 and flopped.

Caswell's vocal career was blunted, though he later recorded for Colossus it was left to the music hungry Brits to unearth this gem and then play it to death!

Wonderful major label release, great song, accomplished performance.

Top 500 Position: **153**
Original Label: **ABC Paramount**
Current Value: **£300**

'Bigger than ever in 2000'

Karen Singer, Soul Fan, Scotland

Holly St. James

That's Not love

A common theme runs through the veins of the scene with songs such as this pop outing from Holly, who no doubt is a failed actress or something.

Straight out of the Beverly Ann, Joanie Sommers, Paula Durante charm school, the girl wallows in 60's naïvety, as the Spectorish backdrop suits the little miss perfectly.

Hey, I am not mocking the disc, it is one which I honestly don't like, but boy is it big.

Our loyalties to these little chicky love grooves is legendary, one can't help thinking though that if the track was by Jackie Trent or Tammy Wynette, we would use it as the customary ashtray.

Top 500 Position: **154**
Original Label: **Canterbury**
Current Value: **£40 Issue £50 Demo**

'One of my own perennial favourites'

Keith Minshull, DJ, Stoke-on-Trent, UK

The Tempos

Countdown (Here I Come)

The Tempos, have nothing to do with the Detroit group of the same name, they were in fact the Younghearts, who's 'A Little Togetherness' is also a Northern classic.

I myself recorded a dance version of the song by Kofi and the Lovetones - which became a monster in Asia!

Back to the original, the falsetto lead is delectable as is the ecstatic intro which sets the scene for what is one heck of a 60's classic that became one of the first Blackpool Mecca spins following its reopening in 1973.

Top 500 Position: **155**
Original Label: **Chess**
Current Value: **£10 Issue**
£15 Demo

'The first major instrumental'

Chrissie Jones, Soul Fan, Nantwich, UK

Ramsey Lewis
Wade In The Water

Chicago keyboard legend Lewis has a long association with the scene.

That apart, his instrumental contribution would easily make a top 5 if we were only concentrating on '67-72.

Just about as effortless as you can get, with the man simply laying down the track as he plays.

A superb rhythm with Young/Holt in attendance creating the atmosphere for a legendary jam session.

Top 500 Position: **156**
Original Label: **Brunswick**
Current Value: **£200 Issue**
£125 Demo

'The group's name is off-putting, the track certainly isn't'

Paul Leka, Songwriter, USA

Adam's Apples
Don't Take It Out On This World

The New York connection of Paul Leka and Brunswick records, saw psyche-soul band Adams Apples turn in a gutsy performance from '67. Later that year they recorded 'You are the one I love', which got it's fair share of play.

The chorus on this stomper makes it, with the backing vocals sounding black while the lead certainly has visions of being the next Felix Cavaliere (Young Rascals).

Sometimes the unusual gets to you, and this is certainly in that category.

Top 500 Position: **157**
Original Label: **Bell**
Current Value: **£6 Issue**
£10 Demo

'A song with distinctly crude overtones!'

Mark Wales, Soul Fan, Sheffield, UK

James and Bobby Purify

Shake A Tail Feather

The Duo who hail from Pensacola, Florida have a long association with the scene starting with Wheel classics 'Let Love Come Between Us', 'Do Unto Me' and 'Wish You Didn't Have To Go'.

Originally a hit for Chicago group the Five Dutones the Purify's version surfaced at the Casino's Mr M's and more recently got a boost courtesy of the Blues Brothers - but either way a good time was had by all!

Top 500 Position: **158**
Original Label: **Back Beat**
Current Value: **£15 Issue**
£25 Demo

'The Boy Wonder of Soul?'

Carl Carlton, Artist, USA

Little Carl Carlton

Competition Ain't Nothin'

No stranger to the scene is the ever-youthful Mr. Carlton, a Detroit vocalist who recorded for Lando in 1964, then Golden World and on to Don Robey's Back Beat label and a real career lift-off on the latter in the 70's before moving to 20th Century.

The youthfulness of Carlton is uncanny as he sounds the same on 'Bad Mama Jama' as he did on his earliest performances.

A totally uplifting commercial slab of 60's soul that one never tires of. Due to a lack of rarity it probably doesn't get enough attention today, but it should, this is a total killer.

Top 500 Position: **159**
Original Label: **Top Ten**
Current Value: **£100 Issue**
£150 Demo

'Harmonies to die for!'

Mark Rosenbourg, Soul Fan, Ohio, USA

The Dynamics
Yes I Love You Baby

With voices flying here, there and everywhere, this is a Wigan anthem that has really stood the test of time... Even its weird 'B' side, 'Soul Sloopy' got plays a few years ago!

With an irresistible tempo and a superb falsetto lead riding high on the Ernstat production this stunning dancer was ripe for national release and was picked up by New York's Laurie records from the Detroit based Top Ten label, it is a real shame that it just didn't make it for the boys.

Lovers of the track will be interested to know that there is an unusual out take and instrumental version that were released on a Goldmine/Soul Supply CD.

Top 500 Position: **160**
Original Label: **Mary Jane**
Current Value: **£75**

'A top-notch discovery and perfect for the scene

Donald Moore, Soul Fan, Michigan, USA

Edward Hamilton and the Arabians
Baby Don't You Weep

Back to credibility with collectors' champion Edward Hamilton and the Arabians. Recording as early as 1960 with the group, Edward waxed lyrical on some great sides for Le Mans, Carrie and Mary Jane, as well as working solo - as did the Arabians who featured other lead singers.

Although I personally plum for 'I'm gonna love for you' for danceability factor, I can understand the popularity of 'Weep' as the song is far stronger.

There is a whole heap of Detroit male vocalists who would have made a fantastic 'revue', guys like Gino Washington, Joe Matthews, etc, and Hamilton would probably have topped the bill in this second tier fantasy of mine.

Major Harris
Call Me Tomorrow

Top 500 Position: **161**
Original Label: **Okeh**
Current Value: **£125 Issue**
£200 Demo

'Cool as you like... The Major does the business'

Bri Mosely, Soul Fan, Lancashire, UK

When the first copy arrived in 1974 the label, artist and title looked 'bob on' for a smasheroo. The reality is collectors loved it, but dancers denounced it as "too slow".

After hanging around for 15 or so years and refusing to lie down, it sort of got its second wind.

Harris of course has a totally credible career, he was one one of the Impacts along with Herb Johnson, cut 'Call Me Tomorrow' during his contract with Okeh before joining the Delfonics, topped off nicely with a worldwide smash on Atlantic with 'Love Won't Let Me Wait' and 'After Loving You'.

Duke Browner
Crying Over You

Top 500 Position: **162**
Original Label: **Impact**
Current Value: **£150 Issue**
£200 Demo

'The intro alone makes it a winner'

Carol Harvey, Soul Fan, Stafford, UK

First played at Tunstall's Torch, the instrumental and vocal sides gained equal exposure.

Barney 'Duke' Browner was responsible for many productions whilst working for Impact owner Harry Balk but this is by far the strongest. The first 4 bars are really infectious and state clearly the disc's intentions - this is a mean Detroit groove that typifies the scene.

Extensively played by DJ Tony Jebb.

Top 500 Position: **163**
Original Label: **Soul Clock**
Current Value: **£15 Issue**
£50 Demo

'A super niter goodie from '72'

John Thomas, Soul Fan, Nottingham, UK

The Fuller Brothers
Time's A Wasting

Deliciously self satisfying romper from the early 70's featuring Los Angeles based Fuller Brothers.

We often forget the validity of such discs in today's big money scene, but ask yourself this question, what price would you put on this if discovered today?

Quite simply this is the type of record that made Northern Soul what it is... a stunning opening few bars, a feel good song, a terrific hook and a dancers delight!

YES I am biased, not to the cache of oldies I seem to be raving over, but simply towards records bathed in pure magic!

Sure the act had visions of going head to head with Sam and Dave. Fellas don't shatter my ellusions, you'll do for me!

Top 500 Position: **164**
Original Label: **Modern**
Current Value: **£30**

'Long forgotten but an inspiration to many'

Keith Alexander, Soul Fan, Fife, Scotland

Mel Williams
Can It Be Me

Originally played at the Mecca, 'Can It Be Me' found major status at the Casino's Mr M's before going on to be a 6T's classic at the 100 Club.

Fast and furious, this is the business as far as all nighters are concerned. Also recording a demo of Wally Cox's 'This Man', Mel's other giant 'Burn Baby Burn' commands some serious money these days.

One of the best intros ever!

April Stevens
Wanting You

Top 500 Position: **165**
Original Label: **MGM**
Current Value: **£25 Issue**
£35 Demo

'Sending girlie dance sounds soaring to new heights!'

Paula Rose, Soul Fan, Stoke-on-Trent, UK

A stunning dance favourite that actually got a UK release circa 1967. Yep that's right - it's that old standard reworked into a Motown style groove.

Born Carol Lo Tempio at Niagra Falls, April had already achieved chart success working with her brother Nino Tempo - but, in terms of Northern popularity, this one is one of THE all-time greats!

Initially exposed at the Torch in 1972 the track was important in putting MGM on the map amongst Northern collectors.

Jodi Mathis
Don't You Care Anymore

Top 500 Position: **166**
Original Label: **Capitol**
Current Value: **£20**

'Straight out of the top drawer'

Keith Fielding, Soul Fan, Warwick, UK

Difficult to understand the thinking behind record executives at a major label such as Capitol.

Firstly, Mathis is a fine vocalist. The song too is great, and bang on the money during that period of time - but who the hell let her use a name like that? Imagine the ensuing confusion on radio shows of the time - therefore it just got lost in the rush.

The creativity of Ian Levine brought the 45 to the fore far earlier than other more traditional dancers. In terms of floor appeal, it simply has an all round coolness about it, building quickly out of a teasing intro and following the great string arrangement is young Jodi giving the performance of her life.

Top 500 Position: **167**
Original Label: **RCA Victor**
Current Value: **£30**

'Light the blue touch paper and stand well back!'

Jeremy Wright, Soul Fan, London, UK

The Exciters
Blowing Up My Mind

Dynamite and nitro glycerine wails Brenda Reid, as the Exciters make their second entrance into our chart.

Taken from the 'Caviar and Chitlins' album, the subsequent 45 release became a massive club hit.

The group were excellent and had it not been for a volatile relationship between Brenda and the late Herb, the act may have gone even further than the mini revival under Ian Levine.

As a quartet in the early 60's they had a million seller with 'Tell Him', covered in the UK by Billie Davies, and in the US by Dean Parrish slightly changing the lyrics to answer 'Tell Her'.

Top 500 Position: **168**
Original Label: **Calla**
 Issue
 £40 Demo
Current Value: **£30**

'INSTANT'

Tina Royce, Soul Fan, London, UK

Doris Troy
I'll Do Anything

Doris Payne together with Gamble and Huff... It just had to be sensational and IT IS!

First hitting paydirt in 1963 with the original version of 'Just One Look' which was covered by the Hollies, plus of course 'Whatcha Gonna Do About It' this time done over by the Small Faces. A perennial artist she went on to record for the Beatles ill-fated Apple records as well performing backing vocals on Pink Floyd's 'Dark Side Of The Moon' album.

The lady who's life story was documented in the hit West End musical 'Mama I Want To Sing' has here produced a true Northern classic, a record so good in fact that even DJ Tony Blackburn covered it!

Top 500 Position: **169**
Original Label: **HIB**
Current Value: **£150 Issue**
£200 Demo

'Both sides are monumental'

Mick Chesterton, Soul Fan, The Wirral, UK

Luther Ingram

Exus Trek / If It's All The Same To You

Both sides of this Wylie/Hestor gem have fulfiled their potential on the Northern scene.

Ingram from Jackson, Mississippi, made his mark with Stax prior to a short lived association with the legendary writers. Strangely enough he also recorded the song 'I Spy For The FBI' which Wylie and Hestor also penned, but hit for Jamo Thomas.

Rare these days to see a vocal and instrumental getting the same amount of plays, but the backing track is one of the greatest instrumentals ever.

Top 500 Position: **170**
Original Label: **Dynovoice**
Current Value: **£40**

'This is the real deal'

Gaynor Forrest, Soul Fan, Hampshire, UK

The Invitations

What's Wrong With Me Baby?

Although running second to 'Ski-ing in the snow', the maturity of 'baby' has the scene buzzing again.

Released here on Stateside, it has the typical Curtis Mayfield links and though it may be a New York recording it does have the Windy City feel to it.

The clip-clop backbone, faultless harmony and solid hook helps it to cross the finish line in record time.

The band hail from NYC, and recorded for Diamond, MGM, Dyno Voice, Big Tree, Red Greg and Silver Blue. They toured the UK in the 60's masquerading as the 'original' Drifters with Herman Colefield as the front man. Lew Kirton who is no stranger to the scene took over as lead in 1972.

Top 500 Position: **171**
Original Label: **Capitol**
Current Value: **£20 Demo**
£10 Issue

'As someone remarked at the time 'they're playing a record by Shirley Bassey"

Noel Barrington, Soul Fan, Wales, UK

Nancy Wilson
The End Of Our Love

An unusually brilliant offering from the legendary Nancy Wilson. It is the type of 45 you would never look for, until exposure of course.

The 'this is the end' chorus makes it, accompanied by the slick Vine Street production.

'Ms. Jazz' from Columbus, Ohio was recording as early as 1956 and surprisingly had only two hits, the flip 'Face It Girl It's Over' being one of them.

The lady herself was the 'all hidden treasure' that the majors were unfocused on, however the great director Don Siegel used two of her tracks in the 'B' movies The Killers and Charley Varrick, which raised her profile.

Top 500 Position: **172**
Original Label: **Ric-Tic**
Current Value: **£8 Issue**
£50 Demo

'JJ's finest Soul sound'

Dennis Coffey,
Guitar Legend, Artist and Producer, USA

JJ Barnes
Please Let Me In

'Please Let Me In' has the distinction of being one of the first Solid Hitbound productions supervised by Don Davis, Pat Lewis and George Clinton.

Discovered by a young Ian Levine in a New Orleans junk shop in 1968 it was loaned to Les Cokell, resident DJ at the Twisted Wheel. It caused a real stir and this fantastic 1965 recording was quickly picked up by other DJs around the UK. Thousands of over stocks quickly arrived from the States somewhat stunting its financial growth.

This really is a fantastic record!

Top 500 Position:	173
Original Label:	RCA Victor
Current Value:	£300 Issue
	£150 Demo

'That unique Detroit sound again'

Alan Mahoney, Soul Fan, North Wales, UK

Willie Kendrick
Change Your Ways

The GWP/Pied Piper production team settled in at RCA in 1966 and made for the major a series of fantastic sides. The list of artists they handled looks like a who's who of northern, including, The Hesitations, Freddie Butler, The Metros, Lorraine Chandler, etc. Not all were on the 'nipper' logo, but the best certainly were.

Kendrick has two other excellent 45's - but this is the best of 'em with triple tracked backing vocals, tip-top lead and that big Motor City groove.

Top 500 Position:	174
Original Label:	Coral
Current Value:	£125 Issue
	£100 Demo

'A gem of an artist even in the 60's at 15 years old'

Sidney Barnes, Writer, Chicago, USA

Patti Austin
Take Away The Pain Stain

Thank heavens for the French CD retrospective released in 1999. The recordings for Coral are some of the best non-sellers the scene has ever witnessed.

We all have our favourites, but it is this raucous dancer from '66 has been a consistent turntable hit since '73.

Is it any wonder the lady went on to better things being the Goddaughter of Quincy Jones and making her first recordings for adverts at just 4 years old?

She also has a US No. 1 to her credit in 1982 in duet with James Ingram as well a providing vocals for Quincy's legendary 'The Dude' album.

A 'better' offer in 1998 saw Ms. Austin plum for a Carribean jazz festival as opposed to rainy Fleetwood, and though she made the right decision financially, I doubt it emotionally!

Top 500 Position: **175**
Original Label: **Fat Fish**
Current Value: **£75 Issue**
£100 Demo

'One of the first BIG money sounds'

Nick Regan, Soul Fan, Essex, UK

Leon Heywood

Baby Reconsider

Houston born Heywood has had an indifferent career musically. Recording with Arthur Wright and Cliff Goldsmith in the 60's he went on to have a big US hit in '75 with 'I want to do something freaky to you', moving on to a European hit in 1980 with 'Don't Push It Don't Force It'.Certainly lots of innuendo in Leon's songs.

But we concentrate on the Mirwood-esque 'Baby Reconsider.

At the Twisted Wheel this was almost impossible to get and for a time was the UK's rarest in-demander. A forceful performance with all the regular LA instrumentation in place, (which borrows heavily from the Contours' 'Just A Little Misunderstanding') Haywood must be well proud of this US failure as judging by his video performance recently, he positively revels in it.

Top 500 Position: **176**
Original Label: **Karen**
Current Value: **£70 Issue**
£100 Demo

'Sublime D-town soul'

Sharon Colley, Soul Fan, London, UK

The Soul Twins

Quick Change Artist

Many Sam and Dave types came and went during '66-69, sadly Detroit's Soul Twins were another casualty.

They did however leave us this fantastic memory as well as a three other minor releases for Karen records.

As a live act their potential was spotted by label boss and Ann Arbor radio DJ - Ollie Mclaughlin, who quickly signed them to cash in on the 'soul duet' boom, sadly by '68 they were on their way.

Totally 'golden era' and a definite Top 20 song at the Torch, which spawned many a 'cartwheel'. Now, how DO you do that once again!

NF Porter
Keep On Keeping On

Top 500 Position: **177**
Original Label: **Lizard**
Current Value: **£10 Issue**
£30 Demo

'No matter how hard it gets - keep on - keep strong!'

Bob Evans, Soul Fan, Leicester, UK

Featuring strange keyboards that sound like leftovers from Three Dog Night's 'Mama Told Me Not To Come', this odd 45 had all the makings of the monster floorfiller it became.

Released in 1971 and played to death within months of its initial release, it was until just a few years ago the man's most popular waxing of his two tracks on the scene... That is until the equally enigmatic 'If I Could Only Be Sure' surfaced only a few years ago, rising to massive popularity and a No. 91 placing for NF (Nolan) Porter in this chart.

Lee David
Temptation Is Calling My Name

Top 500 Position: **178**
Original Label: **Columbia**
Current Value: **£100 Issue**
£80 Demo

'A 'tempting' offering from Columbia records'

Jon Lomas, Soul Fan, Greater Manchester, UK

It's hard to find records with the pure magic of Lee David today amongst the easy to find 'average' soul records played in clubs.

This is a top-notch one shot wonder from the little known Columbia artist, who also recorded for Bell and Janus.

The girlie chorus chanting over the first few bars gets the engine warmed up for David to do 0-60 in 3 seconds.

Tracks like this used to keep dance floors full for the DJs - and they continue to do so today. Whilst I remain the proverbial fan of the discoveries of the late 60's/early 70's, I cannot see justification in anyone sneering at true 'Northern' records like Lee David's classic.

Top 500 Position: **179**
Original Label: **Arctic**
Current Value: **£25 Issue**
£50 Demo

'A mighty Philadelphia Soul classic'

Tom Marlond, Soul Fan, Philadelphia, USA

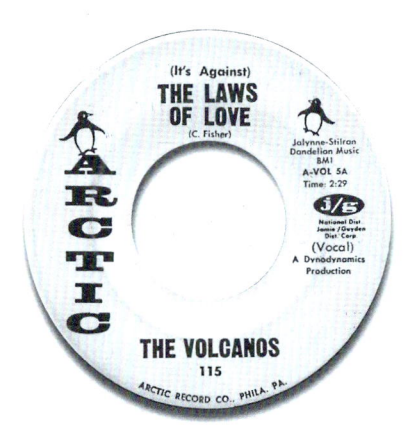

The Volcanos

(It's Against) The Laws Of Love

The Arctic label produced so many excellent singles that it's hard to believe they did not achieve chart success barring Barbara Mason.

The group, featuring Gene Faith on lead, of course evolved into The Trammps and the 70's proved fruitful for the band.

For label owner Jimmy Bishop and distributors Jamie/Guyden this could have been their worst seller. True, 'Help Wanted' and 'Storm Warning' were minor hits but 'Laws' bombed big time!... until a youngster from Bolton acquired a copy while on a buying trip (for former Swan label owner Ed Balbia and his Manchester based Global records) in Philadelphia.

Richard brought it back and played it at Wigan Casino... the rest, as they proverbially say, is history!

Top 500 Position: **180**
Original Label: **Curtom**
Current Value: **£15**

'Superfly power Soul!'

Robert Bentley,
Soul Fan, Bedfordshire, UK

Curtis Mayfield

Move On Up

Surprisingly enough this is not an easy 45 to find on Curtom largely due to the poor sales in the US. In the UK though it was a different story with the constant radio play turning in a high chart position in 1971.

The Northern Soul involvement comes via DJ Dave Evison who played it one night as 'filler' - this became the birth of the oldies and the rest is history.

The artist, well what can you say apart from probably being the finest songwriter of a generation - he is sorely missed. The legacy of Northern hits such as the Five Stairsteps, the Impressions, Leroy Hutson, Marvin Smith, the Fascinations and many more lives with us forever.

Top 500 Position: **181**
Original Label: **UK Mowest**
Current Value: **£10**

'Darkly compelling'
Cliff Moore, Soul Fan, London, UK

Frankie Valli and the Four Seasons

The Night

Switching to Motown after a long and successful period with Philips, Francis Castellucio and the boys returned with two Mowest singles that caused a real stir on the scene.

Wigan perennial 'The Night', a darkly haunting early 70's cut re-invented the group as far as the Northern scene was concerned... for a bunch of white guys they certainly had a 'Soul' following!

The Motown period was generally disappointing for the band, but like Frankie's 'Your Ready Now' this oddity propelled him into the Northern Hall of Fame one more time!

Top 500 Position: **182**
Original Label: **Salsoul**
Current Value: **£40**

'Modernistic happening on the dance floor'
Chris Holmes, Collector, York, UK

Skip Mahoney

Janice (Don't Be So Blind To Love)

Big shortly after it's initial release and huge one more time.

Skip Mahoney and the boys debuted for DC International in 1974, however their best work was for A-Bet a little later.

Salsoul is the unlikeliest label for Northern deemed as 'too disco', but the label scored on the scene with this one, even though it became one of their poorest sellers - though did get UK release on Underworld.

His band were actively touring in the 80's.

Top 500 Position: **183**
Original Label: **Groove City**
Current Value: **£350**

'An awesome Wigan spin'

John Baggaley, Soul Fan, Luton, UK

Sam Ward
Sister Lee

Singing Sammy Ward, who also recorded as Little Sammy Ward, was very much one of the old school R&B singers, with his first recordings in the late fifties. Initially kicked off by the fame of his brother, Billy Ward of the Dominoes fame, he went on to become one of Motown's earliest recording artists, cutting both solos and duets (with Mabel John) as well as working as a staff writer.

From the Groovesville stable this great cut has remained a major player on the golden playlist up North.

Top 500 Position: **184**
Original Label: **Fame**
Current Value: **£200 Issue**
£75 Demo

'A classic Penn/Oldham song'

Bobby Simpson, Soul Fan, Glasgow, Scotland

Art Freeman
Slippin' Around With You

One of two releases on Fame for Art who also worked for 'Jumbo', 'Slippin'' is very much an old school romper from '66 that gained a UK release on Atlantic.

If it does sound a little 'too sweet' for the Fame sound, the Northern scene see that as an advantage.

Girls weaving in and out of Freeman's tale of cheat and lie, the production as you would expect is spot on. I particularly like the synthesiser sound at the beginning, now that <u>was</u> ahead of its time in 1966!

Ronnie McNeir
Sitting In My Class/
Isn't She A Pretty Girl

Top 500 Position: **185**
Original Label: **Deto**
Current Value: **£250**

'O Level Maths at school on a Monday - after a two all-nighters? I just know I'm not going to pass!'

Bob Lowe, Soul Fan, Glasgow, Scotland

The superb 1968 double-sider is Ronnie's first record - and he is of course no stranger to the UK having worked with Ian Levine and Expansion records.

Whilst these Northern Soul gems are held dear by our scene he has risen to become truly legendary on the Modern scene with recordings for RCA, Prodigal, Motown (Berry Gordy had previously wooed him in the sixties hoping to sign him for the short lived Workshop Jazz label) and many others.

This, his inaugural recording, got a reissue in 1978 itself, complete with a remix!

Tony and Tyrone
Please Operator

Top 500 Position: **186**
Original Label: **Atlantic**
Current Value: **£40**

'The telephone ring is just about the best gimmick to be aired on the scene'

Terry Hamilton, Soul Fan, Greater Manchester, UK

From the creative intro, the duet roar through this strange phone routine to great effect.

The duo recorded two fine sides for Columbia as well as working for Ston-Roc and G.M., but it's the commerciality of this Atlantic master that really does the business.

The infectious lyric and rhythm turn the ordinary melody into something else. The single first brought to our attention by DJ Ian Levine is also unique in the fact that the last few seconds are spoken, that in itself is a rarity.

Top 500 Position: **187**
Original Label: **Pandora/ Mohawk**
Current Value: **£400/£40**

'A great 100mph stormer!'
Rachel Twiss, Soul Fan, Manchester, UK

Rita Dacosta
Don't Bring Me Down

Many years ago the late Irv Spice, owner of the Mohawk label told me of his great desire to chart this good but unauthodox effort from 1968.

The timing of the discovery could not have been better as it's tailor made for a 'Casino' type venue the eventual home of its popularity.

A piano and bass intro coupled with Dacosta and wailing gals pleading 'Don't Bring Me Down' was as inspiring as many other 45's with enhanced reputations.

Still immensely popular today at most revivals you can pick up the Mohawk copy (which is still the original) quite inexpensively-the rarer Pandora copy is extremely hard to find.

Top 500 Position: **188**
Original Label: **Neptune**
Current Value: **£20 Issue £35 Demo**

'Just who the hell is 'Ponch' and what IS he going to show her?'
Dave Lee, Soul Fan, South Wales, UK

The Vibrating Vibrations
Surprise Party For Baby

Already featured with the classic 'Cause You're Mine', this later single was practically a new release when exploding onto the scene at the Mecca in 1971.

The intro and subsequent 'Hey, Hey, Hey, Hey'... harmony work a treat in dragging you onto the dancefloor. A further hook, 'Hope She's Going To Show Up' is typical Gamble and Huff, being highly reminiscent of Intruders cuts of a couple of years later.

Absolutely IRRESISTIBLE.

Jimmy Burns
I Really Love You

Top 500 Position: **189**
Original Label: **Erica**
Current Value: **£1,000**

'A galloping Chicago mega-rarity'

Keith Murphy, Soul Fan, Lancashire, UK

A sensational side that gets everybody groovin', if only there were more copies to go around!

Even though it's so obscure many DJ's are only too happy to play the later UK release on Grapevine.

Written by Bobby James, he himself doing a version, the track is a worthy Top 500 entrant.

Burns, a native of the Windy City also recorded for Tip Top, Expo and Minit, but it is this glorious release on Erica that got the all important 'North of Watford' totally soul shakin'.

Laura Lee
To Win Your Heart

Top 500 Position: **190**
Original Label: **Ric-Tic**
Current Value: **£15 Issue**
£25 Demo

'Just unbeatable'

Terry West, Soul Fan, Cornwall, UK

Born Laura Rundless, daughter of a Gospel Choir leader, I must agree with Ian Levine's summation of her roots being buried deep in the Gospel style.

Vocal to 'Festival Time' (chart position 104) 'To Win Your Heart' features male backing vocals by JJ Barnes and Edwin Starr (WOW!).

Laura really is a superb singer who went on to record some great material with for Chess, Cotillion, Hot Wax and Invictus, but it is this great Ric-Tic outing that became a Mecca anthem in 1971.

Top 500 Position: **191**
Original Label: **Gateway**
Current Value: **£10**

'The biggest single of the first wave'

Jim Ryan, Soul Fan, London, UK

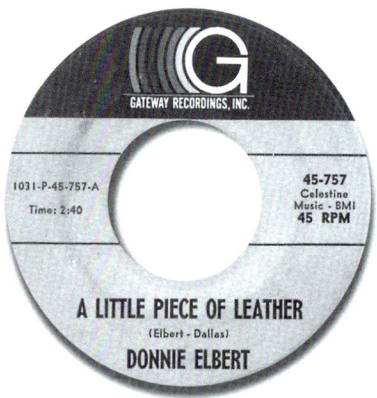

Donnie Elbert
A Little Piece Of Leather

New Orleans born vocalist with a killer falsetto, and although he had established himself as an accomplished R&B virtuoso in the 50's, it was this 1965 recording for Gateway and subsequent re-recording for All Platinum that gave him Euro success.

In fact he moved to the UK in 1964 to get married.

Business wise he was pretty shrewd too becoming A&R director for Polygram in Canada during the 80's.

The track is legendary amongst Mod/Soul boys and along with the driving 90mph beat Elbert wails that highly pitched falsetto onto the half inch master.

He sadly passed away in January 1989, and is sorely missed.

Top 500 Position: **192**
Original Label: **Soul**
Current Value: **£8 Issue**
£30 Demo

'Six by Six' captured everyone at the Wheel'

Gary Sweeger, Soul Fan, Scotland, UK

Earl Van Dyke and the Motown Brass
Six By Six

Apart from being one of the great Motown session guys, Earl scored with several of his own tracks between 1964-67.

The unusual title has a lot to answer for as it became a myth in as much as several people claimed to have 'heard the vocal' by Tony Turner on Musicor.

Kidology aside, I'll stick with this delightful brass bombing instrumental. The groove is sort of Herb Alpert meets Berry Gordy, as the vibrant percussion makes way for the trumpet solos which are so tuneful my Bert Kaempfert loving mother would probably demand the side on her shopping list of easy favourites.

Top 500 Position: **193**
Original Label: **Thomas**
Current Value: **£80**

'Hear the screaming whistle of the Psychedelic Express'

Beth Keating, Soul Fan, London, UK

Saxie Russell

Psychedelic Soul

Born Vernon Taylor, Saxie has made a superb one-off for Eddie Thomas' stable, blowing his horn as if his life depended on it.

There's total dancefloor mania every time this is played and it features excellent vocals to boot! Why this was a one-off recording I will never know!

'Psychedelic Soul' was the ultimate Northern floorshaker at just about every Soul Night in 1974.

Top 500 Position: **194**
Original Label: **Pye**
Current Value: **£60**

'A brilliant British Soul effort'

Gavin Potter,
Soul Fan, Greater Manchester, UK

Kenny Bernard

What Love Brings

Bernard hails from Sydenham in Kent, but is based in Norfolk.

He found himself at the forefront of the scene in 1974 when DJ Richard Searling gave the sound its initial airing, subsequent discoveries such as 'Ain't No Soul', 'The Tracker' and 'Isn't It A Good Idea' failed to make it.

His 'Pity My Feet' recorded for CBS was also popular but it was 'What Love Brings' that was his Northern swan song, massive at Wigan it is today largely forgotten.

As an interesting aside, David Bowie played Sax in his band at one time!

Top 500 Position: **195**
Original Label: **White Label**
Current Value: **£20**

'It's a real surprise that Motown failed to release it at the time'

Robin Chivers, Soul Fan, Suffolk, UK

Brenda Holloway
Reconsider

Brenda Holloway's popularity in the UK has always been a key component for her during the revival years.

When the amazing 'Reconsider' was unearthed Brenda sort of re-invented herself... one more time.

Hailing from Atascadero, California, the history of the lady is one of 'almost, but not quite', with her co-authorship on the standard 'You Made Me So Very Happy'. The brilliance of 'When I'm Gone' and 'Just Look What You've Done' and the real glamour of her live performances show us that Motown lost a real gem.

Top 500 Position: **196**
Original Label: **Parlophone**
Current Value: **£400 Issue**
£150 Demo

'TB Super Soul'

Jimmy Thomas, Artist, London, UK

Jimmy Thomas
The Beautiful Night

Thomas was one of the Ike and Tina Turner Revue who settled in England in the late 60's after a brief recording spell with Mirwood records.

Just when you thought he could never top his immaculate 'Where There's A Will', JT debuts on our side of the Atlantic with a masterpiece.

The song is sexy, and with the amphetamines rolling at the Torch, DJ Tony Jebb with his afghan coat and groupies in tow, this was the disc to 'get off' on!

Jimmy and I made a record with Shirley Lewis in 1983 and my passion for this work of art allowed me to slip out to Highbury to see my beloved SWFC. Jimmy I owe you!

Top 500 Position: **197**
Original Label: **Columbia**
Current Value: **£40**

'Wigan - of course!'

Carol Smith, Soul Fan, London

Wayne Gibson
Under My Thumb

Written by Mick Jagger and Keith Richard this Stones album track found it's way on to the UK Columbia label via Wayne Gibson.

He had several cracks at playing 'superstar' with a career starting in 1963 on Decca, before moving to Pye, Parlophone, Columbia and finally back to Pye.

The latter actually licensed the in-demand 'Thumb' from producer Terry King.

In theory it is a fairly good record, soulfully executed by Gibson before petering out when chart success removed the scene's blinkers. For a time though this was massive.

Top 500 Position: **198**
Original Label: **GSF**
Current Value: **£80**

'Smooth as silk for this nifty New York mover'

Keith Wilson, Soul Fan, Cheshire UK

The Anderson Brothers
I Can See Him Loving You

Written by Ray Dahrouge who recorded the track himself a couple of years later.

Absolute killer new recording in 1974, although never issued. The perfect accompaniment to the changeover from mono to stereo.

DJ Ian Levine who was the master at diversity within the scene, played this floating oddity with real conviction.

Strangely enough I met Lloyd Price then owner of GSF, who vaguely remembered the 'nice bunch of white guys'. Never released commercially, the single got no airplay but has become a firm favourite over the years.

Top 500 Position: **199**
Original Label: **A&M**
Current Value: **£100 Issue**
£40 Demo

'A major adrenaline rush'

Mike Stevenson, Soul Fan, Derbyshire, UK

Towanda Barnes

You Don't Mean It

Recorded in 1968, this New York scorcher is a full on gospel tinged romp over an erstwhile lyric with Barnes and backing vox, yelling 'you don't mean it'. The percussion is immaculate and straight out of the King Errison drum school.

Discovered by DJ Ian Levine at the famed Blackpool Mecca, from the same year you may also remember the Ohio Players' excellent version for Compass.

Top 500 Position: **200**
Original Label: **MGM**
Current Value: **£40**

'Powerful, rhythmic and destined for the scene'

Brian Moore,
Soul Fan, Greater Manchester, UK

Dottie Cambridge

Cry Your Eyes Out

Typical of the time, Cambridge with amplified vocals races through the 60's song with ease.

Though she is none other than Dorothy Moore of Dollettes, Poppies and 'Misty Blue' fame she only had one other attempt as Dottie Cambridge by way of a cover version of 'She's About A Mover'.

One of a clutch of discoveries from Bradford market whereby stall owners Bostocks had acquired thousands of MGM, Verve and other odd American 45's.

1973 was to be the golden year for a good all round Northern Soul single with an anthemic hookline to savour.

Top 500 Position:	**201**
Original Label:	**Legend**
Current Value:	**£25**

'Could have easily been covered by Chicago'

Lester Shaw, Soul Fan, London, UK

A Case Of Tyme
Manifesto

The weirdness on Northern knows no bounds as this rock single from 1970 shook the scene back in '74.

This band who were oblivious to the scene here, must have thought they were on to a real winner, capitalising on the 'rock with horns' sound the US was championing at the time.

Lead singer James Lewis is no David Clayton Thomas or Robert Lamm but he sure delivered excitement to their one and only offering.

In terms of the dancefloor it ranks in the Top 40, although short lived on the scene.

Top 500 Position:	**202**
Original Label:	**Columbia**
Current Value:	**£150 Issue**
	£30 Demo

'A wonderful Motown cover'

Mark Gregson, Soul Fan, Dublin, Eire

George Carrow
Angel Baby (Don't You Ever Leave Me)

I suspect Carrow is a white singer signed by a major label to break more soulful recordings a little more easily.

Still, he serves up a treat, with Stevie Wonder's original put well and truly in the shade.

In fact Darrell Banks' version also emulates the wonderman too. The Columbia man, who later moved to United Artists, though pips it with just a tad more energy and aggression to totally wow all dancers.

The track hurtles at speed (no pun intended!) and has the typical big city feel about it. When playlisted at the Torch alongside the many songs in the book, you can understand why this type of track was so popular. Another cover by the

Another version by the '3 1/2' on Parkway featured none other than Jeff Conaway (Kenicke in Grease!).

The Northern Soul All Time Top 500

Top 500 Position: **203**
Original Label: **Decca**
Current Value: **£150**

'Frighteningly popular for AT LEAST a decade'

Chris Luckett, Soul Fan, Middlesborough, UK

Frankie and Johnny
I'll Hold You

Marvin and Tammi they were not, but as far as the scene goes they outdid the Motowners for a while.

Sounding more like R and J Stone, the duet worked a treat on a European song and licensed to Hickory in the US.

It is basically a boy/girl song with Q and A as it's main content. Recorded in 1966, it has remained very popular, and while I am pleased the commercial sounding 45 that was a real Wigan giant is still being played, it is somewhat looked down upon by serious collectors.

Top 500 Position: **204**
Original Label: **Minit**
Current Value: **£150 Issue**
£100 Demo

'A gorgeous soulful melody'

Steve Smith, Soul Fan, Nottinghamshire, UK

Shawn Robinson
My Dear Heart

A top tune of 1974, 'My Dear Heart' is full of vitality with a cute melody and the customary vibes tinkling about.

More recently a version ostensibly by Diana Ross (it isn't listed in the Jobete publishing catalogue) surfaced courtesy of collector/DJ Gilly. Many will also remember dealer and producer Simon Soussan's US smash hit with the Patti Brooks cut 'After Dark', featured in 'Thank God It's Friday'... Following on from Shalamar's 'Simon's Theme' he did yet another piece of major Northern Soul 'homage' - ie he pinched the tune good and proper!

Top 500 Position: **205**
Original Label: **Wingate**
Current Value: **£10**

'Try saying the title when under the influence'

Gary Chalmers, Soul Fan, Essex, UK

The Dramatics
Inky Dinky Wang Dang Do

The group lead by Ron Banks scored in the early 70's on Volt with some superb singles. We concentrate though on the oddly titled 45 cut in 1966. The appeal is all there to see with an explosive intro followed by bass lead and excitable harmony, topped off with a 'whoooo' at the end of each title line.

That's the cue for the relevant gymnastics, and while this all sounds a little odd, it has to be placed in the context of one of the most credible Soul groups.

Top 500 Position: **206**
Original Label: **Warner Brothers**
Current Value: **£150 Issue £100 Demo**

'Sounding much better than even Kim Weston's version'

Graham Toothill, Soul Fan, Worcester, UK

Alice Clark
You Hit Me (Right Where It Hurt Me)

George Kerr wrote this song while under contract to Jobete publishing. Kim Weston recorded the original but it was never released due to the abundance of great hits that were 'ready to go' at Grand Ave.

The publishing arm were quick to spot any opportunity and when Kerr suggested to Warner Brothers he had found an excellent new singer in Alice Clark the song was born again.

It did not fair too well until the cravings of the north of England discovered the sound in 1973, where it has remained a classic ever since.

Top 500 Position: **207**
Original Label: **Soul Hawk**
Current Value: **£20 Issue**
£50 Demo

'That smouldering intro suddenly erupts into a magnificent dancer'

Gary Marshall, Soul Fan, London, UK

Jimmey 'Soul' Clark
(Come On And Be My) Sweet Darlin'

Clark, who originally recorded as plain Jimmy Clark became a protegé of Detroit producers Richard 'Popcorn' Wylie and Tony Hestor and recorded several undiscovered gems during 66-69. The UK not only found Clark's work, they uncovered a plethora of unreleased material from Wylie.

A long association with the UK has flourished with the Detroit Executives, Tommy Neal, Theresa Lindsay etc.

One-time boyfriend of the great Betty Lavette, Clark's dance anthem is superb with the almost ad-libbed intro leading into the big motortown backbeat of this immensely catchy record.

Top 500 Position: **208**
Original Label: **Decca**
Current Value: **£100**

'Wigan meets a TV ad'

Gary Cole, Soul Fan, Essex, UK

John E Paul
I Wanna Know

A record I had in my collection in 1971 before I had chance to expose it!

Still, DJ Russ Winstanley had the nouse to play it to death in the mid-70's to the rapturous applause of the Casino faithful.

Interestingly enough this British only release has now reached a new audience via the exposure of a 'cat food' commercial. Bizarre or what!

The single is a full-on romp aimed at giving the UK some credibility against the influx of star quality soul that was being played on Radio Caroline, Luxembourg and the discotheques. It sort of works!

Top 500 Position: **209**
Original Label: **Strata East**
Current Value: **£20 (French 45)**

'Changing the course of Northern Soul'

Paula Cole, Soul Fan, Essex, UK

Gil Scott Heron

The Bottle

Played shortly after release on the 'Winter in America' album, Heron, the ever creative poet, eventually caused a worldwide stir with this sensational creation. Initially the preserve of the Northern scene this unique track eventually 'crossed-over' to disco-funk popularity

The value of the 45 is due to the French release, all other copies being the album version which featured a longer mix.

Incredibly successful although it still attracts critics for it's non-Northerness.

Top 500 Position: **210**
Original Label: **Super Sound**
Current Value: **£200**

'Southern Soul at it's very best'

Mike Rogers, Soul Fan, Lancashire, UK

Eula Cooper

Let Our Love Grow Higher

An early 70's single that became an instant smash and, for a time at least, an ultra-rare soaring gospel groove from Georgia that was exclusive to Blackpool's Mecca.

Originally signed to Clintone, Ms. Cooper had other 45s hanging around titled 'Beggars Can't Be Choosey' and 'Standing In For Love' about the same time, but the real winner is 'Higher'. It has a lot of ingredients that many 80's divas used to full effect, with wails and yells throughout.

A real shame there was no accapella flip, then we would see some sampling action.

The Contours
Just A Little Misunderstanding

Top 500 Position: 211
Original Label: Gordy
Current Value: £6 Issue / £15 Demo

'Undoubtedly one of the best records ever'

Guy Stevens (deceased), DJ, London, UK

Possibly one of the first big 'imports' at the time. Unbelievably a non-hit in the US it recovered to secure a UK chart placing in 1970 as a result of its Northern popularity.

Yep, British radio eventually loved it and once again we would have a Top 10 Northern favourite had it not been 'commercialised' so soon. Billy Gordon, Billy Hoggs, Joe Billingsea, Sylvester Potts, Huey Davies and the late Hubert Johnson. The legendary Dennis Edwards joined in late '66 and became the lead prior to his move to the Tempts.

This is the kind of record that paved the way for Northern Soul.

Derek and Ray
Interplay

Top 500 Position: 212
Original Label: RCA Victor
Current Value: £50 Issue / £30 Demo

'The Liberaces of Soul'

Yvonne Parker, Soul Fan, Lancashire, UK

For some, this is about as ghastly as it gets, to others the single represents the time of their lives.

Either way, soul is cast out as this harpsichord led instrumental sounds more at home with curiosity collectors.

To be positive though, this really wowed the dancers and still has a fan base to this day despite the critics.

RCA in 1967 released an updated version of Dragnet to support the TV series, on the flip side they used the throwaway 'Interplay'. As is often the case the other side becomes in-demand, but as quite a few artists have been traced in recent times this pairing can forget that exclusive appearance in Blackburn!

Top 500 Position: **213**
Original Label: **Blue Star**
Current Value: **£700**

'Oh-so sought-after'

Dave Flynn, DJ and Soul Fan, London, UK

Arin Demain

Silent Treatment

Writing a book and charting the most popular northern sides should be easy. I can reveal after six painstaking months I am still rejigging positions due to obscure singles like this coming out of the sub-conscious and staking their claim in the popularity stakes.

Very few own the original, and you could (if on the sidelines) be forgiven for thinking it therefore can't be that popular.

Demain's attempt has worked, people do love it, despite it happening in the wrong country for the guy who also hit the Northern scene with his recordings under the aliases 'Karl Evans' for Skyway (see Louise Lewis) and 'Ernie Lucas' on Okeh.

Top 500 Position: **214**
Original Label: **Philips**
Current Value: **£10 Issue**
£15 Demo

'Raw and dirty 60's Soul'

Brenden Mac, Soul Fan, Merseyside, UK

The Flamingos

Boogaloo Party

Released on Philips in '66, played at the Mojo in Sheffield, Pete Stringfellow's fave rave in '67, and re-released in '69 climbing to No. 26. We could be staring at the first Northern single to ever make the British charts!

Fairly easy to see the popularity, with the party like atmosphere running through at wild animal pace.

The group had been around since '52, launched by Zeke and Jake Carey. Tommy Hunt joined for a while too though despite stories to the contrary, it was Doug McClure and not Tommy who sang lead on 'Party'.

Collectively they will be known for the 50's hits, but this 1966 New York romp put the words 'all nighter' firmly on the map.

Top 500 Position: **215**
Original Label: **Tollie**
Current Value: **£200 Issue**
£150 Demo

'Big Beat ballads and Fletcher go arm in arm'

Tim Garstang, Soul Fan, Sheffield, UK

Sam Fletcher

I'd Think It Over

Acknowledged as the first 'big beat ballad' that was to gain entry level to the scene in the early 80's.

The record is excellent and with timing being everything it helped bring about a change in the persona of many soul nights.

Recording for Vee-Jay subsidiary, Tollie, in 1964 Fletcher was an uncrowned Prince of middle of the road balladeers.

No one at the time could have realised the impact of this marvellous side, and this one will go down in history as the song that changed the mood of the scene.

Surprisingly the UK was not in fact the first European nation to appreciate Sam's talents, this record was very popular on Belgium's 'popcorn' scene of the seventies and spawned a 'lookalike' bootleg that has become the bain of UK collectors.

Top 500 Position: **216**
Original Label: **Chess**
Current Value: **£25 Issue**
£40 Demo

'The instant floor filler to get the groove going

Stuart McKenzie, Soul Fan, Scotland

Marlena Shaw

Let's Wade In The Water

The vocal prowess of Ms. Shaw just shades the classic instrumental from Ramsey Lewis, although intertwined at various junctions of exposure, the vocal wins hands down by almost incessant play in the 80's.

The trend has continued via the scooter enthusiasts with both versions securing major airtime.

Originally recording for Cadet in the US, Marlena has received many accolades, none more so than her version of 'Go away little boy', but in terms of forceful dancefloor action this Richard Evans arrangement could be one of the first ever 'rarities' to attach itself to the scene.

'Let's Wade In The Water' is actually an adaption of an old negro spiritual, listen to the lyrics you'll find them interesting!

Top 500 Position: **217**
Original Label: **SPQR/ LeGrand**
Current Value: **£40 SPQR**
£80 Le Grand

'Soaring Soul from Virginia'

Mark Thompson, Soul Fan, London, UK

Lenis Guess

Just Ask Me

One of the scenes favourite oldies, the oddly named front man evolved out of the SPQR stable which spawned pop artists Jimmy Soul and Gary US Bonds.

Unusually the record hails from Norfolk, Virginia instead of the usual NY, LA or Detroit.

There is a Elsie Strong version, released some years later, and a release on Route in the UK in '75 inspired a cover by Etta Thomas. A good trading name if nothing else.

Incidentally SPQR is, strangely, an abbreviation for the motto of ancient Rome - meaning 'For the senate and the people of Rome' - not perhaps the most obvious source for a record company name!

Top 500 Position: **218**
Original Label: **Decca**
Current Value: **£100 Issue**
£75 Demo

'Delightfully obscure and truly exquisite'

Mick Rogers, Soul Fan, Derby, UK

Lee Roye

Tears (Nothing But Tears)

A track that typifies the scene. Cute vocal and song, unknown singer, and smart dancer to boot!

Lee Roye hails from Burlington, New Jersey and got picked ahead of JR Bailey to record the song. Bailey's version being a one off acetate only.

Rather moorish, if not only for the 'ah tears nothing but tears' hook. It brought together both sexes together on the large maple wooden sprung dance floor.

Definitively Wigan, the 45 is one of a clutch of great obscure soul sides for Decca.

Top 500 Position: **219**
Original Label: **Kent Anniversary Single**
Current Value: **£10**

'THE 80's anthem'

Sean Chapman,
Soul Fan, Buckinghamshire, UK

Melba Moore

The Magic Touch

An unreleased master from 1967, that should have been released by Musicor.

The scene had already sampled Ms. Moore on 'Don't Cry, Sing A Long With The Music', but this, the original version of The Bobby Fuller Four track played at Wigan is far better.

Recorded in New York, Moore was known as an accomplished backing singer working with Aretha, Jerry Butler etc. One of her 'back up' friends was Valerie Simpson who encouraged her to go solo, unfortunately the Musicor deal was unproductive, but try telling that to the Northern faithful who positively adore it!

Top 500 Position: **220**
Original Label: **Sound Stage 7**
Current Value: **£300**

'Richie sounds brilliant for an unknown'

Malc Warman,
Soul Fan, Birmingham, UK

Little Richie

Just Another Heartache

Bass drum intro followed by horns a'plenty and rasping vocal over the John Richbourg production.

John R was a DJ and label owner who nurtured local talent in the hope of gaining lucrative deals.

There seemed to be a couple of 'littles' on SS7 (Hank and Richie) and ironically they both found fame not in Nashville but England.

Despite the authentic Soul sound, Richie turns out to be a white artist... I mean what self respecting black singer would have a name like that - well apart from Little Richard!...

Rufus Lumley
I'm Standing

Top 500 Position: **221**
Original Label: **Holton**
Current Value: **£75**

"S-T-O-M-P-E-R"

Bob Harris,
Soul Fan, London, UK

Discovered on UK Stateside, later followed by the US copies on Holton. The track is simply full on excitement with Rufus wreaking havoc over the unbelievable brass arrangement.

This white boy, who looked suspiciously like Billy Idol, later weighed in with a cut called 'Stronger Than Me' for his RCA album, which became briefly popular and a version of Fats Domino's 'I'm In Love Again' on Skyscraper - mis-credited as Rufus Lunley.

Discovered by 60s collector Bob Stevens.

The Magnetics
Lady In Green

Top 500 Position: **222**
Original Label: **Bonnie**
Current Value: **£1,500**

'The group display all the characteristics of the 50's'

Rod Keene,
Soul Fan, Belfast, Northern Ireland, UK

Both sides of this ultra rare 45 for Bonnie of Detroit are exquisite. The top side has been around the scene now for over 20 years and although the single is almost impossible to get, it has connected well with the dancers and probably has benefited from the real scarcity.

The group recorded in the 60's as The Volumes for Twirl, American Arts, Inferno and Impact, sometimes featuring Duke Browner and are definitely not to be confused with the groups who recorded for Ra-Sel, Sable, JV and Sound Trip.

Top 500 Position: **223**
Original Label: **Hem**
Current Value: **£1,000**

'Vocally this track is truly exceptional'

Eddie Singleton, Label Owner, USA

The Cashmeres
Show Stopper

Recording for Hubba Hubba, Hem and Ninandy, the group from Washington lead by Eddie Jefferson recorded this delightful single in 1967, produced by Shrine supremo Eddie Singleton.

Breaking big at the Casino in 1979 for Richard, I'm not sure if I actually discovered it, but when I came across it in a basement in Baltimore I absolutely flipped.

This wonderful sound's popularity, together with it's flip, 'Don't Let The Door Hit Your Back' (though this has been more popular in its unissued alternate version), has seen unbroken dancefloor and collector popularity ever since its first spins even though few DJs own a copy.

Top 500 Position: **224**
Original Label: **Andre**
Current Value: **£100**

'An annoyingly exciting production'

Miles Grayson, Producer, Los Angeles, USA

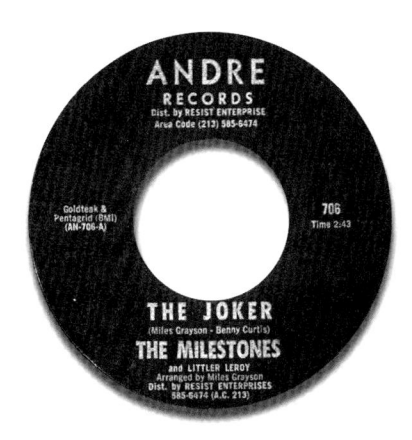

The Mylestones
The Joker

During the last 30 years any underground scene needs a little quirkiness to draw attention to itself. LA producer Miles Grayson drew upon the soul rhythms of '66 with the fascination of TV hit 'Batman'. The result being a wild 'freak out' dancer that was lying in the warehouse gagging to be heard.

Timing is everything in business and cue record dealer Simon Soussan who discovered the single in '74, sent dubs over under the guise of 'Butch Baker' and ka-pow an instant Northern Soul hit.

Cover versions were instantaneous with UK labels Creole and Casino Classics racing for the novelty hit.

I, together with fellow Casino DJ Richard Searling played it 'til the grooves wore out (you had to!), but it was our 'team leader' Russ Winstanley who really hammered it. Club goers cheekily still call him 'the Wigan Joker', that in itself compliments the size of this 45!

Prince Phillip Mitchell
I'm So Happy

Top 500 Position: **225**
Original Label: **Atlantic**
Current Value: **£50**

'Replacing his other giant is a feat in itself'

Robert Harrison, Soul Fan, Chester, UK

Leapfrogging over his mammoth 'Free For All' is the 1979 single 'I'm So Happy'. The reason for the overtaking is that 'Happy' has quite simply fast tracked on two fronts. Firstly it has been constantly played since the early 80's while his original biggie for Shout has dipped over the years.

Secondly, the scooterist crowds totally dig it, and many a rally will have witnessed the ditching of the Lambretta to race to raid the dancefloor!

Mitchell started out in the 60's with Smash recording 'Keep On Talking' which is featured in the top 500 by James Barnett.

Top notch recordings for Event and Ichiban have made the 'Prince' a sought after commodity in collector circles with 'I'm So Happy' being particular sought after, it seems that because collectors opted for the album rather than the single in '79 that it is pretty scarce.

Tony Middleton
Paris Blues

Top 500 Position: **226**
Original Label: **Amy**
Current Value: **£150**

'The odd sounding title is enough to turn anyone off, the fact is, it is excellent'

Nick Turner, Soul Fan, London, UK

The first of two entrants for The Willows' lead singer, Tony Middleton.

Following a brief hit on Melba in 1956, Middleton remained one of the great unsung heroes of rhythm and blues.

The 45 hit the scene at a strange but opportunist stage, as pop dancers were infiltrating big style. Paris Blues and its somewhat 'middle-of-the-road' big-voiced vocal made an almost idiosyncratic impact on the scene which lit the touch paper for the man's other recordings.

Top 500 Position: **227**
Original Label: **La-Cindy**
Current Value: **£500 Issue**
£1,500 Demo

'Massive first play'

John Atkinson, Soul Fan, Burnley, UK

Ernest Mosley

Stubborn Heart

Producer Eddie La Shea from Chicago cut two versions of the song, the commoner Sheppards was leased to Mirwood in LA, and then the ridiculously hard to find cut on La-Cindy (his wife?).

If any 45's have made giant strides in both play and value look no further than Moseley's one shot wonder.

Major backing vocals wail 'ohhhhh ohhhhhhh I love you' throughout the song with the unknown lead doing a sterling job, unfortunately to no avail commercially.

An Ian Levine discovery.

Top 500 Position: **228**
Original Label: **GM**
Current Value: **£20**

'The rock edge gave the Northern Scene a new twist'

Gary Griffin, Soul Fan, Shropshire, UK

Mr. Flood's Party

Compared To What

Ray Charles, Les McCann and others have put their own mark on this underground Jazz classic. The unusual version by Mr. Floods Party saw a UK release in 1971 and within a year of the Ember issue it became a cult at the Torch all nighter.

Possibly the youthfulness of the recording and a touch of soul realised a winner for the Northern scene. Excellent brass throughout, the song has the stop and start routine which dancers love. Still, a strange sound at the side of a Frank Beverly or Frank Wilson, but immensely popular.

Top 500 Position: **229**
Original Label: **Genuine**
Current Value: **£1,500**

'One of the last major cover-ups'

Derek Whiting, Soul Fan, Lincolnshire, UK

Mr. Soul / Al Scott

What Happened To Yesterday?

Amazingly credited to two different artists this late 60's monster was covered as 'Maurice McAllister' by DJ Richard Searling. Truly speaking, had it not been for discoveries of this magnitude, the scene may have petered out after the closure of Wigan Casino in 1981. Smooth Garland Green type vocals, nice big city sounding back beat, and a hook that repeats the line 'your love is slipping away', which of course is not the title. You can understand the mystery concerning the single, firstly two credited acts, then the title/hook dilemma, all adding up to a real rarity of some repute.

Top 500 Position: **230**
Original Label: **Kapp**
Current Value: **£50 Issue**
£50 Demo

'These boys were definitely 'Soul Supermen"

Tony Hunt, Soul Fan, London, UK

The Hesitations

I'm Not Built That Way

This was first single on the great Kapp label for the Hesitations, their are unconfirmed reports of a preceding 1965 release for the legendary D-Town label entitled 'Remember'.

'I'm Not Built That Way' was taken from the sought-after 'Soul Superman' album (which also spawned a scarce French EP featuring another classic 'She Won't Come Back') and indeed features that title track on the reverse. The group was led by George 'King' Scott (deceased) and remained together until 1969 when their final release for GWP featured Debbie Taylor on lead.

Top 500 Position: **231**
Original Label: **Sue**
Current Value: **£200**

'One of my favourites, it's pleasing to see the UK enjoying it too'

Sidney Barnes, Songwriter, New York

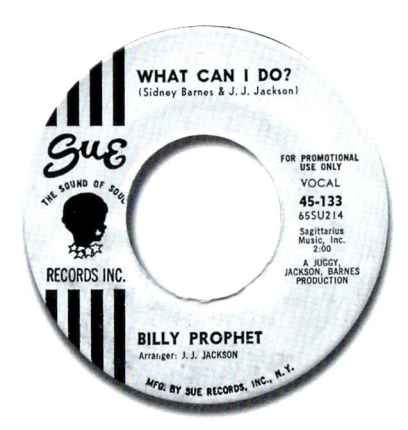

Billy Prophet
What Can I Do?

Prophet's attempt on Sue quickly petered out, as had his previous release on Barry in '65. The track suitably placed for the artist by Sidney Barnes and JJ Jackson (who met while working as writers for Motown's publisher Jobete) and had a taste for the Motor City coupled with the singers New York vocal styling.

Sadly it flopped for Billy (sometimes credited on other 45s as Billy Profit and also an ex-member of the Jive Five) but some nine years later Midlands DJ Pep took his latest find and cultivated another 'top sound'.

Top 500 Position: **232**
Original Label: **Tuff**
Current Value: **£400**

'The catchiness of the record does not detract from the Soul quality'

Ron MacKenzie, Soul Fan, London, UK

Little Joe Roman
When You're Lonesome (Come On Home)

Arguably the same vocalist as Billy Joe Young on Paula with 'I've Got You On My Mind Again' - leastways all the production credits are the same on this unashamed piece of Little Anthony plagiarism.

The Chicago based Tuff Label released some absolute pearlers including Bobby Treetop, E. Rodney Jones etc. With Romans' outing certainly the rarest on the label and most different in production style.

Reminiscent of the California Soul indies such as Danny Monday on Modern, the track has all kinds of 'hooks' rippling through the track without anyone really identifying the title. Maybe that was the problem in the US, making for an instant rarity for us to walk into over in the UK.

James Bounty
Prove Yourself A Lady

Top 500 Position: **233**
Original Label: **Compass**
Current Value: **£100**

'You could offer me your drugs on a silver platter - but I won't take them baby!'

John Gooding, Soul Fan, London, UK

Philadelphia based Bounty was written and produced for by Bobby Eli. Collectors may have come across the dreadful mutant cover version under the name Bryson Bay Brass entitled 'Permanent Injury' - a side swipe at producer Simon Soussan!

With a strong intro that rips straight into an ultra-danceable powerhouse sound, James Bounty's opus was guaranteed to go massive at the Torch.

Other great sides on the label include Helena Ferguson and the Adventurers.

Johnny Sayles
I Can't Get Enough

Top 500 Position: **234**
Original Label: **St. Lawrence**
Current Value: **£25 Issue**
£50 Demo

'Simply the best Northern record ever!'

Tim Brown,
The World's Leading Northern Soul Collector

As a business colleague of mine Tim Brown said 'It's hard to beat this - I can't believe that such a tremendous record failed to sell at the time', and he's right. A superstar on the underground with efforts for Chi-Town, Mar-V-Lus, Minit and the sensational St. Lawrence.

The production is fantastic, starting with a smouldering intro before erupting into a cymbal crashing, horn blasting frenzy, completed with Sayles sending out a clear message to messrs. Pickett and Womack that a new star has emerged.

As a short footnote, the now-deceased Sayles went on to become quite a smash live act in Alaska!

Top 500 Position: **235**
Original Label: **Four Brothers**
Current Value: **£50**

'To achieve legendary status a 45 has to have atmosphere similar to Sam and Kitty'

Gail Macy, Soul Fan, Stoke-on-Trent, UK

Sam and Kitty

I've Got Something Good

A short lived duet from Chicago, although Singin Sam had a solo 45. Without doubt one of the finest all-nighter records ever. Storming brass intro, bubbling bass line and the duo wail 'I've Got Something Good' with the entire dance floor at the Torch in '72 chanting a replacement for Got with Dropped.

Ah youth! but seriously this is the type of single that raised awareness and to this day keeps us very much young at heart.

Top 500 Position: **236**
Original Label: **Warner Brothers**
Current Value: **£35**

'A Northern legend, Sheen delivers something new to savour...'

Mark Smith, Soul Fan, County Durham, UK

Bobby Sheen

Something New To Do

The Dr. Love man is in fine fettle as his short Warner's career debuts with a fabulous beaty smoocher. A song recorded in Alabama in 1972, it caved in under the weight of the sweet ballads and James Brown influence happening at the time.

The artist has been the lead voice of one of the revived Coasters groups, and is currently living in Los Angeles.

Smooth as you like, this sought after 45 brings most Soul Nights to a classy ending.

Top 500 Position: **237**
Original Label: **Columbia**
Current Value: **£8**

'Pop kitsch - lovely!'

Martin Raynor, Soul Fan, Bretton, UK

Spiral Starecase

More Today Than Yesterday

A sprightly chart outing from a Sacramento outfit which was lead by Pat Upton.

DJ Ian Levine had the nerve to play it and why not - it's superb in its own right.

Rare 45 collectors would ask-why? The fact is this song is about dancing and having a good old sing a long.

Further singles such as 'She's Ready', 'No One For Me To Turn To' and 'Baby What I Mean' stirred up some interest too, but the female sounding male lead coupled with the delightful song makes you feel glad to be part of the 60's and 70's.

Top 500 Position: **238**
Original Label: **Atlantic**
Current Value: **£40**

'The emergence of this B side in the last few years has been something else'

Philip Lee, Soul Fan, Cornwall, UK

The Soul Brothers Six

I'll Be Loving You

The A side 'Some Kind of Wonderful' during the 60's was a regular play at most discos (not all nighters), however the truly remarkable flip 'I'll Be Loving You' has turned into a veritable monster during the past decade even surpassing the popularity of the top side.

The group hailed from Philadelphia and were led by John Ellison recording for Fine, Lyndell, Atlantic and Phil-LA of Soul before disbanding in the 70's, Ellison himself taking the name to his new Canadian base.

Top 500 Position: **239**
Original Label: **Acetate**
Current Value: **£1,000**

'The Monitors?... it turned out to be Freddie Gorman and the boys - delivering a superb unissued classic'

Chris Little, Soul Fan, Scotland

The Originals
Suspicion/Baby Have Mercy On Me

Led by Freddie Gorman, himself famed for his early work on Ric-Tic, the Originals have had a long and illustrious career that has spawned a host of sixties and seventies classics. Cuts ranging from Twisted Wheel standard, 'Goodnight Irene' to the Mecca/Ritz disco monster 'Down To Love Town' and current floorpacker 'Don't Stop Now', taken from their 'Portrait' album, have earned them a special place in the hearts of Motown freaks and Northern fans alike.

Famed as being Marvin Gaye's favourite group (he wrote and produced many tracks for them), the vocal talents of the boys are one of Motown's highlights.

The Holland Dozier Holland written 'Suspicion', produced by William Robinson and recorded May 1966, was first spun at Wigan in the late seventies by Richard Searling covered as the Detroit Prophets and since has risen to become a true floor packing standard.

Top 500 Position: **240**
Original Label: **Phil-LA-of-Soul**
Current Value: **£10 Issue £20 Demo**

'The alternate Philly sound'

John Byers, Soul Fan, Leviltown, USA

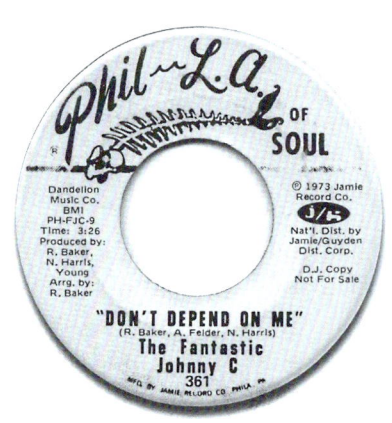

The Fantastic Johnny C
Don't Depend On Me

60's legend who left the decade on a high with such classics as 'Hitch it to the Horse' and 'Boogaloo Down Broadway' re-invented himself with a Baker-Harris-Young production of immense quality.

Johnny Corley was born in Greenwood, South Carolina and managed by Jesse James. Together they formed a formidable partnership securing a long term deal with Phil LA of Soul in Philadelphia.

His main contribution to the Northern scene lies with this 1973 recording which undoubtedly has 'Philadelphia Sound' written all over it.

The official A side 'Waitin' For The Rain' is pretty good, but Jamie's A&R team got it wrong on this occasion.

Top 500 Position: **241**
Original Label: **Festival**
Current Value: **£150 Issue**
£100 Demo

The Flirtations
Stronger Than Her Love

A song influenced by a TV commercial(toothpaste if my memory serves me correct). Sidney Barnes and JJ Jackson were contracted by label owner the late Herb Abramson, a founder member of Atlantic records. Herb and I met at his office on Broadway in 1978, and he played a variety of demos to me by another Flirtations member Charlotte Stokes.

Now the rub... This is NOT the same group that recorded as the Gypsies who later signed for Deram and featured Pearly Gates. This is the act who went on to sign for Josie, and while 'Stronger' is about as commercial as you can get, it sold poorly, citing the demise of girl groups in late '66.

'Thorough and professional, the girls perform to perfection'

Herb Abramson (deceased),
New York, USA

Top 500 Position: **242**
Original Label: **ABC**
Current Value: **£100**

The Natural Four
I Thought You Were Mine

Well it was bound to come good in the end. A cliché most commonly used on the scene, strangely enough on records of immense quality such as this. Originally a minor turntable hit at Blackpool Mecca, the song has spent the last 25 years fighting for survival. The original take of the song issued on Boola Boola is also a sought after item, but the 1970 remix for ABC is the one most loved. Formed in 1969 and led by Chris James; Lonnie Cook the band's mentor once said 'If any soul act have missed out on the big time, it has to be the N4'

I am sure that with the volume of product released daily in the US, the words often fall on deaf ears. Many years later no self respecting soul fan would argue with Cook's appraisal.

A majestic offering from the irrepressible Nat. 4'

Lonnie Cook,
Writer, Los Angeles, USA

Top 500 Position: **243**
Original Label: **Keymen**
Current Value: **£40**

'Sensational mid 60's 45 that has everything'

Tim Ashibende, Collector, Stoke-on-Trent, UK

The Fi-Dels
Try A Little Harder

A group formed by Fred Smith, who had previously recorded on Dore and later signed to Maverick. A record that has been played in just about every Northern club at some stage since it's discovery in 1971.

From a collectability point of view, I rank this among many £2/300 singles, unfortunately the demand is fairly non-existent (why?), and therefore represents the given value.

Coming from the Mirwood stable, the single looks fantastic, never mind the sound. Produced by the great Bob Relf.

Top 500 Position: **244**
Original Label: **Dial**
Current Value: **£15 Issue**
£25 Demo

'Tex scores again with another amusing and original tale'

Mick Allen, Soul Fan, London, UK

Joe Tex
Under Your Powerful Love

Apart from his other book entry 'Show Me',there was a time when another classic might have replaced this 70's racer. 'You Better Believe It' was on everyone's lips for a short time, that is until the 70's collectable started to gather momentum.

'Powerful Love' is now known to be the man's definitive Northern hit, although 'Show Me' slightly edges it in mass appeal. Strictly downhome 'Southern Soul', you can't help but check out the spoken intro, as Tex cheekily listens at the adjoining motel room door to a argument between man and woman, hoping she becomes the damsel in distress. Fellas, we would never do such a thing!

Suddenly as Joe has set the scene for us, he, together with a string arrangement frenzy, tears down the motel room door and... A totally original dance floor smash.

Top 500 Position: **245**
Original Label: **GSF**
Current Value: **£75 (Album)**
£10 Reissue 45

'The week the Northern Scene got real funky'

Bernie Golding, Soul Fan, Lancashire, UK

The Skullsnaps
I'm Your Pimp

You may own a 45 on this 1973 cult classic, which is in fact a late 70's reissue, the original remains the album. The group had minor success on the scene with 'My Hang Up Is You' a UK released single which was a 'Back Stabbers' type effort from this talented NY outfit.

When the oddly sounding 'Pimp' received the inaugural play at Blackpool Mecca in 1975, the usual raised eyebrows were evident as the fresh new groove mingled with the Salvadors etc. Boy, were we creative and brave!

A group formed out of the 60's act the Diplomats.

Top 500 Position: **246**
Original Label: **Roulette**
Current Value: **£40 Issue**
£30 Demo

'The boopity boop intro sent pulses racing'

Geoff Laidlaw,
Soul Fan, Renfrewshire, Scotland

Ila Vann
Can't Help Lovin' That Man Of Mine

DJ Ian Levine gets more than his fair share of adulation in this book, and not surprisingly so, when from the creativity of the last chart entry he skillfully slipped in another 60's recording that is more in line with the roots of the scene.

So, what do we have here, well, the song is the old Rogers and Hammerstein standard, given the full mid 60's soul treatment. Ila Vann was a competent young thing who later went on to release a killer for P.I.P in '73.

Shortly after she found herself with a UK release on Pye Disco Demand, DJ Richard Searling hammered a new 60's version by 'Navy Blue' hitmaker Diane Renay, which at the time was covered up as 'Laura Greene' and even issued as such on UK Grapevine.

Carl Douglas
Serving A Sentence Of Life

Top 500 Position: **247**
Original Label: **United Artists**
Current Value: **£200 Issue**
£100 Demo

'One of my least successful but certainly a more pleasurable one!'

Carl Douglas, Artist, London, UK

Jamaican born, raised in California, and became an engineer before meeting Pierre Tubbs who produced his first single for UA. A UK only release, Douglas later found fame recording with producer Biddu with the worldwide smash 'Kung Fu Fighting' preceded by another drift into the Northern scene with the UK-recorded 'Marble and Iron' which originally only saw light in the US on Buddah.

Discovered with the centre bashed out at Shudehill Market in 1971 by a long-haired and youthful Richard Searling, as a young 'un I found my own in Tottenham Court Road, London in Jan '73 - along with the Cherry People in Bethnal Green! Both songs had not been played before, and one I am certainly glad did, the other, well...

Herb Ward
Honest To Goodness

Top 500 Position: **248**
Original Label: **RCA**
Current Value: **£100 Issue**
£80 Demo

'Ward is another nearly man with a cache of tracks he can be proud of'

Gary Lester, Soul Fan, Lincoln, UK

Ward, from Philadelphia made various attempts as a soul star with three Northern great tracks for Argo, Buddy and RCA.

'Honest to Goodness' was first played at the Mecca.

It's all Philadelphia, with Tommy Bell doing the business as usual with a heavy but lethargic intro before the beat really kicks in and the girlies back up Herbie a treat.

Originally released in the UK on a compilation LP.

Top 500 Position: **249**
Original Label: **Bronco**
Current Value: **£40**

'About as entertaining as it gets on the dancefloor'

Barry Stone, Soul Fan, Sussex, UK

Johnny Wyatt
This Thing Called Love

Call this favouritism, but if confronted by someone who asked the question 'What is Northern Soul?',I would instantly think of this Barry White penned masterpiece from 1966.

Stomping beat, girls, vibes, sax break, and awesome lead vocal who gave us a couple of great Soul sides for Challenge. During my part in the revival of the scene, I have come to the conclusion that the majority of punters want what I want, to enjoy top notch records without any interference from any sort of 'politics of Soul'.

Wyatt, who died in 1983, provides the perfect answer to any critic who refuse to judge a record by the music alone.

Top 500 Position: **250**
Original Label: **Argo**
Current Value: **£80 Issue**
£100 Demo

'A wonderful change of direction for the Northern Scene'

Rob Perry, Soul Fan, West Midlands, UK

Doug Banks
I Just Kept On Dancing

One of the new Soul discoveries of the 80's was Philadelphia's Doug Banks. The artist was in the doo-wop group The Dreamlovers, and recorded for Guyden in 1963.

Simply speaking, the R&B groove has been pretty much the 'norm' over the past few years and due to an influx of copies in recent years this Chess group 45 (which was one of the first really big sounds to emerge in the 80's when the scene was at its least successful) has rocketed in popularity.

Top 500 Position: **251**
Original Label: **ABC**
Current Value: **£60 Issue**
£40 Demo

'I don't know about a Slow Fizz - at this pace you just go off pop!'

Derek Foster, Soul Fan, North Wales, UK

The Sapphires
Slow Fizz

Carol Jackson leads the Philly group to yet another triumphant storming Northern classic. A cornerstone of the Torch sound, there is an alternative version played by Chris 'I Got It From The Vaults' King which has found subsequent release on the Sapphires CD compiled by producer Jerry Ross, and limited edition 7" vinyl.

Another group tracked down recently by ace act detective Ian Levine.

Top 500 Position: **252**
Original Label: **Cadet**
Current Value: **£200**

'A smooth sultry recording by a new legend'

Brian Astle, Soul Fan, Nottinghamshire, UK

Terry Callier
Look At Me Now

Recording for Chess, Elektra, Prestige among new Acid Jazz workouts, Callier's folk roots have lead the man down a completely different avenue to the northern scene. That is until the focus turned to this former £1 - 70's find.

Suddenly both Northern and Modern scenes embraced the man and we find several of his sides getting played including 'Ordinary Joe' which just missed the big chart.

I well remember coming across at least 100 copies of the single in 1978 in a Baltimore warehouse - languishing simply because no one wanted them!

Top 500 Position: **253**
Original Label: **20th Century**
Current Value: **£60**

'A once highly fashionable item... rather like the tank top - never to be seen again!'

Karen Riding,
Soul Fan, Wrexham, Wales, UK

Jeanette Harper

Put Me In Your Pocket

Without wishing to be too unkind in reminding you this claimed victory at many a gig north of Watford during the 70's. Today, it barely gets a spin, due to the change of direction the scene has took.

A super fashionable item in '75 with the cutesy vocal dribbling over a mock Motown beat. Personally, for me it is everything that relegates Northern Soul to the back woods, but that is part of the magic and mystery of the scene.

Top 500 Position: **254**
Original Label: **Pye**
Current Value: **£40**

'Cultivated by the youth clubs and Mod discos'

Chris Collins, Soul Fan, Mansfield, UK

Jason Knight

Our Love Is Getting Stronger

In 1969 I ventured to my first 'official' club, where among the pop hits of the day were the customary Motown spins topped off with a few regional tracks. This 1967 single from Pye was still available and to hear it alongside The Marmalade- 'Lovin' Things' seemed fairly natural (hey I was 13!).

Imagine my surprise, when at the Torch a crowd of regular gymnasts were getting off to this UK - only romp. Obviously a stage name conjuring up visions of a Peter Wyngarde type character all donned out with matching cravat and moustache!

Seriously, the 45 is pretty good, and one of the top British discoveries of all time.

The Northern Soul All Time Top 500

Top 500 Position: **255**
Original Label: **Goldmine**
Current Value: **£10**

'Even the demos from Popcorn's stable became monsters!'

Gail Parker, Soul Fan, Widnes, UK

Tony Hestor
Down In The Dumps

Originally an alternate studio demo to Stanley Mitchell's 'Get It Baby'. John Anderson of Soul Bowl tracked down Richard 'Popcorn' Wylie in Detroit in the late 70's and unearthed a treasure trove of Wylie/Hestor unreleased goodies. From Betty Boo to Willie Harvey to work by the two producers themselves, there is a huge diversity of Wylie and Hestor material.

Even though you can sense the rawness of the rehearsal, Hestor had the knack of positioning a song right where the public wanted it to be. DJ Richard Searling got behind it and Wigan Casino claimed another exclusive.

Top 500 Position: **256**
Original Label: **Mercury**
Current Value: **£150 Issue**
£100 Demo

'A refreshing start to the 80's when the 'faith'less pronounced Northern - 'dead''

Gary Fletcher, Soul Fan, Midlothian, Scotland

Alfie Davison
Love Is A Serious Business

A release from '79 which in some quarters is unthinkable.

The great mystery of Northern soul is the 'yes and no' trials and tribulations of clubbers.

Sure, the DJ himself has influence and can often nurture a track along, this modernistic dancer, sailed through the cloud of nostalgic fog with ease, and allowed newcomers to experience a fresh sound during a period when Northern was at its nadir.

The 45 itself percolated on the New York disco scene too, but the longevity will always remain 'up North'.

Top 500 Position: **257**
Original Label: **Back Beat**
Current Value: **£60**

'It says exactly what I was thinking back in 1974'

Mike Wilson, Warrington, UK

Jeanette Williams
All Of A Sudden

A fantastic gritty performance from Texan Williams. We know her for 'Something Good Gotten' A Hold Of Me' and prior to that dance favourite, dabbled with 'Stuff' a meaty soul cut from 1968. I played the heck out of this acquiring the single from Simon Soussan, who at the time went British label collecting crazy. OK so I swapped a copy of the Carrolls on Polydor for it, let ME at least get the edge sometimes!

The gal is quite superb, and from a group of labels headed by Don Robey, she ought to have had better promotion, as Back Beat could have been onto something.

Top 500 Position: **258**
Original Label: **Giant**
Current Value: **£30 Issue**
£75 Demo

'The first Northern 45 I bought and still my all time favourite

Rod Moore, Perth, Western Australia

Jo Armstead
I Feel An Urge Coming On

Josephine Armstead has many classic soul singles to her credit, including the Motown period as a writer alongside Ashford and Simpson.

Her Northern output includes 45's on Giant and Gospel Truth and productions for Wise World, most notably the Salvadors.

Born in Yazoo City, Mississippi and a former member of the Ikettes, 'Joshie' as she is known took the Northern scene by storm in '71 when it was first aired at the legendary Blackpool Mecca.

The Northern Soul All Time Top 500

Top 500 Position: **259**
Original Label: **Twirl**
Current Value: **£500**

'My favourite dancer of all time'

Cynthia Morgan, Soul Fan, Wales, UK

JoAnn Courcy
I Got The Power

I had the good fortune of discovering this powerhouse of a dancer in, of all places, a newsagents. Just prior to my selection as a Wigan Casino DJ (August, 1973), I strolled into my father's newsagents to collect the local rag when a large box of 45's had been placed on the counter with the sign attachment 'ex-juke box' only 25p each.

Supplied by a greeting card firm from Derby, they obviously thought having no centres meant the above. How wrong they could be, as I perused over around 80 discs, nearly all were soul and cutting to the chase, I found 'You're Not My Kind' - Paula Durante and this absolute dynamite dancer from Detroit.

Sadly, I never managed to play it at the Casino, as I traded it for around £40 worth of essentials I needed to play!...

DUMB MOVE KIDDO!

Top 500 Position: **260**
Original Label: **Eastern**
Current Value: **£10**

'A stomping time was had by all!'

Jeff Lincoln, Soul Fan, Hertfordshire, UK

Eddie and Ernie
I Can't Do It (I Just can't Leave You)

Eddie Campbell and Ernie Johnson were very much cast in the Sam and Dave mould. As a live act they regularly opened for the Ike & Tina Turner Review, whilst their Mod classic 'Outcast' was covered by the Animals and was mutated into Jesse Johnson's 'Left Out' for Old Town.

Back to this chart entry - well it's a stomper time as the duo work up Richard Tee's arrangement a treat. Interestingly enough the pair's manager is none other than Hadley Murrell one-time producer of Northern Soul hitmakers the Servicemen.

Top 500 Position: **261**
Original Label: **Grapevine**
Current Value: **£15**

'We could have sworn the 45 was just another cover up!'

Gail Marchant,
Soul Fan, Greater Manchester, UK

Betty Boo
Say It Isn't So

When a DJ exposes a new 'rarity' and reveals the artist as Betty Boo, you get the feeling you are being had, even if the side is an excellent dancer. The fact is producer Richard 'Popcorn' Wylie can't remember the lady's real name, but does admit to the pseudonym simply to add a little sexiness to the track.

History out of the way as Wylie supplied a tape to Soul Bowl, who wisely dubbed an acetate for long serving Wigan Casino DJ Richard Searling and the rest IS history. The usual suspects are evident —Wylie, Hestor etc, complete with new female talent looking 'for a break'.

Top 500 Position: **262**
Original Label: **Sound Stage 7**
Current Value: **£20 Issue**
£30 Demo

'To hear this and see the man live, was a dream come true'

Rick Foster, Anglo American, Todmorden, UK

Roscoe Shelton
Running For My Life

A Soul and Blues artist of great repute from Lynchburg, Tennesssee. The Nashville label had minor successes with the man in '65/66, and he proved to be key act in the South performing live on many occasions. It must be said that 'Running' is somewhat at odds with most of the man's R&B tinged southern material. Eventually the well ran dry material wise Shelton found a new audience via the lucrative blues scene.

A fantastic singer, which you don't have to be a rocket scientist to ascertain after hearing this Golden Torch anthem from 1972.

The Northern Soul All Time Top 500

Top 500 Position: **263**
Original Label: **Deesu**
Current Value: **£60**

'The stomp stomp intro is totally irresistible'

Jeff Williams, Soul Fan, Humberside, UK

Maurice Williams
Being Without You

Leader of early 60's hitmakers the Zodiacs and preceded by a launch into the music industry as the Gladiolas. Williams, from Lancaster, South Carolina, re-invented himself twice during his career, firstly signing to the New Orleans label Deesu and recording the Motownesque 'Being Without You' which was first brought to the scene's attention by Martin 'Soul Sam' Barnfather.

During the 80's, the hit movie Dirty Dancing popularised his one and only hit 'Stay', where that and other material keeps him working, mainly in Georgia and the Carolinas.

Top 500 Position: **264**
Original Label: **Soul Series**
Current Value: **£10**

'If this ain't the finest Northern discovery ever, I'll quit my 60 a day habit'

Glen Malrose, Collector, California, USA

Spencer Wiggins
Let's Talk It Over

Discovered by true Northern Soul original Brian Rae on an obscure US CD, this 1967 unreleased cut is of absolute stunning quality. Made for the scene - well not quite - but it's as if producer Quinton M Claunch 'knew something'.

Quite how this was unreleased is an intriguing mystery, with Writers Penn/Oldham protegee Wiggins tearing the roof off with a corking piano riff which weaves in and out of a New York type back track.

Spencer does his usual 'Southern style' and delivers a 'creature from the deep', ready and waiting to suck you in. After hearing it, I would not mind in the slightest!

Top 500 Position: **265**
Original Label: **Mo-Groov**
Current Value: **£800**

'You guys in England still looking for that Nomads record?'

John Hook, DJ, North Carolina, USA

The Nomads

Somethings Bad

A North Carolina 45 that even the locals are searching for, so tear up the plane tickets to Charlotte!

Sunny Threatt and Phyllis (Brown?) recorded the 1967 side for the ridiculously obscure Mo-Groov label. The duo also made music with Major Bill Smith for his Texas based Charay label.

Very much Richard Searling's baby, the price tag has slightly diluted the potential of the side, but the minute you do hear it, you are up and dancin'... they certainly were at Wigan!

Top 500 Position: **266**
Original Label: **Maverick**
Current Value: **£100 Issue**
£60 demo

'Terrible Tom for me represents the true meaning of Northern Soul'

Ginger Taylor, DJ, Todmorden, UK

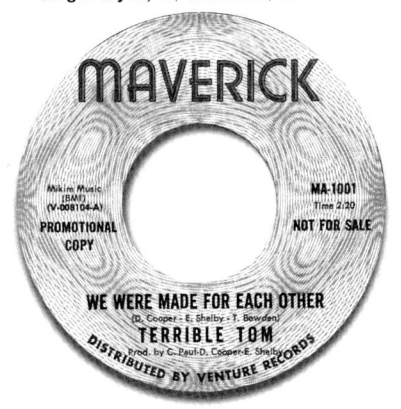

Terrible Tom

We Were Made For Each Other

Terrible Tom, real name Tom Bowden, recorded for Mickey Stevenson and Ernie Shelby's Maverick label in early '68. The unknown Tom is by know means Terrible as the lead vocalist rips through the 100 mph track like a buzz saw. In the heady days of '74 the scene thrived on such discs and captured the very essence of soul that only a dance enthusiast could describe.

Owning a copy back then would have set you back £20, and if you are lucky enough to own the 'B' side (most are double sided promos), you could name your price. Discovered by DJ Ian Levine, and played initially at Blackpool Mecca, the 45 was made for Wigan Casino!

Top 500 Position:	**267**
Original Label:	**Goldwax**
Current Value:	**£15 Issue**
	£25 Demo

'Its raunchiness, coupled with Carr's fantastic delivery, make it one of THE top sounds ever'

Brian Mottram, Soul Fan, Greater Manchester, UK

James Carr

That's What I Want To Know

The man with the unique sound from Memphis started out as a gospel singer with O. V. Wright. Carr, being spotted by Goldwax supremo Quinton Claunch was signed to the company in 1964.

During the four years the company operated, he recorded a wealth of Chips Moman, Dan Penn, Spooner Oldham material. In later years he recorded for River City before re-appearing to record two albums in the early 90's.

Totally underrated, this B side, found it's way onto UK Stateside, before its discovery a couple of years later whereupon it became a Twisted Wheel anthem.

Top 500 Position:	**268**
Original Label:	**Smash**
Current Value:	**£125 Issue**
	£100 Demo

'Country-meets-Soul-meets-Northern'

Keith Alton, Soul Fan, London, UK

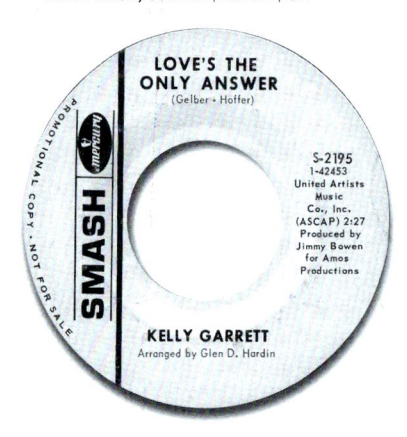

Kelly Garrett

Love's The Only Answer

One of those typical pop dancers predictably massive for at the Casino, Kelly Garrett therefore caught the imagination of the ever faithful,.

Released in 1968, the song didn't sell a bean in the US, which is surprising, as the feel of it suggests it ought to be some kind of TV sitcom theme.

There is also a version by pop artist, Margaret Whiting, even more akin to Tammy Wynette, it came out on Canadian London.

Top 500 Position: **269**
Original Label: **Revilot**
Current Value: **£10**

'Sweet soul without a hint of P-Funk'

Will Davis,
Groovesville, Detroit, USA

The Parliaments
Don't Be Sore At Me

Due to the thousands of imported copies in the early 70's, you are staring at a ten pound record, the fact is, the quality of such a single ought to be commanding 100 times that!

Superb from the outset, George Clinton and company ride the Detroit groove perfectly and deliver the right hook, amazingly not connecting with the chart in 1965. Clinton from Kannapolis, North Carolina formed the group as far back as 1955, releasing their first single on ABC 12 months later. Moving to an independent in '63, New records, they auditioned for Motown and after recording several demos, Clinton stayed in Detroit and hooked up with Don Davis at Solid Hitbound productions.

His status over the past 25 years is legendary by way of the P-Funk interest. In Northern Soul terms he is one name that appears on many rare soul discs.

Top 500 Position: **270**
Original Label: **Unity**
Current Value: **£350**

'One seriously hard record to find!'

Barry Hollingsworth,
Soul Fan, Bedfordshire, UK

Candi Staton
Now You've Got The Upper Hand

The darling of all eras, with this her first 45. In 1968 right through to her one liners being sampled to create a variety of dance hits in the 80's and 90's. In between, why she was recording the best material of her life with producer Dave Crawford in Alabama, with hits such as 'Young Hearts Run Free'.

Just prior to her first recording contract with Fame in the summer of '68, the lady from Hanceville, Alabama recorded a great single for Unity that failed to get any interest even in her home state.

Married for a time to Clarence Carter who's kinky 45 'Strokin' certainly reaffirmed the divorce courts as Staton moved into the gospel field. A super groove that never quite hit the ultimate heights, largely due to it's scarcity.

The Northern Soul All Time Top 500

Top 500 Position: **271**
Original Label: **Decca**
Current Value: **£250 Issue**
£100 Demo

'Pure danceability'

Lisa Holliman, Soul Fan, San Francisco, USA

Lada Edmund Jnr

The Larue

When DJ Ian Levine first played this at Blackpool Mecca it raced to the top of my wants list, I knew that if I could track it down that it would become the new No. 1 sound at the Casino...

Lada was in actual fact an all-round talent. A singer and dancer, she recorded for Coral and Roulette as well as producing two 45's for Decca. Shrine supremo Eddie Singleton was the man behind 'The Larue' a cash-in dance tune which nonetheless has fiery appeal!

Amazingly Lada Edmund also appeared on the big screen in the 70's blaxploitation movie 'Savage' (1973) before fading into obscurity. The promotional picture of her was one fronted by a white model!

Top 500 Position: **272**
Original Label: **Kyser**
Current Value: **£1,000**

'The story of Robby Lawson is legendary and we still know nothing about him'

Stan Krause, Store Owner, Jersey City, USA

Robbie Lawson

Burning Sensation

One of the scenes great discoveries. The story is as follows, a collector from San Francisco Bob Cattaneo discovered it in 1974, and being aware of the Northern scene sold it to a collector. DJ Soul Sam was the first to play it who then promptly sold it to DJ Colin Curtis who then moved it on to me!

The total exchange deals constituted a mere £100, with each of us finding the sound a little unresponsive with the dance floor. Moving on, the 45 well and truly matured and has the distinction of being the first northern 45 to sell for £1, 000.

A busy production by Paul Kyser who released this as his first single on his own label. Trivia wise, here's an absolute peach. An old friend of mine Stan Krause, owner of the Catamount label in Jersey City, distinctly remembers putting the labels on the wax as the record was being made at his fathers pressing plant in Little Ferry, New Jersey in 1967!

The flip side is 'I Have Searched', if only Lawson knew!

Top 500 Position: **273**
Original Label: **A&M**
Current Value: **£100**

'If this is disco then I'm John Travolta!'

Rick Foster, Manager, Anglo-American, UK

Collins and Collins
Top Of The Stairs

A 1980 release in a Northern Soul book?... Well in recent times this disc has moved from the Modern Rooms into the cavernous All-nighter halls as a result of massive popularity. Nor is the original quite the obscurity often demanded - hitting number 68 on the US Black Music Top 100 chart. You may then gauge from a price into three figures that this is a hot ticket item.

Collins and Collins were a brother and sister outfit (Bill and Tonee) whose recorded career would appear to be brief. 'Top Of The Stairs' is an Ashford and Simpson song (they did in fact also record it) and with Philly Disco-General John Davis behind the production it is perhaps no surprise that a small amount of commercial success ensued. It *is* a surprise that it should become such a big record on an essentially 60's based music scene though!

Top 500 Position: **274**
Original Label: **Mala**
Current Value: **£25**

'The whiplash effect distinguished this single from others and proved to be its trump card'

Steve Davies, Soul Fan, Merseyside, UK

Reparata and the Delrons
Panic

So easy to score at Wigan Casino in '74 with such a large and eager audience. Panic represents the 60's well, without a hint of soul. Mary 'Reparata' Aiese from New York had minor US success with 'When A Teenager Cries' in '65.

The UK became the group's next port of call with 'Captain Of Your Ship' in '68. She also recorded for Polydor in the 70's, but it is this lightweight but effective racer from '68 that most folk on the scene remember.

You definitely needed stimulants to be able to dance to this!

Benny Troy
I Wanna Give You Tomorrow

Top 500 Position: 275
Original Label: De-Lite
Current Value: £30

'Disco dross in some quarters - considered a Northern classic in others'

Liz Crowley, Soul Fan, Oxford, UK

Every so often a 45 appears that has little to do with Northern soul. However that very statement adds mystique to the unique movement we are investigating. Troy is a East Coast 'lounge' type singer. A sort of Tony Christie type full of frilly shirts and platforms. Joking apart, the label De-Lite released many soul 45's and was the home for Kool and the Gang.

Checking out the single further, it slips in well to 'North of Watford' playlists, with the sing-a-long chorus and soft disco beat.

The unfortunate thing I remember about the single is, that I traded a now £600 single for it 20 years ago!

Thelma Houston
Baby Mine

Top 500 Position: 276
Original Label: Capitol
Current Value: £75 Issue
£50 Demo

'Even though the song is her first attempt the performance is still there'

Carolyn Hart, Soul Fan, Yorkshire, UK

Many years later in her career she recorded a song titled 'Saturday Night, Sunday Morning' which could somehow be a cryptic message to the northern scene. OK so I'm imagining things, the brilliant female singer from Leland, Mississippi is probably oblivious to the fact that her first single ever is really popular here. Please, someone show her this book!

Accomplished singer with a US No. 1 to her credit with 'Don't Leave Me This Way', the Capitol single from 1966 is perfect Motownesque. Appearing in movies too, the lady is now legendary, and if there was anyone I would like to see live (currently) it's Thelma. If you have never heard it before, try and do so, it's a 'play it on CD and remember the good times' type of single.

Top 500 Position: **277**
Original Label: **New Voice**
Current Value: **£8 Issue**
£20 Demo

'You can feel the excitement in the recording'

Peter Harrison,
Soul Fan, Northamptonshire, UK

Mitch Ryder and the Detroit Wheels

Breakout

Ryder, born William Levise Jnr. had a knack of treating the studio session as a live one. His other Northern winners including ' You Get Your Kicks','Devil With The Blue Dress' and 'Sock It To Me Baby' had that very same feel. His poorest US seller has turned out to be his most fondly remembered UK dancer.

'Breakout', produced by Bob Crewe in 1966, was released on Stateside here and did not take long to become a nighter favourite, gaining regular turntable action as early as 1968. Known originally as Billy and the Rivieras, Ryder is still a cult figure among many celebs, most notably Bruce Springsteen.

Top 500 Position: **278**
Original Label: **Scepter**
Current Value: **£25**

'Another vintage career 45 for THE girl group of the 60's'

Steve Ellis,
Soul Fan, Northamptonshire, UK

The Shirelles

Last Minute Miracle

In the US the group from Passaic, New Jersey had bottomed out as early as 1963. After a string of hits, it was a case 'where to next'. Label boss Florence Greenburg held faith with the quartet and matched them with a variety of happening producers such as George Kerr.

The track was originally written for Linda Jones on Loma, but who could doubt the sheer brilliance of lead singer Shirley Alston. Sure, Jones was a magnificent vocalist too, but Alston knew how to add a little extra gloss. Put that down to chart experience and without diversifying too much the girls output during this period (1965-68) was exemplary.

Originally discovered by DJ Ian Levine it fought for plays in 1973 and, if discovered today, collectors would be talking about it for years.

Top 500 Position: **279**
Original Label: **Musicor**
Current Value: **£80 Issue**
£60 Demo

'A plodding intro - and then WALLOP!'

Jeff Martin, Soul Fan, Australia

Porgy and the Monarchs

My Heart Cries For You

Lead by Porgy Williams. Recorded originally for Mala, Sylves onto Musicor then Verve, the act from Chicago. The focus is on the second of two releases for Musicor with a monster from Wigan!

This old standard becomes highly infectious in the hands of this competent vocal group as they harmonise the hook line with great accuracy and ferment. It is just pitiful that the US had all these fabulous groups (too many in fact) and in Europe we got the 'watered down' copyists.

Top 500 Position: **280**
Original Label: **PAP**
Current Value: **£100**

'One of the first big money 70's anthems

Dennis Turner, Soul Fan, South Wales, UK

Daybreak

I Need Love

One of the most active and talented producers in soul music during the last 25 years, Patrick Adams was a melody maker who was cut from the same cloth as the Philly and Salsoul producers.

Daybreak did little apart from a few plays by Jeff Troy on WWRL in New York. During my time as a record dealer the song was nothing more than a sweet soul sound that I remember as a new release. The UK however latched onto the side which received plays from Richard Searling at Wigan covered up as 'Tyrone Edwards'. The mystery of cover-ups is of course is common place in England, but totally confused Pat when I told him!

Incidentally, as an aside, Adams 'cut his teeth' in the studio in 1967 working for Bobby Robinson on The Carletts- 'I'm Getting Tired', which locally came out on BR, before being leased to Capitol. Patrick went on to produce Four Below Zero plus really making his name as Disco King with Fonda Rae and many others. His real soul connections with Black Ivory make the man a totally unsung hero of Soul.

Top 500 Position: **281**
Original Label: **Ashford**
Current Value: **£30 issue**
£300 Demo

'A bad dancer you might be, but this is the 45 to help you find some rhythm

Dave Evison, DJ, Stoke-on-Trent, UK

Eddie Parker
Love You Baby

Recorded by Jack Ashford for his Ashford label in 1968, the song ridicules the need for a different approach á la 'Cloud Nine' and other hits of the year. Ashford and his wife Lorraine Chandler were accomplished musicians and had worked for Kapp, RCA amongst others. Parker had a single on Awake called I'm Gone', which is a massive rarity.

The history? Well it was discovered at the Golden Torch in 1972, and the Exciters covered it at the request of Ian Levine. Dave Evison has since 'adopted' the tune has his own anthem. Absolutely ferocious in tempo, but forsaking a great melody, Parker was a real screamer and pretty damn good too.

Top 500 Position: **282**
Original Label: **Verve**
Current Value: **£10 Issue**
£15 Demo

'The duo are legendary, but the band more so on the scene'

Keith Wallers, Soul Fan, Merseyside, UK

The Righteous Brothers Band
Rat Race

Talk about unusual! The rhythm band for Bobby Hatfield and Bill Medley chose the old Richard Maltby track to cover in 1966. The influx of copies at Bradford market allowed the single to be exposed at nearly every soul night in the early 70's thus rapidly gaining a toe hold on the scene. This is pure stomp and with instrumentals in general falling from grace it's nice to hear it occasionally.

Yet another Wigan Casino great - this one was absolutely tailor-made for Station Road!

The Northern Soul All Time Top 500

Top 500 Position: **283**
Original Label: **Rouser**
Current Value: **£5,000**

'RARER than rare'

Steve Mikowski, Soul Fan, USA

The Butlers with Frankie Beverly

Because Of My Heart

Very expensive today on Fairmount, 'Because Of My Heart' was in fact originally released on local label Rouser, however there is only one known copy. The reverse 'I Want To Feel I'm Wanted' is yet another classic, if underplayed track, from the Maze front man whose voice just seems to get better and better with age.

The Rouser release is arguably the rarest Northern Soul 45 on its original imprint.

Top 500 Position: **284**
Original Label: **Toxsan**
Current Value: **£300**

'An exceptional 60's dancer with anthemic overtones'

Mark Liddell, Soul Fan, West Midlands, UK

Herb Johnson and the Impacts

I'm So Glad

Although better known on the nationally released Brunswick label, Johnson recorded this in '66 for Wally Osborne's indie label from Philadelphia - his backing group, the Impacts, featured Major Harris - who appears earlier in the chart.

The artist had a few cracks at success with further singles on the label and one for Arctic. What makes this 45 stand out is 'oh whoa whoa oh' hook that ripples through the track. The beat to is irresistible and was one of many classics first aired at the Golden Torch all-nighter.

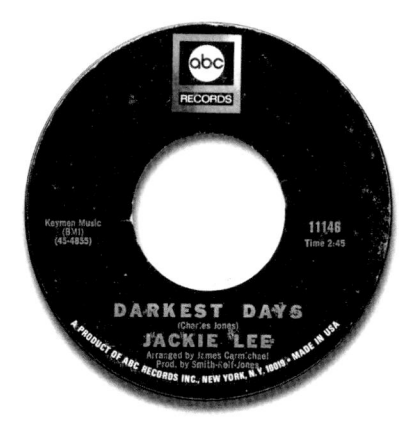

Jackie Lee
Darkest Days

Top 500 Position: **285**
Original Label: **ABC**
Current Value: **£25 Issue**
£50 Demo

'The multi-talented Earl Nelson I presume?'

Tom Levin, Chicago, USA

The Mirwood production team leased this 1967 rarity to ABC, but sadly the act couldn't repeat the success of 'The Duck'. Picked up by the Twisted Wheel DJs, the scene was still in its infancy when we were first treated to this most uplifting of Soul sounds.

At one time it could be counted as the country's biggest in-demander. Regarded now as a 'cheapie' it is typical of the kind of disc that is, in fact no longer knocking around in the States - so that if demand again rises you can expect the value to rocket!

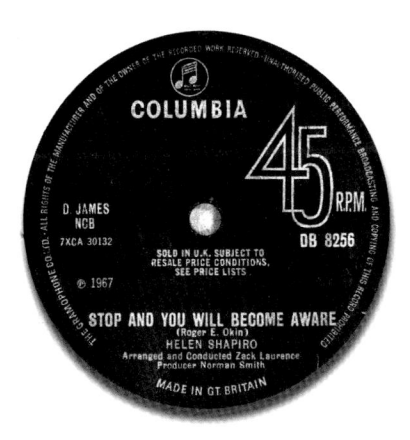

Helen Shapiro
Stop And You'll Become Aware

Top 500 Position: **286**
Original Label: **Columbia**
Current Value: **£70**

'It was only a matter of time before Helen's obscurities surfaced'

Andrew Topping, Soul Fan, London, UK

One of the better pop discoveries at Wigan Casino, Shapiro was the youngest female chart topper when at 15 years of age she had realised two No. 1 hits!

She headlined the first UK tour on which the Beatles appeared as her support act. Outside of the hitmaking period, Shapiro flirted with all manner of releases and this mock-Motown groove is one of the results of the singers' attempts to gain favour with EMI who stayed faithful to her throughout the 60's, despite her having no hits after 1964.

The all-nighters loved this in the 70's and she certainly is one act to have remained in the hearts of a large number of fans with widely-differing musical tastes.

Top 500 Position: **287**
Original Label: **Verve**
Current Value: **£25 Issue**
£40 demo

'To some this was THE Torch anthem'

Gary Holland, Soul Fan, Sheffield, UK

The Shalimars
Stop And Take A Look At Yourself

From a label conception by Norman Granz and distributed by MGM from 1958, Verve mixed Jazz, Folk, Pop and Soul together with many failures. Here is just one that for me is one of the best Northern sides ever. The group from New York were fronted by 'Sari' who later used herself as the official leader on a single for Veep in 1968.

The commerciality of the 45 is glaringly obvious with a piano riff to die for, stunning background vocals and a lead reminiscent of Shirley Alston.

Top 500 Position: **288**
Original Label: **Skyway**
Current Value: **£50**

'Another storming dancer from Miles Grayson'

Brenda Smith,
Soul Fan, West Midlands, UK

Louise Lewis, Miss LL
Oo Wee I'll Let It Be You Babe

A great track to DJ with in the 70's. The single from 1966 is pure Motown meets Mirwood with former opera singer Lewis squealing over a delicious Miles Grayson groove.

A Simon Soussan find with yours truly and Russ Winstanley on it big style at the Station Road venue.

Maybe out of step today, but the catchiness of the melody makes this a worthwhile chart edition for Miss Double-L. A simultaneous release by Karl Evans faired no better commercially.

Top 500 Position: **289**
Original Label: **Canterbury**
Current Value: **£10 Issue**
£25 Demo

'Just a little understanding - it was bound to succeed!'

Bob Crichton, Soul Fan, Los Angeles, USA

The Younghearts
A Little Togetherness

This group also features in the chart under their alternate name, the Tempos.

A monster Torch anthem and now used as the theme tune for the increasingly popular Togetherness Allnighters at Stoke's King George's Hall.

The Los Angeles group led by James Moore later gave up their dual identity and went on to record as the New Younghearts.

'A Little Togetherness' was also released later on the Zea label credited to the 'King Of Hearts'.

Top 500 Position: **290**
Original Label: **United Artists**
Current Value: **£100 Issue**
£25 Demo

'It started out as a theme tune for a TV car commercial'

Robin Holland, Soul Fan, Leicester, UK

The Steve Karmen Band featuring Jimmy Radcliffe
Breakaway

Karmen was a new generation band leader, who later composed the 'I Love New York' promotion theme when the city was considered by some to be unsafe during the 70's. Radcliffe on the other hand was a first class vocalist famous for his work on Musicor and others.

Here we have a big production matched by a mammoth vocal and a blaxploitation type song that Isaac Hayes would have approved of. DJ Colin Curtis was first out of the trap with this one and, it sort of allowed more non-traditional sides to get played. An innovative but unusual record.

Top 500 Position: **291**
Original Label: **Col-Soul**
Current Value: **£300**

'On hearing this I realised Northern Soul could always hold it's head high'

Tom Luccino, Collector, Maryland, USA

The Chandlers
Your Love Makes Me Lonely

Ohio's attempt at group Soul harmony and certainly bagging a few thousand listeners here in the UK. Sadly, the single from 1966, was far too dated for the US market.

They recorded a further single on local label Bleu Rose in 1969, but that too sank without a trace.

Amazingly this record started its rise to fame in Accrington at the British Legion/Band Club nights there - an unglamorous but typically truthful beginning for a Northern Soul record!

Top 500 Position: **292**
Original Label: **Impact**
Current Value: **£75 Demo**
£100 Issue

'Popularised in the 70's, soaring upwards today'

Leanne Holly, Soul Fan, USA

The Lollipops
Loving Good Feeling

This cutesie girl group recorded for Smash, RCA, Motown's V.I.P and Detroit's Inferno.

Label owner Harry Balk had a great production partner in Duke Browner and together they made the label one of the most sought after in Britain.

This is the group's best dancer with a typical young lead joined by a nice chorus.

Drifting in and out of popularity since 1973.

Top 500 Position: **293**
Original Label: **Volt**
Current Value: **£30**

'I'd like to have a Pow-Wow with this lady!'

Kev Sowerby, Soul Fan, Cumbria, UK

Linda Lyndell

Bring Your love Back To Me

A stunning effort from Lyndell, a full-blood American Indian, which allegedly was recorded in Texas with the Crazy Cajun production team. It was released on Volt in 1968 with a UK release here on Stax. She later found minor fame with the much sampled 'What A Man' before disappearing into further obscurity.

A perfect Motown type waxing that made its mark at the tail end of the Twisted Wheel and played extensively by its last DJ, the late Les Cokell.

The groove is insatiable and would make an ideal song to cover today.

Top 500 Position: **294**
Original Label: **Harthon**
Current Value: **£20**

'Lovingly produced by the legendary Harthon crew'

Gary Allen, Soul Fan, Philadelphia, USA

The United Four

She's Putting You On

As I play back my answer phone a voice appears 'hey Kev this is Weldon Arthur McDougall the third, calling from Philadelphia'.

Weldon is one of Philly's great mouthpieces, championing the great music from the city. Why, he should get into politics, but he's too modest for that, simply going about his business recording the local black talent of the day. His association with Styles, Randolph, Holman, Gamble, Huff is well documented, and on this occasion we turn to a 45 first played in 1974 by DJ Ian Levine.

The track is probably the most energetic and entertaining of all the productions he made. Vocals coming at you from all directions, typical Virtue type groove cooking in the background and the quality hook you come to expect from the team.

A thousand pound sound for twenty - the stockbroker says BUY!

Top 500 Position: **295**
Original Label: **American Arts**
Current Value: **£75 Issue**
£50 Demo

'Increasingly popular internationally'

Joe Roccini, Soul Fan, New Jersey, USA

Bobbie Smith
Walk On Into My Heart

The 45 produced by the Balk/Browner tie up, has steadily grown into one of the definitive sounds of the last 20 years. Picking up the slack on the scene from the likes of Lainie Hill, Dena Barnes etc, the 1965 recording did poorly in the US except for Pittsburgh where it became a minor hit.

The disc strolled into Stafford becoming one of their first monster sounds - even generating a 'lookalike' reissue that caught many a collector out.

Bobbie was originally part of a girl group called Bobby and the Dream Girls.

Top 500 Position: **296**
Original Label: **Jay Boy**
Current Value: **£6**

'Massively in-demand with dancers, despite having no collector appeal'

Rob Jeffries,
Soul Fan, Northamptonshire, UK

The Bob and Earl Band
My Little Girl (Instrumental)

Released in the UK when sister company President held the UK rights to Mirwood, the backing track amazingly overtook the popularity of the already released vocal by Bobby Garrett. The scene makes it's 'own' sounds and while DJ's suggest and coerce, the dancer will have the final word.

Record company and punter forced the turntable terrors to play it, and why not, the groove is irresistible with Fred Smith and company doing the usual. Randy Wood's production line was simply sensational and it's a real shame he's not alive to still see the enthusiasts 'go to work'.

Top 500 Position: **297**
Original Label: **ABC**
Current Value: **£80**

'In the scheme of things this is pretty awful - unless of course you are an expert dancer'

Mark Welsh, Soul Fan, Kent, UK

August and Deneen
We Go Together

Major labels issued 'what's happening at the time' one shot wonders. The obvious Sonny and Cher influence via the lyrics and concept is evident. The 45 became another statistic, failing to arouse anyone outside of the promo team at ABC. Years later and the scenes thirst for new 'stompers' saw this manic pastiche become a major part of the culture at Wigan Casino.

Today's DJ's of course frown on such a single, but hang on guys, you were not playing to crowds of 2,000 week after week.

In those days the bigger the dance floor, the faster the tempo, and this little romp from '67 was for a time on everyone's wants list.

Top 500 Position: **298**
Original Label: **Loma**
Current Value: **£100 Issue**
£60 Demo

'Mythology again, as one wag insisted it was the vocal to Bok to Bach'

Chris Lever, Soul Fan, Northamptonshire, UK

Ben Aiken
Satisfied

Ben Aiken had a minor hit with an alternate version to Brenda and The Tabulations 'Stay Together Young Lovers' in 1965 on Roulette. Following his departure and new signing to Warner Brothers, he saw himself on their new Loma label (a soulish spin-off).

The vibe and harp tingling 'Satisfied' exploded onto the scene in May 1973, the reason for the accurate account of 'first play' comes as I was at the Top Rank, Hanley the night of discovery.

For many years Aiken was hailed as a genuine blue-eyed soulster - due to a mix up with Ben Atkins of Memphis. Aiken is of course the genuine article - 'Satisfied' now?

Top 500 Position: **299**
Original Label: **Green Dolphin**
Current Value: **£250 'L' Allen**
£300 as 'Larry'

'A thin, but infectious production'

Steve Harris, Soul Fan, Wiltshire, UK

Larry/L. Allen
Can't We Talk It Over

Larry Allen from Pittsburgh hoped to catch on with a thinly disguised attempt at a real Soul record. Critics aside, it really works in the North of England, or rather the South - it was first popular at Yate, possibly due to the tuneful piano riff.

Collectors love it of course, and while I personally remain unconvinced, the single has survived the variety of directions the scene has gone.

A single that sounds unfinished.

Top 500 Position: **300**
Original Label: **Paula**
Current Value: **£10 Issue**
£25 Demo

'Stunning'

Stan Lewis, Label Owner, Louisiana, USA

The Montclairs
Hung Up On Your Love

Phil Perry is without a doubt one of the Soul's most accomplished singer/songwriters. Even back in 1968 recording for Arch records in St. Louis the signs of greatness were emerging.

With two 'biggies' on Paula, the other being 'I Need You More Than Ever' penned by Bobby Patterson, it was 'Hung Up' that did it for the Montclairs getting the dancers 'at it' in the UK several months after its American release.

The bass riff intro and Perry's killer falsetto sell it magnificently!

Top 500 Position:	**301**
Original Label:	**ABC**
Current Value:	**£300 Issue**
	£200 Demo

'Lightweight pop with just enough vocal expertise to see it through'

Allan Pollard, Soul Fan, Stockport, UK

Jay Traynor
Up And Over

Blue-eyed John 'Jay 'Traynor was an early member of Doo-Wop group the Mystics. Furthering his career he formed Jay and the Americans and left in 1964 to pursue a solo career with ABC. The group which spawned the Northern hit 'Livin' Above Your Head' had new lead Jay Black fronting the group.

Wigan DJ, Richard Searling purchased 'Up And Over' in 1976 from Mecca main man Ian Levine, it subsequently went massive at the Casino, becoming a 70's turntable legend.

Today it continues to become even more popular and expensive to buy!

Top 500 Position:	**302**
Original Label:	**Kent**
Current Value:	**£10**

'A superlative cover-up that became folk law for 20 years or so'

Brian Harris, Soul Fan, Lancashire, UK

Little Ann
What Should I Do

Recording for Dave Hamilton's Topper label before signing to Ed Wingate's Ric-Tic, Ann Bridgforth could never imagine the intensity surrounding her unreleased track (at the time) 'What Should I Do'.

The fact is that the 'master of cover-ups' Richard Searling created one of the scene's best kept secrets. According to the former Casino DJ, the acetate was supplied by record dealer John Anderson. Searling promptly covered the title and artist (it revealed Ann Bridgforth on the label) and exposed it to the all-nighter faithful, under the guise of Rose Valentine - 'When He's Not Around', showing the DJ's smartness and the scene's willingness to embrace the mystery surrounding it!

Top 500 Position: **303**
Original Label: **Crimson**
Current Value: **£100 Issue**
£70 Demo

'A storming dancer with full-on commerciality'

Jeff Hollis, Soul Fan, Australia

Lee Andrews and the Hearts

I've Had It

Put together by Tommy Bell and Billy Jackson, the five piece from Philadelphia lead by Arthur Lee Thompson recorded this fabulous fingersnapper in 1968.

Released on Lost Nite's Crimson label as the follow up to the equally remarkable 'Nevertheless' the side was picked up by DJ Pep who popularised it in the Midlands.

In fact it is one of the first regional-regional hits!

The group were a remarkable 50's act and kept on going through the 60's on RCA and Lost Nite before fading away in 1969.

Top 500 Position: **304**
Original Label: **Smash**
Current Value: **£6**

"Ready or not here I come', they sang, and I flipped'

Jerry Ross, Producer, Philadelphia, USA

Jay and the Techniques

Apples, Peaches, Pumpkin Pie

This is a tale of two countries.

Firstly, in the US, where the song became a million seller in August, 1967. Then in the UK, where it became a cult rarity after bombing out when released on Philips.

As the Twisted Wheel revellers loved it, the song crossed over to more mainstream clubs and, while the scene today is fairly dismissive of the song, it was incessantly played for around 5 years.

I met Jay Proctor in the 80's and he was amazed of the discs failure to hit in the UK and the interest in a few other oddities that definitely did not sell in the US.

For the group from Allentown, PA this was their finest hour, and another success for the prolific production team of Ross/Renzetti.

Top 500 Position: **305**
Original Label: **Marton**
Current Value: **£1,000**

'A tempestuous offering from young Tamala'

Harry Crossley, Soul Fan, Greater Manchester, UK

Tamala Lewis
You Won't Say Nothing

George Clinton had been in Detroit for a spell while still keeping a variety of recording contacts in New Jersey. He captured the whole Motown thing with youngster Tamala Lewis, who probably looked and sounded good but obviously did not have the Gordy conveyer belt at her disposal.

Still, we have an incredibly energetic 45 here, and I for one am still yet to own a copy even though my last offer for one in 1981 (£80) was considered a 'little' too low!

Discovered in the US by former record dealer George Greco.

Top 500 Position: **306**
Original Label: **Page One**
Current Value: **£30**

'Up to the peak of popularity and straight back down again!'

John Grover, Soul Fan, Southampton, UK

Muriel Day
Nine Times Out Of Ten

Larry Page was bemused when I told him how popular this 1969 ditty had been. The Troggs and Kinks manager vaguely remembers the flip 'Optimistic Fool' as an Irish Eurovision entry. Imagine the pauses on the phone as I am describing a back drop, cartwheel, maple wooden floors and a £30 single!

Page remained unconvinced and promptly dismissed the conversation as nothing more than a minor fad. He ought to be right, except the song has filtered into the mainstream and while presenting a daily show for EMAP's 'Magic 828' in Leeds, I dread to think of the amount of requests we had from West Yorkshire. Soul NO - Northern Soul YES !

Top 500 Position:	**307**
Original Label:	**Compass**
Current Value:	**£100**

'Rough and ready - and coming 'atcha like a driverless car!'

Keith Hunt,
Soul Fan, Greater Manchester, UK

The Adventurers

Easy Baby

A Va-Va's discovery, championed by resident DJ Richard Searling. Had the need for pop stompers had not been upon us in 1974 then the 45 would have been right up there in our chart.

The group from New York featured Greg Perry who later recorded for Chess, Alfa and Casablanca. They had great 45's on Ran-Dee, Music World and Blue Rock.

Unusually, the intro starts with a sort of bagpipe effect before launching into a really good soulful offering laced with a rolling back beat.

Top 500 Position:	**308**
Original Label:	**Riverside**
Current Value:	**£30 Issue**
	£50 Demo

'One of the best starts to a 60's floorshaker, ever'

Ian Ryles, Soul Fan, Yorkshire, UK

The Gems

I'll Be There

A 'toot-toot' intro rips into a dancer of some repute from Manchester's legendary Pendulum nights. Here the New York based Riverside label attempts to gain some soulful credibility, with the Gems masterpiece and their stable mate, Lou Courtney, to an otherwise Jazz oriented label.

Originally known as the Lovettes, Minnie Ripperton became lead singer before joining Rotary Connection. The girls originally recorded for Chess, and folded shortly after this last ditch, furious attempt at success.

In 1966 this was too fast for its own good, but a few years later - across the Atlantic the kids loved it!

Top 500 Position: **309**
Original Label: **Decca**
Current Value: **£40**

'The Cindy Scott cover-up name at least gave it a purpose...'

Martin Vincent, Soul Fan, Montreal, Canada

Joey Heatherton
When You Called Me Baby

It is as if this 45 has followed me around permanently for over 20 years! Originally played by Richard Searling on a Belgian Brunswick copy he had covered as Cindy Scott.

I found my own copy shortly after in New Jersey, from a flea market dealer who revealed he knew the writer John Madara (Formations, Len Barry etc). Tracking him down, I discovered that Johanna from New York had a brother who he believed was a Disc Jockey.

Four years later (anorak that I am) I visit WCBS in NYC, and, after a brief introduction to the programming department, I visit the studio to find afternoon drive jock Dick Heatherton in full throttle. Expecting me to 'have the hood totally up' Dick and I chatted, the conversation predictably turned to Northern Soul whereby the link was established. Dickyboy, as he was affectionately known, tried to call his sister Joey, to no avail. She now realises at least someone likes her 1966 effort. She did in fact have a minor chart flurry in the early 70's with a song called 'Gone'. OK, can I take down the hood now?

Top 500 Position: **310**
Original Label: **Decca**
Current Value: **£20 Issue**
£40 Demo

'The revealing intro of... 'where is my baby', sets the scene for a truly frantic jaunt'

Philip Smith, Soul Fan, Leicestershire, UK

Earl Grant
Hide Nor Hair

The cool keyboard player and actor saw this song as his final attempt at major success. He did have a No. 7 hit in 1958, but further chart action was to elude him, and he died in a car accident in 1970.

The disc is pure Soul beat and totally in keeping with what was happening in 1966, it tells quite a story and in that respect can be likened to 'The Snake'.

A Blackpool Mecca spin in '73, the 45 proved real popular until the pop dross of twelve months later froze it out.

Top 500 Position: **311**
Original Label: **Ric-Tic**
Current Value: **£5**

'One of the first big Ric-Tics'

Brian Rae, DJ, North Wales, UK

Al Kent
You Got To Pay The Price

Born Al Hamilton, Al Kent, along with Edwin Starr, put the Ric-Tic label right on the map, with many eager collectors searching for every number.

The UK sought fit to release the side on Track in 1967.

A nifty guitar lead groove that Duane Eddy would be proud of, Kent recorded a few worthwhile tracks with Ed Wingate and even managed a tour with the Ric-Tic revue in the early 80's.

Massive at the Wheel, the tune even realised a vocal version too by Gloria Taylor on King Soul and Silver Fox.

Top 500 Position: **312**
Original Label: **ABC Paramount**
Current Value: **£150 Issue £100 Demo**

'A lounge classic long before the new cult revival'

Gavin Lacey, Soul Fan, London, UK

Eddie Bishop
Call Me

During the 70's the all nighters certainly tested all formats of dance. From the new releases more in keeping with London, to off-the-wall pop stompers, Soul temporarily went on the back burner... Cue oddities such as saxophonist Eddie Bishop's 'Call Me'. The Tony Hatch thingy covered for about the thirtieth time, but the dance floor had it sewn to the holdall and Bishop did at least score somewhere.

Perennially popular amongst the Scooter scene, quite what this Hatch composition that was even recorded by Lulu has to do with Northern Soul, I am still trying to work out!

Top 500 Position: **313**
Original Label: **Brunswick**
Current Value: **£10 Issue**
£15 Demo

'A hazy, fuzzy dancer that seemed to work hand-in-hand with the pills'

Bob Tinsley, Soul Fan, West Midlands, UK

Johnny Jones and the King Casuals

Purple Haze

Hendrix rock masterpiece given a full Soul workout by Atlanta's Johnny Jones.

The year 1972, and with the Torch firmly installed as the top venue, a mixed bag of weird 45's were still knocking around (Scratchy, Put It Where You Want It etc), Purple Haze was no exception!

It really does work though, with the group chanting the lyrics almost demanding audience participation. Remember back in those days the Casino 'clobber' had not yet fully surfaced and it was not uncommon to be standing outside the Hose Street venue with an afghan coat or two!

Top 500 Position: **314**
Original Label: **Tower**
Current Value: **£25**

'The enormity of the first few bars will live forever'

Tony Michaelaides, Soul Fan, London, UK

World Column

So Is The Sun

Not too many 45's are massive on the scene at first play... this Soul single with a distinct Sly Stone flavour was for Ian Levine.

The hook and lyrics are fairly meaningless, it's the 'pap pap pap pap pap pap pa pa' that whips the dancers to a frenzy. The original 'b' side is a Deep Soul classic incidentally, but the mayhem created by 'sun' makes it one of the scenes most exciting discoveries ever.

Northern fans of a younger generation will no doubt remember UK Mod revival band the Jam's shameless rip-off, (or is that 'tribute' or 'homage'?) 'Trans Global Express'.

Top 500 Position:	**315**
Original Label:	**Tay-Ster**
Current Value:	**£500**

'What is Northern Soul?... Look no further!'

Sharon Levesly, Soul Fan, London, UK

Lillie Bryant
Meet Me Halfway

Coming straight out of The Isley's - 'This Old Heart Of Mine', Bryant debuts for Jack Taylor's Tay-Ster label with a masterpiece.

Originally with New York pop duo Billie and Lillie who had two top twenty hits in the US during the late 50's, she tried the solo route with a really good commercially sounding Soul side. Instigated by DJ Barry Tasker at Manchester's short lived Pendulum venue, it failed to attain greater popularity due to the lack of originals in circulation, the one illustrated is in fact the original copy spun by Barry all those years ago!

Top 500 Position:	**316**
Original Label:	**Wind-Hit**
Current Value:	**£1,000**

'The true original is SO hard to find!'

Mark Levesly, Soul Fan, London, UK

Servicemen
Need A Helping Hand

The value may look odd considering many DJ's had it at their disposal in the mid 70's! The fact is the original on Wind Hit featuring the excellent flip 'Are You Angry' is very rare.

Danceability-wise this is the business and to be honest I can't understand why the group never made it after supplying us with 3 excellent 45's - the further 2 are on Chartmaker and Patheway.

DJ Colin Curtis got this one away in 1974. An irresistible vibe intro leaps into a frenzied groove that no self respecting dancefloor should be without!

The Embers
Watch Out Girl

Top 500 Position: **317**
Original Label: **MGM**
Current Value: **£150 Issue**
£75 Demo

'The Soul of the Carolinas'

John Swain (deceased), Hillsborough, North Carolina, USA

In 1978 I visited Raleigh, North Carolina to meet up with record dealer John Swain (deceased) who appeared to be the main contact for Soul outside of the Wax Museum in Charlotte. I certainly knew I was in the right town when the following morning of my arrival, I was subjected (while eating eggs benedict) to a background tape of 'Watch Out Girl', 'I've Been Hurt', 'Be Young, Be Foolish, Be Happy'. I noticed a distinct wiggle from the waitress (who obviously knew the tunes) and asked if she liked the music. As straight faced as you like she hollered 'ah love to shag'. Napkins were quickly ordered as the coffee spill was burning a hole in my Soul!

The Carolinas obviously have a scene that is parallel with our own and thoroughly enjoyable, with DJ's discovering dance sides that sit well within their parameters. The Embers, who are white, are legendary down there and Jackie Gore's outfit are not without a spin or two here with rarities on Bell, Atlantic and EEE. The stock copy incidentally appears to be incredibly rare although it sold fairly well in the South Eastern part of the US. Maybe, that's where they all are!

Dean Courtney
Love, You Just Can't Walk Away

Top 500 Position: **318**
Original Label: **MGM**
Current Value: **£150**

'A great double header from a massive artist on our scene'

Bernie O'Brien, Soul Fan, Lancashire, UK

Courtney could be forgiven for thinking that he was making singles for the north of England during his 60's career.

The RCA and MGM efforts are terrific and outside of his other anthem 'I'll Always Need You', this late 70's spin has been nearly as popular in some quarters. A very well produced disc it would appear not to have actually been issued for some strange reason.

On a recent visit to the UK combining a licensing deal for some of his unissued RCA material with a PA at the 1999 Northern Soul Convention in Blackburn he was a great hit with the Soul crew.

Top 500 Position: **319**
Original Label: **Brunswick**
Current Value: **£30 Issue**
£50 Demo

'A groovy irresistible dancer that just about EVERYBODY loves'

Weldon Arthur McDougall III, Harthon Records

The Cooperettes
Shing-A-Ling

Allnighter classic from 1972, and very difficult to quantify against other more unusual but popular discoveries of recent times. Everything is here, the Harthon groove, great lead, commercial song and lotsa gloss!

The unreleased demo by Irma titled 'You Need Love' received a few plays in the 80's and remains the collectors choice, but the old timer is the one that wins hands down.

Snare drums, strings and that hook, turn it into something special.

Top 500 Position: **320**
Original Label: **Constellation**
Current Value: **£15 Issue**
£30 Demo

'I'm proud to have the contributed to Northern Soul...'

Gene Chandler, Artist, USA

Gene Chandler
I Can Take Care Of Myself

Two different eras of popularity for this monumental mid tempo side from the ever popular Eugene Dixon. Firstly towards the tail end of the Wheel returning as a monster revival spin at the Casino.

A terrific double sider with the classier 'Care' just ahead of 'I Can't Save It', it saw a British label release on Action in 1969 two years after its original US outing on Constellation in '67.

Today it is massive once again following a much needed revival by DJ Richard Searling.

Top 500 Position: **321**
Original Label: **Brunswick**
Current Value: **£10 Issue**
£15 Demo

'Haunting, slick vocals turn an average lyric into something special'

John Moore, Soul Fan, Leeds, UK

Fred Hughes
Baby Boy

Not to be confused with Freddie Hughes who recorded for Wee in California the Chicago based singer recorded a few sides for Brunswick during the 60's. Born in Arkansas, he quickly established himself as a quality Soul singer signing to Vee-Jay in 1965, and scoring a major R&B hit with 'OO Wee Baby I Love You'.

The 1968 recording 'Baby Boy' took off at the Torch all-nighter and has been a classic revival tune ever since.

Top 500 Position: **322**
Original Label: **Sure-Shot**
Current Value: **£50**

'The bass intro is enough for dancers to start the movements'

Steve Roberts,
Soul Fan, Gwent, Wales, UK

The Malibus
Gee Baby (I Love You)

Lead by Monroe Powell. From the Duke/Peacock stable comes this 1967 record from Houston. A dark sort of production with the group groovin' along to an irresistible rhythm track, leaving the hook to sink into your subconscious. DJ Ian Levine discovered and played the first copy in late '73.

The band went on to record three other singles for the label, as well as one for Duke.

Top 500 Position: **323**
Original Label: **Nite Life**
Current Value: **£300**

'You must experience this at an all nighter to fully enjoy it'

Jeff Holland, Soul Fan, Australia

The Jades

I'm Where It's At

Attempting to establish the band's origins has drawn a blank. Groups with the same name have seen releases on MGM, Cherry Red (definitely not them), Mode, Tower, Poncello, Imperial and Verve!

Anyway, whoever the Jades really are they should 'take a bow' as this is their entrance to Northerndom. A frantic pop dancer, with a startling intro popularised by Richard Searling and, in its day, his biggest spin as a one-off at the Casino. In a fit of generosity he loaned it out to be copied for a fanzine, the publisher of which proceeded to leave it on top of the hot range in a Fish and Chip on the way home with dire consequences - Ooops!

Top 500 Position: **324**
Original Label: **Breakthrough**
Current Value: **£4,000**

'Rare, rarer... and nearly the rarest'

Mark Villiers, Soul Fan, Suffolk, UK

The Inspirations

No One Else Can Take Your Place

A fabulous group 45 that everyone wants - on both sides of the Atlantic.

Discovered in 1974 by dealer Bob Cattaneo in San Francisco, the record (a one sided demo) started at the customary £100 and turned in one mighty investment for some.

Producer and label owner Joey Jefferson did remix the record in the late 70's and added the instrumental on the flip, but this is a true collector's dream - that has only ever turned up on 3 or 4 occasions.

The group are not to be confused with other bands of the same name, although it is likely they had involvement with other acts on main label Mutt and Jeff.

Top 500 Position: **325**
Original Label: **Verve**
Current Value: **£30 Issue**
£40 Demo

'The gospel feel makes it a worthy addition to the scene'

Tony Lee, Soul Fan, Yorkshire, UK

Clara Ward
The Right Direction

Absolutely fantastic, taken from the acclaimed 'Hang your tears out to dry' album. Jackson had one the best Gospel choirs in the land 40 years ago, and in 1966, decided to be more contemporary and signed to Verve to make a Soul album. Following minor success on the label with a cover of Lennon and McCartney's 'Help' (a good northern 45 too) Verve had a stab with 'Direction' and suddenly found themselves the purveyors of new gospel, releasing the Robert Banks classic 'A Mighty Good Way' in the same vein.

Direction was the operative word for we niter goers in 1972 as the real Soul of 'Gospel Hummingbird' Ward rippled through the Torch perfectly after a dose of Sam and Kitty! A rare version by Herman Griffin and Gerry Jackson exists on the Stone Blue label.

Top 500 Position: **326**
Original Label: **CBS**
Current Value: **£250**

'Northern Soul from the Lake District!'

Gary White,
Soul Fan, Barrow-in-Furness, Cumbria

Chapter Five
You Can't Mean It

The Barrow-in-Furness (yes that Barrow), UK-based R&B band, signed with Mervyn Conn who in turn produced two singles for them on CBS.

One is a cover of Maxine Brown's 'One In A Million', preceded by this original composition by group leader Dave Girty. Discovered in Manchester at Granada's great Music Library by legendary 'Junk Shopper' Arthur.

It has had a reasonable amount of play dating back to 1978 and was especially popular amongst the Scooter Boys of the eighties - rising to ever greater heights at every Soul night over the next decade.

Top 500 Position: **327**
Original Label: **Tuff/Karisma**
Current Value: **£30 Tuff**
£300 Karisma

'Could this be the first unofficial rap?'

Tom Hooper, Soul Fan, Northamptonshire, UK

E Rodney Jones
R'n'B Time (Part 1)

As popular as the official sung version by Bobby Treetop ('Wait 'Til I Get To Know Ya'), former 60's DJ on WVON in Chicago was invited to 'cut a record', the idea being that he would play it on his show. Well, in certain quarters it worked with Jones backing up the disc all over the 'Windy City'. Latterly his other Tuff release, the considerably rarer 'Peace Of Mind' has found its own popularity.

It was common practice for DJ's to get in on the action with Tom Clay and Frankie Crocker recording potentially good sellers. Years later we got Chris Hill's 'Renta Santa'!

Top 500 Position: **328**
Original Label: **Date**
Current Value: **£40 Issue**
£50 Demo

'Northern Soul never sounded so good'

Steve Ripley, Sony, London, UK

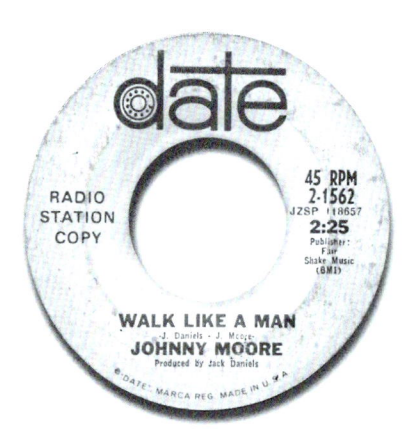

Johnny Moore
Walk Like A Man

One of the very best records from the Torch era. DJ Tony Jebb played the song with real conviction almost weekly around the same time. A ferocious backbeat with Moore's yelling intro 'I may be down - I may be out' is a true delight.

Not to be confused with the Drifters' front man, Moore recorded for Blue Rock, Bright Star, Larry-O, Jadan and Brunswick.

You can now buy the song on the classic Sony CD 'Soul Time' Vol. 1, I urge everyone to own the it!

Top 500 Position: **329**
Original Label: **Date**
Current Value: **£50**

'Vibes and more vibes - the key ingredient of an all nighter classic'

Gill Warner, Soul Fan, Staffordshire, UK

The Sweet Things
I'm In A World Of Trouble

A spate of fabulous recordings on the Columbia spin-off Date in the 60's, meant the scene could get it's teeth into the excitement they created. A girl group sound from '66 with a typical New York production and oh-so-heavenly vocals.

Lead by Francine Barker who later became Peaches (and Herb) thus embarking on a successful career. The girls recorded two singles for Date with this being the undoubted winner. Tailor made for 60's dancing, the sax break, vibes and altogether polished production separate the side from other less obvious 45's.

A true Golden Torch anthem with DJ's Tony Jebb and Keith Minshull leading the way.

Top 500 Position: **330**
Original Label: **MGM**
Current Value: **£150 Demo**
         £250 Issue

'Re-discovered in the 80's, which captured the texture of it perfectly'

Brian Wilks, Soul Fan, Manchester, UK

Andrea Henry
I Need You Like A Baby

Impossible to play this during the 70's due to the down tempo though the subtlety made it a great listen in any era. Detroit was the recording base for the Herman Griffin production at United Sound in March, 1966.

A cover by Janice on Roulette failed to stir any competition and Henry is just Tammi Terrellish enough to win the interest of a crowd who no longer expected (or indeed wanted) 100 mph stompers by the 1990's. If any record epitomises Northern Soul's new wave then this is it.

Top 500 Position:	**331**
Original Label:	**Brunswick**
Current Value:	**£6 Issue**
	£15 Demo

'The lead vocal is the man's finest hour'

Peter Rose, Soul Fan, Hong Kong

The Artistics
I'm Gonna Miss You

Fronted by Marvin Smith, this in all probability is the classiest smoocher to arrive at the Twisted Wheel. A reasonable sized hit in the US, it failed on all fronts here, until Whitworth Street became the focal point for such brilliant music. Smith shows off his vocal range with a lovely falsetto that Eddie Kendricks would have been proud of.

The flip, 'Hope We Have', has also become a perennial oldies favourite in its own right.

The group also recorded for Okeh.

Top 500 Position:	**332**
Original Label:	**Despenza**
Current Value:	**£200/**
	£600 Wand

'60's Chicago that never goes out of fashion'

Brian Allen,
Soul Fan, Nottinghamshire, UK

The Ivorys
Please Stay

Lead by Anita Anderson and an excellent example of a record the 'never-quite-made-it' years ago soaring in demand and therefore price as the UK found out just how rare it really was.

Talking of value, the single was picked up for national release by Wand in 1966, but try finding that release!

A long time in the making, today 'Please Stay' is far bigger than when first it broke in the 70's at the Cleethorpes Allnighter.

A superb single from Chicago.

Top 500 Position: **333**
Original Label: **Caravelle**
Current Value: **£150**

'Swamped by better records during the golden era, it has now matured into a fine adult - albeit 25 years later'

Stefan Kryzwicki, Soul Fan, USA

The Chaumonts
I Need Your Love

Also on Bay Sound. A sort of love-hate relationship exists with this 1967 obscurity from Baltimore, MD.

The label had the great Nicky C record too, but the Chaumonts, probably due to the irritating girl chorus 'ooing and wowing', had the most commercial sounding cut of the label's releases amongst their 8 outings.

The Chaumounts is generally considered have been most popular on the East Coast of England and two of their Bay Sound releases have also had plays on the scene.

Top 500 Position: **334**
Original Label: **Veep**
Current Value: **£10 Issue**
　　　　　　　　£25 Demo

'This is a Randazzo-Pike composition, enough said!'

Simon Wakely, Soul Fan, Australia

Little Anthony and the Imperials
Gonna Fix You Good

Although Mr. Gourdine from Brooklyn, New York is undoubtedly famous here for 'Better Use Your Head', this '66 outing was the first introduction to the group for the Northern scene.

The US No. 4 in '58, 'Tears On My Pillow' did not sell here hence the unknown quantity of the act. . Our first main all-night venue unearthed the gem from it's UK base of United Artists, and the disc became an absolute monster even getting bootlegged as early as 1970!

Top 500 Position: **335**
Original Label: **Share**
Current Value: **£8 Issue**
£15 Demo

'Writer Dave Godin's cementation with the North'

Tony Hallsworth, Soul Fan, Derby, UK

The Ad-Libs
Nothing Worse Than Being Alone

As a youngster reading Blues and Soul magazine, the tales of Northern Soul as portrayed by writer Dave Godin convinced me to investigate further and leave the mining town that had been my world for 14 years.

Godin was fully aware of the demand for obscure uptempo North American 45's, so, upon his inaugural visit to Whitworth Street in early 1970, he offered DJ Les Cokell 'first play' on a 1968 recording for Van McCoy's Share label by '65 hitmakers the Ad-Libs. Lead singer Mary Ann Thomas had lead the act successfully with the initial recordings on Blue Cat, with one release on Karen and the mighty 'New York In The Dark' on A.G.P. before a tie up with Van the man!

Oozing with class the production seems spot on and lyrically par excellence, surprisingly though as good as it is it did not become the monster that DG thought it should have been.

Top 500 Position: **336**
Original Label: **Soul**
Current Value: **£50**

'Superb Motown from the early days of Northern'

Richard Layton, Soul Fan, Worcester, UK

Frances Nero
Keep On Loving Me

Frances was a teenage singer who had one shot at success with Motown subsidiary, Soul, it failed despite - gaining radio airtime, especially in the Philadelphia area.

'Keep On Loving Me' is yet another gem of classy production from Berry Jnr's recording empire which is so 'happening' that it just mystifies me why it didn't hit!

This lady's story continues though courtesy of our own Ian Levine who tracked the lady down in Detroit and recorded 'Footsteps Following Me' which became a big hit some 25 years later, ironically as it happens because Ian who was one of the people responsible for the Northern popularity of her first release!

The Del-Larks
Job Opening

Top 500 Position: **337**
Original Label: **Queen City**
Current Value: **£1,500 Issue**
£2,000 Demo

'My worst seller - yet so popular'...

Sammy Campbell,
Lead Singer, Newark, New Jersey, USA

Discovered by DJ Ian Levine who not only turned his discovery into a monster floor filler but also went on to record the lead singer, Sammy Campbell, under his stage name of Tyrone Ashley on several disco cuts in the 70's.

Remaining very rare, yours truly found a black and silver demo in a store in Newark, New Jersey, in 1977... I sold it for £100 - I'll never make a stockbroker!

This is a superb East Coast group 45 that sounds unlike any other and that just about EVERYBODY wants!

Jerry Cook
I Hurt On The Other Side

Top 500 Position: **338**
Original Label: **Capitol**
Current Value: **£50**

'After hearing this I knew the meaning of 'keep the faith'

R, Soul Fan, Doncaster, UK

One of those Soul obscurities that makes you wonder how it failed to hit!

Written by Sidney Barnes who performed it on the Blue Cat label, the unknown but fantastic Jerry Cook (I feel this must be a pseudonym) became one of the most crucial discoveries after the Torch closed and Wigan opened. The scene, in a sort of limbo at the time, needed various new finds and this certainly fitted the bill.

A much better production than Barnes' version with a gloss and vivacity missing from the original take.

Top 500 Position: **339**
Original Label: **Wand**
Current Value: **£10 Issue**
£20 Demo

'Vibrant and compelling'

Ken Holmes, Soul Fan, Leeds, UK

Chuck Jackson

These Chains Of Love (Are Breaking Me Down)

'Chains' was originally a Country recording by BJ Thomas (remember 'I Don't Have A Mind Of My Own'?) on Hickory, but our man wins through in the end. Released here on Pye International it became one of the first big all-nighter sounds via the Twisted Wheel.

Much has been written and said about Jackson, suffice to say this is undoubtedly his best 60's Northern dancer.

Top 500 Position: **340**
Original Label: **Quinvy**
Current Value: **£700**

'One of the most talked about and least successful floor fillers'

Rob Whitton, Soul Fan, Hertfordshire, UK

Don Varner

Tear Stained Face

When a record is discovered and pre-promoted as was this when Ian Levine played it as early as 1974, the dance floor expectancy was high to say the least. In real terms the song was a failure. During the 80's and 90's with more record collector involvement, the 45 from Alabama realised its true potential.

Varner hailing from the state, was produced by Quin Ivy, a local DJ and label owner. He recorded for Diamond, Downbeat, House Of Orange, Quinvy and sister label South Camp.

Top 500 Position: **341**
Original Label: **Sound Stage 7**
Current Value: **£40 Issue**
£30 Demo

'A vibrant piece of Soul group machinery'

Carol Frederick,
Soul Fan, Stoke-on-Trent, UK

The Valentines

Breakaway

Another 45 totally out of focus, with dealers finding it a tough cookie to sell. Try explaining that to the traders of rare singles 25 years ago!

A terrific sound from Nashville, that is simply a dancer of some repute. The group are not the ones who recorded for Rama in the 50's, but a quartet who cut two singles for Sound Stage 7 in 1969.

Once again, the fun element of the side takes centre stage as 'Breakaway' was an absolute giant 1972-74 and it is tricky to find original copies that do not jump!

Maybe a little too 'boppy' for today's market, but an important jigsaw piece in the make up of Northern Soul.

Top 500 Position: **342**
Original Label: **Sonday**
Current Value: **£20 Issue**
£30 Demo

'The energy level of this fresh sounding Northern side is second to none'

Bev Chalmers, Soul Fan, Coventry, UK

Leslie Uggams

Love Is A Good Foundation

The first time the UK had encountered Ms. Uggams was via DJ Ian Levine who yet again sniffed out a winner. Released on Dionne Warwick's label Sonday, the actress/singer from New York performed well on a dynamic song and arrangement. Later, the scene heard from the lady again with the 1966 recording for Atlantic - 'Don't You Even Care'. I foolishly asked Atlantic to re-press it for the UK market (which they did) only to discover it really wasn't that popular! Best return to the Highland Room circa '73 and the exhilaration of 'Love Is A Good Foundation'!

Top 500 Position: **343**
Original Label: **Verve**
Current Value: **£10 Issue**
£15 Demo

'Wild and crazy instrumental'

Dave Owen, Soul Fan, Doncaster, UK

The Triumphs
Walkin' The Duck

The Duck of course was a Soul dance craze among African Americans in '65 and many producers jumped on the bandwagon with their own interpretation of it. Chips Moman a key figure on the Memphis music scene, took local combo The Triumphs to the task and record an instrumental variation of Jackie Lee's hit.

Scorching brass and neat lead guitar are perfect for dancing, helped on enormously by a reasonable supply of copies from the famous Bradford market in '72. The Golden Torch was the outlet for this thoroughly enjoyable romp.

Top 500 Position: **344**
Original Label: **Cadet**
Current Value: **£150**

'Another cut from the incredible Chess stables'

Bob Richards, Soul Fan, North Wales, UK

George Kirby
What Can I Do

A stylish sound that caught on in the 80's, this wonderful Chicago string laden cooler is perfect for the variety the scene now demands.

Kirby is obviously another gem that has not yet heard of our movement as he would I'm sure be amazed at the fond affection we have for this superlative side.

Sadly a further release for the Chess subsidiary Argo records also failed to make any impact in the American charts.

Top 500 Position: **345**
Original Label: **NYCS**
Current Value: **£30**

'Refreshing to hear even today'

Colin Dilnot, Soul Fan, Merseyside, UK

Flame 'N' King

Ho Happy Day

An unusual sort of Gospel/Soul/Disco 45 from New York, '77. DJ Richard Searling played the single approximately two years after release, but even then it was impossible to get.

Developing out of the Fatback Band, the group were simply seeking to cash in on the delicate balance between Soul and disco of the time. As early as '68 the outfit were distributing their own label from their Queens, New York base (Gerry and Paul, The Puzzles), and this feel gooder seemed a natural throwback. The lead singer incidentally is Oscar Richardson.

Top 500 Position: **346**
Original Label: **Dejac**
Current Value: **£75**

'One of only a small group of latin 45's on the scene'

Stan Forbes, Collector, Dublin, Eire

Tommy Navarro

I Cried My Life Away

El Watusi by Ray Baretto ventured into Club Soul back in the mid-60's, Tommy Navarro continued that brief tradition.

The Top Of The World monster from the early 80's along with Bobby Valentin's Fania stormer 'Use It Before You Lose It' helped pave the way for more originality and diversity in the scene.

Unlike more overtly latin sounds of the period, Tommy Navarro's classic remains a favourite, having today spread from its more southerly following to be a nationwide floorfiller.

Top 500 Position: **347**
Original Label: **Lloyd**
Current Value: **£40**

'One of the first real Northern sounds'

Mick Roberts, Soul Fan, Nottingham, UK

Paul Kelly
Chills And Fever

Miami based Kelly recorded the song in 1965 for a local Florida label before gaining a national release on Dial, which was distributed by Atlantic.

A reasonable success with sales over 10, 000, the single was released here on Black Atlantic and an immediate hit at the Twisted Wheel club. Kelly, became a revered vocalist in the States with product for Phillips, Happy Tiger and Warner Brothers amongst others.

More recent times have seen the prior release to 'Fever' break on the scene. 'The Upset' is a very rare item from a very well known artist - proving that there are still surprises in store for our scene!

Top 500 Position: **348**
Original Label: **Golden World**
Current Value: **£400 Issue**
£80 Demo

'Just impossible to get for many years'

Jan Smith, Soul Fan, London, UK

Tamiko Jones
I'm Spellbound

Born Barbara Tamiko Ferguson. First recording contract with Chess. Her first Detroit 45 was for Ed Wingate's Golden World in '66, later recording for Bell subsidiary December before a career with UK based Contempo finding a husband in the shape of label boss and founder member of Blues and Soul John Abbey. I found a yellow stock issue of the single in '78 and to this day can't remember why I would sell such a fantastic and super rare release.

Mostly, the singles are white demo copies, largely from a Soul Bowl haul some 20 years ago. The discovery was unearthed outside of Wigan/Blackpool by Midlands DJ Pep and became one of his 'exclusives', adding to the mystery and collectability at the time.

Written by Rosemary McCoy especially for Jones, it reflected what McCoy saw as her distinctly 'Witchy' sex appeal!

Top 500 Position: **349**
Original Label: **Thelma**
Current Value: **£35 Issue**
£100 Demo

'A Detroit Soul brother that helped expose the great Thelma label to the UK

Richard Allinson, Collector, Detroit, USA

Emanuel Laskey

I'm A Peace Loving Man

Recording for NPC, Wild Deuce and Thelma, Lasky was the top drawer singer who sadly did not breakout of the local scene, turning to Gospel instead. The 45 we are focussing on is the first play of any Thelma release, gaining minor plays at the Golden Torch.

The act himself was around the Don Davis set up as far back as '63 with a song called 'Welfare Cheese', and whilst a reasonable hit ensued, it is his later material on Thelma which saw his reputation grow in the UK.

Top 500 Position: **350**
Original Label: **Atlantic**
Current Value: **£20 Issue**
£30 Demo

'I couldn't believe it! seeing Barbara Lewis performing at a flea market in Orlando!'

Ray at Rock 'n' Roll Heaven, Orlando, USA

Barbara Lewis

I Remember The Feeling

A great cover exists too by Deon Jackson. This is one of Lewis' sleepers airing periodically over 25 years, but increasing of late.

Barbara was born in South Lyon, Michigan and discovered by WHRB DJ and later Karen (named after his daughter) records boss Ollie McLaughlin.

Written by Rose McCoy and recorded at Atlantic studios in June '66 the track is about as professional as you can get. Her earlier works including 'Someday We're Gonna Love Again' from '64 often included backing vocals from the mighty Dells.

Top 500 Position:	**351**
Original Label:	**Jamie**
Current Value:	**£15 Issue**
	£30 demo

'Cool as you like for the newcomer'

Tony Leggett, Soul Fan, North Wales, UK

Marke (Chris) Jackson
I'll Never Forget You

Released in the US as Marke and here as Chris. The single recorded by Van McCoy in 1968 was the first in a series of demos recorded by Van and Billy Jackson. What happened to the Billy Jackson sessions we are not exactly sure, except according to (Billy) Jackson the singer 'skipped town' during a dispute. McCoy recorded a demo too titled 'Since there's no doubt' which did surface on acetate but never came out despite being scheduled to be released on the UK '444' label.

The single is as classy as you would expect from Van, and forgotten by a few, when reminded of it's existence, big smiles fill the room.

Top 500 Position:	**352**
Original Label:	**Theoda**
Current Value:	**£150**

'My northern Soul roots started with this fantastic Detroit dancer'

Cath Lubinski, Soul Fan, London

Ann Perry
That's The Way He Is

First spun by DJ Pep, at Wolverhampton's Catacombs, the super quick tempo, fresh sounding female vocal (we know of no other record by her) and a glorious hook line make for an incredible dancer.

The record was released twice, once locally in Detroit and again in Los Angeles (identifiable by the Circa Distribution rosette on the light green, rather than light blue label).

Originally popular as an instrumental - famed for the way its beat ricocheted off the back wall at Wigan - today the vocal is a monstrous all nighter favourite!

Top 500 Position: **353**
Original Label: **Musicor**
Current Value: **£6**

'I sincerely hope you have as much fun dancin' to it as I did creating it'

Richard 'Popcorn' Wylie, Producer, Detroit, USA

The Platters

Washed Ashore
(On A Lonely Island In The Sea)

When Sonny Turner replaced Tony Williams in the group everybody said 'what are they going to do now?', the answer was to start making top quality Soul music!

The traditional balladeers donned dancing shoes as they teamed up with Wylie and Hestor to make a new album in early 1967. Recording in New York and at the Terra Shirma studios in Detroit, Turner pulled in some of his best performances with the above, 'I Love You 1,000 Times' and 'With This Ring', as well as the cover of John Hampton's Northern monster 'Not My Girl' (unreleased at the time).

'Washed Ashore' has become the dancer even outsmarting the energetic 'Sweet Sweet Lovin', itself a major Northern item at the Wheel. While remembered as one of the first major Black groups, their 60's period for Soul lovers was by far the best.

Top 500 Position: **354**
Original Label: **Sidra**
Current Value: **£100 Red**
£60 Blue

'Just made for the Northern Soul dancers'

John Kirsten, Soul Fan, London, UK

'Instrumental' (Ronnie and Robyn)

Sidra's Theme

The more popular instrumental to a vocal by Ronnie and Robyn was discovered in 1974 and its popularity surged as both major venues at the time (Wigan Casino and Blackpool Mecca) were on it like a shot.

The vocal as you would expect is pop, but the instrumental is pure Detroit and pretty good too. The unusual harp intro builds to a great orchestral performance (the invoice for musician participation must have been staggering) and the beat relentlessly kicks throughout. To anyone hearing it from outside the UK, you might think you were listening to 'two way family favourites on short wave'. To the North it's another chapter in this most remarkable scene.

Incidentally Robyn went on to record for Motown subsidiary, VIP, as part of 'Rick, Robyn and Him'.

Top 500 Position: **355**
Original Label: **Hickory**
Current Value: **£8 Issue**
£15 Demo

'Still a terrifically exciting track'

Chris Johnson, Soul Fan, Hong Kong

The Newbeats

Run Baby Run

From the first wave of rare 45's to be played this major Stateside hit from 1966 shook the Twisted Wheel in the late 60's and everyone wanted it - so much so it charted in '71 and crossed over to every teen disco. The group assembled in Nashville featured the high falsetto of Texas born Larry Henley. the act also scored on the scene with 'Crying My Heart Out' .

Very forgotten and far too commercial to play in these times the track was on everyone's lips for around 2 years and was popularised by mobile discos everywhere.

Top 500 Position: **356**
Original Label: **Goldspot /GAR**
Current Value: **£200 Goldspot**
£100 GAR Issue
£50 GAR Demo

'A tricky intro but with enough panache to be a true original'

Kev Sowerby, Soul Fan, Cumbria, UK

Kenny Smith

Lord What's Happening To Your People

Originally in doo-wop group Otis Smith and the Charms. The disc had two almost simultaneous releases for the Cincinatti, Ohio labels.

The first on Goldspot has a church organ intro, the latter a more contemporary version in keeping with the time, 1972. Smith had recorded for RCA in the late 60's without any success and this great gospel groover was to become an anthem at Blackpool Mecca largely due to plays by resident DJ Colin Curtis.

The copies on Goldspot and the blue stock issue on GAR are incredibly rare, so check those collections immediately.

Top 500 Position: 357
Original Label: Soft/Coral
Current Value: £50 Soft
£10 Coral

'This side displays all the hallmarks of a monster Northern sound'

Tom Wilkinson, Soul Fan, Scotland, UK

The Sons Of Moses
Soul Symphony

Major Bill Smith of the US Air force, upon retirement, eagerly wanted to get into the business and sources report over 3,000 recordings were produced by the man in less than 15 years. With hits from Bruce Chanel and Paul and Paula under his belt he ventured into Soul music mainly inspired by Randy Wood of Mirwood whom he had met when Wood was owner of Dot records. During the period '65-69, Smith had Pic and Bill, Robert Thomas, Sunny and Phyllis (aka The Nomads) and others, recording alternate versions in many cases. In fact during '74 a collector from the Burnley area was almost being sent weekly new versions of the song by Ede Robin (a vocal) plus the Hammond Bros and Maggie(an instrumental).

Smith, ever the entrepreneur latched on to the Northern market custom pressing his 'rarities' to meet demand. Initially released on his own 'Soft' label, and later leased to Coral, 'Symphony' is simply a tuneful play on the works of Ramsey Lewis and, whilst largely forgotten, the 45 is still a floor filler when played.

Top 500 Position: 358
Original Label: Sound Stage 7
Current Value: £20 Issue
£30 Demo

'Capturing the very essence of the 60's perfectly'

Tom Brewer, Soul Fan, Leicester, UK

Little Hank
Mister Bang Bang Man

First plays in the UK were as far back as '68 and, is credited as being one of the first rare 45's to be reissued. The UK release on London is incredibly rare and although acknowledged by the Record Collector price guide at £35, sources reveal it is more likely to be £100 as the single was withdrawn after only a week!

The US copy didn't fair much better, but the underground loved it. Coming off like a cross between 'Shotgun' and 'Shotgun Wedding' the song is heavy with metaphors of a different kind, Hank sounds pretty good with his one of only two releases on the label.

Saxes blaring all over the place, it programmes perfectly with the Willie Mitchell's and Robert Parker's. Very southern in it's feel, very Northern as an end result!

Top 500 Position: **359**
Original Label: **Columbia**
Current Value: **£300 YOP**
£200 JF Demo
£300 JF Issue

'The title may well have put dealers off even playing it'

Chris Little, Soul Fan, Lancashire, UK

Youth Opportunity Programme / Jimmy Fraser

Of Hopes And Dreams And Tombstones

A promo only from Columbia originally credited to the 'Youth Opportunity Programme', featuring sleeve notes by Senator Hubert Humphrey, it was subsequently issued as Jimmy Fraser.

Not surprisingly when you listen to the lyrics the song in fact has a strong social message, and indeed it was part of the same US government sponsored campaign that produced Brenda Holloway's 'Play It Cool, Stay In School'

The record originally surfaced in the late seventies with the instrumental side in favour. Twenty years later it was the R&B tinged vocal that had the dancers clapping to this memorable tune's perfectly timed breaks.

Top 500 Position: **360**
Original Label: **Brunswick**
Current Value: **£8 Issue**
£15 Demo

'A brilliant duet packed full of Marvin and Tammi overtones'

Gail Smith, Soul Fan, Hampshire, UK

Gene Chandler and Barbara Acklin

From The Teacher To The Preacher

Both hugely successful at Brunswick with Chandler already being charted in the Northern hall of fame.

Now we look at the late Ms. Acklin who enjoyed healthy sales on many 45's for the label, not least 'Love Makes A Woman' which peaked at no. 15 in '68 stateside. Barbara who recently passed away was cousin to Monk Higgins who recorded her both as Barbara Allen and Acklin for his Special Agent label out of Chicago. She married Eugene Record of the Chi-Lites and co-wrote 'Have You Seen Her' before signing to Capitol.

The classic 'Teacher' is an old school Wheel sound with a certain classiness that both artists generated on most of their recordings.

Top 500 Position: **361**
Original Label: **Okeh**
Current Value: **£75 Issue**
£100 Demo

'Okeh was undoubtedly the scenes' backbone, product wise'

Barry Wain, Soul Fan, London, UK

The Triumphs

I'm Coming To Your Rescue

Ferocious mover from the scene's favourite label. The group from Los Angeles were brought to Okeh by producer Arthur Wright and released another goodie 'Memories',but the winner is undoubtedly 'Rescue'.

Played extensively at the Golden Torch,'I'm Comin' To Your Rescue' takes a well earned position in the top 500 for the Triumphs, a group often mistakenly associated with the Verve combo of the same name who hailed from Memphis and also appear in the chart.

Top 500 Position: **362**
Original Label: **Imperial**
Current Value: **£40 Demo**
£100 Issue

'Blue Eyed Soul at its very best'

Brian Lea, Soul Fan, Greater Manchester, UK

Danny Wagner and the Kindred Soul

I Lost A True Love

After playing this and his version of Johnny Wyatt's 'This Thing Called Love', from the Kindred Soul Album, I discovered 'I Lost a True Love' was indeed a single too!

Fortunately this invigorating side was a instant hit at Wigan Casino when I first played it in March 1974. Barry White had a hand in the production and the record company saw Wagner as a new Johnny Rivers, who at the time had left the company and formed the U. S. Soul City label.

Top 500 Position: **363**
Original Label: **Bareback**
Current Value: **£150 Issue**
£200 Demo

'One of the happiest Northern sounds you're ever likely to hear'

Tony Gioe, DJ, New York, USA

Will Collins and Will Power

Is There Anything I Can Do?

A good friend of mine Tony Gioe was the A&R man for Midland International and had scored hits in the U. S. with Carole Douglas and Silver Convention, as well as the great Marboo 45 'What About Love'.

After lunch one afternoon in the late seventies, Tony asked if I wanted to take a few boxes of some new releases from their new sister label Bareback. I politely declined as I though what the heck am I going to do with new 70's releases! You can imagine how I felt when I discovered that DJ Richard Searling was playing a cover up by The Love Committee known to be by Will Collins on Bareback.

Somehow I wish the record was poor - fat chance! This one is straight from the top deck! Collins went on to record for Capitol and gave our spin off scene Jazz Funk the classic 'Where You Gonna Be Tonight'.

Top 500 Position: **364**
Original Label: **Music Merchant**
Current Value: **£10**

'It was amazing to hear this sampled so heavily in a new track by Fat Boy Slim'

Dave Carne, Soul Fan, Cumbria, UK

The Just Brothers

Sliced Tomatoes

This 1972 instrumental recorded for Music Merchant records first came to Northern Soul's attention courtesy of the Torch, remaining popular throughout the 70's.

Played as an almost brand new release, 'Sliced Tomatoes' with its twangy guitar reminiscent of a Surf instrumental soon became a major dancefloor filler in the Stoke venue already famed for such legendary instrumentals as 'Thumb A Ride' and 'Tracks To Your Mind'.

In more recent years, despite a bizarre burst of interest resulting from heavy sampling of the track by dance supremo Norman 'Fat Boy Slim' Cook, it is the duo's earlier vocal recording for Garrison 'Carlena', also an excellent (and today very pricey) dancer, that has supplanted the popularity of 'Sliced Tomatoes'... Though it will be sometime before it attains the longevity of its younger brother!

Top 500 Position: **365**
Original Label: **Tetragramatton**
Current Value: **£10 Issue**
£15 Demo

'The performance in Blackburn is discussed almost as much as his music'

Terry Mould, Soul Fan, South Wales, UK

Bobby Paris

Per-son-ally

Let's establish some interesting facts on New Yorker Paris who moved to California in the late 60's. On three different labels he has a trio of absolute hot-to-trot 45's of which this 1968 recording was his first actual play on the scene.

The excitement factor at the Golden Torch was paramount, and the one line hook followed by 'I Don't Give A Hang' (substituting 'Damn' which was still considered swearing at the time) has become one of the biggest Northern hits.

The single got a UK release on Polydor in 1968 which is much rarer than the U.S. copy (weighing in at around £60) and was covered by both the notorious Wigan's Ovation and Strawberry Jam - weak versions by comparison with our man Paris of course!

Top 500 Position: **366**
Original Label: **Verve**
Current Value: **£100**

'A total adrenaline rush hitting 9. 9 on the Richter scale!'

Martin Grimes, Soul Fan, Northampton, UK

Youngblood Smith

You Can Split

A total one-off from the man and sheer athleticism from the audience made it a top dancer during the Wigan era.

Re-issued far too early (1974) and with the misleading title 'Walk On Baby', which was it's original cover up name.

Unless you know otherwise, the 45 was never actually issued, whilst most of the demos ended up in the UK... No change there then!

An intro similar to 'I Can't Help Myself' by the Four Tops.

Top 500 Position:	**367**
Original Label:	**KKC**
Current Value:	**£300**

'Many slants on the Philly Dog craze have appeared, Jimmy's interpretation is right up there'

Bill Esplen, Soul Fan, Northumberland, UK

Jimmy Raye
Philly Dog Around The World

Sticks Evans a New York session drummer, owned two labels Hype and KKC. The 1966 single on KKC is an earth shattering 45 that didn't click initially when played by DJ Ian Levine at Blackpool Mecca and it was down to Soul Sam to popularise the record at St. Ives and other venues of the time. Wigan eventually took its cue for a piece of dance ephemera almost tailor-made for its cavernous dancehall.

Owning an original copy is not quite as easy as you may think as a lookalike counterfeit is still floating around and in many cases masquerading as the original.

Top 500 Position:	**368**
Original Label:	**United Artists**
Current Value:	**£70 Issue**
	£100 Demo

'The epitome of big-beat'

Cal Sutton, Soul Fan, London, UK

Ray Pollard
The Drifter

As tastes have changed over the years, the appreciation of total quality has never lapsed. 'The Drifter' was also competently recorded by Long John Baldry on British United Artists.

Well turning full circle we can now honour the side which now ranks as one of the Top 5 'enders', and at least brings Pollard in from the cold.

Largely unknown here, he was the voice behind 50's/early 60's group The Wanderers, moving on to record for UA, Decca, with a version of Elvis' 'Wanderlust', and Shrine. 'It's A Sad Thing', also recorded for UA, also continues to receive attention, but the sheer craft of 'The Drifter', which received a British release, ensures it's popularity long into the new millennium.

Interestingly Ray has only one arm as a result of service in the Korean war, but that hasn't hindered a burgeoning career as a film extra - look closely and you'll see him in 'Ghostbusters'!

Top 500 Position: **369**
Original Label: **Mercury**
Current Value: **£6 Issue**
£10 Demo

'The all 'original' oldie that refuses to lie down!'

Gary Marsh, New Jersey, USA

Jerry Butler

Moody Woman

From Sunflower, Mississippi and the older brother of Billy, the 'Ice Man' started out life with the Northern Jubilee Gospel singers before joining The Quails and of course The Impressions in 1957.

'Moody' was his third to last hit which started back in 1958. The link with Gamble and Huff was a prudent move as the hits trawled out from '67 and continued until '72 before a second wind with Philadelphia International in the mid 70's - then off to Motown.

A remarkable career, with the UK embracing this minor hit from 1969 almost from initial release. However the 'scene' has championed the side in more recent times-to full effect.

Top 500 Position: **370**
Original Label: **Phoof**
Current Value: **£15 Issue**
£25 Demo

'A short lived Wigan anthem, that you either love or hate'

Barbara Teal, Soul Fan, Australia

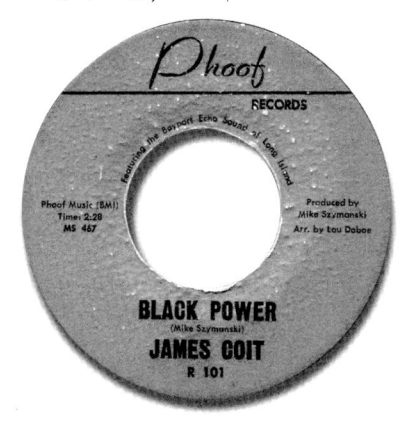

James Coit

Black Power

When you are on a record buying trip and you find the most in demand single at the time of your enterprising venture it certainly puts a spring in your step.

During a trip to Long Island, New York in 1977, I had James Coit at the top of my wants list. Entering a store I had never been to before imagine my surprise at finding it there. Literally this became a triple figure record for about two months, and while the collector interest has waned over the years I have to reveal that on a closer listen it's not bad at all.

Wigan Casino was the obvious venue to test the water with such a frantic effort and the dancers were equal to it.

Top 500 Position:	**371**
Original Label:	**Keymen**
Current Value:	**£40**

'Great as an instrumental or as a vocal'

Jeff Barry,
Soul Fan, Greater Manchester, UK

The Furys
I'm Satisfied With You

Led by Jerome Edwards the group was handled by James McKeachin (Jimmy Mack - not to be confused with the Palmer artist). A fantastic 1966 recording for an act who tried desperately for a hit via Mark IV and Liberty among others.

James Carmichael's arrangement is awesome as the strings and bass link with the lead's intro 'Hey Girl' into one of the all-time greats. By the way the instrumental take which was massive at the Casino in its own right is only to be found on the various reissues.

A note to collectors - this is a vastly underrated 45!

Top 500 Position:	**372**
Original Label:	**Capitol**
Current Value:	**£20**

'A spate of 'kid' Soul started to infiltrate the scene in early 74, Garner was at the forefront'

Robert Taylor, Soul Fan, London, UK

Reggie Garner
Hot Line

Child TV star Reggie Garner had a brief career musically, scoring with a minor hit for Capitol titles 'Teddy Bear', before departing for ABC and the Northernesque 'Half A Cup'.

Slotting in to a new youthfulness that DJ Ian Levine was implementing i.e. Mark Copage, Leonard Kaigler, Garner's 'Hotline', was unashamedly commercial for an all-nighter monster in the first part of 1975.

Unfortunately he didn't hit the heights TV wise either, and Garner returned to singing under the identity of Reginald.

Top 500 Position: **373**
Original Label: **Impact**
Current Value: **£250 Issue**
£200 Demo

'A real sleeper from where else? - Detroit!'

Barry James, Soul Fan, Detroit, USA

Jock Mitchell
Not A Chance In A Million

Jock recorded two singles for Impact and one for local label Golden Hit which is extremely sought after. The clubs up North plumped for the danceable 'Not A Chance In A Million'.

Certainly a record in the 70's that could not get past around the £10 mark in saleability, the mid-eighties saw this disc recognised as a true classic of non-Motown Detroit Soul - with perhaps one of the greatest changes in tempo ever committed to vinyl!

Top 500 Position: **374**
Original Label: **Verve**
Current Value: **£100 Issue**
£80 Demo

'A superb vocal'

Gary Fisher, Soul Fan, Indiana, USA

Howard Guyton
I Watched You Slowly Slip Away

Former lead singer of Festival group, the Top Notes which also featured Derek Martin, Howard Guyton, recorded this terrific beat shuffler for Verve in 1966. Fellow New York recording artist Lou Courtney cut it for Philips too, but even though Courtney was the writer Guyton's version just edges it.

Amazingly this was the original 'cheap' 45 until the 80's, when tempos changed and the disc became a seriously sought after item, it now takes its place as something of a latter day classic.

Top 500 Position: **375**
Original Label: **UK Spring**
Current Value: **£10**

'A Mr M's classic'

Richard Thomas, Welling, UK

Millie Jackson
A House For Sale

Another delicious almost new release from Jackson who recorded it for her 1976 LP 'Free And In Love'.

A total Mecca play it caught on instantly with the scene as the transition from mono to stereo was well and truly under construction.

Settling in New York in the late 60's Ms. Jackson recorded her 1st single for MGM titled 'My Heart Took A Licking' which is now being taken seriously by collectors. 'House For Sale' meantime has become a household phrase at most commercial Soul Nights.

Top 500 Position: **376**
Original Label: **Imperial (LP)**
Current Value: **£30**

'To this day, hardly anybody knows the original name and title'

Alan Loxley, Soul Fan, Inverness, UK

Total Eclipses
6 O'Clock

The creativity of record dealer Simon Soussan, was arguably a turning point in the scene's makeup. Discovering odd 45's like 'Footsee' and adding instrumentation to Soul it up a little, gave the scene additional excitement. The Lovin' Spoonful recorded the vocal version and the orchestral cover by Total Eclipses sat on a obscure LP, until SS speeded it up, and gave it a new identity as 'Supertime' by the Golden World Strings.

A little cheeky perhaps, but an improvement on the bland original. This is where only the dancers become appreciative and is considered non-descript by collectors.

Top 500 Position: **377**
Original Label: **Goldmine**
Current Value: **£5**

'Many of my fans rate this as my best - yet it was only a demo!'

Eddie Holman, Artist, USA

Eddie Holman
Where I'm Not Wanted/Hurt

Eddie is a legend of the scene, a writer of a host of classics for Philadelphia's finest, from Larry Clinton to Bernard Williams, he is of course most widely respected for his own golden voice and enormous solo recording output for Parkway, ABC, GSF, Silver Blue and Salsoul.

First finding favour in the North with the ultimate Mod feelgood sound 'Eddie's My Name', his 'Hey There Lonely Girl' became one of the first Northern driven pop hits in 1970.

'Where I'm Not Wanted' and 'Hurt' (also enormously popular by the Victors on Philips) were first played from a double sided Harthon studio demo acetate that still featured the count-ins. Broken by Richard Searling, both deservedly became all-time Station Road dancefloor classics.

Top 500 Position: **378**
Original Label: **Mirwood**
Current Value: **£10 Issue**
£15 Demo

'Stunningly original and atmospheric, and certainly energising'

Jim Moorhead, Soul Fan, Glasgow, UK

Jackie Lee
Do The Temptation Walk

Synonymous with the scene is Louisiana's Earl Nelson, better known as Lee. The period of 64' to 67' had Nelson working a conveyor belt of dance crazes and uptempo Soul nuggets.

He was possibly the most played artist in Soul Clubs during the late 60's, and we could easily have listed the 'B' side 'Shotgun And The Duck' as this also received adulation from the dancefloor.

His relationship with Randall Wood was critical and historically he was certainly the dance master of the mid sixties in the Los Angeles area.

Top 500 Position: **379**
Original Label: **Solid Hit**
Current Value: **£800**

'The most in demand 45 from the Detroit based Solid Hit label'

Pat Lewis, Artist, Detroit, USA

Pat Lewis
No One To Love

First recording 'Deep Freeze' as part of the Adorables along with sister Diane and another set of sisters called Jackie and Betty (surname unknown). Pat and Diane became two thirds of Isaac Hayes' backup group Hot Buttered Soul. She featured on many Golden World releases and productions by George Clinton, Parliament and Funkadelic. Pat is still active today performing in clubs, in and around the greater Metropolitan Detroit area.

At first sight of the gaudy label you might assume this record was trashy 70s pop, but this sound which took a good while to break is a massively popular Northern Soul classic today.

Lewis recorded three other worthy releases for Solid Hit but for some reason this is by far the rarest.

Top 500 Position: **380**
Original Label: **Vee Jay**
Current Value: **£10 Issue**
£15 Demo

'A great platform for the lady to discover the UK, and see first-hand the interest in her'

Brenda Hollings, Soul Fan, Manchester, UK

Betty Everett
Getting Mighty Crowded

Born 61 years ago in Greenwood, Mississippi, typical gospel performer who moved to Chicago in the late 50's, recording for Cobra the Vee-Jay. Following the international smash hit of the 'Shoop Shoop Song' and 'Let it Be Me' with Jerry Butler, she recorded the very atmospheric 'Getting Mighty Crowded', which has been revived more recently after a cult following at the Twisted Wheel club.

She later recorded for Uni, with her album track 'You're Falling In Love' being a monster sound and 'Fantasy', she most certainly is an act who's work is cherished by Soul fans worldwide.

Top 500 Position: **381**
Original Label: **Champion/Doc**
Current Value: **£20 Champion**
£250 Doc

'Now it's been re-discovered as a Motown acetate, interest is riding high again'

Kath Jones, Soul Fan, Sanbach, Cheshire, UK

Sandy Wynns

A Touch Of Venus

Professionally known as Edna Wright and former Honey Cone member. Originally in the Blossoms along with her sister Darlene Love, she recorded for Champion, Simco and Canterbury. The single released with its incredibly rare UK Fontana issue became a huge Catacombs, Mecca and Torch favourite.

A Jobete published song written by Motown staffer Ed Cobb (who produced it for Sandy), 'A Touch Of Venus' was in fact created for the great Marvin Gaye! Whilst Marvin never released it, a demo by Patrice Holloway is doing the rounds at this very moment. Mary Love did also record this classic, though it sadly remained in the can.

Top 500 Position: **382**
Original Label: **Swan**
Current Value: **£10 Issue**
£25 Demo

'The General commands attention, whenever I hear his sublime voice'

Paul Simpson, Record Dealer, UK

The Showmen

Our Love Will Grow

From one of the best double siders of it's generation. Norman Johnson powers a lead that others dare to follow.

Roaming like a stealth bomber, this side has weaved continuously around the scene, though generally suffering from being 'too easy to get' during the heady 70's.

Finally, we all latched on and bravely played the 'cheapie' until mass overkill turned it underground once more.

The flip 'You're Everything' is now starting to draw attention and not a day too soon. One of the old Swan masters, cut at Virtue studios. Enough said!

Top 500 Position: **383**
Original Label: **Verve**
Current Value: **£100 Issue**
£80 Demo

'Listen to this when you've just split with the missus - it'll slay you!'

Dave Greenhill, Collector, UK

The High-Keys
Living A Lie

The group led by Troy 'Love Explosion' Keyes was typical of its big city production.

A Golden Torch discovery and fairly easy to find throughout the 70's. Eventually the constant demand for copies has forced the price up to reflect its quality as a dancer.

The flip is one of the all-time great 'Soul' sides too but 'Living A Lie' is the one that will never die.

Top 500 Position: **384**
Original Label: **Soozi**
Current Value: **£20**

'How I would love to tell the group what a fabulous track this is'

Julie Roberts, Soul Fan, Nottingham, UK

The Velvet Hammer
Happy

The 70's and Chicago are linked heavily to the charts with the Chi-Lites keeping the Windy City alive. Eugene Record may have been top dog but what about the wannabees such as Velvet Hammer?

Typical falsetto lead in an attempt to challenge the Russell Thompkins of their time, what makes this one shot wonder is the originality of the arrangement. The strings are superb, the song excellent, so one can derive from that, the record company were simply under financed, even more amazing then that this 45 was culled from an album!

One of the better 70's singles to still warm the cockles of many a true Northerner.

Top 500 Position: **385**
Original Label: **Crazy Horse**
Current Value: **£10**

'The second Northern hit for this Blue Eyed outfit"

Ed Philips, Soul Fan, Derby, UK

David and the Giants
Ten Miles High

Following on from their other chart entry, David Huff and The Giants who sound as if they are from New York (that Brooklyn accent gives it away). The Muscle Shoals, Alabama recorded single also failed to make it. DJ Ian Levine quickly found the single off the back of his initial play of 'Superlove'.

Although not quite as big as the former, it certainly did the business in 1974, and prompted Capitol in the UK to re-issue both sides back to back following the big oldies revival of 1975/76.

Top 500 Position: **386**
Original Label: **Minit**
Current Value: **£10 Issue**
£25 Demo

'The real meat 'n' potatoes of the scene'

Bill Snow, Soul Fan, Doncaster, UK

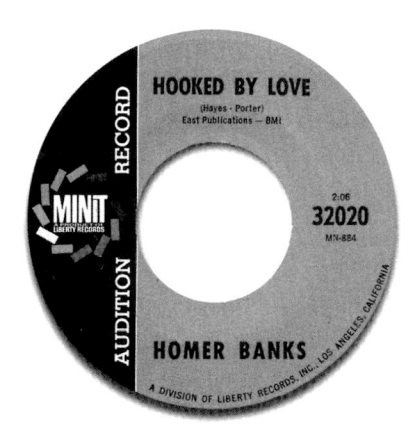

Homer Banks
Hooked By Love

Legendary song writer who provided much of the material for the Stax roster after 1968. He was born in Memphis in 1941, and made his debut on the Genie label recording 'Lady Of Stone'. As well as writing classics such as 'Who's Making Love' for Johnny Taylor, he signed to the Minit label and recorded some absolute dynamite stuff.

The Twisted Wheel club is credited with discovering the disc, and it's getting more plays today as newcomers realise the emotional attachment he had to all his performances- not bad for a singer with a lisp!

His other classic 'A Lot Of Love', also recorded and popular by Taj Mahal, was recently a major hit when covered by Simply Red.

Top 500 Position: **387**
Original Label: **AGC**
Current Value: **£30, £250 with rare flip**

Joe Hicks
Don't It Make You Feel Funky

Amazingly enough the record was played on radio by Wolfman Jack (American Graffiti), during his stint out in California. The record sold very little though.

Two separate releases with different flip sides exist, and the record was discovered in 1974 by DJ Ian Levine. Hicks went on to record for the Stax subsidiary Enterprise for whom he made an album, and listening closely to the largely unknown singer from LA he had much too offer.

'The Funk element is certainly missing, Northern Soulers are grateful for that'

Brian Hall, Soul Fan, North Wales, UK

Top 500 Position: **388**
Original Label: **St Lawrence**
Current Value: **£10 Issue / £30 Demo**

Mamie Galore
It Ain't Necessary

Outstanding 45 from April 1966, that was written by Jerry Butler and almost made the U. S. charts bubbling under at No. 132. Discovered by Monk Higgins, Mamie, born Mamie Davies, recorded for Sack, Thomas and Imperial (with Dee Erwin).

A cover version exists by The Embers on Bell and one by Brandy Alexander on Tangerine titled 'Do Right Man'.

Allnighter-wise it was one of the Top 5 discoveries of 1971.

'My personal introduction to the Northern scene, and what a record to start me off.'

Ann Roberts, Soul Fan, Stafford, UK

Top 500 Position: **389**
Original Label: **Soul**
Current Value: **£25**

'This one really gets them going at most venues'

Tim Greensmith, Soul Fan, Sheffield, UK

Junior Walker and the Allstars

Tune Up

Audrey deWalt Jnr. was discovered by Johnny Bristol. 'Tune Up' is one of Junior's first recordings for Motown after being signed to the company's Soul subsidiary. Junior joined the Hitsville roster after Berry Gordy bought out 'Harvey', the label owned by Harvey Fuqua on which the Allstars released 'Twist Lackawanna' and the incredible 'Brainwasher', a cut that makes 'Tune Up' sound like a stroll in the park!

The Northern of scene of late has been experimenting with earlier R&B sides and this unbelievable sax workout quite rightly is one of his most played tunes, even surpassing most of his mid-60's output.

Top 500 Position: **390**
Original Label: **Island**
Current Value: **£20**

'One of the first Mod records to cross over to the Northern Scene'

Rob Glass, Soul Fan, Essex, UK

Wynder K Frog

Green Door

Michael Weaver from Colchester with a surprising Northern Soul hitster. The 60's instrumental version of Jim Lowe's 1956 hit was very popular in the late 60's and became a Wigan giant a decade or so later.

He recorded an album titles 'Out Of The Frying Pan' and worked with the Spencer Davis Group around the same time.

Very little to do with Soul, but a terrific dancer nonetheless.

Top 500 Position: **391**
Original Label: **Excello**
Current Value: **£100**

'Discovered as early as 1969, the collector confined the masterpiece to his bedroom'

Barry Kendrick, Soul Fan, Midlands, UK

Roger Hatcher
Sweetest Girl In The World

Brother to Willie Hatcher and cousin to Edwin Starr.

I was visiting a childhood friend in 1969 and he promptly played a few Twisted Wheel purchases made by his elder brother. Amongst them he spun this 45 which he had got from a Soul pack (very fashionable for collectors at the time), it was years before I actually heard this in a club and even longer before it approached anything like its enormous current popularity.

The Nashville label formed by Ernie Young had boasted some terrific blues music and amazing enough had licensed the flip side 'I'm Gonna Dedicate This Song To You' to UK President. The British indie sadly left off the real winner. Staking it's claim in our hall of fame, this Soul man recorded other 45's In his home town of Detroit on the Dotty's and aptly titled Northern De-La label and finally in the 70's released a very rare and obscure album for the Guiness label.

Top 500 Position: **392**
Original Label: **RCA Victor**
Current Value: **£60 Demo**
£300 Issue

'Chandlers' discs escalated in popularity during the 70's, here's another milestone'

Robert Steele, Soul Fan, Los Angeles, USA

Lorraine Chandler
I Can't Change

Despite the famous discussion on 'is she - or isn't she singing flat?' her superbly emotional deliveries ensure that her vinyl output really is top-notch.

The three singles recorded for RCA are quite simply mind blowing and long after the oddities have burned themselves out, these exquisite Jack Ashford productions will still be going strong.

This track also recorded by Yvonne Baker on Junior was first aired by Catacombs DJ and Midlands main man Pep.

Top 500 Position: **393**
Original Label: **Wand**
Current Value: **£150**

'Just one of a multitude of incredible Soul sounds from the boys'

Dallas Frazier, Producer, Texas, USA

The Masqueraders
Do You Love Me Baby?

The Masqueraders from Dallas, Texas are one of the great Soul groups, led by the wonderful voice of Lee W Jones and later by Lee Hatim, their recording career for a wide range of labels including Stairway, AGP, Bell, LaBeat, Amy, ABC and Bang, started with Soul Town, for whom their incredibly rare and extremely popular 'That's The Same Thing' was waxed.

This is yet another 45 that didn't quite make it in the venues of the 70's - it took another decade to appreciate the sheer quality of the recording - a tenfold increase in price has of course ensued.

Top 500 Position: **394**
Original Label: **Date**
Current Value: **£20 Issue**
£12 Demo

'An old-style girl group with a big city production and a lightning quick beat'...

Mitchell Waring, Soul Fan, Bedford, UK

The Charmaines
Eternally

Some 45's take your breath away during a particular time frame. One Saturday morning in February 1974 I received a package from record dealer Simon Soussan with this inside. The second the stylus hit the vinyl I just knew this would be tonight's number one at the Casino, I was not wrong.

Unfortunately the track petered out too early and was promptly re-issued. A mini revival is taking place for records of this ilk at the moment and I am pleased to say the single is once again the centre of attention.

Produced in Detroit by Herman Lewis, the record was quickly picked up by Columbia subsidiary Date for release in 1966.

Top 500 Position: **395**
Original Label: **Parkway**
Current Value: **£400 Issue**
£250 Demo

'A legendary 'cover-up'

Mark Leadbetter, Soul Fan, Sussex, UK

Vickie Baines
Country Girl

When DJ Richard Searling covered over this exquisite 45 on Parkway as Christine Cooper, the mystery became so wrapped up in 'scene euphoria' perhaps only the 'who shot JR 'saga on Dallas was bigger in the 80's.

The single saved Wigan from ridicule in the late 70's, with a subsequent uncovering in 1980.

Baines had two outings for Cameo Parkway both of which failed miserably being unsupported by the label and she moved on to Warner Brothers Soul label, Loma.

To this day the exposure of those initial plays has propelled the side to even greater heights.

But in the mire of 'Joe 90' and Muriel Day, thank heavens for the discovery.

Top 500 Position: **396**
Original Label: **United Artists (UK)**
Current Value: **£50**

'The second of three Northern discoveries by the man'

Alex Philpott, Soul Fan, Staffordshire, UK

Bobby Goldsboro
Too Many People

In similar vein to Paul Anka it was inevitable that Goldsboro from Marianna, Florida would sidestep his pop-country roots to go uptempo in the mid-60's. Strangely his biggest northern hit never saw the light of day in the US, and this is surprising because the 'Honey' man revels with the Soul groove of 1967.

As you would expect Wigan Casino was the stomp outlet for this nifty mover. An investigation of his 60's output reveals a surprising number of similar cuts.

Top 500 Position: **397**
Original Label: **Columbia**
Current Value: **£75 Issue**
£30 Demo

'Another 70's 45 that helped cement a new style within the scene'

Paul Veerhorn, Soul Fan, Holland

Lou Edwards

Talkin' 'Bout Poor Folks (Thinking 'Bout My Folks)

This single was the first sign of a totally new groove that was about to infiltrate the scene in 74'. Looking back the whole shaft style which in theory had nothing to do with Northern was beginning to impose it's style.

The record from 1972 absolutely bombed in the US probably due to an uncompromisingly 'black' style. Originally played by DJ's Ian Levine and Colin Curtis at the famed Highland Room, its Soulful style was very much in vogue at Blackpool Mecca though it is rarely heard these days.

Top 500 Position: **398**
Original Label: **Bell**
Current Value: **£10 Issue**
£20 Demo

'A classic from the early days of the scene'

Jeffrey Mitchell, Soul Fan, London, UK

The O'Jays

I Dig Your Act

A blockbusting side penned by the Poindexter brothers for one of the finest acts ever!

Eddie Levert leads the original Ohio group into ecstacy as they tear into this George Kerr production from late 1967.

Discovered by DJ Eddie O'Jay, their remarkable career dates back to 1958 when they were known as the Mascots. The group recorded for Apollo, Wayco, King, Imperial, Minit, Bell, Neptune and Philadelphia International (the start of their real success), before some cool stuff for EMI's Manhattan.

A real good Northern night can't be complete without hearing this, or one of their many other floorfillers such as 'Hold On' 'I'll Never Forget You' 'Deeper (In Love With You)'.

The Northern Soul All Time Top 500

Top 500 Position: **399**
Original Label: **Candi**
Current Value: **£1,200**

'The introductory church organ makes way for a fantastic Doo-wop, Soul beat'

Mick Plant, Soul Fan, Cumbria, UK

The Empires
You're On Top Girl

James Chavis the label owner, dumped around 1, 000 45's to a thrift store near Willmington, Delaware in 1976. I managed to find multiple copies of the in-demand 'Like A Bee' by The Spidells, I also found a copy of this wonderful mover from 65, did I leave a bulk quantity?...

An absolute stormin' dancer far too dated even at the time for success but cherished by collectors and dancers alike resulting in today's massive price tag.

Top 500 Position: **400**
Original Label: **Liberty**
Current Value: **£50 Issue**
£75 Demo

'The emotion ripples through the dance halls as this great balladeer really delivers'

Gary Holland, Soul Fan, Leeds, UK

Gene McDaniels
Walk With A Winner

Eugene McDaniels has just celebrated his 65th birthday.

Originally from Kansas City he moved to Omaha and sang in choirs before signing to Liberty in 1961. In his first two years he had no less than six hits, he also recorded a good follow up to 'Winner' with 'Hang On', before disappearing and performing as Universal Jones in 1972.

Popular for many years, this record is still one of the truly great 'enders'.

Top 500 Position: **401**
Original Label: **Palmer**
Current Value: **£300**

'Firing on all cylinders'

Keith Leadbetter, Soul Fan, Norfolk, UK

The People's Choice

Savin' My Lovin' For You

Not to be confused with the Philadelphia group who recorded for Philips, Phil-LA-Of Soul, PIR etc. Rumours abound that in fact Al Green was in the group, though a recent interview with writer/producer 'Popcorn' Wylie revealed that he certainly didn't remember such a famous minister in the lineup!

In terms of quality, well it's yet another powerhouse group sound that features that rolling Detroit groove made the way only Wylie and Hester know how!

Top 500 Position: **402**
Original Label: **Buttercup**
Current Value: **£30**

'A real Casino anthem'

Graham Leavitt, Soul Fan, Scotland

Sheila Anthony

Livin' In Love

From a label owned by Teddy 'You Don't Need A Heart' Randazzo, comes this Soul beater that doesn't sit too well with any audience except for northern England.

I am as surprised as anyone at the popularity of such an obscurity and DJ Russ Winstanley played the single with a conviction which finally got it a UK release on Route records after Ian Levine broke it at Blackpool Mecca.

Top 500 Position: **403**
Original Label: **Swan**
Current Value: **£10**

'The condensation from the walls of the Twisted Wheel went straight on my mohair suit'

Ray Monks, Soul Fan, Merseyside, UK

Mickey Lee Lane
Hey Sah-Lo-Ney

From Pittsburgh, PA comes this 1965 dancer in similar vein to Mitch Ryder's outings. The record sold fairly well in the states as it slipped out almost unnoticed on UK Stateside. There was talk of Itzy being it's first label, this is false as Swan bought the master from Itzy who then promptly manufactured some copies a couple of years later, Lane went on to have another mediocre hit pop wise with 'Shaggy Dog'.

Also recorded by UK Mod group the Action (who performed at the Mojo), Mickey's original was first played at the legendary Twisted Wheel by Les Cokell - who had tracked it down after he heard it one Sunday afternoon on Radio Luxembourg!

Curiously, Cobblestone a subsidiary of Buddah, best known for the Vonnettes, released a remixed instrumental version in 1968, entitled 'Tracks To Your Mind' by the Sounds of Lane, which was so popular at The Golden Torch.

Top 500 Position: **404**
Original Label: **Soul**
Current Value: **£10 Issue**
£30 Demo

'Resurfacing again after all these years'

Gary Shelton, Soul Fan, West Midlands, UK

Gladys Knight and the Pips
Just Walk In My Shoes

One of the first rare Motown plays from the Twisted Wheel. Almost impossible to get in the late 60's, it quite simply sold nowt on Soul or on the UK TMG logo.

Several covers exist too including Gary Glenn (CO & CE) and the Outsiders (Capitol) which were both played at the Casino. Eventually the one true stunning version is back on the turntables from where the professional singer of some 48 years can well and truly be saluted.

A fantastic record that everyone adores!

Top 500 Position: **405**
Original Label: **Kent (UK)**
Current Value: **£10**

'The unreleased tracks now being played are as good as the classics of yesteryear'

Robert Lee, Soul Fan, New York, USA

Carla Thomas
I'll Never Stop Loving You

Daughter of Rufus, she recorded with her father as early as 1960.

The wonderful Carla Thomas needs very little introduction to Soul fans. Although her material has always been considered a little too harsh for the Northern scene, the fantastic tape discovery by Kent records as licensor of Stax in the UK is a truly remarkable find.

The vibes and strings are not in any way in the tradition of the Memphis label, but quite frankly who cares, Thomas puts in a performance as if to outdo her massive 'Gee Whiz' hit. How on earth did it fail to gain release?

Top 500 Position: **406**
Original Label: **Ric-Tic**
Current Value: **£10**

'Our Edwin just keeps on coming up with them!'

Peter Whitney, Soul Fan, Cumbria, UK

Edwin Starr
I Have Faith In You

The flip to 'Stop Her On Sight' - and what a performance from the UK's favourite Soul man.

A truly wonderful sound, 'I Have Faith In You' has traditionally been an 'ender' though today its quality makes it a popular spin at any time of the night!

Also covered by 'Bari Track' man Doni Burdick on Sound Impression, in recent times the unissued 'Detroit Sound' instrumental has also been enormously popular.

Top 500 Position: **407**
Original Label: **St. Lawrence**
Current Value: **£10 Fatman**
£75 Batman

'Working off the hit TV series the obscurity works well'

Kerry Holmes, Soul Fan, Scunthorpe, UK

Butch Baker
The Fat Man/Batman At The Go-Go

Like the Mylestones 'The Joker', Monk Higgins tried his hand with this play on the Batman series. In fact the single came out twice using first using 'Bat Man', which is very scarce indeed, and then 'Fat Man' as the lead words in the title.

Played at most of the all-niters in 73', you usually find that any cash-in on a TV series is necessarily contrived, that is not the case on this young singer's gem from Chicago.

A Blackpool Mecca spin from 1973.

Top 500 Position: **408**
Original Label: **Jamie**
Current Value: **£200 Issue**
£150 Demo

'The heartbeat of a hare'

Kev Sowerby, Soul Fan, Cumbria, UK

Pookie Hudson
This Gets To Me

James 'Pookie' Hudson was the lead with Doo-Wop group the Spaniels. Like all front men he decided to go it alone and teamed up with Jamie's house producer Bob Finiz. The result was this vibe laden groover from 1966.

The song is simple but effective and has a large following dating back to the mid 70's whereby it became a monster tune - largely due to plays from the East Anglia area

Subsequent collector's items by Hudson's band have been unearthed on Calla and North American, whilst Pookie went on to make a career for himself on the oldies revival circuit in the US.

Top 500 Position: **409**
Original Label: **Jubilee**
Current Value: **£10 Issue**
£15 Demo

'Coming off like Reginald Dixon meets Motown'

Tom Tynan, Soul Fan, Tyneside, UK

The Baltimore and Ohio Marching Band

Condition Red

The A side 'Lapland' sold fairly well in the States, enough so that it was released on UK Stateside.

The flip is the dance hit over here, the perfect model for the perverse side of Northern Soul, with the customary 2.5 minutes of pumping base lead track with a whistling organ.

Absolutely monstrous in 1974, long forgotten now it is a track guaranteed to confuse those trying to understand our music from outside the scene.

Top 500 Position: **410**
Original Label: **Kent (UK)**
Current Value: **£10**

'This song ought to have been on her album 'The Fabulous Sound Of...''

Ben Chambers, Soul Fan, London, UK

Maxine Brown

It's Torture

Discovered by Tony Bruno who signed her to his Nomar label, and scored immediately with 'All In My Mind'. The fan base for the lady from Kingstree, South Carolina has never been more evident, largely due to the unearthing of this track from the Wand vaults and her appearance at The Cleethorpes Weekender a few years ago.

Total Big City, a great singer, and an instant four figure single had it been released on some tiny label somewhere.

Top 500 Position: **411**
Original Label: **Fame**
Current Value: **£150 Issue**
£100 Demo

'A drum roll, an infectious beat combine with Barnett's bragging vocal'

Roger Wilson, Soul Fan, London, UK

James Barnett

Keep On Talking

The first single on Fame created by Dan Penn and Spooner Oldham in the company's Florence, Alabama studios.

The sensational backing vocals and the chorus is bouncy. Arthur Conley and Philip Mitchell also covered it, but here's by far the best version whose popularity is founded on the spins it first saw at the Torch in 1972.

The intro is about as dynamic as you can get.

Top 500 Position: **412**
Original Label: **Minit**
Current Value: **£20**

'The 'Heatwave' beat kicks'

Bev Thatcher, Soul Fan, California, USA

Jimmy Holiday and Clydie King

Ready Willing And Able

Jimmy Holiday rewrote a song that he had produced for Pamela Beatty called 'Talkin' Eyes' twelve months prior.

This potent item comes from two top quality singers with Holiday a seasoned pro recording for Everest, Diplomacy, Minit, crossover to name but a few, and the delightful Clydie King who made a series of great solo records for Imperial, Lizard, Speciality and Philips before assuming the identity of Brown Sugar on Polydor.

Top 500 Position: **413**
Original Label: **Verve**
Current Value: **£40 Issue**
£50 Demo

'Production hero from New Jersey who tells it like it is'

Robert Jackson, Soul Fan, West Midlands, UK

Robert Banks

A Mighty Good Way

Robert Banks is a legendary Soul producer who worked with a variety of quality performers, on this occasion he turns to his gospel roots to record a thrilling single for Verve.

Almost too Soulful for the drug fuelled all-niters of the early 70's, this 45 made its way high up the Golden Torch playlist in 1972.

Collectors will find the man's name on many east coast rarities.

Top 500 Position: **414**
Original Label: **Smash**
Current Value: **£30 Issue**
£50 Demo

'A fantastic double sider'

Fred Willars, Soul Fan, Newark, USA

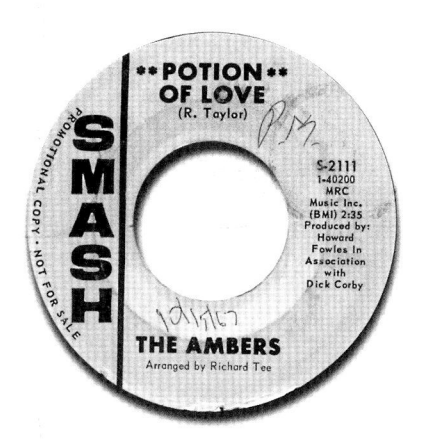

The Ambers

Potion Of Love

Robert Rhoney and Billy Chinn from New Jersey led the group to a nine year recording career without a hit. Signing for Greezie, New Art, Verve, Smash (Mercury) and finally Jean.

DJ Ian Levine discoverer of so many of the scenes' top sounds turned this into an absolute giant first play at Blackpool Mecca in 1973, today its flip 'Another Love' is also getting plays.

Top 500 Position: **415**
Original Label: **Fee**
Current Value: **£75**

'One of the hottest almost new releases'

Martin Evans,
Soul Fan, Cardiff, Wales, UK

Carol Anderson
Sad Girl

Carol who died tragically young was a bit part player on the Detroit music scene, recording for Big Tree, Whip, Expansion, Mid Town, Soulsonic and Fee. UK based Soul Bowl records made the discovery and supplied DJ Richard Searling 'who made the record his own'.

Interestingly this enormously popular sound was regularly selling at mid-eighties all nighters for up to £10 a copy on John Anderson's Grapevine label - when his import business, Soul Bowl, still had loads of genuine Fee originals for the same price! It just goes to show - check those record lists!

Top 500 Position: **416**
Original Label: **Hawk Sound**
Current Value: **£10 Issue**
£25 Demo

'Short lived and long overdue a revival'

Pete Haigh, DJ, Blackpool, UK

The Mylestones
Sexy Lady

An early 70's sweet Soul performance with a beat.

Championed by DJ Ian Levine at Blackpool Mecca the record failed to make an impact in the states despite being on former hitmaker Johnny Otis' Hawk Sound label.

Whilst possibly having a connection to producer Myles Grayson, the group are not the ones who recorded 'The Joker'.

In fact this group have one hell of a falsetto lead.

Joe Matthews
Ain't Nothing You Can Do

Top 500 Position: **417**
Original Label: **Kool Kat**
Current Value: **£350 Issue**
£400 Demo

'A great stomping classic'

Carl Matthews, Soul Fan, Warrington, UK

DJ Colin Curtis was the first to expose this Detroit rarity to the ever faithful Blackpool Mecca crowd in 1974. Matthews was no stranger to the scene recording excellent sides for Thelma.

The scarcity of the original has somewhat stumped its growth on the revival circuit but it is a masterpiece among collectors. The 'no no no no baby' intro reveals a slick bass bomber that becomes a joyous groove on the floor.

The one factor against the classic is that it was discovered in the 'Golden Era' (71-75) when there were too many fantastic discoveries. Today though it has risen to be a 45 of some repute.

Gene Toones
What More Do You Want

Top 500 Position: **418**
Original Label: **Simco**
Current Value: **£1,000 Issue**
£700 Demo

'Massively popular after failing in the 70's'

Glyn Smith, Soul Fan, Warrington, UK

An obscure spin by Ian Levine, Gene Toones took a good many years to gain mass popularity.

The New York based Toones following his departure from the independent Simco label he formed a group called Chapter IV and released a single on Wand titled 'Baby Boy' in 1975.

Just about everyone is searching for this single today, including many who, like me, sold the darn thing for £5 twenty five years ago!

Top 500 Position: **419**
Original Label: **Wheel City**
Current Value: **£700**

'A class act at the controls of that drivin Detroit rhythm'

Chris Fletcher, Soul Fan, Warwickshire, UK

Melvin Davis
Find A Quiet Place

Melvin who later joined Invictus group 8th Day recorded a variety of singles including product for Mike Hanks in the mid-60's. Melvin indeed almost made it in 1968 with 'Save It' for Mala which garnered a lot of airplay in the States.

Davis recorded this single in 1965 for Hanks' Wheel City label. Those lucky collectors who snapped up this rarity in the 70's for around £10 are now smiling sweetly as it will now set you back around £700!

A fabulous Detroit rarity!

Top 500 Position: **420**
Original Label: **Mar-V-Lus**
Current Value: **£10 Issue**
£25 Demo

'One of the first big girl group singles from Blackpool Mecca'

Nick Moore, Soul Fan, Preston, UK

The Du-ettes
Every Beat Of My Heart

Barbara Livsey later formed Barbara and The Uniques (Arden) and together with Mary Francis Hayes made several singles for the Chicago Mar-V-Lus group of labels.

Initially discovered and played at Blackpool Mecca in 1971, the record was re-issued in England on President therefore dampening DJ enthusiasm but leaving a melodic legacy which never quite leaves the subconscious.

The group's only success was 'Please Forgive Me' in 1965.

Top 500 Position: **421**
Original Label: **Ric-Tic**
Current Value: **£10 Issue**
£100 Demo

'An underrated act'

Jimmy Knowles, Soul Fan, St Helens, UK

Al Kent
The Way You Been Acting Lately

First propelled into the Northern limelight by his instrumental 'You've Got To Pay The Price', Al Kent Hamilton and the Ric-Tic label have become permanent fixtures on the scene and whilst his Wheel sound was the first played, it is 'The Way You've Been Acting Lately' that has proved the most popular and enduring. Discovered as early as 1971 it became a massive Blackpool Mecca spin and went on to become a key sound in the Casino oldies revival of '77.

Al's performance in the early 80's at Chris King's Hinkley Allnighter as part of the Ric-Tic revue is still talked about today... forget the instrumental - this guy can really sing!

Al is apparently working with 'Popcorn' Wylie in the States - we await the results with interest!

Top 500 Position: **422**
Original Label: **Fraternity**
Current Value: **£400 Issue**
£200 Demo

'A fabulous group and the scene relished it'

Steve Andrews, Soul Fan, North Wales, UK

Imaginations
Strange Neighborhood

First spun as a cover up at Wigan's Casino by key player, Richard Searling, this is another one of those singles that was 'recorded too late'. Released in 1967 when the whole Detroit/Group thing was already disappearing, the record sold poorly, even in it's Ohio locality.

The Imaginations, not be confused with the group from Philadelphia or the 70's outfit on Twentieth Century, did record another single on Fraternity in 1968, but this bombed out too - a pity for such a soulful combo.

Top 500 Position: **423**
Original Label: **Scepter**
Current Value: **£600**

'THE beat ballad anthem'

Mark Cosgrove, Soul Fan, York, UK

Johnny Maestro

I'm Stepping Out Of The Picture

Former lead singer of The Crests who recorded another fantastic Northern record twelve months after this on Parkway with 'Heartburn'. Later he had hits with the group Brooklyn Bridge on Buddah.

New York through and through, this Brooklyn born white singer is held in high esteem by Soul and Doo-Wop fans alike and this somewhat late (1980's) discovery is still extremely popular resulting in the high value of this scarce 45.

Top 500 Position: **424**
Original Label: **Pye**
Current Value: **£5**

'The record companies had finally discovered Northern Soul'

Dave McAleer, Soul Fan, London, UK

Nosmo King/The Javells

Goodbye/Goodbye Nothing To Say

Sitting in the Pye records A&R department one day in 1974 Dave McAleer discovered a single that had been released a few weeks previously on their own label by an act called Nosmo King (this was a creation of signing Steve Jameson who had formed a group called No Smoking).

Dave Mac was a Soul fan who knew the Northern scene was hot to trot and subsequently ordered some acetates renaming the group The Javells. Most of us were duped but the kids did not care, hence a UK chart position of No. 26 in 1974 on the Pye Disco demand label.

Top 500 Position: **425**
Original Label: **Motown**
Current Value: **£10**

'White hot right now'

Gavin Hallister, Collector, Arizona, USA

The Supremes
He's All I Got

It was bound to happen, the group originally known as the Primettes, with a number 9 hit 1966 in the US revisit the Northern Soul scene with the B side to 'Love Is Like An Itching In My Heart'.

Amazingly it looks as if they are back in fashion as DJ's are already playing another track by them (Stormy) from the 1987 Motown CD 'Never Before Released Masters'.

When the flipsides of Motown hits can make it over 30 years later in the quest for something 'new' there is proof positive that the scene will last forever!

Top 500 Position: **426**
Original Label: **Fontana**
Current Value: **£50**

'Hideously unfashionable now, but let's remember just how big it really was'

Mark Lethory, Soul Fan, Dublin, Eire

Kiki Dee
On A Magic Carpet Ride

Born Pauline Mathews 53 years ago in Bradford, she was signed to Fontana as early as 1963 and pretty much stayed with the label until a brief excursion to Motown in 1970.

Her international success of course was with Elton John. This is in fact her second Northern single (the first a cover of Tammi Lynn) but certainly the most popular. Totally Wigan it even inspired yours truly to record a cover version on my own Destiny label back in 1979. It didn't sell!

Top 500 Position: **427**
Original Label: **Fontana/ Teri-De**
Current Value: **£75/£1,000**

'A legendary producer and writer with his own song'

James Conwell, Singer, Los Angeles, USA

Len Jewell
Bettin' On Love

Sadly passing away in 1996, Leonard Jewell Smith, sometimes credited as 'His Imperial Highness Sir Leonard Jewel Smith', is highly rated by most Northern Soul fans.

His involvement as partner in the Soulville production company with Leonard Graham and Jimmy Conwell were just part of this very talented guy's output. Fronting various groups in the mid 60's including The Styles on Modern, he recorded this song for his own Teri-De label gaining national release on Fontana and eventually re-issuing the record on a blue Teri-De label due to UK demand.

Top 500 Position: **428**
Original Label: **Columbia**
Current Value: **£10**

'A bizarre instrumental that could only be recognised as a Northern 45'

Phil Woodley, Soul Fan, Carlisle, UK

Phil Coulter
A Good Thing Going

Recorded in the UK but surprisingly released only in the US, Coulter is a Northern Ireland producer who has worked with Billy Connelly and Sandie Shaw amongst others.

Together with partner Bill Martin he wrote the Eurovision hit 'Puppet On A String'.

'Good Thing' represents the obscure side of Coulter's massive output which perversely became one of 'The Heart Of Soul's' biggest sounds in 1978.

Top 500 Position:	**429**
Original Label:	**Veep**
Current Value:	**£100 Issue**
	£80 Demo

'One of the true unsung heroines of 60's Soul'

Rob Thomas, Collector, Lincolnshire, UK

Cindy Scott
I Love You Baby

Simply a great dancer, 'I Love You Baby' is just the tip of the iceberg when it comes to this little lady's talent.

Ben-lee, Arctic and an extensive list of backing vocals as well as 'Time Can Change A Love', also on Veep, have made her a household name in Northern Soul circles.

Despite the widely held belief that she is the vocalist on current unreleased monster sound 'World Of Happiness' this is merely a convenient cover-up name.

Top 500 Position:	**430**
Original Label:	**Constellation**
Current Value:	**£15 Issue**
	£30 Demo

'The Duke of Soul with another Northern hit'

Jenny Galloway, Soul Fan, Suffolk, UK

Gene Chandler
Mr. Big Shot

Gene took his stage surname from the actor Jeff Chandler.

'Mr Big Shot' was probably his worst selling single. DJ Ian Levine promoted the record to the faithful at Sale's Blue Room Soul Night and it became extremely popular across the North until it was overtaken by the rarer discs coming on stream at the time.

In terms of rarity this is possibly his hardest Constellation 45.

Top 500 Position: **431**
Original Label: **Shrine**
Current Value: **£1,500**

'One of the rarest Northern collectors' labels ever'

Jim Moore,
Soul Fan, North Carolina, USA

The Cairos
Stop Overlooking Me

Fantastic discovery around 20 years ago from the wonderful Shrine label.

The group lead by Kenny Lewis who sometimes used Shirley Edwards as female background later formed The Dreams ('They Call Me Jesse James').

Prior to the Shrine output he had a brief period as lead singer of the Enjoyables on Capitol, before a one off on Buddah with 'What's Her Name' and a 45 on De-vel.

In terms of musical content this stomper has a real identity of its own, utilising a burbling bass man in the manner of the Rivingtons a few years before - this Doo-Wop style is further reinforced by an interesting unissued acapella version.

The label has been popularised by the efforts of collector Andy Rix.

Top 500 Position: **432**
Original Label: **Class**
Current Value: **£100 Issue**
£150 Demo

'Raspin' duet that's a real floorshaker'

Jack Bollington, Soul Fan, Derby, UK

Buster and Eddie
Can't Be Still

Buster is Tommy Williams and together with his brother Eddie who starred in some of the great Doo Wop groups such as the Aladins, Velvetones, Fortunes and The Colts recorded this Soul 45 in 1965 in LA.

The recording itself sound remarkably like a lot of the Renfro singles. A Wigan Casino spin in 1974, unjustly it was discarded by DJ's far too early but the plays between 1973 and '81 warrant a chart position.

An immortal sound if only for the unforgettable lyric 'I'm like a man with ants in his pants - I can't be still'.

Top 500 Position: **433**
Original Label: **Shrine**
Current Value: **£1,500**

'The legendary DC label hits the spot again'

Graham Steele,
Soul Fan, West Midlands, UK

Eddie Daye and the Four Bars

Guess Who Loves You

Originally played by DJ Richard Searling during the latter part of Wigan masquerading as Frank Wilson!

Eddie Jasper Daye had knocked around the DC recording scene for many years and was a key lounge act in the area.

Although Shrine was started in order to revive the black music industry in Washington DC along the lines of Motown, the productions have a unique quality. Almost messy and over-busy they win through by virtue of sheer power as is the case case with 'Guess Who Loves You' - despite a complete lack of melody.

Top 500 Position: **434**
Original Label: **Capitol**
Current Value: **£100 Issue**
£75 Demo

'A big late Twisted Wheel discovery, that the whole of Manchester was searching for'

Kelvin Lee, Soul Fan, Greater Manchester, UK

Patrice Holloway

Love And Desire

Sister of Motown diva Brenda who was signed to Capitol and Motown (although until recently the material remained in the vault) and finally back to Capitol.

A topsy turvy career which for a time looked fruitful as she joined the Hanna Barberra cartoon band 'Josie and the Pussycats' working alongside former Charlie's Angel, Cheryl Ladd.

Her final song for the label was 'Black Mother Goose' which is now better known by Sam Nesbitt. Recently 'Stolen Hours' has become a firm favourite too, but the activity surrounding this great double sider from '66 wins the race.

Top 500 Position: **435**
Original Label: **Elf**
Current Value: **£30 Issue**
£25 Demo

'Emerging from the very origins of the scene'

Mark Thatcher, Soul Fan, Reading, UK

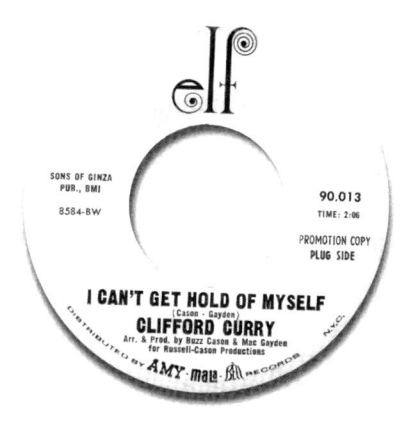

Clifford Curry
I Can't Get Hold Of Myself

Boy has he been around. Formerly with The Five Pennies, Four Jokers, The Chimes, The Hollyhocks, and The Contenders.

The Tenessee singer had a few sides that were relatively popular but this was his finest hour.

An extremely big sound at the Wheel in 1970, a UK release on Pama further added to it's popularity.

A stop-start production and a thoroughly compelling hookline add up to a real charmer that just keeps coming back on the oldies circuit.

Top 500 Position: **436**
Original Label: **Okeh**
Current Value: **£20 Issue**
£30 Demo

'That screaming reverend just sends me Tutti-Fruitti - 'Poor Dog' that I am!'

Frank Waller, Soul Fan, Merseyside, UK

Little Richard
I Don't Want To Discuss It

Born Richard Penniman, the wild man of Rock 'n' Roll recorded a series of 45's for Okeh in 1967. Recorded in California, the official 'A' side 'Hurry Sundown' was the title of a 'B' movie of the same year. The flip though is a fantastic rockin' Soul cut.

'I Don't Want To Discuss It' was a key record in putting the short lived Up The Junction allnighter in Crewe on the map whilst yet another of his Okeh sides, 'A Little Bit Of Something' also created something a stir in the early 70's.

Debonairs
Lovin' You Takes All Of My Time

Top 500 Position: **437**
Original Label: **Solid Hit**
Current Value: **£750**

'Those water damaged labels could be the only ones in existence'

Tom Cottan, Soul Fan, new York, USA

Later becoming Dawn with lead singer Tony Orlando, Joyce, Vincent Wilson and Telma Hopkins were recording for Golden World in Detroit in 1964 before signing to Don Davis at Solid Hitbound productions in 1966.

Originally discovered by record dealer Martin Koppel the scarcity of this disc has somewhat hindered its play. Very commercial and totally Supremes influenced.

The flipside 'Headache In My Heart' was released again and even got release on UK Track, the sheer rarity of 'Lovin' would suggest that it was withdrawn for some specific reason.

Marvin Gaye
Love Starved Heart

Top 500 Position: **438**
Original Label: **Tamla**
Current Value: **£50**

'Belting unreleased Motown that has deservedly been issued in CD'

Chris Jenner, Motown expert, London, UK

Marvin Pence Gaye Jnr, recorded a wealth of material with Norman Whitfield in the mid 60's.

This is one that almost got away until being discovered on a acetate that came into Richard Searling's possession in 1979 with no known title at the time, it became popular as 'It's Killing Me'.

In recent times the persistence of DJ Chris King in his dealings with Motown have seen a fluke US promo release and finally a release on CD in the UK.

Top 500 Position: **439**
Original Label: **Gordy**
Current Value: **£10**

'Motown megalomania'

Sheila Brunt, Soul Fan, Lincolnshire, UK

Martha Reeves and the Vandellas

One Way Out

The flip of 'Love Bug Leave My Heart Alone',and Reeves' top tune on the Northern scene.

Fairly common, it became a massive oldie in the 70's and remains very popular today.

A US hit in '67, the group have weathered all storms and are still performing today. With a track record spanning almost 40 years (dating back to '62 with the Del-Phis) Martha may not have too many more pleasant surprises, the hard driven 'One Way Out' may just be one of them.

Top 500 Position: **440**
Original Label: **Omen**
Current Value: **£150**

'A big beat groover, that never ceases to amaze'

John Givens, Soul Fan, Warley, UK

Brice Coefield

Ain't That Right

In and out of many R&B groups starting with The Savours, Coefield's only solo single was in 1966 recording for the A&M subsidiary Omen.

First popular at venues like the Cats, Torch and Mecca, 'Ain't That Right' is one of the unsung heroes of early 70's playlists that has retained credibility through the years becoming even bigger now then when it was first played.

One of those rarities from the 70's that wasn't reissued, booted ensuring the longevity of a song with such immortal lines as 'money can buy the Mona Lisa and money can straighten the Tower of Pisa'.

Top 500 Position: **441**
Original Label: **Capitol**
Current Value: **£50**

'To old timers this is one of the best Northern records ever!'

Jim Barratt,
Soul Fan, Greater Manchester, UK

Bobby Sheen

Dr. Love

Long, long before his superb Warner Brothers winner was ever thought about, the Twisted Wheel had already embraced this great version of the Whispers' original.

A typical big time West Coast production making full use of the Vine Street orchestration. An immensely popular sound around 1970, part of the legendary Discotheque '66 series this classic British collector's item received a UK reissue in 1972 as a result of its enduring popularity.

In more recent times Sheen has toured with the Coasters and has worked with a variety of top producers including Phil Spector and Terry Woodford.

Top 500 Position: **442**
Original Label: **Liberty**
Current Value: **£5**

'Unashamedly kitsch'

Lee Shanklin, Soul Fan, Dublin, Eire

Gary Lewis and the Playboys

My Heart's Symphony

After being discovered in 1964 as the house band at Disneyland California, the group signed to Liberty and had a spate of hits through to 1968. Gary, born Carie Levitch is the son of comedian Jerry Lewis.

The song was a hit in 1966 in the US and reached the UK Top 40 in February 1975.

Popularised by every DJ on the scene at the time after initial "Play it for a dare" spins by DJ Richard Searling, it is almost certainly the only Allnighter spin to prominently feature a Hawaiian guitar!

Top 500 Position: **443**
Original Label: **Mercury**
Current Value: **£100 Issue**
£75 Demo

'I don't understand what Northern Soul is but this is a good record I didn't want to sell to England'

Steve Kolanjan, Collector, New York, USA

Burning Bush

Keeps On Burning

Championed by DJ Ginger Taylor, this white record from New York, the creation of ace producer Artie Kornfeld, became massive at the tail end of the 70's.

Fast and furious, this one could only have made it in the 70's due to its tempo and blatantly white vocals - so white in fact that this was covered up as the 'Gems' (a female group). Nonetheless one of the real biggies of '76/'77, and in terms of danceability is a first class mover.

Top 500 Position: **444**
Original Label: **Mir-A-Don**
Current Value: **£200**

'That group harmony sells it so well'

Melvyn Christie, Soul Fan, Australia

The Ascots

Another Day

Archie Powell and Pat Thompson are the leaders of this Washington DC group, they also had a popular duet single on the same label, 'Darling, Darling'.

A true sleeper that was around for years prior to taking off in the late 80's. Very quickly it became apparent that copies were not available and the price soared.

Compare the understated production and great harmonies with the previous track by Burning Bush to understand where the scene has gone in recent years.

Top 500 Position: **445**
Original Label: **Wand**
Current Value: **£10 Issue**
£20 Demo

'The London influence surprisingly made this a Northern monster'

Gary Carlton, Soul Fan, Cambridge, UK

Chuck Jackson

Hand It Over

Once a massive influence on the Beatles, with John Lennon sighting Jackson as one of his favourite singers in an interview in NME in 1963.

Chuck is cousin to Walter (yes that Walter Jackson!) and his brother Senator, and perennial black presidential candidate, Jesse Jackson and to Ann Sexton. Following initial success with doo-wop legend The Del-Vikings, he first recorded solo for Beltone in 1960.

'Hand It Over', recorded in 1964 was a US Hot 100 No. 92 hit. This superb Wand recording, was an early favourite at clubs like the Wheel DJ's Rob Bellars & Phil Saxe, and Sheffield's Mojo that disappeared for many years until its deserving resurrection by Harborough Horace and the boys at London's legendary 100 Club.

Top 500 Position: **446**
Original Label: **Jetstar**
Current Value: **£15 Issue**
£25 Yellow vinyl demo

'A solid 45 from one of the scene's favourite artists'

Clive Holland, Soul Fan, London, UK

Bobby Patterson

My Baby's Coming Back To Me

Bobby has recently sprung to prominence via the Blackpool Soul Weekender. Patterson and his band the Mustangs had several great sides for Jetstar which incidentally was the inspiration for UK distributor of the now same name, following owner Carl Palmer having his own UK label - Pama, which in fact released one of the very first UK cover-ups via Wheel DJ Rob Bellars.

The side was Bobby's 'What A Wonderful Night For Love', which is popular again today along with 'Im In Love With You' - a mid tempo lovely from 1970. Writing for the Montclairs and recording for Paula and now his own label, Proud. Bobby is one of R&B's super Soul guys.

Bits 'n Pieces
Keep On Running Away

Top 500 Position: **447**
Original Label: **Nasco**
Current Value: **£15**

'Superb 70's sounding as fresh as the the sea breeze at Cleethorpes'

Bill Hamilton, Soul Fan, Grimsby, UK

Also known as Brothers, Sisters and Cousins. The emergence of the Winter Gardens, Cleethorpes in 1975 posed the first real threat to Wigan Casino and this was one of the key 45's to cement the rivalry.

Like the No. 1 venue they raced out of the trap with new names DJ wise and a fresh playlist which consisted of some obscure new releases. Not all were good, but a gem or two emerged like this Tennessee recording from 1974.

Features an absolutely wild falsetto lead with a thumping bass and rhythm combo.

Ron Holden
I'll Forgive And Forget

Top 500 Position: **448**
Original Label: **Challenge**
Current Value: **£40**

'Longevity never really materialised for what it is ostensibly a true Northern gem'

Carol Lerning, Soul Fan, New Jersey, USA

The R&B vocalist from Seattle later worked as a DJ for Art Laboe and his 'Oldies But Goodies' nights around the East LA area before sadly passing away in 1997.

Without wishing to become an A&R man you can hear the let down in the final mix as the chorus is outstanding and the verse so weak.

Massive at Wigan for a short time it seems likely that 'I'll Forgive And Forget' was never actually released as no one seems to have seen an issue!

Top 500 Position: **449**
Original Label: **Warner Brothers**
Current Value: **£60 Issue**
£80 Demo

'Absolutely brilliant'
Martin Porterhouse, Soul Fan, Canada

Linda Jones
I Just Can't Live My Life (Without You Babe)

Sadly passing away in March 1972, the sheer brilliance of this lady is well documented. Starting her recording career with Cub records she moved on to Atco, Blue Cat, Loma, Warner Brothers, Neptune, Turbo and Stang.

To many she is THE all-time great Soul voice. It was Ian Levine that first treated us to this truly magnificent George Kerr masterpiece.

It is a great dancer, but the rhythm is irrelevant - paling into the background as Linda delivers the vocal of a lifetime!

Top 500 Position: **450**
Original Label: **MGM**
Current Value: **£100 Issue**
£30 Demo

'The ultimate 'countdown' sound!'
Martin Waterfield,
Soul Fan, West Midlands, UK

The Jewels
We Got Togetherness

I hold my hand up to this one! This is where a DJ discovers a single lurking in a colleague's box knowing full well he could make it massive!

It really is a frantic 200 mph dancer that takes no prisoners!

In Max Millward's shop in November 1973 I purchased it from him for £15 - and promptly hammered it at the Casino. It was tailor made for that environment.

The group remain a mystery, sources reveal they were the Jewels on Dimension and Four Jewels on Dynamite and hail from New York. The flip side is a rendition of 'I'm Forever Blowing Bubbles' - I stopped short of airing that one due to my soccer loyalties being in Sheffield and not the East End of London!

The Northern Soul All Time Top 500

Top 500 Position: **451**
Original Label: **Dunhill**
Current Value: **£300 Issue**
£150 Demo

'Perhaps the greatest Northern double-sider of them all!'

Clive Hall, Soul Fan, Yorkshire, UK

Willie Hutch

The Duck/Love Runs Out

One time boyfriend of Brenda Holloway, the former singer in the Phoenetics of 'Just A Boy's Dream' fame, Willie Hutch is a legend on the scene. I first played this in March 1974 after acquiring it from dealer Simon Soussan. Simon ensured that 'The Duck' was to make its debut as Richard Temple on Stephanye - 'Love Runs Out' was left to go massive in '77.

Both sides are simply too good for words and made for a label like Mirwood. Dunhill obviously intended to cash in on Jackie Lee's dance craze.

Two totally different recordings, one a million seller the other sunk without trace. But as far as the scene is concerned Soul hero Willie Hutchinson with his work for Motown and RCA as well as with groups like the Marvellos is OUR choice North of Watford!

Top 500 Position: **452**
Original Label: **Impel/ Seventy 7**
Current Value: **£200 Impel**
£40 Seventy 7

'A really classy dancer'

Ted Jennings, Soul Fan, New Jersey, USA

Ann Sexton

You've Been Gone Too Long

This delicious 70's play from Blackpool Mecca was yet another of DJ Ian Levine's masterstrokes. Smack in the middle of the customary 'stomper' set comes this easy groover which did sell locally around Tennessee.

Originally released on Impel Ann Sexton's classic was later picked up by Seventy 7 records. A relative of Chuck Jackson, Ann went on to become a cult figure in the Southern States, performing at many Soul and Blues concerts.

Top 500 Position: **453**
Original Label: **Gordy**
Current Value: **£10 Issue**
£25 Demo

'Megadacious Motown'

Sharon Davies, Writer, London, UK

Kim Weston

Helpless

If not so easily obtainable we might be looking at the biggest record ever. The scene's obsession with rarity can easily stunt a records' growth!

Born Natalie Wilson, Kim was formerly married to William 'Mickey' Stevenson, the great Motown writer/producer. She has appeared with Marvin Gaye and Johnny Nash on vinyl and has a plethora of immaculate material in and out of the Motown vaults.

Helpless is true M-Town, with a irresistible groove, magnificent vocal and glossy production. Oh, not forgetting one of the best sax breaks ever.

If on a small label with 2 or 3 copies known, say hello to a five grand price tag!

Top 500 Position: **454**
Original Label: **MB**
Current Value: **£500**

'One of my all-time favourites!'

Horace Ott, Arranger, New York, USA

Bobby Kline

Say Something Nice To Me

I secured a few copies of this sublime 45 from the great producer/arranger and label boss Horace Ott in the 70's. Sadly at the time it was considered far too slow and I promptly off-loaded them for £6 each!

During the intervening 20 years tempos have changed and today the popularity of sounds of this quality is at a peak.

The release itself is on the local label MB which was out of Queens, New York, sadly it sold poorly despite the support of local black radio station WWRL who stayed with the cut for a month or-so.

Top 500 Position: **455**
Original Label: **Sedgrick**
Current Value: **£3,000**

'A legendary big ticket item'

Mark Evans, Collector, South Wales, UK

Don Gardner
Cheatin Kind

This is the type of investment we all wish we had made!

Sold for just £50 in the 70's, the price tag raced up to £300 in the 80's, today? Well it's a year's mortgage payments for some to buy this little gem!

This is a terrific piece of Chicago production by Jimmy Vanleer on a song executed to perfection by Gardner who had been kicking around the Windy City scene with a number of creditable 45's to his name.

Ever growing in stature, this is a fantastic haunting mid-60's cut!

Top 500 Position: **456**
Original Label: **Fantasy**
Current Value: **£6 Issue**
£10 Demo

'Totally out there in left field'

Steph Keeley, Soul Fan, Stafford, UK

Roger Collins
You Sexy Sugar Plum

The Bay area produced many a fine recording artist and Roger Collins is up there with the best.

His finest hour is the self penned 'She's Looking Good', later to be covered by Wilson Pickett.

The Northern scene had other ideas when a recent release from '74 set the UK on fire which culminating in a UK hit.

Collins himself is the all original showman, playing guitar even doing comedy!

He still writes material today for Buddy Ace and Sugar Pie Desanto among others, and obviously still receives royalties for his UK one hit wonder!

Top 500 Position: **457**
Original Label: **Mowest**
Current Value: **£10**

'Hey Mr. DJ, have you got the 'animal song'?'

Lionel Richie, Artist, USA

The Commodores
The Zoo (The Human Zoo)

This is about as freaky as you can get within the scene, as a really strange Gloria Jones/Pam Sawyer song capitalised on the changeover from traditional 60's to 70's almost new releases.

Yes, we are talking Lionel Richie here as the 'nighter patrons' warmed to the bizzare feel of the track while still doing the back drop thingy!

The record is good. A mesmerising and totally original Motown single that confirmed a perception of 'oddness' from those of the 'out crowd'. At the time we needed a few sounds of this ilk to confirm their ignorance of the truth!

Either way I love it and surprise, surprise it has been played at a few venues recently. Remember how big this really was.

Top 500 Position: **458**
Original Label: **Capitol**
Current Value: **£8 Issue**
£15 Demo

'Wreckless and totally invigorating'

John Mellor, Soul Fan, Indiana, USA

Human Beinz
Nobody But Me

A US hit in 1968 although written and recorded by the Isley Brothers several years prior. The group from Youngstown, Ohio have always remained somewhat of a cult garage band.

On these shores however they found themselves in the middle of the Ruffin's, Carr's, Mitchell's and other Soul icons to be found at the Twisted Wheel.

Well this IS a strange sort of 'Soul', but how many would be forced to admit having rushed to the dancefloor after that first guitar chord and the clarion call 'No, no, no-no-no, no no-no' from the lead 'Bein'!

The Northern Soul All Time Top 500

Top 500 Position: **459**
Original Label: **Palmer**
Current Value: **£500 Issue**
£400 Demo

'Martha's bloke sure can sing!'

Nick Leeds, Soul Fan, London, UK

Jimmy Mack

My World Is On Fire

Many rumours have circulated as to the identity of this man. It is true that Martha Reeves did comment about a guy who was a friend of Lamont Dozier and the Holland brothers, and yes Jimmy IS from Detroit...

One thing is for sure - he is NOT the Jimmy Mack of the Furys' fame, that's James McKeachin. Palmer A&R boss of the time, Joey Welz once told me he was just some local act that label boss Palmer James had signed up for a one-single deal.

Whatever the answer, if you are out there Jimmy, this is one 45 you can be really proud of!

Top 500 Position: **460**
Original Label: **Soul**
Current Value: **£10 Issue**
£30 Demo

'Yet another class act from the incredible production line'

Peter Jeffries, Soul Fan, Leicester, UK

The Velvelettes

These Things Will Keep Me Loving You

We never seem to be on a level playing field with Motown, they were indeed the Man. Utd of Northern Soul.

Even their poorest sellers are better than your average 'big money rarity'. Quite why this was never a stateside hit I do not know, but the UK saw sense and on re-release it reached the top 40 in 1971. A '66 recording from the stunning Norman Whitfield handled act it demands attention.

The group, originally known as the Barbees, were signed in 1963 and left Motown in '69, before reactivating via Motor City in 1990.

Top 500 Position: **461**
Original Label: **Cameo**
Current Value: **£10 Issue**
£20 Demo

'Discos were never the same after hearing this'

Steve Stone, Soul Fan, Nottingham, UK

Chubby Checker
At The Discotheque

Ernie Evans sure found some club action post-Twist, and he re-confirms his multiple Top 500 entries with the first of his 1965 recordings for Parkway.

The production is all too familiar as are the lyrics, the effortless ease of his vocal is superb. Many doubted Checker's vocal ability maybe possibly because of his fortuitous discovery by Dick Clark. The mid-60's really showed what he could do, and this Feldman-Goldstein-Gottehrer production confirmed his position as a top quality Soul singer.

One of THE Twisted Wheel anthems, the song symbolises the first wave of US imports to hit our scene.

Top 500 Position: **462**
Original Label: **Dotty's**
Current Value: **£800**

'A killer rarity'

Richard Lea, Soul Fan, Coventry, UK

Johnny Hampton
Not My Girl

Also recorded, though unissued, by the Platters, for me Hampton's is the definitive version. Recorded in 1965 at Ernie Stratton's Detroit studio, the label released a few 45's hoping to make their mark with the likes of the great Roger Hatcher.

This sound though was far too raw for the radio and without airplay it promptly sank. The Platters version has cropped up on a few CDs in recent times but had to wait for a 100 Club Anniversary single to hit vinyl at long last, unsurprising then that it is the Dotty's release that continues to receive the most plays at all nighters despite its rarity.

Top 500 Position: **463**
Original Label: **HFMP**
Current Value: **£15**

'THE 70s anthem!'

Mick Kozluk, Soul Fan, Sussex, UK

Larry Houston

Let's Spend Some Time Together

A local Chicago act like so many desperately trying to break out nationally, Houston would no doubt be amused to hear that his 70s classic was covered up as 'Top Cat'!

Quite why the name arose we are not sure - perhaps DJ Richard Searling has a secret love for Hanna Barberra cartoons! But joking apart, this is the type of 70s local Soul release that offered the scene some real passion - very much in the Bobby Hutton - Larry Saunders or Nate Evans bag.

Houston turned in a truly creditable performance that remained very popular for quite a while - but it is definitely now overdue for a revival!

Top 500 Position: **464**
Original Label: **Tamla Motown**
Current Value: **£10**

'Motown once again leading the field'

Johnny Bristol, Producer, USA

The Isley Brothers

Tell Me It's Just A Rumour

Taken from the 'Soul On The Rocks' LP, belatedly issued as a single in 1973 due to demand, this blockbusting stormer saw the veterans convert a new army of fans.

Sure, we all bought the hits, but this nifty dancer recorded in '67, surprised us all with it's phrenetic tempo.

I once interviewed Johnny Bristol who co-wrote it and he not only remembered the track, but liked it too!

The brothers from Cincinnati go back as far as the late 50's, but to us young 'uns it is the Motown period we most cherish.

Ronald Isley is absolutely top notch and belts the song out like he knows it's a smash. Eventually it was - but it took the North of England to make it!

Top 500 Position: **465**
Original Label: **Wand**
Current Value: **£10 Issue**
£15 Demo

'Appearing in Grimsby (Cleethorpes?) made me realise how popular I am!'

Maxine Brown, Artist, New York, USA

Maxine Brown

One In A Million

The great songwriter Rudy Clark was in the middle of a purple patch in his career following the roaring success of 'The Shoop, Shoop Song' with Betty Everett along with several other R&B hits.

His lyrical skills are most certainly evident on this New York production of 'One In A Million', a song which was incidentally covered by a number of UK acts including Karol Keyes and Northern favourites Chapter Five.

Top 500 Position: **466**
Original Label: **Soul**
Current Value: **£10 Issue**
£20 Demo

'A truly unsung Motown heroine'

Eddie Singleton,
Shrine Label Owner, USA

Barbara Randolph

I Got A Feeling

You can identify the backbone of the northern scene quite easily by listening to records like this.

A non-hit from 1967, that surfaced just one year later in the North of England to joyous delight.

We may have eventually concined this one to the local discos, but only after we had worn out the grooves during the early days of the scene!

Randolph sank under Berry Gordy, but later found another Motown connection marrying Eddie Singleton, ex-husband of Berry's first wife Raynoma Gordy.

Top 500 Position: **467**
Original Label: **Mod**
Current Value: **£30**

'This track stayed with me through 13 years of absence from the Northern scene'

Brian Reynolds, Soul Fan, UK

Madeline Bell
Picture Me Gone

It's not often that the cover version outstrips the original, in this case the by former Blue Mink lead singer, instantly recognisable in the UK as a major ('I could do with a 'D'') commercial singer.

'Picture Me Gone' is the flip to her cover of Dee Dee Warwick's 'I'm Gonna Make You Love Me' which became a US hit for Maddy. If we were compiling this chart in 1975, or indeed the days of the Wheel, then we would undoubtedly be saluting the original Evie Sands. However it is the later day popularity of this version both at Soul nights and on the eighties Scooter scene that has pushed Ms. Bell to the fore.

Top 500 Position: **468**
Original Label: **Immediate**
Current Value: **£100**

'Pat gracefully holds the rejected 'Stone' demo together'

Keith Allison, Soul Fan, Newark, UK

PP Arnold
Everything's Gonna Be Alright

Ex-Ikette PP Arnold found herself slap-bang in the middle of London's swinging sixties scene back in '67. Turning to Britain's finest sessioneers she soon scored with 'First Cut Is The Deepest', conversely 'Everything's Gonna Be Alright' did <u>not</u> enjoy 'immediate' (ouch!) success and this joyous pounding number was left in deletion boxes before the Torch club in Stoke-on-Trent made it an anthem some 4/5 years later.

A surprisingly rare non-US release.

Top 500 Position: **469**
Original Label: **Columbia**
Current Value: **£6 Issue**
£15 Demo

'What a mover from the Clapping song girl'

Carol Chadwick, Soul Fan, Oldham, UK

Shirley Ellis
Soul Time

A comeback record following her success with the 'Clapping Song' for mid-sixties hitmaker Shirley Ellis a singer/songwriter from New York.

Her husband (Lincoln Chase) also wrote most of her material and the sexy 'Soul Time' has knocked around the scene for nigh-on 30 years or more.

Simple, infectious with a wonderful brass laden groove, Ellis has a voice that is not too dissimilar to Marlena Shaw and while Shaw has continued recording and retained immense credibility Ellis has disappeared, leaving us with this fine 'bopper' to wipe the dust off occasionally. Hey, I'm not downsizing the appeal, this was super big at one stage.

Top 500 Position: **470**
Original Label: **Karen**
Current Value: **£75 Issue**
£50 Demo

'A haunting Detroit melody from the ever popular 'Popcorn''

Ian Savoury, Soul Fan, London, UK

Richard (Popcorn) Wylie
Rosemary What Happened

Discovered by DJ Ian Levine, Wylie's attempt to cash in on the Roman Polanski movie 'Rosemary's Baby' failed miserably in the American charts.

However the Northern scene of 1974 took it to heart and, with Daddy's kids on backing vocals, the legend adds another cherished collector's item, albeit on the wrong side of the Atlantic!

The Northern Soul All Time Top 500

Top 500 Position: **471**
Original Label: **Dial**
Current Value: **£6 Issue**
£15 Demo

'The sheer energy makes it a dancers dream'

Barry Hart, Soul Fan, Yorkshire, UK

Joe Tex
Show Me

The Commitments was the platform on which the song became immensely popular worldwide with the stage act that developed from the hit film - it also created a bit of a stir on initial release in 1967. However the Northern scene took it to heart via the incredibly popular Mr. M's oldies sessions at Wigan Casino. Never really considered as anything except a good Soul single until DJ Dave Evison re-invented it in the late 70's.

Tex was born Joseph Arrington Jnr in Texas and sadly left us in 1982.

Whilst it was a US hit peaking at No. 35 it bombed here, but since the Commitments launch, the song has become a firm favourite with karaoke fans and Saturday night TV hosts!

Top 500 Position: **472**
Original Label: **Parkway**
Current Value: **£8 Issue**
£15 Demo

'What a great version of Shirley and Lee'

Stefan Kurz, Soul Fan, Austria

Bunny Sigler
Let The Good Times Roll and Feel So Good

Walter (Bunny) Sigler recorded one hell of an album for Parkway in 1967. With at least 3 Northern monsters to his credit, the Philly man took on these two old standards and made them work second time around.

One of the great pioneers of Northern Soul, Sigler together with Leon Huff created many Soul classics of which this is definitely one.

One of the first real dancers at the Twisted Wheel.

Top 500 Position: **473**
Original Label: **Hot**
Current Value: **£200**

'The song that kick-started the Casino'

Mike Rollo (deceased),
DJ, Wigan Casino, UK

The Sherrys
Put Your Loving Arms Around Me

The first record played at Wigan, this was a popular wartime hit given the makeover by the daughters of Little Joe Cook, who had his own popular alternate take entitled 'I'm Falling In Love With You Baby' which was credited as 'Against My Will' on its subsequent reissue.

The girls had a minor 1962 hit on Jamie with 'Pop, Pop, Pop-Pie' but unfortunately this 1966 release featuring lead vocal by Dina Cook failed miserably and indeed proved to be their last recording.

Top 500 Position: **474**
Original Label: **Goodway**
Current Value: **£400**

'A delight to open the album and find it in there!'

Rich Rosen,
Record Dealer, Las Vegas, USA

The Silhouettes
Not Me Baby

A promo only 45 that was distributed with the group's 1967 comeback album, this single is absolutely top-notch. Whilst Doo-Wop fans remember the group for their 1958 classic 'Get A Job', it is the Motownesque Goodway recording that we view as the peak of the group's recording career - Northern Soul-wise.

A great dancer, 'Not Me Baby' features a wonderfully controlled lead vocal by Bill Horton that at time soars up to total perfection!

Originally played by DJ Colin Curtis.

Top 500 Position: **475**
Original Label: **Tamla**
Current Value: **£25 Issue**
£50 Demo

'Big-boss Motown in full effect'

Lol Charles, Soul Fan, Detroit, USA

The Marvellettes
I'll Keep Holding On

Working it's way into the chart is the totally credible 'I'll keep holding on', which has ventured in and out of Northern play for the last 32 years!

The group from Inkster, Michigan, also recorded as the Darnells, and have the distinction of having a no. 1 in the US.

In terms of Northern action, the group are near the top of the tree with absolute stunners such as 'Reachin' For Something I Can't Have', 'Only Your Love Can Save Me' amongst many others.

This 1965 Ivy Joe Hunter/Mickey Stevenson penned goodie, totally rocks your world if you are a true Motown and Northern fan.

Top 500 Position: **476**
Original Label: **Palmer/LaBeat**
Current Value: **£1,200 Palmer**
£900 LaBeat
£1,500 LB Demo

'One of the ultimate Northern SOUL records'

Clive Jones, Soul Fan, Warwickshire, UK

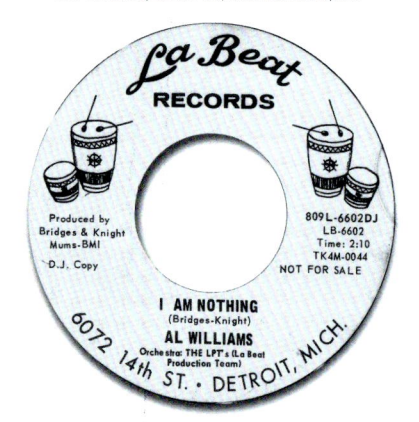

Al Williams
I Am Nothing

A Lou Beatty production as Detroit reigns supreme once again with a 45 that was issued on two separate labels - but either is rarer than snake's ears!

The vocal is typical of the time within R&B but the groove - like so many from Michigan is irresistible! DJ Richard Searling first aired the single in the late 70's and it was released in the UK on grapevine in 1979.

At most Northern Soul nights this is one of the most credible singles you're ever likely to come accross!

Top 500 Position: 477
Original Label: **Magic City**
Current Value: **£125 Issue**
£200 Demo

'A thundering Detroit Express Train sound'

Alan Riding, Soul Fan, Barnsley, UK

Thelma Lindsey

Prepared To Love You

A stupendous romper from Detroit that Blackpool Mecca unleashed on us in 1973 - although the Casino revelled in the tempo for longer.

The flip 'Why Weren't You There' is a pearl too! - Making the disc a fairly unbeatable double header. Brass and bubbling bass line force Lindsey into overdrive and her performance surely warranted an album?

Today the side is very sought after with the DJ copies in particular fetching a high price.

Top 500 Position: 478
Original Label: **A&M**
Current Value: **£200 Issue**
£125 Demo

'A gifted white artiste from LA'

Ed Cobb, Producer, Los Angeles, USA

Toni Basil

Breakaway

A lady who went on to become an ultra-famous choreographer, she had her own bubblegum punk hit with 'Mickey' in 80s.

Toni's career started with US TV's 'Shindig' series and it was in her cheerleader influenced dance style that she really made her mark, eventually being appointed as Janet Jackson's choreographer in the 80's.

'Breakaway', a 1965 recording credited to Ed Cobb and Lincoln Mayorga is typical of the period's white Teen-Soul with a Motown beat - but with that little bit extra!

Discovered languishing in a forgotten corner of Ian Levine's massive collection when Ian first sold some of his records, it was first exposed to the scene by Soul Sam in 1978.

Top 500 Position: **479**
Original Label: **Gordy**
Current Value: **£10**

'One of Edwin's true greats'

Keith Randolph, Soul Fan, Delaware, USA

Edwin Starr

My Weakness Is You

Edwin was originally in the Futuretones This is undoubtedly his best 'feel good' dancer of the 60's but was a poor seller!

Quite why Gordy released this as a 'B' side is anyone's guess

If you are a dancer, then listening to the first eight bars of this song conjure up thoughts of the spectacular twists and turns that have everybody in the club reeling with admiration.

If you are a record buyer, then the next announcement from you is SOLD! Tom Toms, girlie back up and Edwin's inimitable style all add up to another winner.

Yes we have seen him a hundred times but he is like no other. The biggest Northern Soul act ever - END OF STORY!!!.

Top 500 Position: **480**
Original Label: **MGM**
Current Value: **£150 Issue**
£75 Demo

'A neat working'

Jim Smith, Soul Fan, Michigan, USA

The Velours

I'm Gonna Change

Though originally by the Four Seasons, for whom it was bigger on the scene in 1973, the Velours' version of 'I'm Gonna Change' has been far more popular ever since.

Changing their name to the Fantastics, the Velours embarked on a brief but successful career in the UK scoring with 'Something Old Something New' in 1971 having previously recorded in the UK for MGM.

This is a brilliant version of the song which was discovered by respected Midlander - Pep, a regular DJ at the Catacombs, Wigan and a host of other classic venues.

The Tymes
What Would I Do?

Top 500 Position: **481**
Original Label: **MGM**
Current Value: **£20 Issue**
£30 Demo

'Can I have half a pound of Victory Vs... Oh and a copy of the Tymes!'

Nick Moore, Soul Fan, New York, USA

The group led by George Williams, who apparently now lives in Kent, hit the chart for the first time (see 490) with this remarkable dancer.

The appeal of this Tommy Bell penned MGM Torch monster was undoubtedly bolstered by a wealth of copies that appeared on Bradford market in 1972 so allowing every aspiring DJ to spin it in his local Soul Night!

The hook 'What would I do without you baby' makes it.

Nancy Ames
I Don't Want To Talk About it

Top 500 Position: **482**
Original Label: **Epic**
Current Value: **£10 Issue**
£15 Demo

'A love song with great depth'

Brenda Halley, Soul Fan, Winchester, UK

Out of the same stable as Lainie Hill, Lynne Randell and the like, comes a lightweight pop singer who after two other near-misses nosedived into obscurity.

A key fashion item in the 70's, 'I Don't Want To Talk About It' gave the girls a chance to twirl their flared skirts to Ames' heartfelt plea to 'I don't wanna talk about it, now we are thru'.

Totally unfashionable today, it was a veritable monster back in the mid-70's.

The Northern Soul All Time Top 500

Top 500 Position: **483**
Original Label: **Jay Boy**
Current Value: **£125**

'A late-comer to the scene, how on earth did we miss it?'

Mick Glover, Soul Fan, Gloucester, UK

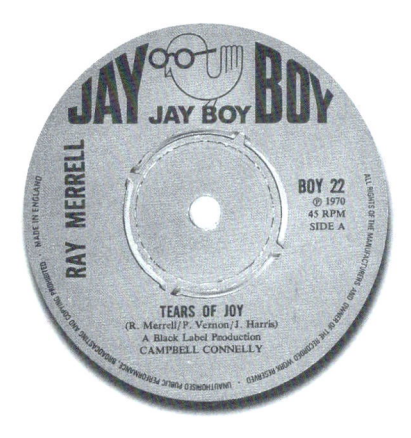

Ray Merrell

Tears Of Joy

Another unlikely Northern hitmaker as a contemporary performer of Irish Folk music! He joined Pye in 1964 moving to the indie label Windsor in 1966 before a brief career with Columbia in 1968, finally arriving at Jay Boy for his finest hour in 1970.

The 45 slots into the big beat movement well and imagine how surprised I was to receive a call from the man recently.

A massive British collector's item.

Top 500 Position: **484**
Original Label: **MGM**
Current Value: **£150 Issue**
£100 Demo

'Paris Blues and this - there's nothing more to say!'

Jimmy Smith, Soul Fan, London, UK

Tony Middleton

To The Ends Of The Earth

The old Nat King Cole number, also covered by Frank Sinatra, is really given the treatment by former Willows lead singer Tony Middleton.

Amazingly it actually received an excruciatingly rare UK Polydor release which weighs in at around the £400 mark.

Claus Ogerman's 1966 production is typical of New York R&B of the time and whilst this great cut was pretty much a non-starter in the 70's it has become one of the scene's most loved sounds in more recent times.

Eddie Parker
I'm Gone

Top 500 Position: **485**
Original Label: **Awake**
Current Value: **£1,000**

'Hopelessly pricey today'

Jeff Lealing, Soul Fan, London, UK

A frighteningly rare record that has emerged as a major player both on and off the turntable.

First discovered in the mid-70's it somehow became caught up in the plethora of quality nighter sounds. Finally when the euphoria of the time died down it was the Soul 45's like this Detroit outing that remained to take their rightful place in the Northern Soul Hall of Fame.

If you are determined to own 'I'm Gone' on vinyl but don't get paid like a professional footballer, and don't want a reissue you'll find that Billy Sha-Rae's version is pretty good as well (he also recorded a very good alternative vocal to the equally sought after September Jones track entitled 'Do It').

The Metros
Since I Found My Baby

Top 500 Position: **486**
Original Label: **RCA**
Current Value: **£50**

'The 'Sweetest One' by a great vocal group'

Gary Leeds, Soul Fan, London, UK

This is the group's second release from their 'Sweetest One' album which also includes a brilliant cover of the O'Jays' 'I'll Never Forget You' which has become very popular in its own right.

This is the group led by Percy L. Williams and should not be confused with the combo who worked for 1-2-3 and Ra-Sel. A Detroit based outfit, the group actually had a 80's outing for Soul King, but further investigation reveals this to in fact be a 1970 recording. Tracked down by Goldmine Soul Supply recently, this later recording can be heard on 'Detroit Soul From The Vaults'.

Top 500 Position: **487**
Original Label: **Money**
Current Value: **£10**

'To many this is the finest Soul record EVER'

Dave Godin,
Journalist and Soul Fan, Sheffield, UK

Bettye Swann
Make Me Yours

Simply irresistible. The single released here on CBS, didn't fair too well although it attained a Top 30 hit in the US in 1967.

The Wheel were the first to champion the classic, not without comment from journalist Dave Godin who went on record to say that it is his favourite 45 ever. Born Betty Jean Champion in Louisiana, she found fame recording for Money an independent label from Los Angeles.

Prior to the 1967 sessions in LA, she was a member of The Fawns who had recorded for Chancellor at the time. Scene wise it's now played regularly, although impossible to find a place for it during the stompified 70's. Bobby Montgomery, ZZ Hill and High Inergy have all done covers of the vintage song.

Top 500 Position: **488**
Original Label: **Argo**
Current Value: **£250**

'A stunning vocalist'

Trevor Wheatstone, Soul Fan, Yorkshire, UK

Herb Ward
Strange Change

Discovered by the legendary Harthon team of Randolph Styles and Weldon McDougall III, Philadelphian Ward recorded for Argo in 1965 before moving onto Buddy and of course RCA Victor where he released another true Northern classic 'Honest To Goodness'. A recent revelation is that Herb is in fact Herb Johnson who recorded for Toxsan, Brunswick, Tyler and Arctic and the like.

Fans of Herb's wonderful voice will find some interesting alternate versions of his City of Brotherly Love output on Goldmine Soul Supply CD 'The Northern Soul Of Philadelphia Vol. 2'.

Top 500 Position: **489**
Original Label: **Impact**
Current Value: **£200**

'A real oddity from Detroit'

Mick Bradley, Soul Fan, Derbyshire, UK

Nabay
Believe It Or Not

Odd is being kind to this real esoteric piece of nonsense.

I believe the rarity of the disc to be the platform for it's popularity, however I confess to loathing it.

The Impact waxing, recorded in 1966 - where else but Detroit, is still one of THE choice collectors' items and with the constant harmonized chant it has become a perennial favourite.

Nabay was in fact a Lebanese singer who was finally released from Impact records because owner Harry Balk owed him a favour!

Top 500 Position: **490**
Original Label: **Parkway**
Current Value: **£15 Issue**
£30 Demo

'Terrific group harmony'

Billy Jackson, Producer, USA

The Tymes
Here She Comes

From 1964 one of the 'old' sounds is saluted as George Williams, the lead singer, follows the beat to the anthemic conclusion that 'here she comes walking down the street'.

The label was certainly on a hot streak at the time with masses of hits from Dee Dee Sharp, The Orlons, Chubby Checker etc.

Maintaining a positive association with producer Billy Jackson, the band had a stop start career but did make some wonderful records on Cameo, Winchester and Columbia.

Sadly the band finally split up in the 80's, shortly after their comeback which produced 'You Little Trustmaker' and 'Miss Grace' for RCA.

Top 500 Position: **491**
Original Label: **Duke**
Current Value: **£10 Issue**
£20 Demo

'Mr Blue with arguably his best Soul 45'

Bob Hall, Soul Fan, Manchester, UK

Bobby Bland
Shoes

Robert Calvin Bland from Rosemark, Tennessee is no stranger to the scene despite being world renowned as a Blues master. His recordings go back as far as 1949, and with several other classic Duke singles ('Call On Me', 'Yum Yum Tree', 'Good Time Charlie' and 'I'm Not Myself Anymore') he has a fair fan base within our world too.

'Shoes' represents his true anthem, after originally becoming a constant play at the 100 Club, London in the 80's.

Top 500 Position: **492**
Original Label: **La Beat**
Current Value: **£1,500**

'A meaty Detroit bounder'

Barry Williams,
Soul Fan, Greater Manchester, UK

Lester Tipton
This Won't Change

Lou Beatty formed a label par excellence in 1965. Nearly all the releases are sought after, and as for the talent, well try these for size, Al Williams, Nelson Sanders, The Masqueraders, Don Hart and James Shorter, who all contributed to the labels creativity. Club wise, Tipton's effort is first class, with the usual Detroit backtrack and a strong vocal.

As usual, great record, but with no promotion - thank heavens for Northern Soul. Tipton moved to LA later where he was unfortunately the victim of a murder in the late 80's.

Top 500 Position: **493**
Original Label: **Oliver**
Current Value: **£50 Issue**
£60 Demo

'Vintage Wigan'

Beth Stevens, Soul Fan, Wigan, UK

The Steinways

My Heart's Not In It Anymore/ You've Been Leading Me On

Yvonne Gearing, who went on to front the Glories, here sings lead with New York group The Steinways on this fabulous double sider.

'My Heart's' was the official Wigan A-spin but in recent years the flip has become the main play. Backed by abundant rich male harmonies the underrated Gearing really is firing on all cylinders on this one!

Top 500 Position: **494**
Original Label: **Smoke**
Current Value: **£300**

"Misery has finally trapped me and it's tearing me apart'... Just brilliant!'

Dave Makin, Soul Fan, Stafford, UK

George Blackwell

Can't Lose My Head

A truly massive New Jersey Soul beater from local legend and label owner George Blackwell.

Discovered by the Frost brothers in Loughborough of all places, it was promptly sold on to Ian Levine for the princely sum of £3! Of course Ian turned it into pure Northern Soul gold - the rest is history!

Smoke is a sought after collector's label, recorded in 1966 in Newark, N.J. 'Can't Lose My Head' is a real jewel in this label's crown.

Top 500 Position: **495**
Original Label: **Motown**
Current Value: **£10 Issue**
£20 Demo

'About as sublime as you can get'

Gary Walsh, Soul Fan, Wichita, Kansas, USA

The Spinners
Sweet Thing

It is all too easy to compile Motown 45s, they single handedly inspired the scene. The Spinners have their contributions well aired by the North and this 1964 recording is one of many. Bobby Smith breezes through the song (probably in one take) without breaking sweat, Henry Famborough, Pervis Jackson and Billy Henderson routinely perform the background.

The rhythm as you can imagine is 'top drawer', with Earl Van Dyke and the Soul Brothers rhythmically creating another 'hot ticket'.

The Twisted Wheel grabbed hold of it and not surprisingly the 45 is one of the first you might manage to own as your collection builds.

Top 500 Position: **496**
Original Label: **Roulette**
Current Value: **£6 Issue**
£10 Demo

'A slick female groover'

Mark Mason, Soul Fan, Derby, UK

The Fuzz
I'm So Glad

Formerly the Passionettes on Path records and hanging around the scene as a 'B list' item in 1974, the Blackpool Mecca was its official home with DJ Ian Levine working to death. Far too slick for the stomp-stomp niters, it's the groove that makes this a single that helped change the course of the scene.

The group's other single for Calla was 'I Love You For All Seasons' which became a big US Soul hit.

Top 500 Position: **497**
Original Label: **Atco**
Current Value: **£10 Issue**
£15 Demo

'Pioneering the youth culture'

Wayne Kennedy, Collector, UK

Tami Lynn
I'm Gonna Run Away From You

Recorded in 1964 it took 7 years to finally make it, peaking at No.4 in '71. Old hand Bert Berns took control of the typical girl group outing and engaged 19 year old Tami a young New Orleans singer to smother the song in kisses.

The ultimate 'dance 'round yer 'andbag' 45 which every disco in town got behind when re-released on Mojo.

Amazingly it also got a release on UK Atlantic in 1965.

Lynn was first discovered by Harold Battiste and signed to his AFO label, fronting a studio band called the AFO Executives. In more recent times a new discovery entitled 'Runaway' from a rare French EP has simmered along, and with an obvious connection to her longer title, it reprises the massive hit which we adore so much.

Top 500 Position: **498**
Original Label: **Spring**
Current Value: **£40 Issue**
£20 Demo

'The big sing-a-long song of '75'

John Matthews, Soul Fan, Birmingham, UK

Flower Shoppe
You've Come Along Way Baby

Phil Flowers from Washington, DC was a noted performer, writer, manager etc. He recorded a couple of killers for Dot in 1966 amongst many other labels.

Resurfacing in the early 70's, he secured a deal for his new band the aptly named Flower Shoppe. Recording one single for the Spring label with very risqué lyrics about 'the hairs below your waist' - no-wonder it totally bombed leaving the way open for us to once again at least give it a good funeral!

Top 500 Position: **499**
Original Label: **Mirwood**
Current Value: **£6 Issue**
£12 Demo

'One of the true 60's dance crazes'

Karen Grayson, Soul Fan, Upminster, UK

The Olympics
Baby Do The Philly Dog

From the great Mirwood label, 50's hitmakers The Olympics from Compton, California, rip it up with this 'club classic' from 1966.

Fred Smith the chief architect behind the great Mirwood sound cultivates a terrific performance from lead singer Walter Ward.

The song is typical of the time, and I find it difficult to understand how it missed the boat, especially after the success of 'Cool Jerk' among other dance anthems.

Whenever I hear it, fond memories of the legendary Rick Ricardo's record store in San Francisco spring to mind, with shop owner Rick executing the dance to perfection!

Top 500 Position: **500**
Original Label: **Evolution**
Current Value: **£50**

'A pumping bass treat'

Jon Maxtead, Soul Fan, London, UK

Larry Santos
You Got Where You Want Me

This typical Bobby Paris type stomper from 1970 is a pure one-off for Santos.

The intro makes it and, combined with gravelly vocal and killer hook we have the perfect scenario for the one shot wonder.

Though first popular when baggy trousers, bowling shirts were the order of the day, the song still receives a healthy following, but 1975 was undoubtedly it's golden year. Larry himself went on to record for legendary disco label Casablanca in the Seventies.

A reasonable cover version exists by Jon Ford on Philips, but if you can't get enough of Santos, get the LP version - it's a whole verse longer!

bubbling under

Every Soul Boy and Girl has their favourite sounds, I'm sure that as you read the Top 500 that you were surprised not to see a record that is particularly close to your own heart, I have my own personal favourites many of which didn't make it either, however you may well find it in this list of 100 spins that nearly made the chart...

1.	Billy Arnell	Tough Girl	Holly
2.	Bob Brady and the Concords	Everybody's Going To A Love In	Chariot
3.	Marsha Gee	Baby I Need You	Uptown
4.	Jackie Wilson	I Get The Sweetest Feeling	Brunswick
5.	George Lemons	Fascinating Girl	Gold Soul
6.	Tommy Ridgley	My Love Is Getting Stronger	International City
7.	George Pepp	The Feeling Is Real	Coleman
8.	Ollie Jackson	The Day My Heart Stood Still	Magnum
9.	Gwen Owens	You're Wanted (And Needed)	Velgo
10.	Linda Jones	My Heart Needs A Break	Loma

Below: Linda Jones considered by many to be the greatest Soul singer of them all.

The Northern Soul All Time Top 500

11.	**Bob Wilson**	Suzie's Serenade	Sound Stage 7
12.	**Channel 3**	The Sweetest Thing	Dakar
13.	**Dee Edwards**	All The Way Home	D-Town
14.	**Paris**	Sleepless Nights	Doc
15.	**The Four Larks**	Groovin' At The Go-Go	Tower
16.	**Donna Coleman**	Your Love's To Strong	Avin
17.	**Elbie Parker**	Please Keep Away From Me	Veep
18.	**Joanie Sommers**	Don't Pity Me	WB
19.	**Benny Spellman**	Fortune Teller	Minit
20.	**The Ellusions**	You Didn't Have To Leave	Lamon
21.	**JJ Barnes**	Sweet Sherry	Volt
22.	**Steve Flannagan**	I've Arrived	Era
23.	**Marv Johnson**	I Miss You Baby	Gordy
24.	**John Leach**	Put That Woman Down	Lawn
25.	**Danny Monday**	Baby Without You	Modern
26.	**Marvin Holmes**	You Better Keep Her	Brown Door
27.	**Jimmy Ruffin**	He Who Picks A Rose	Motown Acetate
28.	**The Brooks Brothers**	Looking For A Woman	Tay
29.	**Lorraine Chandler**	I Cant Hold On	RCA
30.	**The Trammps**	Hold Back The Night	Buddah
31.	**The Fiestas**	Think Smart	Old Town
32.	**Jnr Walker and the Allstars**	I Ain't Going Nowhere	Tamla Motown
33.	**Edwin Starr**	Backstreet	Ric-Tic

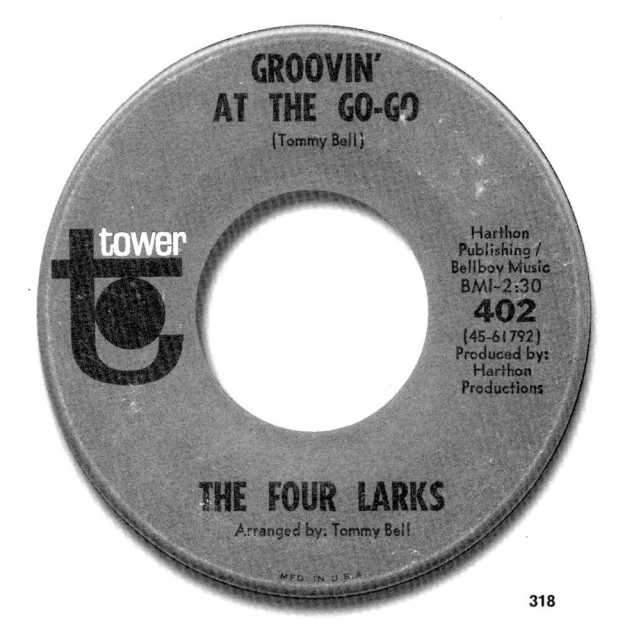

Opposite: Bob and Earl, the Mirwood duo who recorded many Northern classics. Earl Nelson (left) was of course also Jackie Lee and recorded a host of Northern Soul sounds of his own, including 'Would You Believe' and the wonderful 'Darkest Days'.

Left: Another great Harthon production... 'Groovin At The Go-Go' from the Four Larks also features 'I Still Love You (From The Bottom Of My Heart)' on the reverse which has also become popular in recent years.

The Northern Soul All Time Top 500

The Northern Soul All Time Top 500

34.	**Terry Callier**	Ordinary Joe	Chess
35.	**Dalton Boys**	I've Been Cheated	VIP
36.	**Johnny Honeycutt**	I'm Coming Over	Triode
37.	**The Twans**	I Can't See Him Again	Dade
38.	**The Trends**	Thanks For A Little Lovin	ABC
39.	**Bobby Womack**	So Many Sides Of You	Beverly Glenn
40.	**Bunny Sigler**	Follow Your Heart	Parkway
41.	**Jackie Wilson**	I Don't Want To Lose You	Brunswick
42.	**Danny Woods**	You Had Me Fooled	Correc-Tone
43.	**Martha Starr**	Love Is The Only Solution	Thelma
44.	**The Belles**	Don't Pretend	Mirwood
45.	**International GTOs**	I Love You Baby	Rojac
46.	**Jimmy Robins**	I Just Can't Please You	Jerheart
47.	**Just Brothers**	Carlena	Garrison
48.	**The Elgins**	Heaven Must Have Sent You	VIP
49.	**Williams & Watson**	A Quitter Never Wins	Okeh
50.	**Lew Kirton**	Heaven In The Afternoon	Alston
51.	**Charles Johnson**	Never Had A Love So Good	Alston
52.	**The Construction**	Hey Little Way Out Girl	Sync 6
53.	**Jay D Martin**	By Yourself	Tower
54.	**The Magnificents**	My Heart Is Calling	Dee Gee

Left: The Magnificents' 'My Heart Is Calling' has been 'bubbling under' in the popularity stakes for many years. Its was co-written by Marc Gordon and Frank Wilson and despite the misspelling of Jobete it was in fact a Motown published tune.

The Doo-Wop influenced 'B' side 'On Main Street' has also received plays over the years.

55.	**Lynne Vernado**	Wash And Wear Love	Gator
56.	**Yvonne Vernee**	Just like You Did Me	Sonbert
57.	**Mickey Moonshine**	Name It You Got It	Decca
58.	**The Gypsies**	It's A Woman's World	Old Town
59.	**Moses Dillard**	I'll Pay The Price	Mark IV
60.	**Major Lance**	Investigate	Okeh
61.	**Florence Devore**	Kiss Me Now	Phi-Dan
62.	**Benzine**	Village Of Tears	Parkway
63.	**Norma Jenkins**	The Airplane Song	Maltese
64.	**Bud Harper**	Wherever You Were	Peacock
65.	**Little Eddie Taylor**	I Had A Good Time	Peacock
66.	**Margaret Mandolph**	Something Beautiful	Planetary
67.	**The Parliaments**	Heart Trouble	Revilot
68.	**Barbara Lynn**	Take Your Love And Run	Jetstream
69.	**Vala Regan**	Fireman	Atco
70.	**Phil Terrell**	Love Has Passed Me By	Carnival
71.	**André Brasseur**	The Kid	Palette
72.	**The Wonderettes**	I Feel Strange	Ruby
73.	**Damon Fox**	Packin' Up	Fairmount
74.	**Rita and the Tiaras**	Gone With The Wind Is My Love	Dore
75.	**Mandrill**	Never Die	Polydor
76.	**The Formations**	At The Top Of The Stairs	Bank
77.	**Donald Lee Richardson**	You Got Me In The Palm Of Your Hand	Soulville
78.	**Jean Carter**	Like One	Decca
79.	**First Choice**	This Is The House (Where Love Died)	Scepter

Left: Moses Dillard, the man behind 'I'll The Price', 'Pretty As A Picture' and many more great tracks both common and very rare.

Opposite: Edward Hamilton who with the Arabians recorded many Soul gems for the likes of Grand Prix and Mary Jane. Note that though this is a Mary Jane release it is written by Melvin Davis and produced by Lou Beatty of La Beat fame.

Left and Below: Marvin Smith, lead singer of the Artistics

80.	**The Whispers**	Remember Me	Soul Clock
81.	**Donna King**	Take Me Home	Hot Line
82.	**Edward Hamilton and the Arabians**	I'm Gonna Love You	Mary Jane
83.	**Jesse Johnson**	Left Out	Old Town
84.	**Yvonne and the Violets**	Cross My Heart	Barry
85.	**Marvin Smith**	Have More Time	Brunswick
86.	**The Soul Brothers Six**	Thankyou Baby For Loving Me	Atlantic
87.	**Debbie Dean**	Why Am I Lovin' You	VIP
88.	**Sandra Philips**	World Without Sunshine	Broadway
89.	**The Petals**	You Can't Close The Windows To Your Heart	Mercury
90.	**Bobby Williams**	I've Only Got Myself To Blame	Sure-Shot
91.	**Bobby Jason**	Wall To Wall Heartaches	Ranwood
92.	**Cajun Heart**	Got To Find A Way	Warner Brothers
93.	**Cliff Nobles**	My Love Is Getting Stronger	Atlantic
94.	**The Isley Brothers**	My Love Is Your Love	MFP LP
95.	**The Inspirations**	Your Wish Is My Command	Midas
96.	**Charles Sheffield**	It's Your Voodoo Working	Excello
97.	**The Ambassadors**	Too Much Of A Good Thing	Pee-Vee
98.	**William Powell**	Heartache Souvenirs	Power House
99.	**Bobby Treetop**	Wait 'Til I Get To Know Ya	Tuff
100.	**Lorraine Silver**	Lost Summer Love	Pye

The Northern Soul All Time Top 500

essential cd purchases

If you are returning to Northern Soul after a break or are new to the scene and wish to learn more you will no-doubt be wanting to track down those sounds that give you a buzz. But if you have looked in a sales box recently you'll probably have had a shock! Today records that cost a few cents each when they were first pressed are frequently, tens, hundreds and sometimes even thousands of pounds each!

If you are a serious vinyl junkie this is of course of no surprise and will probably just slow you down a little! However for the majority of us most rare vinyl is today beyond our means, however in recent years an enormous amount of classic Northern Soul, rare and not-so rare, has become available not as the notorious bootlegs of old but as legitimate releases on top quality CDs from companies like Kent and Goldmine/Soul Supply as well as the Majors who have at last woken up to the true quality of those subsidiary label 'turkies' they have buried in their vaults!

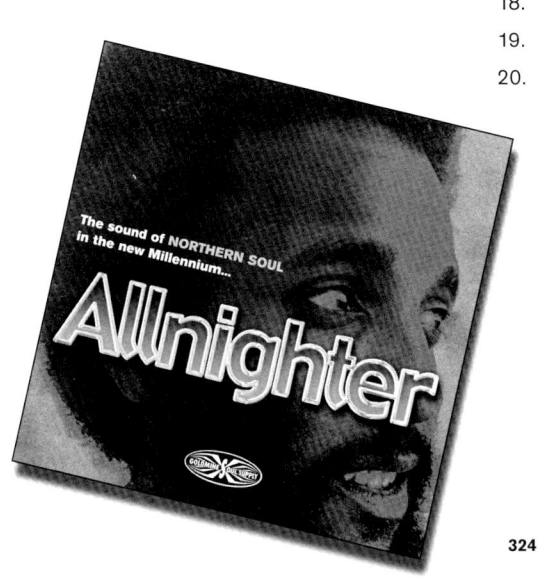

Here's 20 excellent CD purchases that contain most of the Top 500 - to get you started!...

1. Out On The Floor (GOLDMINE/SOUL SUPPLY)
2. The Wigan Casino Story (GOLDMINE/SOUL SUPPLY)
3. The Golden Torch Story (GOLDMINE/SOUL SUPPLY)
4. Big In Wigan (KENT)
5. Jumping At The Go-Go (BMG)
6. Soul Self Satisfaction (UNIVERSAL)
7. Gettin' To Me (KENT)
8. This Is Northern Soul (DEBUTANTE)
9. Soul Time (SONY)
10. The Wigan Casino 25TH (GOLDMINE/SOUL SUPPLY)
11. Rare, Collectable And Soulful (KENT)
12. The Essential Northern Soul Story (GOLDMINE/SOUL SUPPLY)
13. Turning My Heartbeat Up (BMG)
14. Northern Soul Floorshakers (BMG)
15. Shrine, The Rarest Soul Label (KENT)
16. It's Okeh Up North (XCLUSIVE)
17. The Twisted Wheel Story (GOLDMINE/SOUL SUPPLY)
18. Out on The Floor Again (GOLDMINE/SOUL SUPPLY)
19. For Millionaires Only (GOLDMINE/SOUL SUPPLY)
20. Soul Underground (SEQUEL)

Left: Northern Soul continues to develop and grow, 'Allnighter' from Goldmine/Soul Supply captures the essence of today's scene with a host of top current sounds including the massively popular unissued Harthon version of Cliff Nobles' 'Love Is All Right' by Jesse James.

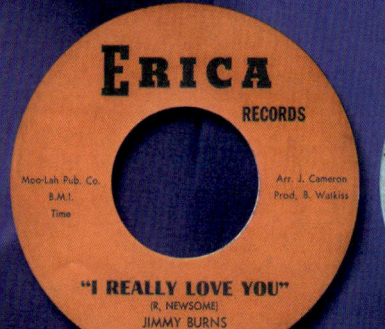

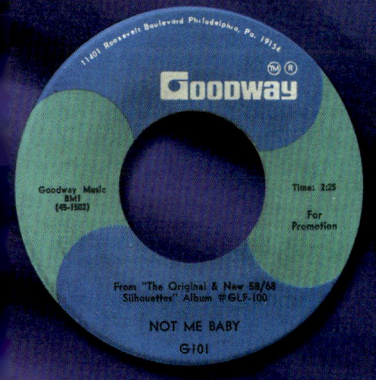

Wonderful rarities!... Classic floorpackers that cost a king's ransom!

Above: 'Ciao Baby' grooving with hip white Australian Ms. Lynne Randell!

Right: The wonderful Barbara Lynn, her first ever UK performance at Blackpool Weekender 1999, supported by Snake Davies and his band.

Wonderful rarities!... Classic floorpackers that cost a king's ransom!

Above: The wonderful Dynamics, famed on our scene for their Top Ten release 'Yes I Love You Baby', also re-issued on Laurie records.

Left: Dee Dee Sharp, famous for 'What Kind Of Lady', her first great Northern sounds from the Wheel 'Standing In The Need Of Love' backed with 'I Really Love You'. She went on to marry the 'boss', Kenny, becoming Dee Dee Sharp-Gamble.

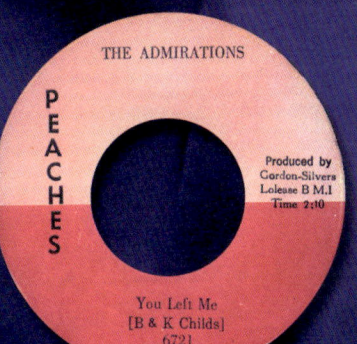

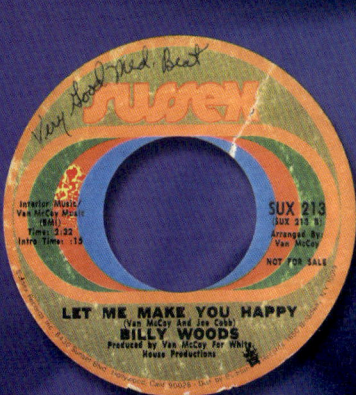

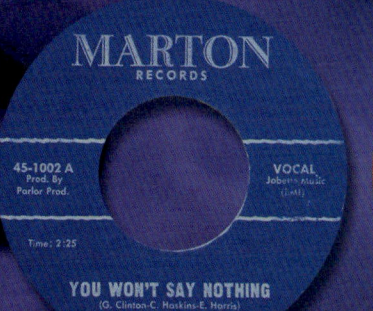

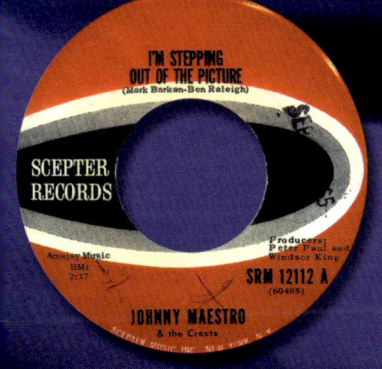

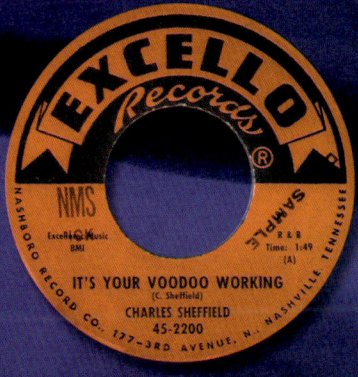

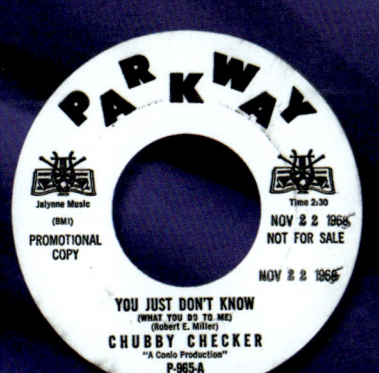

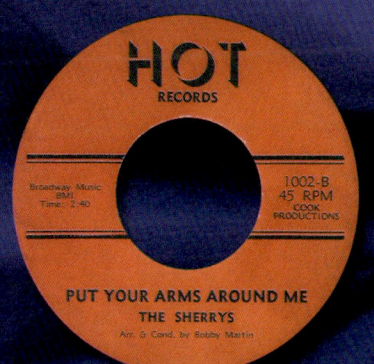

Wonderful rarities!... Classic floorpackers that cost a king's ransom!

THE HIT SOUNDS

SHOTGUN
Junior Walker and the All Stars
Soul 35008

ASK THE LONELY
The 4 Tops
Motown 1073

STOP IN THE NAME OF LOVE
The Supremes
Motown 1074

WHEN I'M GONE
Brenda Holloway
Tamla 54111

NOWHERE TO RUN
Martha and the Vandellas
Gordy 7039

Hits Are Our Business

TAMLA MOTOWN RECORDS
2640 W. GRAND BLVD., DETROIT, MICHIGAN

Above: Brenda Holloway (here live at Burnley Mechanics). A very likeable lady, when she finally performed on these shores courtesy of promoter Chris King in 1997 she took the scene by storm.

Left: Motown - responsible for an incredible number of Northern sounds - here on this one ad we see four classics (not counting Ms. Ross' effort!).

Left: Not you might think the most likely of Soul fans! Chris Tarrant, Bob Carolgees and the Phantom Flan Flinger seen here with Kev at a Soul Alldayer in Nottingham in the 1980.

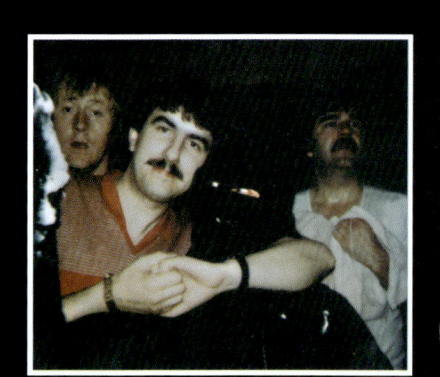

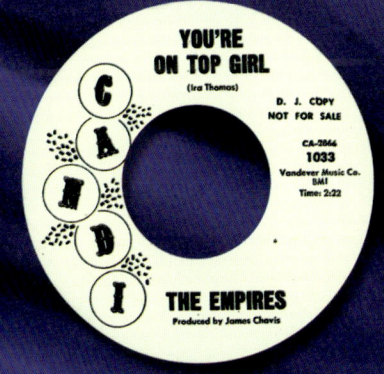

Wonderful rarities!... Classic floorpackers that cost a king's ransom!

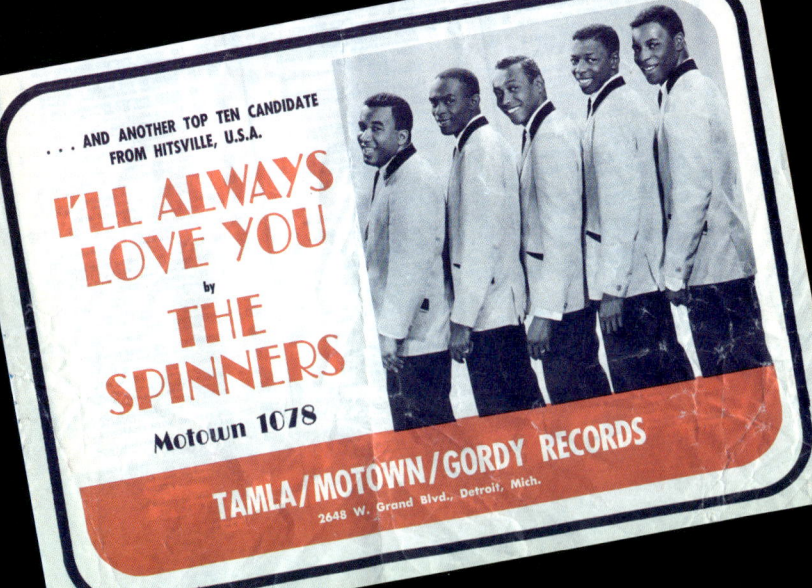

Above: The incomparable Jackie Wilson turns in a thunderous performance.

Left: Perennial favourites the Spinners with their alltime classic 'I'll Always Love You' which is placed right up at number 64 in our chart.

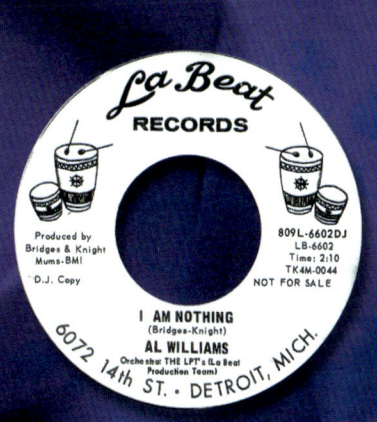

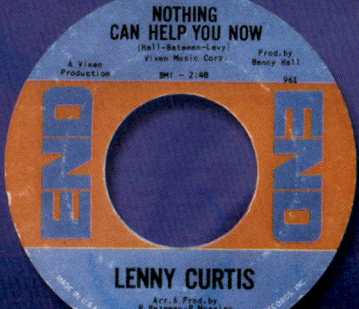

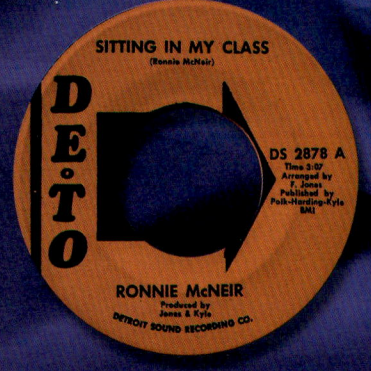

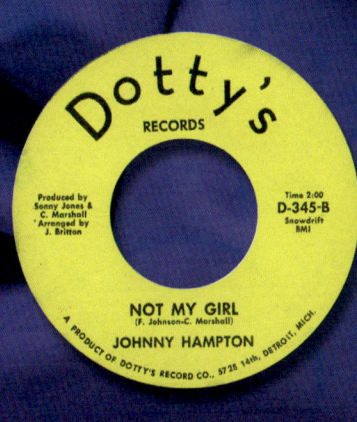

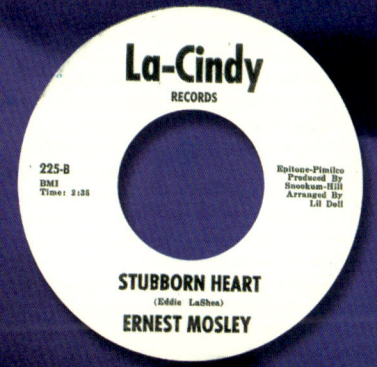

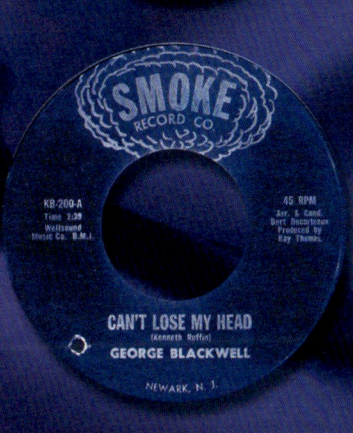

Wonderful rarities!... Classic floorpackers that cost a king's ransom!

The late, great Junior Walker making his sax sing sax live on stage in 1970.

TOP TENS
northern soul over the years

Over the years the scene has resonated to 1000s of different sounds, many like PJ Proby's 'Nicky Hoeky' or Elvis' 'Rubberneckin' popular at the Wheel in the late 60's or Spirogyra - played at Blackpool Mecca in the late 70's are completely out of step today. Massive in their day (though especially in the early days perhaps only locally as with Billy Stewart's 'Exodus' - the number one sound at the Mojo but little played at the Wheel), some do remain popular, but others are completely unplayable today.

Though the Twisted Wheel in fact opened in 1963 in Brazenose Street, Manchester, and only moved to the end of Whitworth Street in mid-1966, I have chosen 1967 as the starting point of the charts. This was a key year in the history of Northern (or rather at the time 'Rare') Soul with the move perhaps being the catalyst it became the period of sea change when in general the scene moved away from the hardcore R&B of Bo Didley and John Lee Hooker and, driven by Motown Stax/Atlantic and Mirwood, towards concentration on Soul. 1967 was basically the first year of recognisable Northern Soul.

This year by year series charts the most popular dancefloor sounds, as established by careful research and the recollections of fans and DJs of the time - it is as accurate as possible.

1967 THE TWISTED WHEEL/THE MOJO - The Inaugural Dance Chart

WADE IN THE WATER	RAMSEY LEWIS	(CHESS)
YOU'VE BEEN CHEATIN'	The IMPRESSIONS	(ABC)
DON'T MESS WITH MY MAN	IRMA THOMAS	(RON)
IT KEEPS RAININ'	FATS DOMINO	(IMPERIAL)
THE FIFE PIPER	The DYNATONES	(ST. CLAIR)
HEY-SAH-LO-NEY	MICKEY LEE LANE	(SWAN)
AT THE DISCOTHEQUE	CHUBBY CHECKER	(PARKWAY)
CALL ON ME	BOBBY BLAND	(DUKE)
LA DE DA I LOVE YOU	INEZ and CHARLIE FOX	(SYMBOL)
KICK THAT LITTLE FOOT SALLY	ROUND ROBIN	(DOMAIN)

Storming the floor, dancefloor top tens over the years...

1968 THE TWISTED WHEEL - We're Off And Runnin'!

GIRLS ARE OUT TO GET YOU	The FASCINATIONS	(MAYFIELD)
NOTHING CAN STOP ME	GENE CHANDLER	(CONSTELLATION)
LET THE GOOD TIMES ROLL	BUNNY SIGLER	(PARKWAY)
MR BANG BANG MAN	LITTLE HANK	(SOUND STAGE 7)
A LITTLE PIECE OF LEATHER	DONNIE ELBERT	(GATEWAY)
THE BEAT	MAJOR LANCE	(OKEH)
DUST MY BROOM	IKE and TINA TURNER	(TANGERINE)
EVERYBODY'S GOING TO A LOVE IN	BOB BRADY	(CHARIOT)
SOMEDAY WE'RE GONNA LOVE AGAIN	BARBARA LEWIS	(ATLANTIC)
GOOD TIME TONIGHT	The SOUL SISTERS	(SUE)

1969 THE TWISTED WHEEL - Getting Bigger...

THE RIGHT TRACK	BILLY BUTLER	(OKEH)
A LIL' LOVIN' SOMETIMES	ALEXANDER PATTON	(CAPITOL)
AT THE TOP OF THE STAIRS	The FORMATIONS	(BANK)
DO THE TEMPTATION WALK	JACKIE LEE	(MIRWOOD)
BREAKOUT	MITCH RYDER and the DETROIT WHEELS	(NEW VOICE)
SHE BLEW A GOOD THING	The POETS	(SYMBOL)
WHAT'S WRONG WITH ME BABY	The INVITATIONS	(DYNO VOICE)
AGENT DOUBLE-O SOUL	EDWIN STARR	(RIC TIC)
DR LOVE	BOBBY SHEEN	(CAPITOL)
THERE'S NOTHING ELSE TO SAY	The INCREDIBLES	(AUDIO ARTS)

Opposite: Laying the foundations... a selection of some of the pioneering sounds of our scene.

Left: Twisted Wheel Memberships came in an assortment of colours year by year, from Green to Purple, Orange and Red etc.

Below: Fontella Bass turning it on at the Wheel in 1970, though she had a limited number of Northern tracks she was always a very popular performer.

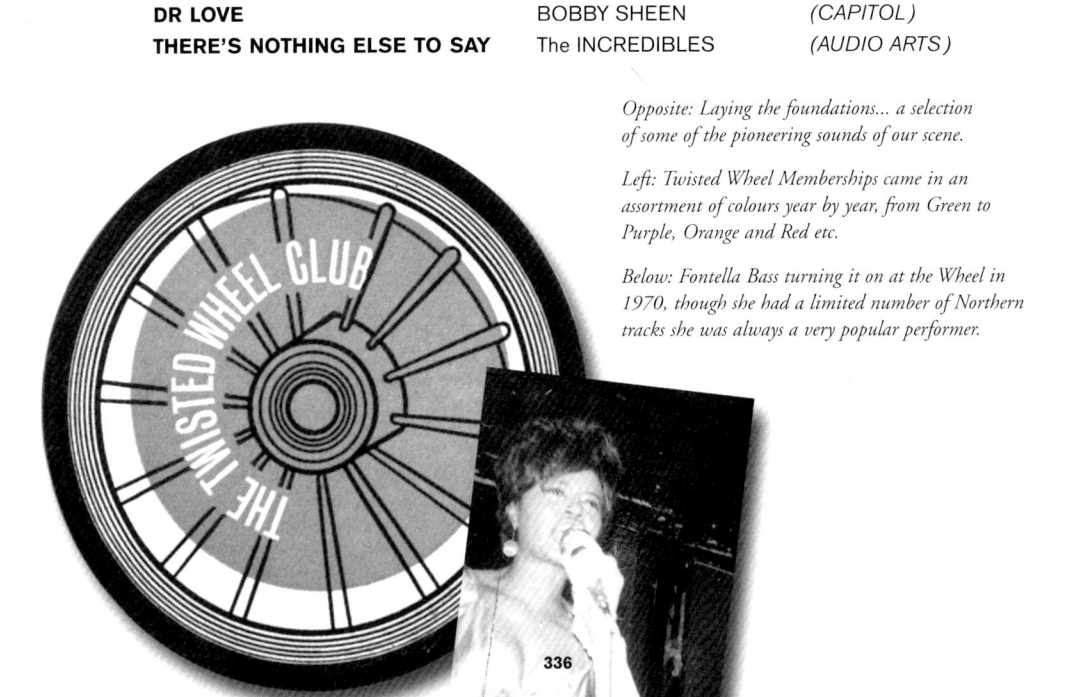

BOOM
RECORDS
Dreamland Music, Inc. - Doraflo Music, Inc. BMI - 2:56
BM 60,038
AMP 45-60,016-B
Produced by Richard Gottehrer for Sire Productions
PROMOTIONAL COPY NOT FOR SALE
SKATE (Part I)
(Gottehrer, Parrish)
DEAN PARRISH
Arranged and Conducted by: BURT KEYES
DISTRIBUTED BY ABC-PARAMOUNT RECORDS, INC. MADE IN U.S.A.
Hi
45-2116
Time: 2:31
LOVE IS AFTER ME
(Porter; Hayes)
CHARLIE RICH
Producer: Natalie Rosenberg
DISTRIBUTED BY LONDON RECORDS, INC.
PaMeLiNe
PAM-100-A
Ala King Music BMI Time: 2:30
Produced By Richard "Popcorn Wylie" Arranged By Mike Terry
GOIN' TO A HAPPENING
(Richard Wylie-T. Hester)
TOMMY NEAL
© 1967
ROMUR RECORDS
Scoebert Music Co. (BMI) Phy-4721A
R0011
Produced by Roscoe Murphy, Jr. Time: 2:27
D.J.
D.J.
LET'S COPP A GROOVE
(R. Murphy & R. Murphy)
BOBBY WELLS
Arranged by Leon Mitchell
ROMUR RECORD CO. © 1967 Phila.
YEW
N-1001-A
SIDE A
45 RPM
ODOM & NEIBURG (BMI)
TIME: 2:50
IN A MOMENT
(THE INTRIGUES)
THE INTRIGUES
PROD. & ARR. BY MARTIN AND BELL
DIST. BY A. A. RECORDS, INC.
NEW YORK, N. Y. 10019
abc
RECORDS
45-10831
AMP 45-13412
PROMOTIONAL COPY NOT FOR SALE
CAN'T SATISFY
(Curtis Mayfield)
THE IMPRESSIONS
Arranged and Conducted by: JOHNNY PATE
A PRODUCT OF ABC-PARAMOUNT RECORDS INC., A SUBSIDIARY OF AMERICAN BROADCASTING COMPANIES, INC.
★★ AIN'T NO SOUL LEFT IN THESE OLE SHOES ★★
(Arthur Resnick - Joe Levine)
SCEPTER RECORDS
T. M. Music (BMI) Time: 1:57
SCE 12161 A
(60761)
RONNIE MILSAP
Produced by Huey P. Meaux
SCEPTER MUSIC INC., NEW YORK, N. Y.
GALAXY
Promotional
Not For Sale
TIME: 2:16
Cireco - BMI
Arranged by Ray Shanklin
750
(F-2587)
SHE'S LOOKING GOOD
(Collins)
RODGER COLLINS
MY WEAKNESS IS YOU
(Whitfield, McMullen, Grant)
GORDY
G-7071
Produced By N. Whitfield
EDWIN STARR
A TRADEMARK OF MOTOWN RECORD CORP. © 1966
LIKE
RECORDS
LK-10226
301
INSTRUMENTAL
SOCK IT TO 'EM J. B. - PART I
REX GARVIN
(And The Mighty Cravers)
DISTRIBUTED BY ATLANTIC RECORD SALES, 1841 BROADWAY NEW YORK, N.Y.
NORTH STATE
RECORDS
Box 183
Goldsboro, N. C. 27530
1001
(SoN 56641)
Time — 2:35
North State Music ASCAP 45 RPM
GIRL WATCHER
(Buck Trail-Wayne Pittman)
THE O'KAYSIONS
BILLY'S BAG
(Billy Preston)
BILLY PRESTON
45
VJ
VEE-JAY RECORDS
PROMOTIONAL COPY
VJ 653
64-6743 — Time 2:30
Greene Music Inc.
ASCAP
Arranged by Rene Hall

1970 THE TWISTED WHEEL / THE BLUE ORCHID-
The Imports Come Rolling In!

YOU GOT TO PAY THE PRICE	AL KENT	*(RIC TIC)*
LOVE, LOVE, LOVE	BOBBY HEBB	*(PHILIPS)*
FOLLOW YOUR HEART	BUNNY SIGLER	*(PARKWAY)*
GOING TO A HAPPENING	TOMMY NEAL	*(PAMELINE)*
YOU GET YOUR KICKS	MITCH RYDER and the DETROIT WHEELS	*(NEW VOICE)*
BACK STREET	EDWIN STARR	*(RIC TIC)*
NEVER FOR ME	The MILLIONAIRES	*(PHILIPS)*
TAKE YOUR LOVE AND RUN	BARBARA LYNN	*(ATLANTIC)*
COMPETITION AIN'T NOTHING	CARL CARLTON	*(BACKBEAT)*
THAT BEATIN' RHYTHM	RICHARD TEMPLE	*(MIRWOOD)*

1971 BLACKPOOL MECCA AND THE CATACOMBS -
Spreading The Word

HERE I GO AGAIN	ARCHIE BELL and the DRELLS	*(ATLANTIC)*
OUT ON THE FLOOR	DOBIE GRAY	*(CHARGER)*
LOVE ON A MOUNTAIN TOP	ROBERT KNIGHT	*(RISING SONS)*
CIGARETTE ASHES	JIMMY CONWELL	*(MIRWOOD)*
I'LL NEVER FALL IN LOVE AGAIN	BOBBY FREEMAN	*(AUTUMN)*
QUEEN OF FOOLS	BARBARA MILLS	*(HICKORY)*
YOUR GONNA MAKE ME LOVE YOU	SANDI SHELDON	*(OKEH)*
IN ORBIT	JOY LOVEJOY	*(CHECKER)*
THE NEXT IN LINE	HOAGY LANDS	*(LAURIE)*
THE WAY YOU BEEN ACTING LATELY	AL KENT	*(RIC-TIC)*

Opposite: Laying the foundations... Further sounds from the early days of Northern Soul.

Right: Inez and Charlie Foxx's frequent live appearances across the UK at clubs like the Wheel, the Mojo and the Blue Orchid helped ensure the popularity of their many cuts, 'Tightrope' was of course particularly popular, but 'Come By Here' is a classic that is largely forgotten today.

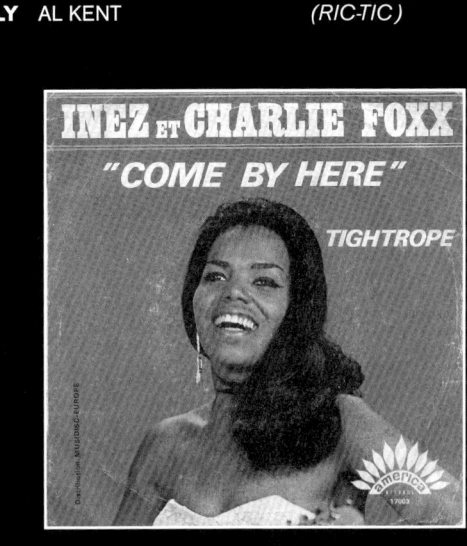

PHILIPS
FOR BROADCAST ONLY NOT FOR SALE
40400
PHW1-38236
Champion Music Co. & Double Diamond Music Co. (BMI) 2:50
Vocal Producer: Jerry Ross From PHILIP'S Album, SUNNY PHM-200-212
LOVE LOVE LOVE
(Ross-Renzetti)
BOBBY HEBB
Arranged by Joe Renzetti
Ric-Tic
RECORDS
Myto Music BMI Time: 2:42 ZTSC-107342
RT-107 Arranged by: Sanders & Starr Production Supervisor: Richard Parker
BACK STREET
(C. Hatcher & B. Sharpley)
EDWIN STARR
A Solid Hitbound Production
Capitol
LOVE AND DESIRE
(Billy Page)
PROMOTION RECORD
NOT FOR SALE
September II Music BMI—2:30
Produced by: Billy and Gene Page
PATRICE HOLLOWAY
Arranged and Conducted by Gene Page
5778
(45-56590)
JERK AND TWINE
(Smith - Davis - Allison)
Chevis Music BMI (13609) Time 2:38
CHESS
JACKIE ROSS
1920
MANUFACTURED BY CHESS PRODUCING CORP., CHICAGO, ILLINOIS, U.S.A.
SHARE
RECORDS
Van McCoy Music Inc. T.M. Music (BMI)
SR 102 A Time: 2:35
SWEET AND EASY
(J. Cobb, V. McCoy)
THE VAN McCOY STRINGS
Arr. Prod. & Cond. By Van McCoy
"HAPPY"
Taken From Album "Bound To Happen" STS-2014
(B. T. Jones, W. Bell)
stax
STA-0038 ST-0157-PL East/ Memphis Music, BMI Time: 2:31 June, 1969
WILLIAM BELL
Prod. by Booker T. Jones
Mirwood
RECORDS
Hangra Music (BMI) (67-3091-B)
5532 Time 2:22
THAT BEATIN' RHYTHM
(Smith, Cornwell, Graham, Colbert)
RICHARD TEMPLE
Produced by Leonard Jewell Smith & Sir Graham
A Soundville Production
LONDON
AMERICAN RECORDINGS
DEMONSTRATION SAMPLE NOT FOR SALE
MADE IN ENGLAND
A
45 RPM
Recorded by PHIL OF SOUL Philadelphia
Pedro Music
TIME 2.42
HL 10212
℗ 1968
RELEASE DATE: 26—7—68
HITCH IT TO THE HORSE
(Jesse James)
THE FANTASTIC JOHNNY C
WHAT'S WRONG WITH ME BABY!
(Linzer - Randell)
dynoVoice
210 6540 Saturday Music, Inc. (BMI) Time: 2:35
PLUG SIDE
THE INVITATIONS
Arr. & Cond. By CHARLES CALELLO
Prod. by DENNY RANDELL and SANDY LINZER
DISTRIBUTED BY BELL RECORDS INC., N.Y.C.
FROM THE TEACHER TO THE PREACHER
(Eugene Record-Barbara Acklin-Carl Davis)
Brunswick
MANUFACTURED BY BRUNSWICK RECORD CORP., NEW YORK, U.S.A.
GENE CHANDLER And BARBARA ACKLIN
Vocal With Orchestra Directed By GERALD SIMS
PRODUCED BY CARL DAVIS
ARRANGED BY WILLIAM SANDERS
(2:24)
mala
RECORDS
MALA 575 8283-BW Tree Publishing BMI Time: 2:17
PROMOTION COPY PLUG SIDE
A PAPA DON PRODUCTION
MY ELUSIVE DREAMS
(C. Putman - B. Sherrill)
Moses & Joshua Dillard
Arr. by Moses Dillard
A PRODUCT OF BELL RECORDS, INC., N.Y.C.
NOLA RECORDS
Bonatemp Pub. Co. BMI - 2:28 Arr. by Wardell Quezergue
721 174-1594 Whorley-Burley Prod.
LET'S GO BABY (Where The Action Is)
Robert Parker
ROBERT PARKER
Dist. by DOVER RECORDS, INC., N.O.LA. 70130

Storming the floor, dancefloor top tens over the years...

1972 THE GOLDEN TORCH AND THE CATACOMBS - All-Nighter Fever

SLICED TOMATOES	The JUST BROTHERS	(MUSIC MERCHANT)
ONE WONDERFUL MOMENT	The SHAKERS	(ABC)
WHAT WOULD I DO	The TYMES	(MGM)
WANTING YOU	APRIL STEVENS	(MGM)
TIMES A WASTING	FULLER BROS	(SOUL CLOCK)
BOK TO BACH	FATHERS ANGELS	(MGM)
I'VE GOT SOMETHING GOOD	SAM and KITTY	(FOUR BROTHERS)
LIKE ONE	JEAN CARTER	(DECCA)
THUMB A RIDE	EARL WRIGHT	(CAPITOL)
I'M IN A WORLD OF TROUBLE	The SWEET THINGS	(DATE)

1973 THE TORCH, BLACKPOOL MECCA, WIGAN CASINO AND VA VA'S - Boom Time!

THERE'S A GHOST IN MY HOUSE	R DEAN TAYLOR	(VIP)
WHAT'S IT GONNA BE	SUSAN BARRETT	(RCA)
BABY HIT AND RUN	The CONTOURS	(TAMLA MOTOWN)
TEMPTATION IS CALLING MY NAME	LEE DAVID	(COLUMBIA)
TAKE AWAY THE PAIN STAIN	PATTI AUSTIN	(CORAL)
STRANGER IN MY ARMS	LYNN RANDELL	(EPIC)
I HURT ON THE OTHER SIDE	JERRY COOK	(CAPITOL)
WAIT TILL I GET TO KNOW YA	BOBBY TREETOP	(TUFF)
PUT YOUR ARMS AROUND ME	The SHERRYS	(HOT/JJ)
TAINTED LOVE	GLORIA JONES	(CHAMPION)

Left: Torch membership, basically they hoped it would last until January 31st!

Opposite: The Torch - only all-nighter in the country! And Edwin on New Year's eve - It was twenty-past twelve before people noticed it was January 1st 1973!

Inset Right: 'Show me the back street', so sad to see... The site of the Golden Torch in a Tunstall side street, awaiting demolition.

THE TORCH - TUNSTALL Stoke-on-Trent
The Country's only...
ALL-NIGHTER
TWELVE SO FULL - SOULFUL HOURS.... 8-30 pm - 8-30 am

JANUARY LINE UP...
Saturday, January 6th
"Our Thank You All-Nighter" featu[ring]
Keith Minshull - Alan Day - Mart[yn Ellis]
AND TO JOIN US AT THE No. 1 EVERY W[EEK]
The North's No. 1 Spinner
TONY JEBB
Free Tickets available from pay desk on request

[Satu]rday, January 13th
[T]he Kingspinners
[Ad]mission 50p Members Guests 60p (before [...])

[Saturda]y, January 20th
[...] Heat Soul Dancer '73 Competit[ion]
[PRI]ZE £50
[Admissio]n 50p Members 60p Guests

[Saturday,] January 27th
[...] All-Nighter
[PROCE]EDS TO LOCAL CHARITIES
[5]0p Members 60p Guests

[MAJO]R LANCE, ROY C, SAM [...]

Verve
SPECIAL DISC JOCKEY REC[ORD]
THE SHALIMARS
STOP AN[D]
TAKE A
LOOK AT
YOURSELF
2:12
VK-10388
(66-VK-224)
Tender Tunes/Marlinda Music
BMI
Arr., Cond. & Prod. by
Hal Wess
A Kama Sutra
Production
(Jackson-Barnes)
MGM RECORDS—A DIVISION OF METRO-GOLDWYN-MAYER INC.—MADE IN U.S.A.

THE TORCH - Tunstall - Stoke-o[n-Trent]
New Year's Eve All Night Ball
8-30 pm to 8-30 am
SUNDAY, DECEMBER 31st

EDWIN STARR
John McFlair Band
Keith Minshull
Martyn Ellis
Alan Day

£1-50 Members & Guests
January 13th ... A[...]

The Torch - Tunstall Stoke-on-Trent
The Country's No. 1
All-Nighter
TWELVE SO-FULL SOULFUL HOURS
NOW OPEN EVERY SATURDAY
8-30 p.m. to 8-30 a.m.

341

FEBRUARY
Programme Details

RIGHT ON [...]

Storming the floor, dancefloor top tens over the years...

1974 WIGAN CASINO AND BLACKPOOL MECCA - The Ultimate Year?

AFTERNOON OF THE RHINO	MIKE POST COALTION	(WARNER BROS)
IF THAT'S WHAT YOU WANTED	FRANKIE BEVERLY and the BUTLERS	(SASSY/GAMBLE)
IF YOU EVER WALKED OUT OF MY LIFE	DENA BARNES	(INFERNO)
I NEVER KNEW	EDDIE FOSTER	(IN)
DOUBLE COOKIN	CHECKERBOARD SQUARES	(VILLA)
YOU DON'T LOVE ME	The EPITOME OF SOUND	(SANDBAG)
I GOT TO FIND ME SOMEBODY	The VEL-VETS	(20TH CENTURY)
I'LL ALWAYS NEED YOU	DEAN COURTNEY	(RCA)
I CAN'T HELP LOVIN YOU	PAUL ANKA	(RCA)
GOODBYE NOTHING TO SAY	NOSMO KING/JAVELLS	(PYE)

1975 WIGAN CASINO AND BLACKPOOL MECCA - More Golden Years

BETTER USE YOUR HEAD	LITTLE ANTHONY and the IMPERIALS	(VEEP)
SEVEN DAY LOVER	JAMES FOUNTAIN	(PEACHTREE)
JOB OPENING	The DEL-LARKS	(QUEEN CITY)
COOL OFF	The DETROIT EXECUTIVES	(PAMELINE)
GET OUT	HAROLD MELVIN	(LANDA)
THE CHAMPION	WILLIE MITCHELL	(HI)
CASHING IN	VOICES OF EAST HARLEM	(JUST SUNSHINE)
LANDSLIDE	TONY CLARKE	(CHESS)
PLEASE OPERATOR	TONY and TYRONE	(ATLANTIC)
I CAN'T CHANGE	LORRAINE CHANDLER	(RCA)

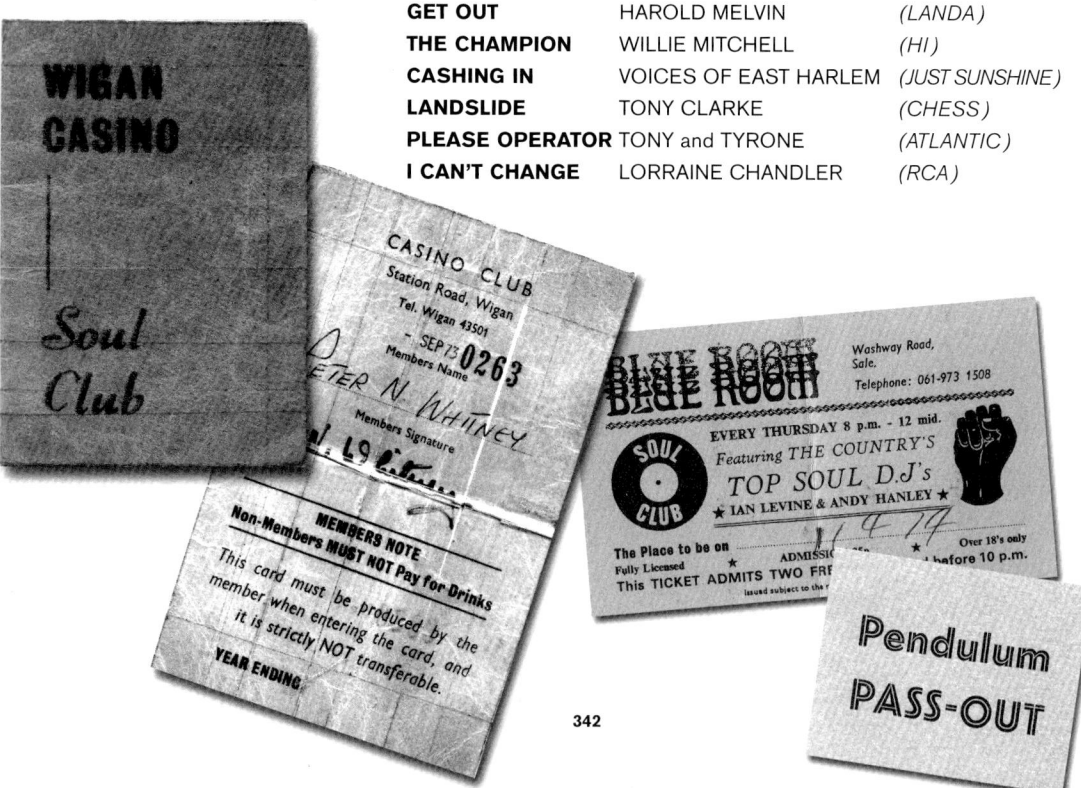

BLACKPOOL MECCA

The place that's established beyond any shadow of doubt as the Country's No. 1 Soul Place
SOLID SOUL SENSATIONS

As promised here are the fabulous details of our Soul attractions in the month of December.

EVERY SATURDAY
as usual
The Highland Room
open 7-30 p.m. — 2-00 a.m.
D.J.s
IAN LEVINE
COLIN CURTIS

There is nowhere to compare to the Mecca and this bumper Xmas Soul Fiesta proves it.

News soon of our coming January attractions

SUNDAY, DECEMBER 9th
our very first
ALL-DAYER
12-00 noon — 12-00 midnight
D.J.s: IAN LEVINE, COLIN CURTIS
Live on stage—straight from the U.S.A.
THE HEARTS OF SOUL
doing two performances

Monday December 24th
Christmas Eve
The Highland Room
is open from 7-30 p.m. — 2 a.m.
with the best and rarest Soul Sounds in the Country
presented by
D.Js: IAN LEVINE, COLIN CURTIS

SUNDAY, DECEMBER 23rd
our second
ALL-DAYER
12-00 noon — 12-00 midnight
D.J.s: COLIN CURTIS
IAN LEVINE
and live on stage, not only
DON DOWNING
but also
BIG AL DOWNING
and their entire Revue doing two shows

MONDAY, DECEMBER 31st
NEW YEAR'S EVE
Let the New Year in with Soulful style in the
Highland Room
open from 7-30 p.m. — 2-00 a.m.
and letting in the New Year are the Country's top two Soul Spinners
IAN LEVINE and COLIN CURTIS

Don't miss this Soulful Christmas and New Year at the Mecca

Storming the floor, dancefloor top tens over the years...

1976 WIGAN CASINO, BLACKPOOL MECCA AND CLEETHORPES WINTER GARDENS - The Crowds Just Kept On Coming...

SEND HIM BACK	The POINTER SISTERS	(ATLANTIC)
I'M COMUN' HOME IN THE MORNUN'	LOU PRIDE	(SUEMI)
SO IS THE SUN	WORLD COLUMN	(TOWER)
MY WORLD IS ON FIRE	JIMMY MACK	(PALMER)
BURNING SENSATION	ROBBY LAWSON	(KYSER)
YOU DON'T KNOW WHERE YOUR INTEREST LIES	DANA VALERY	(COLUMBIA)
EVER AGAIN	BERNIE WILLIAMS	(BELL)
YOU GOT ME WHERE YOU WANT ME	LARRY SANTOS	(EVOLUTION)
COCHISE	PAUL HUMPHREY	(BLUE THUMB)
HEAVEN MUST BE MISSING AN ANGEL	TAVARES	(CAPITOL)

1977 WIGAN CASINO, BLACKPOOL, THE RITZ, CLEETHORPES, ST IVES - But Will It Last?

SHAKE A TAIL FEATHER	JAMES and BOBBY PURIFY	(BELL)
WHEN I'M GONE	BRENDA HOLLOWAY	(TAMLA)
7 DAYS 52 WEEKS	CODY MICHEALS	(MERBEN)
IF YOU LOVED ME	PEGGY MARCH	(RCA)
GIVE UP GIRL	CONNIE QUESTALL	(DECCA)
HEY LITTLE GIRL	MISS DD PHILLIPS	(EVOLUTION)
THIS GETS TO ME	POOKIE HUDSON	(JAMIE)
YOU DON'T KNOW WHERE YOUR INTEREST LIES	FIVE and a PENNY	(POLYDOR)
A LOT OF LOVE	TAJ MAHAL	(COLUMBIA)
GET IT OFF MY CONSCIENCE	The LOVELITES	(LOVELITE)

Left: The Mecca, Colin Curtis and Ian Levine's interest in more than just stompers led to the development and change of the Blackpool sound.

S.O.S.
(HEART IN DISTRESS)
Parkway 971

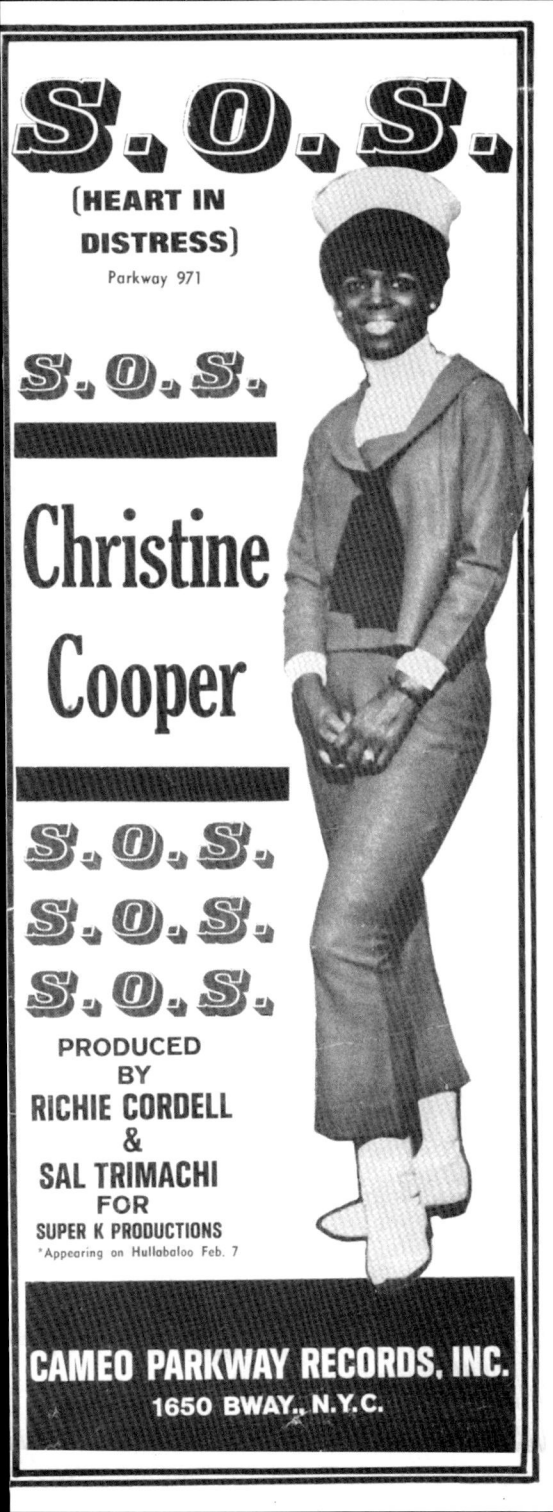

S.O.S.

Christine Cooper

S.O.S.
S.O.S.
S.O.S.

PRODUCED BY
RICHIE CORDELL
&
SAL TRIMACHI
FOR
SUPER K PRODUCTIONS
*Appearing on Hullabaloo Feb. 7

CAMEO PARKWAY RECORDS, INC.
1650 BWAY., N.Y.C.

Brunswick IS BEAUTIFUL

BABY BOY
755419

FRED HUGHES

BEAUTIFUL FROM BRUNSWICK

AFTER YOU
755421

BARBARA ACKLIN

Brunswick RECORDS

Storming the floor, dancefloor top tens over the years...

1978 WIGAN CASINO, PETERBOROUGH, THE RITZ
- Strange Times...

DO I LOVE YOU	FRANK WILSON	(SOUL)
THAT'S WHY I LOVE YOU	The PROFFESSIONALS	(GROOVE CITY)
TIME	EDWIN STARR	(GORDY)
TAKE MY HEART	MARY SAXTON	(QUALITY)
WHY DID YOU PUT IT TO ME BABY	The SHORT PEOPLE	(GUSTO)
MY LIFE WITH YOU	The TRADITIONS	(BAR CLAY)
SPRING RAIN	SILVETTI	(SALSOUL)
DON'T PITY ME	SUE LYNN	(RCA)
SAY GIRL	LONNIE RUSS	(KERWOOD)
THE ICE MAN	BILLY WATKINS	(ERA)

1979 WIGAN CASINO, MORECAMBE AND PETERBOROUGH -
The Dreaded Pop Influence!

NINE TIMES OUT OF TEN	MURIEL DAY	(PAGE ONE)
COUNTRY GIRL	VICKIE BAINES	(PARKWAY)
STOP	BOBBY DIAMOND	(COLUMBIA)
STOP AND YOU'LL BECOME AWARE	HELEN SHAPIRO	(COLUMBIA)
THIS MAN IN LOVE	The NEW WANDERERS	(READY)
THEME FROM JOE 90	RON GRAINER	(PYE)
SHE SAID GOODBYE	BILLY HAMBRIC	(DRUM)
I CAN'T STAND TO LOSE YOU	EJ CHANDLER	(SOS)
THE WHO WHO SONG	JACKIE WILSON	(BRUNSWICK)
MOVE ON UP	CURTIS MAYFIELD	(CURTOM)

Left: The Apollas who produced many Northern hits on the Warner Brothers owned Loma label, (and later for Warner themselves). Most notably the wonderful, storming 'Mr. Creator' for WB which appears in the Top 500 chart and 'I Just Can't Get Enough Of You' for Loma.

Right: David and the Giants' Mecca monster 'Superlove' was quickly followed by the popularity of 'Ten Miles High'. Though both were very poppy they at least had a Muscle Shoals pedigree - giving them a degree of credibility not shared by the likes of Muriel Day or Ron Grainer's 'Joe 90' theme.

DAVID AND THE GIANTS

TEN MILES HIGH!

Debut disc with HIT written all over it! Out of Rick Hall's Fame Productions, Muscle Shoals, Alabama. Capitol's Crazy Horse. Get it now through your CRDC guy.

Crazy Horse. 1300 b/w "I'm Down So Low"

CRAZY HORSE

Capitol Records

Storming the floor, dancefloor top tens over the years...

Below and Left: The Casino just made its 500th all-nighter, but its closure in 1981 and demolition became a powerful image that symbolised the need for the scene's re-birth. Ironically this sea change had already started in the last days of Station Road.

1980 WIGAN CASINO AND ST.IVES -
A Time Of Great New Discoveries - At Last!

BORN A LOSER	DON RAY	(RCA)
BROKEN HEART ATTACK	The SWEET	(SMASH)
I DON'T LIKE TO LOSE	CECIL WASHINGTON & The GROUP	(PROPHONICS)
WHAT HAPPENED TO YESTERDAY	MR SOUL	(GENUINE)
YOU KNOW HOW TO LOVE ME	PHYLLIS HYMAN	(ARISTA)
I'LL PAY THE PRICE	MOSES DILLARD	(MARK IV)
NO SECOND CHANCE	The DEADBEATS	(STRATA)
I NEED MY BABY	JACKIE BEAVERS	(REVILOT)
RAINING TEARDROPS	The DEMURES	(BRUNSWICK)
YOU WON'T SAY NOTHING	TAMALA LEWIS	(MARTON)

1981 THE TOP OF THE WORLD, STAFFORD, THE 100 CLUB
and the death of WIGAN CASINO - The End Of The 2nd Era

I LOVE HER SO MUCH	The MAJESTICS	(LINDA)
I'M LOSING AGAIN	RAY AGEE	(SOULTOWN)
CAN'T GET OVER THESE MEMORIES	JON and the WEIRDEST	(TIE)
I HAVE A GIRL	The MAGNETICS	(RA-SEL)
NOTHING'S TOO GOOD FOR MY BABY		
	The SPRINGERS	(WHALES)
I'LL BE YOUR CHAMPION	JIMMEY 'SOUL' CLARKE	(SOULHAWK)
LOST AND FOUND	KENNY CARLTON	(BLUE ROCK)
HEARTACHE SOUVENIRS	WILLIAM POWELL	(POWERHOUSE)
PLEASE KEEP AWAY FROM ME	ELBIE PARKER	(VEEP)
LADY IN GREEN	The MAGNETICS	(BONNIE)

1982 STAFFORD - Birth Of A New Generation

I'D THINK IT OVER	SAM FLETCHER	(TOLLIE)
LOVE IS A SERIOUS BUSINESS	ALFIE DAVISON	(MERCURY)
I GOT A GOOD THING GOING	The EXECUTIVE FOUR	(JULMAR)
HEARTACHES I CAN'T TAKE	The GAY LETTES	(BLACK JACK)
DON'T LET HIM HURT YOU	Les CHASONETTES	(SHRINE)
UNDER YOUR POWERFUL LOVE	JOE TEX	(DIAL)
SOMETHINGS BAD	The NOMADS	(MO-GROOVE)
BABY WHAT HAPPENED TO OUR LOVE	The RINGLEADERS	(M-PAC)
GUESS WHO LOVES YOU	EDDIE DAYE and 4 BARS	(SHRINE)
OH YEAH YEAH YEAH	VIVIAN CAROL	(MERBEN)

Capturing perfectly Stafford's fresh new attitude, Sam Fletcher's incredible 'beat ballad' 'I'd Think It Over' would simply have never been played a couple of years earlier.

The Northern Soul All Time Top 500

Storming the floor, dancefloor top tens over the years...

1983 STAFFORD - A Time Of Real Innovation

SUSPICION	The ORIGINALS	(UNISSUED MOTOWN)
I JUST KEPT ON DANCING	DOUG BANKS	(ARGO)
DOWN AND OUT	GEORGE FREEMAN	(VALIANT)
I WON'T BE COMING BACK	JD BRYANT	(SHRINE)
SHOWSTOPPER	The CASHMERES	(HEM)
ALL OF MY LIFE	(UNISSUED VIRTUE ACETATE)	
I'M CATCHING ON	BETTY LLOYD	(BSC)
IT'S TOO LATE FOR YOU AND ME	GLADYS NIGHT and the PIPS	(SOUL ACETATE)
NAUGHTY BOY	JACKIE DAY	(PHLECTRON)
THINK SMART	The FIESTAS	(OLD TOWN)

1984 STAFFORD - 60's Newies - Collector's Heaven!

NO OTHER WAY	The CAUTIONS	(SHRINE)
LET LOVE LIVE	The VELVELETTES	(VIP UNRELEASED)
THE ONLY WAY IS UP	OTIS CLAY	(ECHO)
WHAT DIFFERENCE DOES IT MAKE	KENNY SHEPPARD	(MAXX)
STOP OVERLOOKING ME	The CAIROS	(SHRINE)
GIRL I LOVE YOU	The TEMPTONES	(ARCTIC)
JUST A FOOL	JERRY GAINEY	(VERVE)
I CAN'T LET YOU GO	JOHNNY SUMMERS	(YORK TOWN)
DON'T ACCUSE ME	The SQUIRES	(GEE)
LOOKY LOOKY	The BROTHERS GRIMM	(MERCURY)

Left: Vocal genius Emanuel Laskey, a hero to the 60's Newies scene for his variety of superlative recordings.

Opposite: A selection of Stafford sounds - though some had previously been known generally they were very different from their Wigan counterparts.

CORTLAND
SOMEBODY HELP ME
(Granger - Jenkins - Strong)
C-112 B
BMI – 2:29
DONALD JENKINS & THE DELIGHTERS
112
a B. C. Production
SHRINE RECORDS
SR 111-2
2:21
Produced by Eddie Singleton
STOP OVERLOOKING ME
(Keni Lewis)
THE CAIROS
Arranged by Dale Warren
TURNTABLE
RECORDING CORP. N.Y., N.Y.
LAN-6004
Time: 2:20
45 RPM
TT-713
I'VE HAD IT
(B. Benjamin - S. Marcus)
GEORGE SMITH
TOP DOG
JUST AS MUCH
(G. Terry & M. Terry)
2:25
A - 102
KRIS PETERSON
(Producer: Artie Fields)
TOP DOG RECORD CO.
9430 Woodward Ave.
Detroit, Mich. 48202
ME-O
RECORDS
M-1005-A
45 RPM
"GIVE ME LOVE"
(Thurman Hollis)
TOOTSIE ROLLERS
PENTAGON
RECORDS
P 1112-11
I BEAR WITNESS
(J. Stevenson)
VINCE APOLLO
Vocal Assist by The Okay Sisters
GEMINI
STAR RECORDS
30.005
Time: 2:34
I DIDN'T KNOW HOW TO
(David Henry)
THE CONSTELLATIONS
Produced by Pat Jaques
Arr. by Richie Tee
LOOK AT ME
(Wright-Baxter-Hanson)
blue rock
B-4034
R 570
THE DELETTS
FOR BROADCAST ONLY · NOT FOR SALE
PEAK
SAINTMO
Side 2
16456 B
BMI
45 RPM
Time 2:53
IF I KNEW
(Arr: C. Warren)
Fabulous Four
TARX
RECORDS
1639 BROADWAY, R-310, N.Y.C. 10019
45 RPM
1011-S
THAT WAS WHISKEY TALKIN'
(Ronnie McCain)
RONNIE FORTE
Arr. and Cond. by BEN SMITH
REG. U.S. PAT. OFF.
ERA RECORDS
PROMOTIONAL COPY
NOT FOR SALE
I'VE ARRIVED
(Steven Howard)
STEVE FLANAGAN
3186
ISN'T IT JUST A SHAME
Arranged & Conducted by: HERB BERNSTEIN
812
Promotion Copy
NEW VOICE
RECORDS
KENNY WELLS

Storming the floor, dancefloor top tens over the years...

1985 STAFFORD - Still Leading The Field...

MAGIC TOUCH	MELBA MOORE	(MUSICOR UNRELEASED)
ENVY	The ORLONS	(CAMEO)
NEVER LET ME GO	MONIQUE	(MAURCI)
I WANNA GIVE YOU TOMORROW	BENNY TROY	(DE-LITE)
IT TAKES HEART	GREG PERRY	(ALFA)
JANICE	SKIP MAHONEY	(SALSOUL)
I'M COMING OVER	JOHNNY HONEYCUTT	(TRIODE)
TEARS OF JOY	RAY MERRELL	(JAYBOY)
TWO LOVES HAVE I	BIG JOE TURNER	(BLUESTIME)
CHEATIN KIND	DON GARDNER	(SEDGRICK)

1986 100 CLUB - Oldies And Newies Together

I NEED YOU LIKE A BABY	ANDREA HENRY	(MGM)
USE IT BEFORE YOU LOSE IT	BOBBY VALENTIN	(FANIA)
LONELY GIRL	ERIC MERCURY	(SACK)
SILENT TREATMENT	ARIN DEMAIN	(BLUE STAR)
KEEP ON LOVING ME	FRANCES NERO	(SOUL)
I CRIED MY LIFE AWAY	TOMMY NAVARRO	(DE JAC)
FIND A QUIET PLACE	MELVIN DAVIS	(WHEEL CITY)
PLEASE STAY	The IVORYS	(DISPENZA)
DON'T TURN YOUR BACK ON ME	JACK MONTGOMMERY	(BARRACUDA)
FOREVER IN MY HEART ('COME ON BACK TO ME BABY')	The TEMPTATIONS	(MOTOWN UNRELEASED)

Opposite and Inset: The wonderful Maxine Brown whose many Wand recordings, from 'One Step At A Time' and 'Let Me Give You My Lovin'' through to unissued material like 'It's Torture' form part of the backbone of what is the 6T's - 100 Club sound.

The Northern Soul All Time Top 500

353

Storming the floor, dancefloor top tens over the years...

Police swoop on soul fans

NORTHERN SOUL fans have hit out at police who swooped on punters in a drugs blitz outside a Chesterfield nightclub last week.

More than 100 people were held for questioning, some strip-searched, during the massive operation near the Winding Wheel club. Only two people were arrested and charged under the Misuse Of Drugs Act.

Eyebrows were raised at police tactics in the area, which included stopping minibuses full of fans travelling to the all-nighter at a motorway service station.

Club promoter Danny Everard told *NME* that police also tried to block the Winding Wheel's application for an entertainment licence on the grounds that the all-nighters would encourage large scale drug abuse, burglary, car thefts, public disorder, and lead to more cases of missing persons. Their objections were thrown out by Chesterfield Council's licensing committee.

"We've told the police that we've nothing to hide but they're not interested," said Everard.

"I don't want drugs in my venue, there is no dealing inside. To my knowledge, the police pulled two people out of about 350 – and they weren't even in the club! That's hardly many for a weekend."

Chesterfield police confirmed that two people were arrested for drugs-related offences. A spokesman added that the normal quota of 20 to 25 officers were on duty on the night in question, but refused to comment on the number of people searched.

"Policing was normal and necessary for the occasion. I'm not willing to define those terms."

Only three people have been arrested during the four all-nighters the Winding Wheel has held since October.

Some things never change... The rabid vendetta of the squad towards Soul fans continues. The Council owned Winding Wheel in Chesterfield was an excellent and very popular venue run by Danny Everard and Dave Thorley (Stafford promoter), it looked set to take on the torch after the closure of Stafford's legendary Top Of The World. But through the police's underhand tactics and harassment the local council was FORCED to revoke its licence.

1987 100 CLUB / CHESTERFIELD / VARIOUS

SOMETHING NEW TO DO	BOBBY SHEEN	(WARNER BROS)
I STILL LOVE YOU	The SEVEN SOULS	(OKEH)
I'LL NEVER FORGET YOU	The METROS	(RCA LP)
LOVED STARVED HEART	MARVIN GAYE	(TAMLA)
MY BABY'S GOT E.S.P.	FOUR BELOW ZERO	(PAP)
THE SWEETEST THING	CHANNEL 3	(DAKAR)
GIRLS ARE AGAINST ME	The UTOPIAS	(LA SALLE)
STOLEN HOURS	PATRICE HOLLOWAY	(CAPITOL)
WALK ON INTO MY HEART	BOBBIE SMITH	(AMERICAN ARTS)
WHAT MORE CAN A BOY ASK FOR	The DETROIT SPINNERS	(MOTOWN LP)

1988 KEELE / BLACKBURN - Big Crowds On The Horizon

LONELY FOR YOU BABY	SAM DEES	(SSS INTERNATIONAL)
PACKING UP	DAMON FOX	(FAIRMOUNT)
YOU'RE ON TOP GIRL	The EMPIRES	(CANDI)
ONE WAY OR ANOTHER	TINA ROBERTS	(SECURITY)
SAVIN' MY LOVIN' FOR YOU	The PEOPLES CHOICE	(PALMER)
YOU'RE MY LEADING LADY	TOMMY FRONTERA	(ALL-RITE)
DON'T SEND ME AWAY	GARFIELD FLEMMING	(BECKETT)
SOMEONE TELL HER	The IMPERIAL C'S	(PHIL LA OF SOUL)
I NEED LOVE	DAYBREAK	(PAP)
YOU HAD ME FOOLED	DANNY WOODS	(CORREC-TONE)

1989 KEELE - Northern Re-invents Itself

I WATCHED YOU SLOWLY SLIP AWAY	HOWARD GUYTON	(VERVE)
YOU SHOULD O' HELD ON	The 7TH AVE AVIATORS	(CONGRESS)
IF THIS AIN'T LOVE	JOHNNY BARTEL	(SOLID STATE)
I STAND ACCUSED	TONY COLTON	(PYE)
WELCOME TO DREAMSVILLE	SAMMY AMBROSE	(MUSICOR)
YOU LEFT ME	The ADMIRATIONS	(PEACHES)
I BEAR WITNESS	VINCE APOLLO	(PENTAGON)
OUR LOVE WILL GROW	The SHOWMEN	(SWAN)
OF HOPES AND DREAMS AND TOMBSTONES	JIMMY FRASER	(COLUMBIA)
ISN'T IT JUST A SHAME	KENNY WELLS	(NEW VOICE)

Storming the floor, dancefloor top tens over the years...

1990 TWISTED WHEEL REVIVIALS / BRADFORD
- The Revival About To Take Off!

I DON'T LIKE IT	TOMMY BUSH	(RIKA)
HEY GIRL	The VONDELLS	(AIRTOWN)
WHEN YOU LOSE THE ONE YOU LOVE		
	BUDDY SMITH	(BRUTE)
I'M TAKING ON PAIN	TOMMY TATE	(OKEH)
I'LL NEVER STOP LOVING YOU	CARLA THOMAS	(STAX UNISSUED)
PLEASE DON'T GO	WILLIE TEE	(GATUR)
MY FIRST LONELY NIGHT	JEWEL AKENS	(ERA)
YUM YUM TREE	BOBBY BLAND	(DUKE)
AIN'T THAT TRUE LOVE	OSCAR TONEY JUNIOR	(BELL)
I WON'T LET YOU SEE ME CRY	BIG FRANK and the ESSENCE	(BLUE ROCK / PHILLIPS)

1991 BRADFORD / DROYLESDON / AVANT, OLDHAM - Revival Time

SWEET SHERRY	JJ BARNES	(VOLT)
SET MY HEART AT EASE	MIKKI FARROW	(KARATE)
PUT THAT WOMAN DOWN	JOHN LEACH	(LAWN)
QUEEN OF THE GO-GO	REX GARVIN	(TOWER)
I CAN'T HOLD ON	LORRAINE CHANDLER	(RCA)
WHAT A WONDERFUL NIGHT FOR A LOVE		
	BOBBY PATTERSON	(JET STAR)
I'VE HAD IT	LEE ANDREWS	(CRIMSON)
I STILL LOVE YOU	The 4 LARKS	(TOWER)
FRIDAY NIGHT	JOHNNIE TAYLOR	(STAX)
STORM WARNING	The VOLCANOES	(ARCTIC)

Left: During the late 80's and early 90's Brian Rae's enormously popular Twisted Wheel revivals (concentrating on the mid-60's period) at the original Whitworth Street site were a major factor in the development of today's popular R&B styled dancers.

1992 BURY / AVANT / VARIOUS - The Revival Starts To Roll

WHAT CAN I DO?	LORRAINE CHANDLER	(GIANT)
DO I LOVE YOU (INDEED I DO)	CHRIS CLARK	(MOTOWN UNISSUED)
VILLAGE OF TEARS	BENZINE	(PARKWAY)
NEVERTHELESS	LEE ANDREWS	(CRIMSON)
WAIT 'TIL I GIVE THE SIGNAL	The SHIRELLES	(SCEPTER)
HONEY BOY	NELLA DODDS	(WAND)
WISHES	The METRICS	(CHADWICK)
THE LIVELY ONE	BROOKS O'DELL	(COLUMBIA)
PRETTY AS A PICTURE	MOSES DILLARD	(MARK IV)
SOMETHING'S BOTHERING YOU	The DALTON BOYS	(VIP)

1993 THE RITZ - Rebirth of the big venue

THANKS FOR A LITTLE LOVIN'	The TRENDS	(ABC)
SLIPPIN' AROUND	ART FREEMAN	(FAME)
I GO OUT OF MY MIND	CHRIS BARTLEY	(ACETATE)
I WANT MY BABY BACK	EDWIN STARR	(GORDY)
TRIPPIN' ON YOUR LOVE	The STAPLE SINGERS	(KENT)
I'M THE ONE WHO LOVES YOU	DARRELL BANKS	(VOLT)
ASK THE LONELY	The FOUR TOPS	(MOTOWN)
CANDLE IN THE WINDOW	DONI BURDICK	(UNISSUED)
IT'S BETTER	REGGIE ALEXANDER	(BOSS)
I'M A BIG MAN	BIG DADDY ROGERS	(MIDAS)

1994 LOWTON / WINSFORD

THAT'S MY GIRL	DEE CLARK	(CONSTELLATION)
LOOK AT ME NOW	TERRY CALLIER	(CADET)
MY HEART'S BEATIN' STRONGER	ANDY FISHER	(FAT FISH)
ALL OVER THE WORLD	CHUCK JACKSON	(DEBUT)
I'M SO HAPPY	PRINCE PHILIP MITCHELL	(ATLANTIC)
SAY SOMETHING NICE TO ME	BOBBY KLINE	(MB)
COME SEE	BOBBY HUTTON	(PHILLIPS)
SPECIAL KIND OF WOMAN	PAUL THOMPSON	(VOLT)
THE WRONG GIRL	The SHOWMEN	(MINIT)
ABRACADABRA	ERMA FRANKLIN	(EPIC)

Storming the floor, dancefloor top tens over the years...

1995 NORMANTON / WINSFORD / 100 CLUB

RECONSIDER	BRENDA HOLLOWAY	*(MOTOWN UNISSUED)*
TOO LATE TO TURN BACK NOW	CORNELIUS BROTHERS	
	and SISTER ROSE	*(UNITED ARTISTS)*
REACH OUT FOR ME	LOU JOHNSON	*(BIG TOP)*
YOU HIT ME	KIM WESTON	*(MOTOWN UNISSUED)*
I CAN'T BREAK THE NEWS TO MYSELF		
	BEN E KING	*(ATCO)*
TUNE UP	JNR WALKER and	
	the ALLSTARS	*(SOUL)*
YOU AIN'T SAYING NOTHING NEW	VIRGIL HENRY	*(TAMLA/COLOSSUS)*
THINK IT OVER	LIZ VERDI	*(COLUMBIA)*
I WONDER WHY	BILLY ECKSTINE	*(MOTOWN)*

1996 THE RITZ

GONNA BE A BIG THING	The YUM YUMS	*(ABC)*
MY LOVE IS GETTING STRONGER	TOMMY RIDGLEY	*(INTERNATIONAL CITY)*
MAN O MAN	WALTER and	
	the ADMIRATIONS	*(LA CINDY)*
DON'T START NONE	MAYFIELD PLAYERS	*(MAYFIELD)*
I DON'T DO THIS	SYDNEY JOE QUALLS	*(20TH CENTURY)*
KEY TO MY HAPPINESS	The CHARADES	*(MGM)*
NOTHING CAN HELP YOU NOW	LENNY CURTIS	*(END)*
CALL ME	EDDIE BISHOP	*(ABC)*
TOP OF THE STAIRS	COLLINS and COLLINS	*(A&M)*
TOO LATE	MANDRILL	*(ARISTA)*

1997 WINSFORD AND THE RITZ

NO ONE CAN LOVE YOU MORE	GLADYS KNIGHT	*(MOTOWN)*
LUCKY NUMBER	RONNIE M^{c}NEIR	*(MOTOR CITY)*
HAS IT HAPPENED TO YOU YET	EDWIN STARR	*(GROOVESVILLE UNRELEASED)*
THAT'S NOT LOVE	HOLLY ST JAMES	*(ABC)*
RECIPE	LV JOHNSON	*(GROOVESVILLE UNRELEASED)*
LET MY HEART AND SOUL BE FREE	The TANGEERS	*(OKEH)*
PRESSURE	DRIZABONE	*(ISLAND)*
THESE MEMORIES	ALMETA LATTIMORE	*(MAINSTREAM)*
TAKE A GIANT STEP	The PROFILES	*(GOLD TOKEN)*
GETTIN' TO ME	BEN E KING	*(ATLANTIC UNRELEASED)*

Yvonne Vernee, the quality of her recordings for Correc-Tone and Sonbert and a short stint as lead singer with the Elgins have ensured her enduring popularity.

Storming the floor, dancefloor top tens over the years...

1998 THE RITZ AND LOWTON

TRYING TO LOVE TWO	BARBARA LYNN	*(ICHIBAN)*
YOU'VE BEEN AWAY	RUBIN	*(KAPP)*
JEANETTE	WADE FLEMONS	*(RAMSEL)*
WHAT DOES IT TAKE	The BAY BROTHERS	*(MILLENNIUM)*
TOWER OF STRENGTH	GLORIA LYNN	*(EVEREST)*
I'VE HAD IT	GEORGE SMITH	*(TURNTABLE)*
I'M COMING HOME	SEPTEMBER JONES	*(KAPP)*
WHAT'S THAT ON YOUR FINGER	KENNY CARTER	*(UNRELEASED RCA)*
HE'S ALL I GOT	The SUPREMES	*(MOTOWN)*
BABY, BABY DON'T WASTE MY TIME	GLADYS KNIGHT and the PIPS	*(COLUMBIA)*

1999 TOGETHERNESS AND CLEETHORPES

A LOT OF LOVIN GOIN' ROUND	CLARENCE HILL	*(MAINSTREAM)*
HE WHO PICKS A ROSE	JIMMY RUFFIN	*(MOTOWN UNISSUED)*
STORMY	The SUPREMES	*(MOTOWN)*
KISS MY LOVE GOODBYE	BETTYE SWANN	*(ATLANTIC)*
TOUCH OF VENUS	BRENDA HOLLOWAY	*(MOTOWN UNISSUED)*
BABY A GO GO	BARBARA McNAIR	*(MOTOWN UNISSUED)*
PIECES OF MY BROKEN HEART	GLADYS KNIGHT and the PIPS	*(MOTOWN UNISSUED)*
I JUST WANT TO FALL IN LOVE	DETROIT SPINNERS	*(ATLANTIC)*
LOVE IS ALRIGHT	JESSE JAMES	*(VIRTUE ACETATE)*
IF YOU DON'T COME	PATIENCE VALENTINE	*(SAR)*

2000 TOGETHERNESS - Northern storms into the new Millennium

WORLD OF HAPPINESS	ARTIST UNKNOWN	*(UNISSUED HARTHON)*
POOR SIDE OF TOWN	RICHARD STREET	*(UNISSUED MOTOWN)*
KEEPS ON ROLLING	BRENDA HOLLOWAY	*(MOTOWN UNISSUED)*
HE'S THE ONE THAT RINGS MY BELL	SHERRY TAYLOR	*(GLORECO)*
THIS THING CALLED LOVE	JOHNNY WYATT	*(BRONCO)*
IT'S YOUR VOODOO WORKING	CHARLES SHEFFIELD	*(EXCELLO)*
DON'T STOP NOW	THE ORIGINALS	*(MOTOWN LP)*
MY BABY'S BEEN CHEATIN' (I KNOW)	AC REED	*(COOL)*
I JUST CAN'T SPEAK	JIMMY 'BO' HORNE	*(DADE)*
HAVE LOVE WILL TRAVEL	RICHARD BERRY	*(FLIP)*

Right: Richard Berry and the Pharoahs' 'Have Love Will Travel', one of several very different versions, it was released twice on Flip, the second issue is coupled with 'Louie Louie', the group's only real claim to musical stardom it is the original version of the Kingsmen's Doo-Wop classic.

CHARTING
HIGH... northern soul
to enter the UK pop charts

We have carefully selected the ones that charted purely due to 'Northern' demand, resulting from plays on the scene. Many, such as 'Rescue Me', 1-2-3, 'Mockingbird', 'Joe 90', 'This Old Heart Of Mine', 'Tainted Love' (by Soft Cell), 'The Only Way Is Up' (by Yazz and the Plastic Population) or 'Breakin' Down The Walls Of Heartache' have a loose connection to the Rare Soul scene and are similar sounding, but were NOT in demand on the scene from the outset. Sure, tracks such as Barry Gray's 'Joe 90' did receive minor spins but the real demand came from within the Gerry Anderson/TV 21 fan base.

The scene has direct links to the charts too with former Coventry DJ Pete Waterman peaking at no.33, 1975 as 14-18 with a song titled 'Goodbyee'. Nottingham DJ Chris King went one better than Waterman (even though the former has millions of sales as a writer/producer) by scoring with a No.1 in 1992 with 'Please Don't Go'. Arguably the strangest could be producer Simon Soussan who actually made an appearance at Wigan Casino as a DJ, and then went on to create The Sharonettes and Shalamar!

Many would argue that Freda Payne's 'Band Of Gold' is Northern, but not at the time, neither is Edwyn Collins 'A Girl Like You', although the influence is obvious (especially when you look at the picture sleeve which features Northern Soul patches and dancers). The Showstoppers' 'Ain't Nothing But A Houseparty' is an interesting call, peaking at no.11 in 1968, one could be forgiven for thinking it was born 'North of Watford', although the trademark is there, it was merely an international club record.

Northern Soul finds itself being in the frame for sampling. The dance experts have in recent years been active with 'Sliced Tomatoes', 'I'm On My Way', 'The Duck' all finding their way into other releases. TV is getting in on the act too with John E. Paul's 'I Wanna Know' and Rubin's 'You've Been Away' fronting highly original Cat food commercials!

Watch Out!!- For The Best DISCO SPECIALS from BLACK MAGIC RECORDS

The first three singles on our new label aimed at the disco market –

BM 101
BOB RELF
Blowing My Mind To Pieces
PAULA ROUSSELL
Blowing My Mind To Pieces

Two superb versions of this great song on one record. A very in-demand dancer and a sure fire hit.

BM 102
THE SHARONETTES
Papa Ooh Mow Mow (Vocal)
Papa Ooh Mow Mow (Instrumental)

The biggest ever in-demand record from the discos, this is the one they've all been asking for – just watch it GO!!!

BM 103
FATHERS ANGELS
Bok To Bach
Disco Trucking

The original disco Hit Version. ACCEPT NO SUBSTITUTES!!!

Radio advertising on Capital, BRMB, Piccadilly, Hallam and Metro.

Available from CBS and Selectadisc

BLACK MAGIC RECORDS 162-176 Canal Street, NOTTINGHAM.
A part of SELECTADISC

Anyway... here's those charts!

Archie Bell and The Drells	Here I Go Again	*(Atlantic, No.11, 1972)*
George Benson	Supership	*(CTI, No.30, 1975)*
Bob and Earl	Harlem Shuffle	*(Island, No.7, 1969)*
Gene Chandler	Nothing Can Stop Me	*(Soul City, No.41, 1968)*
The Contours	Just A Little Misunderstanding	*(Tamla Motown, No.31, 1970)*
Petula Clark	A Sign Of The Times	*(Pye, No.49, 1966****)*
Guy Darrell	I've Been Hurt	*(Santa Ponsa, No.12, 1973)*
Donnie Elbert	A Little Piece Of Leather	*(London, No.27, 1972*)*
The Elgins	Heaven Must Have Sent You	*(Tamla Motown, No.3, 1971)*
The Exciters	Reaching For The Best	*(20TH Century, No. 31, 1975)*
The Fascinations	Girls Are Out To Get You	*(Mojo, No.32, 1972)*
The Flamingos	Boogaloo Party	*(Phillips, No.26, 1969)*
The Formations	At The Top Of The Stairs	*(Mojo, No.28, 1971)*
Four Seasons	The Night	*(Mowest, No.7, 1975)*
Marvin Gaye	Lucky Lucky Me	*(Motown, No.67, 1994)*
Wayne Gibson	Under My Thumb	*(Pye, No.17, 1974)*
Dobie Gray	Out On The Floor	*(Black Magic, No.42, 1975)*
Bobby Hebb	Love, Love, Love	*(Phillips, No.32, 1972)*
Tommy Hunt	Crackin' Up	*(Spark, No.39, 1975**)*
Tommy Hunt	Loving On The Losing Side	*(Spark, No.28, 1976)*
Tommy Hunt	One Fine Morning	*(Spark, No.44, 1976)*
Millie Jackson	My Man Is A Sweet Man	*(Mojo, No.50, 1972)*
The Javells	Goodbye Nothin' To Say	*(Pye Disco Demand, No.26, 1974)*
L.J Johnson	Your Magic Put A Spell On Me	*(Phillips, No.27, 1976)*
Marv Johnson	I Miss You Baby	*(Tamla Motown, No.25, 1969)*
Robert Knight	Love On A Mountain Top	*(Monument, No.10, 1974)*
Gary Lewis and the Playboys	My Heart's Symphony	*(United Artists, No.36, 1975)*

Left: The Sharnnettes' 'Papa Ooh Mow, Mow', a version of the Rivingtons' Doo-Wop classic became a massive hit. 'Watch Out' as the Black Magic advert says - was this intended as a warning to real Soul fans to avoid this dreadful record?

Hitting the heights... Northern Soul in the British Pop Charts

Ramsey Lewis	Wade In The Water	(Chess, No.31, 1972)
Little Anthony and the Imperials		
	Better Use Your Head	(United Artists, No.42, 1976)
Tami Lynn	I'm Gonna Run Away From You	(Mojo, No.4, 1971)
Harold Melvin and the Blue Notes		
	Get Out	(Route, No.35, 1975)
Mistura feat. Lloyd Michels	The Flasher	(Route, No.23, 1976)
Willie Mitchell	The Champion	(London, No.47, 1976)
The Newbeats	Run Baby Run	(London, No.10, 1971)
Dean Parrish	I'm On My Way	(UK, No.38, 1975)
Gene Pitney	She's A Heartbreaker	(Stateside, No.34, 1968***)
Mike Post Coalition	Afternoon Of The Rhino	(Warner Bros, No.47, 1975)
Jimmy Radcliffe	Long After Tonight Is All Over	(Stateside, No.40, 1964****)
San Remo Strings	Festival Time	(Tamla Motown, No.39, 1971)
The Sharonettes	Papa Ooh Mow Mow	(Black Magic, No.26, 1975)
The Sharonettes	Going To A Go Go	(Black Magic, No.46, 1975)
The Tams	Hey Girl Don't Bother Me	(Probe, No.1, 1971)
R.Dean Taylor	There's A Ghost In My House	(Tamla Motown, No.3, 1974)
Evelyn Thomas	Weakspot	(20TH Century, No.26, 1976)
Evelyn Thomas	Doomsday	(20TH Century, no.41, 1976)
Jamo Thomas	I Spy For The FBI	(Polydor, No.44, 1969)
Trammps	Hold Back The Night	(Buddah, No.5, 1975)
Frankie Valli	You're Ready Now	(Phillips, No.11, 1970)
The Velvelettes	These Things Will Keep Me Loving You	
		(Tamla Motown, No.34, 1971)
Wigan's Chosen Few	Footsee	(Pye Disco Demand, No.9, 1975*****)
Wigan's Ovation	Skiing In The Snow	(Spark, No.12, 1975**)
Wigan's Ovation	Per-so-nally	(Spark, No.38, 1975**)
Wigan's Ovation	Superlove	(Spark, No.41, 1975**)
Al Wilson	The Snake	(Bell, No.41, 1975)
Jackie Wilson	I Get The Sweetest Feeling	(MCA, No.9, 1972)
Betty Wright	Where Is The Love	(RCA, No.25, 1975)

Key to the above the above chart entries:

*   Re-recording of original track.

**   A cover version of the original in-demander.

***   The official B side.

****   Associated with Northern, although NOT at the time of entry into the UK charts.

*****   Based upon a 45 on US Roulette, Footsee by The Chosen Few. The track was re-created by producer Simon Soussan and retitled 'Footsee - The Sounds of Soul'. Pye records, never short on the uptake singles-wise, copied Soussan's arrangement, having obtained the rights from US label Roulette. Employee and Soul fan Dave McAleer instigated the recording, promotion and it's subsequent success. Soccer fans note: The crowd noises are actually overdubs of the 1966 FA Cup Final, Everton versus Sheffield Wednesday!

Below: 'Da, Da, Da - Da Da - Da - Da Da, La - La La'... etecetera, etcetera. The Chosen Few reworked by Simon Soussan then re-recorded by Dave McAleer, give me 'Birth Of A Playboy' any day of the week!

the strange world

Paul Humphrey
'Cochise'
For 12 months this was the scene's biggest hit!

The Playthings
'Stop What You're Doing'
A monster new release cover-up from 1973!

Johnny Jones
'Honey Bee'
A 1972 new release it had a superlative 60's sound!

Tommy Hunt
'Loving On The Losing Side'
One of the few 'tailor-mades' with real credibility!

The Northern Soul All Time Top 500

f northern soul

Robert Knight
'Love On A Mountain Top'
Every British collector, Pop and Mobile DJ was scrambling for this one in 1971!

PJ
'TLC (Tender Loving Care)'
This lightweight 1971 release became number one in the country - for seven days!

Barnaby Bye
'Can't Live This Way'
I discovered it and passed it on to Ian Levine who made it a monster - but where's the Soul?

Jimmy Cliff 'Waterfall'
When the Casino went pop-crazy this track by the 'Rude Boy' fitted the bill perfectly! Produced by Muff Winwood, member of the Spencer Davis Group!

MAJOR LANCE
"Everybody Loves a Good Time" 4-7233

TEACHO
"Chills and Fever
(With The Students) c/
"Same Old Bea
4-723

TED TAYLOR
"Stay Away From My Baby" 4-7231

THE ARTISTICS
"This Heart of Mine"
4-7232

The hits are happening on OKeh

The Northern Soul All Time Top 500

Remember when.... Whether you haven't been involved in Northern Soul for years or are a regular today, your past will be packed with special memories. The following pages are filled with some of those strange and uniquely 'Northern' people, places, records and ephemera that go to form our unique and wonderful scene...

TEN
key northern soul venues

1. WIGAN CASINO (1973 - 1981)
2. BLACKPOOL MECCA (1971 - 1980, with a short break during the days of the Torch)
3. THE TWISTED WHEEL, Whitworth Street, Manchester (1967 - 1971)
4. THE GOLDEN TORCH, Tunstall, Stoke-on-Trent (Allnighters 1972 - 73)
5. THE RITZ, Manchester (Alldayers 1976 - 1979, Allnighters 1993 - Present)
6. THE CATACOMBS, Wolverhampton (1971 - 1974)
7. WINTER GARDENS, Cleethorpes (1975 - 1979)
8. KEELE, Staffordshire (1986 - Present)
9. KINGS HALL, Stoke (1995 - Present)
10. 100 CLUB, London (1981 - Present)

Top ten things you want to remember - or forget!

TEN ultra-collectable rare soul labels

1. **RIC - TIC**, owned by Ed Wingate and Joanne Jackson, sold in 1966 as part of the Golden World package to Motown who continued to run it 'til 1968.

2. **SHRINE**, the ultimate 'rare' Soul label, was owned by Eddie Singleton and Raynoma Gordy, the name and logo represent a 'shrine' to the memory of John F Kenedy also closely related to the HEM and Jet Set labels.

3. **REVILOT**, formed in Detroit by the great Don Davis in partnership with Lebaron Taylor, this legendary label, home to so many classics is 'Toliver' (Taylor's real name) backwards.

4. **THELMA**, yet another Don Davis set up, this time in partnership with Hazel Coleman, based in Detroit, home to Emanuel Laskey, Joe Matthews, The Fabulous Peps, Billy Kennedy and Martha Starr.

5. **OKEH**, the oldest record label in America, had been dormant for many years before it was reactivated by Columbia records. Supported by the likes of Carl Davies, Curtis Mayfield and Van McCoy it has produced many many Northern classics from the Carstairs to the Seven Souls and Major Harris.

6. **GOLDEN WORLD**, parent company of Ric-Tic it was owned by Ed Wingate and Joanne Jackson.

7. **MOTOWN** group and SUBSIDIARIES, founded in 1959 by Berry Gordy Jnr, the group consisted of some 20 different labels, it included unlikely titles like 'Jazz Forum' and 'Weed'.

8. **CAMEO/PARKWAY**, the seminal Philadelphia labels that, with their subsidiaries, have produced countless Northern sounds from artists like Chubby Checker, Bunny Sigler, Yvonne Baker and Christine Cooper.

9. **CHESS/CADET/CHECKER/ARGO**, owned and operated by Leonard Chess and family, it was the powerhouse behind the great Chicago sound from the early Wheel sounds Ko Ko Taylor and Billy Stewart through to Terry Callier and the Dells.

10. **MIRWOOD**, operated by Randall Wood, this Los Angeles based label with close links to Keymen records boasted the writing and production talents of Len Jewell, Fred Smith, James Carmichael, Bob Relf and Earl Nelson. The label's rosta included the Olympics, Bob and Earl, Richard Temple (Jimmy Conwell) and the Belles amongst others and has produced many great Northern classics.

Opposite: Don Robey's Duke/Peacock setup, distributed by ABC, was the home to many great performers including Bobby Bland, Eddie Taylor, Buddy Lamp and Carl Carlton. It has produced many Northern classics, particularly from the days of Northern Soul at the Wheel, when many were played on UK releases like Vocallion and Sue.

DUKE/PEACOCK
IS THE OLDEST NEW COMPANY IN THE WORLD

DUKE/PEACOCK IS AN ESTABLISHED "OLD" COMPANY WITH GREAT STARS LIKE:

- BOBBY BLAND
- O. V. WRIGHT
- CARL CARLTON
- PAULETTE PARKER
- BUDDY LAMP
- JEANETTE WILLIAMS
- AL BRAGGS
- THE LAMP SISTERS
- EDDIE TAYLOR
- THE SOUL TWINS
- JOHN ROBERTS
- FRANKIE LEE
- EDDIE WILSON
- CHARLES McCLEAN
- ERNIE K. DOE
- THE AUGUSTINE TWINS
- THE MALIBUS
- THE INSIGHTS

DUKE/PEACOCK IS AN EXCITING NEW COMPANY WITH CONSISTANT HIT MAKERS LIKE:

- BOBBY BLAND
- O. V. WRIGHT
- CARL CARLTON
- PAULETTE PARKER
- BUDDY LAMP
- JEANETTE WILLIAMS
- AL BRAGGS
- THE LAMP SISTERS
- EDDIE TAYLOR
- THE SOUL TWINS
- JOHN ROBERTS
- FRANKIE LEE
- EDDIE WILSON
- CHARLES McCLEAN
- ERNIE K. DOE
- THE AUGUSTINE TWINS
- THE MALIBUS
- THE INSIGHTS

DUKE/PEACOCK GROWING NEWER WITH EACH GENERATION

Top ten things you want to remember - or forget!

TEN
collectable soul artists

Most people collect what they like, some people collect just one label, the work of only one producer or the work of only one artist. Whether you are a completeist label fanatic or simply wish to own the sounds that take your fancy, the following Soul singers would grace any record box, we've also listed some of the labels on which they produced their best work...

1. **RAY POLLARD**, Shrine, United Artists, Decca and Cub
2. **ROY HAMILTON**, RCA and MGM
3. **MAJOR LANCE**, Okeh
4. **CHUCK JACKSON**, Wand and Motown
5. **MARVIN GAYE**, Motown and CBS
6. **THE HESITATIONS**, Kapp and D-Town
7. **GENE CHANDLER**, Chess, Brunswick and Constellation
8. **JAMES CARR**, Goldwax
9. **BOBBY WOMACK**, Keyman, Liberty, Minit and Beverly Glenn
10. **JJ BARNES**, Revilot, Ric-Tic, Volt

Right: 'Nothing Can Stop' the Duke of Chicago Soul. Highly collectable Gene Chandler has produced many great Northern sounds including 'Mr. Big Shot' and 'There Was A Time'.

truly classic live performances

1. **BETTY WRIGHT**   (Wigan Casino, 1975)
2. **MAJOR LANCE**   (The Torch, 1972
3. **JIMMY RUFFIN**   (The Wheel, 1970)
4. **RIC - TIC Revue** (Hinkley, 1983)
5. **JACKIE WILSON**   (Wigan Casino, 1975)
6. **JJ BARNES**   (The Torch, 1972)
7. **RAY POLLARD**   (100 Club, 1988)
8. **EDWIN STARR**   (The Wheel last night, January 1970)
9. **BARBARA LYNN**   (Togertherness Weekender, September 1999)
10. **TAVARES**   (The Ritz, 1976)

Everybody's favourite lady - with everybody's favourite doorman. Bubbly Brenda Holloway having a laugh with Big Ron at Blackpool's Togetherness Weekender in September 1998.

At their specific request, Brenda toured with the Beatles in 1964. Watching footage of her Shea stadium performance the power of her voice is staggering.

Top ten things you want to remember - or forget!

TEN
four figure classics

1.	**MR. SOUL/AL SCOTT**	What Happened To Yesterday	(GENUINE)	£1,500
2.	**FRANK WILSON**	Do I Love You (Indeed I Do)	(SOUL)	£15,000
3.	**DON GARDNER**	Cheatin Kind	(SEDGRICK)	£3,000
4.	**THE BUTLERS WITH FRANKIE BEVERLY**			
		Because Of My Heart	(ROUSER)	£5,000
5.	**BERNIE WILLIAMS**	Ever Again	(BELL)	£1,500
6.	**INSPIRATIONS**	No One Else Can Take Your Place	(BREAKTHROUGH)	£4,000
7.	**JD BRYANT**	I Won't Be Coming Back	(SHRINE)	£3,000
8.	**JACKIE DAY**	Naughty Boy	(PHLECTRON)	£1,500
9.	**THE MASQUERADERS**	(Mis-spelt as Masquaders on label)		
		That's The Same Thing	(SOUL TOWN)	£2,000
10.	**DENNIS EDWARDS**	Johnny On The Spot	(SOULVILLE)	£2,000

Damned expensive it may be, and very popular amongst collectors, but JD Bryant's Shrine rarity 'I Won't Be Coming Back' won't be making it into our all time Top 500!

The Northern Soul All Time Top 500

TEN
current in-demand singles that **nobody** wanted in the 70's

1.	**CELESTE HARDIE**	You're Gone	(REYNOLDS)
2.	**HANK JACOBS**	Elijah Rockin' With Soul	(CALL ME)
3.	**CONNIE LAVERNE**	Can't Live Without You	(GSF)
4.	**NOLAN PORTER**	If I Could Only Be Sure	(ABC)
5.	**SEVEN SOULS**	I Still Love You	(OKEH)
6.	**GENE TOONES**	What More Do You Want	(SIMCO)
7.	**TOMMY RIDGLEY**	My Love Is Getting Stronger	(INTERNATIONAL CITY)
8.	**THE DYNELLS**	Call On Me	(ATCO)
9.	**ROY HAMILTON**	The Panic Is On	(MGM)
10.	**CLAUDE 'BABY' HUEY**	Why Did You Blow It	(GALAXY)

Right: Though popular for a while during the 80's amongst Scooter riding Soul fans 'Elijah Rockin' With Soul' was never a big mainstream sound in the 70's. However recent years have seen it become sought after and prices have risen accordingly.

Top ten things you want to remember - or forget!

in-demanders from the 70's that **nobody** wants today!

Left: Lloyd Michels, the man behind Mistura.

Their 'Flasher' on Fusion or Route in the UK, once incredibly popular, is now very rarely played and is today a perennial inhabitant of the '50p Cheapies Box' alongside the likes of James Coit, Joe Frazier and Jimmy Cliff.

Lloyd Michels

1.	**T.D VALENTINE**	Love Trap	(EPIC)
2.	**MISTURA**	The Flasher	(FUSION)
3.	**REPARATA AND THE DELRONS**	Panic	(MALA)
4.	**JAMES COIT**	Black Power	(PHOOF)
5.	**JIMMY CLIFF**	Waterfall	(A&M)
6.	**AL FOSTER BAND**	The Night Of The Wolf	(ROULETTE)
7.	**JOE FRAZIER**	First Round Knockout	(MOTOWN)
8.	**BABE RUTH**	Elusive	(CAPITOL)
9.	**SNOOPY DEAN**	Shake 'N' Bump	(TK)
10.	**BAJA MARIMBA BAND**	Along Comes Mary	(A&M)

Top ten things you want to remember - or forget!

TEN
worst records EVER - my choice!

Take note that our old friend the Soul Fox features in almost EVERY case. Simon Soussan had an incredible gift when it came to tracking down new discoveries, unfortunately it didn't extend to a talent for making NEW vinyl (for Black Magic, Soul Galore and Soul Fox, though his work with Shalimar and Casablanca records did produce some passable disco sounds).

1.	THE FLOORSHAKERS	Six by Six	(SOUL FOX)
2.	SOUL FOX STRINGS	Mountain Top Theme	(SOUL FOX)
3.	THE DYNAMITES	Ain't No Soul	(SOUL GALORE)
4.	THE TERRIFICS	I Can't Get Enough	(SOUL GALORE)
5.	THE DYNAMITES	Bok To Bach	(SOUL GALORE)
6.	THE HOTSHOTS	Run Baby Run	(SOUL GALORE)
7.	LESTER LANIN	Dizzy	(METROMEDIA)
8.	HUGO MONTENEGRO	Sherry	(TIME)
9.	RAIN	Out Of My Mind	(BELL)
10.	THE SHARONETTES	Papa Oom - Mow Mow	(BLACK MAGIC)

You would undoubtedly do yourself an injury if you attempted to dance to Lester Lanin's insanely fast instrumental take on Tommy Roe's 60's hit. Also featured 'Oh Bla De, Oh Bla Da' on the reverse!...

It was quite literally 'Mad, Bad and Dangerous to Know' - DREADFUL!

Top ten things you want to remember - or forget!

TEN legendary cover-ups

Over the years our scene has been much criticised for the practice of 'covering-up' records, outsiders often see it as some form of arrogant elitism. However over the years this practice has been important in maintaining exclusivity for a certain DJ which has paradoxically improved the longevity of many records by saving them from mass over-playing.

Where tracks are unissued or 'one-offs' this has not been a problem, but for a relatively easy record to track down like the Coaster's 'Crazy Baby' on Atco which was covered-up for some years as Freddie Jones it has been an important factor in raising the record to the status of respected classic that it holds today before it was swamped out by a flood of copies from the States.

Little Ann whose unissued Topper cut 'When He's Not Around' remains very popular today. It was a particularly long-lived cover-up as 'Rose Valentine'.

1. **ROSE VALENTINE** WHEN HE'S NOT AROUND (actually by LITTLE ANN, unissued Topper)
2. **PHANTOM JANITOR** NO SECOND CHANCE (actually by THE DEADBEATS on Strata)
3. **FREDDIE JONES** MY HEARTS WIDE OPEN (actually by THE COASTERS on Atco)
4. **JOE MATTHEWS** I DON'T LIKE TO LOSE (actually by THE GROUP feat. CECIL WASHINGTON on Prophonics)
5. **MICKY VALVANO** SHE'S FIRE (actually by THE C.O.D.'s on Kellmac)
6. **CHRISTINE COOPER** COUNTRY GIRL (actually by VICKIE BAINES on Parkway)
7. **HB BARNUM** THE ICE MAN (actually by BILLY WATKINS on Era)
8. **JAMES LEWIS** THAT'S THE WAY (actually by THE Q on Hound)
9. **MAURICE McCALLISTER** WHAT HAPPENED TO YESTERDAY (actually by MR. SOUL/AL SCOTT on Genuine)
10. **GENE McDANIELS** SLEEPLESS NIGHTS (actually by PARIS on Doc)

Top ten things you want to remember - or forget!

TEN
northern soul 'buzz' words

In common with every underground scene Northern Soul has developed its own langauge to describe our special interests, differing terms come and go ('dubes' and 'circles', 60's terms for pills would be met with blank faces today!), there are many more but here are a few commonly used ones.

1. **GEAR** — Drugs, usually amphetamines (bombers, blues, dexies etc - uppers, downers - the addictive opiates and barbiturates - are generally frowned upon).

2. **COVER-UP** — A ficiticious title and/or artist attributed to a record to protect its exclusivity (and therefore usually longevity) for a particular DJ.

3. **NEWIE** — A recent discovery, usually from the 60's, hence the term '60's Newie'.

4. **SMASHED** — The desirable/undesirable (depending on your viewpoint) effect of too much amphetamine ('blocked' is ideal, the next stage is 'hammered' - too wrecked to do anything).

5. **THE SCENE** — Definitive term given to the Northern Soul culture - a hang-over from Mod days, an allnighter regular (ie weekly adherent) often being termed as 'on the scene'.

6. **BACK DROP** — One of the acrobatic dance moves, literally dropping back onto your hands, others include 'Russian Rolls', 'Swallow Dives', 'Back Springs' and of course assorted high kicks, somersaults and splits.

7. **SHUFFLING** — An excruciatingly difficult dance (usually to fast 70's sounds) where the feet move at great speed as if bearing no body weight, incredible to see - but **very few** can do it well!

8. **OLDIES** — A movement started in 1974 when Dave Evison did a short spot at Stafford (courtesy of yours truly locking my record box and leaving the stage mid-spot). Dave quickly joined Wigan on the opening of the now legendary Mr. M's, essentially concentrating on long-gone cheapies his 'Oldies' spots fulfilled the need to hear the sounds of our past (primarily those of the Wheel) - at this time the scene was obsessed with rapid turnover of new sounds. Today variants include 'forgotten oldies' (usually referred to by people arguing for their reactivitation) and 'overplayed oldies' (condemned by most regulars, though they usually still love them and just want them to get a rest!).

9. **MODERN** — More recent Soul releases, ranging from 70's to 90's, but usually refering to sounds released post - the late 70's.

10. **CROSSOVER** — Late 60's/early 70's down tempo, frequently collector oriented sounds.

Top ten things you want to remember - or forget!

TEN
venues with amazing attendences

Although many bemoan the passing of the glory days of Northern Soul in the 70's and whilst it is true that the average attendance at an allnighter today is around 500 it is interesting to note that some of the big attendances listed below are from more recent years. All night venues like Manchester's Ritz and Togetherness' events at the King's Hall Stoke regularly play host to 1,000 or more Souls. Today Soul nights in Blackburn and Prestwich, Manchester expect a minimum of 600 for the evening, whilst the weekenders in Blackpool and Cleethorpes both sell out weeks or even months in advance!

1.	**QUEENS HALL (Allnighter)**	Leeds	(1974)	7,000
2.	**WIGAN CASINO (Allnighter)**	Wigan	(1974/75)	2,500
3.	**TOGETHERNESS (Allnighter)**	Stoke-on-Trent	(1998)	1,700
4.	**THE RITZ (Alldayer)**	Manchester	(1977)	1,500
5.	**THE RITZ (Allnighter)**	Manchester	(1998)	1,200
6.	**THE MECCA (Alldayer)**	Blackpool	(1976)	1,400
7.	**THE TORCH (Allnighter)**	Tunstall, Stoke-on-Trent	(1973)	1,300
8.	**THE PALAIS (Alldayer)**	Nottingham	(1975)	1,200
9.	**THE PIER (Allnighter)**	Morecambe	(1984)	1,300
10.	**THE WIRRINA STADIUM (Alldayer)**	Peterborough	(1978)	1,100

Tram Lines (!) in the flagstone floor, loose boards put down to dance on, nowhere to sit and a dreadful sound system...

In 1974 the Queens Hall in Leeds had it all, plus Major Lance live on stage and SEVEN THOUSAND PUNTERS!

Opposite: The International Soul Club put on many well attended events around the UK during the 70's.

The INTERNATIONAL SOUL CLUB
2 Marsh Parade · Newcastle · Staffs ST5 1BT
Over 40,000 Members

---

800 SEATS ONLY
WEEKEND IN MAJORCA
£45 (INCL)

In association with Clarksons

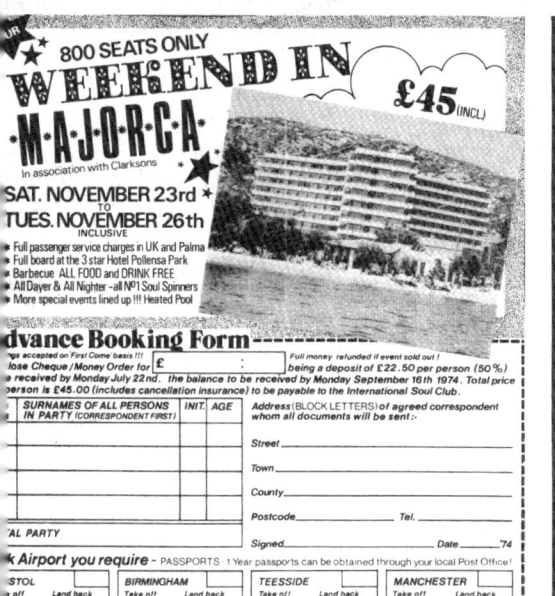

SAT. NOVEMBER 23rd TO TUES. NOVEMBER 26th INCLUSIVE

- Full passenger service charges in UK and Palma
- Full board at the 3 star Hotel Pollensa Park
- Barbecue ALL FOOD and DRINK FREE
- All Dayer & All Nighter — all Nº1 Soul Spinners
- More special events lined up!!! Heated Pool

Advance Booking Form

...accepted on First Come basis !!!
...lose Cheque /Money Order for £ _____ : being a deposit of £22.50 per person (50%)
...received by Monday July 22nd. the balance to be received by Monday September 16th 1974. Total price ...erson is £45.00 (includes cancellation insurance) to be payable to the International Soul Club.

Full money refunded if event sold out !

SURNAMES OF ALL PERSONS IN PARTY (CORRESPONDENT FIRST)	INIT.	AGE

Address (BLOCK LETTERS) of agreed correspondent whom all documents will be sent to:-

Street _____
Town _____
County _____
Postcode _____ Tel. _____
Signed _____ Date _____ '74

...AL PARTY

...Airport you require ____ - PASSPORTS : 1 Year passports can be obtained through your local Post Office!

...STOL	BIRMINGHAM	TEESSIDE	MANCHESTER
...off	Take off	Take off	Take off
...HRS	09-00 HRS	16-20 HRS	18-00 HRS	23-15 HRS
23 NOV	SAT. NOV 23	SAT. NOV 23	TUES. NOV 26	FRI. NOV 22
Land back	Land back	Land back	Land back
22-05 HRS	01-30 HRS	18-00 HRS	22-10 HRS
TUES. NOV 26	WED. NOV 27	TUES. NOV 26	TUES. NOV 26
			Extra Supplement of £2.50ea. on flight

Pollensa Park is featured in current Clarksons Summer Holidays Brochure. BOOK NOW to avoid disappointment.

"WHERE IT'S AT"!!

THE INTERNATIONAL SOUL CLUB ROADSHOW

FEATURING:- KEV ROBERTS AND GUEST DJ's

★ Every Sunday 7-0 — 12-0 Midnight ★ Admission 50p
THE VILLAGE BOURNEMOUTH

★ Every Monday 7-30 — 1-0 am ★ Admission 30p
TOP OF THE WORLD — STAFFORD

★ Every Wednesday 8-0 — 1-0 am ★ Admission 30p
SAMANTHAS — LEEK — STAFFS

★ Every Thursday 8-0 — 1-0 am ★ Admission 30p
THE BLUE DUCK — SMETHWICK — STAFFS
(Opening mid August)

★ Every Friday 9-0 — 2-0 am ★ Admission 40p
THE SPEAKEASY — CREWE — CHESHIRE

"More new I.S.C. "Super Soul Shows" on the way"
Plus Plus Plusssssssssssssssss!!

★ Every Sunday 7-30 — 11-30 ★ Admission 30p
THE STEAM MACHINE — SOUL-ON-TRENT

SEE YOU THERE!! WHERE?? — EVERYWHERE!!

★ ★ ★ ★ ★ ★ ★ ★ ★ ★ ★ ★ ★ ★ ★ ★ ★ ★ ★

Monday Aug. 26th
Champagne All-Dayer
12 till 12pm

Our BIG thank you to you!
Free Bottle Champagne FOR EVERYONE !!

Advance Tickets NOW ON SALE £1.10
From I.S.C. 2 Marsh Parade, Newcastle, Staffs.
Steam Machine Box Office and all I.S.C. Ticket Agents

A COMPETITION
with a 1st Prize of
7 DAY ALL EXPENSES PAID TO THE SOUL CENTRE OF DETROIT, U.S.A.
will be announced soon !!

INTERNATIONAL SOUL CLUB
(SOUTHERN)

PROUDLY PRESENTS

AT THE VILLAGE
Glen Fern Road, Bournemouth, Hants. England.

The INTERNATIONAL SOUL CLUB ROAD SHOW

EVERY SUNDAY 7 PM ~ 12 MIDNIGHT
Commencing July 14th

★ GT BRITAIN
★ FRANCE
★ GERMANY
★ SWEDEN
★ SOUTH AMERICA
★ SWITZERLAND
★ NORWAY

Featuring **'Kev Roberts'** AND THE COUNTRIES TOP SOUL SPINNERS.

ADMISSION TO MEMBERS & BONA FIDE GUESTS ONLY.
Members 50p Guests 60p
All I.S.C. Card are valid.

Top ten things you want to remember - or forget!

TEN
gone but not forgotten venues

Every all-nighter goer will remember names like The Twisted Wheel, Wigan Casino, The Torch and Blackpool Mecca, but there have been countless other clubs that have each had their own input to the scene, in the 60's clubs like Derby's Blue Orchid had their own adherents who were equally into soul as those who attended the Wheel.

In the 70's there were countless other venues like the Winter Gardens in Cleethorpes and the Ivo Centre in St Ives, whilst the 80's saw a massive shake-up from Stafford's Top Of the World... All were important to the scene, here are a few more key venues that are gone, but certainly NOT forgotten...

1. **STARS AND STRIPES,** Yate
2. **THE HOWARD MALLETT,** Cambridge
3. **THE ASSEMBLY ROOMS,** Derby
4. **VA-VA'S,** Bolton
5. **SAMANTHAS,** Sheffield
6. **THE 76 CLUB,** Burton-on-Trent
7. **THE CROMWELIAN,** Bolton
8. **CENTRAL,** Leeds
9. **THE KING MOJO,** Sheffield
10. **THE CHATEAU IMPNEY,** Droitwich

CATACOMBS CLUB Wolverhampton 28682	LEADING R & B SOUL DISCOTHEQUE			
	WEDNESDAY	THURSDAY	FRIDAY	SATURDAY
	BLUE MAX Members Only 12p	CARL DENE Members FREE	BARMY BARRY Members 30p Name D.J's once a month	ALAN DAY BLUE MAX PEP Members 40p

TEN
gone and **sadly missed** characters

1. **Les Cokell** — (The last DJ at the Twisted Wheel)
2. **Andy Lee** — (Collector)
3. **Nev Wherry** — (DJ and collector)
4. **The Mighty Bub** — (DJ, character - comedian!)
5. **Roger Eagle** — (The first DJ at the Twisted Wheel)
6. **Pete Lawson** — (Key collector, legendary for having the words to Jerry Williams' classic 'If You Ask Me' tattooed on his chest!)
7. **'Flash' Atkinson** — (Collector)
8. **Kenny Spence** — (Mr M's and allnighter character)
9. **Mick Kowalski** — (Early allnighter character and collector)
10. **Mike Walker** — (Casino Manager - known by everyone as a 'nice' guy)

Top ten things you want to remember - or forget!

TEN
influential promoters
of the golden era and beyond!

1. **CHRIS BURTON** — The Torch, Queens Hall - Leeds, International Soul Club
2. **TERRY SAMSON** — KGB, Sheffield
3. **MARY CHAPMAN** — Winter Gardens, Cleethorpes
4. **NEIL RUSHTON** — The Ritz Alldayers
5. **MICK FLELLO** — West Midlands Soul Club
6. **NITA ANDERSON** — Wulfrun/Civic Hall, Wolverthampton
7. **CHRIS KING** — Hinckley, Loughborough, Bretby and many live acts
8. **ADY CROASDELL** — The 100 Club, London/Cleethorpes Weekender
9. **DAVE THORLEY** — Top Of The World, Stafford
10. **ALAN SENIOR** — Clifton Halls, Rotherham

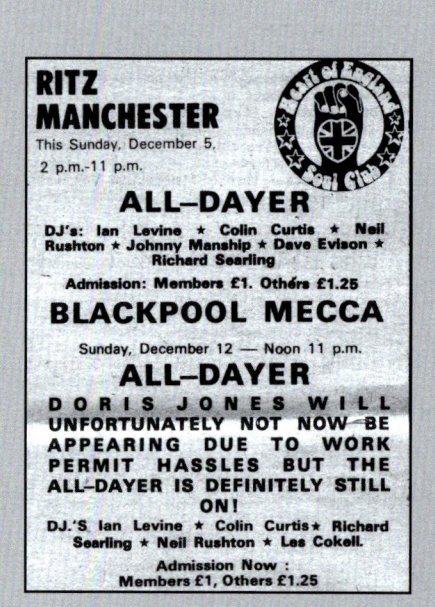

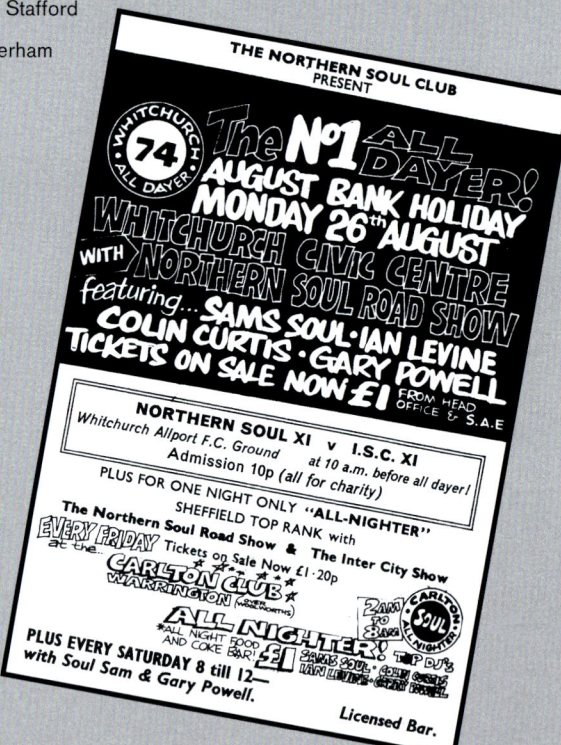

The Northern Soul All Time Top 500

TEN
insatiable record hounds

1.	**JOHN ANDERSON**	Soul Bowl and Grapevine Records
2.	**MARTIN KOPPEL**	Kopp's Collectables, Anglo American, an ex-Pat. based in Canada
3.	**JOHN MANSHIP**	Record Dealer
4.	**ADY PIERCE**	Record Collector and Dealer
5.	**DAVE RAISTRICK**	Record Collector and Dealer
6.	**PAT BRADY**	DJ, Record Collector and Dealer
7.	**TIM BROWN**	Anglo American and the Collector to end them all!
8.	**GARY CAPE**	Record Dealer
9.	**MARK DOBSON**	The DJ 'Butch', Record Collector and Dealer
10.	**TIM ASHIBENDE**	Occasional DJ, Record Collector and Dealer

Right: Toronto based ex-pat Martin Koppel, the North American partner in Anglo-American Records. Martin was on the UK scene in the late 60's before moving to Canada in 1971. Together with British associate Tim Brown he has been responsible for supplying UK based collectors with some staggering rare vinyl - including a copy of Frank Wilson's 'Do I Love You (Indeed I Do)'.

Top ten things you want to remember - or forget!

TEN
venues to hear the top 500

1. **THE RITZ,** Manchester
2. **THE RITZ,** Brighouse
3. **SAMANTHAS,** Sheffield
4. **LEISURE CENTRE,** Alfreton
5. **GRASSHOPPERS,** Preston
6. **THE PALAIS,** Nottingham
7. **TOGETHERNESS,** Fleetwood Weekender/Stoke Allnighter
8. **KEELE UNIVERSITY,** Newcastle Under Lyme
9. **CIVIC HALL,** Winsford
10. **LEISURE VILLAGE,** Kettering

COLUMBIA
Recording Artists

THE SPELLBINDERS

DOSHAWNS Mgt. Inc.
BU-8-1375 UN-5-9795
NEW YORK CITY

Top ten things you want to remember - or forget!

TEN
old monsters out of step today

1.	**TRAVIS WAMMACK**	Scratchy	(ARA)
2.	**PAUL HUMPHREY**	Cochise	(BLUE THUMB)
3.	**WIGAN'S CHOSEN FEW**	Footsee	(PYE DISCO DEMAND)
4.	**THE HOLIDAYS**	Makin' Up Time	(GOLDEN WORLD)
5.	**JAMES COIT**	Black Power	(PHOOF)
6.	**MOOD MOSAIC**	A Touch Of Velvet - A Sting Of Brass	(UK COLUMBIA)
7.	**REX GARVIN AND THE MIGHTY CRAVERS**	Sock It To 'Em JB	(LIKE)
8.	**BOBBY GOLDSBORO**	Too Many People	(UK UNITED ARTISTS)
9.	**AUGUST AND DENEEN**	WE GO TOGETHER	(ABC)
10.	**KIKI DEE**	ON A MAGIC CARPET RIDE	(PHILIPS)

Right: Alice Clarke whose classic Warner Brothers recording 'You Hit Me' remained popular for many years. It is largely forgotten today NOT because the sound ha become unpopular but simply because Kim Weston's incredible original unissued version (unearthed in the Motown vaults by Chris King) has totally overshadowed it!

The Northern Soul All Time Top 500

Pictured: Nolan Porter whose 'Keep On Keeping On' on Lizard and 'If I Could Only Be Sure' for ABC have both been important musical groundbreakers on the scene.

TEN
northern ground breakers

1.	CARSTAIRS	It Really Hurts Me Girl	*(RED COACH)*
2.	JAMES FOUNTAIN	Seven Day Lover	*(PEACHTREE)*
3.	MIKE POST COALITION	Afternoon Of The Rhino	*(MERCURY)*
4.	MR. FLOODS PARTY	Compared To What	*(GM)*
5.	NOLAN PORTER	If I Could Only Be Sure	*(ABC)*
6.	TOMMY NAVARRO	I Cried My Life Away	*(DEJAC)*
7.	TERRY CALLIER	Look At Me Now	*(CADET)*
8.	CHARLES SHEFFIELD	It's Your Voodoo Working	*(EXCELLO)*
9.	N F PORTER	Keep On Keeping On	*(LIZARD)*
10.	JAMES LEWIS AND THE CASE OF TYME	Manifesto	*(LEGEND)*

Top ten things you want to remember - or forget!

interesting lines of **northern** trivia

1. Newsreader **ANNA FORD**, was a regular visitor to WIGAN CASINO

2. Former soccer sensation **GEORGE BEST** was spotted at THE TWISTED WHEEL

3. **ROB DICKENS**, Warner Music Chief and close friend to CHER, acquired the publishing rights to 'THE FLASHER' in 1976.

4. **'REACHING FOR THE BEST'** was originally a ficticious title of a 'single' by BOB RELF, before becoming a reality for THE EXCITERS

5. **PETE WATERMAN** once had a hit as 14/18, while still playing Northern in Coventry.

6. **PATRICE HOLLOWAY** of 'LOVE AND DESIRE'/'ECSTACY' fame was the lead singer of 70's Hanna - Barbara cartoon girl group 'Josie and the Pussycats'.

7. **CAROL DECKER**, singer with T'PAU was a regular at the Whitchurch Alldayers in the 70's.

8. **ROBERT PALMER** was an occasional visitor Wolverhampton's Catacombs, so it's unsurprising to hear his obsession with Soul coming out in all those cover versions of Marvin Gaye.

9. **FRANK WILSON**, Northern Soul legend, has sold over 35 million singles worldwide as a writer and producer.

10. **STUART COSGROVE** former Wigan Casino regular and occasional DJ at venues like Peterborough's Fleet Allnighter is now a senior executive at Channel 4.

'No Honest Bob mate, I've got a copy!' over the years Simon Soussan's capers have become legendary, Exciters eat your heart out! Here's one we 'made earlier'!

The Northern Soul All Time Top 500

It's been around for nigh-on twenty five years, but there's still ONLY ONE COPY!

The wonderful 'No One Else Can Take Your Place' by the Inspirations - AS RARE AS IT GETS!

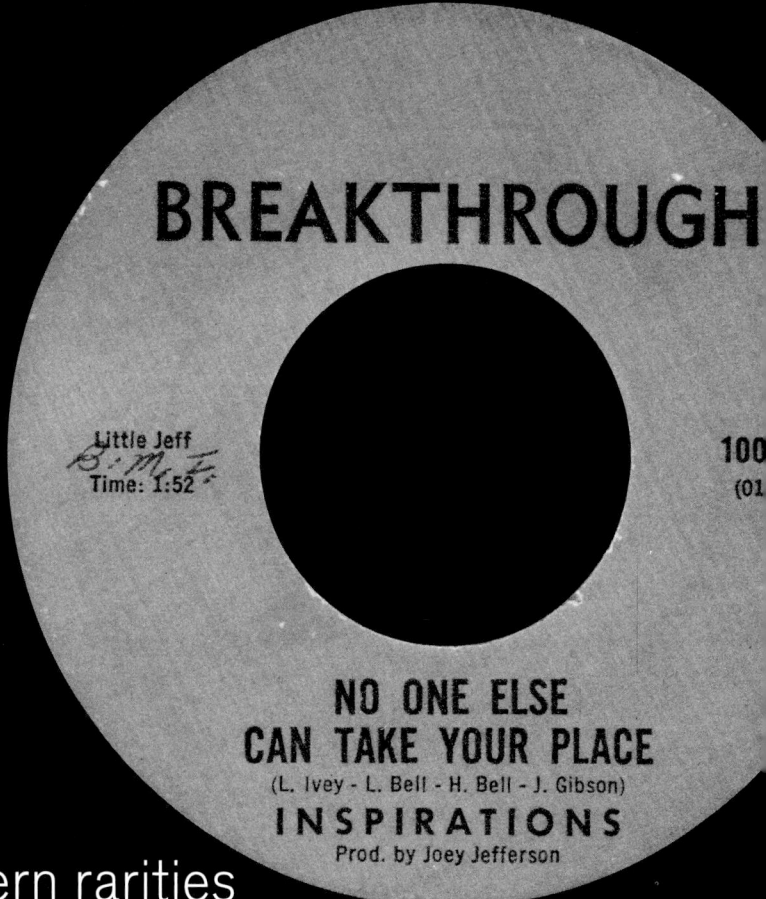

TEN
planet northern rarities

1.	**FRANK WILSON**	Do I Love You (Indeed I Do)	*(Soul)*
2.	**INSPIRATIONS**	No One Else Can Take Your Place	*(Breakthrough)*
3.	**THE BUTLERS WITH FRANKIE BEVERLY**		
		Because Of My Heart	*(Rouser)*
4.	**THE ANDANTES**	Like A Nightmare	*(VIP)*
5.	**DON GARDNER**	Cheatin' Kind	*(Sedgrick)*
6.	**UNKNOWN**	A World Of Happiness	*(Virtue Acetate)*
7.	**JD BRYANT**	I Won't Be Coming Back	*(Shrine)*
8.	**THE PROPHETS**	One Gold Piece	*(Shrine)*
9.	**NATHAN WILLIAMS**	What Price	*(Tru-Gems)*
10.	**BUDDY SMITH**	When You Lose The One You Love	*(Brute)*

Top ten things you want to remember - or forget!

TEN
unlikely northern soul hitmakers

1. **GARY LEWIS AND THE PLAYBOYS**
2. **PAT WILLIAMS ORCHESTRA**
3. **MIKE POST COALITION**
4. **AL DELORY**
5. **BOBBY GOLDSBORO**
6. **PAUL ANKA**
7. **PEGGY MARCH**
8. **SPIRAL STARECASE**
9. **LEN BARRY**
10. **THE VENTURES**

Left: Dusty Springfield, we tend to forget that her Colonial upbringing as a wealthy Irish Catholic was a particulalry unlikely route into Soul music.

However alongside her version of 'What's It Gonna Be' which is of course well known on the scene and a host of Motown covers, she also recorded some more unlikely tracks including 'Bring Him Back' and 'Long After Tonight Is All Over'.

The 'Dusty In New York' EP featured here contains another great forgotten nighter sound - 'Live It Up'.

TEN famous rare soul fans

1. **PETE WATERMAN**
   Ex-Coventry area DJ, now record mogul behind PWL and acts such as Steps.

2. **BELLE AND SEBASTIAN**
   A massive indie-pop act.

3. **PAUL WELLER**
   Top pop star.

4. **ERIC KNOWLES**
   Antiques Roadshow presenter.

5. **PETER STRINGFELLOW**
   Ex-Promoter and DJ of the Mojo, now Nightclub Owner.

6. **STEVE DAVIES**
   Snooker and Pool legend.

7. **JOHN SMITH**
   A prominent football agent.

8. **TREVOR EAST**
   Key SKY TV Sports executive.

9. **DALE WINTON**
   TV personality/presenter.

10. **NORMAN COOK**
    DJ, mixer and artist Fatboy Slim.

Below: Pete Waterman, pop-hit production supremo - and Northern Soul DJ! Pete and I worked together regularly in and around Coventry during the 70's.

Top ten things you want to remember - or forget!

great blue eyed northern tracks

PAUL ANKA	I Can't Help Lovin' You	RCA
BOBBY GOLDSBORO	Too Many People	United Artists (UK)
RUFUS LUMLEY	I'm Standing	Holton
THE CROW	Your Autumn Of Tomorrow	Right On
THE CONSTRUCTION	Hey Little Way Out Girl	Sync 6
LYNNE RANDELL	Stranger In My Arms	Epic
BOBBY PARIS	I Walked Away	Capitol
TONI BASIL	Breakaway	A&M
HELEN SHAPIRO	Stop And You'll Become Aware	Columbia (UK)
BARBARA MILLS	Queen Of Fools	Hickory

Like a cross between Val Doonican and Billy Idol! Rufus Lumley is best known for 'I'm Standing' recorded for Holton records. Nice pullover by the way!

The Northern Soul All Time Top 500

TEN
quality uk only northern

1.	**CARL DOUGLAS**	Serving A Sentence Of Life	*(UNITED ARTISTS)*
2.	**KENNY BERNARD**	What Love Brings	*(PYE)*
3.	**JIMMY THOMAS**	The Beautiful Night	*(PARLOPHONE)*
4.	**TIMI YURO**	It'll Never Be Over For Me	*(LIBERTY)*
5.	**RAY MERRELL**	Tears Of Joy	*(JAY BOY)*
6.	**JACKIE EDWARDS**	I Feel So Bad	*(ISLAND)*
7.	**LEVI JACKSON**	This Beautiful Day	*(COLUMBIA)*
8.	**KENNY BERNARD**	Pity My Feet	*(PYE)*
9.	**MARK LLOYD**	When I'm Gonna Find Her	*(PYE)*
10.	**KENNY LYNCH**	Movin' Away	*(HMV)*

Right: British artist Carl Douglas' 'Serving A Sentence Of Life' very rare, it was only released in the UK unlike his 'Marble And Iron' which only came out Stateside!

Top ten things you want to remember - or forget!

TEN major northern soul cities or areas

1. STOKE ON TRENT
3. WOLVERHAMPTON / BLACK COUNTRY
6. NOTTINGHAM / THE EAST MIDLANDS
5. SOUTH /WEST YORKSHIRE
9. COUNTY DURHAM
3. GREATER MANCHESTER
6. LONDON
7. NORTHAMPTONSHIRE
8. BEDFORDSHIRE
10. CAMBRIDGESHIRE

TEN important northern soul towns

1. BOLTON
3. PONTEFRACT
5. BURNLEY
7. NEWTON AYCLIFFE
9. PRESTON
2. DUDLEY
4. MANSFIELD
6. BURY/RADCLIFFE
8. WIGAN
10. KETTERING

Though traditionally associated with the North West, Northern Soul has many centres around Britain. Though they have never had big Soul venues of their own, towns like Kettering in Northamptonshire and Newton Aycliffe in the North East have been the homes of large and dedicated groups of Soul fans who have had to habitually travel some way to the great Allnighter venues around Manchester and along the M6. Conversly a town like Dudley has very few nighter goers today (Dave Rimmer of Soulful Kinda Music fame - and that's about it!), but boasts long standing Soul venues like Dudley Zoo.

397

Top ten things you want to remember - or forget!

TEN essential northern questions

1. **GOT ANY GEAR?** / KNOW ANYONE WHO'S GOT ANY GEAR? / IS IT ANY GOOD?

2. **IF THE CLOCKS GO BACK, DOES IT STILL FINISH AT 8?**
   (MAY BE FOLLOWED BY THE HAPPY REALISATION THAT THE CLOCKS HAVE ACTUALLY GONE FORWARD AND ITS GOING TO BE A 9 HOUR NIGHTER!)

3. **HAVE YOU GOT A PEN?** / HAVE YOU SEEN WHAT HAPPENED TO MY PEN?

4. **HAVE YOU SEEN** (INSERT NAME)? (BEST ASKED WHEN YOU CAN'T REMEMBER THE NAME)

5. **IS IT** (INSERT NAME) **NEXT WEEK?** (USUALLY SEVERAL WEEKS EARLY/LATE)

6. **WHERE'S THE CLOAKROOM?** (WATCH IT! THIS IS JUST A RUSE TO START VERBALLING!)

7. **WILL YOU TAKE £30?** (FOR THE £50 RARITY ON SALE FOR ONLY £40)

8. **DO YOU NEED ANYTHING?** (IF THEY OFFER IT THEY'RE PROBABLY SQUAD - OR IT'S CRAP!)

9. **WHAT TIME DOES THE BAR SHUT?** (WHETHER OR NOT THE VENUE HAS A LICENSE - SEE NUMBER 6 - REFERENCE THE DREADED VERBALS)

10. **CAN YOU LOOK AFTER MY COAT, OH AND PLAY SOMETHING GOOD!**
    (TO THE DJ, PUTTING IN REQUESTS 2 RECORDS FROM THE END OF A SPOT IS ALSO A POPULAR, IF POINTLESS PASS TIME)

Opposite: The brilliant Isley Brothers, artists behind such Northern greats as 'Why When Love Is Gone', 'Tell Me It's Just A Rumour' and 'My Love Is Your Love', all recorded during their period with Motown.

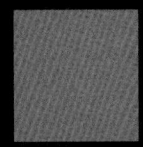

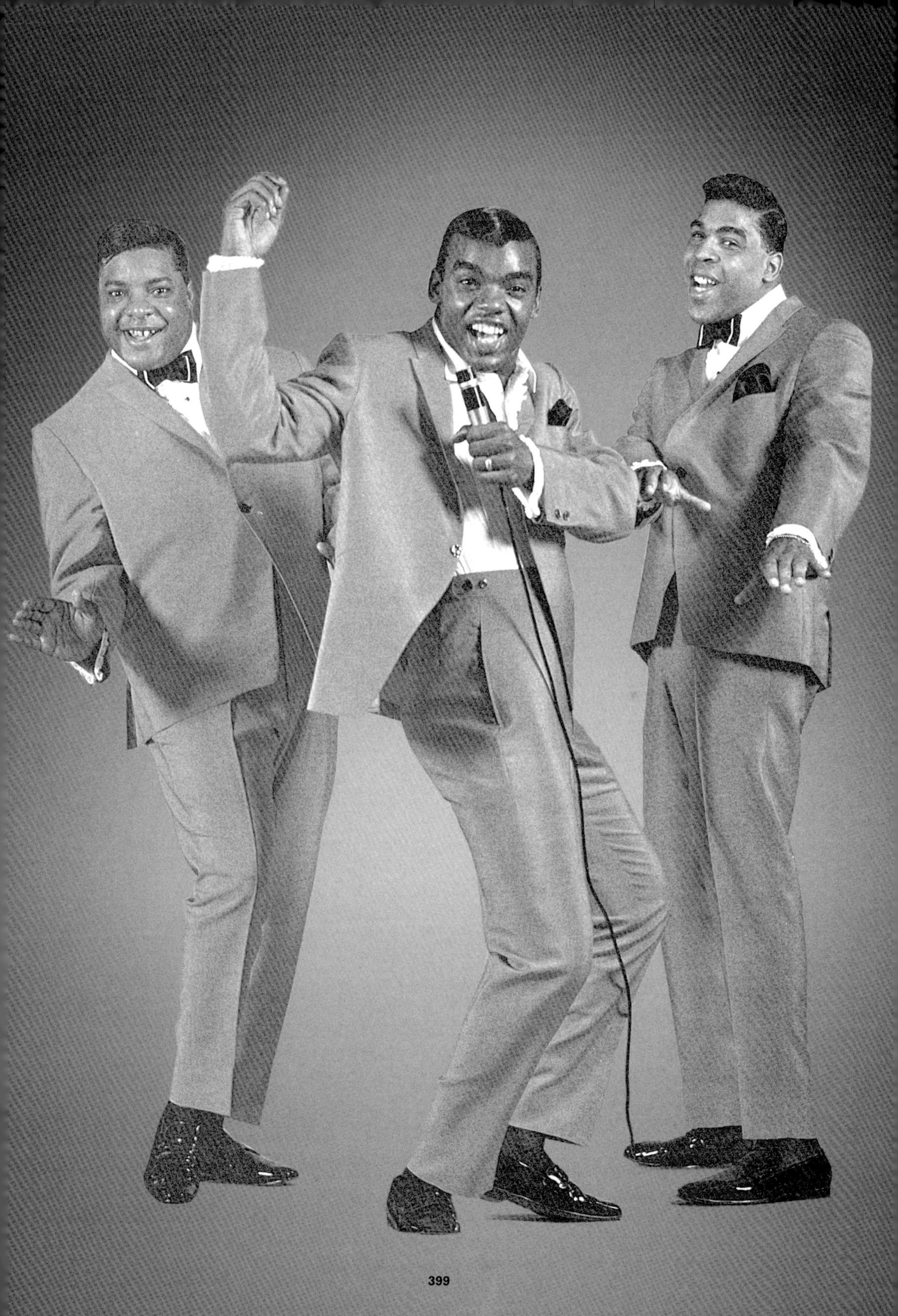

Top ten things you want to remember - or forget!

TEN
classic re-issue labels

1. **ACE/KENT**
2. **RHINO**
3. **WESTSIDE**
4. **SEQUEL**
5. **GOLDMINE/SOUL SUPPLY**
6. **CHARLY**
7. **MOTOWN**
8. **CONNOISSEUR COLLECTION**
9. **EXPANSION**
10. **DEMON/EDSEL**

The Northern Soul All Time Top 500

TEN
great dancers

1. **FRANK BOOPER**
2. **ANGELA LAWRENCE**
3. **MATCHIE**
4. **SOULIE**
5. **SNOWY**
6. **SANDY**
7. **JC**
8. **PHIL WALMSLEY**
9. **CRAIG WESTWOOD**
10. **GIGSY**

Picture: Drilling a hole in the dancefloor at Blackpool Weekender!... Spinning's easy, it's not falling over that's the hard bit!

Top ten things you want to remember - or forget!

TEN
innovative dj's of the 60's

1. **LES COKELL**
   The Twisted Wheel

2. **'FARMER' CARL DENE**
   Catacombs, Chateau Impney.

3. **BRIAN PHILLIPS**
   The Twisted Wheel

4. **GUY STEVENS**
   The Scene, London

5. **BRIAN WALKER**
   The Twisted Wheel

6. **PETE STRINGFELLOW**
   The Mojo

7. **TONY BANKS**
   Leeds Central

8. **JEFF KING**
   Leicester Area

9. **BRIAN RAE**
   The Twisted Wheel

10. **BARRY TASKER**
    Various , later Pendulum

Right: JJ Barnes whose 'Please Let Me In' was a major ground breaker at the Wheel, it was first played by Les Cokell who had borrowed it off a young Blackpool collector called Ian Levine.

TEN
giant dj's of the 70's

Above: Wigan anchormen; Russ, Kev and Richard in the early days of the Casino.

1. **IAN LEVINE**
2. **COLIN CURTIS**
3. **RICHARD SEARLING**
4. **MARTYN ELLIS**
5. **RUSS WINSTANLEY**
6. **PEP**
7. **SOUL SAM**
8. **ALAN DAY**
9. **TONY JEBB**
10. **KEITH MINSHULL**

Right: Messing about at the Mecca, Judith Searling, Ian Levine, Bernie Golding, Len Glab and the late Les Cokell (crouched) in a light hearted mood.

Top ten things you want to remember - or forget!

TEN
movers and dj's of the 80's

1. **CHRIS KING**
2. **DAVE EVISON**
3. **GUY HENNIGAN**
4. **KEB DARGE**
5. **SHAUN GIBBONS**
6. **DAVE THORLEY**
7. **PAT BRADY**
8. **TED MASSEY**
9. **ALAN SENIOR**
10. **ADEY CROASDELL**

TEN
turntable terrors of the 90's

1. **GINGER TAYLOR**
2. **BOB HINSLEY**
3. **TERRY DAVIES**
4. **DEREK ALLEN**
5. **SHIFTY**
6. **KENNY BURRELL**
7. **TOT JOHNSON**
8. **KEV MURPHY**
9. **CARL WILLINGHAM**
10. **BARRY MALEADY**

Right: Dancefloor terrorist, the much loved Ginger Taylor.

north american record dealers

The Northern Soul scene has long honored the talents of the legendary DJs for breaking classic vinyl at allnighters like Wigan, the Torch and the Wheel, but these great spinners have had to track down that vinyl. In many cases key figures like John Anderson have been the supplier but they in turn have had to obtain the vinyl as have those intrepid characters who trawl the States for new vinyl. Whilst America is looked upon as largely ignorant of Rare Soul there are a number of key dealers across America have turned up some of the great finds going right back to the earliest days of imports. Here are ten key figures in the search for elusive vinyl.

1. **VAL SHIVELY** (Philadelphia)
2. **SIMON SOUSSAN** (Los Angeles)
3. **JOHN LAMONTE** (Philadelphia)
4. **MARTIN KOPPEL** (Toronto)
5. **FRED KAPLAN** (New York)
6. **RAY AVERY'S** (Los Angeles)
7. **RADIO CENTRE** (Baltimore)
8. **BERNIE BINNICK** (Philadelphia)
9. **RICH ROSEN** (Las Vegas)
10. **DOWNSTAIRS** (New York)

The Northern Soul All Time Top 500

TEN
essential 70's northern accessories

1. **HOLDALL,** big, shapeless and ideal for dumping in a corner to be left untouched all night.
2. **BOWLING SHIRT,** big, baggy and light in colour to show off the stains from dripping condensation!
3. **FLARED SKIRT,** flared skirts or box skirts look dead good for spinning in, just like those enormous 40" Spencer baggies we like to forget about!
4. **DISCATRON,** the potable 45 player that was perfect for ruining your newly purchased vinyl before you even got it home!
5. **SPEED,** bombers, dexies, blues, daps, green and clears, red and browns but not powder or pondies - unless you'd been let down, or you were a 'div'!
6. **TALCUM POWDER,** Brut was the powder of choice - in a bag hanging from your belt.
7. **BEER TOWEL,** hanging next to your talc bag, additional tennis sweat bands and a couple of strategically placed plasters to stop 'jogger's nipple' were optional!
8. **SEW ON PATCHES,** anniversary patches, label patches, Soul Shetland patches (?) you name it!
9. **FORD CAPRI,** 'cos you couldn't afford a tan Scimitar!
10. **WIGAN CASINO MEMBERSHIP CARD,** older the better! Always in your wallett and preferably next to a gold Torch card, a round Wheel 'beer mat' and a couple of choice others like the Va-Va or Mecca.

Opposite and right:
'Get them while they're hot - they're lovely'... The massive explosion in Northern of the mid-70's kicked of a frenzy of commercialisation.

From a new take on traditional anniversary patches to the more bizarre 'Fully Adjustable' belts (ONLY £1 - and ideally suited for holding up those 40" baggies) it was easy to become a 'bona-fide' Soul fan (just like that 'Wigan's Ovation') by mail order - without ever going to an allnighter!

Today thankfully all the tourists are long-gone!

The INTERNATIONAL SOUL CLUB

2 Marsh Parade
Newcastle
Staffs ST5 1BT

Over 40,000 Members

BADGES Due to increase in manufacturing costs all badges are now **35p**

1. INTERNATIONAL SOUL CLUB
2. SOUL STOKE-ON-TRENT
3. SOUL LINCOLN
4. SOUL LEEDS
5. NORTHERN SOUL HUMBERSIDE
6. SOUL LONDON
7. SOUL GLOUCESTER
8. THE YOGI BEAR CLUB
9. SOUTH WEST INTERNATIONAL SOUL CLUB
10. SOUL BIRMINGHAM
11. RIGHT ON J.J. BARNES
12. SOUL WARWICKSHIRE
13. DETROIT EMERALDS FEEL THE NEED IN ME
14. SOUL WOLVERHAMPTON
15. SOUL BLACKPOOL
16. RIGHT ON THE TORCH
17. SOUL NORTH WALES
18. SOUL YORKSHIRE
19. SOUL LANCASHIRE
20. OKeh
21. THE TWISTED WHEEL LIVES ON
22. INTERNATIONAL SOUL CLUB 1974 LEEDS FESTIVAL
23. SOUL NOTTINGHAMSHIRE
24. VA VA LIVES ON THE NITE NIGHTER BOLTON
25. FOREVER THE TORCH
26. SOUL WIGAN CASINO
27. THE TORCH STOKE-ON-TRENT
28. SOUL U.S.A
29. TORCH FOREVER NORTHERN SOUL
30. THE TORCH RULES
31. KEEP THE FAITH
32. THE DRIFTERS
33. KEEP THE FAITH THE CATACOMBS
34. SOUL STAFFORD
35. SOUL DERBY
36. SOUL CHESHIRE
37. SOUL LEICESTER
38. SOUL SCOTLAND

BADGES Each **35p** +S.A.E.

CAR STICKERS

1. INTERNATIONAL SOUL CLUB
2. KEEP THE FAITH SOUL WIGAN

A great offer - Still only **15p** Each +SAE

MEMBERS NOTICE

SATURDAY, 24th MAY

THE EVENT AT THE
NORBECK CASTLE HOTEL,
QUEENS PROMENADE,
BLACKPOOL

IS **POSTPONED**
UNTIL FURTHER NOTICE

DUE TO THE NEW MANAGEMENT OF THE HOTEL,
WILL NOT PERMIT EVENT TO TAKE PLACE

VOUCHER HOLDERS RETURN TO I S C HEAD OFFICE FOR FULL REFUND

MAIL ORDER DEPARTMENT

ORDER FORM

Print clearly your name, address, requirements, enclosing cheque/P.O. for correct amount to : I.S.C. Mail Order Dept. 2 Marsh Parade, Newcastle, Staffs. ST5 1BT.   remember your s.a.e.

Name: _____

Address: _____
_____

Please send me :-
Badges No's. _____

Key Ring No's. _____

_____ Car Stickers _____

☐ 1975 MEMBERSHIP RENEWAL !!!
put cross in box and send 10p   plus S.A.E

Top ten things you want to remember - or forget!

TEN
venues that are very busy TODAY

Northern Soul is very much alive and kicking! Not only on the traditional home turf, but throughout the UK a wide range of promoters old and new are finding that their venues are regularly full to capacity. Even in London Capitol Soul Club's Friday night Soul Night expects attendences of 650 for an event that finishes at 1.00am! If you're not back on the scene yet you'd better get your dancing shoes polished quick - you may not be able to get in!

1. **TOGETHERNESS EVENTS** — Blackpool Weekender and the King's Hall, Stoke, Allnighter

2. **CLEETHORPES WEEKENDER** — Run by Ady Croasdell and the 6T's crew

3. **THE RITZ,** MANCHESTER — Cellar Full of Soul Bank Holiday Allnighters run by Richard Searling

4. **LOWTON CIVIC HALL** — Soul Nights/occasional Allnighters run by Kev Murphy

5. **PRESTON GRASSHOPPERS** — Classic Soul Nights

6. **100 CLUB,** LONDON — The longest running allnighter by far run under the 6T's banner by Adey Croasdell

7. **ALBRIGHTON** — Soul Nights and occasional Allnighters

8. **LONGFIELD SUITE,** PRESTWICH — Terry Davies promoted Soul Nights and occasional Allnighters

9. **THE RITZ,** BRIGHOUSE — Classic Soul Nights

10. **THE DOME,** LONDON — Soul Nights run by the Capitol Soul Club

TEN journalists to chronicle our scene

Over the years there have been many fanzines to cover Northern Soul, today there are perhaps more than ever, they have all had writers who have captured our scene in print, both as fans and journalists. Here are a selection of influential writers, though the Number 1 slot could go to only one man - Dave Godin. Father of British Soul, he of course christened our unique brand of dance music.

1. **DAVE GODIN**
2. **FRANK ELSON**
3. **RICHARD SEARLING**
4. **NEIL RUSHTON**
5. **PAUL PHILIPS**
6. **TONY CUMMINGS**
7. **MARK BICKNELL**
8. **DAVE RIMMER**
9. **CHRIS SAVOURY**
10. **DAVE NOWELL**

TEN northern soul fanzines

There have been many fanzines to cover Northern Soul. Though they are not necessarily entirely devoted to Northern (usually including Deep or Modern Soul) the following, which are mostly still in print, have been particularly long running, informative and influential.

1. **TOGETHERNESS**
2. **SOULFUL KINDA MUSIC**
3. **SOUL UNDERGROUND**
4. **IN THE BASEMENT**
5. **ECHOES**
6. **BLUES AND SOUL**
7. **SHADES OF SOUL**
8. **SOUL SURVIVOR**
9. **VOICES FROM THE SHADOWS**
10. **SOUL UP NORTH**

Right: Edited by Russ Winstanley, the short-lived Wigan Casino fanzine 'Northern Noise' ran to just 4 issues.

Top ten things you want to remember - or forget!

SIXTIES
northern soul producers - a selection

Here are a selection of important producers and their 60's addresses, it is interesting to note that many producers were officially based in New York even though they may have worked in Detroit, Philadelphia or the like...

Herb Bernstein Enterprises
39 West 55th Street, New York, New York

Quinton Claunch & Rudolph Russell
2445 Chelsea Avenue, Memphis, Tennessee

Tommy Coghill & Chips Moman
827 Thomas Street, Memphis, Tennessee

Bob Crewe
1841 Broadway, New York, New York

Steve Cropper
926 East McLemore Street, Memphis, Tennessee

Don Davis
13640 Pembroke, Detroit, Michigan

Fame Productions (Rick Hall)
603 East Avalon, Muscle Shoals, Alabama

GWP Productions
210 East 55th Street, New York, New York

Marc Gordon Productions Inc.
1022 North Palm Avenue, Los Angeles, California

Ellie Greenwich & Mike Rashkow
1414 Avenue Of the Americas, New York, New York

HB Barnum Productions
1239 North Highland Avenue, Hollywood, California

Leon Haywood
2426 1/2 Lucerne Street, Los Angeles

Quin Ivy & Marlin Breene
101 East 2nd Street, Sheffield, Alabama

Just Productions (Lorraine Chandler)
6097 Whitewood Street, Detroit, Michigan

Kama Sutra Productions Inc. (Phil Steinberg, Arie Ripp)
1650 Broadway, New York, New York

Levine - Resnick Productions
1619 Broadway, New York, New York

John Madara Productions
250 South Broad Street, Philadelphia, Pennsylvania

Jessie Mason - Willie Hutch
8350 Wilshire Boulevard, Los Angeles, California

Curtis Mayfield
8543 Stoney Island Avenue, Chicago, Illinois

Van McCoy Music Inc.
1619 Broadway, New York, New York

Lizard Productions
1826 Canyon Boulevard, Hollywood, California

Mira Productions (Randall Wood)
9025 Sunset Boulevard, Hollywood, California

Willie Mitchell
306 Poplar Street, Memphis, Tennessee

Jerry Murray (Jerryo)
1830 South Karlov, Chicago, Illinois

Music Enterprises (Huey P Meaux)
PO Box 206, Winnie, Texas

Bobby Paris
8358 Sunset Boulevard, Los Angeles, California

A. Mike Terry - Joe Armstead Productions
5622 South Maryland Avenue, Chicago, Illinois

Johnny Rivers - Marc Gordan
8923 Sunset Boulevard, Los Angeles, California

Sidrian Productions
18292 Wyoming, Detroit, Michigan

Shelby Singleton Productions
1817 16th Avenue South, Nashville, Tennessee

Fred Smith
7400 Fountain Avenue, Los Angeles, California

Soulville Records (Horace Parks, James Frazier)
1640 Broadway, Gary, Indiana

Tangerine Records
2107 West Washington Boulevard, Los Angeles, California

Tran-San Productions (George Kerr)
66 Telford Street, East Orange, New Jersey

Teddy Vann Productions
1619 Broadway, New York, New York

Andre Williams
67412 Cornell, Chicago, Illinois

Jimmy Wisner
888 8th Avenue, New York, New York

Charles Wright - Fred Smith
4219 Normal Street, Los Angeles, California

Richard 'Popcorn' Wylie
3044 Taylor Avenue, Detroit, Michigan

410

Laura Lee the 'Rip Off' girl who recorded a number of Northern tracks including 'To Win Your Heart', vocal to 'Festival Time' and an influential Ric-Tic recording that was very popular in the early 70's

412

TEN songwriters dear to our scene

The following writers and partnerships, many of whom were also key producers, account for a staggering chunk of the very best Northern Soul sides... I personally nominate Don Davis as the official God of our scene, with Hester/Wylie and the Harthon boys as first reserves!

1. **HOLLAND/DOZIER/HOLLAND** — Motown, Westbound and Invictus
2. **RANDAZZO/PIKE** — Veep, including Little Anthony, and many others
3. **VAN McCOY** — Okeh, Share, Motown and a host of others.
4. **GEORGE KERR** — The man behind Northern Hits by the Perigents, the O'Jays and Norma Jenkins.
5. **RANDOLPH/STYLES/MCDOUGALL** — Harthon productions, licensed to a wide range of labels from Philadelphia and beyond.
6. **FREDDIE PERREN** — Washington DC based writer on many Northern rarities.
7. **JOHNNY BRISTOL** — Particularly working for Motown in collaboration with many others, notably Harvey Fuqua.
8. **RELF/NELSON** — Mirwood/Keyman.
9. **WYLIE/HESTER** — Independent Detroit for SO MANY labels - pretty much everything that wasn't written by Don Davies! (below)
10. **DON DAVIS** — Thelma, Groovesville, Revilot, Volt and Stax - you name it!

Opposite: Eddie Holland who in common with many writers and producers of 60's Soul music had an notable career as a recording artist himself. 'Candy To Me' and 'I'm On The Outside Looking In' have both been big sounds on the Northern scene - though from opposite ends of our history!

Left: Richard 'Popcorn' Wylie whose londstanding partnership with Tony Hester (and for some time Luther Dixon) produced an incredible number of Northern classics for a whole host of Detroit based labels.

CBS
ANDRE BRASSEUR
2557
Side A
2557A
Good Music Ltd./B.I.E.M.
℗ 1967
2.24
45
THE KID
(Andre Brasseur)
Produced by Roland Kluger
A Palette Recording
MADE IN ENGLAND
TRAIN, KEEP ON MOVIN'
(Willie Hutchison)
LIBERTY
℗ 1966
LBF 15356
Side 2
Carlin Music
Time: 2.33
5TH DIMENSION
Produced by Gordon-Hutch
date
45 RPM
2-1523
ZSP 115337
2:20
Produced by Kapralik/McCoy
WE'RE IN THIS THING TOGETHER
-V. McCoy-
PEACHES & HERB
Arr. & Cond. by Van McCoy
A Daedalus Production
GOLDWAX Records
Lyn-Lou Music & Partner Music (BMI)
(8902)
338
Time: 2.16
FREEDOM TRAIN
(Rogers - Bogard - Wells)
JAMES CARR
Prod. by Quinton Claunch & Rudolph Russell
DISTRIBUTED BY BELL RECORDS INC. NYC
Action
ACT 4535
Time 3.15
RIDE YOUR PONY
(Naomi Neville)
BETTY HARRIS
Producers: Marshall Sehorn & Allen Toussaint
A SANSU Recording
CBS
GUY DARRELL
202082
A5384
Lowery Music
℗ 1966
2.09
45
I'VE BEEN HURT
(Ray Whitley)
Acc. by Des Champ
Production: Irving Martin
MADE IN ENGLAND
island
WIP-6004-A
℗ 1967
Island Music
GIVE AND TAKE
(G. Chambers)
JIMMY CLIFF
Produced by Chris Blackwell & Jimmy Miller
Arranged & Conducted by Les Condon
ATLANTIC
MADE IN GT. BRITAIN
45 RPM
United Artists
584065
℗ 1966
Under licence from Atlantic Recording Corpn., U.S.A.
Produced by Bob Gallo & Tom Dowd
BABY WHAT I MEAN
(Hamilton/Sheldon)
THE DRIFTERS
Arranged by Bob Gallo
POLYDOR RECORDS LIMITED
ATLANTIC
MADE IN ENGLAND BY THE DECCA RECORD CO. LTD. UNDER LICENCE FROM ATLANTIC RECORD CORP.
45 RPM
℗ 1965
Shapiro Bernstein
AT.4056
SEESAW
(Covay, Cropper)
DON COVAY & THE GOODTIMERS
STAY CLOSE TO ME
(Mayfield)
STAIRSTEPS
Produced by Curtis Mayfield for Curtom Records USA
2011-092 A
Camad Pubs.
℗ 1968
Time: 2.07
BUDDAH RECORDS
PRESIDENT
FELICE TAYLOR
PT 193
℗ 1968
45 RPM
SIDE B
I CAN FEEL YOUR LOVE (COMING DOWN ON ME)
(Flanagan-Taylor)
(A Kent Records Production, Los Angeles, California)
COPYRIGHT CONTROL
MAJOR MINOR
MM
45RPM
D434-A
℗ 1967
GET ON YOUR KNEES
(E. Bautista)
LOS CANARIOS
A Barclay Recording

The Northern Soul All Time Top 500

TEN
wonderful motown non-hits

1.	KIM WESTON	HELPLESS	Gordy
2.	THE SPINNERS	WHAT MORE CAN A BOY ASK FOR	Motown
3.	BARBARA RANDOLPH	I GOT A FEELING	Soul
4.	THE ORIGINALS	SUSPICION	Unreleased Soul
5.	THE CONTOURS	BABY HIT AND RUN	UK Tamla Motown /MFP
6.	JUNIOR WALKER AND THE ALLSTARS	I AIN'T GOING NOWHERE	Motown
7.	BRENDA HOLLOWAY	RECONSIDER	Unreleased Tamla
8.	GLADYS KNIGHT AND THE PIPS	JUST WALK IN MY SHOES	Soul
9.	ISLEY BROTHERS	TELL ME IT'S JUST A RUMOUR BABY	UK Tamla Motown only on 45
10.	FRANCES NERO	KEEP ON LOVIN' ME	Soul

Opposite: Remember? Most of us on the Soul scene started at Youth Clubs and small local halls. The sounds we heard were the 'cheapies', frequently reissues or bootlegs, they were the ones which we ourselves would go on to buy when we first started collecting.

Gladys Knight and the Pips, despite their now superstar status, found 'Just Walk In My Shoes' sold very poorly at the time of release.

Top ten things you want to remember - or forget!

TEN
northern soul favourites of the author

1.	**JOHNNY WYATT**	THIS THING CALLED LOVE	Kapp
2.	**JOHNNY TAYLOR**	FRIDAY NIGHT	Stax
3.	**EDDIE FOSTER**	I NEVER KNEW	In
4.	**RUBIN**	YOU'VE BEEN AWAY	Kapp
5.	**BOBBY FREEMAN**	I'LL NEVER FALL IN LOVE AGAIN	Autumn
6.	**ERNEST MOSELY**	STUBBORN HEART	La Cindy
7.	**TAMALA LEWIS**	YOU WON'T SAY NOTHING	Marton
8.	**LOU JOHNSON**	UNSATISFIED	Big Top
9.	**PATTI AND THE EMBLEMS**	I'M GONNA LOVE YOU A LONG, LONG TIME	Kapp
10.	**SANDY WYNNS**	THE TOUCH OF VENUS	Doc

Left: The author's all-time favourite, Johnny Wyatt's 'This Thing Called love' which also came out on UK President and was covered by Danny Wagner on his 'Kindred Soul' album.

The Northern Soul All Time Top 500

TEN chart hits played first on the **northern scene**

1	**TAVARES**	HEAVEN MUST BE MISSING AN ANGEL	*Capitol '76*
2.	**VICKI SUE ROBINSON**	TURN THE BEAT AROUND	*RCA '76*
3.	**ESTHER PHILLIPS**	WHAT A DIFFERENCE A DAY MAKES	*Kudu '75*
4.	**BETTY WRIGHT**	WHERE IS THE LOVE	*RCA '75*
5.	**TAVARES**	DON'T TAKE AWAY THE MUSIC	*Capitol '76*
6.	**GEORGE BENSON**	SUPERSHIP	*CTI '75*
7.	**THE MOMENTS**	I'VE GOT THE NEED	*All Platinum '75*
8.	**SILVETTI**	SPRING RAIN	*Salsoul '77*
9.	**THE O'JAYS**	I LOVE MUSIC	*PIR '75*
10.	**THE MIRACLES**	LOVE MACHINE	*Tamla '76*

Right: Betty Wright's chart topper 'Where Is the Love' - (here on the US release) despite essentially having only this one biggie to sing, her performance at Wigan is considered one of the great live shows of the Northern scene.

Top ten things you want to remember - or forget!

TEN
chart hits played later on the northern scene

1.	**CURTIS MAYFIELD**	MOVE ON UP	*Buddah '71*
2.	**THE SHOWSTOPPERS**	AIN'T NOTHING BUT A HOUSEPARTY	*Beacon '68*
3.	**FONTELLA BASS**	RESCUE ME	*Chess '65*
4.	**DON COVAY**	IT'S BETTER TO HAVE	*Mercury '74*
5.	**THE MIRACLES**	GOING TO A GO-GO	*Tamla '66*
6.	**THE MIRACLES**	COME ROUND HERE I'M THE ONE YOU NEED /SAVE ME	*Tamla '66*
7.	**GRAHAM BONNEY**	SUPER GIRL	*Columbia '66*
8.	**JNR. WALKER**	HOW SWEET IT IS	*Soul '66*
9.	**GENE MCDANIELS**	TOWER OF STRENGTH	*Liberty '61*
10.	**JIMMY RADCLIFFE**	LONG AFTER TONIGHT IS ALL OVER	*Musicor '64*

Below Right: James 'Jimmy Mac' (NO not THAT Jimmy Mack!)' McKeachin, manager and producer of the Furys - a great yet sadly unsuccessful group, he was also responsible for production on Alexander Patten's legendary 'A Little Lovin' Sometimes' - another criminal failure.

The Northern Soul All Time Top 500

TEN
most hyped tracks that never made it!

1.	**REACHING FOR THE BEST**	BOB RELF	*
2.	**SIX BY SIX**	TONY TURNER	*
3.	**MESSING WITH MY MIND**	BARBARA CARR	*(BARR-CARR)*
4.	**HUNG UP ON YOU**	ROY ORBISON	*(MERCURY)*
5.	**OUR LOVE IS IN IN THE POCKET**	INSTRUMENTAL	*
6.	**LANDSLIDE**	INSTRUMENTAL	*
7.	**SHERRY**	HUGO MONTENEGRO	*(TIME)*
8.	**DIZZY**	LESTER LANIN	*(METROMEDIA)*
9.	**SOCIAL TRAGEDY**	DAUGHTERS OF EVE	*(CHECKER)*
10.	**MR MISERY**	PADDED CELL	*(TODDLIN' TOWN)*

*These records do NOT exist!... Despite being MEGA-HYPED in the 70's!

Right: Perhaps it's the relative obscurity of most Northern sounds and therefore information about them, perhaps it's just the gear... But the Northern scene has always been rife with stories of records that just don't exist.

Tony Turner's 'Six By Six' vocal - supposedly on Musicor is a prime example. Much talked of in the 70's - for some unknown reason no-one ever managed to track down a copy - I wonder why?!!! Anyway for all you frustrated would be owners - here at last it is (we'll also be glad to supply a copy of the label of Elvis' version of 'My Sugar Baby' to anyone interested! (please specify preferred label)).

Top ten things you want to remember - or forget!

TEN
brilliant tracks that never really made it!

1.	**LOOK AT ME LOOK AT ME**	VERNON GREENE	(MINIT)
2.	**AIN'T GONNA DO YOU NO HARM**	NEW WANDERERS	(READY)
3.	**WISHES**	The METRICS	(CHADWICK)
4.	**CAN YOU REMEMBER**	RHONDA DAVIES	(DUKE)
5.	**I MUST LOVE YOU**	TIMOTHY WILSON	(SKY DISC)
6.	**I DON'T WANNA GET AWAY FROM YOUR LOVE**		
		YVONNE DANIELS	(STERLING SOUND)
7.	**JUST DO THE BEST YOU CAN**	DUKE and LEONARD	(STOMP TOWN)
8.	**HEY GIRL**	The TOPICS	(CHADWICK)
9.	**WISHIN' AND HOPIN'**	BILLY KEENE	(PAULA/VAULT)
10.	**I KNOW I'M IN LOVE WITH YOU**	GEORGE 'JUKE' BYRD	(PAY-TONS)

'Not the kind of guy to give in and give up', a young Ian Levine, already established as one of the scene's most important DJs, with Mirwood Soul man Jimmy Thomas on a 'Beautiful Night' at Tunstall's legendary Torch club in 1972.

Ian's unparallelled knowledge of Soul music and personal vision for the development our scene not only resulted in his launching a staggeringly high proportion of the greatest Northern classics, but was also responsible for the introduction of almost brand new 70s releases. In the heyday of the screaming stomper these new and utterly different shuffling Mecca sounds were so opposed to the norm that it is hard to appreciate their shattering impact and the controversy surrounding them. Today our scene would be almost unrecognisable without their pervasive and, in retrospect, highly positive influence.

and finally...

For over 30 years Northern Soul has remained a unique form of youth culture that continues to unearth many superb and totally unknown 60s and 70s dance sounds from the States even after so many years of searching. Today many Soul fans who started 'Living The Nightlife' in the scene's earliest days are still regulars on the scene - after 30 years only wishing they had started going sooner! Whether you are a past member of the Soul fraternity, or are just starting to learn about our music, remember that the incredible vinyl featured throughout this book is on the turntables at at least one Allnighter and dozens of Soul Nights every week throughout the country, you'll find there's a space reserved for you on the dancefloor!

ADVERTISEMENT FEATURE

togetherness
the magazine... love soul? subscribe now

From the earliest sounds to all our tomorrow's, building bridges in the Soul scene. Each big issue is packed with the latest news, reviews of top venues, new discoveries, hot new releases, imports and authoritative contributions from the leading names in Northern, Modern and Deep Soul. PLUS FREE with every issue an EXCLUSIVE TOGETHERNESS CD featuring top current Northern sounds from Goldmine Soul Supply and the cream of Modern from Expansion records. Togetherness magazine is total coverage for the UK Soul scene in one essential publication.

ONLY £10.00 incl. P&P for a yearly two-issue subscription (Europe £14.00, Worldwide £15).
Send your details with a cheque a P/O or your credit card details (Visa, Switch, Mastercard or Solo) today:
KRL, PO Box 909, Worksop, Nottinghamshire S80 3YZ, UK.   Tel: 01909 515150   Fax: 01909 774200
You can now order TOGETHERNESS MAGAZINE online too: www.firstnet.co.uk/goldsoul or e-mail: goldsoul.firstnet.co.uk.

ADVERTISEMENT FEATURE

GOLDMINE SOUL SUPPLY

Soul for the Soulful

Covering the full spectrum of Deep, Modern and Northern Soul from the latest dancefloor monsters to in-demand connoisseur classics, Goldmine Soul Supply are the leading music, video and book publishers working exclusively in the Soul music field. Send your address and £1.50 to the above address for your copy of our comprehensive Millennium Soul Catalogue.

Available through all good record stores, or direct from the Goldmine Soul Supply website, www.firstnet.co.uk/goldsoul/.

Goldmine Soul Supply Limited, PO Box 4, Todmorden OL14 6DA, UK

Trade enquiries ONLY to Vital Distribution, 01454 886423.

index

1-2-3 Records	309
3 1/2, the	167
5th Dimension	412
6 O'Clock	254
7 Days 52 Weeks	344
7th Avenue Aviators, the	120, 355
20th Century Records	53, 127, 193, 242, 277, 358, 363
100 Club/6Ts Allnighter, London	289, 297, 312, 242, 352, 408
444 Records	283
A Girl Like You	361
A Good Thing Going	280
A Lil' Lovin' Sometimes	67
A Little Bit Hurt	6, 65
A Little Bit Of Something	284
A Little Piece Of Leather	336, 363
A Little Togetherness	143, 211
A Lot Of Love	259, 344
A Lot Of Love Goin Round	360
A Love Reputation	69
A Love That Never Runs Cold	136
A Man Like Me	6, 140
A Mighty Good Way	229, 273
A Quitter Never Wins	320
A Touch Of Velvet - A Sting Of Brass	389
A Touch Of Venus	257
A&M Records	122, 286, 305, 358, 376
A-Bet Records	157
ABC/ABC Paramount Records	62, 102, 114, 117, 134, 135, 215, 217, 220, 255, 258, 263, 335, 320, 358, 370, 375, 388, 389
AFO Records	81
AGC Records	260
AGP Records	234, 263
Abbey, John	34, 240
Abracadabra	357
Ace Records	400
Ace, Buddy	294
Acklin, Barbara	246, 345
Action Records	226, 414
Action, the	268
Ad-Libs, the	234
Adam's Apples	144, 341
Admirations, the	355
Admirations, the, Walter and	358
Adorables, the	258
Adventures, the	220, 248
Advertisement Features	421, 422
Afternoon Of The Rhino	45, 342, 364
Against My Will	303
Agee, Ray	348
Agent Double-O Soul	121, 336
Aggisald, Steve	46
Ainsworth, Leonard	18
Ain't Gonna Do You No Harm	420
Ain't No Soul	377
Ain't Nothing You Can Do	275
Ain't Nothin' But A Houseparty	361
Ain't That Right	286
Airtown Records	356
Aitken, Ben	215

Al Foster Band	376
Aladins, the	282
Alexander, Brandy	260
Alexander, Reggie	357
Alfa Records	220, 248
Alfreton, Leisure Centre	396
All In My Mind	271
All Of My Life	350
All Over The World	357
All Rite Records	355
All The Way Home	318
Allbrighton	408
Allen, Barbara	246
Allen, Derek	5, 141
Allen, L./Larry	216
Allen, Tony	70
Allnighter CD	324
Alston Records	320, 417
Alston, Shirley	210
Altern 8	5
Ambassadors, the	317, 323
Ambers, the	273
American Arts Records	214
Ames, Nancy	109, 307
Amy Records	30, 74, 131, 263
Andantes, the	391
Anderson Brothers, the	165
Anderson, Anita	232
Anderson, Carol	274
Anderson, John	39, 105, 194, 217, 274, 385, 405
Andrews, Lee, and the Hearts	218, 356, 357
Andrews, Ruby	63
André Brasseur	321, 414
Angelle, Bobby	84
Anglo American Records	385
Anka, Paul	94, 264, 342, 392, 394
Ann, Beverly	123, 143
Ann, Little	217, 378
Another Day	288
Another Love	273
Anthony, Little, and the Imperials	55, 182, 233, 364, 413
Anthony, Sheila	267
Apollas, The	137, 346
Apollo Records	265
Apple, Peaches Pumpkin Pie	138, 218
Apollo, Vince	355
Ara Records	388
Arch Records	215
Arctic Records	208, 281, 310, 350
Arden Records	276
Are You Angry	224
Argo Records	238, 350, 310, 370
Arista Records	51, 348, 358
Arnell, Billy	317
Arnold, PP	300
Arrington, Joseph, Jnr	302
Arthur, 'Junk Shopper'	229
Artistics, the	232, 322
Artistics, the	368, 288
Ashford, Jack	263
Ashford, Nick	137
Ashibende, Tim	385
Ashley, Tyrone	235

Ask The Lonely	357
At The Discotheque	335
At The Top Of The Stairs	336, 363
Atac Records	29
Atco Records	81, 91, 291, 321, 358, 375, 378
Atkens, Ben	215
Atkinson, 'Flash'	383
Atlantic Records	37, 64, 81, 108, 225, 237, 240, 241, 323, 335, 338, 342, 344, 357, 358, 360, 363, 367, 414
Attractions, the	133
Audio Arts Records	138, 336
August and Deneen	215
Autumn Records	117, 416
Avant, the, Oldham	357
Avin Records	318
Awake Records	309
Axelrod, Dave	113
BMG	5, 324
BR Records	206
Babe Ruth	376
Baby A Go-Go	42
Baby Boy (Chapter IV)	275
Baby Boy (Fred Smith)	227, 345
Baby Do The Philly Dog	316
Baby Don't You Weep	146
Baby Have Mercy On Me	186
Baby Hit And Run	78, 340
Baby I Need You	317
Baby Mine	204
Baby Reconsider	6, 154
Baby What Happened To Our Love	349
Baby What I Mean	185
Baby Without You	318
Bacharach and David	21, 48
Back Beat Records	145, 195, 338
Back Drop	379
Back In My Arms Again	98
Back Stabbers	189
Backstreet	318, 338
Bailey, JR	175
Baines, Vickie	264
Baja Marimba Band, the	376
Baker, Butch	178, 270
Baker, Yvonne	19, 262
Baker-Harris-Young	186
Balbia, Ed	156
Baldry, Long John	250
Balk, Harry	147, 212, 214, 311
Baltimore and Ohio Marching Band, the	271
Band Of Gold	7, 361
Bang Records	263
Banks, Darrell	14, 49, 79, 134, 167, 357
Banks, Doug	191, 350
Banks, Homer	256
Banks, Robert	126, 229, 273
Banks, Ron	169
Banks, Tony	69
Bar Clay Records	346
Barbara and The Uniques	276
Barbees, the	296
Bareback Records	248

423

Index

Barefootin'	10
Baretto, Ray	239
Bari Track	38, 71, 269
Barker, Francine	231
Barkesdale, Chuck	101
Barnes, Dena	35, 109, 214, 342, 348, 354
Barnes, JJ	49, 122, 152, 161, 318, 356, 402
Barnes, Sidney	153, 182, 187, 235
Barnes, Towanda	166
Barnett, James	179, 272
Barnfather, Martin 'Soul Sam'	198
Barnum, HB	39, 378
Barracuda Records	57, 352
Barrett, Richard	100
Barrett, Susan	340
Barry Records	182, 323
Barry, John	18
Barry, Len	72, 142, 221, 392
Bartel, Johnny	355
Basil, Toni	305
Bass, Fontella	336, 418
Batiste, Rose	38, 71
Batman At The Go-Go	270
Battiste, Harold	81
Bay Brothers, the	360
Bay Sound Records	233
Be Young, Be Foolish, Be Happy	225
Beach Girls, the	86
Beat, The	336
Beatles, the	32, 90, 150, 208, 289
Beatty, Lou	304, 312, 394
Beatty, Pamela	272
Beauty Is Just Skin Deep	122
Beavers, Jackie	136, 348
Because Of My Heart	208, 374
Beckett Records	355
Beggars Can't Be Choosey	171
Being Without You	198
Believe It Or Not	311
Bell Records	30, 74, 131, 145, 155, 225, 240, 260, 265, 344, 364, 374, 377
Bell, Archie, and the Drells	37, 338, 363
Bell, Madeline	300
Bell, Tommy	66, 190, 218
Bell, William	22
Bellamy, Glenn	5, 61
Bellars, Rob	289
Belles, the	320, 370
Beltone Records	289
Bendinelli, Frank	54
Benlee Productions	281
Benzine	321, 357
Bernard, Kenny	163, 395
Berns, Bert	81
Berry, Richard	360
Better Use Your Head	55, 233, 342, 364
Bettin On Love	280
Beverly Glenn Records	320
Beverly, Frankie and the Butlers	25, 180, 208, 374, 391
Biddu	140, 190
Big In Wigan CD	324
Big Top Records	48, 358, 416
Big Tree Records	151, 274
Bill Black's Combo	141
Billie and Lillie	224
Billingsea, Joe	172
Binnick, Bernie	405
Bishop, Eddie	222, 358
Bishop, Jimmy	156

Bits 'n Pieces	290
Bizarre Inc	5
Black Ivory	206
Black Magic Records	18, 84, 362, 363
Black Mother Goose	283
Black Power	251, 376, 388
Black, Cody	241
Black, Jay	217
Blackburn, Tony	150
Blackpool Mecca	13, 28, 60, 72, 82, 133, 139, 143, 161, 166, 171, 187, 189, 195, 199, 202, 243, 244, 250, 265, 273, 274, 275, 276, 277, 292, 305, 335, 340, 342, 343, 344, 369, 380, 384
Blackwell, George	313
Bland, Bobby	312, 335, 356
Blavat, Jerry	5
Bledsie, Fern	102
Bleu Rose Records	212
Blood Sweat and Tears	93
Blossoms, the	257
Blowing My Mind To Pieces	84
Blowing Up My Mind	150
Blue Cat Records	234, 235, 291
Blue Mink	300
Blue Notes, the	136
Blue Orchid, the	13
Blue Rock Records	82, 220, 230, 348, 356
Blue Room, Sale	281, 342
Blue Star Records	173, 356
Blue Thumb	344, 366
Blues and Soul Magazine	10, 234, 240, 409
Bluestime Records	352
Bob and Earl	84, 124, 363, 370
Bob and Earl Band, the	214
Bob and Fred	115
Bobby Fuller Four, the	176
Bobby and the Dream Girls	214
Bok To Bach	127, 340
Bolan, Marc	119
Bond, Ann	5
Bonds, Gary US	175
Bonney, Graham	418
Bonnie Records	177, 348
Boo, Betty	194, 197
Boogaloo Down Broadway	186
Boogaloo Party	173, 363
Boola Boola Records	187
Boom Records	77, 140
Boss Records	357
Bounty, James	183
Bowden, 'Terrible' Tom	199
Bowie, David	163
Brady, Bob, and the Concords	317, 336
Brady, Pat	385
Bragg, Johnny	132
Brainwasher	261
Breakaway (Steve Karmen)	211
Breakaway (Toni Basil)	305
Breakaway (Valentines)	237
Breakin' Down The Walls Of Heartache	361
Breakout	205, 336
Breakthrough Records	228, 374, 391
Brenda and The Tabulations	215
Bridgforth, (Little) Ann	217
Bright Star Records	230
Brill Building, the	89
Bring Your Love Back To Me	213
Bristol, Johnny	261, 298, 315, 413
Britt, Mel	44, 329

Broadway Records	323
Bronco Records	191, 360, 416
Brooklyn Bridge	278
Brooks Brothers, the	318
Brooks, Patti	168
Brothers Grimm, the	350
Brothers, Sisters and Cousins	290
Brown Door Records	318
Brown Sugar	272
Brown, James	139
Brown, Maxine	91, 229, 271, 299, 353
Brown, Oscar, Jnr	20
Brown, Tim	5, 13, 15, 16, 17, 183
Browner, Duke	35, 147, 177, 212, 214
Bruno, Tony	120, 271
Brunswick Records	33, 139, 144, 208, 221, 223, 226, 230, 232, 246, 311, 317, 320, 322, 323, 341
Brute Records	356, 391
Bryant, Don	251
Bryant, JD	374, 391
Bryant, Lillie	224
Bryson Bay Brass	183
Buddah Records	51, 190, 268, 278, 282, 318, 364, 414, 418
Buddy Records	190, 310
Bunky Records	69
Burdick, Doni	71, 269, 357
Burn Baby Burn	148
Burning Bush	288
Burning Sensation	126, 199
Burns, Jimmy	161
Burrell, Kenny	16, 17, 404
Burton, Chris	384
Burton, Dave	97
Bush, Tommy	356
Buster and Eddie	282
Butch	385
Butler, Billy	9, 27
Butler, Freddy	153
Butler, Jerry	27, 37, 99, 176, 251, 256, 260
Buttercup Records	267
Bye, Barnaby	133, 367
Byrd, George 'Juke'	420
C, Nicky	233
C, the Fantastic Johnny	186
CBS Records	89, 91, 163, 229, 310, 414
CODs, the	378
CTI Records	363
Cadet Records	174, 192, 238, 357, 389
Cairos, the	282, 343, 350
Caiton, Richard	105
Cajun Heart	323
Call Me	222, 358
Call Me Records	375
Call Me Tomorrow	147
Call On Me	312, 335
Calla Records	47, 132, 150, 270, 314
Callier, Terry	192, 357, 389
Cambridge, Dottie	166
Cameo Parkway Records	68, 70, 110, 264, 297, 302, 311, 336, 352, 370
Campbell, Eddie	196
Campbell, Mike	115
Campbell, Sammy	235
Can It Be Me	148
Can You Remember	419
Candi Records	266, 341, 355
Candle In The Window	357

424

Candy and the Kisses	137	Change Your Ways	153	Col-Soul Records	212
Canterbury Records	143, 211, 257	Channel 3	318	Cole, Nat King	308
Can't Be Still	282	Chansonettes, Les	349	Coleman Records	317
Can't Get Over These Memories	125, 325, 348	Chapman, Mary	105, 384	Coleman, Donna	318
Can't Help Lovin' That Man Of Mine	189	Chapter Five	229, 299	Collins and Collins	203, 358
Can't Lose My Head	313, 343	Chapter IV	275	Collins, Edwyn	361
Can't We Talk It Over	216	Charades, the	122, 358	Collins, Roger	294
Cape, Gary	385	Charay Records	199	Collins, Will, and Will Power	248, 343
Capitol Records	67, 70, 110, 113, 149, 152, 204, 206, 235, 248, 252, 259, 268, 283, 282, 287, 295, 336, 340, 347, 354, 376, 417	Charger Records	18, 338	Colossus Records	142, 358
		Chariot Records	317, 336	Colton, Tony	355
		Charles, Ray	122, 180	Colts, the	282
		Charly Records	400	Columbia Records	27, 33, 119, 133, 155, 159, 165, 167, 185, 209, 231, 246, 263, 265, 280, 301, 308, 311, 344, 355, 357, 358, 360, 388, 395, 418
Captain Of Your Ship	203	Charmaines, the	263		
Caravelle Records	233	Charms, the	244		
Carey, Jake	173	Chartmaker Records	224		
Carlena	320	Chaumonts, the	233	Come Go With Me	119
Carletts, the	206	Chavez, Freddie	75	Come On And Be My Sweet Darlin'	170
Carlton, Kenny	82, 348	Chavis, James	266	Come On Train	50
Carlton, Little Carl	145, 338	Cheatin Kind	294	Come See (What's Left Of Me)	62, 357
Carmichael, James	7, 252	Checker Records	338	Comer, Mary Love (See Mary Love)	129
Carnival Records	321	Checker, Chubby	68, 297, 311, 329, 335, 344, 346	Commitments, the, film	302
Carol, Vivien	349			Commodores, the	15, 295
Caroline, Radio	170	Checkerboard Squares, the	15, 17, 45, 342	Compared To What	180, 389
Carr, James	200, 372	Cherry People, the	190	Compass Records	166, 183, 220, 248
Carrie Records	146	Cherry Red Records	228	Competition Ain't Nothin'	145, 338
Carrolls, the	195	Chess Records	31, 69, 88, 101, 121, 144, 161, 174, 192, 220, 238, 240, 248, 320, 335, 342, 364, 370, 418	Conaway, Jeff	167
Carrow, George	167			Condition Red	271
Carstairs, the	46, 389			Congress Records	120, 355
Carter, Clarence	201	Chesterfield Allnighter	354	Conley, Arthur	272
Carter, Jean	321, 340	Chevrons, the	120	Conn, Mervyn	229
Carter, Kenny	360	Chi-Lites, the	246, 258	Connoisseur Collection	5,400
Casablanca Records	220, 316	Chi-Town Records	183	Constellation Records	61, 69, 226, 281, 336, 357
Case Of Tyme, the	93, 167	Chicory Records	27	Construction, the	320, 394
Cashing In	60, 342	Chills And Fever	240	Contempo Records	240
Cashman and Pistilli	135	Chimes, the	284	Contenders, the	284
Cashmeres, the	178, 325, 350	Chinn, Billy	273	Contours, the	78, 154, 172, 340, 363, 415
Casino Classics Records	132, 178	Chris Clark	4, 15, 17, 59	Conwell, Jimmy	124, 280, 338
Casino, Wigan	5, 13, 17, 19, 28, 30, 40, 56, 59, 60, 74, 77, 94, 103, 111, 112, 125, 132, 137, 138, 139, 145, 148,156, 160, 170, 178, 194, 196, 197, 199, 200, 202, 203, 207, 209, 215, 217, 223, 226, 228, 243, 247, 251, 252, 263, 264, 268, 277, 282, 290, 291, 302, 303, 305, 340, 342, 343, 344, 346, 348, 361, 369, 373, 380	Christie,Tony	204	Cook, Dina	303
		Cigarette Ashes	124, 338	Cook, Jerry	235, 340
		Circa Distribution	242	Cook, Little Joe	303
		Clapping Song	301	Cook, Lonnie	187
		Clark, Alice	169, 388	Cook, Norman	393
		Clark, Connie	15, 17, 59	Cooke, Sam	121
		Clark, Dee	61, 357	Cool Off	139, 342
		Clark, Dick	297	Cool Records	360
Castellucio, Francis	112, 157	Clark, Jimmey 'Soul'	170, 348	Cooper, Christine	98, 264, 344, 378
Castles In The Sand	3	Clark, Petula	363	Cooper, Eula	171
Casualeers, the	56	Clark, Rudy	297	Cooperettes, the	226
Caswell, Johnny	142	Clarke, Tony	31, 342	Coral Records	153, 202, 245, 340
Catacombs, the	13, 242, 257, 262, 286, 306, 369, 382	Class Records	282	Cordell, Richie	98
		Claunch, Quinton M	198, 200	Cornelius Brothers and Sister Rose	358
Catamount Records	202	Clay, Tom, Radio DJ	230	Correc-Tone Records	320, 355
Cattaneo, Bob	202, 228	Cleethorpes Weekender	271, 408	Cosgrove, Stuart	390
Cause You're Mine	64, 160	Cleethorpes, Winter Gardens	105, 232, 290, 369	Cotillion Records	41, 161
Cavaliere, Felix	144	Cliff, Jimmy	367, 376	Coulter, Phil	280
Caviar and Chitlins	150	Clinton, George	152, 201, 219, 256	Countdown (Here I Come)	143
Central, Leeds	382	Clinton, Larry	73, 255	Country Girl	264, 346, 378
Chadwick Records	357, 419	Clintone Records	171	Courcy, JoAnn	196
Challenge Records	8, 191, 290	Coachman Records	13	Courtney, Dean	72, 225, 342
Champion Records	40, 257, 340	Coasters, the	97, 185, 287, 378	Courtney, Lou	220, 252
Champion, Mickie	128	Cobb, Ed	40, 119, 257, 305	Cover-Up	378, 379
Champion, The	126, 251, 342, 364	Cobblestone Records	268	Covey, Julian	65
Chance, Nolan	69	Cobra Records	256	Cowboys to Girls	66
Chancellor Records	310	Cochise	367, 388	Cox, Wally	148
Chandler, EJ	346	Coefield, Brice	286	Crackin' Up Over You	58, 363
Chandler, Gene	139, 226, 246, 281, 336, 363, 372	Coefield, Herman	86, 151	Crawford, Dave	201
		Coffey, Dennis	57, 115, 122, 152	Crazy Baby	97, 378
Chandler, Lorraine	19, 153, 262, 318, 342, 356, 357	Coghill, Nigel	5	Crazy Cajun Productions	213
		Coit, James	251, 376, 388		
Chandlers, the	212	Cokell, Les	6, 25, 152, 213, 234, 268, 383, 402, 403		
Chanel, Bruce	245				

425

Index

Crazy Horse Records	142, 259, 347	Debutante Records	324	Don't Cry, Sing A Long With The Music	176
Creation	96	Decca Records	87, 142, 165, 168, 170, 175, 202, 221, 250, 321, 340, 344, 372	Don't Depend On Me	186
Creole Records	178			Don't It Make You Feel Funky	260
Crests, the	278			Don't Knock It	127
Crewe, Bob	89, 109, 205	December Records	240	Don't Leave Me This Way	204
Crimson Records	218	Dee Gee Records	320	Don't Let Him Hurt You	349
Croasdell, Ady	384, 404, 408	Dee, Kiki	3, 279	Don't Let The Door Hit Your Back	178
Crocker, Frankie, Radio DJ	230	Deep Freeze	256	Don't Mess With My Man	335
Cromwellian, Bolton	382	Deep Soul	223	Don't Pity Me	318, 346
Cross My Heart	323	Deeper (In Love With You)	264	Don't Pretend	320
Crossover	379	Dees, Sam	355	Don't Push It Don't Force It	154
Cry Baby	24	Deesu Records	198	Don't Send Me Away	355
Cry Me A River	120	Dejac Records	239, 389	Don't Start None	358
Crying My Heart Out	244	Del-Larks, the	235, 340	Don't Stop Now	186, 360
Crying Over You	35, 147	Del-Phis, the	286	Don't Take Away The Music	417
Cub Records	291	Del-Satins, the	45	Don't Take It Out On This World	144
Cummings, Tony	409	Del-Vikings, the	119, 289	Don't Turn Your Back On Me	352
Cuppy Records	137, 327	Deletts, the	351	Don't You Care Anymore	149
Curry, Clifford	284	Delfonics, the	147	Don't You Even Care	237
Curtis, Colin, DJ	202, 211, 224, 244, 265, 275, 303, 403	Dells, the	101, 241, 370	Doo Wop	130, 217, 270, 278, 282, 303, 320, 360
		Demain, Arin	173, 325		
Curtis, Lenny	138, 343, 358	Demon/Edsel Records	400	Doomsday	364
Curtom Records	82, 156, 346	Demures, the	348	Dore Records	188, 321
C'mon and Swim	117	Dene, 'Farmer' Carl	402	Dot Records	245, 315
		Deram Records	187	Dotty's Records	262, 297, 332
		Derek and Ray	172	Double Cookin'	45
D-Town Records	181, 318, 372	Desanto, Sugar Pie	294	Douglas, Carl	190, 395
DJM Records	50	Despenza Records	232	Douglas, Carole	248
Dacosta, Rita	160	Destiny Records	279	Down And Out	350
Dade Records	136, 320, 333, 360	Determination	140	Down In The Dumps	130, 194
Dahrouge, Ray	165	Deto Records	159, 332	Down To Love Town	186
Dakar Records	318	Detroit Executives, the	139, 170, 340	Downbeat Records	236
Dale, Syd	18	Detroit Prophets, the	186	Downstairs Record Shop	405
Dance, Dance, Dance	56	Detroit Sound	269	Dozier, Lamont	296
Danny and the Juniors	142	Detroit Spinners, the	80, 331, 354, 360, 415	Dr. Love	184, 287, 336
Dark Side Of The Moon	150	Devil With The Blue Dress	205	Dramatics, the	169
Darkest Days	209, 318	Devore, Florence	321	Dreamlovers, the	191
Darling, Darling	288	Dial Records	188, 240, 302, 349	Dreams Band, the	282
Darnells, the	304	Diamond Records	151, 236	Dreams, the	120
Darrell, Guy	363, 414	Diamond, Bobby	346	Drifter, The	250
Date Records	230, 231, 263, 340, 413	Diamond, Ron, Radio DJ	95, 132	Drifters, the	85, 230
Daughters Of Eve	419	Discatron	406	Drifters, the 'Original'	151
David and Reuben	130	Diddley, Bo	335	Driving Beat	126, 356
David and the Giants	142, 259, 348	Dieperro, Tom	16	Drizabone	358
David, Lee	155, 340	Dillard, Moses	321, 348, 357	Drum Records	346
Davies, Billie	150	Dimension Records	291	Du-ettes, the	276
Davies, Huey	172	Dionn Records	41	Duck, The	209, 292
Davies, Mamie (See Mamie Galore)	260	Diplomacy Records	272	Dude, The	153
Davies, Rhonda	420	Diplomats, the	189	Duke And Leonard	420
Davies, Terry	404	Discotheque '66, Capitol	287	Duke/Peacock Records	227, 312, 321, 335, 356, 370, 371, 420
Davis, Arnold	56	Dixon, Eugene (See Gene Chandler)	139, 226		
Davis, Don	38, 121, 134, 136, 152, 201, 241, 285, 413	Dixon, Luther	131	Dunhill Records	292
		Dizzy	377	Durante, Paula	143, 196
Davis, John	203	Do I Love You (Indeed I Do)	4, 15, 16, 17, 59, 346, 357, 374, 391	Dust My Broom	122, 336
Davis, Melvin	276, 322, 329, 352			Dyke and the Soul Brothers	314
Davison, Alfie	194	Do Right Man	260	Dynamics, the	146, 328
Dawn	285	Do The Temptation Walk	255, 336	Dynamite Records	291
Day, Alan, DJ	5, 27, 403	Do Unto Me	145	Dynamites, the	376
Day, Jackie	333, 350, 374	Do You Believe It	57	Dynamo Records	57, 130, 131
Day, Muriel	219, 264	Do You Love Me	78	Dynatones, the	335
Daybreak	206, 355	Do You Love Me Baby?	263	Dynells, the	375
Daye, Eddie, and Four Bars	283, 348	Do-De-Ri Records	29	Dyno Voice Records	86, 151, 336, 355
De-Lite Records	204, 352	Dobson, Mark 'Butch'	385		
De-Lites, the	137	Doc Records	257, 318, 378, 416		
De-vel Records	282	Dodds, Nella	357	EEE Records	225
Deadbeats, the	348, 378	Doggett, Bill	121	EMI Records	133, 209, 265
Dean, Debbie	323	Domain Records	335	Eagle, Roger	383
Dean, Snoopy	376	Domino, Fats	177, 265	Eastern Records	196
Dearly Beloved	57	Don't Accuse Me	350	Easy Baby	220, 248
Debonairs	285	Don't Be Sore At Me	201	Echo Records	350
Debut Records	357	Don't Bring Me Down	160	Echoes (Black Echoes)	409

The Northern Soul All Time Top 500

Echoes Magazine	409	Fairmount Records	208, 321, 355	Foxx, Inez and Charlie	131, 335, 338
Echoes, the	24	Faith, Gene	156	Frank, Big, and the Essence	356
Eckstine, Billy	358	Famborough, Henry	314	Frankie and Johnny	168
Eddie and Ernie	196	Fame Records/Studios	158, 201, 272, 357	Frankie and the Classicals	132
Eddie's My Name	255	Fania Records	239, 352	Fraser, Jimmy	246, 355
Eddy, Duane	222	Fantastics, the	306	Fraternity Records	277
Edmund Jnr, Lada	8, 192	Fantasy	256	Frazier, Joe	276
Edwards, Dee	318	Fantasy Records	294	Free For All	179
Edwards, Dennis	78, 172, 374	Farrow, Mikki	356	Freeman, Art	158, 357
Edwards, Jackie	118, 395	Fascinating Girl	317	Freeman, Bobby	117, 416
Edwards, Jerome	252	Fascination Records	31	Freeman, George	350
Edwards, Lou	265	Fascinations, the	102, 156, 336, 363	French EPs	76, 81, 171, 181
Edwards, Tyrone	206	Fat Fish Records	154, 357	Friday Night	356, 416
El Watusi	239	Fat Man, The	270	Frog, Wynder K	261
Elbejay Records	132	Fatback Band, the	239	From The Teacher To The Preacher	246
Elbert, Donnie	162, 336, 363	Father's Angels	127	Frontera, Tommy	355
Elektra Records	192	Fawns, the	310	Fuller Brothers, the	148, 340
Elf Records	284	Fee Records	274	Fuller, The Bobby, Four	176
Elgins, the	320, 363	Feldman-Goldstein-Gottehrer Productions	7, 297	Funkadelic	256
Eli, Bobby	183	Ferguson, Barbara Tamiko (See Tamiko Jones)	240	Fuqua, Harvey	136, 261, 413
Elijah Rockin' With Soul	7, 375	Ferguson, Helena	183	Furys, the	67, 252, 296, 418
Ellis, Martyn	403	Festival Time	118, 161, 363	Fusion Records	133, 376
Ellis, Shirley	301	Fi-Dels, the	188	Futuretones, the	121, 306
Ellison, John	185	Fiestas, the	318, 350	Fuzz, the	314
Ellusions, the	318	Fife Piper, The	335		
Ember Records	180	Find A Quiet Place	276		
Embers, the	10, 225, 260	Fine Records	185	GAR Records	244
Empires, the	266, 355	Finiz, Bob	270	GM Records	159, 180, 389
End Records	138, 332, 358	Fireman	321	GSF Records	165, 189, 255, 375
Enjoyables, the	282	First Choice	321	GWP Records/Productions	153, 181
Enterprise Records	260	First Cut Is The Deepest	300	Gainey, Jerry	350
Entertainer, The	31	Five Dutones, the	145	Gaitors, the	24
Envy	352	Five Pennies, the	284	Galaxy Records	337, 375
Epic Records	89, 117, 307, 340, 357, 376, 394	Five Stairsteps, the	156, 414	Galore, Mamie	260
		Five and a Penny	344	Gamble Records	25, 66, 340
Epitome Of Sound	23	Flame 'N' King	239	Gamble and Huff Producers	37, 66, 150, 160
Era Records	318, 346, 351, 378	Flamingo Club, the	13	Gamble, Kenny	
Eric Records	96	Flamingoes, the	173, 363	(See also Gamble and Huff)	213
Erica Records	161	Flannagan, Steve	318	Gardner, Don	7, 294, 352, 370, 391
Ernstat Productions	146	Flasher, The	133, 364, 376	Garner, George	114
Errison, King	166	Flello, Mick	384	Garner, Reggie	252
Erwin, Dee	62, 260	Flemming, Garfield	355	Garrett, Bobby	214, 319
Eskee Records	325	Flemmons, Wade	360	Garrett, Kelly	200
Eternally	263	Fletcher, Sam	174, 349	Garrison Records	320
Eubanks, Darrell (See Banks, Darrell)	79	Flip Records	360	Garvin, Rex	130, 337, 356, 388
Evans, Ernest (See Checker, Chubby)	68, 297	Flirtations, the	187	Gateway Records	162, 336
Evans, Karl	173, 210	Follow Your Heart	320	Gator Records	321
Evans, Nate	298	Fontana Records	257, 279, 280, 332	Gatur Records	356
Evans, Ray	46	Footsee	26, 56, 254, 363, 365	Gay Lettes, the	349
Evans, Richard	174	Footsteps Following Me	234	Gaye, Marvin	3, 16, 17, 186, 257, 285, 354, 363
Evans, Sticks	250	For Millionaires Only, CD	324		
Event Records	179	Ford Capri	406	Gear	379
Ever Again	136, 344, 374	Ford, Jon	316	Gearing, Yvonne	313
Everard, Danny	354	Forever In My Heart	352	Gee Baby (I Love You)	227
Everest Records	272, 360	Formations, the	221, 321, 363	Gee Records	350
Everett, Betty	256, 299	Forte, Ronnie	351	Gee Whiz	269
Every Beat Of My Heart	276	Fortune Teller	318	Gee, Marsha	317
Everybody's Going To A Love In	317, 336	Fortunes, the	282	Gemini Records	351
Everything's Gonna Be Alright	300	Foster, Al, Band	376	Gems, the	220, 288
Evil One	114	Foster, Eddie	16, 103, 340, 416	General American Records	90
Evison, Dave	13, 111, 157, 207, 302, 404	Foster, Rick	13	Genie Records	259
Evolution Records	316, 344	Fountain, James	22, 340	Genuine Records	11, 181, 329, 348, 374, 378
Excello Records	262, 323, 329, 360, 389	Four Below Zero	206	Gerry and Paul	239
Exciters, the	127, 150, 207, 363	Four Brothers Records	184	Get A Job	303
Expansion Records	159, 274, 400	Four Jokers, the	284	Get It Baby	130, 194
Expo Records	161	Four Larks, the	318	Get It Off My Conscience	344
Exus Trek	151	Four Perfections, the	95	Get On Your Knees	414
		Four Seasons, the (See also Valli, Frankie and the) 112, 306, 363		Get Out	100, 340, 342, 364
FIP Records	44, 329	Four Tops, the	3, 249, 329, 357	Getting Mighty Crowded	256
Face It Girl It's Over	152	Fox, Damon	321	Gettin' To Me	10, 358
				Giant Records	115, 195, 357

427

Index

Gibson, Wayne	165, 363	Greenburg, Florence	205	Heatherton, Dick	3, 221
Gigsy	400	Greene, Laura	189	Heatherton, Joey	221
Giles, Leola	137	Greezie	273	Heaven In The Afternoon	320
Gilly, DJ	168	Griffin, Herman	229, 231	Heaven Must Be Missing An Angel	417
Gilmer, Jimmy	61	Groove City Records	129, 158, 327, 346	Heaven Must Have Sent You	320
Ginger, Taylor, Raymond, DJ	199, 288, 404	Groovesville Records	158, 201, 358	Hebb, Bobby	83, 338, 363
Gioe, Tony	248	Groovin' At The Go-Go	318	Help Me	7, 141
Girl I Love You	350	Group, the	348	Help Me (Get Myself Back Together Again)	119
Girl Watcher	6, 10, 337	Guess Who Loves You	283, 325, 349	Help Wanted	156
Girls Are Against Me	354	Guess, Lenis	175	Helpless	293, 415
Girls Are Out To Get You	102, 336	Guiness Records	262	Hem Records	178, 325, 350
Girty, Dave	229	Guy, Billy	97	Henderson, Billy	314
Give Up Girl	344	Guyden Records (See also Jamie/Guyden Records)	191	Hendley, John	125
Gladiolas, the	198			Henry, Andrea	231, 352
Glasser, Dick	137	Guyton, Howard	253, 355	Henry, Virgil	358
Glenn, Gary	268	Gypsies, the	187, 321	Here I Go Again	6, 37, 363
Global Records	156			Here She Comes	311
Glorico Records	360			Heritage Records	127
Glories, the	313	HBR Records	335	Heron, Gil Scott	171
Go Away Little Boy	174	HFMP Records	298	Hesitations, the	153, 181, 372
Godin, Dave	13, 234, 310, 409	HIB Records	151	Hestor, Tony	129, 139, 151, 170, 194,
Going To A Go-Go	364	HMV Records	114, 395		197, 243, 267, 411, 413
Going To A Happening	337, 338	Haley, Bill	137	Hey Girl	356
Gold Soul Records	317	Half A Cup	252	Hey Girl (Topics, the)	420
Gold Token Records	358	Hall, Rick	142	Hey Girl Don't Bother Me	8, 92, 364
Golden Hit Records	253	Hambric, Billy	346	Hey Little Girl	344
Golden Torch Story, the, CD	324	Hamilton, Al (See Kent, Al)	222, 277	Hey Little Way Out Girl	320
Golden World Records	134, 145, 240, 256, 370, 388	Hamilton, Dave	30, 217	Hey Sah-Lo-Ney	268, 335
Golden World Strings	254	Hamilton, Edward and the Arabians	146, 323	Hey There Lonely Girl	277
Goldmine/Soul Supply	5, 15, 16, 129, 146, 194,	Hamilton, James	26	He's All I Got	279, 360
	255, 309, 324, 400, 423	Hamilton, Roy	21, 58, 372, 375	He's Coming Home	123
Goldsboro, Bobby	264, 388, 392, 394	Hammond Bros	245	He's The One That Rings My Bell	360
Goldsmith, Cliff	154	Hampton, Johnny	243, 297, 333	Hi Records	126, 141, 251, 337, 342
Goldspot Records	244	Hand It Over	289	Hickory Records	128, 168, 236, 244, 338
Goldwax Records	200, 372	Hang On	266	Hicks, Joe	256
Gone With The Wind Is My Love	321	Hang Your Tears Out To Dry	229	Hide Nor Hair	221
Gonna Be A Big Thing	106	Hanks, Mike	276	Higgins, Monk	246, 260, 270
Gonna Fix You Good	233	Hanna Barberra	283, 298	High Inergy	310
Gonna Hang On In There Girl	9	Happy	339	High-Keys, the	258
Good Time Charlie	312	Happy (Velevet Hammer)	258	Highland Room, the	
Good Time Tonight	336	Happy Tiger Records	240	(See also Blackpool Mecca)	94, 237, 265, 344
Goodbye/Goodbye Nothing To Say	278, 340	Harlem Shuffle	363	Hill, Clarence	360
Goodnight Irene	186	Harper, Bud	321	Hill, Lainie	109, 307
Goodway Records	303, 325	Harper, Jeanette	193	Hill, ZZ	310
Gordon, Billy	172, 320	Harris, Major	147, 208	Hit And Run	38, 71
Gordon, Marc	134	Hart, Don	312	Hitch It To The Horse	186, 339
Gordy Jnr, Berry	3, 17, 36, 42, 118, 159,	Harthon Productions/Records	73, 213, 226, 277, 310	Hitsville, USA	3, 80, 129, 261
	162, 172, 261, 299	Harvey Records	261	Ho Happy Day	239
Gordy Records	118, 219, 286, 293, 306,	Harvey, Willie	194	Hoggs, Billy	172
	318, 337, 346, 357	Has It Happened To You Yet	358	Hold Back The Night	318, 364
Gordy, Raynoma	299, 370	Hatch, Tony	222	Hold On	265
Gore, Jackie	225	Hatcher, Charles (See also Starr, Edwin)	121	Holden, Ron	8, 290
Gorman, Freddie	186	Hatcher, Roger	262, 297	Holiday, Jimmy	272
Gospel Truth Records	195	Hatcher, Willie	262	Holland Dozier Holland	135, 186, 413
Got To Find A Way	323	Hatfield, Bobby	207	Holland, Eddie	412
Gotta Have Your Love	114	Hatim, Lee	263	Hollies, the	150
Gotta See Jane	36	Have Love Will Travel	360	Holloway, Brenda	3, 15, 129, 164, 246,
Graham, Larry	117	Have More Time	322, 323		292, 358, 373, 415
Graham, Leonard	280	Have You Seen Her	246	Holloway, Patrice	257, 283, 354, 360
Grand Prix Records	322	Hawaii 5-0	72	Holly Records	317
Grant, Earl	221	Hawk Sound Records	274	Hollyhocks, the	284
Granz, Norman	210	Hayes, Isaac	93, 211, 256	Holman, Eddie	213, 277
Grapevine Records	161, 189, 197, 274	Hayes, Mary Francis	276	Holmes, Marvin	318
Grasshoppers, Preston	386, 408	Haywood, Leon	6, 154	Holmes, Rupert	85
Gray, Dobie	18, 338, 363	He Who Picks A Rose	318	Holton Records	177
Grayson, Miles, Producer	178, 210, 274	Headache In My Heart	285	Honest To Goodness	190, 310
Greco, George	219	Heartache Souvenirs	323, 333	Honey Bee	366
Green Dolphin Records	216, 333	Heartaches Away My Boy	98	Honey Cone	135, 257
Green Door	6, 261	Heartaches I Can't Take	349	Honeycutt, Johnny	320, 352
Green, Al	126, 251, 267	Heartburn	278	Hooked By Love	259
Green, Garland	181	Heathcote, John 'Hector	135	Hope We Have	232

428

Hopkins, Telma		285	I Get The Sweetest Feeling		364	Imperial Cs, the	355
Horne, Cleveland		46	I Go Out Of My Mind		357	Imperial Records	84, 228, 247, 254, 260,
Horne, Jimmie 'Bo'		331, 360	I Got A Feeling		299		265, 272, 335
Horse, The		6	I Got A Good Thing Going		349	Impressions, the	99, 335, 337
Horton, Bill		303	I Got The Fever		96, 196	In A Moment	337
Hose Street (See the (Golden) Torch)		48, 223	I Got To Find Me Somebody		53, 342	In Orbit	88, 338
Hot Line		252	I Have A Girl		348	In Records	103, 342, 416
Hot Line Records		323	I Have Faith In You		269	In The Basement Magazine	409
Hot Potato		61	I Have Searched		202	In-Crowd, The	18
Hot Records		303, 329, 340	I Hurt On The Other Side		235, 340	Incredibles, the	138, 336
Hot Wax Records		161	I Just Can't Please You		320	Indiana Wants Me	36
Hotshots, the		377	I Just Can't Live My Life (Without You Babe)		291	Inferno Records	35, 177, 212, 342
House Of Orange		236	I Just Can't Speak		331, 360	Ingram, Luther	151
Houston, Larry		298	I Just Kept On Dancing		191, 350	Inky Dinky Wang Dang Do	169
Houston, Thelma		204	I Just Want To Fall In Love		360	Inspirations, the	228, 323, 326, 374, 391
How Sweet It Is		418	I Lost A True Love		247	Instrumental (Ronnie and Robyn)	243
Howard Mallet, the		382	I Love Her So Much (It Hurts Me)		130, 348	International City Records	317, 358, 375
Howe, Derek		13, 48	I Love Music		417	International GTOs, the	320
Hubba Hubba Records		178	I Love You 1,000 Times		243	International Soul Club	380, 393, 407
Hudson, Pookie		270	I Love You Baby		281	Interplay	172
Huff, David		142, 260	I Love You Baby (International GTOs)		320	Intrigues, the	337
Huff, Leon			I Love You For All Seasons		314	Intruders, the	160
(See also Gamble and Huff		37, 66, 142, 213, 302	I Miss You Baby		318, 363	Invictus Records	161, 276
Hughes, Fred		227, 345	I Must Love You		420	Invitations, the	86, 151, 336, 339
Human Beinz, the		295	I Need Love		206, 355	Is There Anything I Can Do?	248
Humphrey, Paul		344, 388	I Need My Baby		136, 348	Island Records	65, 118, 261, 361, 363
Humphrey, Senator Hubert		246	I Need You		9, 91	Isley Brothers, the	80, 224, 295, 298, 323, 399,
Hung Up On You		417	I Need You Like A Baby		231, 352		415
Hung Up On Your Love		216	I Need You More Than Ever		216	Isn't It A Good Idea	163
Hunt, Tommy		173, 363, 366	I Need Your Love		233	Isn't It Just A Shame	351, 355
Hunter, Ivy Joe		304	I Never Knew		103, 342, 416	Isn't She A Pretty Girl	159
Hurt		277	I Really Love You		29, 161	It Ain't Necessary	260
Hutch, Willie		76, 292	I Really Love You/Standing In			It Keep Rainin'	335
Hutson, Leroy		60, 99, 156	The Need Of Love (Dee Dee Sharp)		328	It Really Hurts Me Girl	46, 389
Hutton, Bobby		62, 298, 357	I Remember The Feeling		241	It Takes Heart	248, 352
Hyman, Phyllis		348	I Spy For The FBI		10, 151, 364	Itzy Records	268
Hype Records		250	I Stand Accused		355	It'll Never Be Over For Me	395
			I Still Love You		76, 126, 354, 375	It's A Sad Thing	250
			I Still Love You (From The Bottom Of My Heart)		356	It's Against The Laws Of Love	156
I Ain't Going Nowhere		318	I Thought You Were Mine		187	It's Better	357
I Am Nothing		304, 333	I Took An Overdose		64	It's Better To Have	418
I Bear Witness		355	I Travel Alone		74	It's Killing Me	285
I Can Feel Your Love (Comin Down On Me)		414	I Walked Away		70, 110	It's Needless To Say	136
I Can See Him Loving You		165	I Wanna Give You Tomorrow		204, 352	It's Okeh Up North, CD	324
I Can Take Care Of Myself		226	I Wanna Know		170, 361	It's Too Late For You And Me	350
I Cant Hold On		318	I Want My Baby Back		357	It's Torture	10, 271
I Can't Break The News To Myself		358	I Want To Feel I'm Wanted		208	It's Your Voodoo Working	9, 323, 329, 360, 389
I Can't Change		19, 262, 342	I Watched You Slowly Slip Away		253, 355	Ivorys, the	232, 352
I Can't Do It (I Just Can't Leave You)		196	I Wonder Why		358	Ivy, Quin	236
I Can't Get Enough		183, 377	I Won't Be Coming Back		350, 374, 391	I'd Think It Over	174, 349
I Can't Get Hold Of Myself		284	I Won't Let Her See Me Cry		356	I'll Always Love You	80, 332
I Can't Help Lovin' You		94, 342	I'll Never Forget You		265, 309	I'll Always Need You	72, 225
I Can't Help Myself		249	I've Only Got Myself To Blame		323	I'll Be Lovin' You	185
I Can't Hold On		356	Ice Man, The		378	I'll Be There	220
I Can't Let You Go		350	Ichiban Records		179, 360	I'll Be Your Champion	348
I Can't Make It Anymore		111	Ideals, the		139	I'll Do Anything	150
I Can't Save It		226	If I Could Only Be Sure		107, 154, 375, 389	I'll Forgive And Forget	8, 290
I Can't See Him Again		320	If I Knew		351	I'll Hold You	168
I Can't Stand To Lose You		346	If It's All The Same To You		151	I'll Keep Holding On	304
I Cried My Life Away		239, 352, 389	If That's What You Wanted		25, 342	I'll Never Fall In Love Again	118, 338, 416
I Didn't Know How To		351	If This Isn't Love		355	I'll Never Forget You	242, 354
I Dig Your Act		265	If You Ask Me		47	I'll Never Forget You (Marke Jackson)	242
I Don't Have A Mind Of My Own		236	If You Don't Come		360	I'll Never Stop Loving You	269, 356
I Don't Like It		356	If You Ever Walk Out Of My Life		35, 342	I'll Pay The Price	348
I Don't Wanna Get Away From Your Love		420	If You Loved Me		344	I'm A Big Man	357
I Don't Want To Discuss It		284	Ikettes, the		3, 300	I'm A Peace Loving Man	241
I Don't Like To Lose		348	Imaginations		277	I'm Catching On	350
I Don't Want To Lose You		320	Immediate Records		300	I'm Coming Home	360
I Don't Want To Talk About It		307	Impact Records		147, 177, 212, 253, 331	I'm Coming Over	320, 352
I Feel An Urge Coming On		195	Impacts, the		147	I'm Comin' To Your Rescue	247
I Feel So Bad		118, 395	Impel Records		292, 331	I'm Comun' Home In The Morn'un	93, 344

Index

Entry	Page
I'm Falling In Love With You Baby	303
I'm Getting Tired	206
I'm Gone	207, 309
I'm Gonna Change	306
I'm Gonna Dedicate This Song To You	262
I'm Gonna Love You	146, 323
I'm Gonna Love You A Long, Long Time	54, 416
I'm Gonna Make You Love Me	300
I'm Gonna Miss You	138, 232
I'm Gonna Run Away From You	81
I'm In A World Of Trouble	231, 340
I'm In Love Again	177
I'm In Love With You	289
I'm Losing Again	9, 348
I'm Not Built That Way	181
I'm Not Myself Anymore	312
I'm Not Strong Enough	95
I'm On My Way	77, 364
I'm Satisfied With You	252
I'm So Glad	208, 314
I'm So Happy	179, 357
I'm Spellbound	240
I'm Standing	177
I'm Stepping Out Of The Picture	278, 329
I'm Taking On Pain	356
I'm The One Who Loves You	14, 357
I'm Where It's At	228
I've Arrived	318
I've Been Cheated	320
I've Been Hurt	225, 363, 414
I've Got Something Good	184, 340
I've Got The Need	417
I've Got You On My Mind Again	182
I've Had It	218, 351, 356
I've Had It (Smith, George)	355, 360
JC, Dancer	401
JJ Records	340
JV Records	87, 177
Jack, Wolfman, Radio DJ	260
Jackson, Billy	218, 242, 311
Jackson, Carol	114, 192
Jackson, Chuck	21, 232, 289, 292, 357, 372
Jackson, Deon	241
Jackson, Earl	81
Jackson, Gerry	229
Jackson, JJ	182, 187
Jackson, Jesse	289
Jackson, Levi (See also Solomon King)	133, 395
Jackson, Marke (Chris)	242
Jackson, Millie	116, 254, 363
Jackson, Ollie	317
Jackson, Pervis	314
Jackson, Walter	289
Jacobs, Hank	375
Jadan Records	230
Jades, the	228
Jagger, Mick	165
Jam, the	223
Jamerson, Ella	137
James, Bobby	161
James, Elmore	122
James, Holly St.	8, 123, 143
James, Jesse	186, 323, 360
James, Jimmy	6, 140
James, Palmer	296
James, Tommy	98
Jameson, Steve	278
Jamie/Guyden Records	156, 186, 242, 270, 303, 344
Janice	231
Janice (Don't Be So Blind To Love)	157, 352
Janus Records	155
Javells, the	47, 56, 278, 342, 363
Jay Boy Records	214, 308, 352
Jay and the Americans	217
Jay and the Techniques	218
Jean Records	273
Jeanette	360
Jebb, Tony, DJ	5, 49, 147, 164, 230, 231, 403
Jefferson, Eddie	178
Jefferson, Joey	228
Jenkins, Donald, and the Daylighters	351
Jenkins, Norma	321
Jerheart Records	320
Jerk And Twine	339
Jerry-O	130
Jet Stream Records	321, 356
Jewell, Len	280
Jewels, the	291
Jimmy Mack (See also McKeachin, James)	252, 418
Jive Five, the	182
Job Opening	235, 342
Jobete Publishing	129, 134, 168, 169, 182, 257
John Lee's Groundhogs	117
John and the Wierdest	125, 325, 348
John, Mabel	158
Johnson, Charles	320
Johnson, Ernie	196
Johnson, Herb, and the Impacts	147, 208, 310
Johnson, Hubert	172
Johnson, Jesse	196, 323
Johnson, Jimmy and Ollie	56
Johnson, LJ	363
Johnson, Lou	48, 358, 416
Johnson, Marv	318, 363
Johnson, Norman	257
Johnson, Syl	251
Johnson, Tot	404
Joker Records	59, 326
Joker, The	178, 270, 274
Jones, Brenda Lee	77
Jones, E. Rodney	182, 230
Jones, Freddie	97, 378
Jones, Gloria	40, 119, 295, 340
Jones, Johnny, and the King Casuals	223, 366
Jones, Lee W	263
Jones, Linda	205, 291, 317
Jones, Marvin	57
Jones, Quincy	153
Jones, September	309, 360
Jones, Tamiko	240
Josie Records	187
Jubilee Records	271
Juliet Records	131
Julmar Records	349
Jumbo Records	158
Jumping At The Go-Go CD	324
Junior Records	262
Junior, Marvin	101
Just A Boy's Dream	292
Just A Fool	350
Just A Little Misunderstanding	154, 172, 363
Just Another Heartache	176
Just As Much	351
Just Ask Me	175
Just Brothers, the	320, 339
Just Do The Best You Can	420
Just Like Romeo And Juliet	6, 134
Just Like The Weather	69
Just Look What You've Done	164
Just Loving You	63
Just One Look	150
Just Sunshine Records	60, 342
Just Walk In My Shoes	268, 315
Just Walking In The Rain	132
KKC Records	250
Kaigler, Leonard	252
Kaplan, Fred	405
Kapp Records	43, 54, 181, 207, 360, 372, 416
Karate Records	356
Karen Records	154, 234, 241, 301
Karisma Records	230
Karl, Frankie, and the Chevrons	120, 326
Karmen, Steve, Band featuring Jimmy Radcliffe	211
Keele Allnighter	369, 386
Keene, Billy	420
Keep On Keeping On	107, 155
Keep On Loving Me	234, 289
Keep On Running Away	290
Keep On Talking	179, 272
Keeps On Burning	288
Keeps On Rolling	360
Kellmac Records	378
Kelly, Paul	240
Kemp, Sgt., Army Bill	5
Kendrick, Willie	153
Kendricks, Eddie	3, 104, 232
Kennedy, Wayne	5
Kent (Ace) Records	176, 217, 269, 271, 324, 357, 400
Kent (Modern) Records	122
Kent, Al	222, 277, 338
Kerr, George	169, 205, 265, 291, 413
Kerwood Records	346
Key To My Happiness	123, 358
Keyes, Troy	258
Keymen Records	124, 188, 252, 370, 413
Kick That Little Foot Sally	335
King Of Hearts	211
King Records	129, 265, 331
King Soul	222
King, Chris, DJ	56, 277, 285, 315, 384, 404
King, Clydie	272
King, Jeff, DJ	402
King, Jonathon	77
King, Nosmo	278, 342
King, Solomon (See also Levi Jackson)	133
King, Terry	165
King's Hall, Stoke	369, 380, 386, 408
Kinney, Fern	117
Kirby, George	238
Kirton, Lew	151, 320
Kiss My Love Goodbye	360
Kline, Alan	89
Kline, Bobby	293, 357
Knight, Gladys, and the Pips	268, 350, 360, 415
Knight, Jason	193
Knight, Marie	1, 120
Knight, Robert	338, 339, 363, 367
Kool Kat Records	275
Kool and the Gang	204
Koppel, Martin	5, 13, 16, 17, 130, 285, 385, 405
Kornfeld, Artie	288
Kudu Records	417
Kung Fu Fighting	190
Kyser Records	202
Kyser, Paul	126, 202, 344

La Beat Records	263, 304, 312, 327, 333	Lewis, Gary, and the Playboys	287, 363, 392	Love Won't Let Me Wait	147
La De Da I Love You	335	Lewis, Herman	263	Love You Baby	207
La Salle Records	354	Lewis, James	167, 378, 389	Love, Darlene	257
La-Cindy Records	180, 333, 358, 416	Lewis, Kenny	282	Love, Isiah	56
Laboe, Art	290	Lewis, Linda	129	Love, Love, Love	83, 338, 339, 363
Lady In Green	177, 327, 348	Lewis, Louise, Miss LL	173, 210	Love, Mary	17, 129
Lady Of Stone	259	Lewis, Pat	152, 256, 333	Love, You Just Can't Walk Away	225
Lamon Records	318	Lewis, Ramsey	144, 174, 245, 335, 364	Lovejoy, Joy	88, 338
Lamonte, John	405	Lewis, Ronnie	87	Lovelite Records	344
Lance, Major	82, 139, 321, 336, 368, 373, 380	Lewis, Shirley	164	Lovelites, the	344
		Lewis, Tamala	219, 348, 416	Lover	137, 326
Landa Records	100, 342	Liberty Records	252, 266, 287, 372, 395, 414, 418	Lovetones, the	143
Lando Records	145			Lovett, Leroy (See also Ben-Lee Productions)	54
Lands, Hoagy	108, 338	Lightly, Paul	5	Lovettes, the	220
Landslide	31, 342	Like A Bee	266	Love's The Only Answer	200
Lane, Mickey Lee	268, 335	Like A Nightmare	391	Loving Good Feeling	212
Lanin, Lester	377	Like Adam And Eve	134	Loving On The Losing Side	364, 366
Larry-O Records	230	Like One	340	Lovin' You Takes All Of My Time	285
Larue, The	202	Linda Records	129, 331	Lowton Civic Centre	408
Lasalle, Denise	69	Lindsay, Theresa	170	Lucas, Ernie	173
Laskey, Emanuel	241, 350	Lindsey, Thelma	305	Lucky Lucky Me	363
Last Minute Miracle	205	Little Hank	245, 336	Lucky Number	358
Lattimore, Almeta	358	Little Queenie	141	Lumley, Rufus	177, 394
Laurie	5	Little Richard	284	Lynch, Kenny	395
Laurie Records	77, 108, 140, 146, 338	Little Richie	176	Lyndell Records	185
Lavette, Betty	170	Living A Lie	258	Lyndell, Linda	213
Lawn Records	73, 318, 356	Livingston, Joe	114	Lynn, Barbara	321, 326, 356, 373
Lawrence, Angela	401	Livin' Above Your Head	217	Lynn, Gloria	360
Laws, Eloise	135	Livin' In Love	267	Lynn, Tami	279, 315, 364
Lawson, Robbie	126, 202, 329, 344	Livsey, Barbara	276		
Le Grand Records	175	Lizard Records	155, 272, 389	M-Pac Records	349
Le Mans Records	146	Lloyd Records	240	M.V.P.'S, the	51
Leach, John	318, 356	Lloyd, Betty	350	MB Records	357
Leavell, Joann	102	Lloyd, Mark	395	MCA Records	364
Lee, Andy	383	Locarno	369	MGM Records	108, 111, 116, 123, 127, 149, 151, 166, 210, 228, 231, 254, 291, 306, 307, 308, 336, 340, 352, 358, 372, 375
Leedham, Dave	2	Loma Records	122, 134, 137, 205, 215, 264, 291, 317		
Lee, Jackie (See also Earl Nelson)	84, 124, 209, 238, 292, 319, 336	London Records	141, 245, 339, 364		
		Lonely For You Baby	355	MS Records	31
Lee, Laura	118, 161, 411	Lonely Girl	352	Machine, the	65
Left Out	196, 323	Long After Tonight Is All Over	21, 364, 418	Mack, Jimmy	296, 331, 344
Legend Records	167, 389	Longfield Suite, Prestwich	408	Maconie, Stuart	6
Legend, Tobi (See also Lark, Tobi)	30, 42	Look At Me	351	Madara, Johnny	142
Leka, Paul	144	Look At Me Now	192, 357, 389	Maestro, Johnny	278, 329
Lemons, George	317	Look At Me, Look At Me	420	Maggie	245
Lend A Hand	62	Look Records	75	Magic City Records	305
Lenita Productions	140	Looking For A Woman	318	Magic Touch, The	176, 352
Lennon and McCartney	229	Looking For You	24	Magnetics, the	177, 327, 348
Let Her Go	125	Looky Looky	350	Magnificents, the	320
Let It Be Me	256	Lord What's Happening To Your People	244	Magnum Records	317
Let Love Come Between Us	145	Lost And Found	347	Mahal, Taj	259, 344
Let Love Live	350	Lost Nite Records	218, 329	Mahoney, Skip	157, 352
Let Me In	19	Lost Summer Love	323	Mainstream Records	358, 360
Let Me Make You Happy	124, 329	Love And Desire	283, 339	Majestics, the	130, 331, 348
Let My Heart And Soul Be Free	358	Love Bug Leave My Heart Alone	286	Major Minor Records	412
Let Our Love Grow Higher	171	Love Child	36	Make Me Yours	310
Let The Good Times Roll and Feel So Good	302, 336	Love Committee, the	248	Makin' Up Time	388
Let's Copp A Groove	337	Love Control	248	Mala Records	104, 203, 206, 276, 339
Let's Go Baby (Where The Action Is)	339	Love Explosion	258	Maleady, Barry, DJ	404
Let's Spend Some Time Together	298	Love Factory	135	Malibus, the	227
Let's Talk It Over	198	Love Is A Good Foundation	237	Maltby, Richard	207
Let's Wade In The Water	144, 174	Love Is A Serious Business	194, 349	Maltese Records	321
Levert, Eddie	265	Love Is All Right	360	Mama I Want To Sing, musical	150
Levine, Ian	3, 22, 44, 46, 127, 131, 133, 135, 149, 150, 152, 159, 161, 165,166, 180, 185, 189, 192, 199, 202, 205, 207, 213, 217, 223, 227, 234, 235, 236, 237, 250, 252, 255, 259, 260, 265, 267, 273, 274, 275, 281, 291, 292, 301, 305, 313, 314, 403, 420	Love Is Like An Itching In My Heart	279	Mama Told Me Not To Come	155
		Love Machine	417	Man O Man	358
		Love Makes A Woman	246	Man Without A Woman	115
		Love On A Mountain Top	338, 363, 367	Mandolph, Margaret	321
		Love Runs Out	292	Mandrill	321, 358
		Love Starved Heart	285, 354	Manhattan Records	265
Levise, William Jnr. (See Mitch Ryder)	205	Love The Life I Live	134	Manifesto	93, 167, 389
Lewis, Barbara	241, 336	Love Trap	376	Manship, John, record dealer	13, 385

Index

Mar-V-Lus Records	183, 276
Marboo Records	248
March, Peggy	344, 392
Mark IV Records	252, 321, 348, 357
Martin, Bobby	66, 96
Martin, Derek	253
Martin, Shane	91
Marton Records	329, 348, 414
Marvellettes, the	3, 304
Mary Jane Records	146, 323
Masqueraders, the	263, 312, 374
Massey, Ted, DJ	404
Matchie, dancer	401
Mathis, Jodi	149
Matthews, Joe	275, 370, 378
Maurci Records	352
Maverick Records	188, 199
Maxx Records	350
Mayfield Players	358
Mayfield Records	102, 336, 358
Mayfield, Curtis	60, 99, 139, 151, 156, 346, 370, 416
Mayorga, Lincoln	119, 305
Maze	25, 208
McAleer, Dave	365
Mc Daniels, Gene	378, 416
McAllister, Maurice	181, 378
McCoy, Rosemary	240, 241
McCoy, Van	52, 119, 124, 234, 242, 411
McCutcheon, Les	16, 17
McDaniels, Gene	266
McDougall III, Weldon Arthur	13, 213, 310
McEwan, Patsy	117
McKeachin, James 'Tenafly'	67, 252, 296
McLaughlin, Ollie	154
McNair, Barbara	42, 120, 360
McNeir, Ronnie	159, 333, 358
Me-O Records	351
Medley, Bill	207
Meet Me Halfway	327
Melba Moore	352
Melba Records	179
Melvin, Harold and the Blue Notes	342
Memories	247
Merben Records	344, 349
Mercury Records	96, 112, 192, 273, 288, 323, 349, 350, 389, 416, 417
Mercury, Eric	352
Merrell, Ray	308, 352, 395
Messing With My Mind	417
Metrics, the	357, 418
Metromedia Records	377, 419
Metros, the	153, 309, 354
Michael and Raymond	115
Michaels, Cody	344
Michaels, Tony	134
Michels, Lloyd	133, 376
Mickey	305
Mid Town Records	274
Midas Records	323, 357
Middleton, Tony	179, 308
Mighty Bub, the	383
Mike Post Coalition	45, 342, 389, 392
Millward, Max, record dealer	291
Millenium Records	360
Miller, Bob	5
Millionaires Only, for, CD	324, 324
Millionaires, the	338
Mills, Barbara	128, 394
Mills, Jackie	53
Mimms, Garnett	24
Minit Records	161, 168, 183, 258, 265, 272, 318, 357, 372, 418
Minshull, Keith, DJ	13, 231, 403
Mir-A-Don Records	288
Mira Records	124
Miracles, the	415, 416
Mirwood Records	154, 124, 209, 210, 245, 255, 316, 320, 336, 338, 370
Miss Grace	311
Miss You Baby	318
Mister Bang Bang Man	9, 245, 336
Mistura	5, 133, 376
Misty Blue	166
Mitchell, Jock	253
Mitchell, Prince Phillip	179, 272, 357
Mitchell, Stanley	130, 192
Mitchell, Willie	126, 245, 295, 342, 356
Mo-Groov Records	197, 349
Mockingbird	361
Mod Records	300
Mode Records	228
Modern Records	122, 129, 148, 182, 280, 318
Modern Soul	379
Mohawk Records	160
Mojo Records	81
Mojo Records	363
Mojo, the (King), Sheffield	13, 173, 289
Moman, Chips	200, 238
Moments, the	415
Monday, Danny	182, 318
Monette, Raymond	115
Money Records	84, 310
Monique	352
Montenegro, Hugo	377, 419
Montgomery, Bobby	310
Montgomery, Jack	57, 352
Monument Records	363, 367
Mood Mosaic	388
Moody Woman	37
Moonshine, Mickey	321
Moore, Dorothy	166
Moore, James	211
Moore, Johnny	85, 230
Moore, Melba	176
More Today Than Yesterday	185
Mosley, Ernest	180, 333, 414
Motor City Records	358
Motown Records	3, 9, 16, 17, 38, 42, 80, 88, 104, 120, 149, 158, 159, 164, 182, 193, 209, 210, 234, 243, 257, 261, 268, 279, 283, 285, 293, 299, 303, 314, 315 ,318, 350, 352, 354, 357, 358, 360, 370, 372, 376, 400, 413
Mountain Top Theme	377
Move On Up	156, 346, 416
Movin' Away	395
Mowest Records	157, 295, 363
Mr Big Shot	281
Mr Creator	137
Mr Flood's Party	180, 389
Mr Misery	419
Mr M's, Wigan Casino	145, 302
Mr Soul (See also Scott, Al)	11, 181, 329, 348, 374, 378
Murphy, Kev, DJ	404
Murphy, Ron, collector	17
Murrell, Hadley	194
Muscle Shoals	142
Musette Records	128
Music For Pleasure Records (MFP)	323, 413
Music Merchant Records	135, 340
Musicor Records	1, 21, 120, 176, 206, 243, 352, 355, 416, 419
Must Love You	418
Mutt and Jeff Records	228
My Baby Came From Out Of Nowhere	125
My Baby's Been Cheatin' (I Know)	360
My Baby's Coming Back To Me	289
My Baby's Got ESP	354
My Dear Heart	168
My Elusive Dreams	339
My First Lonely Night	356
My Heart Cries For You	206
My Heart Is Calling	320
My Heart Needs A Break	317
My Heart Took A Licking	254
My Hearts Symphony	72
My Heart's Beatin' Stronger	357
My Heart's Not In It Anymore	313
My Heart's Symphony	287, 363
My Heart's Wide Open	97, 378
My Life With You	346
My Little Girl (Instrumental)	214
My Love Is Getting Stronger	317, 323, 358, 375
My Love Is Your Love	323, 323
My Man Is A Sweet Man	116, 363
My Sugar Baby	59, 327
My Weakness Is You	306
My World Is On Fire	296, 331 344
Mylestones, the (1)	178
Mylestones, the (2)	274
NUVJ Records	50
NYCS Records	239
Nabay	311, 331
Name It You Got It	321
Nasco Records	290
Nash, Johnny	293
Natural Four, the	187
Naughty Boy	331, 350, 374
Navarro, Tommy	239, 352, 389
Navy Blue	189
Neal, Tommy	170, 337, 338
Nelson, Earl (See also Jackie Lee)	7, 84, 255, 319, 370
Neptune Records	160, 265, 291
Nero, Frances	234, 352, 413
Nesbitt, Sam	283
Never Die	321
Never For Me	338
Never Had A Love So Good	320
Never Let Me Go	352
Nevertheless	357
New Art Records	273
New Voice Records	109, 205, 336, 338
New Wanderers, the	346, 418
New York In The Dark	234
Newbeats, the	244
Newie (60's Newie)	379
Newman, Dave	75
Next In Line, The	108, 338
Nic-Nacs, the	128
Night Owl	70
Night, The	112, 157, 363
Nine Times Out Of Ten	346
Nite Life Records	228
Nives, Dave	5
No One Can Love You More	358
No One Else Can Take Your Place	228, 327, 374, 391
No One For Me To Turn To	185
No One To Love	256, 333
No Other Way	350
No Second Chance	348, 378

Nobody But Me		295
Nola Records		34, 339
Nomads, the		197, 245, 349
North State Records		337
Northern De-La Records		262
Northern Soul Floorshakers, CD		324
Northern Soul Of Philadelphia Vol. 2, CD		310
Northern Soul Story, the Essential, CD		324
Not A Chance In A Million		253
Not Me Baby		303
Not My Girl		243, 297, 333
Nothing Can Compare To You		90
Nothing Can Help You Now		138, 333, 358
Nothing Can Stop Me		336, 363
Nothing Worse Than Being Alone		234
Nothing's Too Good For My Baby		348
Now You've Got The Upper Hand		201
Nowell, Dave, writer		409
Nowhere To Run		330
OO Wee Baby I Love You		227
Okeh Records	9, 27, 32, 52, 76, 82, 147, 173, 232, 247, 284, 320, 336, 338, 354, 356, 358, 370, 375	
Okeh Soul Promotions (Keele)		355
Okeh Up North, it's, CD		324
Old Town Records		196, 318, 321, 323, 350
Oldham, Spooner		198, 200, 272
Oliver Records		313
Olympics, the		316, 370
Omen Records		287
On A Magic Carpet Ride		279, 388
One Fine Morning		363
One In A Million		229, 299
One Way Or Another		355
One Way Out		286
One Wonderful Moment		135, 340
Only Your Love Can Save Me		304
Oo Wee I'll Let It Be You Babe		210
Open The Door To Your Heart		79
Orbison, Roy		419
Ordinary Joe		320
Originals, the		3, 186, 360, 413
Orlons, the		311, 352
Osbourne, Wally		208
Otis, Johnny		274
Ott, Horace		293
Our Love Is In The Pocket		49, 419
Our Love Will Grow		257, 355
Out Of My Mind		377
Out Of The Frying Pan		261
Out On The Floor		118, 338, 363
Out On The Floor, CD		324
Out on the Floor Again, CD		324
Outsiders, the		268
Owens, Gwen		317
O'Dell, Brooks		357
O'Jay, Eddie, radio DJ		265
O'Jays, the		309
O'Kaysions, the		10, 337
PAP Records		206, 354, 355
PIP records		189
PJ		367
Packin' Up		321, 355
Padded Cell		419
Page One Records		346
Paladino, Robert		23
Palais, Nottingham		380, 386

Palette Records		321, 321
Palmer Records	252, 267, 296, 304, 327, 331, 344, 355	
Palmer, Carl		289
Pama Records		289, 284
Pameline Records		139, 338, 337, 342
Pandora Records		160
Panic		203, 376
Papa Ooh Mow Mow		362, 364, 377
Paris		318, 378
Paris Blues		179
Paris, Bobby		70, 75, 110, 249, 394
Parker, Eddie		207, 309
Parker, Elbie		318, 348
Parker, Robert		245, 339
Parkway Records (See also Cameo/Parkway)	19, 68, 98, 167, 264, 278, 297, 302, 311, 320, 321, 327, 329, 335, 336, 338, 346, 357, 378	
Parliament(s), (the)		201, 256, 321
Parlophone Records		164, 395
Parrish, Dean		77, 140, 150, 337
Party Time Records		95, 325
Pat Williams Orchestra		392
Patches (Sew On)		406, 407
Patten, Alexander		67, 336
Patterson, Bobby		216, 289, 356
Patti and the Emblems		54, 416
Paul and Paula		245
Paul, John E		170, 361
Paula Records		182, 216, 289, 418
Pay-Tons Records		418
Payne, Doris (See Troy, Doris)		150
Payne, Freda		361
Peaches Records		329, 355
Peaches and Herb		231
Peachtree Records		22, 342, 389
Peak Records		351
Pee-Vee Records		323
Peebles, Ann		251
Pendulum Allnighter, Manchester		342
Penn, Dan		198, 200, 272
Penniman, Richard (See Little Richard)		284
Pentagon Records		351, 355
People's Choice, the		267, 327, 355
Pep, DJ		182, 240, 242, 262, 306
Pepp, George		7, 317
Per-son-ally		70, 249, 364
Perception Records		125
Permanent Injury		183
Perren, Freddie, Productions		411
Perry, Ann		242
Perry, Greg		248, 352
Petals, the		323, 323
Peterson, Kris		351
Phantom Janitor		378
Phelectron Records		331, 350, 374
Phi-Dan Records		321
Phil Town Records		120, 327
Phil-LA Of Soul Records		185, 186, 267, 355
Philadelphia IR		267
Philadelphia International Records (PIR)	265, 267, 415	
Philips Records	65, 83, 157, 173, 240, 253, 267, 272, 316, 337, 338, 339, 357, 356, 363, 388	
Philips, Brian, DJ		402
Philips, Paul, writer		409
Philips, Sandra		323
Phillips, Esther		415
Phillips, Miss DD		344
Philly Dog Around The World		250

Phoof Records		251, 376, 388
Pick Me Up And Put Me In Your Pocket		193
Pickett, Wilson		183, 294
Picture Me Gone		300
Pieces Of My Broken Heart		360
Pied Piper Productions		115, 153
Pier, the, Morecambe		380
Pierce, Ady, record dealer		385
Pipkin, Chester		129
Pitney, Gene		21
Pity My Feet		163, 395
Planetary Records		321
Platters, the		243, 297
Play It Cool, Stay In School		246
Playthings, the		366
Please Don't Go		34, 356
Please Forgive Me		276
Please Keep Away From Me		318, 348
Please Let Me In		152
Please Operator		159, 342
Please Stay		232, 352
Poets, the, (American)		87, 336
Pointer Sisters, the		105, 344
Pollard, Ray		250, 372, 373
Polydor Records	193, 203, 247, 308, 321, 344	
Polygram Records		17, 162
Pompeii Records		122
Poncello Records		228
Poor Side Of Town		360
Pope Brothers		92
Poppies, the		117
Porgy and the Monarchs		206
Porter, Nolan (NF)		107, 155, 375, 389
Potion Of Love		273
Potts, Sylvester		172
Powell, Archie		288
Powell, Monroe		227
Powell, William		323, 333, 348
Power House Records		323, 333, 348
Prepared To Love You		305
President Records		276, 262, 412
Pressure		358
Prestige Records		192
Preston Billy		337
Pretty As A Picture		357
Price, Lloyd		164
Pride, Lou		93
Prince, Tony		5
Prisonaires, the		132
Probe Records		364
Prodigal Records		159
Professionals, the		129, 327, 346
Profiles, the		358
Profit, Billy		182
Prophet, Billy		182
Prophets, the		96, 391
Prophonics Records		325, 348, 378
Prove Yourself A Lady		183
Psychedelic Soul		7, 163
Purify, James and Bobby		145, 344
Put That Woman Down		318, 356
Put Your Loving Arms Around Me		303, 340
Pye (Casino Classics, International, Disco Demand)	163, 132, 189, 193, 278, 308, 323, 342, 346, 355, 363, 365, 388	
Q, the		378
Quails, Sidney Joe		358
Quality Records		346

Index

Queen City Records	234, 342		372	SOS Records	346
Queen Of Fools	128, 338	Ric-Tic Revue, the	277, 373	SPQR Records	175
Queen Of Fools	394	Ricardo, Rick, record dealer	316	SSS International Records	355
Queen Of The Go-Go	356	Rich, Charlie	337	Sack Records	260, 352
Queens Hall, Leeds	380	Richardson, Donald Lee	321	Sad Girl	274
Questall, Connie	344	Richardson, Oscar	239	Salsoul Records	157, 255, 346, 352, 415
Quezergue, Wardell	105	Richie, Lionel	295	Salvadors, the	28, 189
Quick Change Artist	154	Richie, Little	176	Sam and Kitty	184, 229
Quick Joey Small	98	Rick, Robyn and Him	243	Sam and Kitty	340
Quinvy Records	236	Ride Your Poney	412	Samantha's Allnighter, Sheffield	382, 386
		Ridgley, Tommy	317, 358, 375	Samson, Terry, promoter	384
		Right Direction, The	229	San Remo Golden Strings, the	118
RCA (Victor) Records	58, 72, 94, 115, 123, 150, 153, 159, 172, 177, 190, 207, 213, 244, 262, 309, 311, 318, 340, 342, 344, 346, 348, 354, 356, 360, 364, 372, 394, 415	Right On Records	394	Sandbag Records	23, 342
		Right Track	9, 27, 336	Sanders, Nelson	312
		Righteous Brothers Band, the	207	Sandi Sheldon	52, 338
		Rika Records	356	Sands, Evie	300
		Rimmer, Dave, writer	409	Sandy, dancer	401
RPM Records	128	Ringleaders, the	349	Santa Posa Records	363
Ra-Sel Records	177, 309, 348	Rising Sons	338	Santos, Larry	316, 344
Radcliffe, Jimmy	21, 416	Rita and the Tiaras	321	Sapphires, the	114, 192
Radio Centre, record dealer	405	Ritson, Mike, writer	13	Sar Records	121, 360
Rae, Brian, DJ	198, 402	Ritz, the, Brighouse	386, 408	Sassy Records	25, 342
Ragland, Lou	74	Ritz, the, Manchester	369, 380, 384, 386, 408	Satisfied	215
Rain	377	River City Records	200	Saunders, Larry	298
Raining Teardrops	348	Rivers, Johnny	20, 247	Save Me	416
Raistrick, Dave, record dealer	385	Rivingtons, the	282	Save My Love For A Rainy Day	104
Rampart Records	130	Rix, Andy	431	Savin' My Lovin' For You	267, 327, 355
Ramsel Records	360	Roberts, Tina	355	Savours, the	286
Ramsey, Dorothy	137	Robey, Don	145, 193	Savoury, Chris, writer	409
Randazzo/Pike Productions	57, 411	Robin, Ede	245	Sawyer, Pam	119, 295
Randell, Lynne	8, 89, 109, 307, 326, 340, 394	Robins, Jimmy	320	Saxe, Phil	289
Randolph, Barbara	299, 413	Robinson, Shawn	168	Saxton, Mary	346
Randolph, Luther	213	Robinson, Vicki Sue	415	Say Girl	346
Randolph, Styles, McDougall Productions	411	Robinson, William 'Smokey'	3	Say It Isn't So	197
Ranwood Records	323	Rogers, Big Daddy	357	Say Something Nice To Me	293, 357
Rare, Collectable And Soulful, CD	324	Rojac Records	320	Sayles, Johnny	183
Rat Race	207	Rollers, Tootsie	351	Scepter Records	57, 69, 205, 278, 321, 329, 337, 357
Ray, Don	348	Romancers, the	117		
Ray, Johnny	132	Romans, Little Joe	182	Scooter Boys/Scene	61, 229, 248, 300
Raye, Jimmy	250	Rome, Richie	45	Scott, Al (See also Mr Soul	7, 181, 374
Reach Out For me	358	Romur Records	337	Scott, Cindy	281
Reaching For The Best	127, 363, 390, 419	Ron Records	335	Scott, George 'King'	181
Reachin' For Something I Can't Have	304	Ronnie and Robyn	243	Scratchy	388
Ready Records	346, 418	Rosemary What Happened	301	Searling, Richard, DJ	5, 13, 73, 125, 136, 163, 178, 181, 189, 192, 195, 197, 206,, 226, 228, 248, 255, 264, 274, 283, 285, 287, 298, 304, 403, 409
Ready Willing And Able	272	Rosen, Rich, record dealer	405		
Real Humdinger	122	Ross, Diana	3		
Recipe	358	Ross, Jackie	339		
Reconsider	164, 358, 413	Ross, Jerry	106, 114, 192	Security Records	355
Record, Eugene	246, 258	Roulette Records	56, 26, 189, 202, 215, 231, 376	Sedgrick Records	294, 325, 352, 374, 391
Red Coach Records	46, 389	Round Robin	335	Seesaw	412
Red Greg Records	151	Rouser Records	208, 325, 374, 391	Send Him Back	105, 344
Redd, Gene	46	Route Records	267, 364	Senior, Alan, promoter	384, 404
Redding, Otis	26	Roy 'C'	361	Sensations, the	19
Reed, AC	361	Roye, Lee	175	Sequel Records	400
Reeves, Martha, and the Vandellas	286, 330	Rubin	43, 360, 414	Serving A Sentence Of Life	190, 395
Reflections, the	134	Ruby Records	321	Set My Heart At Ease	356
Regan, Vala	321	Ruffin, Jimmy	3, 295, 318, 360, 373	Seven Day Lover	22, 342, 389
Relf, Bob	84, 188, 362, 370, 390, 419	Run Baby Run	244, 377	Seven Days Too Long	26, 365
Relf, Nelson Productions	411	Rundless, Laura (See Lee, Laura)	161	Seven Souls, the	76, 354, 370, 375
Remember	181	Running For My Life	197	Seventy 7 Records	292
Remember Me	323	Rushton, Neil	384, 409	Sexton, Ann	289, 292
Renay, Diane	189	Russ, Lonnie	346	Sexy Lady	274
Renfro Records	282	Russell, Patty	54	Sha-Rae, Billy	309
Renzetti, Joe	106	Russell, Saxie	163	Shades of Soul Magazine	409
Reparata and the Delrons	203, 376	Russell, Stuart, writer	13	Shaggy Dog	268
Rescue Me	416	Ryder, Mitch, and the Detroit Wheels	205, 336, 338	Shakatak	16
Revilot Records	38, 49, 79, 134, 136, 201, 321, 329, 348, 370, 372	R'n'B Time (Part 1)	230	Shake A Tail Feather	145, 344
				Shakers, the	135, 340
Reynolds Records	375			Shalamar	168
Rhino Records	400	SOS (Heart In Distress)	98, 344	Shalimars, (Sari and) the	210, 341
Ric-Tic Records	118, 121, 122, 152, 161, 269, 277, 318, 336, 338, 339, 370, 372				

434

Shapiro, Helen	209, 346, 394	Skyway Records	173, 210	Soul Survivor Magazine	409
Share Records	234, 339	Sleepless Nights	318, 378	Soul Symphony	245
Sharonettes, the	362, 377	Sliced Tomatoes	340, 361	Soul Time	301
Sharp, Dee Dee	66, 311, 328	Slippin' Around With You	158, 357	Soul Time' Vol. 1 CD	230, 324
Shaw, Marlena	301	Slow Fizz	114, 192	Soul Town Records	263, 348, 374
She Blew A Good Thing	9, 87, 336	Smash Records	96, 112, 200, 212, 273, 348	Soul Twins, the	154
She Said Goodbye	346	Smashed	379	Soul Underground Magazine	409
She Won't Come Back	181	Smith, Bernadine	102	Soul Underground, CD	324
She's Ready	185	Smith, Bobbie	214, 354	Soul Up North Magazine	409
Sheen, Bobby	184, 287, 336, 354	Smith, Bobby	315	Soulful Kinda Music Magazine	409
Sheffield, Charles	389, 323, 360	Smith, Buddy	356, 391	Soulie, dancer	401
Shelby, Ernie	199	Smith, Fred	7, 188, 370	Soulsonic Records	274
Sheldon, Sandi	52	Smith, George	351, 360	Soulville Records	321, 374
Shelton, Roscoe	197	Smith, John, collector	393	Sound Impression Records	71, 325
Shepperd, Kenny	350	Smith, Major Bill	197, 245	Sound Stage 7 Records	176, 197, 237, 245, 318, 336
Shepperd, 'Bunky' Bill	69	Smith, Marvin	156, 232, 322, 323	Sound Trip Records	177
Shepperds, the	180	Smith, Moses	41	Soundmasters, the	131
Sherill, Billy	117	Smith, Otis	125, 244	Sounds of Lane, the	268
Sherry	377, 419	Smith, Pete	13	Soussan, Simon	16, 17, 127, 168, 178, 183, 193, 210, 254, 263, 377, 405
Sherrys, the	303, 329, 340	Smith, Rob	5
She'll Come Running Back	44, 329	Smith, Tom	13	South Camp Records	236
She's About A Mover	166	Smith, Youngblood	249	Spaniels, the	270
She's Fire	378	Smoke Records	313, 333	Spark Records	363, 364
She's Looking Good	294, 337	Snake, The	6, 20, 364	Special Kind Of Woman	357
She's Putting You On	213	Snow, Bill	13	Speciality Records	272
She's Wanted	73, 331	Snowy, dancer	401	Spector Records	122
Shirelles, the	32, 357, 205	So Is The Sun	344	Spector, Phil	287
Shively, Val, record dealer	405	So Many Sides Of You	320	Speed	406
Shives, Robert	119	Social Tragedy	419	Spellbinders, the	119, 387
Shoes	312	Sock It To Em JB (Part 1)	337, 388	Spellman, Benny	318
Shoop Shoop Song	256, 299	Sock It To Me Baby	205	Spence, Kenny	383
Short People, the	346	Soft Cell	39, 40, 361	Spencer Davis Group, the	261
Shorter, James	312	Soft Records	245	Spidells, the	266
Shotgun	245, 330	Solid Hit Records	256, 285, 333	Spinners, the (Detroit)	80, 314, 332, 354, 360, 413
Shotgun And The Duck	255	Solid Hitbound Productions	121, 201	Spiral Starecase	185, 392
Shotgun Wedding	245, 361	Solid State Records	355	Spring Rain	346, 415
Show Me	188, 302	Some Kind of Wonderful	185	Spring Records	116, 254, 315
Show Stopper	178, 325, 350	Somebody (Somewhere) Needs You	134	Springers, the	348
Showmen, the	257, 355, 357	Someday We'll Be Together	136	Springfield, Dusty	392
Showstoppers, the	416	Someday We're Gonna Love Again	241, 336	Squires, the	350
Shrine Records	8, 202, 250, 282, 283, 325, 333, 349, 350, 352, 370, 372, 374, 391	Someody Help Me	351	St James, Holly	8, 140, 358
	Someone Tell Her	355	St Lawrence Records	183, 260, 270
	Something Beautiful	321	Stackhouse, Ruby (See also Ruby Andrews)	63
Shrine, The Rarest Soul Label, CD	324	Something Good Gotten' A Hold Of Me	193	Stairsteps, the (Five)	156, 412
Shuffling, dance	379	Something New To Do	184, 354	Stairway Records	263
Sidra Records	243	Something Old Something New	306	Standing In For Love	171
Sidra's Theme	243	Somethings Bad	197, 349	Stang Records	291
Sigler, Bunny	302, 320, 336, 338, 370	Something's Bothering You	357	Staple Singers, the	357
Sigma Studios	66	Sommers, Joanie	8, 123, 143, 318	Starr, Edwin	5, 12, 121, 161, 262, 269, 306, 318, 336, 337, 338, 339, 346, 357, 338, 373
Silent Treatment	173, 325, 352	Sonbert Records	321
Silhouettes, the	303, 325	Sonday Records	237
Silver Blue Records	151, 255	Sons Of Moses, the	245	Starr, Martha	320, 370
Silver Convention Records	248	Soozi Records	258	Stars and Stripes Allnighter, Yate	216, 382
Silver, Lorraine	323, 323	Soul Bowl, record dealer	105, 197, 240, 274	Stateside Records	79, 96, 102, 108, 131, 138, 140, 151, 205, 366
Silvetti	346, 415	Soul Brothers Six, the	185, 323
Simco Records	257, 275, 375	Soul City Records	20, 247, 363	Staton, Candi	201
Simon Says	98	Soul City Records (UK)	27	Stax Records	151, 213, 269, 280, 339, 356, 414
Simon and Garfunkel	33	Soul Clock Records	148, 323, 340
Simpson, Valerie	193	Soul Fox Records	377	Stay Close To Me	412
Sinatra, Frank	308	Soul Fox Strings	377	Stay Together Young Lovers	215
Since I Found My Baby	309	Soul Galore Records	377	Steele, Don	5
Singin' Sam	184	Soul Hawk Records	170, 348	Steinways, the	313
Singleton, Eddie	8, 299, 370	Soul King Records	309	Sterling Sound Records	418
Sister Lee	158	Soul On The Rocks, LP	298	Steve Karmen Band, the, feat. Jimmy Radcliffe	211
Sitting In My Class	159, 333	Soul Records	3, 15, 162, 234, 261, 296, 299, 346, 350, 352, 358, 374, 391, 413, 416	Stevens, April	149, 340
Six By Six	162, 377, 419		Stevens, Bob, collector	177
Skate (Part 1)	337		Stevens, Guy, DJ	402
Skiing In The Snow	86, 151, 364	Soul Sam, Barnfather, Martin, DJ	198, 202, 248, 403	Stevenson, William 'Mickey'	199, 293, 304
Skullsnaps, the	189	Soul Self Satisfaction	324	Stewart, Billy	370
Sky Disc Records	418	Soul Series Records	198	Stewart, Roger	13
Skyscraper Records	177	Soul Sisters, the	336	Stewart, Sly	117

Index

Stick By Me Baby	28
Stolen Hours	283, 354
Stomp Town Records	418
Ston-Roc Records	159
Stone Blue Records	229
Stone, Sly	117, 135
Stop	346
Stop And Take A Look At Yourself	210
Stop And You'll Become Aware	209, 346, 394
Stop Her On Sight	269
Stop In The Name Of Love	330
Stop Overlooking Me	282, 333, 350, 351
Stop What You're Doing	366
Stop, Take A Look At Yourself	341
Storm Warning	156, 356
Stormy	360
Strange Neighborhood	277
Stranger In My Arms	89, 326, 340, 394
Strata East Records	171
Strata Records	348, 378
Stratton, Ernie	297
Strawberry Jam	249
Street Corner Symphony	131
Street, Judy	39
Street, Richard	360
Strider Records	39
Stringfellow, Pete, DJ	173, 393, 402
Strings-A-Go-Go	45
Strong, Elsie	175
Stronger Than Her Love	187
Stronger Than Me	177
Stubborn Heart	180, 333, 414
Styles, Randolph	213, 310
Styles, the	280
Sue Records	122, 182, 336
Sue Records (UK)	102, 335
Suemi Records	93, 331, 344
Sugar Shack	61
Summers, Johnny	350
Sunny and Phyllis (See also Nomads, the)	245
Super Girl	416
Super Sound Records	171
Superlatives, the	126
Superlove	142, 364
Supership	363, 415
Supertime	254
Supremes Never Before Released Masters CD	279
Supremes, the	4, 15, 36, 279, 285, 330, 360
Sure-Shot Records	227, 323
Surprise Party For Baby	1
Suspicion	186, 350, 413
Sussex Records	124, 329
Suzie's Serenade	318
Swan Records	156, 257, 268, 335, 355
Swann, Bettye	310, 360
Sweet And Easy	339
Sweet Honey Baby	122
Sweet Sherry	318, 356
Sweet Thing	314
Sweet Things, the	231, 340
Sweet, the	348
Sweeter Than The Day Before	15, 121
Sweetest Girl In The World	262
Sweetest One	309
Sylves Records	206
Symbol Records	87, 335, 336
Sync 6 Records	320, 394
TK Records	376
TKO Records	84
TLC (Tender Loving Care)	367
Tainted Love	40, 340, 361
Take A Giant Step	358
Take Away The Pain Stain	153, 340
Take Me Home	323
Take My Heart	346
Take Your Love And Run	321, 338
Talkin' Eyes	272
Talkin' 'Bout Poor Folks (Thinking 'Bout My Folks)	265
Tamla Motown Records (TMG)	79, 268, 298, 318, 330, 332, 340, 363, 364, 413, 415, 416
Tamla Records	285, 304, 344, 354, 358, 367
Tams, the	92
Tangeers, the	358
Tangerine Records	122, 260, 336
Tarx Records	351
Tasker, Barry, DJ	402
Tate, Tommy	356
Tavares	344, 373, 415
Tay Records	318
Taylor LeBaron	38, 370
Taylor, Debbie	181
Taylor, Felice	412
Taylor, Johnny	259, 356, 414
Taylor, Ko Ko	370
Taylor, Little Eddie	321
Taylor, R Dean	36, 40, 56, 340
Taylor, Raymond 'Ginger', DJ	404
Taylor, Rosemary	117
Taylor, Sherry	360
Taylor, Ted	368
Taylor, Vernon (See Russell, Saxie)	163
Tayster Records	327
Teacho	368
Tear Stained Face	236
Tears (Nothing But Tears)	175
Tears Of Joy	308, 352, 395
Tears On My Pillow	70, 233
Teasin' You	34
Teddy Bear	252
Tee, Richard	197
Tee, Willie	34, 356
Tell Me It's Just A Rumour	298, 413
Tempio, Carol Lo	149
Temple, Richard (See also Conwell, Jimmy)	124, 338, 339, 370
Tempo, Nino	149
Tempos, the	143, 211
Temptation Is Calling My Name	155, 340
Temptations, the	78, 104, 352
Temptones, the	350
Ten Miles High	142, 259, 347
Teri-De Records	280
Terra Shirma Studios	243
Terrell, Phil	321
Terrell, Tammi	231
Terrible Tom	199
Terrifics, the	377
Tetragramatton Records	70, 110, 249
Tex, Joe	188, 302, 349
Thank God It's Friday	168
Thank You John	34
Thanks For A Little Lovin	320, 357
Thankyou Baby For Loving Me	323
That Beatin' Rhythm	124, 338
That Driving Beat	251
That Was Whiskey Talking	351
That's My Girl	61, 357
That's No Way To Treat A Girl	1, 120
That's Not Love	7, 143, 358
That's The Same Thing	263, 374
That's The Way He Is	242
That's What I Want To Know	9, 200
That's Why I Love You	129, 327, 346
The Beautiful Night	164, 395
The Day My Heart Stood Still	317
The End Of Our Love	152
The Girl Across The Street	41
The Lively One	357
The Night Of The Wolf	376
The Only Way Is Up	350
The Panic Is On	375
The Sweetest Thing	318, 354
The Way You've Been Acting Lately	338
The Wrong Girl	357
Thelma Records	241, 275, 320, 370
Theme From Joe 90	264, 346
Theoda Records	242
There Is Nothing Else To Say	138
There Was A Time	139
There's A Ghost In My House	6, 36, 340, 364
There's A Pain In My Heart	177
There's Nothing Elso To Say	336
These Chains Of Love (Are Breaking Me Down)	236
These Heartaches I Can't Stand	35
These Memories	358
These Things Will Keep Me Loving You	296
They'll Never Know Why	75
They're Talking About Me	132
Think It Over	358
Think Smart	318, 350
This Beautiful Day	133, 395
This England, documentary	10
This Gets To Me	344
This Is Northern Soul, CD	324
This Is The House (Where Love Died)	321
This Man	148
This Man In Love	346
This Old Heart Of Mine	80, 361
This Thing Called Love	191, 360, 416
This Won't Change	312, 327
Thomas Records	69, 163, 260
Thomas, BJ	236
Thomas, Carla	269, 356
Thomas, Don	50
Thomas, Eddie	163
Thomas, Irma	335
Thomas, Jimmy	164, 395
Thomas, Robert	245
Thompkins, Russell	258
Thompson, Pat	288
Thompson, Paul	357
Thorley, Dave, DJ	384
Three Dog Night's	155
Thumb A Ride	7, 113, 340
Tie Records	125, 325, 348
Tiffany's, Coventry	393
Tighten Up	37
Tightrope	131
Time	346, 377
Time Can Change A Love	281
Time Marches On	109
Time Records	419
Time Will Pass You By	30
Times A Wasting	340, 148
Tip Top Records	161
Tipton, Lester	312, 327
To The Ends Of The Earth	308
To Win Your Heart	161

436

Toddlin Town Records	419	Twisted Wheel Story, the, CD	324	Vernee, Yvonne	321, 359
Togetherness Promotions, Allnighter and Weekender	211, 373, 380, 408	Twisted Wheel, the, Manchester	12, 13, 86, 87, 117, 138, 162, 186, 209, 232, 240, 243, 244, 246, 251, 256, 262, 268, 284, 289, 295, 297, 302, 336,, 370, 373, 390	Verve Records	123, 206, 207, 210, 228, 229, 238, 247, 249, 253, 258, 273, 355
Togtherness Magazine	409, 421			Vibrations, the (Vibrating)	64, 160
Toliver (See Taylor, LeBaron)	38, 370			Villa Records	45, 327, 342
Tollie Records	174, 349			Village Of Tears	321, 357
Tomangoes, the	29, 327			John, Vincent	126
Tony and Tyrone	159, 342	Two Loves Have I	352	Virtue Acetate	360, 391
Too Darn Soulful	131	Tyler Records	310	Virtue, Frank	213
Too Late	32	Tymes, the	307, 311, 340	Vocaleers, the	117
Too Late (Mandrill)	358			Voices From The Shadows Magazine	409
Too Late For You And Me	315	Uggams, Leslie	237	Volcanoes, the	156, 356
Too Late To Turn Back Now	358	Unchained Melody	58	Volt Records	14, 213, 169, 318, 356, 357, 372
Too Many People	264, 388, 394	Under My Thumb	164		
Too Much Of A Good Thing	323	Under Your Powerful Love	188, 349	Volumes, the	177, 356
Toones, Gene	275, 375	Underworld Records	157		
Top Dog Records	351	Undisputed Truth, the	104		
Top Notes, the	253	Uni Records	256	Wade In The Water	144, 335, 364
Top Of The Stairs	203, 358	United Artists Records (UA)	24, 122, 190, 211, 250, 264, 233, 358, 364, 372, 388, 394, 395	Wagner, Danny and the Kindred Soul	247
Top Rank, Hanley	119, 215			Wait 'Til I Get You Into My Arms	82
Top Ten Records	146, 328			Wait 'Til I Get To Know Ya	230, 323, 340, 357
Topics, the	418	United Four, the	213	Waitin' For The Rain	186
Topper Records	30, 378	United Sound Studios	49, 134, 231	Walk Like A Man	230
Torch, the (Golden)	13, 48, 49, 113, 125, 126, 133, 140, 149, 154, 164, 167, 182, 183, 184, 197, 207, 227, 229, 230, 231, 235, 238, 241, 247, 249, 257, 258, 268, 272, 273, 286, 300, 307, 340, 341, 369, 373, 380	Unity Records	201	Walk On Baby	249
		Universal Records	324	Walk On Into My Heart	214, 354
		Unsatisfied	48, 414	Walk With A Winner	266
		Upset, The	240	Walker, Junior, and the Allstars	261, 318, 330, 334, 358, 413, 415, 416
		Uptite Records	126		
		Upton, Pat	185	Walker, Mike	383
Total Eclipses	254	Uptown Records	119, 317	Walking The Dog	115
Touch Of Venus	360	Use It Before You Lose It	239, 352	Walking Up A One Way Street	34
Tough Girl	317	Utopias, the	354	Walkin' The Duck	238
Tower Of Strength	360			Wall To Wall Heartaches	323
Tower Of Strength (McDaniels, Gene)	416			Walmsley, Phil, dancer	401
Tower Records	318, 320, 344, 356	VIP Records	36, 213, 320, 323, 340, 350, 357, 391	Walter and the Admirations	358
Toxsan Records	208, 310			Walter, Shirley	102
Track Records	285	Va-Va's, Bolton	25	Wammack, Travis	388
Track, The	163	Valentin, Bobby	352	Wand Records	140, 236, 263, 275, 289, 299, 357
Tracks To Your Mind'	268	Valentine, Patience	360		
Traditions, the	346	Valentine, Rose	378	Wanderers, the	250
Train Keep On Moving	412	Valentine, TD	376	Wanderlust	250
Trammps, the	156, 318, 364	Valentines, the	237	Wanting You	340
Trampoline	6	Valentinos, the	121	Ward, Billy	158
Trans-American Records	84, 390	Valery, Dana	33	Ward, Clara	229
Travellin' Man	74	Valetin, Bobby	239	Ward, Herb	190, 310
Treetop, Bobby	182, 230, 323, 340	Valiant Records	350	Ward, Sam (Singing Sammy)	158
Trends, the	320, 357	Valery Dana	344	Warner Brothers Records (WB)	130, 137, 169, 184, 240, 287, 291, 318, 287, 323, 342, 354, 388
Triode Records	320, 352	Valli, Frankie	112, 364		
Trippin' On You Love	357	Valli, Frankie, and the Four Seasons	157		
Triumphs, the	238, 247	Valvano, Mickey	378	Warwick, Dionne	48, 237
Troy, Benny	204, 352	Van Dyke, Earl, and the Motown Brass	162	Wash And Wear Love	321
Troy, Doris	150	Van Dyke, Earl, and the Soul Brothers	315	Washed Ashore (On A Lonely Island In The Sea)	243
Tru-Gems Records	391	Van Dykes, the	104	Washington, Dinah	19
Try A Little Harder	188	Van McCoy Strings, the	339	Washington, Geno	29
Trying To Love Two	360	Vance, Paul	85	Washpan Records	29, 327
Tuff Records	182, 230, 323, 340	Vann, Ila	189	Watch Out Girl	10
Tune Up	261, 358	Varner, Don	236	Waterfall	367, 376
Turbiton, Willie (See Tee, Willie)	34	Vault Records	418	Waterman, Pete, DJ	361, 390, 393
Turbo Records	291	Vee Jay Records	256, 337, 174	Watkins, Billy	346, 378
Turn The Beat Around	415	Veep Records	55, 210, 233, 281, 318, 342, 348	Wayco Records	265
Turner, Big Joe	352			Waymon, Cal	138
Turner, Ike and Tina	3, 122, 164, 196, 336	Vel-vets, the	53, 342	We Go Together	215, 388
Turner, Sonny	243	Velgo Records	317	We Got Togetherness	291
Turner, Spyder	111, 125, 134	Velours, the	306	We Were Made For Each Other	199
Turner, Tony	419	Velvelettes, the	296, 350	Weaver, Michael (See also Frog, Wynder K)	261
Turning My Heartbeat Up, CD	324	Velvet Hammer, the	258	Webb, Jim	20
Turnin' My Heartbeat Up	51	Velvet Satins, the	90	Weed Records	370
Turntable Records	360	Velvetones, the	282	Welcome To Dreamsville	355
Twans, the	320	Ventures, the	392	Welfare Cheese	239
Twirl Records	177, 196	Verdi, Liz	358	Wells, Bobby	337
Twist Lackawanna	261	Vernado, Lynne	321	Wells, Kenny	351, 355

Index

Wells, Mary	121
Welz, Joey	296
We're In This Thing Together	412
Weston, Kim	129, 293, 358, 413
Westside Records	400
Westwood, Craig, dancer	401
Whales Records	348
What	39
What A Difference A Day Makes	415
What A Man	213
What A Wonderful Night For Love	289, 356
What About Love	248
What Can I Do	238
What Can I Do?	182, 357
What Difference Does It Make	350
What Does It Take	360
What Good Am I?	128
What Happened To Yesterday	11, 181, 329, 348, 374, 378
What Kind Of Lady	66
What Love Brings	163, 395
What More Can A Boy Ask For	354, 413
What More Do You Want	275, 375
What Price	391
What Shall I Do?	132
What Would I Do	340, 307
Whatcha Gonna Do About It	150
What's Her Name	282
What's It Gonna Be	340
What's That On Your Finger	360
What's Wrong With Me Baby	86, 151, 336, 339
Wheel City Records	276, 329, 352
When He's Not Around	378
When I'm Gone	164, 330, 344
When I'm Gonna Find Her	395
When You Lose The One You Love	356, 391
When You're Lonesome (Come On Home)	182
Where Is The Love	364, 415
Where I'm Not Wanted	255
Where There's A Will	164
Where Were You	23
Where You Gonna Be Tonight	248
Wherever You Were	321
Wherry, Nev, DJ	383
Whip Records	274
Whispers, the	323
White, Barry	191, 247
White, Graham 'Docker'	6, 383
Whitfield, Norman	104, 285, 315
Whiting, Margaret	200
Whitney, Pete	13
Who Do You Love	114
Who Who Song, The	346
Who's Making Love	259
Why Am I Lovin' You	323
Why Did You Blow It	375
Why Did You Put It To Me Baby	346
Why Weren't You There	305
Wigan Casino Story, the, CD	324
Wigan's Chosen Few	47, 364, 365, 388
Wigan's Ovation	86, 142, 247, 364
Wiggins, Spencer	198
Willams, Tommy and Eddie (See Buster and Eddie)	282
Williams and Watson	320
Williams, Al	304, 312, 333
Williams, Bernie (Bernard)	136, 255, 333, 344, 374
Williams, Bobby	320
Williams, Jeanette	195
Williams, Jerry	47
Williams, Ken	119
Williams, Larry	76

Williams, Larry, and Watson, Johnny	32
Williams, Maurice	198
Williams, Mel	148
Williams, Porgy	206
Williams, Tony	243
Willingham, Carl, DJ	404
Willows, the	179, 308
Wilson, Al	20, 141, 364
Wilson, Bob	318
Wilson, Frank	3, 15, 16, 17, 45, 59, 180, 346, 374, 390, 391
Wilson, Jackie	132, 346, 317, 320, 332, 364, 373
Wilson, Nancy	152
Wilson, Natalie (See Weston, Kim)	293
Wilson, Obrey	76
Wilson, Timothy	418
Winchester Records	311
Winding Wheel Allnighter, Chesterfield	354
Wingate Records	169
Wingate, Ed	118, 240, 370
Winstanley, Russ, DJ	77, 210, 267, 403
Winter Gardens Allnighter, Cleethorpes	290
Winter Gardens, Cleethorpes	105, 369
Winton, Dale	10, 393
Wirrina, Peterborough	380
Wiseworld Records	28
Wish You Didn't Have To Go	145
Wishes	357, 418
Wishin' And Hopin'	418
With This Ring	243
Womack, Bobby	183, 320, 372
Womack, Cecil	121
Wonder, Stevie	3, 167
Wonderettes, the	321
Wood, Brenton	118
Wood, Chuck	26, 365
Wood, Randall	214, 255, 245
Woodbury, Gene	136
Woodford, Tery	287
Woodliffe, Jonathon, DJ	16, 17
Woods, Billy	124, 329
Woods, Danny	320, 355
Woods, Gilda	41
World Column	344
World Of Happiness	281, 360, 391
World Without Sunshine	323
Wrapped Around Your Finger	87
Wright, Arthur	247
Wright, Betty	364, 373, 415
Wright, Earl	113, 340
Wright, Edna	257
Wright, OV	200
Wyatt, Johnny	191, 360, 416
Wylie, Richard 'Popcorn'	13, 130, 151, 170, 192, 197, 243, 267, 277, 301, 413
Wynns, Sandy	257, 414
Yes I Love You Baby	146, 328
Yew Records	337
York Town Records	350
You Ain't Saying Anything New	358
You Better Believe It	188
You Better Keep Her	318
You Can Split	249
You Can't Close The Windows To Your Heart	323
You Can't Mean It	229
You Didn't Have To Leave	318
You Didn't Say A Word	6, 19
You Don't Know Where Your Interest Lies	33, 344

You Don't Love Me	23
You Don't Love Me Anymore	142
You Don't Mean It	166
You Don't Want Me No More	82
You Get Your Kicks	205, 338
You Got Me In The Palm Of Your Hand	321
You Got To Pay The Price	338
You Got To Pay Your Dues	85
You Got Where You Want Me	316
You Had Me Fooled	320, 355
You Hit Me (Right Where It Hurt Me)	169, 358
You Just Don't Know (What You Do To Me)	68, 329
You Know How To Love Me	348
You Left Me	329, 355
You Lie So Well	1
You Little Trustmaker	311
You Made Me So Very Happy	164
You Sexy Sugar Plum	294
You Shook Me Up	58
You Should 'O Held On	120, 327, 355
You Turned My Bitter Into Sweet	129
You Want to Change Me	83
You Won't Say Nothing	329, 348, 414
You're Not My Kind	196
Young, Billy Joe	182
Young/Holt	144
Younghearts, the	143, 211
Your Autumn Of Tomorrow	394
Your Love Makes Me Lonely	212
Your Love's Too Strong	318
Your Magic Put A Spell On Me	363
Your Wish Is My Command	323
Youth Opportunity Programme	246
You'll Never Walk Alone	58
You're Everything	257
You're Falling In Love	256
You're Gone	375
You're Gonna Love My Baby	42
You're Gonna Make Me Love You	52, 338
You're My Leading Lady	355
You're On Top Girl	266, 331, 355
You're Ready Now	7, 112, 157, 364
You're The Love Of My Life	77
You're Wanted (And Needed)	317
You've Been Away	43, 360, 361, 414
You've Been Cheatin'	99, 335
You've Been Gone Too Long	292, 331
You've Been Leading Me On	313
You've Come Along Way Baby	315
You've Got Your Mind On Other Things	123
Yum Yum Tree	312, 356
Yum Yums, the	106, 358
Yuro, Timi	8, 42, 395
Yvonne and the Violets	323
Zea Records	211
Zodiac Records	63
Zoo, The (The Human Zoo)	295

Northern Soul Top 500

charting the tracks that put the ultimate underground sound on the map - complete with values

KEV ROBERTS

Over 400 fascinating illustrated pages charting the sounds that put Northern Soul on the map...

Priced at just £19.99 in Paperback or £29.99 for a Limited Edition Collector's Hardback edition signed by the Author and chart entrants Frank Wilson, Kenny Bernard, Bobby Patterson and Jimmy Thomas, add £4.95 P&P

Available by mail order direct from: Goldmine/Soul Supply Limited, PO Box 4, Todmorden, OL14 6DA, UK   www.firstnet.co.uk/goldsoul

Classic Soul Sites !

www.firstnet.co.uk/goldsoul
The official Goldmine/Soul Supply site and lots more!
CDs, Vinyl, Magazines, Books, Events

www.raresoulvinyl.co.uk
The worlds rarest vinyl and much more

www.beatinrhythm.com
Mega stock of CDs from the US & UK + vinyl delights.

www.togethernessonline.com
The largest Northern Soul events in the UK